MILADY
STANDARD
MAKEUP

MILADY
STANDARD
Michelle D'Allaird
Brooke Boles
Gina Boyce
Sheila McKenna
Sandra Alexcae Moren
Suzanne Mulroy
Aliesh Pierce
Denise Podbielski
Susanne Schmaling
MAKEUP
CENGAG
Learning
tralia Brazil Japan Korea Mexico Singapore Spain United Kingdom United States

Milady Standard Makeup, First Edition
Michelle D'Allaird, Brooke Boles, Gina Boyce, Sheila McKenna, Sandra Alexcae Moren, Suzanne Mulroy, Aliesh Pierce, Denise Podbielski, and Susanne Schmaling

President, Milady: Dawn Gerrain

Director of Content and Business Development: Sandra Bruce

Acquisitions Editor: Martine Edwards

Senior Product Manager: Jessica Mahoney

Editorial Assistant: Sarah Prediletto

Editorial Assistant: Elizabeth A. Edwards

Director of Marketing and Training: Gerard McAvey

Senior Production Director: Wendy A. Troeger

Production Manager: Sherondra Thedford

Senior Content Project Manager: Nina Tucciarelli

Senior Art Director: Benjamin Gleeksman

Cover Photo
© Laurie and Charles, Getty Images Inc.

Library of Congress Control Number: 2011943909

ISBN-13: 978-1-111-53959-7

ISBN-10: 1-111-53959-6

Milady
Executive Woods
5 Maxwell Drive
Clifton Park, NY 12065
USA

Cengage Learning is a leading provider of customized learning solutions with office locations around the globe, including Singapore, the United Kingdom, Australia, Mexico, Brazil, and Japan. Locate your local office at **www.cengage.com/global**

Cengage Learning products are represented in Canada by Nelson Education, Ltd.

To learn more about Milady, visit **milady.cengage.com**

Purchase any of our products at your local college store or at our preferred online store **www.cengagebrain.com**

Printed in the United States of America
2 3 4 5 6 7 16 15 14 13 12

Contents in Brief

Table of Contents

Part 2 Makeup Foundation / 123

Part 3 Specialty Makeup / 205

Part 4 Advanced Makeup / 351

Part 5 Business Skills / 445

Procedures at a Glance

Mini-Procedures

Preface

You are about to begin a journey into a career that can be filled with success and personal satisfaction. The need for professional makeup artists continues to grow in new and exciting ways, providing numerous opportunities for personal triumph in a variety of career paths.

As your school experience begins, consider how you will approach your course of study through attitude, study skills and habits, and perseverance—especially when the going gets tough. Stay focused on your goal: to become a Makeup Artist and embark on your career. Never hesitate to talk to your instructor should any problems arise that might prevent you from reaching your destination.

A Message from the Author

Michelle D'Allaird

Michelle D'Allaird

The business of beauty has been in existence for what seems to be decades. Where all was once considered the "beauty" business, today each element has evolved into specific categories of professions; each specialty has its own credentials, education, and standards: *Cosmetology, Esthetics, Nail Services, Waxing*—and the driving force behind this textbook… ***Makeup***.

The multibillion-dollar industry of Makeup has long been carving out a place for itself as a profession; a profession in need of certain standards, expectations, skills, and accountability. Meeting these demands and establishing standards, expectations, skills, and accountability is the principle function of this textbook.

You will find tens, if not hundreds, of Makeup books on the shelves in bookstores, libraries, and classrooms—all with unique ideas, tricks, techniques, trade secrets, and insight into the amazing world of Makeup. This textbook has bits and pieces of all of it: input from top makeup leaders, experts, and professionals compiled together as a whole to deliver one source with a magnitude of information that takes the new makeup artist from the very first application all the way to the glitz and glamour of High Fashion and the Runway.

The majority of this textbook is about creating works of art; masterpieces that are as unique to each makeup artist as they are to each individual client. The technical chapters begin with the fundamentals of working with facial shapes and their features, creating the perfect canvas with preparation, foundations, concealers, powders, and blushes and then move directly into techniques to work with the features of the vast array of people that you will have access to, each unique and beautiful in their own way.

Subsequent chapters delve into makeup application for specific settings and situations: everything from working with teens, men, and mature skin to wedding, photography, runway, and high-definition makeup techniques. Each chapter includes step-by-step procedures to walk you through the entire application process.

This textbook has been designed to act as the guidebook for the novice makeup artist and as a reference for the seasoned artist. Its contents came from many of the most elite in the industry—all of them with the passion, experience, and desire to provide you with their knowledge to set you off and running, if not sprinting, into the amazing World of Makeup.

A special thank-you to Denise Podbielski and Sherry Weiczhowski, licensed estheticians and makeup artists in New York, that provided me with their knowledge and expertise to add to many of the basic procedures. I also thank my family and employees that supported and dealt with my crazy schedule through this process.

Please take time to review the features of this text that immediately follow; spend a few more minutes reviewing the career profiles and backgrounds of all of our amazing contributing authors; and then take a few more to visualize the limitless opportunities that the Makeup Profession has to offer, and imagine just where you might find yourself next year, in 5 years, and in 10 years down the road!

Dream big, and aspire even bigger. The sky is the limit, and you are entering the most limitless, creative, inspirational profession that has ever existed. Let your mind run free and allow your artistic techniques to emerge into something new with every day, every new face, and every new opportunity!

Dream on...and make it happen,

Michelle D'Allaird

Features of this Edition

This edition includes many features and learning tools that will help you master key concepts and techniques.

Pre-and Post-Service Procedures

To drive home the point that pre-service cleaning, disinfecting, and preparing for the client are important, you will find that a unique Pre-Service Procedure has been created in Chapter 7, "Creating the Canvas," to specifically address setting up your makeup station and for meeting, greeting, and escorting your client to your service area. Additionally, this chapter also contains a Post-Service Procedure created to address cleaning, disinfecting, and organizing after servicing a client.

Why Study This?

Milady knows, understands, and appreciates how excited students are to delve into the newest and most exciting products and equipment, and we recognize that students can sometimes feel restless spending time learning the basics of the profession. To help you understand why you are learning each chapter's material and to help you see the role it will play in your future career as a makeup artist, Milady has added this new section to each chapter. This section includes three or four bullet points that tell you why the material is important and how you will use the material in your professional career.

Did You Know?

Clients with aging skin will often refer to their skin as "losing the glow" or looking very "dull." This is a common result of the declining rate of cellular turnover.

Activity

Communication

Makeup artists should always perform a complete consultation with mature clients prior to each makeup application. (See Chapter 6, Client Consultation, for more information on performing effective consultations.) Active listening is one of the most important skills to develop in this process. To practice active listening try this activity:

In a group of two or more people, have one person describe the skin concern that bothers her the most.

1. Without precisely repeating the speaker's statement, have the listeners state their names and then describe the speaker's concern.
2. Have the speaker repeat the names of the listeners.
3. Evaluate the active listening skills of the speaker and the listeners. Discuss how to improve listening skills.

CHALLENGES OF AGING SKIN

Understanding the challenges of aging skin is the first step in learning makeup application techniques that will work well for this segment of your clientele. Prepping the skin prior to makeup application is essential, and an effective daily home skin care routine, along with monthly facial treatments, is part of this process.

Thorough consultation and appropriate skin analysis is critical before the application of makeup to mature skin. To make proper product choices for mature makeup applications, you must determine the client's specific skin type and product usage. LO2

Determing Stages of Aging Skin

Determining the correct skin type is important in order to prep the skin and choose appropriate makeup formulations. It is also important to understand the stages that aging skin goes through and to determine where the client is in the aging process. Although it is simple to categorize stages of aging skin based upon a client's age, it is important to know that environmental factors, lifestyle, and genetics all play an important role. Different ages can easily fall into different stages. Each stage requires unique application techniques to minimize the appearance of aging.

Stage 1: Fine Wrinkles/Mild Loss of Firmness/Mild Pigment Discolorations

The first visual signs of aging are (Figure 14–1):

- Lines (appearing with facial movement) at the sides of the eyes and at the upper lip.
- Mild pigment discoloration, or uneven skin color, that appears in two types:
  - Hyperpigmentation—dark spots caused by sun damage and hormonal changes.
  - Hypopigmentation—light spots caused by a loss of pigment.
- Mild smile-line depth.
- Fine visible capillaries, or small blood vessels.
- Rough skin texture, increased fine wrinkles, and dark circles under the eyes.
- General dull skin color.
- Fading hair or eyebrow color.

Figure 14–1 Stage 1 aging can start as early as 35.

324 Chapter 14 Makeup for Aging Skin

These features provide interesting information that will enhance your understanding of the material in the text and call attention to special points.

The **Activity** boxes describe hands-on classroom exercises that will help you understand the concepts explained in the text.

CREATING YOUR PERSONAL PORTFOLIO

The Internet is a world unto itself and the number of on-line users is increasing daily. There is a saying in marketing: "If you are not on the Web, then you don't exist." Your on-line portfolio or Web site will be a personal calling card where you display your talents and work for potential customers and employers to evaluate your professional skills. The Internet and your Web site is also where potential employers and clients will be able to find you. In the makeup profession, your on-line portfolio is just as important, and often times more important, than your resume, client list, and physical portfolio. Your on-line portfolio is a visual representation of your talent and skill and contributes as much to your professional image as your "toolbox" and the display of professional qualities you selected.

Think of a portfolio as an exhibit of your work on display for potential clients and employers that allows them to evaluate your professional skills and makeup artistry. Your portfolio should contain a wide range of photos and diverse makeup applications, as well as a list of clients and productions you have worked on (the bigger the better of course, but everyone has to start somewhere). Start an on-line portfolio right away, even while you are still in school. The progression of your skills and expertise will be clearly represented in a portfolio that originates with the beginning of your career. The important thing is to establish your presence in the industry as soon as you can.

Do your homework, research carefully, and think long-term—you, your portfolio, and Web address want to be around for years to come. Investigate and discover what top makeup artists are doing with their on-line portfolios by viewing the Web sites of the artists profiled throughout this book.

If creating a Web site is currently not in your budget, then create a "Fan Page" on Facebook to showcase your work. Remember: Your fan page is your business page and is not just a professional representation of your work, but it is also a representation of your professional image.

Portfolio Photos

When you are starting out as a makeup professional, compiling quality photos can be a challenge. Create your own design "dream team" for a photoshoot consisting of a photographer, hairdresser, clothing stylist/designer, and fledgling models. Contact cosmetology students, photography schools, fashion institutes, and modeling agencies as novices are always in need of great photos. Come together as a team and collaborate on the look and feel of each shot you will take in your photoshoot. This will not only help you acquire photos, but it will also teach you how to work on a team with other creative professionals in the industry.

By taking photos of your best work you will have a true representation of your talents, artistry, and skills. Your photo selection should be diverse:

WEB RESOURCES

The following is a list of "Portfolio Hosting Sites" to help get you started in establishing your on-line portfolio:

- www.bigblackbag.com
- www.viewbook.com
- www.getparade.com
- www.styleseat.com

fyi

theEDGE video (Metroluxe and Muse editions) by Milady, a part of Cengage Learning, deconstructs the creative process of design from concept to completion and will give you the tools and insights of what it takes to design a collection and produce a photoshoot. Find theEDGE at www.milady.cengage.com.

Chapter 19 Your Professional Image 453

FYIs offer important, interesting information related to the content. Often, **FYI** boxes direct you to a Web site or other resource for further information.

The **Web Resources** provide you with Web addresses where you can find more information on a topic and references to additional sites for more information.

HERE'S A TIP

These helpful tips draw attention to situations that might arise and provide quick ways of doing things. Look for these tips throughout the text.

This feature alerts you to check the laws in your region for procedures and practices that are regulated differently from state to state and province to province. It is important, while you are studying, to contact state boards and provincial regulatory agencies to learn what is allowed and not allowed. Your instructor will provide you with contact information.

CAUTION

Some information is so critical for your safety and the safety of your clients that it deserves special attention. The text directs you to this information in the **CAUTION** boxes found in the margins.

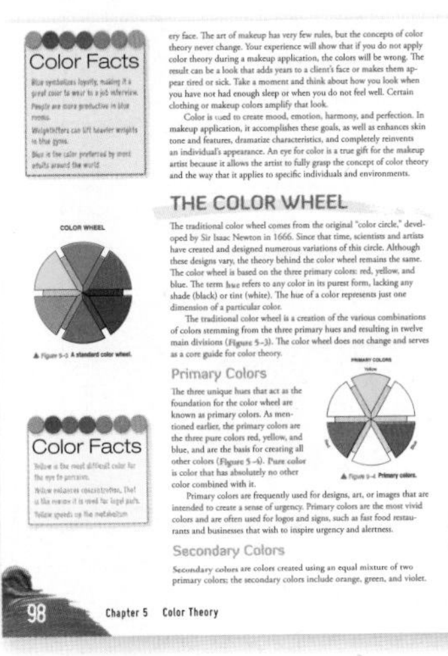

The **Color Facts** appears in Chapter 5, "Color Theory," to provide you with interesting facts related to the symbolism and meaning behind popular colors.

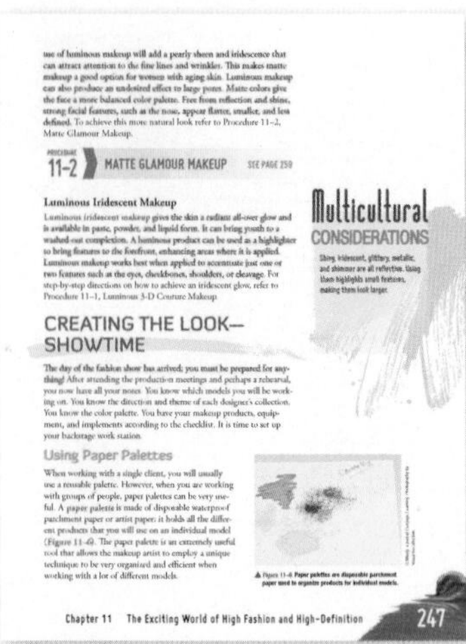

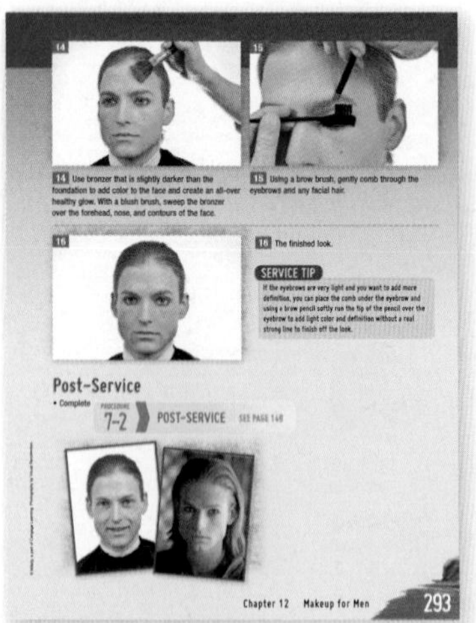

Multicultural CONSIDERATIONS

The **Multicultural Considerations** addresses makeup tips for a range of skin tones and women of color, written by professional makeup artists Shimika Kennison and Aliesh Pierce.

Each chapter includes a **CAREER PROFILE** featuring incredible makeup experts from around the world. Twenty successful artists share their triumphs, challenges, and the opportunities they encountered starting their career in the Makeup Business. The profiles give an overview of the artist's background, and the artist's personal success story of how they made it in the competitive Makeup Business, along with tips for future artists like yourself.

SERVICE TIP

Service Tips draw attention to situations that might arise while performing a service and provide quick ways of doing things. Look for these tips in the procedures.

Educational Chapter Formatting

Each chapter of *Milady Standard Makeup* includes specialized formatting and strategies for the presentation of material to enhance your experience while working with the chapter and to facilitate the learning process.

Learning Objectives

At the beginning of each chapter is a list of learning objectives that tell you what important information you will be expected to know after studying the chapter. Throughout the chapter you will see a special icon that indicates you have finished reading the material that corresponds to each of these Learning Objectives. **✓ L01**

Key Terms

The words you will need to know in a chapter are given at the beginning in a list of **Key Terms**. When the word is discussed for the first time within the chapter, it appears in **boldface** type. If the word is difficult to pronounce, a phonetic pronunciation follows it in parentheses.

Procedures

All step-by-step procedures offer clear, easy-to-understand directions and multiple photographs for learning the techniques. At the beginning of each procedure, you will find a list of the needed implements, materials, and supplies along with any preparation that must be completed before the procedure begins.

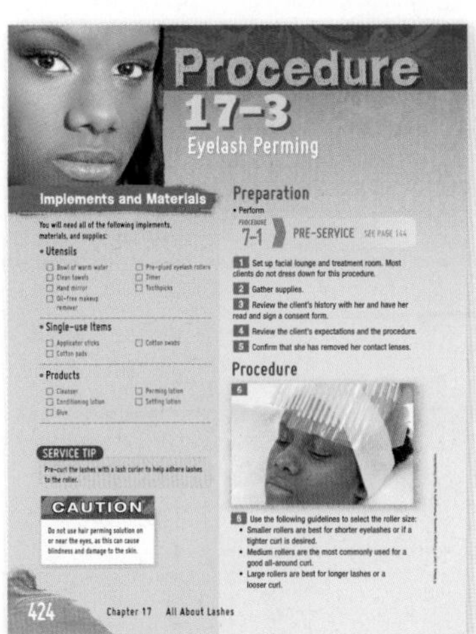

Procedure 17-3 *(continued)*

11 Using the applicator, carefully press the lashes on the roller one at a time to avoid overlapping or crossing of lashes.

11a Make sure that the lower lashes are not curled onto the rod.

12 Apply perm solution with a cotton swab or manufacturer's applicator across the lashes that are adhered to the rod. Avoid contact with the skin. Carefully follow manufacturer's instructions for processing; depending on the kit, timing ranges anywhere from 8 to 15 minutes.

13 Check lashes by separating one or two from the roller with a toothpick. If you do not yet see the curl you are trying to achieve, leave the lashes on the roller for 2 to 3 minutes longer. Wipe off any excess perming lotion and rinse thoroughly following manufacturer's guidelines.

14 Apply setting or neutralizer lotion to the lashes with the application stick. Leave neutralizer on according to manufacturer's instructions, generally 5 to 10 minutes.

15 Remove setting lotion with wet cotton-tipped swabs or wet cotton rounds, rinsing thoroughly.

16 If the kit includes a post-treatment lotion, apply it now with an applicator stick or cotton swab. Let lotion set for 5 minutes or according to manufacturer's instructions.

17 Use cleanser and gently swipe the upper part of the roller, touching the eyelid. Using a damp cotton-tipped swab, clean the eyelid from side to side. Slowly roll the rod downward with the cotton swab, freeing the lash from the rod.

CAUTION

Do not let any perming solution enter the client's eyes or touch her skin.

18 Clean lashes with warm, damp cotton or gauze pads.

19 The finished look.

Post-Service LO10

- Complete PROCEDURE 7-2 POST-SERVICE SEE PAGE 148
- Provide the client with home-care instructions. It is best to let the lashes rest for 24 hours prior to applying mascara.
- Be sure to dispose of perm rods.

426 Chapter 17 All About Lashes

Chapter 17 All About Lashes 427

All of the procedures appear in a special **PROCEDURES** section at the end of the chapter.

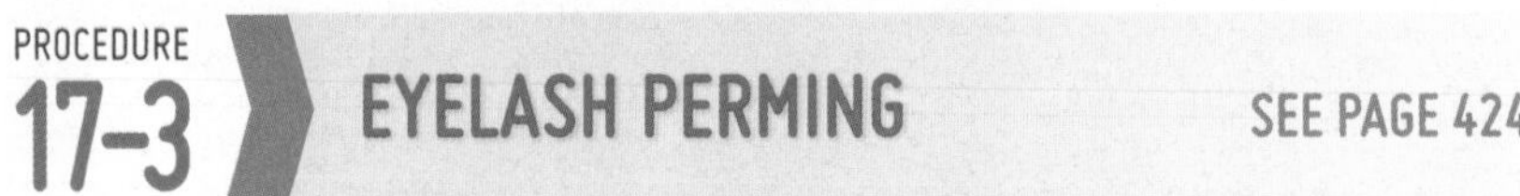

Some students will want to review a procedure at the time it is mentioned in the main content. To make it easy for you to find the procedure you are looking for at these times, Milady has added Procedural Icons. These icons appear where each procedure is mentioned within the main content of the chapter, and they direct you to the page number where the entire procedure appears.

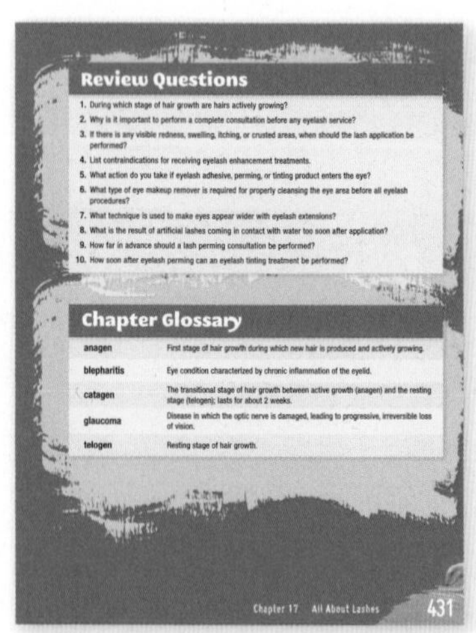

Review Questions

1. During which stage of hair growth are hairs actively growing?
2. Why is it important to perform a complete consultation before any eyelash service?
3. If there is any visible redness, swelling, itching, or crusted areas, when should the lash application be performed?
4. List contraindications for receiving eyelash enhancement treatments.
5. What action do you take if eyelash adhesive, perming, or tinting product enters the eye?
6. What type of eye makeup remover is required for properly cleansing the eye area before all eyelash procedures?
7. What technique is used to make eyes appear wider with eyelash extensions?
8. What is the result of artificial lashes coming in contact with water too soon after application?
9. How far in advance should a lash perming consultation be performed?
10. How soon after eyelash perming can an eyelash tinting treatment be performed?

Chapter Glossary

anagen	First stage of hair growth during which new hair is produced and actively growing.
blepharitis	Eye condition characterized by chronic inflammation of the eyelid.
catagen	The transitional stage of hair growth between active growth (anagen) and the resting stage (telogen); lasts for about 2 weeks.
glaucoma	Disease in which the optic nerve is damaged, leading to progressive, irreversible loss of vision.
telogen	Resting stage of hair growth.

Chapter 17 All About Lashes 431

Review Questions

Each chapter ends with questions designed to test your understanding of the chapter's content. Your instructor may ask you to write the answers to these questions as an assignment or to answer them orally in class. If you have trouble answering a chapter review question, go back to the chapter to review the material and then try again.

Chapter Glossary

All key terms and their definitions are included in the **CHAPTER GLOSSARY** at the end of each chapter, as well as in the **GLOSSARY/ INDEX** at the end of the text.

Extensive Learning and Teaching Package

While *Milady Standard Makeup* is the center of the curriculum, students and educators have a wide range of supplements from which to choose.

Student Supplements

SUPPLEMENT TITLE	SUPPLEMENT DESCRIPTION
Milady Standard Makeup Student Workbook	• Designed to reinforce classroom and textbook learning. • Helps students recognize, understand, and retain the key concepts as covered in the textbook. • Provides fill-in-the-blank, multiple-choice, matching, labeling exercises, and face charts that reinforce practical applications.

Educator Supplements

Milady proudly offers a full range of innovative products created especially for makeup educators to make classroom preparation and presentation easy, effective, and enjoyable.

SUPPLEMENT TITLE
Milady Standard Makeup Course Management Guide CD
Milady Standard Makeup DVD Series
Milady Standard Makeup Instructor Support Slides CD

Thank you for choosing Milady as your Total Learning Solutions Provider. For additional information on the above resources or to place an order please contact your Milady Sales Representative or visit us online at www.milady.cengage.com.

About the Authors

Michelle D'Allaird

Michelle D'Allaird

Michelle began her career as an educator and trainer for an East Coast skin care franchise where she hired and trained estheticians in over 12 locations. Michelle is a licensed esthetician, cosmetologist, and CIDESCO Diplomat. Her passion and desire for superior education motivated her to open her own esthetics school in 2003, the Aesthetic Science Institute, a New York state esthetics school in Latham, NY.

With over 20 years of experience in the skin care and beauty industry, Michelle's expertise spans teaching; curriculum development for esthetics, nails, medical aesthetics, and laser; speaking; test development; and authoring. She is the coauthor of *Salon Fundamentals: Esthetics Textbook* (2007), a regular contributing author to *les nouvelles esthétique & spa* and *Dermascope* magazines, as well as a host and guest speaker at esthetics conferences across the United States.

Since 2006, Michelle has acted as a consultant for an international cosmetic company providing education and training in over 18 countries around the world. She is the Director of Education for Aesthetics International Association and a member of AIA, AACS, and BSA. Michelle was voted Woman of the Year 2011 in the skin care profession by the National Association of Professional Women.

Her passion for the skin care industry and raising the bar for education has been a driving force behind her success and continued satisfaction in providing others with the tools to grow, change, and emerge into a new level of professionalism.

Hot Pants Cosmetics Model Brooke Boles Courtesy of HedLux

Brooke Boles

Brooke Boles, creator of Hot Pants Cosmetics and president of HedLux Premium School Products, has a wide range of accomplishments including a successful career as a model, actress, philanthropist, motivational speaker, makeup artist, mother, and most notably: entrepreneur. Brooke's first entrepreneurial venture started in college with Boo-Boos, a fashion accessory which sold in over 300 stores nationwide, including Nordstrom's. Brooke officially entered the market with Op Art Mineral Shadows and also created the makeup line Hot Pants in 2004, which currently sells to salons, spas, and cosmetology schools nationwide. Brooke is also notable for launching the first volumizing "light up" lip gloss, Lip Lust. Most recently, she developed the first complete professional collection of High Definition Makeup that optically airbrushes the skin without the use or expense of an airbrush machine.

Brooke and her products have been featured on QVC, CBS's *The Early Show*, *Good Day LA*, the *Grammy Awards*, and in the *LA Times* to name a few. Additionally, Brooke has served as a spokesperson for the American Association of Cosmetology Schools (AACS) and the Cut It Out initiative to fight domestic abuse and appeared as a guest speaker for the Cosmetology Educators of America (CEA).

© GEGI Fashion

Gina Boyce

Fashion designer Gina Boyce has had a lifelong love affair with the Fashion and Beauty industry. Her creative approaches revolve around the learned techniques of the visual arts. Creating and working with color has evolved into a full-fledged love of fashion, hair, and makeup. Starting out as a licensed hairstylist, Gina then began to pursue her interest in makeup application.

Working with top cosmetic companies, Gina developed her skills and repertoire as a makeup artist and progressed to feature films, television, and print. Reinventing herself once again, Gina has moved her focus to fashion. Her innate talent for color and design make for a solid understanding of transformative makeup.

In addition to her broad range of experience, skill, artistry, and expertise, Gina's natural talent along with her eye for color and design inspired her to create her own fashion label. GEGI is a contemporary collection of fashion with a classic edge. To this day, Gina continues to work in the World of Fashion—always open to creating something fresh, new, and innovative. You can find Gina behind the scenes of the fashion industry working on a team with other makeup artists, involved in the production of a show or event, or off showcasing the GEGI collection on Fashion's "catwalk."

Sheila McKenna

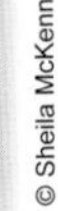

© Sheila McKenna

Sheila McKenna, president and founder of Kett Cosmetics, is an industry veteran with over 20 years of experience in Makeup Artistry. Her work has been seen in film, television, print, theater, and on the runway. She is an expert in the field of Airbrush Makeup and founded the Kett line of products and airbrush equipment in 2000. Today, Kett Cosmetics is globally recognized and considered an essential brand for professional artists, makeup academies, studios, and television networks.

Sandra Alexcae Moren

© Sandra Alexcae Moren, www.kyronspaconsulting.com

Sandra Alexcae Moren, B.Ed., is an educator, Salon/Spa Consultant, author, Makeup & Image Consultant with Kyron Spa & Salon Consulting (a division of Chiron Marketing Inc.), and has over 35 years of experience in the professional beauty industry.

As a cosmetologist, educator, Master Judge with the Judges Panel of Canada, member of the Cosmetology Industry Association of British Columbia, former spa director, and author it was a natural evolution to assist individuals in their personal and business transformations.

Sandra has experienced many exciting opportunities working in the Modeling and Fashion venues as a stylist, makeup artist, image consultant, events co-coordinator, and mature model. Living, working, and traveling internationally have allowed Sandra to personally encounter and research the marketplace diversity within the salon/spa, education, makeup, fashion, and modeling industries.

Sandra's books *Spa & Salon Alchemy: The Ultimate Guide to Spa & Salon Ownership* and *Spa & Salon Alchemy: Step by Step Spa Procedures* are a must for anyone in the industry.

Suzanne Mulroy

© Suzanne Mulroy

Suzanne Mulroy brings 25 years of experience in the beauty and wellness industry to her current position as Market Development Manager for Milady. She began her career as a makeup artist in Chicago—building a diverse and extensive clientele—and continues to share her extensive knowledge and commitment to the industry by helping hundreds of people achieve their dreams. Some of her contributions include: producing workshops at Fred Segal Beauty for professional and novices alike interested in pursuing a career in film, TV, and fashion; Director of Operations for 2 multimillion-dollar Beverly Hill's spas; overseeing a 5 million-dollar sales territory; and traveling the world as an international speaker. Her passion and inspiration come from developing programs and products designed to revolutionize the industry.

Photography by Neil France

Aliesh Pierce

Aliesh Pierce has a diverse educational background which includes studying Business Management at Fisk University. She is a licensed esthetician, a makeup artist, and a beauty advisor to cosmetic manufacturers. Aliesh shares her expertise with estheticians at various conventions/conferences such as the ICES Long Beach and ICES Philadelphia, The Spa and Resort Expo in Los Angeles and New York, as well as the CEA National Conference. Her makeup has appeared in Italian *Elle*, *Vogue*, *Essence*, and *les nouvelles esthétique & spa*.

As a consultant, she helped Jafra Cosmetics International expand their color range for the African American market and launched the entire color range in the U.S. and Europe. She began her writing career interviewing burn survivors for the nonprofit foundation Burn Survivors Throughout the World. Aliesh continues to work as a Freelance Beauty Analyst, lending her expertise to various marketing projects.

© Making Faces

Denise Podbielski

Denise Podbielski has been in the rewarding business of Beauty and Wellness since 1988, when she began as a cosmetologist and makeup artist. In 1993, Denise became a Trucco Educator with Sebastian International where she taught educational makeup classes for artists. Denise also freelances with various companies such as Lancôme, Chanel, and Ultima II. She apprenticed her hair skills under Giulio Veglio.

In 2001, Denise became a New York state licensed esthetician and began focusing on education. In 2003, she began teaching at an esthetics school. As her passion for makeup evolved, she began teaching advanced makeup trainings for students and other licensed professionals. In 2007, Denise opened her own practice, Making Faces, where she practices as a holistic and clinical esthetician, makeup artist, and wellness and nutrition consultant.

During 2010, Denise continued her education by studying herbalism under Rosemary Gladstar. In July of 2011, Denise became a certified herbalist and is now incorporating natural herbs into skin care for consumers and clients. She is currently continuing her holistic education and studying aromatherapy for the skin at The East-West School for Herbal & Aromatic Studies and is in the process of developing her own aromatherapy skin care line.

Susanne Schmaling

Sadie Williams Photography

Susanne Schmaling, L.E., is the National Director of Education for Associated Skincare Professionals and the former founder and director of the Pacific Institute of Esthetics located in Northwest Oregon as well as a licensed esthetician, makeup artist, nail technician, and instructor. Susanne is the author of the critically acclaimed *Milady's Aesthetician Series: The Comprehensive Guide to Esthetic Equipment* (2009) and *Milady's Aesthetician Series: Aging Skin* (2012).

With a focus on skin science, dynamic measurable antiaging skin therapies, and holistic skin care techniques, Susanne's expertise and extensive experience make her a popular presenter at conferences and seminars throughout the world. The former creator and owner of an award-winning day spa, her career includes extensive experience in all aspects of esthetics, spa body therapies, makeup, and nail technology as well as spa consulting, school curriculum planning, and spa design.

Acknowledgments

Milady recognizes, with gratitude and respect, the many professionals who have offered their time to contribute to this edition of *Milady Standard Makeup* and wishes to extend enormous thanks to the following people who have played a part in this edition:

- Michelle D'Allaird, esthetician, school owner, and consultant for her invaluable assistance throughout the development process of the textbook and for sharing all of her time and makeup knowledge during the *Milady Standard Makeup* photo shoot.
- Daesha Harris and Thomas Dragonette from **Visual Recollection**, professional photographers, whose photographic expertise helped bring many of these pages to life. Website: www.visualrecollection.com
- James Piraino, Cheri Rivette and the entire staff at **Hair & Body Essentials** in Clifton Park, NY, for welcoming Milady's staff, models, and crew for the *Milady Standard Makeup* photoshoot.
- Thom Cammer and Kim Collea, professional makeup artists, for sharing their energy and passion for makeup and performing men's makeup, contouring, eye makeup application, and special effect makeup at the photo shoot. **Thom Cammer**, www.thomcammer.com and **Kim Collea**, www.kimcollea.com.
- Alayne Curtiss, professional makeup artist and owner of **Make Me Fabulous** in Ballston Spa, NY, for her artfully inspired makeup applications. A big Thank-You to her entire team of talented artists and hairstylists: Amy Bath, Kara Geske, Susan Truax, Angela Nickels, and Kyle Garcia.
- Diane Casey, Owner of **Esthetiques** in Saratoga Springs, NY, for generously performing the eyelash tinting service at the photoshoot.
- Faith Maus, owner of **Ginger Lashes**, for her incredible work applying dramatic eyelash extensions on our model for the Lash chapter.
- Erin K. Longton, professional stylist, at **Artistic Hair Design & Spa**, Malta, NY, for her great work on the eyelash perming services.
- Gina Boyce, designer from GEGI designs, for being such a fashion inspiration and for designing the models outfits and accessories in the Matte and Luminous makeup procedures. She was also instrumental at the photoshoot as the subject-matter expert for the glamour makeup applications.

- Aliesh Pierce, professional makeup artist, for all of her creativity and guidance in managing and even performing makeup applications at the photoshoot along with, her writing and authoring abilities—most especially with regard to the camouflage techniques.
- The owners and staff at the **Adephi Hotel** in Saratoga Springs, NY, for their hospitality and allowing our staff to take photographs at their beautiful downtown location.
- Maria K. Hebert, Cayla Pratt, Sarah Prediletto, and Alyssa Hardy for their hard work in identifying, researching, and editing the "Career Profiles" featuring successful makeup artists in each chapter.

Special thanks to Milady's Infection Control Advisory Panel members that reviewed the manuscript:

- Barbara Acello, M.S., R.N., Denton, TX
- Mike Kennamer, Ed.D., Director of Workforce Development & Skills Training, Northeast Alabama Community College
- Leslie Roste, R.N., National Director of Education & Market Development, King Research/Barbicide, WI

Product Suppliers

- ***Your Name Cosmetics*** for generously providing a wide range of makeup for the photoshoot and Makeup DVD, including beautiful displays. The majority of the brushes and makeup used and pictured in this text were donated by Your Name Cosmetics, www.yournamepro.com.
- ***Kett Cosmetics*** for supplying step-by-step photos for the airbrushing chapter including the product shots, basic makeup application, and camouflaging tattoos.
- ***Temptu Airbrush*** for contributing airbrush equipment and supplies.

Reviewers of Milady Standard Makeup

Linda Bertaut, Bertaut Beauty, CA

Peggy Braswell, Southeastern Technical College, GA

Robin Roberts Cochran, Gadsden State Community College-Ayers Campus, AL

Kimberly Coleman, Aspire Beauty Academy, MO

Rhonda Cummings, Director of Advanced Education, Face Forward Inc., MA

Alayne G. Curtiss, Make Me Fabulous, NY

Pamela Earle, President, Complections International Academy, Ontario, Canada

Bianca Felice, Keiser Career College & High Brow Studio & Skin, FL

Cindy German-Day, Nuance Skin Boutique, GA

Jeanne Healy, Carolina Skin Care Academy, Inc., SC

Kim Jarrett, Instructor, B Street Design, KS

Helen LeDonne, Santa Monica College, CA

Yolanda Matthews, The Cosmetology Connection & Consulting Services, TX

Elizabeth Myron, FL

Denise Podbielski, Making Faces, NY

Denise Sauls, Lurleen B. Wallace Community College, AL

Karen Sutera, Karen Sutera Salon, NY

Madeline Udod, Eastern Suffolk BOCES, NY

Daria Wright, Beauty Aficionado, IL

Tamara Yusupoff, Bellus Academy: The Academy of Beauty and Spa, Advanced Skin Care Training Center, CA

Part 1

Makeup Fundamentals

Chapter 1 The Evolution of Makeup Artistry

Chapter Outline

- Why Study the Evolution of Makeup Artistry?
- The Makeup Image
- A Future in Makeup
- The Evolutionary Timeline
- An Ever-Changing Era

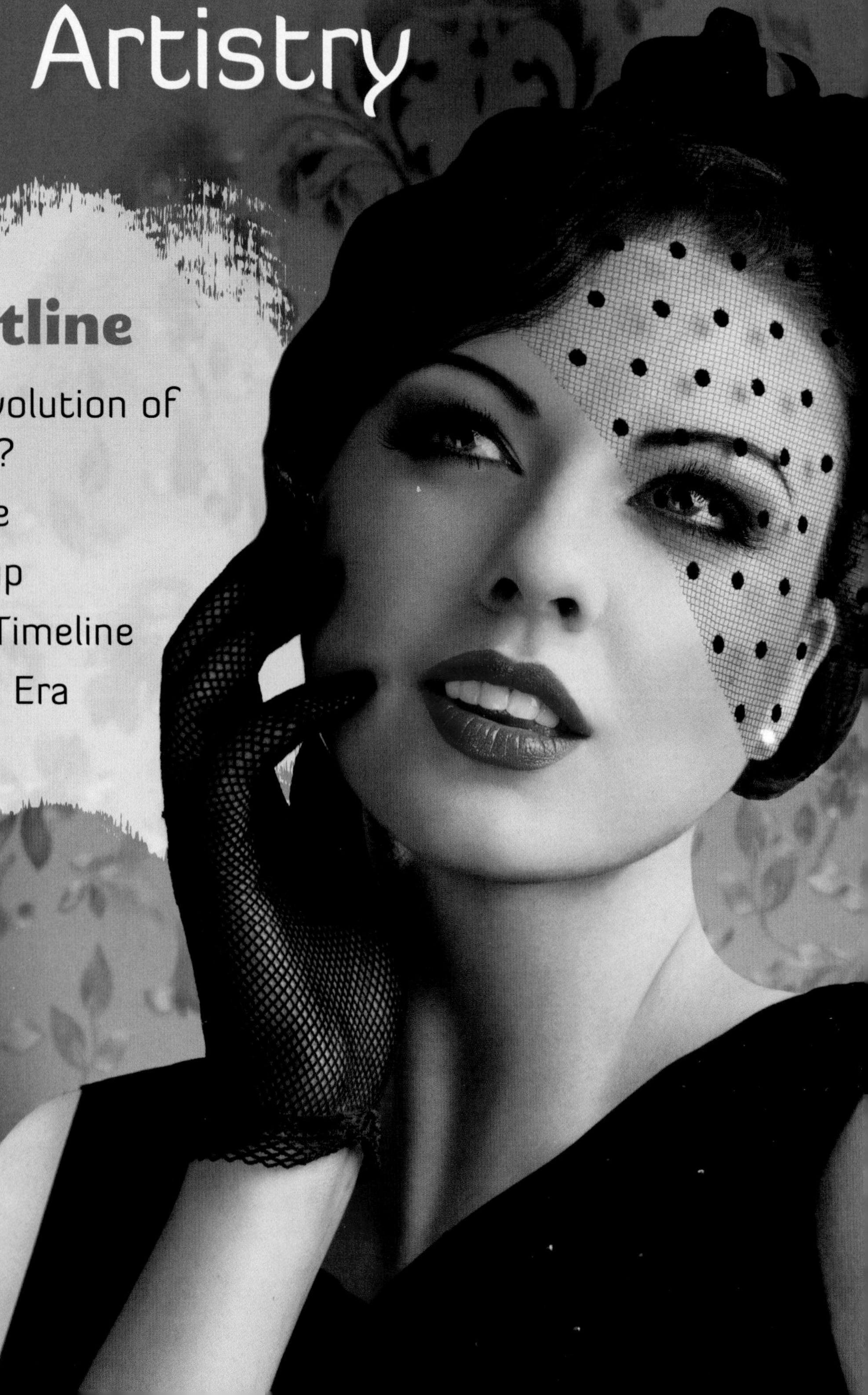

Learning Objectives

After completing this chapter, you will be able to:

- ☑ **LO1** Identify the introduction of the first makeup products.
- ☑ **LO2** Understand the first ingredients used in early makeup formulations.
- ☑ **LO3** Identify key individuals responsible for the innovation and growth of cosmetics.
- ☑ **LO4** Understand the role that makeup has played in beauty, status, and identity since 4000 BC.

Key Terms

Page number indicates where in the chapter the term is used.

carminic acid
pg. 11

Flappers
pg. 13

galena
pg. 7

mesdemet
pg. 7

palor
pg. 10

udju (malachite)
pg. 7

Career Profile

www.stephanienavarro.com.

Stephanie Navarro was uncompromising in her pursuit of a successful career in makeup artistry. When she was just 17 years old, she moved to Los Angeles and worked long hours to support herself and make her dream come true. In recent years she has done makeup for major photographers such as David Christopher Lee and on feature films such as *Redemption*. Currently a freelance artist, Stephanie continues to increase her client list and pursue success.

"When I am working, I love meeting new groups of people, being creative, and getting my brushes dirty. I am a freelance makeup artist and hairstylist in Los Angeles. I am in the beginning stages of my career, but I have already worked on a wide array of projects in film, television, commercials, and photo shoots. If I am not booked, I stay productive by updating my Web site and resume, collecting unpaid invoices, and keeping in touch with contacts.

"I started out in the rough neighborhoods of Chicago, Illinois. I had no idea that applying makeup was something that could be done as a career outside of a salon. When I was only 15 years old, I helped a friend on a student film as an assistant makeup artist. The job came with no pay and long hours; I worked for the 6 days I was asked to assist and ended up staying on for the entire 4 weeks of the project. It was exciting to be a part of the film-making process. I continued to work on student films until I moved to Los Angeles.

"I finished high school early and with my parents' permission moved to Los Angeles, California, at the age of 17 to pursue a career as a makeup artist. I enrolled in cosmetology school before going on to makeup school. Doing both hair and makeup, I was told, would ensure more work in a competitive market. After I graduated, I found a job in a salon doing makeup and eyebrows to support myself. Then I enrolled in makeup school.

"There is something to be learned from every job experience. Sometimes what starts out as a stressful day makes me rise to a new challenge and show new capabilities I didn't know I had. I used to be uncomfortable doing extravagant hairstyles until I was working with a model for a magazine shoot and the photographer decided he wanted a hair change right on the spot. I ended up creating the *Marie Antoinette* look that he wanted, and everyone loved it.

"I've had several mentors throughout my career. I assisted Lauren Lee on my first film, and she taught me the basics before I had any training or experience. I worked for Farrah Moorhouse for a year in a salon; she trained me to meticulously wax and tweeze brows and to sell the makeup I was applying. I assisted Aliesh Pierce, a seasoned makeup artist, who fine-tuned my makeup techniques for people of all colors.

"I am grateful to be able to live in Los Angeles and support myself as a freelance makeup artist. In every passing month, I see that my goals are met and my career continues to move forward. Whether it's contributing to this book or working with someone I have seen on the big screen, I feel that I continue to accomplish my dreams as my career continues to flourish."

(c) Kekoz Photography

Makeup is certainly nothing new to the modern world. Cosmetics and personal hygiene products have been in use since ancient times. As early as 3000 BC, the Egyptians were using cosmetics made of iron oxide, black kohl, powdered green malachite, and ochre. During some of the most tumultuous times in history, only a few items were constantly available, and lipstick was one of them. Current events, entertainment, and famous individuals all have played a role in influencing makeup and fashion trends.

WHY STUDY THE EVOLUTION OF MAKEUP ARTISTRY?

Makeup artists should study and have a thorough understanding of the evolution of makeup artistry because:

- Makeup artistry has been a cultural influence since 4000 BC.
- An understanding of the evolution of makeup will help makeup artists fully understand and appreciate the trends of today.
- With the media pressing the idea that "Image is everything," makeup artists should understand why.

THE MAKEUP IMAGE

In the many centuries that makeup has been in existence, trends, styles, colors, and techniques have continued to morph; creating for makeup a world all its own. Society today places a heavy emphasis on image and appearance. First impressions account for how one person will choose to interact with another. According to business consultant Carol Kinsey Goman, Ph.D., "within 7 seconds a person will establish their impression of another individual" (**Figure 1–1**). Everything from clothing, makeup, and hair to the way a person walks, talks, and stands is evaluated.

▲ Figure 1–1 **First impressions are everything in the makeup industry.**

The media and social pressures reinforce the attitude that "Image is everything," and this idea is evident in the sales figures for cosmetics. According to the market research company, Euromonitor International, worldwide color cosmetics sales exceeded $36 billion in 2007, with nearly $10 billion brought in globally from eye makeup sales alone. The desire for ageless beauty is phenomenal, especially with heightened consumer awareness, antiaging concerns, and publishing materials such as *New Beauty Magazine*. Now is the perfect time to delve into this timeless profession.

STATE REGULATORY ALERT

Some states, such as New York, require that a makeup artist have either a cosmetology license or an esthetics license in order to charge a fee for applying cosmetics to the face. Check with your state to make sure you are not practicing outside of your legal scope of practice.

A FUTURE IN MAKEUP

It is very likely you have been a makeup artist for a long time, practicing makeovers on your friends and your family. Are you in a never-ending search for people who will let you re-create their look? If so, you have talent in your blood, and you are on the right career track. There is a reason that makeup artists are called "artists" and not makeup professionals or makeup technicians; makeup is truly an art. Makeup artistry requires an eye for color, symmetry and definition, and the ability to see and think in an original way.

Skilled makeup artists will find that their career paths can lead in many directions. Right now you may or may not know exactly where you want to take your makeup career, but one thing is certain: if you keep an open mind and work hard, you can find yourself in places beyond your dreams. In Chapter 19, Your Professional Image, and in Chapter 20, Business in Makeup, several possible career tracks will be discussed in detail, but take a look at the many options below.

▲ **Figure 1–2 You could work selling makeup in a department store.**

- **Independent Makeup Artist:**
  - Bridal
  - Photography
  - Video
  - Shows, pageants, proms, special events
- **Spa, Salon, or Skin Care Center Makeup Artist (Figure 1–2)**
- **Makeup Instructor/Trainer**
- **International Makeup Artist**
- **Cosmetic Company:**
  - Makeup Artist
  - Educator/Trainer
- **Mortuary Makeup**
- **Product Developer**
- **Camouflage Specialist**
- **Specialty Makeup Artist:**
  - Runway and High Fashion (**Figure 1–3**)
  - Print
  - Television and HD
  - Video
  - Theater

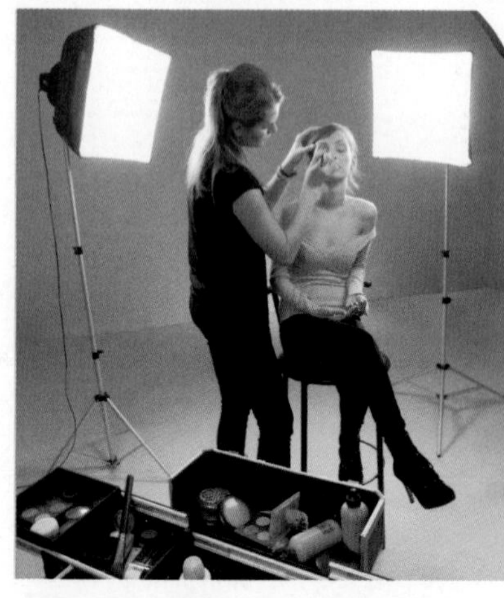

▲ **Figure 1–3 Working in high fashion and photography will always stay exciting.**

The list of opportunities is virtually endless, and new careers and concepts in makeup are being created on a daily basis. You may even have the opportunity to create your own position within the industry.

Most unique and exciting professions have an ever-changing, ever-evolving history that includes inspiration and attitude. The makeup profession has evolved over thousands of years of women and men striving to create status and identity. This striving continues today.

THE EVOLUTIONARY TIMELINE

Makeup artistry has evolved from the use of natural ingredients, such as copper, lead ore, arsenic, mercury, crushed berries, and burnt matches, to the use of the synthetic and mineral products of today. The desire for optimal beauty—and the cosmetic products used to create it—once resulted in the use of life-threatening products such as arsenic, lead, and mercury. Leeches were even used to provide the pale appearance deemed beautiful at one point in history. The history of the cosmetics industry's maturity has been climactic. Fortunately, for the practitioners and clients of today, this multibillion-dollar industry has come a very long way in its products and techniques.

© Eye Ubiquitous/SuperStock

▲ Figure 1–4 One form of African tribal face painting.

African Face Painting

African tribal face painting is an established and historically significant aspect of a tribal culture dating back to ancient times (**Figure 1–4**). Often used during ceremonies or in times of war, natural cosmetics served not only as forms of expression but also as a means of communication between different tribes. Although cosmetics were most commonly applied to the face, some tribes would arrive to battles or ceremonies wearing only a loin cloth with cosmetically produced patterns covering their entire bodies. The typical colors used were red, blue, yellow, and white. These colors were derived from raw materials—such as roots, berries, and clay—gathered from the local environment.

Did You Know?

Many African tribal cultures used face painting for occasions such as the birth of a child, as a sign of love and purity, and to signify a rite of passage into adulthood. These applications are still used today by many tribal cultures across the African Continent.

The Egyptians

Although African tribal cultures had probably been using cosmetics for many centuries before the Eygptians, the first recorded use of cosmetics dates back to approximately 3000 BC during the time of the first Egyptian dynasty. Upper-class Egyptians felt that decorating a person's eyes as well as other facial features was a way to beautify and set themselves apart from the lower classes. Eye makeup was worn by both men and women on a daily basis and was a part of their daily grooming routine (**Figure 1–5**). In fact, the use of eye makeup was spiritually linked, so even the poor did all they could to decorate their eyes. The class separation did not necessarily come from using eye makeup, but from the expense and quality of the products themselves, especially the applicators and jars.

The first eye makeup colors were black and green. **Mesdemet** was the first black eye shadow; it was created by the Egyptians using **galena**, the dark blue-gray ore of lead that in ancient times was mined off the coast of the Red Sea. Egyptians used **udju**, also known as **malachite**, the dark-green ore of copper mined in ancient times from the Sinai Desert, to line their lower eyelids.

© Elen/www.Shutterstock.com

▲ Figure 1–5 Egyptian women's makeup.

Did You Know?

Ancient Egyptians were not the only ones wearing makeup, and makeup was not only focused on the eyes. Ancient Mesopotamian women crushed semiprecious jewels and used them to decorate their lips. Red clay mixed with water was used to color their cheeks, and henna was used to dye their nails orange or yellow.

▲ Figure 1–6 **Ancient Egyptian makeup palette.**

Although Egyptians applied eye makeup for beautification, they believed that their cleanliness and beauty connected them to their spirituality and helped them ward off evil. Interestingly enough, not only was mesdemet used to ward off unwanted spirits, it acted as an insect repellent and disinfectant, keeping bugs away and reducing eye infections. To further darken and outline the eyes, the Egyptians created kohl makeup—a cosmetic product made up of lead, copper ores, burned almonds, ash, and various other ingredients—and used it as an eyeliner (**Figure 1–6**). The kohl had a powder consistency, and using a small stick, it was carefully applied around the eyes in an almond shape, accentuating the size and shape of the eyes. ☑ **LO1**

The term *cosmetae* was used to describe Roman slaves that were responsible for bathing, dressing, and adorning men and women of that era.

The Greeks and the Romans

The Greeks were the next to delve into the use of cosmetics. They were completely taken by the appearance and beauty of the Egyptians and quickly adopted Egyptian cosmetic uses, techniques, and products. However, the Greek use of cosmetics was for aesthetic purposes rather than spiritual purposes.

The Romans adored cosmetics, color, extravagance, and the beautification of the entire body. From lavish baths to eccentric cosmetic formulations (they made nail polish from heated sheep fat and blood), the Romans catapulted cosmetic use into a new era.

The Middle Ages

As the popularity of makeup grew, so did the emergence of cosmetics as a status symbol. From the fifth century to the fifteenth century and beyond, pale skin was a sign of wealth and status. This sought-after appearance led many European women of the sixth century to take drastic measures; they bled themselves to paleness using leeches. In contrast with the upper-class desire for paleness, Spanish prostitutes during this time period wore pink makeup to emphasize their features. Although makeup was a symbol of status, church leaders during the Middle Ages greatly frowned upon the use of cosmetics, believing it to be sinful and immoral.

The Italian Renaissance

The Italian Renaissance, like the Middle Ages, idealized pale complexions. As a sign of wealth and social status, both men and women used lead paint and powder made of arsenic to whiten their complexion (**Figure 1–7**). Women of the thirteenth century accentuated their pale complexions with bright pink lipstick. This more obvious makeup application showed that a family had the means to afford synthetic cosmetics.

Did You Know?

Native Americans also applied natural cosmetics to their horses to communicate rank during times of war.

Native American Cosmetics

Increased fifteenth century trade markets caused expeditions to be funded to discover new trade routes through the seas. It was during one of these expeditions, in the year 1492, that Christopher Columbus traveled to the American continents and the Native American people. Before the written word was first transcribed on surface of stone, Native American tribes covered their bodies in patterns and colors to communicate status and intention. The application of cosmetics to the faces and bodies of the tribal members was used during all special occasions, from religious ceremonies to declarations of war.

© SuperStock/SuperStock

▲ **Figure 1–7 A pale-faced woman of the Italian Renaissance.**

© Wolfgang Kaehler/SuperStock

▲ **Figure 1–8 An example of Native American face painting.**

Did You Know?

During the Elizabethan Era in Europe, the desire for a pale complexion continued (**Figure 1–9**). By the end of the Elizabethan Era and the beginning of the Stuart Era, an outbreak of disease had given people new admiration for rosy cheeks and a healthy color.

© Image Asset Management Ltd./SuperStock

▲ **Figure 1–9 Queen Elizabeth.**

Every tribe had a unique look and style of face painting that followed a ritualistic application, according to the tradition of their ancestors (**Figure 1–8**). Similar to the African tribal culture, the Native American tribal culture had cosmetics made from raw natural materials gathered from their surrounding environment. Some of the most common materials included various plants, berries, clay, and even duck feces.

The Stuart Era

As a new culture was being established in the Americas, the European culture was continuing to evolve. During the Stuart Era and the reign of King Charles II, the desire for a pale complexion took a brief break, with heavier cosmetics and darker foundation becoming popular. During this time, many people had pale skin from spending extended periods of time indoors due to illness or epidemics. The slightly darker complexion and

© The Art Archive/SuperStock

▲ **Figure 1–10 The Wife of King Charles II displaying the application of heavy cosmetics.**

© Exactostock/SuperStock

▲ **Figure 1–11 A young Geisha.**

The well-known courtesan, Catherine "Kitty" Fisher, who died in 1767, was probably killed by her use of toxin-filled, skin-whitening products.

rosy cheeks that became popular during this time signified healthy skin color and tone (**Figure 1–10**).

The Eighteenth Century: French Restoration

In the eighteenth century, people had various views about the use of makeup. Cosmetics used to whiten the face were made from toxic ingredients, including lead and carbonite, and many skin conditions and illnesses were attributed to their use. During this time, rouge and lipstick emerged, but their use was not popular among the higher classes. Healthy, spirited, and fun-loving women were the ones using red rouge and lipstick, and many people of the time considered those qualities a sign of prostitution and debauchery.

The Eighteenth Century: England

Because makeup had such a terrible reputation as a sign of prostitution and moral decay, during the late 1700s the British Parliament passed a law that allowed for a woman to be tried for the practice of witchcraft if she wore lipstick. A second law was passed to allow for the annulment of a marriage if a woman wore lipstick prior to her wedding day.

Geishas

Geishas are recognizable historical figures who wear intricate makeup. From their distinct style of dress (kimono) to their porcelain-white facial makeup, these women have become lasting and iconic figures in the history of makeup artistry.

Geishas endured hours of preparation and application to achieve their profession's desired appearance as entertainers and artisans in Japanese society. The women would first remove their eyebrows, commonly using a technique known as threading. The porcelain-white of their skin was created by using rice- or lead-based powders mixed with water to form a paste. This paste was applied as a thick foundation covering the face and neck. From this foundation the dramatic features could be boldly emphasized. The final cosmetic application included dark eyebrows painted high on the forehead, red lips stained using benibana or safflower juices, and eyes outlined with coal (**Figure 1–11**).

The Regency Era

During the Regency Era, most women wore makeup daily, and most men no longer did. Makeup had been feminized, and the only men who continued to wear it were from the upper class. During this era, **pallor**, a pale, colorless complexion or appearance, continued to be desirable because it represented a life of leisure. Tanned skin was a tell-tale sign of working outside and as such, a sign of being in the lower economic class. Wealthy people—those who could stay inside, out of the sun—came to prize their pale skin as a sign of wealth and class (**Figure 1–12**). When women, even country women, went outside, they tried to cover all exposed areas of their skin: They wore sun bonnets, gloves, and scarves, and they carried parasols. Skin whiteners were still made from toxic ingredients such as lead and mercury and still posed a threat to the wearer's health—nevertheless, many people continued to wear them in an effort to have white skin. Other makeup recipes of this time used herbs, flowers, fat, brandy, vegetables, and crushed strawberries.

Some of the first commercially produced cosmetics were developed in the 1800s by local pharmacists known as apothecaries. Even though apothecaries usually worked to keep people healthy, many of their cosmetic creations contained highly dangerous and poisonous ingredients such as mercury, nitric acid, and belladonna. Today apothecaries are still well known for homeopathic remedies; however, they now use natural ingredients such as herbs, flowers, and plants to produce medicinal creams and remedies for illnesses and skin conditions (**Figure 1–14**).

© iStockphoto/mikeklee

▲ **Figure 1–12** Upper-class woman with a pale complexion.

Did You Know?

Carminic acid, a bright-red acid produced by cochineal insects, was used as a cosmetic color in lipstick as far back as the nineteenth century. Cochineal insects live on cactus in Mexico and Central America and produce the color to keep other insects away (**Figure 1–13**).

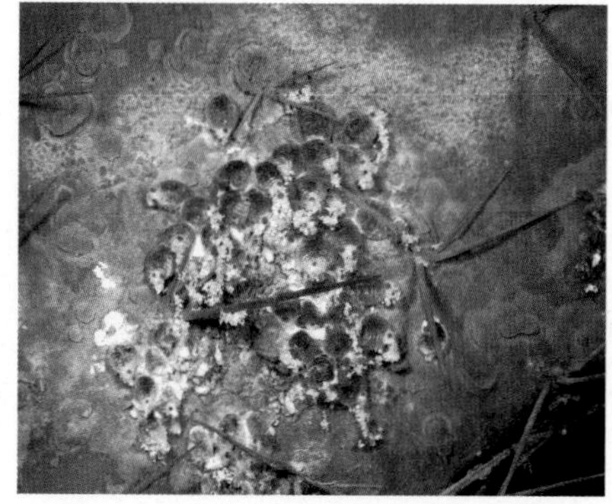
© Dr. Morley Read/www.Shutterstock.com

▲ **Figure 1–13** Cochineal insects on a cactus leaf.

© iStockphoto/halbergman

▲ **Figure 1–14** Apothecary jars.

The Victorian Era

The Victorian Era lasted from 1837–1901. During this time Queen Victoria made several statements linking the use of cosmetics to actresses and prostitutes, two classes of people that were widely considered to be synonymous.

Any alteration in natural skin color was frowned upon, so commercial cosmetics were not widely available. Because of this women would rub red beet juice into their cheeks to create a natural, flushed appearance. Women were also known to tweeze their eyebrows, massage castor oil into their eyelashes, and use rice powder to dust their noses. Although colorful lipstick was not used, clear pomade was applied to the lips to add a glossy sheen. Other, more discreet, women would simply give their cheeks some color with a quick pinch when nobody was looking. Eventually the use of makeup began to regain social acceptance and popularity. Full-faced, full-color makeup was still frowned upon by many and even considered a sign of questionable moral standing, but healthy,

For many centuries, men commonly wore a variety of cosmetics. King George IV, for example, not only wore makeup, but also invested a small fortune in cold creams, powders, and concoctions of paste.

© K. Thorsen/www.Shutterstock.com

▲ Figure 1–15 A woman of the Victorian Era.

The California Perfume Company was founded in 1886 by a former bookseller, David H. McConnell, who wanted to provide individuals the opportunity to get out of agricultural and manufacturing jobs and become their own bosses. In 1939 the California Perfume Company became Avon. Today Avon is sold in 134 countries and does approximately $8 billion in annual sales.

Permanent makeup, which is considered trendy and advanced today, actually got its start over 100 years ago. In the early 1900s, a British man by the name of George Burchette became one of the first widely known professional tattoo artists. Also known as "The Beauty Doctor," Mr. Burchette was one of the first people to tattoo lipstick on women's lips.

pinch-cheeked, natural-looking makeup was quickly gaining acceptance (**Figure 1–15**). ✓ **LO2**

The Nineteenth Century

The turn of the century saw vast changes in the world of beauty and cosmetics. The desire for a healthy, natural, and youthful appearance continued, taking with it a growing investment in personal care and appearance.

In 1896 the first commercial brand of facial cream was produced. An entrepreneurial woman by the name of Mrs. Francis Henning opened one of history's most famous salons, the House of Cyclax, on South Molton Street in London. At this time it was not accepted practice to visit beauty salons, and women would sneak in through back doors so that they would not be recognized or caught getting help to look more natural and beautiful. Mrs. Henning sold her own mixtures of facial creams and cosmetics; soon to be marketed as the Cyclex Cosmetic brand. Not only is the Cyclex Cosmetic brand still in business today, in 1961 it was granted (and still holds) the Royal Warrant by Her Majesty Queen Elizabeth II. The Royal Warrant is a mark of distinction and recognition, and it is given only to companies that supply products to the Royal Family.

The Twentieth Century

During the early twentieth century, the true makeup revolution took off. Makeup became fashionable in the United States and Europe due to the influence of ballet and theater stars, and it became even more popular with the emergence of the movie industry and the stars of Hollywood. These eras laid the foundation for women's creative freedom to amplify their own beauty.

The pale skin of prior eras took a complete turnaround. The wealthy and elite spent their leisure time traveling and basking on the beaches and at newly established premier resorts. As a result, a tanned complexion became a sign of wealth and prosperity.

1901-1920

During the early 1900s advances in cosmetics applications began to rapidly emerge. For years women had been using homemade mascara. This homemade cosmetic staple consisted of hot beads of wax on the tips of their lashes to enhance their length, thickness, and color. In the early 1900s, T.L Williams produced the first retail mascara, named after his sister Mabel. Today this company is known as Maybelline.

During this time, lipstick took the leap into a fancy new metal case that was designed by Maurice Levy, and the first pressed powders were introduced, complete with their own mirror and powder puff applicator—packaging that is still used today.

Women's confidence continued to grow, along with their desire to create a more beautiful and youthful appearance. Cosmetics were no longer secretly sold in private salons; instead, women by the thousands openly used cosmetics. As a result, sales of salon services skyrocketed. The first salon to openly display and retail cosmetics, Selfridges, was opened in 1909 in London by a Wisconsin native, Harry Gordon. Selfridges' flagship store is still open today. It monopolizes 540,000 square feet (50,000 square meters) on Oxford Street and houses everything from a salon and cosmetic products to clothing, shoes, toys, furniture, jewelry, and housewares.

The 1920s

The Roaring Twenties belonged to the Flappers, a brand new woman! **Flappers** were Northern, urban, single, young middle-class women in the 1920s who had their own jobs, disposable income, and independence. Flapper styles—which embraced dark eyes, red lipstick, and red nail polish—contributed to the liberation of women and the beginning of the mass market for cosmetics.

Coco Chanel, a famous designer who spent lavish leisure time in Monte Carlo and the French Riviera, created the widely held belief that tanned skin represented high sophistication. During this time period, fake tanning products were created and became fashionably popular among the wealthy and elite.

Lipstick also took on a whole new role during this decade. New lip colors were created, and various shades of red were widely used. Lipstick was carefully applied to the lips using the "Cupid's Bow" technique, inspired by actress Clara Bow, to create a perfectly shaped feminine lip (**Figure 1–16**).

© Howard Rose/SuperStock

▲ Figure 1–16 **The perfectly formed "Cupid's Bow" lips.**

During the 1920s, much like today, the lips and the eyes received the most cosmetic attention. For years women had been using various ingredients to enhance the eye. This era introduced the first eyelash curler, Kurlash (**Figure 1–17**). Although it was expensive and difficult to use, it instantly earned a position in the marketplace—the price deterred very few customers!

© Underwood Photo Archives/SuperStock

▲ Figure 1–17 **Use of makeup's first eyelash curler.**

The 1930s

Elizabeth Arden opened a beauty parlor in the 1930s. This new type of beauty parlor helped the average woman gain access to an assortment of colors and types of makeup, and this prompted other cosmetic companies to begin to create a wide selection of lipstick colors. The ongoing availability, wide selection, and acceptance of lipstick positioned it as a symbol of female sexuality and maturity (**Figure 1–18**). The use of lipstick by teenage girls at this time was most certainly frowned upon and viewed by many adults as an act of rebellion.

© SuperStock/SuperStock

▲ Figure 1–18 **A beautiful woman applying dark red lipstick, a symbol of maturity in the 1930s.**

© Omer N Raja/www.Shutterstock.com

▲ Figure 1–19 A modern Middle Eastern woman with henna-outlined eyes.

A 1935 edition of *Vogue* magazine featured Turkish women outlining their eyes with a deep-colored henna in an almond shape, much like the ancient Egyptians had done (**Figure 1–19**). The magazine's popularity took off in high fashion and led to the introduction of the term *vamp*, because of similarity between the eyes featured on the magazine's models and dark-lined vampire eyes.

The 1940s

World War II made it necessary for women to work in typically male-dominated professions such as engineering and scientific research. Hazel Bishop, an organic chemist in New York and New Jersey, turned her skills toward cosmetics, and in the late 1940s she created the first long-lasting lipstick, called No-Smear lipstick. With the help of a local advertiser, Raymond Specter, Bishop's lipstick business thrived.

During the war, many people sought escape in film and theater. As a result, movie stars' looks and styles started to set trends for the looks and styles of the general population.

In 1930s Hollywood, individuals began to be hired specifically to apply makeup. This was the introduction of the Makeup Artist.

The 1950s

During the 1950s, cosmetics began to be considered a necessity for many women creating a need for a diverse selection of cosmetic types; and the advertising to go along with it. For a short time, throw-away lipstick cases were used, but the focus quickly shifted from the lips to the eyes as a result of Audrey Hepburn's cat eyes (**Figure 1–20**). Hollywood glamour girls, such as Marilyn Monroe and Elizabeth Taylor, had an enormous impact on beauty styles. Bridget Bardot, a French actress, caught the attention of the world with her sultry, dark, smoky eyes and pale lips. To further accent the eyes, diverse colors of mascara were introduced to the market. Blue, green, and even purple mascara gained popularity over the more common brown and black.

© Science and Society/SuperStock

▲ Figure 1–20 Audrey Hepburn.

The 1960s

The 1960s was a youth-oriented decade, with baby boomers coming of age and defining the era as their own. Each counterculture of the time had its own innovative style. A variety of popular makeup looks were born—from the natural application of the hippie to the heavy and dramatic looks of the Mod trend. For the liberated, fun-loving, freedom-fighting hippies, makeup was intended to look natural (if it was worn at all), but the use of vibrant colors and images painted on the face and body certainly was popular.

The 1960s and 1970s countercultures used makeup as a form of expression, particularly with the growing women's movement. Some people involved in the feminist movement wore very little makeup because they associated cosmetics with the objectification of women as sex objects rather than individuals; they believed that makeup played a role in the second-class status of women. Other feminists felt that makeup could accelerate the revolution, releasing them from the static and subdued roles their mothers played in the 1940s and 1950s.

A larger demographic of women were following the trends of such fashion icons as Twiggy and Edie Sedgwick. A heavy-handed makeup application and dramatic expression of the eyes became popular due to the women associated with the Mod trend. This 1960s trend began in London and crossed borders through fashion magazines, music, art, and celebrities like Edie Sedgwick. British teenager and "it girl" Twiggy, known as the first supermodel, was an icon for this particular look. She perpetuated a look in which the lashes were either false or mascara was applied so heavily that they appeared to be. The lips were left pale, drawing attention to the drama of the eye makeup. The cheeks were given a hollow look, to make the thin models look even thinner.

During the 1960s, the wand applicator for tube mascara was invented and introduced. Before this new application technique, mascara was applied using a wet brush dipped into a colored powder. Once the mascara was applied, the woman would have to wait for the paste to harden.

The 1960s was rich with new trends and new forms of expression, most of which were enhanced by the innovative use of makeup (**Figure 1–21**). ✓ **LO3**

Did You Know?

Max Factor & Company is a cosmetics company founded in 1909 by Maximilian Faktorowicz (1877—1938), a Polish-Jewish cosmetician credited with coining the term *makeup*. He had spent years creating formulations for cosmetics, and when he arrived in Los Angeles he was appalled at the appearance and application of makeup on actors and actresses. As a result, Max Factor created the first makeup designed to not crack or cake even during the longest of performances; this product is known today as pancake makeup.

The 1970s

The hippies' desire for a more natural look continued into the 1970s. Prior to this time the majority of cosmetics were for Caucasian and pale skin tones. During the 1970s, several cosmetic companies began to cater to the cosmetic needs of women with darker skin tones that appeared gray and sallow when using the lighter foundation colors (**Figure 1–22**). Large cosmetic companies saw the untapped market for darker skin tones and launched key cosmetic products such as foundation and powder formulated for darker skin. This trend flourished; today's cosmetic color selection caters to the wide array of skin tones encountered across cultures.
✓ **LO4**

▲ **Figure 1–21 A young woman in 1960s style displaying a Mod trend look.**

The Twenty-First Century

From the end of the twentieth century through the start of the twenty-first century, makeup continues to be among the most rapidly changing products in the consumer market (**Figure 1–23**). It continues to grow as a staple of most women's, and even many men's, daily grooming routines.

Many ritualistic makeup applications are still in practice today with Geishas, Native Americans, and African tribal members still holding onto tradition. Even in these cultures, most makeup is now composed of synthetic materials. However, a worldwide trend toward organic makeup is quickly gaining popularity as a result of growing environmental consciousness. In 2007 the worldwide sales of organic cosmetics soared to $7 billion.

▶ **Figure 1–22 In the 1970s makeup for the African American Woman was specialized.**

© Alena Ozerova/www.Shutterstock.com

▲ **Figure 1–23 In the twenty-first century trends change every day.**

The makeup trends of today change with the seasons. With new developments in technology and social networking, makeup artistry has the unique ability to experience new developments almost daily. The twenty-first century fashion trends and industry goals no longer involve emulating your favorite celebrity; the new trends are all about self-expression. Makeup is applied to accommodate every individual's unique features. The use of makeup is no longer a symbol of status and is worn by many different people in numerous diverse cultural and social groups across the globe.

In terms of annual sales, the United States leads the cosmetic industry with $52.761 billion in annual sales, about 42 percent of the worldwide total. The "Top 100" ranks the world's largest cosmetics manufacturers by beauty sales. In 2004, the total annual sales were $124.539 billion, and the top countries, along with each country's number of top-ranking cosmetic sales companies, were as follows: United States: 34; France: 16; Italy: 11; Germany: 10; Japan: 9; United Kingdom: 6; Russia, South Korea, and Switzerland: 3; Spain and Brazil: 2; Sweden: 1.

As the demand for quality cosmetics continues, a market for prestige and premium-brand cosmetics becomes more established. The 2009 *Euromonitor International Colour Cosmetic Report* stated that annual sales of premium color cosmetics in the US were $3.4 billion, creating a niche market of not only quality ingredients and quality cosmetics, but a higher price-point to match.

AN EVER-CHANGING ERA

In 1963, Mary Kay Ash, an entrepreneur from Dallas, Texas, started a home-based cosmetic sales business. Mary Kay is now sold in more than 33 countries, has over 900,000 independent distributors, and does over $1 billion in annual sales.

Every era and every decade brings with it new trends, styles, products, colors, and techniques for makeup users and makeup professionals. But one thing never changes: every customer is different, and every customer has his or her own individual desired look. Your professional responsibility is to stay informed about cutting-edge trends and colors and learn how to incorporate them into your daily work.

Every day history is being made, and in the makeup profession, you are about to become part of that history. In fact, you are making history in a profession with few hard and fast rules or guidelines. You can make your own rules, inspired by the artist and vision inside you. Your creative gifts and keen eye for color will elevate you and your skills to a unique level; others will also rise, but because no two makeup artists are alike, they too will stand alone. Live your life through the eyes of an artist, and provide the world with the gift of beauty.

This textbook will provide the cornerstone of your skills and the fine-tuning of your unique artistic traits. Use the information and skills in the pages that follow to mold your future in Makeup.

Review Questions

1. As early as 3000 BC, what ingredients did Egyptians use to create makeup?
2. What was the total revenue generated by color cosmetic sales in 2007?
3. List some of the possible career options for a makeup artist.
4. Which cultural look included the application of dark eyebrows painted high on the forehead, red lips, and eyes outlined with coal?
5. Why did Native Americans cover their bodies in patterns and colors?
6. During the European Middle Ages, what look signified wealth?
7. What was used to lighten the face during the Italian Renaissance?
8. In the 1800s local pharmacists made many cosmetics; what were these pharmacists called?
9. In which century did the true makeup revolution begin?
10. What was the first eyelash curler called?
11. What was Clara Bow's name used to describe?
12. During the 1960s and 1970s, what political movement played a key role in minimizing the use of makeup for many women?

Chapter Glossary

carminic acid	A bright-red acid produced by cochineal insects; used as a cosmetic color in lipstick back as far as the nineteenth century. Cochineal insects live on cactus in Mexico and Central America and produce the color to keep other insects away.
Flapper	Northern, urban, single, young middle-class women in the 1920s that had their own jobs, disposable income, and independence.
galena	The dark blue-gray ore of lead that in ancient times was mined off the coast of the Red Sea (used to make mesdemet).
mesdemet	The first black eye shadow; it was created by the Egyptians using galena.
pallor	A pale, colorless complexion or appearance.
udju	Also known as *malachite*, the dark-green ore of copper mined in ancient times from the Sinai Desert and used by Egyptians to line their lower eyelids.

Chapter 2 Infection Control: Principles and Practices

Chapter Outline

Learning Objectives

After completing this chapter, you will be able to:

- ☑ **LO1** Understand regulatory agencies and the differences between them.
- ☑ **LO2** List the types and classifications of bacteria.
- ☑ **LO3** Define hepatitis and Human Immunodeficiency Virus (HIV) and explain how they are transmitted.
- ☑ **LO4** Explain the differences between cleaning, disinfecting, and sterilizing.
- ☑ **LO5** List the types of disinfectants and how they are used.
- ☑ **LO6** Discuss Universal and Standard Precautions.
- ☑ **LO7** List your responsibilities as a makeup artist.
- ☑ **LO8** Describe how to safely clean and disinfect tools and implements.

Key Terms

Page number indicates where in the chapter the term is used.

accelerated hydrogen peroxide(AHP)
pg. 36

acquired immune deficiency syndrome (AIDS)
pg. 30

acquired immunity
pg. 32

allergy
pg. 33

antiseptics
pg. 39

asymptomatic
pg. 43

bacilli
pg. 26

bacteria (microbes or germs)
pg. 25

bactericidal
pg. 25

bioburden
pg. 34

bloodborne pathogens
pg. 30

body substance isolation (BSI)
pg. 40

clean (cleaning)
pg. 25

cocci
pg. 26

contagious disease (communicable disease)
pg. 28

contamination
pg. 29

decontamination
pg. 32

diagnosis
pg. 29

diplococci
pg. 26

direct transmission
pg. 27

disease
pg. 24

disinfectants
pg. 23

Key Terms *(continued)*

Page number indicates where in the chapter the term is used.

disinfection
pg. 25

efficacy
pg. 34

exposure incident
pg. 43

folliculitis
pg. 31

fungi
pg. 31

fungicidal
pg. 25

hepatitis
pg. 30

hospital disinfectants
pg. 23

human immunodeficiency virus (HIV)
pg. 30

immunity
pg. 32

indirect transmission
pg. 27

infection
pg. 24

infection control
pg. 25

infectious
pg. 29

infectious disease
pg. 25

inflammation
pg. 27

local infection
pg. 27

Material Safety Data Sheet (MSDS)
pg. 23

methicillin-resistant staphylococcus aureus (MRSA)
pg. 28

microorganism
pg. 26

mildew
pg. 31

multiuse (reusable)
pg. 37

natural immunity
pg. 32

nonpathogenic
pg. 26

nonporous
pg. 23

occupational disease
pg. 29

parasites
pg. 31

parasitic disease
pg. 29

pathogenic
pg. 26

pathogenic disease
pg. 29

personal protective equipment (PPE)
pg. 40

pus
pg. 27

quaternary ammonium compounds (quats)
pg. 36

sanitize
pg. 25

scabies
pg. 31

single-use (disposable)
pg. 37

sodium hypochlorite
pg. 36

spirilla
pg. 26

Standard Precautions (SP)
pg. 40

staphylococci
pg. 26

sterilization
pg. 33

streptococci
pg. 26

systemic disease
pg. 29

tinea capitis
pg. 31

toxins
pg. 27

tuberculocidal disinfectants
pg. 24

tuberculosis
pg. 24

Universal Precautions (UP)
pg. 43

virucidal
pg. 25

virus
pg. 28

Career Profile

Growing up as a dancer, Krissy Ferro developed a love for makeup at an early age. Following that passion she launched her career in cosmetology. Her affinity for the way in which makeup can transform and affect a woman piqued her interest in everything about makeup, including its composition. Her company, Ferro Cosmetics, was created to address the problems she found in the ingredients of makeup. Using 100 percent natural products, Krissy is continuing to influence the way both clients and makeup artists look at makeup.

"I've been using makeup my entire life, beginning at the age of 3 in my first dance recital. For the next 23 years, I performed professionally. After I left dance, I still loved the beauty and glam of makeup and hair. For that reason I pursued a career in cosmetology.

"After receiving a license in cosmetology, I opened my first salon and day spa. Initially, hair was central. Makeup was a service I offered only for weddings and special occasions. However, I found that many women didn't understand makeup, were afraid of it, or were severely allergic to it. By incorporating makeup consultations into my hair appointments and by utilizing the time clients spent processing as a time to review what they liked and didn't like about their look, I fell in love with makeup artistry. By styling hair I helped women achieve confidence, and with makeup I gave them even more. You can't instantly change the size of your jeans, but with makeup you can instantly change your look—and you can love it!

"I began working for a well-known makeup company in the Buffalo, NY, area, working home parties to sell products; however, I found myself giving everyone makeovers instead. I quickly rose in the ranks of the company and began receiving corporate recognition as a makeup artist. Through the clientele I built with this corporation, I began receiving calls from customers who loved the work I did but were having allergic reactions to the products. After extensive research I found the problem in the composition of the product; it was not 100 percent natural, and it needed to be in order to perform like a professional line. I decided to use my experience as a makeup artist, my knowledge of color theory developed during my work as an educator for two high-profile professional lines, and thousands of hours of research and development to create my very own line of mineral makeup.

I am now an advocate of natural skin care products. I work with high-profile celebrities and photographers along with everyday women. I even did makeup for the 2012 edition of the very book that taught me to be a professional - *Milady Standard Cosmetology*.

Having a thorough understanding of infection control principles and practices is necessary when dealing with the public and coming into direct contact with clients' skin on a daily basis. Responsible professionals in the field of makeup must understand the types of infections they may encounter. Practicing the basics of cleaning and disinfecting and following federal and state rules will safeguard your health as well as the health of your clients.

To do this, you must understand the chemistry of cleaning and disinfecting products, along with the proper methods of use.

WHY STUDY INFECTION CONTROL: PRINCIPLES AND PRACTICES?

Makeup artists should study and have a thorough understanding of infection control principles and practices because:

- Knowledge of products and practices to prevent the spread of infection will ensure a safe work environment for the makeup artist and the client.
- Multiple federal and state agencies have placed regulations on the Cosmetology industry that you need to be aware of.
- As a makeup artist you will have daily contact with your clients' skin and bodily openings such as the eyes, nose, and mouth.
- Practicing universal infection control procedures will be an asset to the makeup artist's professional image.

REGULATION

Many different federal and state agencies regulate the practice of cosmetology and esthetics, and—although few agencies regulate makeup—the practice of makeup application is embedded in the beauty business and therefore falls within the more general rules and regulations. These agencies regulate everything from manufacturing, sales, uses of product, equipment licensing specifications, and professional conduct.

Federal Agencies

Federal agencies set guidelines for the manufacturing, sale, and use of equipment and chemical ingredients. These guidelines also monitor safety in the workplace and place limits on the types of services you can perform.

Occupational Safety and Health Administration (OSHA)

The Occupational Safety and Health Administration (OSHA) was created as part of the U.S. Department of Labor to regulate and enforce safety and health standards to protect employees in the workplace. Regulating employee exposure to potentially toxic substances and informing employees about the possible hazards of materials used in the workplace are key points of the Occupational Safety and Health Act of 1970. Because of these regulations, the Hazard Communication Standard (HCS) was created, requiring that chemical manufacturers and importers assess the potential hazards associated with their products. The Material Safety Data Sheet (MSDS) is a result of the HCS.

The standards set by OSHA are important because they address issues relating to the handling, mixing, storing, and disposing of products; general safety in the workplace; and your right to know about any potentially hazardous ingredients contained in the products you use and how to avoid these hazards.

Material Safety Data Sheet (MSDS)

Both federal and state laws require that, for all products sold, manufacturers supply a **Material Safety Data Sheet (MSDS)**, information compiled by the manufacturer about product safety including the names of hazardous ingredients, safe handling and use procedures, precautions to reduce the risk of accidental harm or overexposure, and flammability warnings. The MSDS also provides useful disposal guidelines and medical and first aid information.

OSHA and state regulatory agencies require that MSDSs be kept available for all products in a place of business. Both OSHA and state board inspectors can issue fines to beauty-related businesses that do not have MSDSs available during regular business hours. MSDSs often can be downloaded from the product manufacturer's or the distributor's Web site. Not having MSDSs available poses a health risk to anyone exposed to hazardous materials and violates federal and state regulations. All employees must read the information included on each MSDS and verify that they have read it by adding their signatures to the sign-off sheet. These sign-off sheets must be available to state and federal inspectors upon request.

Environmental Protection Agency (EPA)

The Environmental Protection Agency (EPA) registers many types of disinfectants sold and used in the United States. **Disinfectants** (dis-in-FEK-tents) are chemical products that destroy all bacteria, fungi, and viruses (but not spores) on surfaces. The two types most frequently used in the makeup profession are hospital disinfectants and tuberculocidal disinfectants.

- **Hospital disinfectants** (HOS-pih-tal dis-in-FEK-tents) are disinfectants that are effective for cleaning blood and body fluids. They can be used on any nonporous surfaces in the workplace. **Nonporous** (nahn-POHW-rus) means that an item is made or constructed of a material that has no pores or openings and cannot absorb liquids. Hospital disinfectants control the

spread of **disease** (dih-ZEEZ), an abnormal condition of all or part of the body, or its systems or organs, that makes the body incapable of carrying on normal function. Chapter 3, Facial Anatomy and Physiology, delves more into skin abnormalities, including those which a makeup artist can continue to work on and those which must be referred to a physician.

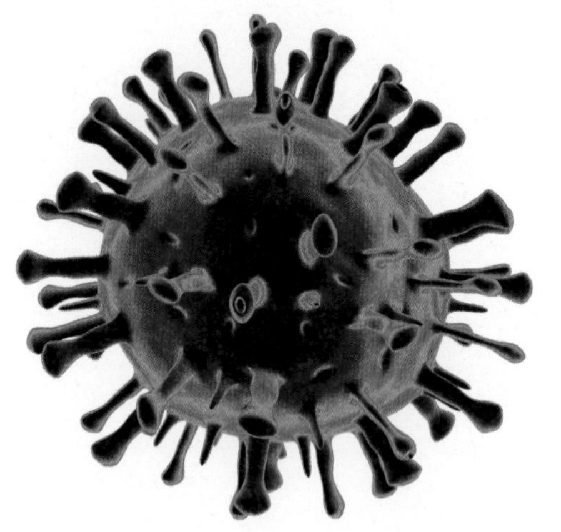

© iStockphoto/Mile Atanasov

- **Tuberculocidal disinfectants** (tuh-bur-kyoo-LOH-sy-dahl dis-in-FEK-tents) are disinfectants that kill the bacteria that cause **tuberculosis** (tuh-bur-kyoo-LOH-sus), a disease that is transmitted through coughing or sneezing. These bacteria are capable of forming spores, so they are difficult to kill. Tuberculocidal disinfectants are one kind of hospital disinfectant. However, the fact that tuberculocidal disinfectants are more powerful does not mean that you should automatically reach for them. Some of these products can be harmful to tools and equipment, and they require special methods of disposal.

It is against federal law to use any disinfecting product contrary to its labeling. Before manufacturers can sell a product for disinfecting tools, implements, or equipment, they must obtain an EPA-registration number that certifies that the disinfectant may be used in the manner prescribed by the manufacturer's label. This means that if you do not follow the label instructions for mixing, contact time, and the type of surface the disinfecting product can be used on, you are not complying with federal law. If there is a lawsuit, you will be held responsible.

STATE REGULATORY ALERT

Check the rules in your state to be sure that the product you choose for disinfection complies with state requirements.

State Regulatory Agencies

State agencies regulate licensing, enforcement, and your conduct when you are working. State regulatory agencies exist to protect professionals and to protect consumers' health, safety, and welfare while they receive makeup services. State regulatory agencies include licensing agencies, state boards of cosmetology, commissions, and health departments. The regulatory agencies require that everyone working in any beauty-related business follow specific procedures. Enforcement of the rules through inspections and investigations of consumer complaints is also part of an agency's responsibility. An agency can issue penalties against the salon or business owner and the makeup artist's license. Penalties vary and include warnings, fines, probation, and suspension or revocation of licenses. It is vital that you understand and follow the rules of your state at all times. Not doing so puts your reputation, your license, and everyone's safety in jeopardy. ☑ LO1

PRINCIPLES OF INFECTION

A career as a makeup professional is exciting and rewarding, but it is also a great responsibility. One careless action could cause injury or **infection** (in-FEK-shun), the invasion of body tissues by disease-causing pathogens. Preventing the spread of infection requires knowing proper infection control procedures and following them at all times. Prevention begins and ends with you (**Figure 2–1**).

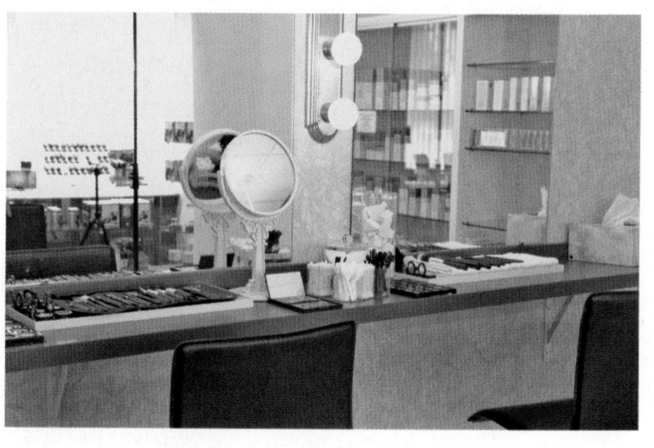

© Milady, a part of Cengage Learning. Photography by Visual Recollection.

▲ Figure 2–1 **A clean, neat makeup work area gains your client's confidence.**

Infection Control

Infection control refers to the methods used to eliminate or reduce the transmission of infectious organisms. There are four types of potentially harmful organisms that can directly affect the makeup environment:

- Bacteria
- Viruses
- Fungi
- Parasites

Under certain conditions, many of these organisms can cause infectious disease. An **infectious disease** (in-FEK-shus dih-ZEEZ) is a disease caused by pathogenic (harmful) microorganisms that enter the body. An infectious disease may or may not be spread from one person to another person.

Professional makeup artists must understand how to properly clean and disinfect tools and equipment so they are safe for both artists and clients. To **clean** (cleaning) is a mechanical process (scrubbing) using soap and water or detergent and water to remove all visible dirt, debris, and many disease-causing germs from tools, implements, and equipment; cleaning also removes invisible debris that interferes with disinfection, and it is required before disinfecting. You will also find that many commercially available products used in the cleaning and disinfecting process continue to use the words *sanitize* and *sanitizing*. The term **sanitize** is defined as a chemical process for reducing the number of disease-causing germs on cleaned surfaces to a safe level.

As a makeup artist you cannot perform services or recommend treatments for infections, diseases, or serious skin conditions. Clients with such problems should be referred to their physicians.

The chemical process of **disinfection** (dis-in-FEK-shun) destroys most, but not necessarily all, harmful microrganisms on environmental surfaces. Disinfection is not effective against all bacterial spores.

Cleaning and disinfecting procedures are designed to prevent the spread of infection and disease. Disinfectants used in salons must be **bactericidal** (back-teer-uh-SYD-ul), capable of destroying bacteria; **virucidal** (vy-ru-SYD-ul), capable of destroying viruses; and **fungicidal** (fun-jih-SYD-ul), capable of destroying fungi. Be sure to mix and use these disinfectants according to label instructions so they are safe and effective.

Contaminated implements and tools can spread infections from client to client if the proper disinfection steps are not taken after every service. You have a professional and legal obligation to protect clients from harm by using proper infection control procedures. If clients are infected or harmed because you performed infection control procedures incorrectly, you may be found legally responsible for their injuries or infections.

Bacteria

Bacteria (bak-TEER-ee-ah) (singular: bacterium, back-TEER-ee-um), also known as **microbes** (MY-krohbs) or **germs**, are one-celled microorganisms

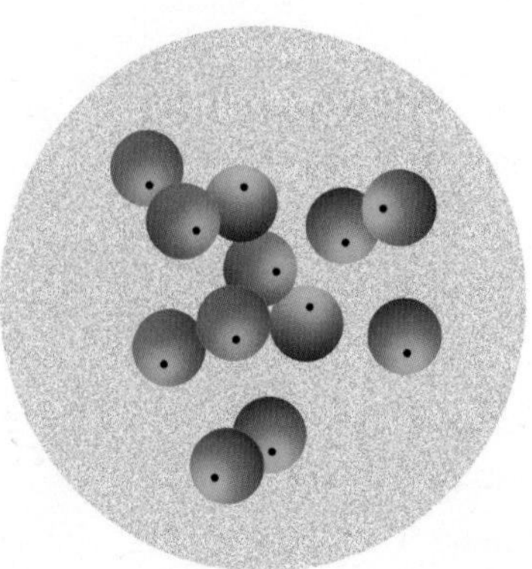

▲ Figure 2–2 Cocci.

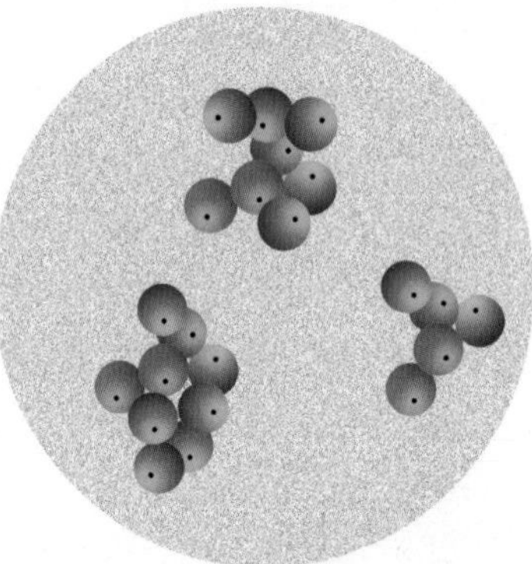

▲ Figure 2–3 Staphylococci.

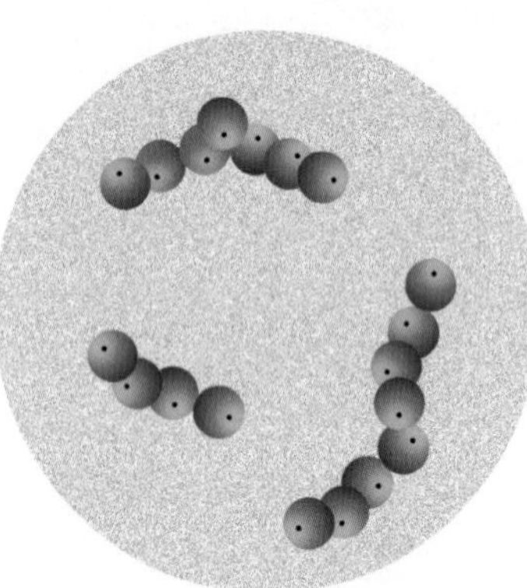

▲ Figure 2–4 Streptococci.

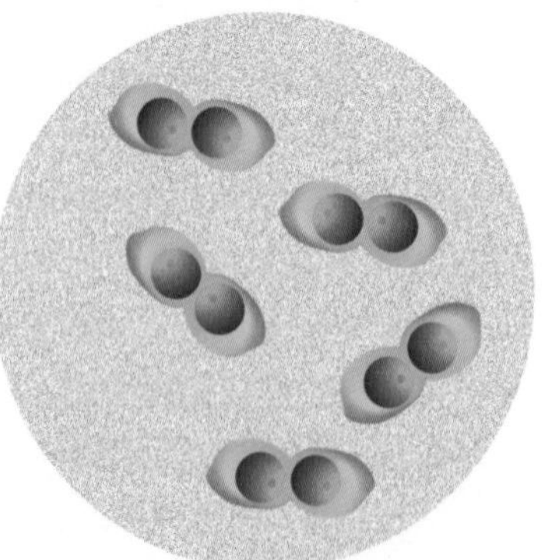

▲ Figure 2–5 Diplococci.

that have both plant and animal characteristics; some are harmful, but most are harmless. A **microorganism** (my-kroh-OR-gah-niz-um) is any organism of microscopic or submicroscopic size. Bacteria can exist almost anywhere: on skin; in water; in the air; in decayed matter; on environmental surfaces; in body secretions; on clothing; on brushes, tools, and implements; and under the free edge of nails. Bacteria are so small they can only be seen by using a microscope.

Types of Bacteria

The thousands of different kinds of bacteria all fall into two primary categories: pathogenic and nonpathogenic. Most bacteria are **nonpathogenic** (non-path-uh-JEN-ik), harmless organisms that may perform useful functions and are safe to come in contact with since they do not cause disease or harm. Nonpathogenic bacteria are used to make yogurt, cheese, and some medicines. In the human body, nonpathogenic bacteria help the body break down food and protect against infection. They also stimulate the immune system.

Pathogenic (path-uh-JEN-ik) bacteria are harmful microorganisms that can cause disease or infection in humans when they invade the body. Following strict standards for cleaning and disinfecting will prevent the spread of pathogenic microorganisms. It is crucial that you, as a makeup artist, learn proper infection control practices while in school to ensure that you understand the importance of following them throughout your career. **Table 2–1**, Causes of Disease, presents terms and definitions related to pathogens.

Classifications of Pathogenic Bacteria

Bacteria have three distinct shapes that help to identify them. Pathogenic bacteria are classified as described below.

- **Cocci** (KOK-sy) are round-shaped bacteria that appear singly (alone) or in the following groups (**Figure 2–2**):
    - **Staphylococci** (staf-uh-loh-KOK-sy) are pus-forming bacteria that grow in clusters like bunches of grapes and are responsible for causing abscesses, pustules, and boils (**Figure 2–3**). Some types of staphylococci (or *staph* as many people call it) may not cause infections in healthy humans.
    - **Streptococci** (strep-toh-KOK-sy) are pus-forming bacteria arranged in curved lines resembling a string of beads. They cause infections such as strep throat and blood poisoning (**Figure 2–4**).
    - **Diplococci** (dip-lo-KOK-sy) are spherical bacteria that grow in pairs and cause diseases such as pneumonia (**Figure 2–5**).
- **Bacilli** (bah-SIL-ee) are short rod-shaped bacteria; they are the most common bacteria and produce diseases such as tetanus (lockjaw), typhoid fever, tuberculosis, and diphtheria (**Figure 2–6**).
- **Spirilla** (spy-RIL-ah) are spiral or corkscrew-shaped bacteria that cause diseases such as syphilis (a sexually transmitted disease or

TABLE 2–1	
CAUSES OF DISEASE	
TERM	**DEFINITION**
BACTERIA	One-celled microorganisms having both plant and animal characteristics. Some are harmful and some are harmless.
DIRECT TRANSMISSION	Transmission of blood or body fluids through touching (including shaking hands), kissing, coughing, sneezing, and talking.
GERMS	Nonscientific synonym for disease-producing organisms.
INDIRECT TRANSMISSION	Transmission of blood or body fluids through contact with an intermediate contaminated object such as a razor, extractor, nipper, or an environmental surface.
INFECTION	Invasion of body tissues by disease-causing pathogens.
MICROORGANISM	Any organism of microscopic to submicroscopic size.
PARASITES	Organisms that grow, feed, and shelter on or in another organism (referred to as the host), while contributing nothing to the survival of that organism. Parasites must have a host to survive.
TOXINS	Various poisonous substances produced by some microorganisms (bacteria and viruses).
VIRUS	A parasitic submicroscopic particle that infects and resides in cells of biological organisms. A virus is capable of replication only through taking over the host cell's reproductive function.

▲ **Table 2–1 Causes of Disease.**

STD) and Lyme disease. They are subdivided into subgroups, such as treponema papillida, which causes syphilis, and borrelia burgdorferi, which causes Lyme disease (**Figure 2–7**).

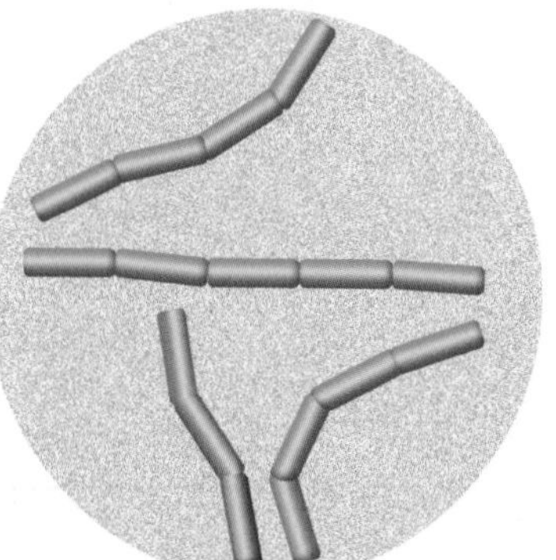

▲ Figure 2–6 **Bacilli.**

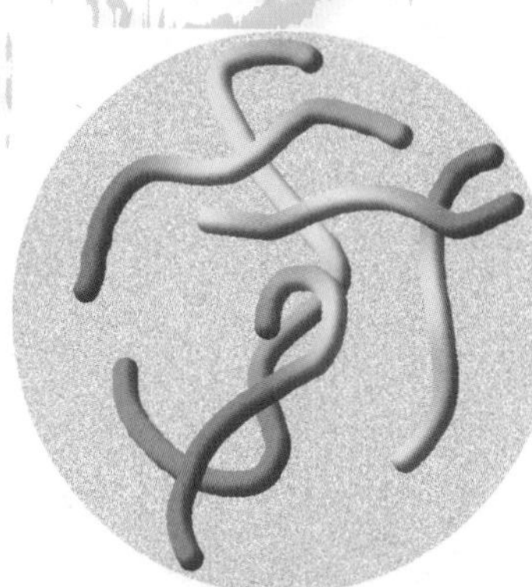

▲ Figure 2–7 **Spirilla.**

Bacterial Infections

There can be no bacterial infection without the presence of pathogenic bacteria. Therefore, if pathogenic bacteria are eliminated, clients cannot become infected. You may have a client who has tissue **inflammation** (in-fluh-MAY-shun), a condition characterized by redness, heat, pain, and swelling as the body reacts to injury, irritation, or infection. **Pus** is fluid created by infection. It contains white blood cells, bacteria, and dead cells. The presence of pus is a sign of a bacterial infection. A **local infection** is confined to a particular part of the body and appears as a lesion containing pus. Examples of local infection include a pimple or an abscess.

Staphylococci are among the most common bacteria that affect humans and are normally carried by about one-third of the population. Staph bacteria can be picked up on doorknobs, countertops, and other surfaces; however, in salons, spas, medical facilities, and medi-spas, they are more frequently spread through skin-to-skin contact (such as shaking hands) or through the use of unclean tools or implements. If these bacteria get into the wrong place, they can be very dangerous. Although lawsuits are rare considering the number of services performed in a salon or spa or medi-spa, every year many facilities are sued for allegedly causing staph infections.

Some types of infectious staph bacteria are highly resistant to conventional treatments such as antibiotics. An example is the staph infection called **methicillin-resistant staphylococcus aureus (MRSA)** (METH-eh-sill-en-ree-ZIST-ent staf-uh-loh-KOK-us OR-ee-us), which initially appears as a skin infection such as pustules, rashes, and boils that can be difficult to cure; without proper treatment, the infection may become systemic and can have devastating consequences. Historically, MRSA occurred most frequently among persons with weakened immune systems or among people who had undergone medical procedures or spent time in hospital settings. Today, it has become more common in otherwise healthy people. Because of these highly resistant bacterial strains, it is important to clean and disinfect all tools and implements used in the workplace. You owe it to yourself and your clients!

A **contagious disease** (kon-TAY-jus dih-ZEEZ), also known as **communicable disease** (kuh-MYOO-nih-kuh-bul dih-ZEEZ), is a disease that is spread by contact from one person to another person, such as the common cold, ringworm, conjunctivitis (pinkeye), viral infections, and natural nail or toe and foot infections. Some contagious diseases that prevent a makeup professional from servicing a client are the common cold, conjunctivitis (pinkeye), and viral infections. The most common way these infections spread is through dirty hands, especially those that are not clean under the fingernails and in the webs between the fingers. Be sure to always wash your hands after using the restroom, before eating, and before and after working on a client. Contagious diseases can also be spread by contaminated implements, cuts, open sores, pus, mouth and nose discharges, shared drinking cups, telephone receivers, and towels. Uncovered coughing or sneezing and spitting in public also spread germs. **Table 2–2**, Terms Related to Disease, lists terms and definitions that are important for a general understanding of disease. ✓ **LO2**

Viruses

A **virus** (VY-rus) (plural: viruses) is a parasitic submicroscopic particle that infects and resides in the cells of a living organisms; a virus is capable of replication only by taking

TABLE 2–2

TERMS RELATED TO DISEASE	
TERM	**DEFINITION**
ALLERGY	A reaction due to extreme sensitivity to certain foods, chemicals, or other normally harmless substances.
CONTAGIOUS DISEASE	Also known as *communicable disease*; a disease that is spread by contact from one person to another person, such as the common cold, ringworm, conjunctivitis (pinkeye), viral infections, and natural nail or toe and foot infections.
CONTAMINATION	The presence, or the reasonably anticipated presence, of blood or other potentially infectious materials on an item's surface or visible debris or residues such as dust, hair, and skin.
DECONTAMINATION	The removal of blood or other potentially infectious materials on an item's surface and the removal of visible debris or residue such as dust, hair, and skin.
DIAGNOSIS	Determination of the nature of a disease from its symptoms and/or diagnostic tests. Federal regulations prohibit salon or spa professionals from performing a diagnosis.
DISEASE	An abnormal condition of all or part of the body, or its systems or organs, that makes the body incapable of carrying on normal function.
EXPOSURE INCIDENT	Contact with nonintact (broken) skin, blood, body fluid, or other potentially infectious materials that is the result of the performance of an employee's duties.
INFECTIOUS	Caused by or capable of being transmitted by infection.
INFECTIOUS DISEASE	Disease caused by pathogenic (harmful) microorganisms that enter the body. An infectious disease may or may not be spread from one person to another person.
INFLAMMATION	Condition in which the body reacts to injury, irritation, or infection. An inflammation is characterized by redness, heat, pain, and swelling.
OCCUPATIONAL DISEASE	Illnesses resulting from conditions associated with employment, such as prolonged and repeated overexposure to certain products or ingredients.
PARASITIC DISEASE	Disease caused by parasites, such as lice and mites.
PATHOGENIC DISEASE	Disease produced by organisms including bacteria, viruses, fungi, and parasites.
SYSTEMIC DISEASE	Disease that affects the body as a whole, often due to under-functioning or over-functioning internal glands or organs. This type of disease is carried through the blood stream or the lymphatic system.

▲ Table 2–2 **Terms Related to Disease.**

over the host cell's reproductive function. A virus is unique in that it requires a host cell in order to replicate and survive. Viruses are so small that they can be seen only under the most sophisticated and powerful microscopes. They are known to cause common colds and other respiratory and gastrointestinal (digestive tract) infections, as well as measles, mumps, chicken pox, smallpox, rabies, yellow fever, hepatitis, polio, influenza, and human immunodeficiency virus (HIV), which causes acquired immune deficiency syndrome (AIDS).

One difference between viruses and bacteria is that a virus can live and reproduce only by taking over other cells and becoming part of them, while bacteria can live and reproduce on their own. Bacterial infections can usually be treated with specific antibiotics, but viruses are not affected by antibiotics. Viruses are very hard to kill without harming the body's own cells in the process. Vaccinations prevent viruses from growing in the body. There are many vaccines available for viruses, but not all viruses have vaccines. A vaccine is available for hepatitis B, and it is recommended that all salon, spa, and medical facility practitioners should receive this vaccine. In fact, health authorities recommend that all service providers in industries involving direct contact with the public—including cosmetologists, estheticians, makeup artists, teachers, florists, and bank tellers—ask their doctor about getting vaccinated for hepatitis B.

Bloodborne Pathogens

Bloodborne pathogens are disease-causing microorganisms carried in the body by blood or body fluids; examples include hepatitis and HIV. The spread of bloodborne pathogens is possible any time that the skin is broken.

Hepatitis

Hepatitis (hep-uh-TY-tus) is a bloodborne virus that causes disease and can damage the liver. In general, it is difficult to contract hepatitis; however, hepatitis is easier to contract than HIV because, unlike HIV, hepatitis can be present in all body fluids of those who are infected and can live on a surface outside the body for long periods of time. For this reason, it is vital that all surfaces that contact clients are thoroughly cleaned and disinfected.

There are three types of hepatitis that are of concern: hepatitis A, hepatitis B, and hepatitis C. Hepatitis B is the most difficult to kill on a surface, so check the label of the disinfectant you use to be sure that the product is effective against hepatitis B. Hepatitis B and C are spread from person to person through blood and, less often, through other body fluids, such as semen and vaginal secretions.

HIV/AIDS

Human immunodeficiency virus (HIV) (HYOO-mun ih-MYOO-noh-di-FISH-en-see VY-rus) is the virus that causes **acquired immune**

deficiency syndrome (AIDS) (uh-KWY-erd ih-MYOON di-FISH-en-see sin-drohm), a disease that breaks down the body's immune system. HIV is spread from person to person through blood and, less often, through other body fluids such as semen and vaginal secretions. A person can be infected with HIV for many years without having symptoms, but testing can determine whether a person is infected within 6 months after exposure to the virus.

The HIV virus is spread mainly through the sharing of needles by intravenous (IV) drug users and by unprotected sexual contact. Less commonly, HIV is spread through accidents with needles in healthcare settings. Less frequently, the virus can enter the bloodstream through cuts and sores. It is not spread by holding hands, hugging, kissing, sharing food, or using household items such as telephones or toilet seats. There are no documented cases that indicate the virus can be spread by food handlers, insects, or casual contact during makeup services.

If you accidentally cut a client who is HIV-positive, the tool will be contaminated. You cannot continue to use the implement without cleaning and disinfecting it. Continuing to use a contaminated implement without cleaning and disinfecting it puts you and others in the salon, spa, or medical facility at risk of infection. ✓ **LO3**

Fungi

Fungi (FUN-jI) (singular: fungus, FUN-gus) are microscopic plant parasites that include molds, mildews, and yeasts; fungi can produce contagious diseases, such as ringworm. **Mildew** (MIL-doo) is a type of fungus that affects plants or grows on inanimate objects but does not cause human infections.

Folliculitis (fah-lik-yuh-LY-tis), also called **folliculitis barbae, sycosis barbae,** or **barber's itch**, is an inflammation of the hair follicles caused by a bacterial infection from ingrown hairs due to shaving or other epilation methods. It is primarily limited to the bearded areas of the face and neck or around the scalp. The infection occurs almost exclusively in older adolescent and adult males. A person with folliculitis may have deep, inflamed or noninflamed patches of skin on the face or the nape of the neck. Folliculitis is similar to **tinea capitis** (TIN-ee-uh KAP-ih-tis), a fungal infection of the scalp characterized by red papules, or spots, at the opening of hair follicles.

Parasites

Parasites are organisms that grow, feed, and shelter on or in another organism (referred to as a host) while contributing nothing to the survival of that organism. They must have a host to survive. Parasites can live on or inside of humans and animals. They also can be found in food, on plants and trees, and in water. Humans can acquire internal parasites by eating fish or meat that has not been properly cooked. External parasites that affect humans on or in the skin include ticks, fleas, and mites.

Scabies (SKAY-beez) is a contagious skin disease and is caused by the itch mite, which burrows under the skin. Contagious diseases and condi-

Pathogenic bacteria, viruses, or fungi can enter the body through:

- Broken or inflamed skin, such as a cut, a scratch, a bruise, or a rash.
- The mouth (contaminated water, food, or fingers).
- The nose (inhaling different types of dust or droplets from a cough or sneeze).
- The eyes or ears (less likely, but possible).
- Unprotected sex.

The body prevents and controls infections with:

- Healthy, unbroken skin—the body's first line of defense.
- Body secretions, such as perspiration and digestive juices.
- White blood cells that destroy bacteria.
- Antitoxins that counteract the toxins.

tions caused by parasites should only be treated by a doctor. Contaminated countertops, tools, and equipment should be thoroughly cleaned and then disinfected with an EPA-registered disinfectant for the time recommended by the manufacturer or with a bleach solution for 10 minutes.

Immunity

Immunity is the ability of the body to destroy and resist infection; immunity against disease can be either natural or acquired and is a sign of good health. **Natural immunity** is immunity that is partly inherited and partly developed through healthy living. **Acquired immunity** is immunity that the body develops after overcoming a disease, through inoculation (such as flu vaccinations), or through exposure to natural allergens such as pollen, cat dander, and ragweed.

PRINCIPLES OF PREVENTION

Proper decontamination can prevent the spread of disease caused by exposure to potentially infectious materials on an item's surface. It also will prevent exposure to blood, visible debris, or residue such as dust, hair, and skin.

Decontamination (dee-kuhn-tam-ih-NAY-shun) is the removal of blood or other potentially infectious materials on an item's surface and the removal of visible debris or residue such as dust, hair, and skin. There are two methods of decontamination.

- **Decontamination Method 1:** Cleaning and disinfecting with an appropriate EPA-registered disinfectant.
- **Decontamination Method 2:** Cleaning and sterilizing.

Many state regulatory agencies believe there is a lower risk of infection in beauty-related businesses than in medical facilities, where sterilizing is a major concern.

Therefore, most regulatory agencies are only concerned with Decontamination Method 1: cleaning and disinfecting. When done properly, Method 2 results in the destruction of all microbes through heat and pressure in an autoclave.

Decontamination Method 1

Decontamination Method 1 has two steps: clean and disinfect. When you clean, you remove all visible dirt and debris from tools, implements, and equipment by washing with liquid soap and water and by using a clean and disinfected nail brush to scrub any grooved or hinged portions of the item.

A surface is properly cleaned when the number of contaminants on the surface is greatly reduced. In turn, this reduces the risk of infection. The vast majority of contaminants and pathogens can be removed from the surfaces of tools and implements through proper cleaning. This is why cleaning is an important part of disinfecting tools and equipment. A surface must be properly cleaned before it can be properly disinfected. Using a disinfectant without cleaning first is like using mouthwash without brushing your teeth. It just does not work properly!

Cleaned surfaces can still harbor small amounts of pathogens, but the presence of fewer pathogens means infections are less likely to be spread. Putting antiseptics on your skin or washing your hands with soap and water will drastically lower the number of pathogens on your hands. However, it does not clean them properly. The proper cleaning of the hands requires rubbing hands together and using liquid soap, warm running water, a nail brush, and a clean towel. Do not underestimate the importance of proper cleaning and hand washing. They are the most powerful and important ways to prevent the spread of infection.

There are three ways to clean your tools or implements:

- Washing with soap and warm water and scrubbing them with a clean and properly disinfected nail brush.
- Using an ultrasonic unit.
- Using a cleaning solvent.

The second step of Decontamination Method 1 is disinfection. Disinfection is the process that eliminates most, but not necessarily all, microorganisms on nonliving surfaces. This process is not effective against bacterial spores. All disinfectants should carry an EPA-registration number, and the label should clearly state the specific organisms the solution is effective in killing when it is used according to the label instructions.

Remember that disinfectants are products that destroy all bacteria, fungi, and viruses (but not spores) on surfaces. Disinfectants are not for use on human skin, hair, or nails. Never use disinfectants as hand cleaners since this can cause skin irritation and **allergy** (AL-ur-jee), a reaction due to extreme sensitivity to certain foods, chemicals, or other normally harmless substances. All disinfectants clearly state on the label that you should avoid having them come into contact with skin. This means avoid contact with your skin as well as the client's. Do not put your fingers directly into any disinfecting solution and be sure that any disinfected implements are completely dried prior to the next use.

Disinfectants can potentially be harmful if absorbed through the skin, which makes following proper mixing instructions critical. If you mix a disinfectant in a container that is not labeled by the manufacturer, the container must be properly labeled with the contents and the date it was mixed. All concentrated disinfectants must be diluted exactly as instructed by the manufacturer on the container's label.

Decontamination Method 2

Decontamination Method 2 also has two steps: cleaning and sterilizing. The word *sterilize* is often used incorrectly. **Sterilization** is the process that completely destroys all microbial life, including spores. Sterilization is required for any tools that puncture the skin or come in contact with bodily fluids.

CAUTION

Read labels carefully! Manufacturers take great care to develop safe and highly effective products. However, when used improperly, many otherwise safe products can be dangerous. Like all products, disinfectants must be used exactly as the label instructs.

© iStockphoto/Nelic

The most effective methods of sterilization use high-pressure steam autoclaves. Simply exposing instruments to steam is not enough. To be effective against disease-causing pathogens, the steam must be pressurized in an autoclave so that the steam penetrates the spore coats of the spore-forming bacteria.

Most people without medical training do not understand how to use an autoclave. For example, dirty implements cannot be properly sterilized without first being properly cleaned. Autoclaves need regular maintenance and testing to ensure they are in good working order. Color indicator strips on autoclave bags can provide false readings, so these strips should never be relied upon as the sole indicator of whether instruments have been sterilized. These strips are only an indication, not absolute verification that the autoclave is working.

The Centers for Disease Control and Prevention (CDC) requires that autoclaves be tested weekly to ensure they are properly sterilizing implements. The accepted method is called a spore test. Sealed packages containing test organisms are subjected to a typical sterilization cycle and then sent to a contract laboratory that specializes in autoclave performance testing. You can find laboratories to perform this type of test by simply doing an Internet search for "autoclave spore testing." Other regular maintenance is also required to ensure the autoclave reaches the correct temperature and pressure. Keep in mind that an autoclave that does not reach the intended temperature for killing microorganisms may create a warm, moist place where pathogenic organisms can grow and thrive. ☑ **LO4**

Choosing a Disinfectant

You must read and follow the manufacturer's instructions whenever you are using a disinfectant. Mixing ratios (dilution) and contact time are very important. Not all disinfectants have the same concentration, so be sure to mix the correct proportions according to the instructions on the label. If the label does not have the word *concentrate* on it, the product is already mixed. It must be used directly from the container and must not be diluted. All EPA-registered disinfectants, even those sprayed on large surfaces, will specify a contact time in their directions for use. Contact time is the amount of time the surface must stay moist with disinfectant in order for the disinfectant to be effective.

Disinfectants must have efficacy claims on the label. **Efficacy** (ef-ih-KUH-see) is the ability to produce an effect. As applied to disinfectant claims, *efficacy* means the effectiveness with which a disinfecting solution kills organisms when the product is used according to the label instructions.

Professionals have many disinfectants available to them and should choose the one best suited for their specialty. The ideal disinfectant would:

- Maintain efficacy in the presence of **bioburden**, the number of viable organisms in or on an object or surface or the organic material on the surface of an object before decontamination or sterilization.
- Be inexpensive.

- Be nontoxic and nonirritating.
- Include strips for checking effectiveness.
- Be readily available from multiple manufacturers.
- Be EPA-approved.
- Be environmentally friendly (can be disposed down the salon drain).
- Have no odor.
- Be noncorrosive.

Makeup artists must be aware of the types of disinfectants that are on the market. Additionally, it is important to learn about new disinfectants that become available because there are constant upgrades and improvements being made in these products.

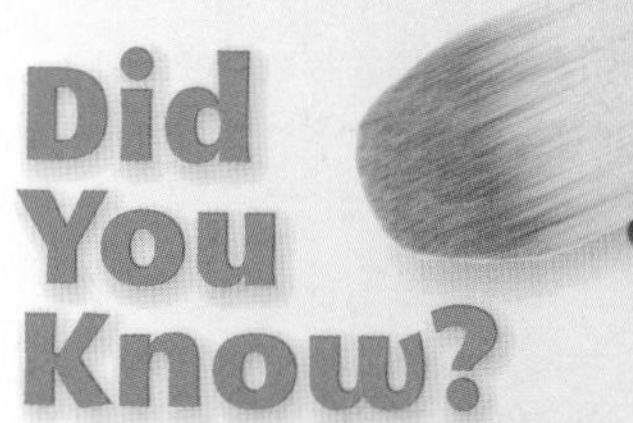

Not all household bleaches are effective as disinfectants. To be effective, bleach must have an EPA-registration number, must contain at least 5 percent sodium hypochlorite, and must be diluted properly to a 10 percent solution—9 parts water to 1 part bleach.

Proper Use of Disinfectant

Implements must be thoroughly cleaned of all visible matter or residue before being placed in disinfectant solution. This is because residue will interfere with the disinfectant and prevent proper disinfection. Properly cleaned implements and tools, free from all visible debris, must be completely immersed in disinfectant solution. Complete immersion means there is enough liquid in the container to cover all surfaces of the item being disinfected, including the handles, for 10 minutes or for the time recommended by the manufacturer

Disinfectant Tips

- Use disinfectants only on precleaned, hard, nonporous surfaces.
- Always wear gloves and safety glasses when handling disinfectant solutions.
- Always dilute products according to the instructions on the product label.
- Always submerge the item in the disinfectant for 10 minutes unless the product label specifies differently.
- To disinfect large surfaces such as tabletops, carefully apply the disinfectant onto the precleaned surface and allow it to remain wet for 10 minutes unless the product label specifies differently.
- Change the disinfectant according to the instructions on the label. If the liquid is not changed as instructed, it will no longer be effective and may begin to promote the growth of microbes.

CAUTION

Disinfectants must be registered with the EPA. Look for an EPA-registration number on the label.

Types of Disinfectants

Disinfectants are not all the same. Some disinfectants should be used on tools and implements that are immersed and some should be used on nonporous surfaces. As stated earlier, a nonporous surface is one that cannot absorb liquid. You should be aware of the different types of disinfectants and the ones that are recommended for use in the makeup environment.

The EPA has recently approved a new disinfectant that is available in a spray and an immersion form, as well as wipes.

- **Accelerated hydrogen peroxide (AHP)** is a disinfectant based on stabilized hydrogen peroxide. AHP disinfectant only needs to be changed every 14 days and is nontoxic to the skin and environment.

Read the labels of all disinfectants closely. Choose the one that is most appropriate for its intended use and safest for you and your clients.

Disinfectant Appropriate for Use

Quaternary ammonium compounds (KWAT-ur-nayr-ree uh-MOH-neeum KAHM-powndz), also known as **quats** (KWATZ), are disinfectants that are very effective when used properly in salon or spa settings. Quats usually disinfect implements in 10 minutes and can be used on makeup implements and tools. These formulas may contain antirust ingredients, so leaving tools in the solution for prolonged periods can cause dulling or damage. Tools should be removed from the solution after the specified period, rinsed (if required), dried, and stored in a clean, covered container. Quats are not recommended for brushes, but they are well suited for tweezers and other metal implements.

Bleach

Household bleach, 5.25 percent **sodium hypochlorite** (SOH-dee-um hy-puh-KLOR-ite), is an effective disinfectant and has been used extensively as a disinfectant in salon and makeup settings. Bleach can be corrosive to metals and plastics and can cause skin irritation and eye damage.

To mix a bleach solution, always follow the manufacturer's directions. Store this solution away from heat and light, mix a new solution every 24 hours, and date the container to ensure that the solution is not saved from one day to the next. Bleach can be irritating to the lungs, so be careful about inhaling the fumes.

CAUTION

Bleach is not a magic potion! All disinfectants, including bleach, are inactivated (made less effective) in the presence of many substances, including oils, lotions, creams, and soaps. If bleach is used to disinfect equipment, it is critical to use a detergent first to thoroughly clean the equipment and remove all debris. Never mix detergents with the bleach.

Disinfectant Safety

Disinfectants are pesticides (a type of poison) and can cause serious skin and eye damage. Some disinfectants appear clear while others are cloudy. Always use caution when handling disinfectants, and follow the safety tips below.

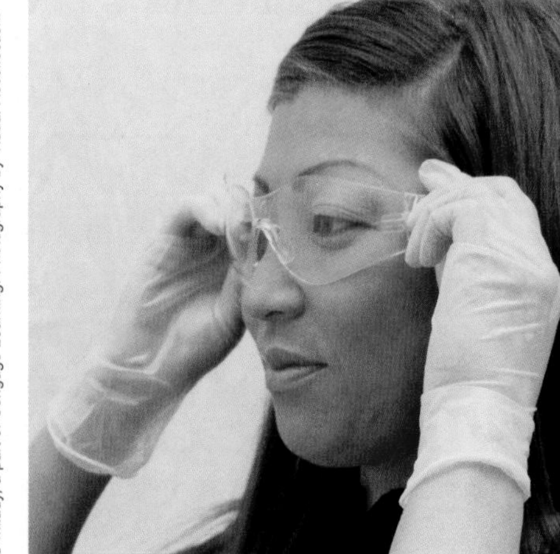

▲ Figure 2–8 Wear gloves and safety glasses while handling disinfectants.

Safety Tips for Disinfectants

Always

- Keep an MSDS on hand for the disinfectant(s) you use.
- Wear gloves and safety glasses when mixing disinfectants (**Figure 2–8**).
- Avoid skin and eye contact.
- Add disinfectant to water when diluting (rather than adding water to a disinfectant) to prevent foaming, which can result in an incorrect mixing ratio.

- Use tongs, gloves, or a draining basket to remove implements from disinfectants.
- Keep disinfectants out of reach of children.
- Carefully measure and use disinfectant products according to label instructions.
- Follow the manufacturer's instructions for mixing, using, and disposing of disinfectants.
- Carefully follow the manufacturer's directions for when to replace the disinfectant solution in order to ensure the healthiest conditions for you and your client. Replace the disinfectant solution every day—more often if the solution becomes soiled or contaminated.

Never

- Let quats, bleach, or any other disinfectant come in contact with your skin. If you do get a disinfectant on your skin, immediately wash the area with liquid soap and warm water. Then rinse the area and dry the area thoroughly.
- Place any disinfectant or other product in an unmarked container. All containers should be labeled.

Jars or containers used to disinfect implements are often incorrectly called "wet sanitizers." The purpose of disinfectant containers is to disinfect, not to clean. Disinfectant containers must be covered, but not airtight. Remember to clean the container every day and to wear gloves when you do. Always follow the manufacturer's label instructions for disinfecting products. ✓ LO5

Another word that is used (most often in marketing and sales copy) to describe multiuse items is *disinfectable*, which means these items can be disinfected and used again.

Disinfect or Dispose?

In the makeup profession, two types of items are used: multiuse (reusable) items, and single-use (disposable) items.

Multiuse, also known as **reusable**, items can be cleaned, disinfected, and used on more than one person even if the item is accidentally exposed to blood or body fluid. These items must have a hard, nonporous surface. Examples of multiuse items are tweezers and some brushes.

Single-use, also known as **disposable**, items cannot be used more than once either because they cannot be properly cleaned so that all visible residue is removed—such as pumice stones used for pedicures—or because cleaning and disinfecting damages or contaminates them. Examples of single-use items are wooden sticks, cotton balls, sponges, gauze, tissues, paper towels, plastic applicators, and some brushes. Single-use items must be thrown out after each use and are an excellent choice whenever possible. Single-use items are the surest way to prevent the spread of disease and to ensure the highest level of infection control practices in the makeup environment.

▲ **Figure 2–9 Carefully pour disinfectant into the water when preparing disinfectant solution.**

Cleaning and Disinfecting Nonelectrical Tools and Implements

State rules require that all multiuse tools and implements must be cleaned and disinfected before and after every service—even when they are used on the same person. Mix all disinfectants according to the manufacturer's directions, always adding the disinfectant to the water, not the water to the disinfectant (**Figure 2–9**).

PROCEDURE **2-1** **CLEANING & DISINFECTING NONELECTRICAL TOOLS AND IMPLEMENTS** SEE PAGE 46

▲ **Figure 2–10 Clean and disinfect makeup stations regularly.**

Disinfecting Work Surfaces

Before beginning every client service, all work surfaces must be cleaned and disinfected (**Figure 2–10**). Be sure to clean and disinfect tables, chairs, arm rests and any other surface whenever a customer's skin has touched them. Clean doorknobs and handles daily to reduce the risk of transferring germs to your hands.

Cleaning Towels, Linens, and Capes

Clean towels, linens, and capes must be used for each client. After a towel, linen, or cape has been used on a client, it must not be used again until it has been properly laundered. To clean towels, linens, and capes, launder them according to the directions on their labels. Be sure that towels, linens, and capes are thoroughly dried. Items that are not dry may grow mildew and bacteria. Store soiled linens and towels in covered or closed containers, away from clean linens and towels, even if your state regulatory agency does not require that you do so. Whenever possible, use disposable towels, especially in restrooms.

CAUTION

Ultraviolet (UV) sanitizers are useful storage containers, but they do not disinfect or sterilize.

Caring for Brushes

Proper care of brushes is important because they are in constant contact with makeup products and various clients. Brushes can be washed with an antibacterial detergent followed by a commercial brush-cleaning solution. Spray-on instant sanitizers are effective, but their high alcohol content can dry the brush hairs over time.

Always clean brushes in running or still water with the ferrule (the metal ring that keeps the brush hairs and handle together) pointing downward. If the ferrule is pointing upward during cleaning, water may dissolve the glue that keeps the brush hairs in place. Rinse brushes thoroughly after cleaning and lay them flat on a clean towel to dry (**Figure 2–11**). An ultraviolet-light sterilizer can also be used to store brushes until the next use.

Handling Single-Use Supplies

All single-use supplies, such as wooden sticks, cotton, gauze, wipes, applicators, and paper towels, should be thrown away after one use. Anything exposed to blood must be double-bagged and marked with a biohazard sticker, separated from other waste, and disposed of according to OSHA standards.

Hand Washing

Properly washing your hands is one of the most important actions you can take to prevent spreading germs from one person to another. Proper hand washing removes germs from the folds and grooves of the skin and from under the free edge of the nail plate by lifting and rinsing germs and contaminants from the surface. Wash hands thoroughly before and after each service. Always follow the hand washing procedure in this chapter.

Antimicrobial and antibacterial soaps can dry the skin, and medical studies suggest that they are no more effective than regular soaps or detergents. Therefore, it is recommended that you minimize the use of antimicrobial and antibacterial soaps. Repeated hand washing can also dry the skin, so using a moisturizing hand lotion after washing is a good practice. Be sure the hand lotion is in a pump container, not a jar.

Avoid using very hot water to wash your hands because doing so can damage the skin. Remember: You must wash your hands thoroughly before and after each service, so do all you can to reduce the possibility of irritation.

PROCEDURE **2-2** **PROPER HAND WASHING** SEE PAGE 48

Waterless Hand Sanitizers

Antiseptics (ant-ih-SEP-tiks) are chemical germicides formulated for use on skin and registered and regulated by the Food and Drug Admin-

TOOL BELTS

Tool belts must be properly cleaned and disinfected between each client. To follow proper infection control procedures, use a different tool belt for each client if there is not time for cleaning and disinfection; or do not place used brushes in the tool belt after use, until they have been thoroughly cleaned and disinfected.

▲ Figure 2–11 Lay brushes on a clean towel to dry after cleaning.

STATE REGULATORY ALERT

Regulations for cleaning brushes vary from state to state. Be sure to closely check your state guidelines for proper procedures.

CAUTION

Bar soap can actually grow bacteria if it is sitting in a dish or on a sink. For hand washing, use liquid soap that is dispensed with a pump.

istration (FDA). Antiseptics can contain either alcohol or benzalkonium chloride (ben-ZAHL-khon-ee-um KLOHR-yd), which is less drying to the skin than alcohol. Neither type of antiseptic can clean the hands of dirt and debris; this can only be accomplished with liquid soap, a soft-bristle brush, and water. Use hand sanitizers only after properly cleaning your hands. Never use an antiseptic to disinfect instruments or other surfaces. They are ineffective for that purpose.

UNIVERSAL AND STANDARD PRECAUTIONS

The Centers of Disease Control and Prevention (CDC) studies diseases and provides guidance to prevent their spread. AIDS was a major public health crisis in the 1980s. In 1985, the CDC responded by introducing Universal Precautions (UP). Using this system, workers evaluated each client-care situation and applied gloves if there was a risk of contact with visible blood. Sometimes blood is present but not visible. If blood was not visible, gloves were not needed. In 1987, a hospital developed a new system called **body substance isolation (BSI)**. The guidelines were published and widely adopted. When using BSI, **personal protective equipment (PPE)** is to be worn for contact with all body fluids, even if blood is not visible.

Standard Precautions (SP) were introduced by the CDC in 1996 to replace Universal Precautions. Workers must assume that all blood and body fluids are potential sources of infection, regardless of the perceived risk. The precautions are used for all clients whenever exposure to bloodborne pathogens is likely. Standard Precautions took information from both Universal Precautions and BSI. The importance of all body fluids, secretions, and excretions was recognized as a factor in the spread of disease. PPE is worn any time contact with blood, body fluid, secretions, excretions, mucous membranes, or nonintact skin is likely. The name *Standard Precautions* was selected to prevent confusion with other types of precautions. One goal was to be as simple and user-friendly as possible.

The most common method for spreading infection is through the hands. In 2002, the CDC published the "Guidelines for Hand Hygiene." Investigators studied different methods of cleansing hands. They found that products containing alcohol were more effective in removing germs than using soap and water, unless the hands were visibly soiled. Most healthcare facilities and many other businesses began using alcohol-based products for routinely cleansing the hands. This includes the operating room, which is the most sterile area in a hospital. Standard Precautions were updated in 2007 by the CDC. The 2002 hand washing guidelines were included, as were precautions to prevent the spread of respiratory infections.

When the CDC publishes a change, it takes several years for the new information to get to everyone who needs it. From 1970 to 1996, infection control changes were frequent. Some workers had a hard time keeping up with all the changes and became confused. Many continue to use a combination of both Universal Precautions and BSI to this day. Many experienced workers consider Standard Precautions the equivalent of Universal Precautions. This is incorrect. They are very different systems. Refer to **Table 2–3** for a brief comparison of Universal and Standard Precautions.

TABLE 2–3

BRIEF COMPARISON OF UNIVERSAL AND STANDARD PRECAUTIONS

UNIVERSAL PRECAUTIONS (UP)	STANDARD PRECAUTIONS (SP)
OVERVIEW	**OVERVIEW**
Everyone is considered a potential threat for transmission of bloodborne pathogens. Workers are expected to evaluate the risk and use Universal Precautions to protect themselves and others. **Universal Precautions apply to:** • Blood • Other body fluids containing visible blood, semen, vaginal secretions • Body tissues • Fluids: cerebrospinal, synovial (knee), pleural (lung), peritoneal (abdomen), pericardial (heart), and amniotic fluid (bag of water that protects the fetus during pregnancy) **Universal Precautions do not apply to:** • Feces • Nasal secretions • Sputum • Sweat • Tears • Urine • Vomitus • Saliva • Breast milk ***Unless these substances contain visible blood.***	Workers must assume that all blood and body fluids are potential sources of infection, regardless of the perceived risk. Workers are expected to use Standard Precautions to protect themselves and others. **Standard Precautions apply to:** • Blood • All body fluids • All secretions (except sweat) • Excretions • Mucous membranes • Nonintact (broken) skin • Breast milk Wear gloves when contact with any blood or body fluid is likely. Wear gloves for all contact with body substances and tissues, even if you cannot see blood. Gloves are not required for contact with perspiration (sweat).

▲ Table 2–3 **Brief Comparison of Universal and Standard Precautions.**

(continued)

TABLE 2–3

BRIEF COMPARISON OF UNIVERSAL AND STANDARD PRECAUTIONS	
UNIVERSAL PRECAUTIONS (UP)	**STANDARD PRECAUTIONS (SP)**
Wear gloves when contact with body fluids containing visible blood is likely.	
GLOVES	**GLOVES**
Changing gloves during care not required. Change gloves after each contact.	Apply gloves when contact with the substances listed above is likely. Change gloves *immediately prior* to contact with mucous membranes and nonintact skin.
ITEMS AND SURFACES IN ROOM	**ITEMS AND SURFACES IN ROOM**
Apply UP to items and surfaces that may have contacted substances to which UP apply.	Apply SP to items and surfaces that may have contacted substances to which SP apply.
Environmental contamination not an issue.	Avoid environmental contamination with used gloves. (This means counters, faucets, door knobs, etc.)
NEEDLES AND SHARPS	**NEEDLES AND SHARPS**
Avoid recapping needles. Place used sharps in a puncture-resistant container near the area of use.	Avoid recapping needles. Handle needles and sharps carefully to prevent injury to the user and others who may contact the soiled device. Place used sharps in a puncture-resistant container near the area of use.
SPLASHING OF BLOOD AND BODY FLUIDS	**SPLASHING OF BLOOD AND BODY FLUIDS**
No guidelines; splashing of blood or body fluids not addressed.	Apply a mask, eyewear, or gown if splashing is likely.
ADDITIONAL INFORMATION	
For additional information, refer to: Hand Hygiene in Healthcare Settings go to: www.cdc.gov/handhygiene/ 2007 Guideline for Isolation Precautions: Preventing Transmission of Infectious Agents in Healthcare Settings go to: www.tinyurl.com/4zxfunz	

▲ Table 2–3 **Brief Comparison of Universal and Standard Precautions. (continued)**

As you can see, infection control procedures change frequently as new information becomes available. Keep up with changes by reading professional journals, looking on-line, and going to continuing education classes. As a makeup artist, you must understand the differences between UP and SP. By using Standard Precautions, you can be sure that you are meeting the highest standards of practice. To protect yourself and your clients, learn all you can and be very diligent with infection control!

© iStockphoto/Stephanie Frey

OSHA and Universal Precautions

OSHA publishes a set of standards for **Universal Precautions (UP)** that require the employer and employee to assume that there are pathogens present in human blood that can spread disease in humans. (These standards can be found in the OSHA publication, *Standard 1910.1030, Bloodborne Pathogens.*) Because it may not be possible to identify clients with infectious diseases, strict infection control practices should be used with all clients. In most instances, clients who are infected with the hepatitis B virus or other bloodborne pathogens are **asymptomatic**, which means that they show no symptoms or signs of infection. Bloodborne pathogens are more difficult to kill than germs that live outside the body.

OSHA sets safety standards and precautions that protect employees in situations where they could be exposed to bloodborne pathogens. Precautions include proper hand washing, wearing gloves, and properly handling and disposing of sharp instruments and any other items that may have been contaminated by blood or other body fluids. It is important that specific procedures are followed if visible blood is present.

An Exposure Incident: Contact with Blood or Body Fluid

You should never perform a service on any client who comes in with an open wound or an abrasion. However, sometimes accidents happen while a service is being performed.

An **exposure incident** is contact with nonintact (broken) skin, blood, body fluid, or other potentially infectious materials that is the result of the performance of an employee's duties. Should the client suffer a cut or abrasion that bleeds during a service, follow these steps for the client's safety, as well as your own:

1. Stop the service.
2. Put on gloves to protect yourself from contact with the client's blood.
3. Stop the bleeding by applying pressure to the area with a clean cotton ball or piece of gauze.

© iStockphoto/Vitalina Rybakova

4. When bleeding has stopped, clean the injured area with an antiseptic wipe. Every workplace must have a first aid kit.
5. Bandage the cut with an adhesive bandage.
6. Clean and disinfect your workstation, using an EPA-registered disinfectant designed for cleaning blood and body fluids.
7. Discard all single-use contaminated objects such as wipes or cotton balls by double-bagging (place the waste in a plastic bag and then in a trash bag). Place a biohazard sticker (red or orange) on the bag, and deposit the bag into a container for contaminated waste.
8. Before removing your gloves, make sure that all multiuse tools and implements that have come into contact with blood or other body fluids are thoroughly cleaned and completely immersed in an EPA-registered disinfectant solution designed for cleaning blood and body fluids or 10 percent bleach solution for at least 10 minutes or for the time recommended by the manufacturer of the product. Be sure that you do not touch other work surfaces, such as faucets and counters. If you do, these areas must also be properly cleaned and disinfected. Remember: Blood may carry pathogens, so you should never touch an open sore or a wound.
9. Remove your gloves and seal them in the double bag along with the other contaminated items for disposal. Thoroughly wash your hands and clean under the free edge of your nails with soap and warm water before returning to the service.
10. Recommend that the client see a physician if any signs of redness, swelling, pain, or irritation develops. ☑ LO6

THE PROFESSIONAL IMAGE

Infection control practices should be a part of the normal routine in order for makeup artists to project a steadfast professional image (**Figure 2–12**). The following are some simple guidelines that will keep the makeup area looking its best.

- Keep floors and workstations dust-free.
- Keep all work areas well-lit.
- Keep restrooms clean, including door handles.
- Provide toilet tissue, paper towels, liquid soap, properly disinfected soft-bristle nail brushes, and a container for used brushes in the restroom.
- Prohibit eating, drinking, and smoking in areas where services are performed.

© Milady, a part of Cengage Learning. Photography by Visual Recollection.

▲ Figure 2–12 **Your professional image is a reflection of you and your work station.**

- Empty waste receptacles regularly throughout the day.
- Never place any tools or implements in your mouth or pockets.
- Store clean and disinfected tools in a clean, covered container. Clean drawers may be used for storage if only clean items are stored in the drawers. Always isolate used implements from disinfected implements.
- Avoid touching your face, mouth, or eye areas during services.
- Clean and disinfect all work surfaces after every client.
- Always properly wash your hands before and after each service.
- Use clean linens and disposable towels on clients. Keep soiled linens separate from clean linens.

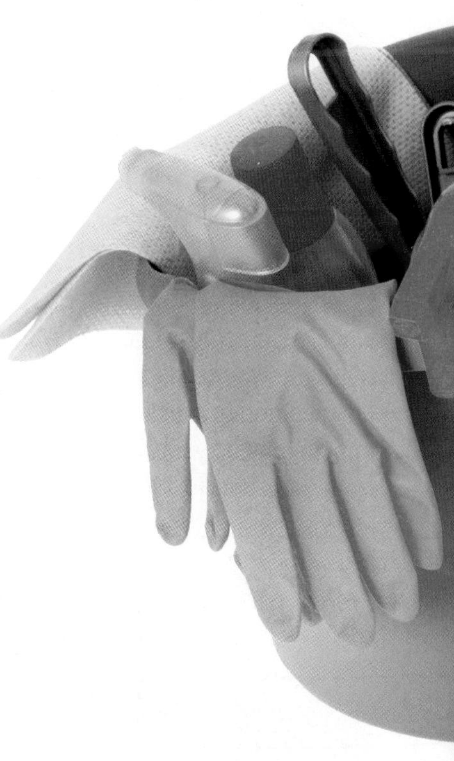
© iStockphoto/Thumb

Your Professional Responsibility

You have many responsibilities as a makeup professional, but none is more important than protecting your clients' health and safety. Never take shortcuts for cleaning and disinfecting. You cannot afford to skip steps or save money when it comes to safety.

- It is your professional and legal responsibility to follow state and federal laws and rules.
- Keep your license current and notify the licensing agency if you move or change your name.
- Check your state's Web site weekly for any changes or updates to rules and regulations. ☑ LO7

Procedure 2-1

Cleaning and Disinfecting Nonelectrical Tools and Implements

Nonelectrical tools and implements include items such as hairbrushes, clips, pencil sharpeners, and tweezers.

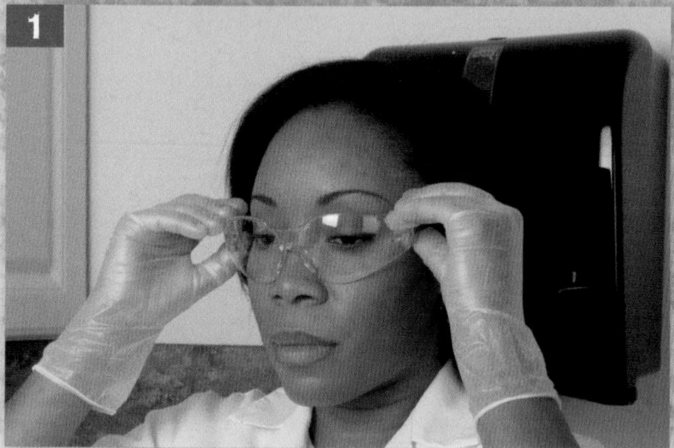

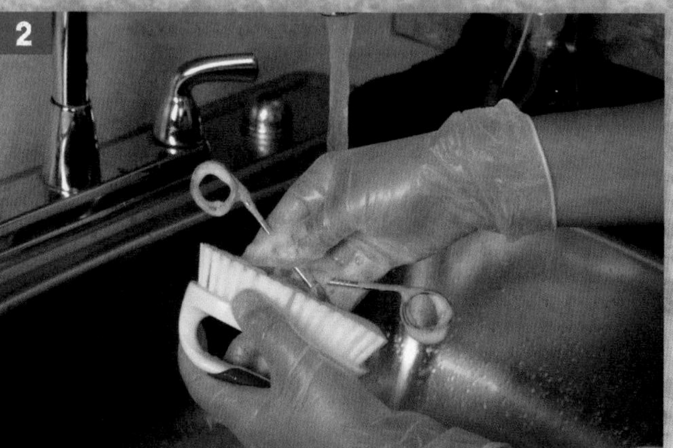

1 It is important to wear safety glasses and gloves while disinfecting nonelectrical tools and implements to protect your eyes from unintentional splashes of disinfectant, to prevent possible contamination of the implements by your hands, and to protect your hands from the powerful chemicals in the disinfectant solution.

2 Rinse all implements with warm running water. Then thoroughly clean them with soap, a nail brush, and warm water. Brush grooved items, if necessary, and open hinged implements to scrub the revealed area.

3 Rinse away all traces of soap with warm running water. The presence of soap in most disinfectants will cause them to become inactive. Soap is most easily rinsed off in warm, not hot, water. Hotter water is not more effective. Dry implements thoroughly with a clean or disposable towel, or allow them to air dry on a clean towel. Your implements are now properly cleaned and ready to be disinfected.

4 It is extremely important that your implements be completely clean before you place them in the disinfectant solution. If implements are not clean, your disinfectant may become contaminated and ineffective. Immerse cleaned implements in an appropriate disinfection container holding an EPA-registered disinfectant for the required time (at least 10 minutes or according to the manufacturer's instructions). Remember to open hinged implements before immersing them in the disinfectant. If the disinfection solution is visibly dirty, or if the solution has been contaminated, it must be replaced.

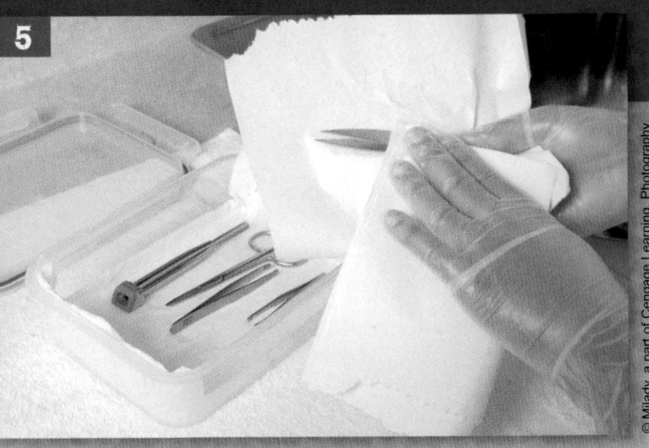

5 After the required disinfection time has passed, remove tools and implements from the disinfection solution with tongs or gloved hands, rinse the tools and implements well in warm running water, and pat them dry.

6 Store disinfected tools and implements in a clean, covered container until needed.

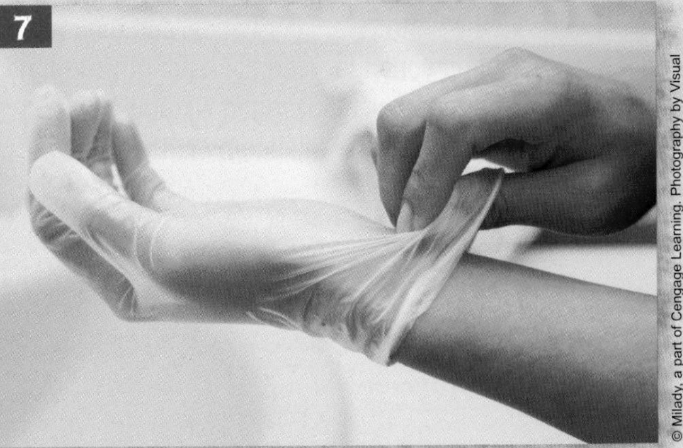

7 Remove gloves and thoroughly wash your hands with warm running water and liquid soap. Rinse and dry hands with a clean fabric or disposable towel.

✓ **LO8**

Procedure 2-2

Proper Hand Washing

Hand washing is one of the most important procedures in the infection control procedure and is required in every state before any service.

fyi

Dirty nail brushes should be stored together in a closed container until you are ready to clean and disinfect them. Then nail brushes should be properly cleaned, rinsed, dried, and immersed for the required disinfection time in a disinfectant that does not harm plastics. After they have been disinfected, rinse the brushes in clean, warm water, dry them, and place them in a clean storage location.

1 Turn on the water, wet your hands, and then pump soap from a pump container onto the palm of your hand. Rub your hands together, all over and vigorously, until a lather forms. Continue for a minimum of 20 seconds.

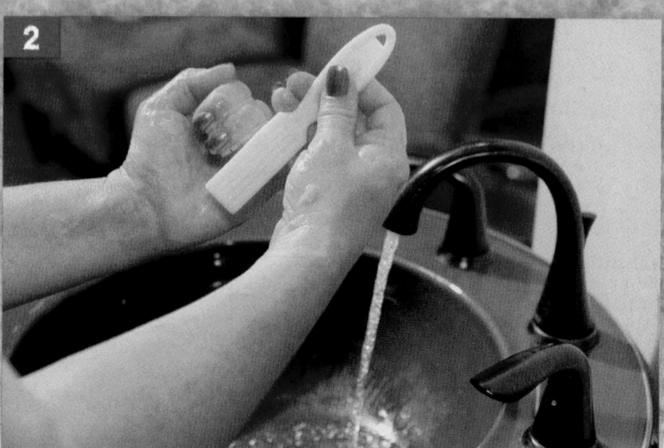

2 Choose a clean, disinfected nail brush. Wet the nail brush, pump soap on it, and brush your nails horizontally back and forth under the free edges. Change the direction of the brush to vertical and move the brush up and down along the nail folds of the fingernails. The process for brushing both hands should take about 60 seconds to finish. Rinse hands in running warm water.

3 Use a clean cloth or paper towel, according to the salon policies, for drying your hands.

4 After drying your hands, turn off the water with the towel and dispose of the towel.

Review Questions

1. What is the primary purpose of regulatory agencies?
2. What is an MSDS? Where can you get it?
3. What are bacteria?
4. Name and describe the two main classifications of bacteria.
5. Name and describe the three forms of pathogenic bacteria.
6. What is a contagious disease?
7. What is the difference between cleaning, disinfecting, and sterilizing?
8. What is the length of time for proper disinfection of tools immersed in solution?
9. What are Universal Precautions?
10. What are Standard Precautions?
11. List two types of disinfectants.
12. What is the reason for practicing infection control standards?
13. What must disinfectants have the ability to destroy?
14. What is the term used to describe the body's inherited ability to destroy or resist infection?
15. What type of tool provides the surest standards of infection control?
16. Identify three professional responsibilities of the makeup artist in order to protect clients' health and safety.

Chapter Glossary

accelerated hydrogen peroxide (AHP)	A disinfectant based on stabilized hydrogen peroxide.
acquired immune deficiency syndrome	Abbreviated AIDS; a disease that breaks down the body's immune system.
acquired immunity	Immunity that the body develops after overcoming a disease, through inoculation (such as flu vaccinations), or through exposure to natural allergens, such as pollen, cat dander, and ragweed.
allergy	Reaction due to extreme sensitivity to certain foods, chemicals, or other normally harmless substances.
antiseptics	Chemical germicides formulated for use on skin; registered and regulated by the Food and Drug Administration (FDA).
asymptomatic	Showing no symptoms or signs of infection.

Chapter Glossary *(continued)*

bacilli	Short rod-shaped bacteria. They are the most common bacteria and produce diseases such as tetanus (lockjaw), typhoid fever, tuberculosis, and diphtheria.
bacteria (singular: bacterium)	Also known as *microbes* or *germs*; one-celled microorganisms that have both plant and animal characteristics; some are harmful and some are harmless.
bactericidal	Capable of destroying bacteria.
bioburden	The number of viable organisms in or on an object or surface or the organic material on the surface of an object before decontamination or sterilization.
bloodborne pathogens	Disease-causing microorganisms carried in the body by blood or body fluids; examples include hepatitis and HIV.
body substance isolation	Abbreviated BSI; personal protective equipment is worn for contact with all body fluids, even if blood is not visible.
clean (cleaning)	A mechanical process (scrubbing) using soap and water or detergent and water to remove all visible dirt, debris, and many disease-causing germs from tools, implements, and equipment; cleaning also removes invisible debris that interferes with disinfection, and it is required before disinfecting.
cocci	Round-shaped bacteria that appear singly (alone) or in groups. The three types of cocci are staphylococci, streptococci, and diplococci.
contagious disease	Also known as a *communicable disease*; disease that is spread by contact from one person to another person, such as the common cold, ringworm, conjunctivitis (pinkeye), viral infections, and natural nail or toe and foot infections.
contamination	The presence, or the reasonably anticipated presence, of blood or other potentially infectious materials on an item's surface or visible debris or residues such as dust, hair, and skin.
decontamination	The removal of blood or other potentially infectious materials on an item's surface and the removal of visible debris or residue such as dust, hair, and skin.
diagnosis	Determination of the nature of a disease from its symptoms and/or diagnostic tests. Federal regulations prohibit salon or spa professionals from performing a diagnosis.
diplococci	Spherical bacteria that grow in pairs and cause diseases such as pneumonia.
direct transmission	Transmission of blood or body fluids through touching (including shaking hands), kissing, coughing, sneezing, and talking.
disease	An abnormal condition of all or part of the body, or its systems or organs, that makes the body incapable of carrying on normal function.
disinfectants	Chemical products that destroy all bacteria, fungi, and viruses (but not spores) on surfaces.
disinfection	Also known as *disinfecting*; the process that eliminates most, but not necessarily all, microorganisms on nonporous surfaces. This process is not effective against bacterial spores.

Chapter Glossary *(continued)*

efficacy	The ability to produce an effect.
exposure incident	Contact with nonintact (broken) skin, blood, body fluid, or other potentially infectious materials that is the result of the performance of an employee's duties.
folliculitis	Also known as *folliculitis barbae*, *sycosis barbae*, or *barber's itch*. Inflammation of the hair follicles caused by a bacterial infection from ingrown hairs. The cause is typically from ingrown hairs due to shaving or other epilation methods.
fungi (singular: fungus)	Microscopic plant parasites that include molds, mildews, and yeasts; fungi can produce contagious diseases such as ringworm.
fungicidal	Capable of destroying fungi.
hepatitis	A bloodborne virus that causes disease and can damage the liver.
hospital disinfectants	Disinfectants that are safe for cleaning blood and body fluids.
human immunodeficiency virus	Abbreviated HIV; the virus that causes acquired immune deficiency syndrome (AIDS).
immunity	The ability of the body to destroy and resist infection. Immunity against disease can be either natural or acquired and is a sign of good health.
indirect transmission	Transmission of blood or body fluids through contact with an intermediate contaminated object, such as a razor, extractor, nipper, or an environmental surface.
infection	The invasion of body tissues by disease-causing pathogens.
infection control	The methods used to eliminate or reduce the transmission of infectious organisms.
infectious	Caused by or capable of being transmitted by infection.
infectious disease	Disease caused by pathogenic (harmful) microorganisms that enter the body. An infectious disease may or may not be spread from one person to another person.
inflammation	A condition characterized by redness, heat, pain, and swelling as the body reacts to injury, irritation, or infection.
local infection	Confined to a particular part of the body and appears as a lesion containing pus.
Material Safety Data Sheet	Abbreviated MSDS; information compiled by the manufacturer about product safety, including the names of hazardous ingredients, safe handling and use procedures, precautions to reduce the risk of accidental harm or overexposure, and flammability warnings.

Chapter Glossary *(continued)*

methicillin-resistant staphylococcus aureus	Abbreviated MRSA; initially appears as a skin infection such as pustules, rashes, and boils that can be difficult to cure. Without proper treatment, the infection becomes systemic and can have devastating consequences that can result in death.
microorganism	Any organism of microscopic or submicroscopic size.
mildew	A type of fungus that affects plants or grows on inanimate objects but does not cause human infections.
multiuse	Also known as *reusable*; items that can be cleaned, disinfected, and used on more than one person even if the item is accidentally exposed to blood or body fluid.
natural immunity	Immunity that is partly inherited and partly developed through healthy living.
nonpathogenic	Harmless organisms that may perform useful functions and are safe to come in contact with since they do not cause disease or harm.
nonporous	An item that is made or constructed of a material that has no pores or openings and cannot absorb liquids.
occupational disease	Illnesses resulting from conditions associated with employment, such as prolonged and repeated overexposure to certain products or ingredients.
parasites	Organisms that grow, feed, and shelter on or in another organism (referred to as a host), while contributing nothing to the survival of that organism.
parasitic disease	Disease caused by parasites, such as lice and mites.
pathogenic	Harmful microorganisms that can cause disease or infection in humans when they invade the body.
pathogenic disease	Disease produced by organisms, including bacteria, viruses, fungi, and parasites.
personal protective equipment	Abbreviated PPE; worn for contact with all body fluids, even if blood is not visible.
pus	Fluid created by infection.
quaternary ammonium compounds	Also known as *quats*; disinfectants that are very effective when used properly in salon or spa settings.
sanitize	A chemical process for reducing the number of disease-causing germs on cleaned surfaces to a safe level.
scabies	Contagious skin disease caused by the itch mite, which burrows under the skin.

Chapter Glossary *(continued)*

single-use	Also known as *disposable*; items that cannot be used more than once. These items cannot be properly cleaned so that all visible residue is removed or they are damaged or contaminated by cleaning and disinfecting in an exposure incident.
sodium hypochlorite	Common household bleach; an effective disinfectant for the salon or spa setting.
spirilla	Spiral or corkscrew-shaped bacteria that cause diseases such as syphilis and Lyme disease.
Standard Precautions	Abbreviated SP; precautions such as wearing personal protective equipment to protect skin and mucous membrane where contact with a client's blood, body fluids, secretions (except sweat), excretions, nonintact skin, and mucous membranes is likely. Workers must assume that all blood and body fluids are potential sources of infection, regardless of the perceived risk.
staphylococci	Pus-forming bacteria that grow in clusters like bunches of grapes and are responsible for causing abscesses, pustules, and boils. Some types of staphylococci may not cause infections in healthy humans.
sterilization	The process that completely destroys all microbial life, including spores.
streptococci	Pus-forming bacteria arranged in curved lines resembling a string of beads. They cause infections such as strep throat and blood poisoning.
systemic disease	Disease that affects the body as a whole, often due to under-functioning or over-functioning internal glands or organs. This type of disease is carried through the blood stream or the lymphatic system.
tinea capitis	A fungal infection of the scalp characterized by red papules, or spots, at the opening of hair follicles.
toxins	Various poisonous substances produced by some microorganisms (bacteria and viruses).
tuberculocidal disinfectants	Disinfectants that kill the bacteria that causes tuberculosis.
tuberculosis	A disease caused by a bacteria that is transmitted through coughing or sneezing.
Universal Precautions	A set of standards published by OSHA that require the employer and the employee to assume that all human blood and body fluids are infectious for bloodborne pathogens.
virucidal	Capable of destroying viruses.
virus (plural: viruses)	A parasitic submicroscopic particle that infects and resides in cells of biological organisms. A virus is capable of replication only through taking over the host cell's reproductive function.

Chapter 3 Facial Anatomy and Physiology

Chapter Outline

Learning Objectives

After completing this chapter, you will be able to:

- ☑ **LO1** Explain the importance of anatomy and physiology of the face and facial skin as it applies to makeup application.
- ☑ **LO2** Identify the bones and muscles of the face.
- ☑ **LO3** Identify the layers of the skin and their functions.
- ☑ **LO4** Describe common skin conditions that a makeup artist would encounter.
- ☑ **LO5** Identify which skin conditions a makeup application may be performed on.

Key Terms

Page number indicates where in the chapter the term is used.

Key Terms

Page number indicates where in the chapter the term is used.

lacrimal bones
pg. 58

lentigines
pg. 69

lesion
pg. 64

levator anguli oris muscle (caninus muscle)
pg. 60

levator labii superioris muscle (quadratus labii superioris muscle)
pg. 60

macule
pg. 65

malignant melanoma
pg. 70

mandible
pg. 59

maxillae
pg. 59

melanocytes
pg. 62

mentalis muscle
pg. 60

milia
pg. 67

nasal bones
pg. 58

nevus (birthmark)
pg. 69

nodule
pg. 70

nonstriated muscles
pg. 59

orbicularis oculi muscle
pg. 59

orbicularis oris muscle
pg. 60

papillary layer
pg. 62

papule
pg. 64

primary lesions
pg. 64

procerus
pg. 60

propionibacterium acnes
pg. 67

pustule
pg. 65

reticular layer
pg. 62

risorius muscle
pg. 60

rosacea
pg. 67

scale
pg. 66

scar
pg. 66

seborrheic dermatitis
pg. 67

secondary skin lesions
pg. 66

squamous cell carcinoma
pg. 70

stratum corneum (horny layer)
pg. 61

stratum germinativum (basal cell layer)
pg. 62

stratum granulosum (granular layer)
pg. 61

stratum lucidum
pg. 61

stratum spinosum (spiny layer)
pg. 62

striated muscles
pg. 59

telangiectasis
pg. 67

triangularis muscle
pg. 60

ulcer
pg. 66

vesicle
pg. 68

vitiligo
pg. 69

wheal
pg. 65

zygomatic bones (malar bones, cheekbones)
pg. 59

zygomaticus major muscles
pg. 60

zygomaticus minor muscles
pg. 60

Career Profile

Courtesy of Alex Byrne.

Looking at makeup artistry as an innate, creative passion, Alex Byrne directed her path in life to pursue that passion. Coupled with years of hard work and schooling, her passion has resulted in her accomplished reputation and jobs with the most important designers in the fashion industry worldwide. Alex Byrne is currently working with clientele in London and New York and continuing on her creative path through makeup.

Courtesy of Benjamin Kaufmann.

"When I was building my career, I had a different perspective on what it meant to be successful. I thought that 'getting there' would be measured by how many *W Magazine* and *Vogue* covers I had in my portfolio. But hours in the photo studio are never as glamorous as they sound. Now I love to work hard investigating formulas, getting calls for quotes, and jazzing up one of my ladies for the red carpet. It's a ball, the party before the party.

"At the start of my college career at the University of Illinois, I was initially drawn to the right brain way of thinking, which led me to study organic chemistry. I soon realized that this major was more of a time commitment than I liked, and I changed my major to English Literature and Art History. During this time, I obtained a campus job at a hair salon that would ultimately solidify the direction of my future vocation.

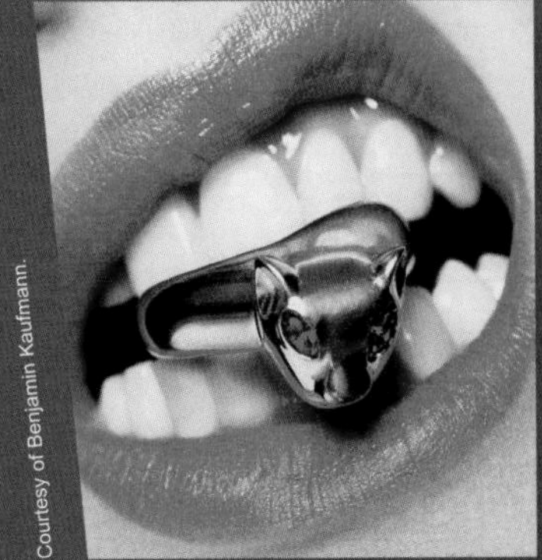
Courtesy of Benjamin Kaufmann.

"After attending the University of Illinois for 4 years, I chose to focus my area of expertise on another domain that I was truly passionate about: makeup artistry. I had the privilege of receiving private instruction with a makeup artist who was formerly the National Training Director for Chanel and Christian Dior. From this beginning, and after receiving further extensive training through the MAC school, I obtained the skills necessary to not only build my own portfolio, but to launch a freelance career.

"Following a move to New York, I had the opportunity to begin assisting world-renowned makeup artists Francois Nars and Stephane Marais for fashion shows and photo shoots. By the late 90s, I had the opportunity to transfer to London, where I continued to assist Francois and Stephane and further develop my craft in makeup artistry. Many new opportunities presented themselves in London, including the privilege to assist other talented artists. After years of hard work, I began leading my own catwalk shows.

Courtesy of Benjamin Kaufmann.

"I am currently working as a makeup artist based in London and New York, supporting a variety of entertainment personalities and leading runway shows, magazine shoots, and red carpet events.

"I couldn't be happier with the choices I've made. I always look forward to sharing my knowledge and experience with up-and-coming artists, and I value each and every opportunity to provide guidance and inspiration to those embarking on this career path."

—Alex Byrne

There is a vast amount of available information about the anatomy and physiology of the human body. It is here, in the structure of the face and in the condition of the skin, that your work as a makeup artist begins. This is your canvas, and the condition of this canvas will help you choose specific products, colors, tools, and techniques for makeup applications

This chapter introduces you to the structure of the face and the function of the skin, and it discusses skin conditions that you are likely to encounter as a makeup artist. Over time and with experience you will see hundreds, if not thousands, of different faces. By understanding the structure of the face and the function of the skin, you will be able to help each of these faces look its best. ☑ LO1

WHY STUDY FACIAL ANATOMY AND SKIN PHYSIOLOGY?

Makeup artists should study and have a thorough understanding of anatomy and skin physiology because:

- Your skill as a makeup artist includes the ability to enhance features that are the result of each client's facial anatomy and physiology.
- Understanding facial anatomy and physiology will help you determine proper product choices and application techniques.
- Understanding skin conditions will make it easier to identify those that makeup can improve and those that indicate that makeup application is inappropriate/contraindicated.

BONES OF THE FACE

The structure of an individual face is completely dependent upon its framework. Therefore, this chapter will begin with that framework: the bones and the muscles of the face.

The facial bones bring distinction and character to the face and to the facial features. As a makeup artist, you will be able to creatively alter the appearance of this framework with contour, highlight, and color. It is often amazing how much the appearance of the face changes after highlight and contour are applied just to one feature.

The following bones create the structure and shape of the front of the face (**Figure 3–1**):

- **Nasal bones** (NAY-zul BOHNS). Two bones that form the bridge of the nose.
- **Lacrimal bones** (LAK-ruh-mul BOHNS). Two small, thin bones located at the front inner wall of the eye sockets.

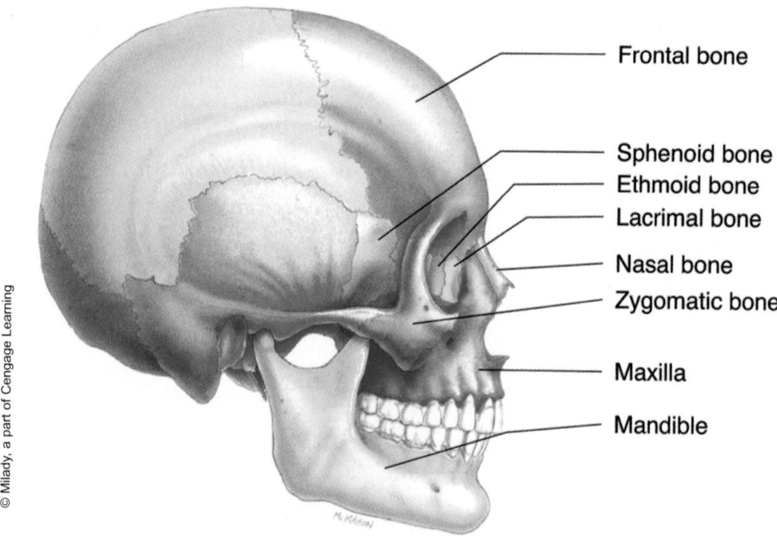

▲ **Figure 3–1 Bones of the cranium and face.**

- **Zygomatic bones** (zy-goh-MAT-ik BOHNS), also known as **malar bones** or **cheekbones**. The two bones that form the prominence of the cheeks.
- **Maxillae** (mak-SIL-ee). The two bones of the upper jaw.
- **Mandible** (MAN-duh-bul). Lower jawbone; largest and strongest bone of the face.

Although it is not considered a bone of the face, but rather a bone of the cranium, the **frontal bone** contributes to the appearance of the face; it forms the forehead.

Did You Know?

Some muscles of the face act as both voluntary and involuntary muscles. Blinking is both voluntary and involuntary. The muscles around our eyes help us blink.

MUSCLES OF THE FACE

Muscle tissue is responsible not only for movement of the face, but for the shape of the face as well (**Figure 3–2**). Facial muscles allow people to make expressions. All muscles are either striated or nonstriated. **Striated muscles** (STRY-ayt-ed MUS-uls) are muscles that are attached to the bones and are voluntary, or consciously controlled; they include the muscles used for smiling and winking.

Nonstriated muscles (nahn-STRY-ayt-ued MUS-uls) are muscles that are involuntary and function automatically, without conscious will; nonstriated muscles include the eyelids when you blink.

Muscles of the Eyebrow and Nose

The eyebrow muscles include the following:

- **Orbicularis oculi muscle** (or-bik-yuh-LAIR-is AHK-yuh-lye MUS-ul). A ring of muscle around the eye socket; enables you to close your eyes.
- **Corrugator muscle** (KOR-oo-gay-tohr MUS-ul). Muscle located beneath the

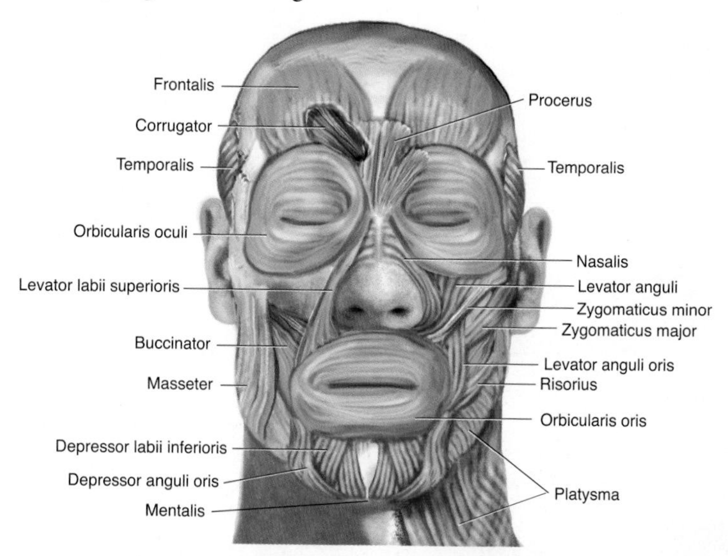

▲ **Figure 3–2 Muscles of the head, face, and neck.**

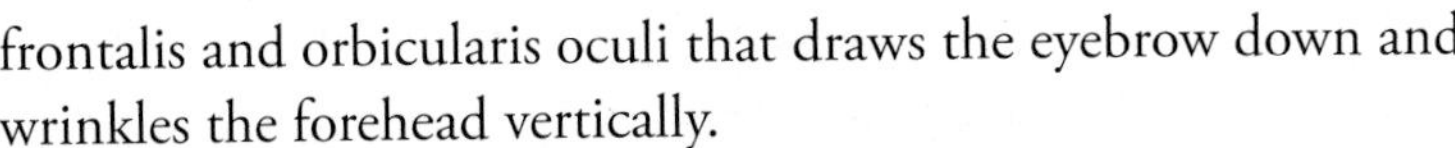

frontalis and orbicularis oculi that draws the eyebrow down and wrinkles the forehead vertically.

- **Frontalis** (frun-TAY-lus) muscle. A muscle of the scalp, it is not considered a muscle of the eyebrow; but is responsible for raising the eyebrows, drawing the scalp forward, and causing wrinkles across the forehead.
- **Procerus** (proh-SEE-rus). Covers the bridge of the nose, lowers the eyebrows, and causes wrinkles across the bridge of the nose.

Muscles of the Mouth

You have over 30 muscles in your face that control your expressions. It actually takes more muscles to frown than it takes to smile.

The muscles of the mouth are active in most facial movements and expressions. From talking and smiling to puckering and blowing, the muscles around the mouth influence the appearance and expression of the entire face. The important muscles of the mouth are the following:

- **Buccinator muscle** (BUK-sih-nay-tur MUS-ul). Thin, flat muscle of the cheek between the upper and lower jaw that compresses the cheeks and expels air between the lips.
- **Depressor labii inferioris muscle** (dee-PRES-ur LAY-bee-eye in-FEER-ee-or-us MUS-ul), also known as **quadratus labii inferioris muscle** (kwah-DRAY-tus LAY-bee-eye in-feer-ee-OR-is MUS-ul). Muscle surrounding the lower lip; lowers the lower lip and draws it to one side, as in expressing sarcasm.
- **Levator anguli oris muscle** (lih-VAYT-ur ANG-yoo-ly OH-ris MUS-ul), also known as **caninus muscle** (kay-NY-nus MUS-ul). Muscle that raises the angle of the mouth and draws it inward.
- **Levator labii superioris muscle** (lih-VAYT-ur LAY-bee-eye soo-peer-ee-OR-is MUS-ul), also known as **quadratus labii superioris muscle** (kwah-DRA-tus LAY-bee-eye soo-peer-ee-OR-is MUS-ul). Muscle surrounding the upper lip; elevates the upper lip and dilates the nostrils, as in expressing distaste.
- **Mentalis muscle** (men-TAY-lis MUS-ul). Muscle that elevates the lower lip and raises and wrinkles the skin of the chin.
- **Orbicularis oris muscle** (or-bik-yuh-LAIR-is OH-ris MUS-ul). Flat band of muscle around the upper and lower lips that compresses, contracts, puckers, and wrinkles the lips.
- **Risorius muscle** (rih-ZOR-ee-us MUS-ul). Muscle of the mouth that draws the corner of the mouth out and back, as in grinning.
- **Triangularis muscle** (try-ang-gyuh-LAY-rus MUS-ul). Muscle extending alongside the chin that pulls down the corner of the mouth.
- **Zygomaticus major muscles** (zy-goh-mat-ih-kus MAY-jor MUS-ul). Muscles on both sides of the face that extend from the zygomatic bone to the angle of the mouth. These muscles pull the mouth upward and backward, as when you are laughing or smiling.
- **Zygomaticus minor muscles** (zy-goh-mat-ih-kus MY-nor MUS-ul). Muscles on both sides of the face that extend from the zygomatic bone to the upper lips. These muscles pull the upper lip backward, upward and outward, as when you are smiling. ☑ LO2

THE SKIN

The skin is the largest organ of the human body, and the human body cannot survive without if it is not functional and intact. It acts as a natural barrier between our bodies and the environment, and it protects the network of muscles, bones, nerves, blood vessels, and everything else inside our bodies. The skin of the face is one of the first things people notice about one another. Most important for you, the skin is the makeup artist's canvas.

Healthy skin should be free of any visible signs of disease, infection, or injury. It is slightly moist, soft, smooth, and flexible. The surface of healthy skin is slightly acidic and contains four appendages that are important for the proper functioning and condition of the skin. Appendages of the skin include the hair, nails, and sudoriferous (sweat) and sebaceous (oil) glands.

As a makeup professional, you will find that clients have various expectations. Some clients will want you to enhance their appearance; others will want you to alter their appearance more noticeably; and still others will want you to completely transform their face. One thing clients often want you to do, but that is beyond your scope of practice or capabilities as a makeup artist, is to change the condition of their skin. The most perfect makeup job in the entire world will not change the condition of the skin, it is actually quite the opposite; the healthier the skin, the more amazing the makeup application will look. Better conditioned skin leads to more beautiful makeup applications.

With a full understanding of the skin's function, you can help clients make proper cosmetic choices in order to accentuate their individual features.

The Layers of the Skin

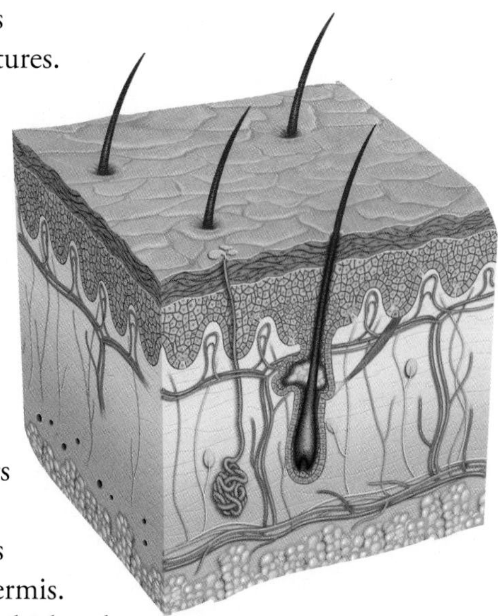

The skin is composed of two main layers, the epidermis and the dermis. Each layer plays an important role in the structure, function, health, and appearance of the skin.

The Epidermis

The **epidermis** (ep-uh-DUR-mis) is the outermost and thinnest layer of the skin (**Figure 3–3** on page 62). It contains no blood vessels but has many small nerve endings. The epidermis is made up of five sublayers that work together to create the visual appearance of the skin.

- The **stratum corneum** (STRAT-um KOR-nee-um), also known as the **horny layer** (HOR-nee LAY-ur), is the outer layer of the epidermis. It is composed of scale-like keratin cells that are continually being shed and replaced by new cells from underneath. **Keratin** (KAIR-uh-tin) is a fibrous protein that is also the principal component of hair and nails. These cells, called corneocytes, combine with lipids (fats) naturally produced by the skin to help make the stratum corneum a protective, water-resistant layer.
- The **stratum lucidum** (STRAT-um LOO-sih-dum) is the clear, transparent layer just under the stratum corneum. It is the thinnest layer, being only one cell thick, of skin on the face.
- The **stratum granulosum** (STRAT-um gran-yoo-LOH-sum), also known as the **granular layer** (GRAN-yuh-lur LAY-ur), is the lowest layer in the

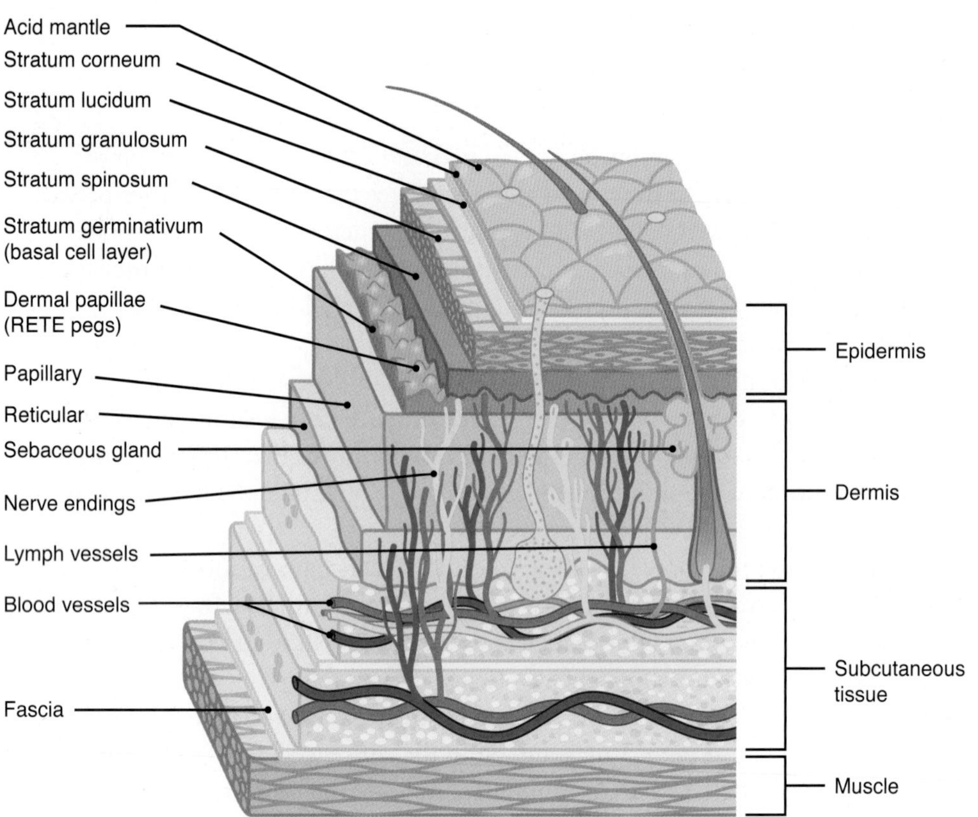

▶ **Figure 3–3 Layers of the epidermis and the dermis.**

epidermis that is composed of cells filled with keratin. These cells are pushed to the surface to replace dead cells that are shed from the stratum corneum.

- The **stratum spinosum** (STRAT-um spy-NOH-sum), also known as the **spiny layer**, lies just below the stratum granulosum. The spiny layer is where live, healthy skin cells begin to harden and become keratinized.
- The **stratum germinativum** (STRAT-um jer-mih-nah-TIV-um), also known as the **basal cell layer** (bay-ZUL CEL LAY-ur), is the deepest layer of the epidermis. This is the live layer of the epidermis that produces new epidermal skin cells. It is responsible for the growth and reproduction of the epidermis. The stratum germinativum also contains special cells called melanocytes. **Melanocytes** (muh-LAN-uh-syts) produce the skin pigment called melanin, which provides skin with its natural color. Melanin is also produced to protect the skin cells in response from the destructive effects of excessive ultraviolet (UV) light, hormonal changes, inflammation, and damage to the skin.

The epidermis is only 0.04 millimeter to 1.5 millimeters (1/1,000 to 1/16 inch) thick. One millimeter is .039 of an inch.

The Dermis

The **dermis** (DUR-mis) is the underlying or inner layer of the skin (refer to **Figure 3–3**). The dermis is about twenty-five times thicker than the epidermis. Within its structure, there are numerous blood vessels, lymph vessels, nerves, sudoriferous (sweat) glands, sebaceous (oil) glands, and hair follicles. The dermis is comprised of two layers: the papillary (upper layer) and the reticular (deeper layer).

The **papillary layer** (PAP-uh-lair-ee LAY-ur) is the upper layer of the dermis that lies directly beneath the epidermis. The papillary layer is rich in blood vessels and capillaries that feed and nourish the epidermal layer above it. The **reticular layer** (ruh-TIK-yuh-lur LAY-ur) is the deeper layer of the dermis that consists of specialized proteins known as collagen and elastin. **Collagen** (KAHL-uh-jen) is a fibrous protein that gives the skin form and strength. This fiber makes up a large percentage of the dermis and provides structural support by holding together all the structures found in this layer. When collagen fibers are healthy, they allow the skin to maintain its firmness. When collagen fibers become weakened due to age, lack of moisture, environmental damage such as UV light, or frequent changes in weight, the skin will begin to lose its tone and wrinkles are formed.

Elastin (ee-LAS-tin) is a protein that forms elastic tissue. Elastin gives the skin its flexibility and elasticity. It helps the skin regain its shape, even after being repeatedly stretched or expanded. Elastin can be weakened by the same factors that weaken collagen: UV exposure, environmental damage, poor skin care, and other types of damage to the skin.

As we age the natural production of collagen automatically decreases.

Functions of the Skin

The skin not only affects appearance; it also has many practical functions. The six principal functions of the skin are protection, sensation, heat regulation, excretion, secretion, and absorption.

- **Protection**. The skin protects the body from injury and bacterial invasion. The outermost layer is resistant to wide variations in temperature, minor injuries, chemically active substances, and many forms of bacteria.
- **Sensation**. By stimulating different sensory nerve endings, the skin responds to heat, cold, touch, pressure, and pain.
- **Heat regulation**. A healthy body maintains a constant internal temperature of about 98.6 degrees Fahrenheit (37 degrees Celsius). As changes occur in the outside temperature, the blood and sudoriferous (sweat) glands of the skin make necessary adjustments to allow the body to be cooled by the evaporation of sweat.
- **Excretion**. Perspiration from the sudoriferous glands is excreted through the skin. Through this process, salt and other chemicals are removed from the body.
- **Secretion**. Sebum (oil) is secreted by the sebaceous glands. This oil lubricates the skin, keeping it soft and pliable. Emotional stress and hormone imbalances can increase the flow of sebum.
- **Absorption**. Some ingredients can be absorbed by the outer layers of the skin, but very few ingredients can penetrate the epidermis. Small amounts of fatty materials, such as those used in many advanced skin care formulations, may be absorbed between the cells and through the hair follicles and sebaceous gland openings to improve the health and appearance of the skin. ☑ LO3

CONDITIONS OF THE SKIN

Like all other organs of the body, the skin is susceptible to a variety of diseases, disorders, and conditions. As a makeup artist, you must be prepared to recognize certain common skin conditions, and you must be able to distinguish between those that you can work on and those that must be referred to a physician. Although you will learn to recognize certain skin conditions, you are not qualified to diagnose them. In some cases, you can continue the makeup application without risking harm to yourself or your client. In other cases, your work might make the condition worse or the condition may pose a health threat to others; in these cases, you must not perform the makeup application.

Lesions of the Skin

A **lesion** (LEE-zhun) is any change in the continuity of the skin in texture, color, or shape. A lesion can be relatively harmless, like a freckle or a bruise, or a lesion can be as dangerous as skin cancer. Lesions can indicate skin disorders or diseases, and they sometimes indicate internal diseases. Being familiar with the principal types of skin lesions will help you distinguish between conditions that prevent perfroming a makeup application and conditions that allow it.

There are two categories of lesions, primary lesions and secondary lesions. **Primary lesions** are lesions that are of a color different than the color of the skin, or lesions that are raised above the surface of the skin (refer to **Table 3–1**). Makeup applications can be performed over primary lesions, but application over open lesions must be avoided.

TABLE 3–1 PRIMARY SKIN LESIONS

FIGURE	NAME OF LESION	DESCRIPTION	TYPICAL DIMENSIONS	EXAMPLES	CAN YOU APPLY MAKEUP?
	Vesicle	Different color than the color of the skin; accumulation of fluid between the upper layers of the skin; elevated mass containing serous fluid.	Less than 0.5 cm	Herpes simplex, herpes zoster, chickenpox	No
	Bulla	Large blister containing a watery fluid; similar to the vesicle but larger	Greater than 0.5 cm	Contact dermatitis, large second-degree burns, bulbous impetigo, blister	No
	Papule	Solid, elevated lesion; contains no fluid, may develop pus; frequently seen in acne.	Less than 0.5 cm in diameter	Warts, acne	Yes

▲ Table 3–1 Primary Skin Lesions.

continued

TABLE 3–1 PRIMARY SKIN LESIONS

FIGURE	NAME OF LESION	DESCRIPTION	TYPICAL DIMENSIONS	EXAMPLES	CAN YOU APPLY MAKEUP?
	Tubercle	Abnormal, rounded, solid lump above, within, or under the skin. Solid and elevated; however it extends deeper than papules into the dermis or subcutaneous tissues	0-5 to 2 cm	Lipoma, erythema, nodosum, cyst	Yes
	Pustule	Elevated lesion that becomes filled with pus and cellular debris. Raised, inflamed, papule with white or yellow center containing pus in the top of the lesion referred to as the head of the pimple.	Usually described as less than 0.5 cm	Acne, impetigo, furuncles, carbuncles, folliculitis	Yes
	Tumor	Abnormal mass varying in size, shape, and color.	Greater than 2 cm	Carinoma (such as advanced breast carcinoma); not basal cell or squamous cell of the skin	Yes
	Macule	Any flat spot or discoloration on the skin, such as a freckle or red spot, left after a pimple has healed.	Less than 1 cm	Freckle	Yes
	Wheal	Itchy, swollen lesion that lasts only a few hours; caused by a blow or scratch, the bite of an insect, urticaria (skin allergy), or the sting of a nettle.		Insect bite or a hive	No

▲ Table 3–1 **Primary Skin Lesions. (continued)**

Secondary skin lesions are characterized by piles of material on the skin surface, such as a crust or scab, or depressions in the skin surface, such as an ulcer (refer to **Table 3–2**). They are generally the result of a primary lesion

▼ Table 3–2 **Secondary Skin Lesions.**

TABLE 3-2 SECONDARY SKIN LESIONS

FIGURE	NAME OF LESION	DESCRIPTION	EXAMPLES	CAN YOU APPLY MAKEUP?
	Scar	Also known as *cicatrix*; Light colored, slightly raised mark on the skin following an injury or healed lesion.	Mark left from a deep cut	Yes
	Crust	A hard buildup of dead cells, blood, pus, and epidermal debris.	Scab	No
	Ulcer	Open lesion on the skin or mucous membrane of the body; accompanied by loss of skin depth and possibly weeping of fluids or pus.	Open wound	No
	Scale	Any thin, dry epidermal skin cells.	Dandruff or flaky skin	Yes
	Fissure	Any thin, dry epidermal skin cells.	Openings in cracked lips or hands.	Yes
	Excoriation	Lesion from scratching or scraping.	Mark left after picking at a pimple	No

Common Sebaceous Gland Disorders

Sebaceous glands are the oil glands that keep the skin moist, supple, and youthful looking. They are also the cause of a variety of common skin conditions.

An open **comedo** (KAHM-uh-doh) (plural: comedones), also known as a **blackhead**, is a hair follicle filled with keratin and sebum. When the sebaceous material is exposed to the environment it oxidizes and turns black. Comedones appear most frequently around the sides of the nose and the center of the chin (**Figure 3–4**). A **closed comedo**, also known as a **whitehead**, is similar sebaceous material trapped beneath a very thin layer of dead skin cells. They appear as a small bump just under the skin surface. Makeup applications can be performed over comedones.

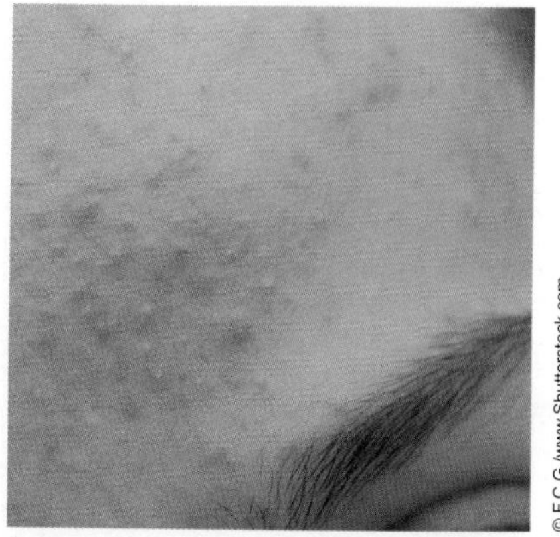

▲ Figure 3–4 **Open and closed comedones.**

Milia (MIL-eel-uh) are benign, keratin-filled **cysts**—closed, abnormally developed sacs containing fluid, semifluid, or morbid matter, above or below the skin—that appear just under the epidermis and have no visible opening. Milia resemble small sesame seeds and are almost always perfectly round. They are commonly found around the eyes, cheeks, and forehead, and they appear as small, whitish masses (**Figure 3–5**). Makeup applications can be performed over milia.

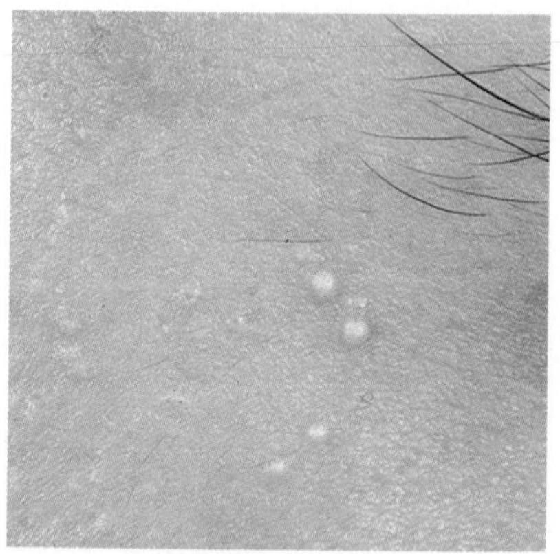

▲ Figure 3–5 **Milia.**

Acne (AK-nee) also known as **acne vulgaris** (AK-nee vull-GAIR-us), is a frequently seen skin disorder characterized by chronic inflammation of the sebaceous glands from retained secretions and bacteria known as **propionibacterium acnes** (pro-PEE-ah-nee-back-tear-ee-um). Characteristics of various stages of acne include open and closed comedones, papules, pustules, and cysts (**Figure 3–6**). Makeup applications can be performed as long as there are no open lesions.

Seborrheic dermatitis (seb-oh-REE-ick derm-ah-TIE-tus) is a skin condition caused by inflammation of the sebaceous glands. It is often characterized by redness, dry or oily scaling, crusting, and/or itchiness. The red, flaky skin often appears in the eyebrows, in the scalp and hairline, at the middle of the forehead, and along the sides of the nose.

Seborrheic dermatitis is a medical condition, but makeup applications can be performed if proper topical treatment products have been prescribed. Clients with this skin condition tend to be sensitive to makeup ingredients.

Rosacea (roh-ZAY-shuh), formerly called acne rosacea, is a chronic inflammatory condition that appears on the cheeks and nose and that is characterized by flushing (redness), **telangiectasis** (tee-lang-jek-tay-shuhz) (distended or dilated surface blood vessels), and in some cases the formation of **papules** (small, solid bumps) and **pustules** (raised lesions containing pus). Certain factors are known to aggravate rosacea such as exposure to heat, sun, and very cold weather; ingestion of spicy foods, caffeine, and alcohol; and stress. Individuals with rosacea tend to be sen-

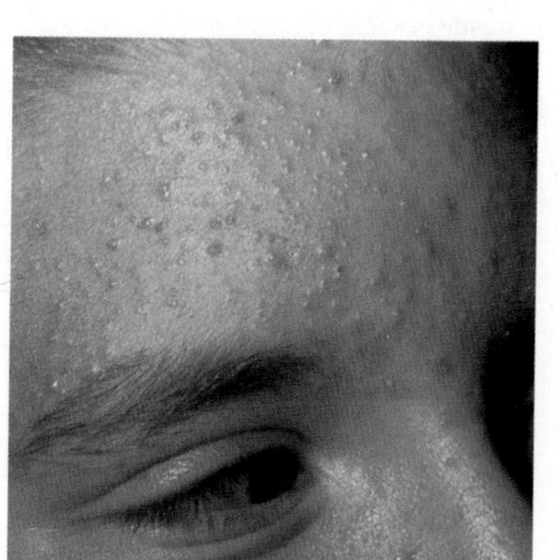

▲ Figure 3–6 **Acne vulgaris.**

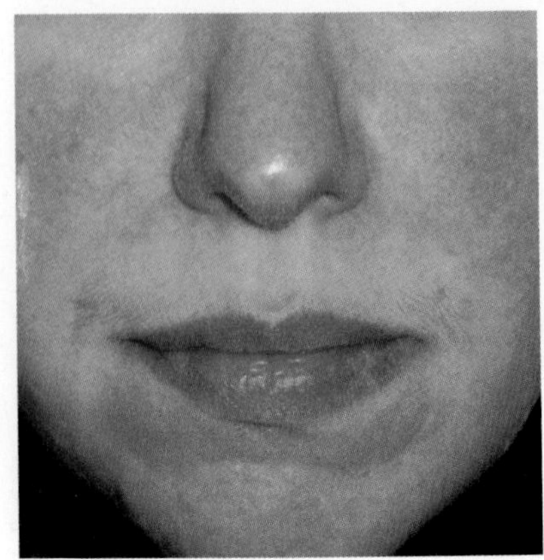
Courtesy of the National Rosacea Society.

▲ Figure 3–7 Classic rosacea.

sitive to makeup ingredients, although proper products help to ease the constant redness (**Figure 3–7**).

Inflammatory Disorders

Inflammatory conditions arise when there is a presence of a foreign substance in or on the skin. They can be linked to bacteria, viruses, or various external stimuli.

Conjunctivitis (kuhn-juhngk-tuh-VAHY-tis), also known as **pink-eye**, is a common bacterial infection of the eyes. It is extremely contagious. Makeup applications should not be performed on clients with conjunctivitis; clients should be politely rescheduled and referred to a physician immediately. Any product or implements that have touched infected eyes must be thrown away.

Dermatitis (dur-muh-TY-tis) is a term broadly used to describe any inflammatory condition of the skin.

Eczema (EG-zuh-muh) is an inflammatory, uncomfortable, and often chronic disease of the skin, characterized by moderate to severe inflammation, scaling, and sometimes severe itching. Eczema is not contagious, and if the condition is being treated with prescribed topical medications, you can apply makeup to affected areas (**Figure 3–8**). Makeup should be completely avoided if there is any moisture or oozing from the area.

CAUTION

Contaminated eye pencils and brushes are a leading cause of the spread of conjunctivitis. It is your professional responsibility to prevent the spread of eye infections. Here are simple tips:

- Sharpen eye pencils before and after each use on every client. While applying makeup, sharpen the eye pencil after you finish the client's first eye, before beginning the second eye.
- Properly cleanse hands, nondisposable utensils, chairs, and counters between clients with approved disinfectant or alcohol.
- Dispose of any product that you suspect may be contaminated.
- Gracefully refuse to perform a makeup service on any client with a suspected eye infection, or any other possible infection on the face.

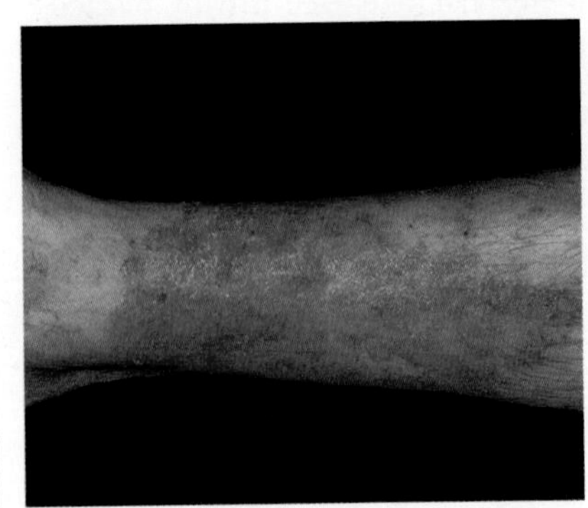
Courtesy of www.dermnet.com.

▲ Figure 3–8 Eczema.

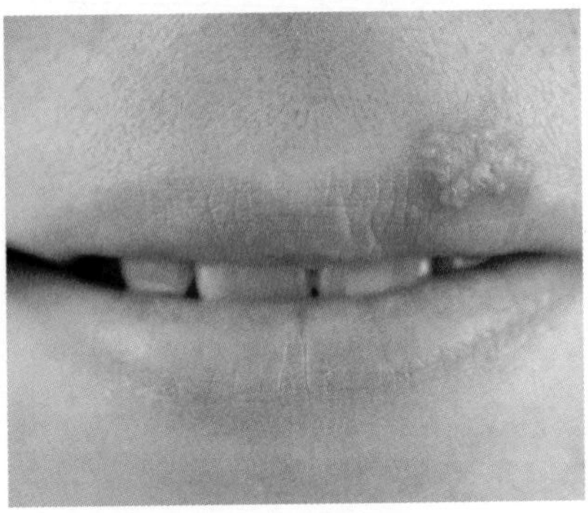
© Levent Konuk/www.Shutterstock.com

▲ Figure 3–9 Herpes simplex I.

Herpes simplex (HER-peez SIM-pleks) is a recurring viral infection that presents as a fever blister or cold sore (**Figure 3–9**). It is characterized by the eruption of a single **vesicle**, a small blister or sac containing clear fluid, lying within or just beneath the epidermis, or group of vesicles on a red swollen base. The blisters usually appear on the lips, nostrils, or other part of the face, and the sores can last up to 3 weeks. Herpes simplex is contagious and makeup application should be avoided.

Impetigo (im-pet-EYE-go) is a contagious bacterial skin infection characterized by weeping lesions. Impetigo normally occurs on the face

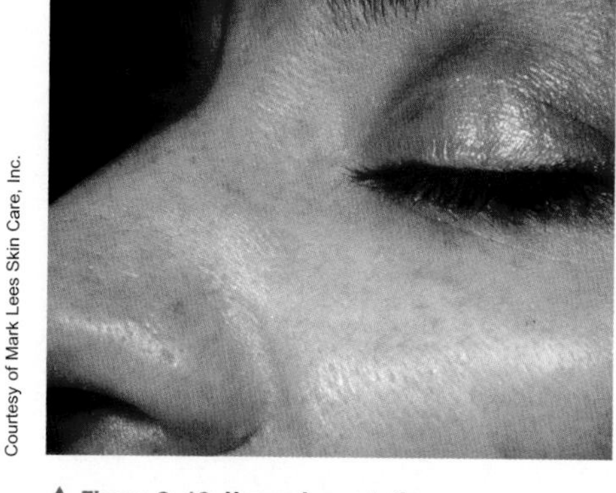

Courtesy of Mark Lees Skin Care, Inc.

▲ Figure 3–10 **Hyperpigmentation.**

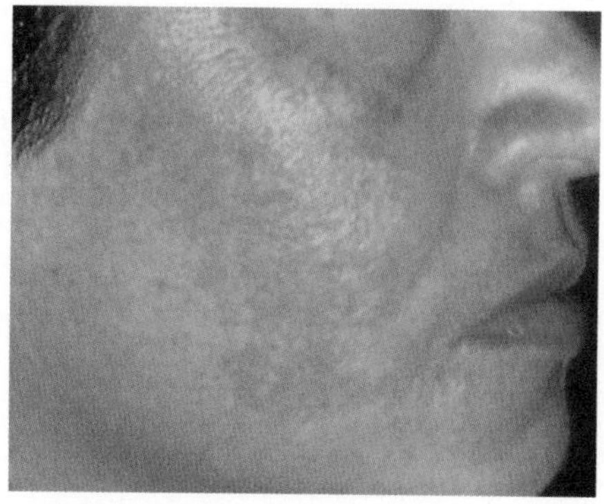

Courtesy Timothy G. Berger, M.D.

▲ Figure 3–11 **Chloasma.**

(especially the chin area) and is most frequently seen in children. Clients with any type of weeping open facial lesions should be politely rescheduled and referred to a physician immediately. Makeup application should not be performed.

Pigmentation Disorders

Pigment can be affected by several factors, including heredity, hormonal fluctuations, UV exposure, medications, systemic disorders, and inflammation. Although sometimes difficult to cover, pigmentation disorders are not contraindications for makeup application, and are frequently a reason that a client seeks a professional makeup artist's advice. The following terms relate to changes in the pigmentation of the skin:

- **Hyperpigmentation** means darker than normal pigmentation, appearing as dark patches (**Figure 3–10**).
- **Hypopigmentation** is the absence of pigment resulting in light or white patches.
- **Albinism** (AL-bi-niz-em) is the absence of melanin pigment in the body, including the skin, hair, and eyes. The technical term for albinism is congenital leukoderma or congenital hypopigmentation.
- **Chloasma** (kloh-AZ-mah) is a condition characterized by hyperpigmentation on the skin in spots that are not elevated. Also called the "mask of pregnancy" or liver spots, chloasma is triggered by hormonal changes (**Figure 3–11**).
- **Lentigines** (len-TIJ-e-neez) (singular: lentigo, len-TY-goh) is the technical term for freckles, small yellow- to brown-colored spots on skin that has been exposed to sunlight.
- **Nevus** (NEE-vus), also known as ***birthmark***, is a small or large malformation of the skin due to abnormal pigmentation or dilated capillaries.
- **Vitiligo** (vi-til-EYE-goh) is a skin condition characterized by hypopigmented spots and splotches on the skin; it may be genetic or related to thyroid conditions (**Figure 3–12**). Heavier camouflage makeup is often needed to even the skin color. ☑ **LO4**

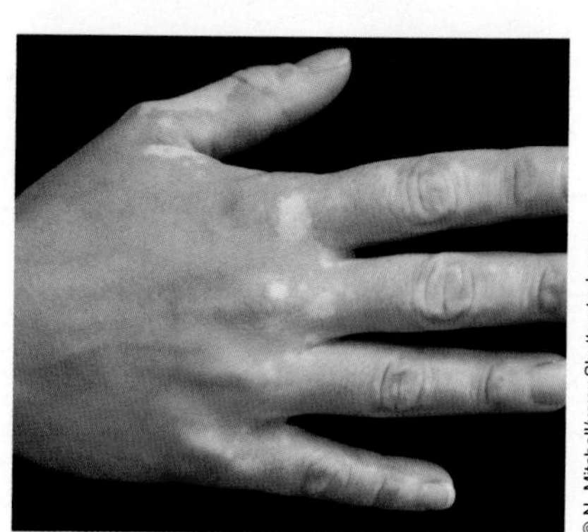

© N. Mitchell/www.Shutterstock.com

▲ Figure 3–12 **Vitiligo on the hand.**

Skin Cancer

Excess exposure to UV light is the primary cause of skin cancer. There are three main types, each named for the type of cells that it affects.

Basal cell carcinoma (BAY-zul SEL kar-sin-OH-muh) is the most common type of skin cancer, but the least severe; it is often characterized by light or pearly **nodules** (**Figure 3–13**). **Squamous** (SKWAY-mus) **cell carcinoma** is more serious than basal cell carcinoma, and often is characterized by scaly red papules or nodules (**Figure 3–14**). The third and most serious form of skin cancer is **malignant melanoma** (muh-LIG-nent mel-uh-NOH-muh), which is often characterized by black or dark brown patches on the skin that may appear uneven in texture, jagged, or raised (**Figure 3–15**). Malignant melanoma is the least common—but also the most dangerous—type of skin cancer. Makeup application need only be avoided if the cancerous lesions are open or moist.

Courtesy of www.dermnet.com.

▲ Figure 3–13 **Basal cell carcinoma.**

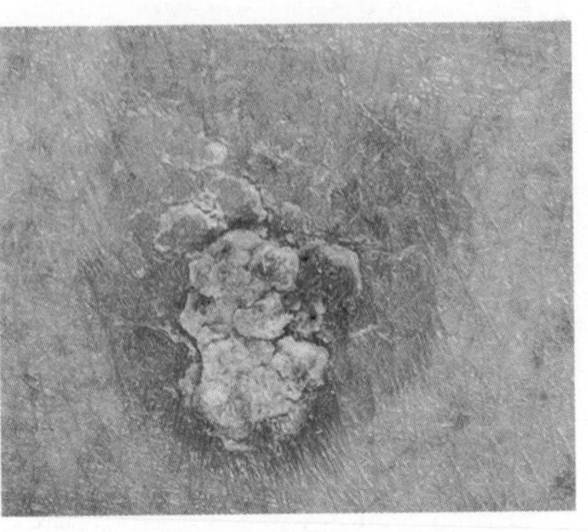

Courtesy of www.dermnet.com.

▲ Figure 3–14 **Squamous cell carcinoma.**

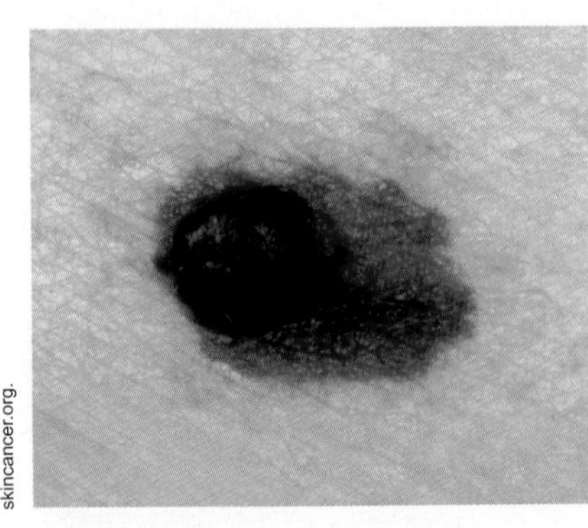

Courtesy of The Skin Cancer Foundation, http://www.skincancer.org.

▲ Figure 3–15 **Malignant melanoma.**

If the cancer is detected early, people with any of these forms of skin cancer have a good chance for survival. As a makeup professional you can play a unique role by recognizing the appearance of serious skin disorders and referring the client to a dermatologist for diagnosis and treatment. ✔ **LO5**

This chapter has provided you with critical information that will enable you to understand the structure of the face and to recognize various skin conditions. Makeup professionals often explain to clients the importance of skin care in general, and they often make recommendations regarding specific products that a client should use, given her particular skin type and facial structure.

As product formulations change and new ingredients enter the marketplace, the makeup industry is closely mimicking the skin care industry. Many cosmetic lines and products now contain active ingredients that improve the condition and functioning of the skin. Sunscreens, antibacterials, and firming and toning ingredients are now an integral part of the makeup world. Your knowledge of skin structure and function will help you to choose and recommend appropriate products for your clients.

Review Questions

1. How many bones create the structure and shape of the face?
2. Explain the difference between striated and nonstriated muscles.
3. What is the name of the bone that creates the cheekbone?
4. List the four appendages of the skin.
5. In which layer of the skin are new cells constantly being reproduced?
6. Which layer of the skin contains the protein structures collagen and elastin?
7. Which protein substance is responsible for providing the skin with strength and firmness?
8. List the six functions of the skin.
9. Define lesion.
10. Describe the differences between the two categories of lesions.
11. What are benign, keratin-filled cysts appearing just under the epidermis without a visible opening called?
12. Define acne vulgaris.
13. Describe the characteristics of rosacea.
14. What term describes darker than normal pigmentation that appear as dark patches?
15. What is the pigmentation disorder that is the result of hormone changes called?
16. What is the lay term for lentigines?
17. Name the most common and the least severe type of skin cancer, which is often characterized by light or pearly nodules.
18. Define eczema.
19. Is eczema contagious?
20. Can a makeup application be performed on a client with conjunctivitis?

Chapter Glossary

acne	Also known as *acne vulgaris*; frequently seen skin disorder characterized by chronic inflammation of the sebaceous glands from retained secretions and bacteria known as propionibacterium.
albinism	Absence of melanin pigment in the body, including the skin, hair, and eyes; the technical term for albinism is congenital leukoderma or congenital hypopigmentation.
basal cell carcinoma	Most common and least severe type of skin cancer; often characterized by light or pearly nodules.
buccinator muscle	Thin, flat muscle of the cheek between the upper and lower jaw that compresses the cheeks and expels air between the lips.

Chapter Glossary *(continued)*

bulla (plural: bullae)	Large blister containing a watery fluid; similar to a vesicle but larger.
chloasma	Condition characterized by increased pigmentation on the skin due to hormonal changes. Sometimes referred to as the "mask of pregnancy" or liver spots.
closed comedo	Also known as a *whitehead*; hair follicle is closed and not exposed to the environment; sebum remains a white or cream color and comedo appears as small bump just under the skin surface.
collagen	Fibrous protein that gives the skin form and strength.
comedo (plural: comedones)	Also known as a *blackhead*; a hair follicle filled with keratin and sebum.
conjunctivitis	Also known as *pinkeye*; common bacterial infection of the eyes, extremely contagious.
corrugator muscle	Muscle located beneath the frontalis and orbicularis oculi that draws the eyebrow down and wrinkles the forehead vertically.
crust	Dead cells that form over a wound or blemish while it is healing; an accumulation of sebum and pus, sometimes mixed with epidermal material.
cysts	Closed, abnormally developed sacs containing fluid, semifluid, or morbid matter, above or below the skin.
depressor labii inferioris muscle	Also known as *quadratus labii inferioris muscle*; muscle surrounding the lower lip; lowers the lower lip and draws it to one side, as in expressing sarcasm.
dermatitis	Inflammatory condition of the skin.
dermis	Underlying or inner layer of the skin.
eczema	An inflammatory, uncomfortable, and often chronic disease of the skin characterized by moderate to severe inflammation, scaling, and sometimes severe itching.
elastin	Protein base similar to collagen that forms elastic tissue.
epidermis	Outermost and thinnest layer of the skin; it is made up of five sublayers that work together to create the visual appearance of the skin.
excoriation	Skin sore or abrasion produced by scratching or scraping.
fissure	A crack in the skin that penetrates the dermis. Examples are severely cracked and/or chapped hands or lips.
frontal bone	The frontal bone forms the forehead.

Chapter Glossary *(continued)*

frontalis	A muscle of the scalp, it is not considered a muscle of the eyebrow; but is responsible for raising the eyebrows, drawing the scalp forward, and causing wrinkles across the forehead.
herpes simplex	Fever blister or cold sore; recurring viral infection.
hyperpigmentation	Darker than normal pigmentation, appearing as dark splotches.
hypopigmentation	Absence of pigment resulting in light or white splotches.
impetigo	Contagious bacterial skin infection characterized by weeping lesions.
keratin	Fibrous protein of cells that is also the principal component of hair and nails.
lacrimal bones	Two small, thin bones located at the front inner wall of the eye sockets.
lentigines (singular: lentigo)	Technical term for freckles. Small yellow- to brown-colored spots on skin exposed to sunlight and air.
lesion	Any change in the continuity of the skin in texture, color, or shape. May indicate an injury or damage that changes the structure of the tissues or organs.
levator anguli oris muscle	Also known as *caninus muscle*; muscle that raises the angle of the mouth and draws it inward.
levator labii superioris muscle	Also known as *quadratus labii superioris muscle*; muscle surrounding the upper lip; elevates the upper lip and dilates the nostrils, as in expressing distaste.
macule (plural: maculae)	Spot or discoloration on the skin, such as a freckle or a red spot left after a pimple has healed.
malignant melanoma	Most serious form of skin cancer; often characterized by black or dark brown patches on the skin that may appear uneven in texture, jagged, or raised.
mandible	Lower jawbone; largest and strongest bone of the face.
maxillae	The two bones of the upper jaw.
melanocytes	Cells that produce the dark skin pigment called melanin.
mentalis muscle	Muscle that elevates the lower lip and raises and wrinkles the skin of the chin.
milia	Benign keratin-filled cysts that can appear just under the epidermis and have no visible opening.

Chapter Glossary *(continued)*

nasal bones	Two bones that form the bridge of the nose.
nevus	Also known as *birthmark*; small or large malformation of the skin due to abnormal pigmentation or dilated capillaries.
nodule	A solid bump larger than .4 inches (1 centimeter) that can be easily felt.
nonstriated muscles	Muscles that are involuntary and function automatically, without conscious will.
orbicularis oculi muscle	Ring muscle of the eye socket; enables you to close your eyes.
orbicularis oris muscle	Flat band of muscle around the upper and lower lips that compresses, contracts, puckers, and wrinkles the lips.
papillary layer	Outer layer of the dermis, directly beneath the epidermis.
papule	A raised bump, often red due to inflammation, and often sore due to the pressure of swelling; papules are frequently seen in acne; large sore bumps that do not have a head of pus.
primary lesions	Lesions of color different than the color of the skin, or lesions that are raised above the surface of the skin.
procerus	Covers the bridge of the nose, lowers the eyebrows, and causes wrinkles across the bridge of the nose.
propionibacterium acnes	Scientific term for acne bacteria.
pustule	Raised, inflamed papule with a white or yellow center containing pus in the top of the lesion referred to as the head of the pimple.
reticular layer	Deeper layer of the dermis that consists of specialized proteins known as collagen and elastin.
risorius muscle	Muscle of the mouth that draws the corner of the mouth out and back, as in grinning.
rosacea	Chronic redness and congestion appearing primarily on the cheeks and nose, characterized by redness, dilation of the blood vessels, and in some cases, formation of papules and pustules.
scale	Any thin dry or oily plate of epidermal flakes. An example is abnormal or excessive dandruff.
scar	A lightly raised mark on the skin formed after an injury or lesion of the skin has healed.
seborrheic dermatitis	Skin condition caused by an inflammation of the sebaceous glands. Often characterized by inflammation, dry or oily scaling, crusting, and/or itchiness.

Chapter Glossary *(continued)*

secondary skin lesions	Characterized by piles of material on the skin surface, such as a crust or scab, or depressions in the skin surface, such as an ulcer.
squamous cell carcinoma	Type of skin cancer more serious than basal cell carcinoma; characterized by scaly, red or pink papules or nodules; also appear as open sores or crusty areas; can grow and spread in the body.
stratum corneum	Also known as *horny layer*; outer layer of the epidermis.
stratum germinativum	Also known as *basal cell layer*; deepest, live layer of the epidermis that produces new epidermal skin cells and is responsible for growth.
stratum granulosum	Also known as *granular layer*; layer of the epidermis composed of cells that look like granules and are filled with keratin; replaces cells shed from the stratum corneum.
stratum lucidum	Clear, transparent layer of the epidermis under the stratum corneum.
stratum spinosum	The spiny layer just above the stratum germinativum layer.
striated muscles	Muscles that are attached to the bones and are voluntary, or consciously controlled.
telangiectasis	Distended or dilated surface blood vessels.
triangularis muscle	Muscle extending alongside the chin that pulls down the corner of the mouth.
ulcer	Open lesion on the skin, accompanied by pus and loss of skin depth.
vesicle	Small blister or sac containing clear fluid, lying within or just beneath the epidermis.
vitiligo	Hereditary condition that causes hypopigmented spots and splotches on the skin; may be related to thyroid conditions.
wheal	Itchy, swollen lesion that lasts only a few hours; caused by a blow or scratch, the bite of an insect, urticaria (skin allergy), or the sting of a nettle. Examples include hives and mosquito bites.
zygomatic bones	Also known as *malar bones* or *cheekbones*; the two bones that form the prominence of the cheeks.
zygomaticus major muscles	Muscles on both sides of the face that extend from the zygomatic bone to the angle of the mouth. These muscles pull the mouth upward and backward, as when you are laughing or smiling.
zygomaticus minor muscles	Muscles on both sides of the face that extend from the zygomatic bone to the upper lips. These muscles pull the upper lip backward, upward and outward, as when you are smiling.

Chapter 4 Tools of the Trade

Chapter Outline

Learning Objectives

After completing this chapter, you will be able to:

- ☑ **LO1** Identify the differences regarding makeup brush-types and makeup bristle-types.
- ☑ **LO2** List various utensils required for every makeup artist's toolkit.
- ☑ **LO3** Identify types of single-use tools for makeup application.
- ☑ **LO4** Describe different types of makeup cases.

Key Terms

Page number indicates where in the chapter the term is used.

blotting paper
pg. 88

brow comb
pg. 87

brow scissors
pg. 87

ferrule
pg. 80

hair
pg. 79

ingrown hairs
pg. 87

Kolinsky sable
pg. 81

makeup tool belts
pg. 91

natural hair
pg. 80

natural-hair brushes
pg. 80

nylon
pg. 82

palette
pg. 88

pointed slant tweezers
pg. 87

pointed tweezers
pg. 87

refillable brush
pg. 86

retractable brushes
pg. 86

slant tweezers
pg. 87

synthetic hair
pg. 82

synthetic-hair brushes
pg. 80

Taklon
pg. 82

train cases (travel cases)
pg. 91

weasel hair (red sable)
pg. 81

Career Profile

Tim Maurer has over 20 years of experience as a master esthetician and internationally renowned makeup artist. Driven by his passion for the art of makeup and the allure of healthy skin, Maurer's mission is to raise the bar on the knowledge and application of makeup products and techniques used at today's leading spas. With the creation of Mukha Essentials, Maurer has realized his vision of makeup as skin care. Today Maurer's name is synonymous with simple beauty.

"As a nationally recognized makeup artist, my work has been featured in leading magazines such as *British Vogue*, on fashion runways around the globe, and in feature films like *Little Man Tate* and *Field of Dreams*. I explored my vision until I reached the obvious conclusion that I should create my own skin care and color lines. Both product collections are oil-free, alcohol-free, and fragrance-free. The mineral-based formulas of the products have been proven to restore the texture and tone of the face, as their main ingredients are accepted transdermally, through the skin. Copper, magnesium, and zinc are known healing agents for scar tissue, acne, and rosacea. The result is makeup that works as skin care.

"I am an apprentice to the world-renowned makeup artist Way Bandy, and I developed my skills working in New York City. I often give seminars on makeup techniques on everything from everyday living to theatrical and stage application. I have worked tirelessly to stay on the cutting edge of new techniques and trends in makeup, and I am often called upon to create fresh new looks for shoots and runway events all around the nation.

"I have served as a Beauty Director of the Mrs. International Pageant System and was a contributor to the article "Beyond Makeup 101" in the international trade magazine *Les Nouvelles Esthétiques*. I am also one of only a handful of Americans ever asked to speak at The International Congress of Esthetics and Makeup Artistry in Paris. It was my honor to appear as a keynote speaker with Deepak Chopra. I spoke to an audience of more than 7,000.

"In 2007, my vision came full circle with the creation of a cosmetic revolution: Mukha Essentials. It is not merely a new product line; it is an entirely new concept in cosmetics and skin health. Mukha Essentials is a collection of cosmetics and skin care that are the basic foundation for achieving healthy, beautiful skin. Truly, this line is makeup as skin care."

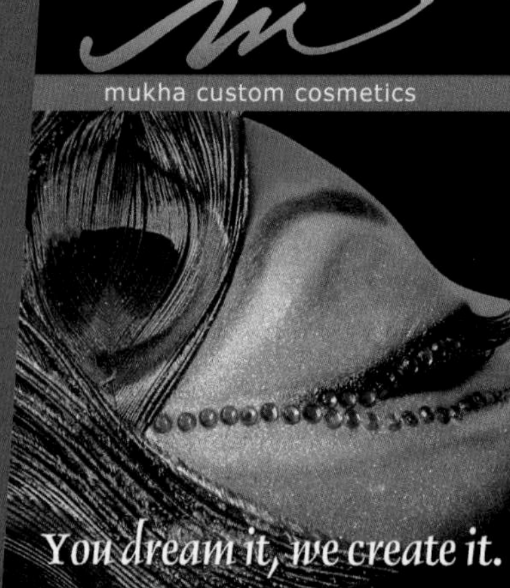

mukha custom cosmetics
You dream it, we create it.

Courtesy of Tim Maurer.

The use of proper tools can make or break the accuracy, perfection, success, and overall outcome of any job. For example, a painter requires the proper canvas, paints, and brushes; an architect requires the proper pencils, measuring tools, and paper; a fashion designer requires the right fabrics, patterns, and sewing machine.

As a professional makeup artist, your choice of tools will directly influence the outcome of every makeup application that you perform, from a simple day-makeover to the most extravagant high-fashion application. This chapter will provide you with the many options available and with insight into the unique features and benefits of each. You will develop personal preferences over time as you become familiar with the purpose of each tool as your experience grows.

Choices include single-use (i.e., disposable) and multiuse (i.e., nondisposable), synthetic and natural, long-handled and short-handled, and so on. Take your time, try all of the options, and fill your toolbox with tools you love so you can master your trade.

WHY STUDY TOOLS OF THE TRADE?

Makeup artists should study and have a thorough understanding of tools of the trade because:

- A working knowledge of all available tools will improve your ability to perform a flawless makeup application.
- The various available applicators create different looks and will allow you to create a custom look for every client.
- Your tool choices will enhance your individuality and style.

BRUSHES

For any makeup artist, the most important tools are the brushes. Brushes vary in size, shape, make, use, cost, and longevity. Preferences for brush styles and types vary dramatically from one makeup artist to another. However, every professional makeup artist agrees that brushes are the artist's most essential tool—anyone who says otherwise has yet to experience the magic of each brush stroke.

Top-quality makeup brushes can last from 10 years to a lifetime. This does not necessarily mean that all of your brushes must be expensive. Even top makeup artists have brush collections that include a range of quality and cost, depending upon personal preference and use. You will be the decision maker in the creation of your own brush collection.

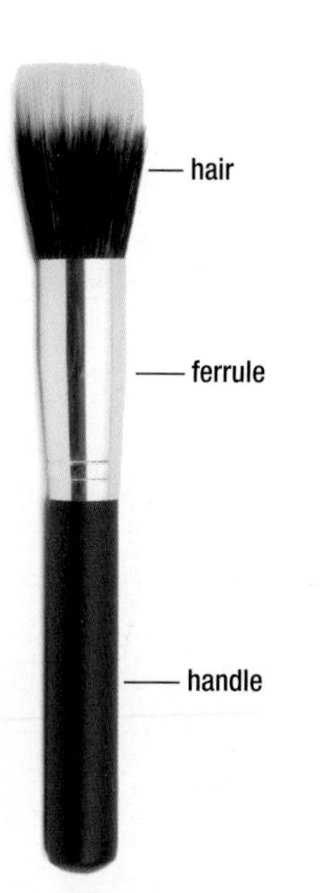

▲ **Figure 4–1 The different parts of a brush: the hair, the ferrule, and the handle.**

Three Brush Parts

A makeup brush is divided into three parts: the hair, the ferrule, and the handle (**Figure 4–1**). Each part affects the quality, efficacy, and lifespan of the brush. **Hair** is the term used for the bristles of makeup brushes. Hair

types are quite interesting and extensive; they are covered in the following paragraphs.

The **ferrule** is the metal part of the brush that attaches the glued bristles to the handle and adds a certain amount of strength to the bristles. The ferrule can be made from aluminum, aluminum alloy, copper, or brass. The ferrule should always be seamless. Regardless of the type of metal used, high-quality brushes will have a double crimp, or ring, around the ferrule to avoid any loosening or wobbling of the handle.

Brush handles can be made of wood, acrylic, plastic, or metal. The handle type you choose will be a matter of personal preference. Wooden handles, although one of the more popular choices, are the most sensitive to chemical brush cleaners and cannot be left in a solution or detergent for any length of time. Brush handles also come in a wide range of lengths. Very short handles are often used on brushes for travel. The most preferred handle length tends to be 7 inches (17.75 centimeters); however, handle length is also a matter of personal preference. Many makeup artists believe that a longer handle gives them more artistic design control. The only way to find your personal preference is to use several different lengths of brushes. What is well suited for one artist may not be so for another.

Brush Hair Types

This topic could well be a chapter all its own. Brush hair types fall into two categories: natural and synthetic. **Natural-hair brushes** are brushes made from animal hairs or blends of animal hairs. **Synthetic-hair brushes** are manmade brushes whose bristles come from fabric and chemical sources. Each type of bristle has distinct features, qualities, and functions. Once again, your personal preference will play an important role in the individual bristle hair choices that you choose to work with. Complete details on both types of brush hair are provided in the following paragraphs.

▲ Figure 4–2 Scales on a natural hair shaft.

Natural-Hair Bristles

Natural hair comes from a variety of animal sources. Natural animal hair, just like human hair, consists of an outer layer called the cuticle. This outer layer is composed of hundreds of small fish-like scales, quite similar to the outer layer of the skin (**Figure 4–2**). When brushes made using natural-hair bristles are pressed into powder cosmetics, the cosmetic gets trapped beneath, around, and between the scales. When the brush is tapped or stroked onto the skin, the particles of cosmetic are released onto their new surface, making natural hair an excellent way to transport cosmetics from a palette or container to the face. Natural-bristle brushes are very much a favorite with makeup artists and tend to get softer with extended use.

Badger Bristles

Badger hair, which usually comes from China, is a popular and widely available choice for brush bristles. The highest quality badger hair comes from the animal's neck area. Each hair varies in color from light to dark and back again. Gray badger hair tends to be the least expensive, but it is not as soft as other colors.

The softness of badger hair makes it an excellent choice for larger makeup brushes, such as powder and blush brushes. Because high-quality badger hair is quite expensive, it is often blended with other types of hair.

Did You Know?

Natural-hair brushes are made from hair that is cut from animals. Not a single brush manufacturer harms animals to manufacture their brushes.

Squirrel Bristles

Squirrel bristles are among the softest natural bristles available and have very fine, delicate tips. They are a favorite among professional makeup artists. Hair used for high-quality squirrel-hair makeup brushes comes only from long-haired squirrels, not the squirrels that run up your trees. Squirrel hair is commonly blended with pony and/or goat hair. Squirrel hair holds water, making it an excellent choice for liquid makeup application.

Goat Bristles

Goat hair is the most common type of hair found in cosmetic brushes because it is widely available and relatively inexpensive. Goat hair is soft and quite strong. It is commonly blended with various, more expensive, types of hair. Handmade goat-bristle brushes are a less expensive alternative to squirrel-bristle brushes and can be found in a range of colors including red, brown, and white (**Figure 4–3**).

▲ Figure 4–3 **Goat hair.**

Pony Bristles

Pony hair is also used to create makeup brushes. Pony bristles have a less delicate, less pointy end. The pony hair used in makeup brushes comes mainly from China. Pony-bristle brushes are less expensive than squirrel-bristle brushes, but more expensive than goat-bristle brushes. Brushes are rarely made of 100 percent pony hair. Pony hair is often mixed with squirrel hair to reduce the cost of squirrel-bristle brushes (**Figure 4–4**).

▲ Figure 4–4 **Pony hair.**

Sable Bristles

Sable is the largest category of makeup brushes, and sable hair is used in almost every type of brush, including powder brushes, blush brushes, and shadow brushes. It is soft and strong, and it holds cosmetic color and product very well (**Figure 4–5**).

Kolinsky sable is a type of natural bristle that comes from mink found in the cold climates of China and Siberia; it is among the finest, softest, and most expensive material from which makeup brushes are made. The bristles are golden brown and unique in that they are both springy and unbelievably soft.

Weasel hair, also known as **red sable**, is not as soft as Kolinsky sable but still very valuable. Although weasel is a common brush material in North America, only weasel hair from Asia is long enough and fine enough to be comparable to Kolinsky.

▲ Figure 4–5 **Sable hair.**

▲ Figure 4–6 Boar hair.

Allergies are becoming more common, so be sure to complete a consultation form so you can review sensitivities with your client. This will allow you to ensure that your client will not have an allergic reaction to your brushes.

▲ Figure 4–7 Taklon bristles.

Boar Bristles

Boar hair is a course hair that is thicker and stronger than other types of hair used in makeup brushes. Due to its firmness, boar hair is commonly used in brow brushes (**Figure 4–6**).

Raccoon Bristles

Raccoon bristles fall right in the middle of all bristle categories. They have a very soft texture, but they still maintain a certain amount of firmness. Raccoon is widely available and very affordable. Raccoon is usually blended with various other natural bristles.

Camel Bristles

Oddly enough, camel-bristle makeup brushes do not contain a single bit of camel hair. Rather, camel-bristle brushes are created using a combination of different hair types. Camel bristles are a mix of pony, ox, goat, squirrel, raccoon, and even boar. They are made in very large quantities and are generally very inexpensive.

Synthetic Brushes

Synthetic hair is a manmade material used to make brush bristles; it comes from fabric and chemical sources. Brushes made with synthetic hair contain no animal hair. Synthetic bristles do not contain an outer layer of scales to trap cosmetic color, and they do not contain any protein or other allergens. Because their basic properties are so different compared with natural-hair brushes, the results they provide are different as well:

- Synthetic brushes are nonabsorbent and are an excellent choice for use with liquid or paste cosmetics such as foundation, concealer, and liquid eyeliner.
- Rather than becoming more flexible with use the way that natural brushes do, synthetic brushes tend to become stiffer and firmer with use.
- Synthetic-bristle brushes are easier to clean and disinfect than natural-bristle brushes. They are therefore considered to be more hygienic than natural-bristle brushes.

Types of Synthetic Bristles

The most common synthetic bristles are nylon and Taklon. **Nylon** is the firmest synthetic fiber that is used in makeup brushes; it is commonly used for eyebrow brushes as well as concealer and eyeliner brushes. **Taklon** is a soft, smooth synthetic fiber that comes from polyester and is often used to make large brushes. Taklon is often orange in color (**Figure 4–7**).
☑ LO1

Brush Types and Uses

Brushes vary in their components, their shape, and their uses. As you get to know the available options, take your time, try as many as you can, and do not feel that you have to buy them all. Your preferences for specific brushes, bristle types, shapes, sizes, and handle lengths will be the result of experience, so experiment, have fun, and enjoy the process of building your toolbox. The following section provides important information and ideas about various brush types.

▲ Figure 4–8 Powder brushes of different shapes.

Powder Brush

The powder brush is a large, round brush with soft bristles. It is used to dust loose powder onto large areas of the face or body and to dust off excess powder. Powder brushes are made from raccoon, squirrel, goat, sable, or badger hair.

Powder brushes come in various shapes including dome, diamond, pointed, and angled tips (**Figure 4–8**). Dome-shaped powder brushes provide the most coverage and are useful for large areas. Diamond-shaped, pointed, and angled powder brushes provide focused coverage and deliver a more highly concentrated amount of product for fuller coverage.

▲ Figure 4–9a Round blush brush.

Blush Brush

Blush brushes are similar to powder brushes but smaller. They have soft bristles made from a wide variety of different hair types. Blush brushes can be either round or angled (**Figure 4–9a and b**).

▲ Figure 4–9b Angled blush brush.

Foundation Brush

Foundation brushes have longer, flatter bristles that end in a round or oval compact shape. They are excellent for applying and blending liquid, cream, and paste foundation. They can be used for shading and highlighting. They deliver complete coverage. Foundation brushes are available in both natural-bristle and synthetic-bristle types (**Figure 4–10**).

▲ Figure 4–10 Foundation brush.

Concealer Brush

The concealer brush is a smaller version of the foundation brush. It has a flat surface with a rounded end. Concealer brushes come in various sizes (**Figure 4–11 a-c**). Small concealer brushes are ideal for small areas, such as under and around the eyes and creases along the nose. Their synthetic bristles allow them to hold, apply, and blend cream-based products for heavy coverage, touch-ups, and flawless blending.

▲ Figure 4–11a Small concealer brush.

▲ Figure 4–11b Medium concealer brush.

▲ Figure 4–11c Large concealer brush.

Eye Shadow Brushes

Eye shadow brushes, also referred to as a small fluff brushes, come in a variety of shapes and sizes. They are soft and rounded, with short bristles that are usually made from goat hair. A typical brush set of eye shadow brushes will contain a small brush, a medium brush, and a large brush. The largest brush has slightly longer bristles and is used to apply eye shadow to the full lid and brow bone or to add highlight to the brow bone (**Figure 4–12**). The medium brush is used for applying shadow to the eyelid (**Figure 4–13**). The smallest brush, which comes to a very slight point on one end, is ideal for creating contour and for applying product perfectly in the crease of the eyelid (**Figure 4–14**).

▲ Figure 4–12 **Large eye shadow brush.**

▲ Figure 4–13 **Medium eye shadow brush.**

▲ Figure 4–14 **Small eye shadow brush.**

Eyeliner Brush

Eyeliner brushes are used for precise application of powder eyeliner or liquid eyeliner. They are small brushes with short, compact bristles that can be made of various materials. The fine-tipped eyeliner brush tapers to a point and is excellent for applying liquid eyeliner (**Figure 4–15a**). A flat, fine-tipped, angled brush can be used to apply either powder or liquid eyeliner (**Figure 4–15b**).

▲ Figure 4–15a **Fine-tipped eyeliner brush.**

▲ Figure 4–15b **Angled eyeliner brush.**

Lip Brush

Lip brushes—which are usually quite small—can have many shapes, depending upon their intended use. Angled lip brushes are used for coverage and control around the lip line (**Figure 4–16**). Fine-tipped lip brushes are excellent for applying lip liner (**Figure 4–17**). Flat-tipped, diamond-shaped lip brushes are designed to apply lipstick and provide smooth, even coverage to the entire lip area (**Figure 4–18**).

▲ Figure 4–16 **Angled lip brush.**

▲ Figure 4–17 **Fine-tipped lip brush.**

▲ Figure 4–18 **Flat-tipped, diamond-shaped lip brush.**

▲ Figure 4–19 Angled small fluff brush.

▲ Figure 4–20 Angled contour brush.

▲ Figure 4–21 Angled eyeliner fluff brush.

Angle Brush

Angle-brush bristles are cut at an angle instead of straight across, creating a chiseled edge and a pointed or rounded end. Angle brushes have various uses. Small, fluffy angle brushes can be used to apply eye shadow to the crease of the eyelid, allowing for contour and flexibility in the application process (**Figure 4–19**). Larger angled fluff brushes are used for contouring the cheekbone area (**Figure 4–20**). Small angled brushes with firmer, stiffer bristles can be used for applying eyebrow color, eyeliner, and lipstick (**Figure 4–21**).

▲ Figure 4–22 Kabuki brush.

Kabuki Brush

Kabuki brushes have short handles and firmly packed bristles (**Figure 4–22**). They vary in size and are exceptionally soft. They usually have round or slightly fan-shaped bristles. They are typically used to apply mineral makeup, but they are also used for facial powder, blush, bronzer, shimmer powders, contouring, and highlighting. Although Kabuki brushes are designed to apply powders and minerals to the skin, they can remove too much product if used as a powder brush.

Contour Brush

The contour brush was mentioned briefly where angled brushes were discussed. Contour brushes look very similar to blush brushes, but the bristles have either a blunt, flat end or an angled cut (**Figure 4–23a and b**). Contour brushes are used to add definition to the face and to create a slimmer, defined look and/or higher cheekbone. They are made from various types of bristles.

▲ Figure 4–23a Flat contour brush.

▲ Figure 4–23b Angled contour brush.

Fiber-Optic Brush

The fiber-optic or dual-fiber brush is an awesome addition to every professional toolkit. This brush is made of black goat bristles and synthetic white, feather-type bristles that extend beyond the goat hair. Intended for the application of powder makeup, the fiber-optic brush allows for a light, beautiful application of powder, shimmer, or blush. The natural bristles hold the powder product, while the synthetic bristles lightly disperse the color onto the face (**Figure 4–24**).

The opposite effect is obtained when using the fiber-optic brush for foundation. The synthetic white bristles are extremely porous and hold a large amount of liquid product. The feather-like bristles can sink product into every nook, cranny, and crease thus creating a flawless, almost airbrushed, foundation look.

▲ Figure 4–24 A fiber-optic brush.

CAUTION

Retractable and refillable brushes are very difficult to properly clean and disinfect between uses. They are best suited for personal home-use and should not be a part of your professional toolkit. However, they are do make an excellent retail product.

© iStockphoto/Juxtagirl

Retractable Brushes

Retractable brushes retreat into the handle of the brush. When you remove the slip-on cover and place it on the handle end of the brush, it pushes the bristled end out from within the handle. These brushes are for personal use only because they cannot be properly cleaned and disinfected. Retractable brushes are most commonly used for applying lipstick and blush. High-quality retractable brushes will actually hold product for multiple applications without re-dipping, which make them perfect for a quick reapplication of lip color during the day or an evening out.

Refillable Brushes

Another excellent brush for personal use is the **refillable brush**, a brush with a reservoir handle that can be refilled with product: product and brush all in one. The refillable brush is commonly used for mineral makeup, blush, powder foundation, bronzer, and shimmer.

The selection of brushes is endless, and the choices are yours. Use, practice, and purpose will help you decide which brushes are critical to your toolkit and which can wait until another time. ☑ LO1

Brush Cleaner

Many types of brush cleaner are available. There are brush cleaners that clean, disinfect, condition, and oil your brushes. There are also fast-drying brush cleaners. As a professional makeup artist, you must use brush cleaners carefully and according to label instructions; it is your responsibility to ensure that bacteria and disease do not spread from one client to another. Conjunctivitis (i.e., pink-eye), Herpes simplex I (i.e., cold sores), and acne bacteria are the most common viral and bacterial conditions encountered by makeup artists. In addition, a wide range of bacteria are likely to be present in an unclean work environment, especially with the ongoing use of dirty brushes.

Choose a brush cleaner that contains hospital-grade disinfectant, which will kill 99.9 percent of bacteria and dry very quickly. Before purchasing any brush cleaner check its efficacy on the ingredient label and be sure to obtain a Material Safety Data Sheet (MSDS) for your records.

CAUTION

Wash your hands before and after every client to protect both yourself and your client from the spread of bacteria.

UTENSILS

Makeup utensils are tools that will allow you to do your job more efficiently and effectively. They are not all required for the application of makeup, but they are critical for perfecting the final desired look.

Brow Accessories

The eyebrows frame the eyes and can completely alter the appearance of the entire face. Such an important feature requires precise grooming and a few very critical tools. (You will learn all about eyebrows in Chapter 8, Facial Features.)

Tweezers

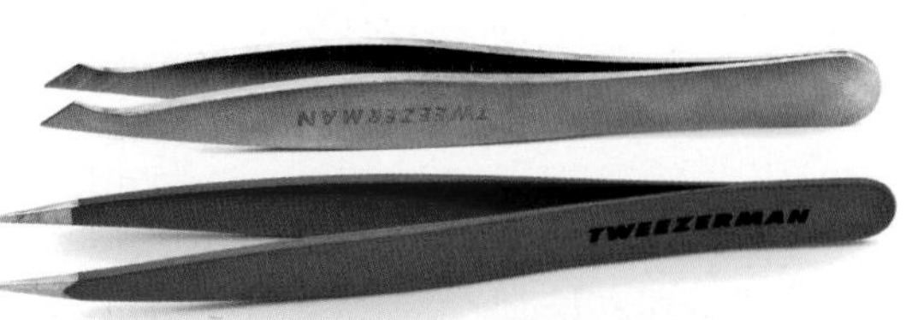

▲ Figure 4–25 **Pointed slant and pointed tweezers.**

Tweezers are used to remove individual hairs from the brow area and to remove stray hairs from above, beneath, and around the eyes. They are also used to remove unwanted hairs from other areas of the face such as the upper lip and chin. **Slant tweezers** are the most common type of tweezers and often the easiest to work with. The tip of slant tweezers is angled, making it very easy to use. **Pointed tweezers** end with a very sharp point and are excellent for removing fine, difficult hairs, as well as ingrown hairs (**Figure 4–25**). **Ingrown hairs** are hairs trapped under the surface of the skin, beneath a layer of dead skin cells. **Pointed slant tweezers** are tweezers that are angled at the end, with a very sharp point at the angle's tip. This allows precise hair removal for shaping, removing difficult hairs, and releasing ingrown hairs. Tweezers are available in many colors and designs, but remember that the colorful, eye-catching prints may end up being removed by disinfecting products. Most professional makeup artists choose plain stainless steel tweezers.

Note: Makeup artists cannot remove ingrown hairs unless you are licensed cosmetologist or esthetician.

HERE'S A TIP

To find the right tweezers for you, try several types and brands. See how the grip feels in your hand and make sure that when you close the tweezers, the sides come into full contact with one another.

Brow Scissors

Brow scissors are very small scissors with short, thin ends; they are used to trim long brow hairs that you do not want to remove completely but that need to be shortened for proper shaping (**Figure 4–26**). Brow scissors are easy to find, very inexpensive, and made of stainless steel.

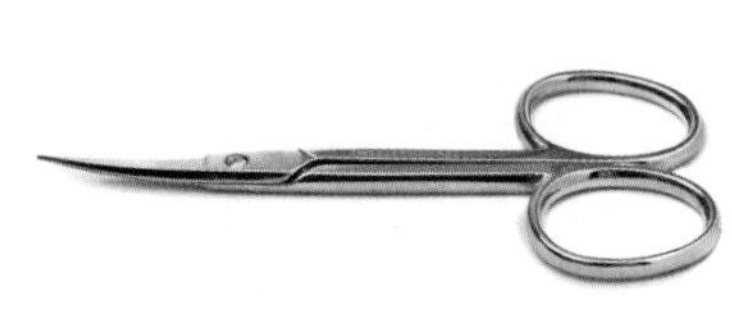

▲ Figure 4–26 **Brow scissors.**

▲ Figure 4–27 **Brow comb.**

Brow Comb

A **brow comb** is a tool used to brush eyebrow hairs into the desired position, creating a finely groomed look (**Figure 4–27**). They are made of either plastic or metal, and they are both easy to find and affordable. In addition to the comb itself, many brow combs have a brush on one side. Brow combs are also ideal for separating lashes after mascara has been applied, but if you use a brow comb in this manner, be sure to clean it thoroughly.

Eyelash Curlers

▲ Figure 4–28 **Eyelash curler.**

You will find an eyelash curler in every makeup artist's toolkit. Eyelash curlers add instant shape and length to lashes by curling them upward before mascara is applied (**Figure 4–28**). Most eyelash curlers are made of stainless steel. They are affordable and easy to find. Battery-operated, heated eyelash curlers are easy to use, very effective, and gentler on the lashes. Heated lash curlers can also be used after applying mascara without causing the mascara to clump. A few manufacturers offer lower lash curlers; and a detailed eyelash curler, which looks like a small tweezers with a flat head, is also available. Detailed curlers are effective for curling closer to the lash root and in tight areas such as the inner and outer eye.

Single-use mascara wands make excellent, affordable brow combs, with the added benefit that they can be thrown away (instead of being cleaned) after one use.

Blotting Paper

Blotting paper is a highly absorbent, thin paper that absorbs excess oil from the surface of the skin, leaving a smooth, matte finish. Blotting papers contain oil-absorbing ingredients such as kaolin or powder, and some brands contain a light fragrance. Remember that the fewer ingredients any product has, the less likely clients are to have allergic reactions or sensitivity.

Blotting paper is an excellent addition to your makeup toolkit when you work with clients who have oily skin, when you work extensive photo sessions that require several reapplications of makeup, or for a quick shine remover between photo or video shots. Blotting paper can be purchased in packs of 50 to 100, or more.

Sharpeners

Makeup sharpeners are pencil sharpeners. They can be either plastic or metal, and they are available with different size sharpening holes to accommodate different-sized pencils (**Figure 4–29**). Sharpening pencils in-between and during use is an excellent way to prevent the spread of bacteria from one eye to another or from one client to another.

▲ **Figure 4–29 Makeup pencil sharpeners.**

Palettes

A makeup **palette** is used to hold makeup that is scraped or removed from its container (**Figure 4–30**). Makeup palettes are the perfect tool for mixing and blending and for a cleaner makeup application. A plastic paint palette from any art or craft store is perfect. It allows you to mix various colors together and to reapply product with the same tool without the worry of contaminating the original container. There are many types and shapes of makeup palettes, and they are made of many materials such as plastic, aluminum, paper, and stainless steel. For jobs with multiple clients, a paper towel acts as an excellent makeup palette; you can label it with a specific client's name and dispose of it after use; you can also fold the edges and keep excess makeup for touch-ups.

▲ **Figure 4–30 Labeled paper palettes.**

Draping

To avoid getting makeup on a client's clothing, proper draping is necessary. Draping is particularly important if your client is dressed in special attire for a special event. Blush on a wedding dress does not make for a happy bride. Step-by-step instructions for proper draping appear in Chapter 7, Creating the Canvas.

Capes

Large, light plastic capes can be found at any beauty supply store. They snap around the neck and are large enough to cover the client's entire upper body and lap. Plastic and nylon capes can be easily wiped down with disinfectant or washed in the washing machine. A single-use neck strip is placed around the neck under the cape; this prevents the cape from coming in contact with the skin.

Headband and Hair Clips

Whether or not you use a headband to hold the client's hair out of the way depends on the situation. If a client has already had her hair styled, she will probably not want to wear a headband. However, if the hair is not an issue, a terry cloth or elastic headband holds the hair completely off the face making for an easy makeup application. Hair clips of various sizes are excellent choices to hold small sections of the hair off the face without ruining the hairstyle. ☑ LO2

HERE'S A TIP

Aside from makeup, every toolkit should have:

- Makeup remover for a quick clean up.
- Toner in a spray bottle for a quick hydrating facial spritz.
- Facial moisturizer to smooth and hydrate the skin.
- Lip moisturizer for plumping and smoothing dry lips.

SINGLE-USE TOOLS

Single-use tools are thrown away after one use. They are excellent to prevent the spread of bacteria or viruses between clients, but not all of them provide the creative possibilities that some multiuse tools offer.

Eye Shadow Applicators

Single-use shadow applicators come in many sizes, shapes, and lengths (**Figure 4–31**). Some are flat and round, while others are oblong or even pointed. Many different sizes and shapes are available, offering the makeup artist many options in eye shadow application. They can be used for full-coverage of the lid, contouring in the crease, and even for liner application. Single-use tools require a different application technique than brushes, but they are certainly cleaner.

▲ Figure 4–31 **Various types of disposable shadow applicators.**

Mascara Wands

Single-use mascara wands, often referred to as a "spooly", are a necessity. A mascara wand should never be dipped into a tube

HERE'S A TIP

Every makeup toolkit should contain a supply of cotton balls, cotton swabs, alcohol wipes, gloves, and tissues.

of mascara following use, and it should never be used on more than one person. The wand that comes with the tube (i.e., adhered to the lid) should never come in contact with a client; however, product can be scraped from the original wand onto a single-use wand. Single-use mascara wands are also excellent for brushing the eyebrows into shape.

Spatulas

Small plastic spatulas are very inexpensive, easy to find, and come in packs of 10 to 100. They are the perfect way to remove product from its original package and place it onto a palette or applicator.

Sponges

Single-use sponges come in various shapes: round, square, and wedged. They are gentle on the skin and hold product without absorbing it. Sponges are used to apply liquid and cream makeup products to the face and are excellent for blending.

Brushes

Many brush companies are now making single-use brushes. Single-use brushes are made of synthetic bristles or inexpensive natural bristles. The brushes come in various sizes and types, from shadow brushes to contour and powder brushes.

Although single-use tools are not most artists' first choice (except for those mascara wands!), they are a clean, neat, inexpensive way to get a job done. Even if you don't use them on a regular basis, a selection of single-use tools comes in handy in a pinch.

HERE'S A TIP

Metal spatulas are another excellent tool option for the makeup kit. However, metal spatulas are not disposable and require proper cleaning and disinfecting between clients.

Single-Use Paper Drape

Single-use drapes are hand-sized towels made of paper. They are inexpensive and easy to use for a quick makeup application or to protect the client's clothing during a touch-up. ☑ LO3

MAKEUP CASES

The makeup cases you use represent you as a professional. Your makeup products and tools must be clean, neat, and organized. This not only represents you well; it also makes your job easier. You can find your gold shimmer shadow, for example, immediately when you need it. You will never have to sift aimlessly through a disorganized bag. Fortunately there are many choices in cases and carriers for products and tools.

▲ **Figure 4–32a Small train case.**

▲ **Figure 4–32b Large train case.**

Train Cases

Train cases, also known as **travel cases**, are lightweight metal, canvas, or leather-type material (**Figure 4–32a and b**); when they are opened, the sides span out displaying one, two, three or more tray-levels to hold various products and tools. The levels and available space depend upon the size of the case. Studio cases are very large cases that have legs that can be opened so that they stand by themselves.

Belts

Makeup tool belts are leather, nylon, or cloth belts that snap or tie around the waist; they come in various sizes. In fact, some tool belts can hold countless brushes and other small tools (**Figure 4–33**). ☑ **LO4**

More makeup tools are available all the time. Brush shapes, sizes, and designs are constantly being updated and fine-tuned to meet the ever-changing needs of makeup professionals.

The makeup tool list is quite extensive from the start, and your personal wish-list will grow as your experience and skills are perfected. As your experience increases and you begin to establish your own identity as a makeup artist, you will develop strong preferences for the tools that help you perform at your best. Nowhere in the makeup profession is it written that one particular tool is necessary for any particular job: Whatever works for you will be the right tool.

▼ **Figure 4–33 Makeup tool belt.**

Review Questions

1. What are the different parts of a makeup brush?
2. How long should a quality makeup brush last?
3. What is the difference between a natural bristle and a synthetic bristle?
4. How do natural boar bristles work so effectively?
5. Define Taklon.
6. What is the most commonly used natural bristle for makeup brushes?
7. What is the finest and most expensive type of sable?
8. List the most common types of hair used for powder brush bristles.
9. What are three important eyebrow utensils?
10. Describe the purpose of an eyelash curler.
11. Explain the benefit of using single-use tools.
12. What is the deciding factor (most important) in choosing types of tools?
13. What length is the most common choice for makeup handles?

Chapter Glossary

blotting paper	A highly absorbent, thin paper used to absorb excess oil from the surface of the skin, leaving a smooth, matte finish.
brow comb	A tool used to brush the eyebrow hairs into the desired position, creating a finely groomed look.
brow scissors	Very small scissors with short, thin ends; they are used to trim long brow hairs that you do not want to remove completely, but that need to be shortened for proper shaping.
ferrule	The metal part of the brush that attaches the glued bristles to the handle and adds a certain amount of strength to the bristles.
hair	The bristles of a makeup brush.
ingrown hairs	Hairs trapped under the surface of the skin, beneath a layer of dead skin cells.
Kolinsky sable	A type of natural bristle that comes from mink found in the cold climates of China and Siberia; it is among the finest, softest, and most expensive material from which makeup brushes are made.

Chapter Glossary *(continued)*

makeup tool belts	Leather, nylon, and cloth belts that snap or tie around the waist; they come in various sizes.
natural hair	Hair from a variety of animal sources.
natural-hair brushes	Brushes made from animal hairs or blends of animal hairs.
nylon	The firmest synthetic fiber that is used in makeup brushes; it is commonly used for eyebrow brushes as well as concealer and eyeliner brushes.
palette	Tool used to hold makeup that is scraped or removed from its containers.
pointed slant tweezers	Tweezers that are angled at the end, with a very sharp point at the angle's tip.
pointed tweezers	Tweezers that end with a very sharp point and are excellent for removing fine, difficult hairs, as well as ingrown hairs.
refillable brushes	A brush with a reservoir handle that can be refilled with product: product and brush all in one.
retractable brushes	Brushes that retreat into the handle of the brush.
slant tweezers	The most common type of tweezers, and often the easiest to work with; the tip of slant tweezers is at an angle, making it very easy to manipulate use.
synthetic hair	A manmade material used to make brush bristles; comes from fabric and chemical sources.
synthetic-hair brushes	Manmade brushes whose bristles come from fabric and chemical sources.
Taklon	A soft, smooth synthetic fiber that comes from polyester and is often used to make large brushes.
train cases	Also known as *travel cases*; lightweight metal or leather-type material; when they are opened, the sides span out displaying one, two, three or more levels of compartments to hold various products and tools.
weasel hair	Also known as *red sable*; not as soft as Kolinsky sable but still very valuable.

Chapter 5 Color Theory

Chapter Outline

Why Study Color Theory?
Color Theory
The Color Wheel
Color Temperature
Color Saturation
Color Harmony
The Real Color Wheel

Learning Objectives

After completing this chapter, you will be able to:

- ☑ **LO1** Identify the components of the color wheel.
- ☑ **LO2** Describe the differences between warm colors and cool colors and provide examples of each.
- ☑ **LO3** Define color saturation.
- ☑ **LO4** Understand color harmony and how it influences makeup color choices.
- ☑ **LO5** Describe the Real Color Wheel and its purpose in color theory.

Key Terms

Page number indicates where in the chapter the term is used.

analogous colors
pg. 100

complementary colors
pg. 99

cool colors
pg. 101

desaturated colors
pg. 102

harmony
pg. 103

hue
pg. 98

neutral colors
pg. 101

primary colors
pg. 97

pure color
pg. 98

saturation
pg. 102

secondary colors
pg. 98

shade
pg. 103

tertiary colors
pg. 99

tint
pg. 102

tone
pg. 103

warm colors
pg. 101

Career Profile

© Golden Lee Makeup Studio.

An affinity for color inspired Golden Lee's career as a makeup artist. Her background in studio art contributes to her perspective on makeup artistry, and inspiration has been the key to her success. She has worked with major commercials, including Coca-Cola and Citibank, and she has worked all around the world. Golden Lee has truly had a diverse and significant career. She continues to be inspired in her ongoing freelance career.

"My interest in makeup started in high school when I took art lessons and realized that I have a strong sensitivity for colors. Upon graduation, I attended beauty school. Just out of school and having a passion for makeup, I set up a studio and started applying makeup for customers. Most of the time, I depended on my own sense of beauty to apply makeup for customers. I knew that I needed more knowledge and experience in order to succeed, so I decided to move to Taipei. It was there that I worked as an assistant for a famous makeup artist. Over the 3 years, I learned a great deal and gained a tremendous amount of experience in the industry.

Courtesy of Golden Lee.

"For the past 16 years of my career, I have worked as a freelance makeup artist. I have done makeup for magazines, advertisements, and weddings, all in different settings. I also teach makeup artistry.

"Some of my greatest work includes applying makeup for television advertisements. I have worked on the sets of the commercials for Citibank, Coca-Cola, and 7-Eleven (Taiwan). I also worked on the advertisements for Volkswagen (Taiwan), Ford (Taiwan), and Casio (Taiwan). I have worked in many fashion shows including the Shanghai Adidas Original Series Fashion Show, the Celine Fashion Show, and the Nokia New Mobile Phone Launch Show.

Courtesy of Golden Lee.

"In my view, makeup artists should know more than just how to apply makeup. They also need to know the art and esthetics of makeup. I feel that observing and appreciating the surrounding designs and architectures contribute to my makeup inspiration.

"My motto is 'learn as much as possible, and never feel enough about learning.'"

Courtesy of Golden Lee.

▲ **Figure 5–1 Color has endless variations.**

Color influences every aspect of our lives. It plays a role in our choices: clothes, cars, foods, furniture, fixtures, makeup. Even our mood is affected by color. The first systematic study of the physiological effects of color dates back to Goethe's *Theory of Colours* in 1810. One cannot escape the amazing impact that color has; we wake each day and see the bursting multitude of colors that surround and saturate our lives. One of the most amazing features about color is the endless variations and perceptions of what color is and the many aspects encompassing it (**Figure 5–1**).

WHY STUDY COLOR THEORY?

Makeup artists should study and have a thorough understanding of color theory because:

- As a professional makeup artist, you will find that color theory is critical to problem solving and creating a harmonious work of art on every face.
- Color theory will guide you as you choose proper makeup colors for clients.
- You will use your knowledge of color theory to enhance clients' skin tone, dramatize clients' features, and completely reinvent clients' looks.

COLOR THEORY

▲ **Figure 5–2 Primary colors: red, yellow, and blue.**

The color of an object is not only a result of the object itself; the environment (including lighting and surrounding colors) and the individual's eye and brain also affect the perception. A particular blue object, for example, will look entirely different when placed against different backgrounds or in different lighting. In addition, five different people could look at the object and describe its color in five completely different ways. As a result of these variations, color theory is a complex subject to understand. On the other hand, the complexity of color is exactly what makes the art of makeup so fascinating.

Although color theory is complex, the fundamentals are constant. The concept of color theory dates back to the 18th century and Isaac Newton's controversial theory. Newton was the first to name the primary colors. Today this concept is widely accepted; we are well aware that the **primary colors**, red, yellow, and blue, are the basis of all other colors (**Figure 5–2**).

As a professional makeup artist, you will need complete knowledge and understanding of color theory. This understanding will be critical to your ability to solve problems and create a harmonious work of art on ev-

Color Facts

Blue symbolizes loyalty, making it a great color to wear to a job interview.

People are more productive in blue rooms.

Weightlifters can lift heavier weights in blue gyms.

Blue is the color preferred by most adults around the world.

ery face. The art of makeup has very few rules, but the concepts of color theory never change. Your experience will show that if you do not apply color theory during a makeup application, the colors will be wrong. The result can be a look that adds years to a client's face or makes them appear tired or sick. Take a moment and think about how you look when you have not had enough sleep or when you do not feel well. Certain clothing or makeup colors amplify that look.

Color is used to create mood, emotion, harmony, and perfection. In makeup application, it accomplishes these goals, as well as enhances skin tone and features, dramatize characteristics, and completely reinvents an individual's appearance. An eye for color is a true gift for the makeup artist because it allows the artist to fully grasp the concept of color theory and the way that it applies to specific individuals and environments.

THE COLOR WHEEL

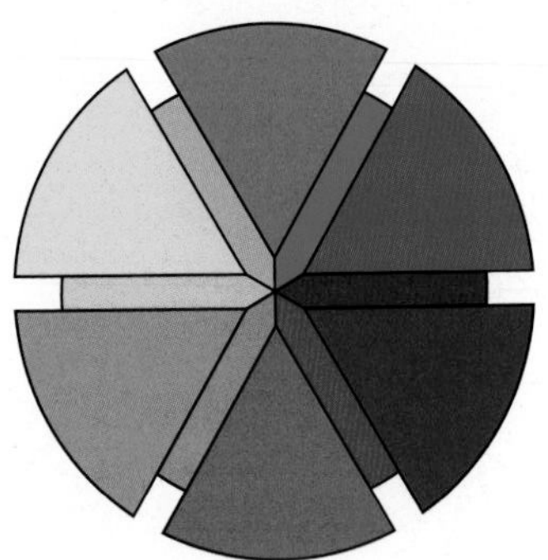

▲ Figure 5–3 A standard color wheel.

The traditional color wheel comes from the original "color circle," developed by Sir Isaac Newton in 1666. Since that time, scientists and artists have created and designed numerous variations of this circle. Although these designs vary, the theory behind the color wheel remains the same. The color wheel is based on the three primary colors: red, yellow, and blue. The term **hue** refers to any color in its purest form, lacking any shade (black) or tint (white). The hue of a color represents just one dimension of a particular color.

The traditional color wheel is a creation of the various combinations of colors stemming from the three primary hues and resulting in twelve main divisions (**Figure 5–3**). The color wheel does not change and serves as a core guide for color theory.

Primary Colors

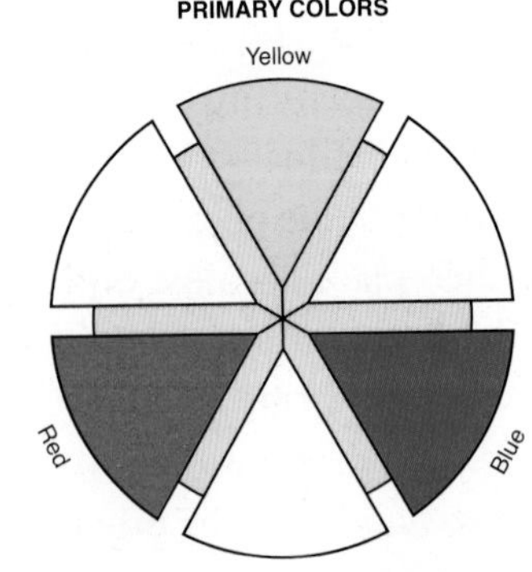

▲ Figure 5–4 Primary colors.

The three unique hues that act as the foundation for the color wheel are known as primary colors. As mentioned earlier, the primary colors are the three pure colors red, yellow, and blue, and are the basis for creating all other colors (**Figure 5–4**). **Pure color** is color that has absolutely no other color combined with it.

Primary colors are frequently used for designs, art, or images that are intended to create a sense of urgency. Primary colors are the most vivid colors and are often used for logos and signs, such as fast food restaurants and businesses that wish to inspire urgency and alertness.

Color Facts

Yellow is the most difficult color for the eye to perceive.

Yellow enhances concentration. That is the reason it is used for legal pads.

Yellow speeds up the metabolism.

Secondary Colors

Secondary colors are colors created using an equal mixture of two primary colors; the secondary colors include orange, green, and violet.

- Orange is a mixture of red and yellow.
- Green is a mixture of yellow and blue.
- Violet is a mixture of blue and red.

Notice on the color wheel the triangular positioning of the primary colors in relation to one another and how the secondary colors fall between them (**Figure 5–5**). Secondary colors are not as vivid as primary colors, and they have less of a tendency to evoke a sense of urgency.

Purple is considered the color of royalty.

Purple represents luxury, wealth, and sophistication.

Tertiary Colors

Tertiary colors are created by mixing a primary color with a secondary color; examples of tertiary colors include blue-green, yellow-green (olive), orange-red (vermillion), blue-violet, red-violet, and yellow-orange (**Figure 5–6**). These are the final six colors of the traditional color wheel. Earth tones, colors such as brown and khaki, are tertiary colors that are created by mixing the three primary colors together.

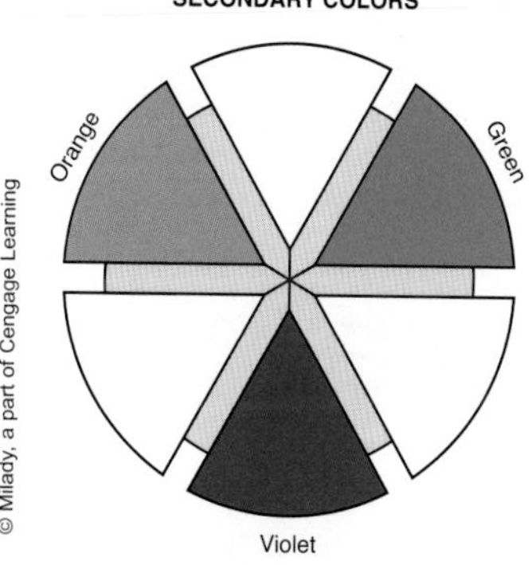

▲ Figure 5–5 **Secondary colors.**

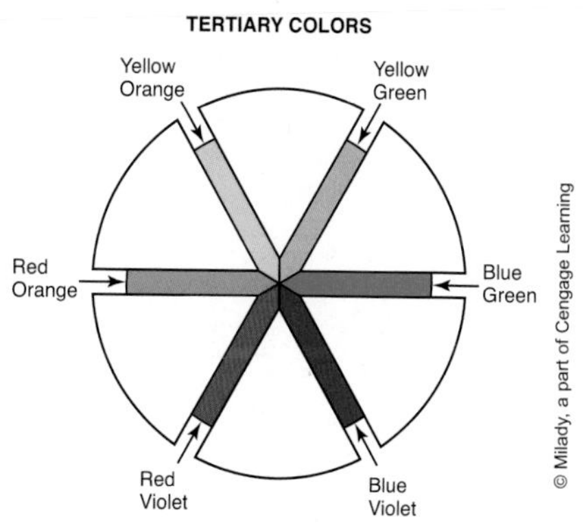

▲ Figure 5–6 **Tertiary colors.**

Color Facts

Decorators suggest that clients stay away from yellow and orange for home kitchens because these colors reportedly stimulate the appetite.

Complementary Colors

Complementary colors are colors that fall directly across from each other on the color wheel (**Figure 5–7**). The name is a bit deceiving, because complementary colors are anything but "complementary." When used next to each other, they create a distinct contrast, with each intensifying the appearance of the other. This can be beneficial when you want a particular color to clearly stand out.

Complementary colors are frequently used when the goal of a makeup application is a vibrant, dynamic, and dramatic look (**Figure 5–8**). When mixed together, complementary colors create neutral, dark hues. This allows a makeup artist to create darker, natural looks without using black.

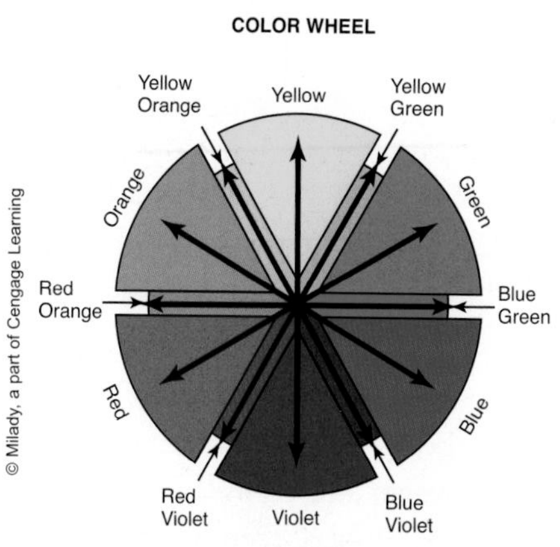

▲ Figure 5–7 **Complementary colors.**

▲ Figure 5–8 **An example of a complementary eye makeup application.**

Analogous Colors

Analogous colors are colors that are located directly next to each other on the color wheel (**Figure 5–9**). They create minimal contrast and therefore match very well. Analogous colors are used in makeup application for soft, subtle looks, such as everyday makeup or many bridal applications; they can also be used to call attention to a specific facial feature, rather than the makeup itself (**Figure 5–10**). **LO1**

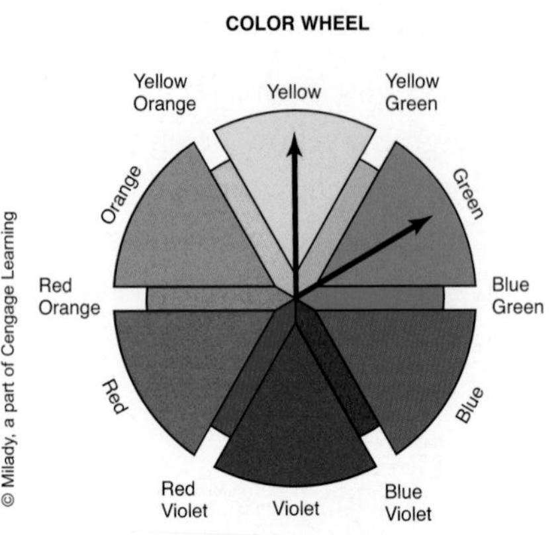

▲ Figure 5–9 **Analogous colors on the color wheel.**

▲ Figure 5–10 **Analogous colors used for an eye makeup application.**

COLOR TEMPERATURE

Up to this point, the discussion of color and the color wheel is quite simple to understand. It is from this point forward that the concept of color begins to get more complex.

Most people have heard colors referred to as warm or cool. Individuals have their own vision of what warm and cool colors look like, but when it comes to makeup, the concept of warm and cool will be critical when determining skin tones and appropriate colors necessary to create a harmonious and flattering look. An improper match between skin tone and foundation is almost always the result of a mismatch between warm and cool colors.

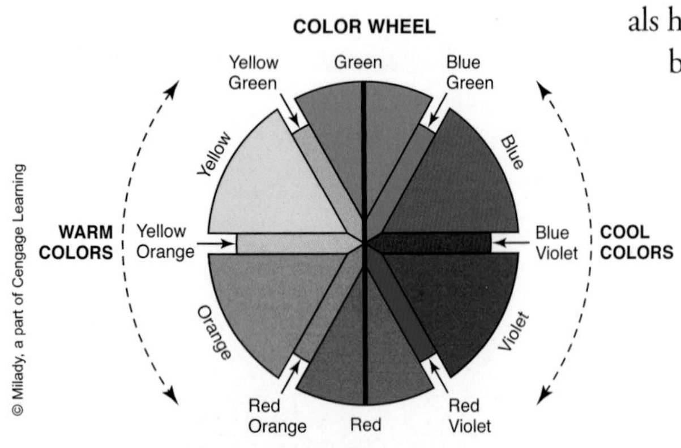

▲ Figure 5–11 **The color wheel divided to represent both warm and cool colors.**

Warm and cool makeup colors can be used to alter and emphasize facial features, especially eye color. They can also dramatize an outfit or a special look.

If you were to divide a color wheel in half down the middle of green and the middle of red, one half would represent warm colors and the other would represent cool colors (**Figure 5–11**).

The red-yellow side of the wheel represents the warm colors and the blue-green side represents the cool colors. The line down the center of both the green and red colors is to show that green and red can be both warm and cool. If red is orange-based, it is warm. If red is blue-based, it is cool. Green is similar. If green is yellow-based it is warm. If green is blue-based, it is cool.

Warm Colors

Warm colors range from yellow and gold through the oranges, red-oranges, most reds, and even some yellow-greens (refer to Figure 5–11). Warm colors get their name because they instantly remind us of heat and warm things, such as the blazing sun or a hot fire. In paintings, décor, and makeup, warm colors represent energy, boldness, vibrancy, excitement, and even anger.

Cool Colors

Cool colors are exactly opposite of warm colors and include blues, greens, violets, and blue-reds (refer to Figure 5–11). Cool colors suggest cool temperatures and remind us of cool things, such as water, grass, air, and ice. In paintings and décor, cool colors tend to evoke a sense of calmness. In makeup application, cool colors (although soothing in nature) can be used to add excitement, as when they are used to accentuate eye colors. ☑ LO2

Neutral Colors

Neutral colors are colors that do not complement or contrast any other color. Examples include brown and gray, along with multiple variations of each (**Figure 5–12**). They are a perfect blend of earthy tones. In makeup they represent natural, soft, flesh colors and are acceptable color choices for any skin tone.

▲ Figure 5–12 **Neutral tones represent natural, soft, flesh colors.**

> **Color Facts**
>
> For years clothing and cosmetic companies have created marketing campaigns to help customers choose colors that are most attractive on them. The concept revolves around categorizing individuals as cool, warm, or neutral based upon their characteristics!

Cool Characteristics (Figure 5–13)

EYE COLOR	Blue or gray
HAIR COLOR	Typically blond, brown, or black
SKIN TONE	Blue and pinkish undertones
CLOTHING	Looks best in colors such as blue, red, pink, or purple, and tend to look best in silver jewelry

▲ Figure 5–13 **Example of a woman with cool color characteristics**

Warm Characteristics (Figure 5–14)

EYE COLOR	Brown, green, or hazel
HAIR COLOR	Brown, black, red, auburn, blond or strawberry blond
SKIN TONE	Yellow/orange or olive undertones
CLOTHING	Look best in earthy-toned clothing, such as browns, yellows, oranges, yellowish green, cream and ecru, and look dazzling in gold jewelry

▲ Figure 5–14 **Example of a woman with warm color characteristics.**

▲ **Figure 5–15 Example of a woman with neutral color characteristics.**

Neutral Characteristics (Figure 5–15)

EYE COLOR	Any
HAIR COLOR	Any
SKIN TONE	Pink, olive, or yellow undertones (difficult to determine)
CLOTHING	Can wear just about any color and look good in both silver and gold.

COLOR SATURATION

Saturation refers to the pureness of a color or the dominance of hue in a color. A fully saturated color is the truest version of that color and is extremely vibrant. To use an example, the hues used for each of the twelve colors on the basic color wheel are saturated. Saturation changes as that hue moves from the outer edge of the color wheel toward the center, where it loses color, becomes desaturated, and begins to appear gray (**Figure 5–16**).

When a color is desaturated, a large amount of pure color has been removed. **Desaturated colors** are colors mixed with white and located toward the inner ring of the color wheel; they contain a large amount of gray and very little remaining pure color, and they are often considered neutral. The degree of saturation is the range from the outer edge of the color wheel (fully saturated) to the center (fully desaturated), perpendicular to the value axis. The various degrees of saturation create tints and shades. ☑ LO3

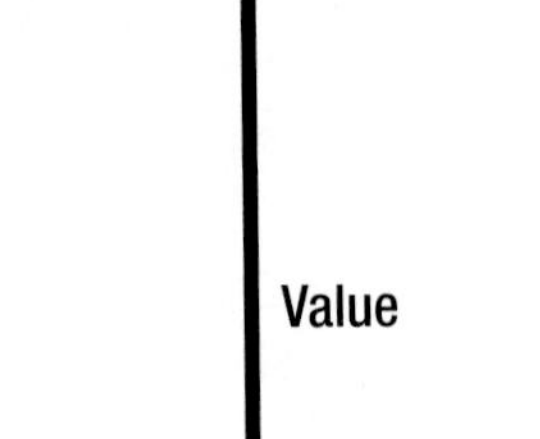

▲ **Figure 5–16 An example of saturated color.**

Tint

The addition of white to any color creates a **tint**. Adding white decreases the hue, the amount of true color. Tint is often referred to as brightness. The more white that is added to a color, the brighter that color becomes (**Figure 5–17**).

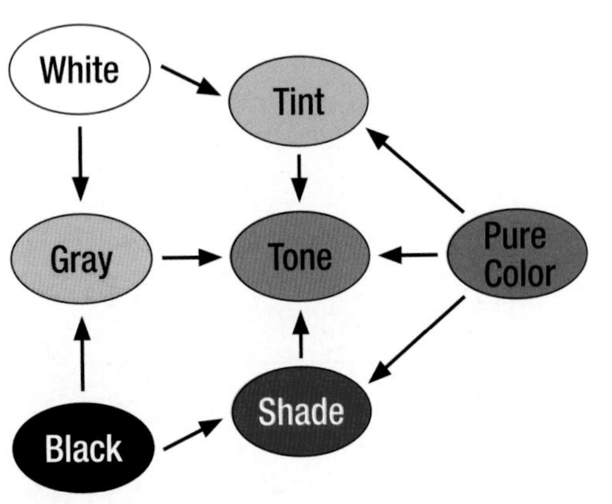

▲ **Figure 5–17 Tint/shade/tone chart.**

Shade

When black is added to a color, the resulting color is called a **shade**. Adding black to a color decreases the hue (the amount of true color) and affects the color's value. The more black that is added to a color, the darker its value.

Tone

The term *tone* is used in many different ways in makeup, such as in discussions of skin tone and color tone. A **tone** is the color that results when gray is added to a color. When gray is added to any color, it creates a different tone.

Color Facts

Red is the most emotionally intense color and stimulates a faster heartbeat and breathing.

Pink, although it is a tint of red, is the most romantic color and is soothing and tranquilizing.

COLOR HARMONY

Harmony is mentioned several times throughout this textbook for many reasons. The goal of a professional makeup artist is almost always to create a harmonious makeup application. **Harmony** is the existence of unity in a design; it is the most important of all artistic principles. Harmony holds together all of the elements of a design. When a makeup application has harmony, it blends, flows smoothly, and is calming or pleasing to the eye.

Harmony applies to all elements of a makeup application: the colors, the application techniques, and the match between the colors and techniques and the client's complexion, facial features, and even a client's personality.

Take a moment to think about a time when you noticed, on first glance, that another person's makeup application negatively affected her attractiveness because it lacked harmony.

The concept of color theory revolves around colors that are either harmonious or not harmonious. Colors that do not blend well together and are not harmonious are referred to as contrasting. Contrasting color can be useful in makeup application when the intent is to emphasize a specific feature or detail.

As important as it is to grasp the concepts of harmony and contrast in makeup application, it is even more important to have a basic understanding of harmony as it applies to an individual's natural coloring. In this respect, you will see the direct link between color harmony and color temperature.

Did You Know?

Within 7 seconds, people will make eleven first impressions of someone. Color alone accounts for between 62 and 90 percent of that first impression!

Color Facts

Black is the color of authority and power.

Black is a popular color in fashion because it slenderizes the appearance.

Black is the most stylish and timeless clothing color.

Warm Harmony

A warm-harmony individual tends to have medium to dark skin, dark hair, and medium to dark eyes. The most harmonious makeup color choices for this individual are shown in **Figure 5–18**.

- Medium to Dark Browns
- Plums/Wines
- Dark Purple/Grape
- Forest Green
- Khaki
- Bronze/Copper
- Charcoal
- Rusts/Deep Reds

Examples of makeup products that would not be harmonious for this individual include light blue eye shadows and pale pink blushes; these are cool colors.

▲ **Figure 5–18 An individual with warm-harmony features and a warm-harmony makeup application.**

Cold Harmony

A cold-harmony individual tends to have very fair skin, light eyes, and light hair. The abundance of light features makes the cold-harmony individual well suited for a variety of bright colors. The most harmonious makeup color choices this individual are shown in **Figure 5–19**.

- Light Blue
- Bright, Light Pink
- Light Green
- Lilac
- Yellow
- Peach
- Bright Reds
- Pastels

A deep plum blush and dark green or charcoal eye shadow would give a hard appearance to the cold-harmony individual. Cold colors can be effectively used on warm-harmonied women when they are used to highlight. A touch of gold or bright blue placed properly on the lid or at the lash line can add sparkle to the eye.

Color Facts

As one matures, skin color and hair color tend to lighten. A woman who was a warm harmony at age 30 will most likely look better in softer, lighter colors at age 50.

▼ **Figure 5–19 An individual with cold-harmony features and a cold-harmony makeup application.**

Neutral Harmony

A neutral-harmony individual tends to have light to medium skin, medium hair (e.g., ash brown, dark blond), and medium colored eyes such as hazel or a light brown. This individual looks good in a wide variety of colors from both the warm and cold harmony selection. Examples even include colors such as those shown in **Figure 5–20**.

- Mauve
- Teal
- Navy
- Tints and shades of pink, blue, and green

© Kurhan/www.Shutterstock.com

▲ **Figure 5–20 An individual with neutral-harmony features and a neutral-harmony makeup application.**

The amazing combinations of primary colors available to neutral-harmony individuals, in conjunction with black, white, and gray, create literally hundreds of different colors.

Although the concept of harmony extends far beyond the three categories of warm, cool, and neutral, these categories can serve as a starting point and a guide as you begin to work with makeup. Keep in mind that placing individuals into any one category can nearly be impossible; hereditary coloring varies greatly, and people can change hair color and eye color anytime they like. Therefore, a bit of cleverness is required on the part of the makeup professional. Harmony can be a creation of color infused with background and light, and remember, the only real rule of harmony is that what you create must be appealing to the eye! ☑ LO4

Did You Know?

Crayola© crayons are currently available in 120 different colors! The selection includes 23 reds, 20 greens, 19 blues, 16 purples, 14 oranges, 11 browns, 8 yellows, 2 grays, 2 coppers, 2 blacks, 1 white, and even 1 gold and 1 silver!

THE REAL COLOR WHEEL

The Real Color Wheel (RCW) was created by Don Jusko and represents 468 colors of various shades and tints (**Figure 5–21**). Jusko found that when painting, photographing, or arranging color on location, it was impossible to memorize all of the analogous and complementary colors along with their tints and shades. The RCW was a quick reference tool for determining which colors were related and what their relationship to one another was.

It bears repeating that as a makeup professional—although a multitude of colors may be required— the final objective is always a harmonious look that is pleasing to the eye. How can it be possible to create harmony when using five, eight, or even ten or more colors? The answer is that practice, study, and commitment will deepen and expand your understanding of color theory and harmony. ☑ LO5

The world of color is fascinating. Realize the impact that color has on every aspect of life, and realize your own influence when it comes to color. Placing a small amount of color onto the tip of a brush and then applying it with the perfect stroke can change a person's appearance in a second.

▼ **Figure 5–21 A replica of the Real Color Wheel.**

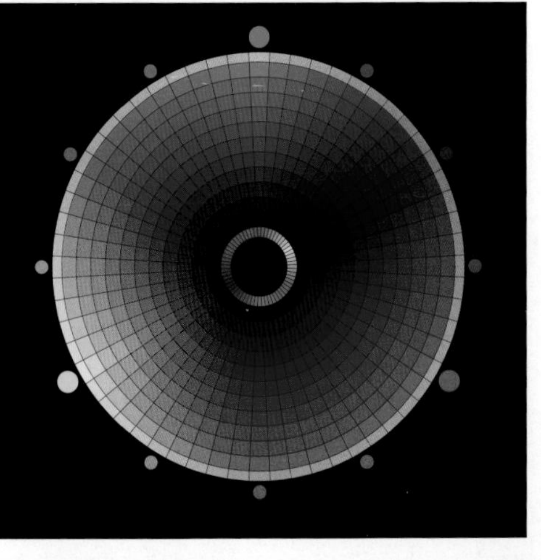

© digital_dreamland/www.Shutterstock.com

Review Questions

1. The traditional color wheel dates back to what year?
2. Define hue.
3. What term is used for colors that blend well together and are pleasing to the eye?
4. List the three primary colors.
5. List the three secondary colors.
6. What are colors directly across from each other on the color wheel called?
7. What are colors directly next to each other on the color wheel called?
8. What are the final six colors of the color wheel and how are they created?
9. What term is used for colors that represent energy, boldness, vibrancy, excitement, and even anger?
10. What is the term for a color that contains gray?

Chapter Glossary

analogous colors	Colors that are located directly next to each other on the color wheel.
complementary colors	Colors that fall directly across from each other on the color wheel.
cool colors	Colors that suggest coolness; they are dominated by blues, greens, violets, and blue-reds.
desaturated colors	Colors mixed with white and located toward the inner ring of the color wheel; they contain a large amount of gray and very little remaining pure color. They are often considered neutral.
harmony	The existence of unity in a design; it is the most important of all artistic principles.
hue	Any color in its purest form, lacking shade or tint.
neutral colors	Colors that do not complement or contrast any other color. Examples include brown and gray.
primary colors	Red, yellow, and blue; the basis of all other colors.
pure color	Color that has absolutely no other color combined with it.
saturation	The pureness of a color or the dominance of a hue in a color.
secondary colors	Colors created using an equal mixture of two primary colors: orange, green, and violet.

Chapter Glossary *(continued)*

shade	Colors that result when black is added to another color.
tertiary colors	Colors created by mixing a primary color with a secondary color.
tint	Colors that result when white is added to another color.
tone	Colors that result when gray is added to another color.
warm colors	Range of colors from yellow and gold through oranges, red-oranges, most reds, and even some yellow-greens.

Chapter 6 Client Consultation

Chapter Outline

Why Study Client Consultations?

Making a Good First Impression

The Consultation Form

The Consultation Process

Evaluating the Client's Features and Characteristics

Documentation

Learning Objectives

After completing this chapter, you will be able to:

- ✓ **LO1** Understand the need for each necessary component of a consultation form.
- ✓ **LO2** Perform the steps necessary for an evaluative consultation process.
- ✓ **LO3** Discuss information from the consultation form as it applies to a specific client's features, needs, and desires.

Key Terms

Page number indicates where in the chapter the term is used.

communication
pg. 117

consultation form
pg. 112

cosmetic treatment card
pg. 119

Physicians' Desk Reference (PDR)
pg. 115

reflective listening
pg. 118

Career Profile

Courtesy of Julia Francis.

As one of the top makeup artists in the United Kingdom, Julia Francis has a long list of credentials. Despite her busy schedule, Julia finds time to collaborate with and educate makeup artists, including established artists, aspiring artists, and students who are just considering the profession. Her company, Good Foundations, was born from hundreds of e-mails and calls from people wanting more advice and information about the industry. At Good Foundations, any makeup artist can find advice about choosing a school as well as useful tips on how to break into the industry. Good Foundations is a consultation service available over the telephone, on Skype, or face-to-face and offers students from all over the world practical, honest advice.

Photography by Paul Winter.

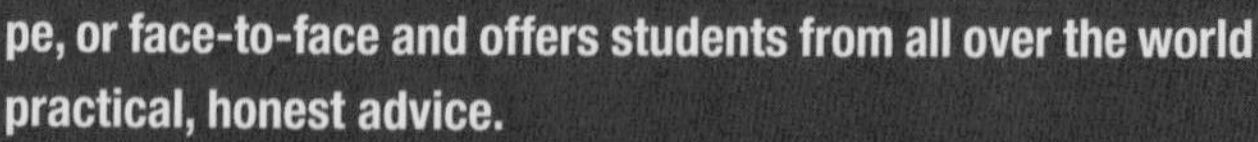

"It had always been my childhood dream to be a makeup artist. Looking back on my life, I don't remember ever wanting to do any other job. I started my training with a 3-year course in Hair and Beauty at The London College of Fashion. Five years later, I did a 3-month intensive course at The Delamar Academy of Makeup and began my successful journey as a makeup artist. I have had the pleasure of working on many high-profile sets where I worked on celebrities and top models from around the world. I have created makeup looks for the stars of famous movies such as *Star Wars, Wimbledon,* and *The Hitchhiker's Guide to the Galaxy*, as well as for models who appeared in magazines such as the *Tatler, Harper's BAZAAR, Glamour, Red,* and *Grazia*. I met George Lucas while working as a body painter on *Star Wars: Revenge of the Sith*. Receiving a nod of satisfaction and appreciation from Mr. Lucas has got to be one of my proudest achievements to date. George Lucas is a legend!

Thomas Seargent Photography.

"One of my most prestigious experiences was working on a 1940s-inspired TV commercial for Head & Shoulders. I did the makeup and nails for eight stunning models. The commercial has gone on to be one of the most iconic campaigns in the shampoo industry.

Courtesy of Mark Cant.

"Makeup artistry is all about being in the right place at the right time and never giving up. Along my journey, I was lucky to meet photographers, directors, and makeup artists who took me on and gave me opportunities to work on high-profile clients."

Julia can be contacted at www.good-foundations.org or www.juliafrancis.co.uk.

Choosing the right shades of makeup for an individual face is one of the most difficult aspects of makeup artistry. The wrong color combination can ruin an entire look, causing people to see the makeup instead of the face itself.

A complete consultation and a completed consultation form are the foundation for a successful makeup application—and, in turn, the foundation for a successful business. Incomplete consults can result in allergic reactions, miscommunication, poor results, and dissatisfied clients. Dissatisfied clients can result in ruined professional reputations.

A thorough consultation demonstrates commitment to your client, your service, and your profession. During the consultation, you will create a personal connection with your client. You will help her become more knowledgeable and skilled with makeup application by teaching her techniques for accentuating favorite features and camouflaging least favorite features.

WHY STUDY CLIENT CONSULTATIONS?

Makeup artists should study and have a thorough understanding of client consultation because:

- The consultation process is the link between your skills and your client's satisfaction.
- A thorough consultation will help you choose products for the individual client.
- A thorough consultation will help you understand your client's goals and concerns.
- A consultation ensures proper communication between the makeup artist and the client.
- The consultation forms document the products and colors used for the makeup service.

▲ **Figure 6–1 A professional makeup artist greets a new client.**

MAKING A GOOD FIRST IMPRESSION

You are your own best advertising. As a professional makeup artist, it is imperative to not only "talk the walk" but also "walk the talk." Be sure your appearance at work is impeccable. You should exude beauty, creativity, fun, and confidence—all characteristics that you want to create for your clients.

First impressions are a topic we have returned to again and again in this textbook. When you present yourself as professionally put-together, you will inspire confidence in your clients (**Figure 6–1**). After all, you wouldn't have your house painted by a painter whose own house had atrocious color choices, shaky seams, and brush strokes mixed with roller marks. For the same reason, makeup artists cannot expect clients to trust them if they look like they just rolled out of bed.

Your body language, confidence, and mannerisms also contribute to your professional presentation. Greet your client with a smile, a firm hand shake, and a warm and meaningful welcome. Place yourself in your client's shoes and think about what you would expect from a top-notch makeup professional.

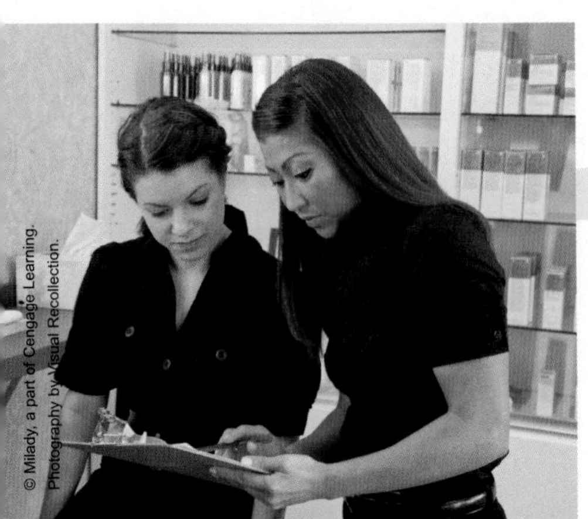

▲ **Figure 6–2 Review a detailed consultation form before the application of makeup.**

THE CONSULTATION FORM

The client **consultation form** is a questionnaire used to gather pertinent information about a client and their needs. This tool will guide your work with the client, and every client should complete the consultation form as the first step upon arriving for their appointment. Explain to your client the importance of the form in determining proper product selection, improving skin imperfections, and determining current makeup concerns (**Figure 6–2**).

Do not simply hand the client a form and ask them to fill it out. The proper procedure is to sit or kneel beside the client and let them know that you need to gather some important information in order to select proper products and avoid complications. By communicating the importance of the consultation form, you will reinforce the client's confidence in your professionalism, skills, and abilities.

There are many different types of consultation forms. You can develop your own or use one provided by a manufacturer or other company. Regardless of the type of form, there are a few categories of information that you will always need to collect (**Figure 6–3**).

General Information

The consultation form should always begin with general information about the client: their name and contact information, the date, the source of the referral, and the reason for the visit. This information, which should be updated for accuracy at every visit, will help you organize your client files. This general information can also act as a key marketing tool for mailings, e-mail campaigns, and specials based on birthdays, anniversaries, new products, and special events.

Purpose of Visit

Determining the purpose of the visit allows you to take control of the consultation process and help your client stay on track toward their goals. If your client says that learning how to choose colors for everyday makeup is the purpose but that she feels makeup is a bit too loud for everyday, your professional responsibility is to redirect her choices. Help to choose basic,

COSMETIC CONSULTATION FORM

Name: ______________________ Date: ______________

Address: ______________________________________

City: ______________________ State: __________ Zip: __________

Phone: ______________ (Work) ______________ (Cellular) ______________

E-mail Address ______________________________________

Purpose of Todays Visit:

☐ Makeup Lesson ☐ Color Choices ☐ Bridal Application ☐ Photography
☐ Special Occasion ☐ Everyday Makeup ☐ Moisturizer ☐ Other ______________

List Three Concerns/Objectives of Today's Makeup Appointment:

☐ ______________________________________
☐ ______________________________________
☐ ______________________________________

Makeup Regimen:

☐ Foundation ☐ Concealer ☐ Powder ☐ Eye Shadow ☐ Eyeliner ☐ Lipstick
☐ Lip Liner ☐ Blush ☐ Mascara ☐ Other______________________
☐ Product Brands ______________________________________
☐ How often do you wear Makeup? ______________________________________

Skin Care Regimen:

☐ Cleanser ☐ Exfoliator ☐ Toner/Astringent ☐ Mask ☐ Eye Products
☐ Sunscreen ☐ Moisturizer ☐ Other ______________________

Are you currently using products containing any of the following?

☐ Glycolic Acid ☐ Salicylic Acid ☐ Lactic Acid ☐ Any hydroxyl acid ☐ Exfoliating Scrub
☐ Vitamin A derivatives (retinol, etc.) ☐ Antibiotics ☐ Acne Medication

Have you had any chemical peels, laser, microdermabrasion, or any other resurfacing treatments?

☐ Yes ☐ No In the last month? ☐ Yes ☐ No

Have you ever had an allergic reaction to any of the following?

☐ Cosmetics ☐ Medicine ☐ Sunscreens ☐ Hydroxyl Acid ☐ Animals ☐ Fragrance
☐ Iodine ☐ Other: ______________________

Your Health

Have you been under a physician's care in the past 12 months? ☐ Yes ☐ No

Have you had in the past or currently have any of the following health issues?

Cancer	Multiple Sclerosis (MS)	Diabetes
Epilepsy	Hormonal Imbalance	Heart Problems
Hysterectomy	Systemic Disease	Thyroid Conditions
Varicose Veins	Spinal Injury	Osteoporosis
Arthritis	Autoimmune Disorder	High Blood Pressure
Lupus	Fibromyalgia	Other ______________

Please list any medications or supplements that you take on a regular basis: ______________

____

▲ Figure 6–3 The consultation form.

(continued)

Do you wear contact lenses? ☐ Yes ☐ No
Do you suffer from cold sores? ☐ Yes ☐ No
Do you suffer from sinus problems? ☐ Yes ☐ No

The Following is to be Completed with Makeup Professional:

☐ Describe your most important makeup concern? ______________________

____

☐ What colors and types of makeup are you most comfortable wearing? ______________________

____

☐ How much time do you spend applying makeup each day? ______________________

____

☐ What would you like to change about your current makeup regimen or look? ______________________

____

☐ If a special event, what is the time of day, season, purpose of the event? ______________________

____

☐ Are there certain colors that you are most comfortable wearing/not wearing? ______________________

____

*The next two lines are for the makeup artists own important questions.

☐ ______________________

☐ ______________________

▲ **Figure 6–3 (continued)**

neutral colors that deliver and create the look the client is seeking and is comfortable wearing. You can then demonstrate some simple ways to jazz-up the look for an after-hours evening out. With the client's goal in mind, you can educate your them on makeup products, looks, and techniques that are best suited to meet their needs and comfort level.

Current Product Use

Before choosing any type of specific makeup product, it is important to first know the client's current skin care and makeup regimens. This information will help you to determine a client's skin type, skin conditions and any possible contributing factors, willingness to commit to a regimen, and the level of care given to thier appearance. This information will direct product choices and application techniques.

An individual's skin changes with age, lifestyle (activeness, outdoor activity), climate, product use, medications, illness, stress, and the seasons. Skin care and makeup choices should change as well.

Medications

You will find it helpful to keep a medical reference book in your place of business. The ***Physicians' Desk Reference*** **(PDR)** (PDR Network, 2011) is a medical book that contains thousands of types of medications, their uses, and their possible side effects. There are hundreds of different medications for hundreds of different conditions, and new ones are developed every day. With a PDR at your fingertips, you can quickly discover the purpose of any medication the client is taking, along with any effects the medication may have on her skin. Several categories of medications are known to have specific effects on the skin. Other reference books of this type are also available, but the PDR is the medical industry's standard.

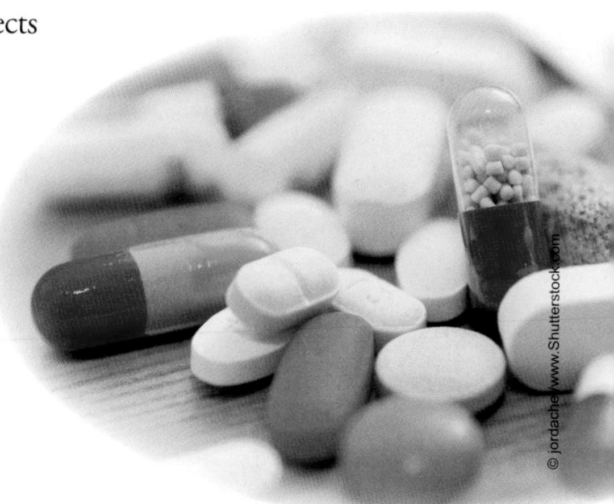

▲ Figure 6–4 **There are many types of antibiotics on the market today.**

Antibiotics

Antibiotics—topical or systemic—are prescribed for a wide variety of bacterial infections (**Figure 6–4**). They are also prescribed to treat a host of skin conditions, such as acne and rosacea. Antibiotics tend to increase overall skin sensitivity, dehydrate the skin, and greatly increase sensitivity to UV exposure.

Antihistamines

Antihistamines are prescribed for environmental and seasonal allergies and for allergic reactions due to contact dermatitis. They are well known for dehydrating the surface layers of the skin.

Steroids

Topical steroids are prescribed for dermatitis and skin inflammation. Oral steroids are prescribed for a host of medical conditions such as allergies and asthma. Steroids typically increase skin sensitivity, and when they are applied topically, they sensitize and thin the stratum corneum, which can result in dehydrating the surface skin and giving it a thin, sensitive, and red appearance.

Medical Conditions

You need to obtain information regarding medical conditions because of possible problems on the surface of the skin or as a result of medications. As a makeup professional, you are not legally able or medically qualified to diagnose medical conditions; doing so is clearly outside your scope of practice. However, you will find it useful to develop an understanding of the impact various conditions have on the function and appearance of the skin. This understanding will help you choose products and techniques for the client.

Heart Conditions

Heart conditions may result in a chronic flushed appearance in the face, neck, and décolleté.

Pregnancy

Pregnancy can influence a wide variety of conditions, and no two pregnancies are alike. Pregnant clients may experience increased skin sensitivity, acne breakouts, hyperpigmentation, dehydration, hair loss, or even excessive hair growth. It is important to remember that most of these conditions are triggered by the enormous hormonal changes within the body and will very likely diminish within a few weeks or months following delivery (**Figure 6–5**).

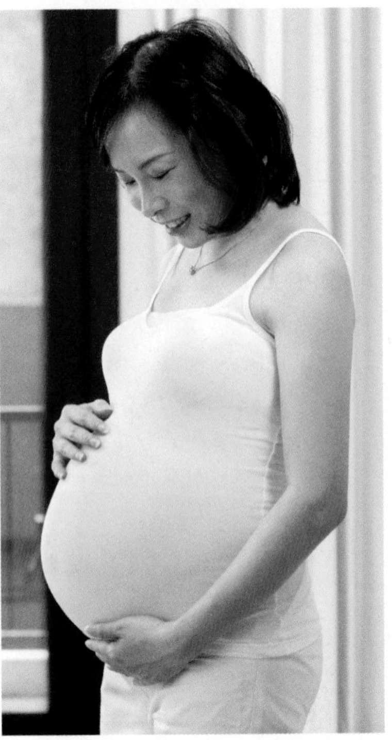

© OtnaYdur/www.Shutterstock.com

▲ Figure 6–5 **A pregnant client can present unique challenges.**

High Blood Pressure

Clients with high blood pressure are often able to regulate their condition properly with medication. This medical condition may result in a flushed appearance to the face, neck, and décolleté.

Immune Disorders

Immune disorders, such as lupus and acquired immune deficiency syndrome (AIDS), create a long list of concerns. When the immune system is strained, the body does not heal properly, so you must treat the skin in a gentle manner. During times of active immune responses, clients with immune disorders may experience a discoloration, a "butterfly" mask across the face, unusual lesions, reoccurring breakouts, and extreme skin sensitivity.

Recent Surgery

In the final stages of healing, wounds created by surgery may appear as green/yellow bruising or very fresh, pink-red skin. Special precautions should be taken to avoid irritating the area or spreading bacteria. The client may wish to make some different, short-term makeup choices, but once the skin is completely healed, she can probably return to her customary products.

© iStockphoto/cclickclick

Allergies

Because you will be using a wide range of cosmetic ingredients, you need to know about their allergies and sensitivities, especially as they relate to ingredients in skin care products and makeup products. The two most common ingredient allergens are sunscreens and coloring ingredients. Product sources and ingredients are constantly changing and can often be formulated from more natural resources. Stay informed about new products that may be right for your clients with allergies.

Milk/Dairy Products containing lactic acid, which acts as a mild exfoliant and hydrating agent, are derived from milk sources. You should not use these products on clients with dairy allergies or sensitivities.

Aspirin Products containing salicylic acid, willow bark, and wintergreen are likely to cause a reaction in clients with aspirin allergies. These ingredients are commonly used as exfoliants and peeling agents. Also, because of their antibacterial properties, they are commonly found in acne and oily skin products.

Environmental Allergies You need to be familiar with environmental allergies and the medications a client is taking to treat them. This information is helpful because the types of medications or even the allergies themselves may be affecting the condition of the skin. Most medications for sinus and allergy conditions are very dehydrating to the skin. ✓ **LO1**

> **HERE'S A TIP**
>
> Depending upon your working environment and your experience, you may want to consider creating your own consultation form. This allows you to gather information that you feel is important and that may not appear on the form used by the facility. For example, if the majority of your makeup clients come to you for special-occasion makeup, you can tailor your form to these events by asking questions about the venue, the event colors, and so on. On the other hand, if most of your clients come in for makeovers, everyday makeup, or lessons, you can target the form toward daily activities, lifestyle, makeup comfort levels, and other preferences.

THE CONSULTATION PROCESS

Once the client consultation form has been completed, the next step is to integrate the consultation form into an interactive communicative consultation. It is your professional responsibility to review each section of the consultation form very carefully with the client. This will guarantee that you and the client have the same goals for the appointment and that the client's desired outcome will be achieved. The information on the consultation form will serve as the groundwork for the rest of the consultation process.

Often a professional will instantly have a vision of what a particular client could or should look like. However, if you give a client a look she does not like or want, she will leave dissatisfied and most likely will not return. One of the biggest mistakes that a makeup professional can make is to not communicate with a client on expectations and needs. The three major complaints often heard from clients following a professional makeup application or makeover are that they don't look like themselves afterward; they would never wear the colors or amount of makeup that was chosen; and that they will never be able to re-create the same look on their own.

Communication

Communication is the act of successfully sharing information between two people, or groups of people, so that the information is effectively and clearly understood. In addition, communication is the cornerstone of success in the beauty business. You cannot deliver results if you do not know what a client wants, so listen to your client very closely. By doing so, you will gain her trust and over time may be able to persuade her to try more creative colors, products, and application techniques.

HERE'S A TIP

The consultation should include a discussion of eyebrow shaping, which may require a separate tweezing or waxing appointment (Figure 6–7). The shape of the eyebrows can alter the entire look of the face, so you should always discuss the importance of proper eyebrow grooming, various ways to accomplish a well-groomed look, and the impact that eyebrow shaping will have on your client's appearance. If you are unable to perform a grooming procedure, develop a relationship with an esthetician you can recommend.

The complete consultation process is a combination of facts obtained from the consultation form and your assessment of the client's physical attributes. As a professional makeup artist, you must develop highly effective communication skills. This includes thoroughly reading and understanding the consultation form, listening to what the client wants, reflecting your understanding back to the client so that she can clarify any confusion, and finally letting the client know how you plan to meet her needs (**Figure 6–6**).

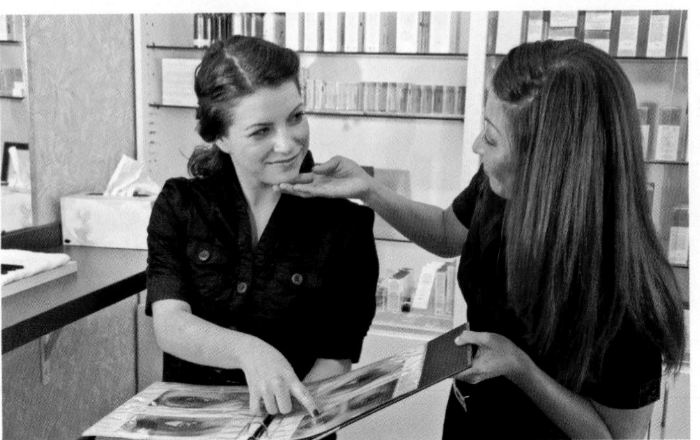

▲ Figure 6–6 **It is important to communicate a desired look with your client.**

Reflective Listening

The best way to ensure that you fully understand your client is to practice reflective listening. **Reflective listening** is a process in which you listen to the client and then repeat back, in your own words, what you think the client is telling you. Here is an example:

> "OK Jessica, let me see if I understand what you are looking for. The most important thing for you is to have a daytime makeup application that is simple but still covers the redness on your chin and cheeks. Is this correct?"

This type of statement gives Jessica the opportunity to confirm your understanding of her goals for the appointment. It also validates for you your understanding of her goal.

As an artist, you have a gift of being naturally creative. Because of this gift, you have the ability to envision a new style or look that a client could never have imagined. Use this important gift during the consultation process. Validate your client's wishes through reflective listening, and then take them to the next level using your expertise and talent. With Jessica, discussed previously, you can explain that there are simple ways to minimize the redness on her chin and cheeks, while at the same time accentuating her beautiful blue eyes. This kind of advice draws attention away from the client's flaws or areas of concern and places emphasis on a source of pride. At the end of such a conversation, Jessica would probably feel pretty good about herself. ✓ LO2

▲ Figure 6–7 **Proper grooming is key to a successful application.**

EVALUATING THE CLIENT'S FEATURES AND CHARACTERISTICS

Another component of the consultation takes place when you use your professional eye to evaluate the client's characteristics. You cannot know which products to use and how to use them until you determine the client's skin tone, which features you will emphasize (highlight), which you will deemphasize (contour), and so on.

A **cosmetic treatment card** is a form used to document the details of the application, including an evaluation of the client's features, the purpose for the visit, the colors and products used, the application techniques, and any other pertinent information that will be useful for future visits (**Figure 6–8**). The card should include space where you can add details about all of the following client features.

HERE'S A TIP

Before clients come in for repeat visits, be sure to review the cosmetic treatment card. This will help you remember what was done in previous visits and what might need to be changed for this visit. Your client will appreciate the fact that you remember her and her issues so clearly.

COSMETIC TREATMENT CARD

Name: ______________________ Date: __________
Purpose of Visit: ______________________
Client Skin Tone: ______________________
Makeup Style: ______________________
Regular Makeup Regimen: ______________________
____

Clothing Style: ______________________

Products/Colors Used:
Eyes: ______________________
Cheeks: ______________________
Lips: ______________________
Foundation: ______________________ Powder: __________
Concealer: ______________________

Special Techniques: ______________________
Unique Facial Features: ______________________
Notes: ______________________

▲ Figure 6–8 **Cosmetic treatment card.**

HERE'S A TIP

The perfect foundation match requires blending from the jawline to the neck, and (when there is a dramatic color difference between the neck and chest) down onto the chest as well.

Once you have established a client's needs and desires, use your professional knowledge and artistic abilities to determine how to deliver results. By evaluating the client's features and characteristics, you will be better able to choose tools, colors, and techniques that will be best for accomplishing your client's goals. There are five client features that should be listed on the cosmetic treatment card and that must be determined before the makeup application can begin:

- Skin Tone
- Dynamic Facial Features
- Facial Shape
- Clothing Style
- Makeup Style

If something is harmonious, it is pleasing to the eye. Harmony is engaging and creates a sense of order and balance as well as intrigue and attention. When something is not harmonious, it is either boring or chaotic. A boring visual experience will not engage the eye. A chaotic visual experience can actually repel the eye. By paying attention to the client's desires and features, you will help her to attain a harmonious and comfortable look. The makeup artist's task is to present a visual experience and color harmony that will deliver visual interest and a sense of order.

Skin Tone

Skin tone is one aspect of makeup that never changes. You must determine the skin tone of the client in order to properly select foundation. Aspects of skin tone to determine are:

- Warm or cool
- Even or uneven
- Ruddy/red
- Sallow/grey
- Imperfections (scars, birthmarks, and so on)
- Differing skin tone on the face, neck, or chest

Dynamic Facial Features

Dynamic features include unique, often prominent, facial features that a client may want to hide/diminish or may want to emphasize/accentuate. Closely assess facial features and talk with your client about their thoughts and feelings. Which features are her favorites? Are there features that are important to emphasize? Deemphasize? Communicate your professional thoughts regarding specific features, but be diplomatic. Your client's opinion might be different from yours when it comes to which features should be highlighted and which should be contoured. Areas to discuss and assess include:

- Overall facial shape
- Size and shape of the nose
- Size and shape of the eyes
- Size and shape of the mouth and lips
- Length of eyelashes
- Shape and color of the eyebrows
- Eye color

Because they are unique to the client, dynamic features will often require unique application techniques (**Figure 6–9**).

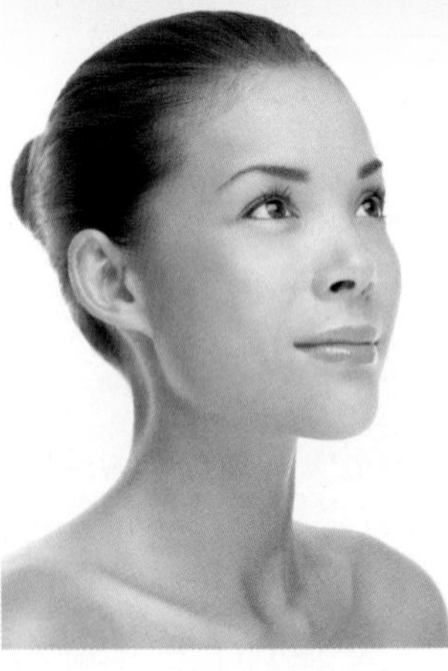

▲ Figure 6–9 Analyze your client's unique features.

Makeup Style

Evaluate your client's current everyday makeup style. Often makeup styles match a client's personality and are expressed in application technique as well as the color choices. Does your client tend to be trendy or conservative? Does her makeup tend toward minimal or toward excessive? Keep in mind, however, that people have different interpretations of words such as *trendy* and *conservative*. A trendy look to a 20-year-old may be completely different from a trendy look to a 50-year-old (**Figure 6–10**). And a look considered to be everyday makeup by one client might be considered an evening-look by another. As a general guideline, you can use the list below as a reference in determining makeup styles:

- Trendy
- Evening
- For work
- Minimal/excessive
- Day
- Conservative/simple
- For play

▼ Figure 6–10 The makeup applications of younger clients and mature clients will vary.

If your client arrived for her appointment wearing makeup, you can evaluate her style based on that look. What colors was she wearing? How many colors did she use? Which features were accentuated? If the client is not wearing any makeup when she arrives, ask her to describe her makeup routine, favorite color choices, application techniques, and how she would describe her own everyday style.

Your job is to listen to what your client wants. Then you can either help the client improve her current style or help her get comfortable with a new tyle. Maintaining some of the client's existing makeup style as part of an updated look will encourage a certain level of comfort.

HERE'S A TIP

For special-occasion makeup be sure to have your client bring along clothing, color swatches, photos, or any image that will give you a "feel" for the event.

Clothing Style

Clothing choices are relevant when a client is seeking makeup for a special event such as a wedding, party, photoshoot, reunion, and so on. Ask your client to describe the attire being worn to the event; this will help you choose colors and application techniques. However, even for an everyday makeup look, it is a good idea to get a feel for how your client dresses on a daily basis. ☑ LO3

© Milady, a part of Cengage Learning. Photography by Visual Recollection.

▲ Figure 6–11 Show your client your professional portfolio.

DOCUMENTATION

As you choose colors, products, and techniques, you should document those choices.The cosmetic treatment card should have space for this information. In fact, this card takes all of the information gathered during the consultation and evaluation process and describes how it was put into action during the makeup application. This card will serve as a starting point for future visits.

Pictures speak a million words. Taking a photo of a client in her own makeup application, one with no makeup at all, and one when you have completed your professional application is a guaranteed way for the client to see and fully appreciate the differences and improvement. Digital photos are simple to place on a computer for quick access or to print out and place in client files for future reference. Photographs are also necessary for building your professional portfolio. Your portfolio contains photographs of your finest work and is one of your most important marketing tools (**Figure 6–11**). Portfolios are discussed further in Chapter 19, Your Professional Image.

The consultation is a necessary part of each and every makeup application. It is designed to ensure that a client's desires and expecatitions are clear and that her needs are met. It is a simple and certain way to become a success (**Figure 6–12**). Never skimp on this all-important part of each and every makeup application.

▼ Figure 6–12 A satisfied client after a consultation.

© PashOK/www.Shutterstock.com

Review Questions

1. Explain why it is important to make a good first impression.
2. What is the purpose of a client consultation form for makeup services?
3. Which part of the consultation form can act as a key marketing tool for mailings, e-mail campaigns, and specials?
4. Name three effects that antibiotics can have on skin.
5. How can pregnancy affect the skin?
6. What is one of the biggest mistakes a makeup artist can make with a client?
7. What is the purpose of the cosmetic treatment card?
8. What is a dynamic feature?
9. What are examples of makeup styles?
10. Define harmony.

Chapter Glossary

communication	The act of successfully sharing information between two people, or groups of people, so that the information is effectively and clearly understood.
consultation form	A questionnaire used to gather pertinent information about a client and her needs.
cosmetic treatment card	A form used to document the details of the application, including an evaluation of the client's features, the purpose for the visit, the colors and products used, the application techniques, and any other pertinent information that will be useful for future visits.
Physicians' Desk Reference	Abbreviated PDR; a medical book that contains thousands of types of medications, their uses, and their possible side effects.
reflective listening	Listening to the client and then repeating, in your own words, what you think the client is telling you.

Part 2

Makeup Foundation

CHAPTER 7
CREATING THE CANVAS

CHAPTER 8
FACIAL FEATURES

CHAPTER 9
THE EVERYDAY APPLICATION

Chapter 7 Creating the Canvas

Chapter Outline

Learning Objectives

After completing this chapter, you will be able to:

- ✓ **LO1** Describe the types of foundations and their uses.
- ✓ **LO2** Describe the types of concealers and their uses.
- ✓ **LO3** Describe the types of powders and their uses.
- ✓ **LO4** Describe the types of blush and their uses.
- ✓ **LO5** Identify the six facial shapes and determine the key objectives in working with their characteristics.
- ✓ **LO6** Identify the Three-Part Procedure and explain why it is useful.

Key Terms

Page number indicates where in the chapter the term is used.

concealer
pg. 132

contour
pg. 131

cream foundations
pg. 130

cross-contamination
pg. 130

emollient based
pg. 130

foundation
pg. 128

highlight
pg. 131

inert substances
pg. 129

line of demarcation
pg. 131

liquid foundation
pg. 129

mineral makeup
pg. 129

mousse foundation
pg. 130

oil-based foundation
pg. 129

parabens
pg. 129

skin tone
pg. 129

stick foundation
pg. 130

toner
pg. 128

translucent
pg. 134

water-based foundation
pg. 129

Career Profile

Jackeline Goh

Jackeline Goh has relied on her passion for makeup artistry to get her through the ups and downs on her career path. Her passion has allowed her to work with both makeup and hair and to fill her portfolio with video and print ads for use within the makeup industry and with the public. She hopes to someday open up a one-stop, head-to-toe makeover salon, and she believes her love of makeup artistry will help her accomplish this goal.

"Over the years I worked at a hairdressing salon, I realized that makeup and hairstyling complement each other, representing a dual service that many customers wanted. As a result, I studied makeup so I could provide the makeup services that my customers desired.

"After some time working as both a hairstylist and a makeup artist, I moved on to work as a freelance makeover artist. An acquaintance of mine offered me opportunities to work for productions, and ever since I have been gradually building up my contacts and reputation in the industry. My reputation has been built mainly by word of mouth, and from the beginning, job offers came my way.

"Many interesting challenges have come along during my career. Once I had to apply makeup on a male model in his 20s for a video sponsored by the Ministry of Community Development, Youth and Sports (MCYS). Using only makeup, I was to illustrate senescence (or biological aging) on the face of the male model. The model was filmed at four stages of aging, and each stage required the male model to "age" by 20 years. Creating these four stages was a true challenge for me.

"My passion for this line of work helps me overcome challenges and keep a positive attitude. One of my most difficult jobs in terms of physical hardship was the SingTel Grid Girls 2008 video shoot. SingTel is Singapore's largest telecommunication operator, and I was hired to do makeup for a video on their Web site. The job sounded simple—do makeup and hair for a few girls. When I arrived, however, there were 11 girls, and I had to do the job alone, over a span of 2 days, working 12 hours each day. The shooting site was an unfurnished workshop, which lacked proper tables and chairs for me and for the models. As a result of the long hours and the uncomfortable working conditions, I experienced severe backaches and over-strained eyes by the end of day one. I still had to complete the job, and I wanted my models to shine on screen. So to avoid discomfort on day two, I brought my own high stool to the site and finished the job without pain.

"My job as a makeup artist and a hair specialist entails not only hard work, but also a fervent passion and dedication to this industry. Passion is the key driver that helps me go the extra mile. My passion creates a beneficial cycle. It inspires high quality in my work, and that quality gives me satisfaction in a job well done, along with compliments from satisfied customers. Smiling, satisfied customers make me feel spiritually accomplished. Such positive experiences, in turn, intensify the passion which I hold dear. I feel that I have found the career to which I can dedicate my life, and the challenge now is to continue raising my skills to the next level."

Courtesy of Jackeline Goh.

One of the most interesting and intriguing aspects of the human face is that every person has unique facial features and characteristics. A makeup artist's goal is to emphasize each individual's most stunning and attractive features. To allow for attention to detail and guarantee spectacular results, makeup application must begin with the ideal canvas. Creating the ideal canvas involves proper prepping of the skin and the selection of appropriate concealer, foundation, powder and blush, along with the correct application of products given the individual's face shape.

WHY STUDY CREATING THE CANVAS?

Makeup artists should study and have a thorough understanding of how to create the ideal canvas for every and any client for several reasons:

- The successful completion of any artistic masterpiece depends upon the quality of the canvas on which it is created. The higher the quality of the canvas, the more brilliant and beautiful the final piece of art.
- To create an ideal facial canvas you must know what products to choose and their purpose.
- Creating the ideal canvas includes choosing the proper products for individual skin type.
- Color selection and matching the foundation to the client's natural coloring is the first step in creating a harmonious makeup application.
- Simple steps early in a makeup application will help accentuate the client's most attractive facial features.

STATE REGULATORY ALERT

Be sure to check with your state regulations. In many states, if you are not a licensed esthetician or cosmetologist you may not be permitted to apply and remove skin care products.

PREPARING THE SKIN

Basic preparation of the skin may seem insignificant to a makeup application; however, skin preparation helps determine the quality of the makeup application, including appearance and longevity. Every makeup application should begin with clean, hydrated skin. If your client arrives already wearing makeup, you must properly cleanse, tone, and moisturize the client's skin before beginning the makeup application. Refer to the client consultation form to determine your client's skin type so that you can choose the proper products. Even though you will be dealing with different skin types, it is not necessary to have a huge selection of skin care products in your kit; a simple, basic selection will be sufficient for every situation.

Toner is also a quick fix when cleanser is not available, when makeup needs to be removed and reapplied, or when oily skin needs refreshing.

Cleanser

Clean skin—free of all dirt, debris, and excess oil—is necessary for proper makeup application. For combination to dry skin types, a gentle cream cleanser with mild foaming abilities is an excellent choice. For normal to oily skin, a gel-based cleanser or foaming cleanser is better suited to remove excess oils.

Toner

Toner serves multiple purposes, and it is a critical skin care product for the makeup kit. Choose a toner that is manufactured to accompany the cleansers you have chosen. **Toner** is a skin care product designed to complete the cleansing process by removing any further excess dirt, oil, makeup, or debris from the surface of the skin. It also balances the pH of the skin, properly preparing it for products that are applied afterward.

Moisturizer

A light moisturizer is excellent for a smooth makeup application. However, too much moisturizer can create a landslide; excess moisturizer can cause makeup to slide and smudge. In fact, some oily skin types may not need a moisturizer at all. If the skin is soft and supple after cleansing and if makeup can be easily applied without pulling at the skin, additional moisturizer is not necessary. In addition, many foundations contain wonderful moisturizing ingredients, so your choice in foundation also affects whether you need to use a separate moisturizer. The best way to determine whether to apply moisturizer is to refer to your client consultation form and to your client's regular skin care regimen. Then base your choice on the client's skin type, as well as your other product choices.

HERE'S A TIP

Many makeup artists use primer in place of moisturizer, especially in the case of combination and oily skin types. Makeup primer has a mild silicone base that allows many types of concealers and foundations to be applied to the skin with an even, smooth, and thorough coverage.

Makeup Remover

Sometimes a client may arrive with a full face of makeup, including waterproof mascara. In such cases, it is necessary to use makeup remover formulated to remove waterproof mascara and eyeliner. Such a product is also an excellent choice for quickly removing makeup from the entire face.

FOUNDATION

Foundation was given its name for a reason. It is the first product used in the actual makeup application, and as such, it provides the "foundation" on which the whole application is built. However, in some instances concealer is applied before foundation; those cases are discussed in the next few paragraphs.

Foundation is a makeup product designed to even out skin tone and mild imperfections and provide a base for the makeup application. With foundation, choosing the proper color is critical and depends on the skin tone of the client. **Skin tone** is the degree of warm color tone or cool color tone in the skin. Determining skin tone improperly can result in a lifeless and dull makeup application. On the other hand, the proper foundation enhances the client's natural skin tone and blends beautifully from the face down the jawline to the neck and chest. Refer to what you learned about color theory to determine a client's skin tone. Is your client warm toned or cool toned? Foundations come in shades from the darkest of brown/black to the palest of flesh-white, so it is always possible to find a perfect match to your client's skin tone.

Types of Foundation

Foundations come in a variety of formulations, textures, and coverage (**Figure 7–1**). Your choice of foundation will depend on your client's skin and the purpose of the makeup application. Many foundations provide benefits such as sunscreen, environmental protection, moisturizing ingredients, or oil absorption. The best foundation choice provides the desired color, consistency, and coverage.

▲ Figure 7–1 **Different types of foundations.**

Liquid Foundation

Liquid foundation is suited for just about any skin type and provides a sheer, light, natural coverage; it can be oil-based, water-based, or mineral-based. **Oil-based foundation** contains more oil than water and is best suited for dry or mature skin types. **Water-based foundation** contains more water than oil; it is better suited for oily skin, blemished skin, or combination to dry skin.

Mineral Foundation

Mineral makeup has gained enormous popularity in recent years, and because of its unique properties, mineral-based foundation is good for all skin types. Minerals are **inert substances**, ingredients that cannot sustain bacterial growth and have no properties that cause allergies. **Mineral makeup** contain fewer ingredients and are less likely to cause allergic reactions on sensitive skin; most are talc-free and paraben-free. **Parabens** are ingredients used as preservatives in cosmetics.

Because of their unique properties, mineral cosmetics are the cosmetic of choice for people with allergies, people with sensitive skin, or clients who have just had a facial procedure. Mineral cosmetics are available in liquid and powder form, are long-lasting, and offer UVA and UVB protection. Even though most mineral cosmetics are hypoallergenic, you should check ingredient labels to be sure that allergy-causing ingredients have not been added.

Mineral makeup in powder form is the most antibacterial because it does not contain water. Liquid mineral foundations are still excellent in preventing bacterial growth since they contain fewer ingredients compared with other types of makeup; however, water (the first ingredient) will make them more susceptible to bacterial growth.

Liquid-to-powder foundations give the coverage of a liquid with the smooth look of a powder. They are light on the skin and create a slightly matte finish with sheer to medium coverage.

Cream-to-Powder Foundation

Many manufacturers produce a Cream-to-Powder Foundation. This product comes in a compact, is applied with a sponge, and transforms from a velvety cream to a micro-fine powder when it comes in contact with the skin.

Cream Foundation

Cream foundations can be either water-based or oil-based; they are thicker in consistency than a liquid foundation and provide overall coverage with a smooth texture and deep tone. However, this does not mean that cream foundations are all heavy. Their specific manufacturer and ingredients determine their weight and coverage. Cream foundations are excellent for dry skin, mature skin, and skin with uneven texture and tone. There are also cream foundations that are formulated specifically for oily skin types.

Mousse Foundation

Mousse foundation is a liquid product that comes in an aerosol or spray can, boosted by air (like whipped cream); it is light, easy to apply, and an excellent choice for any skin type. Many liquid foundations are formulated with ingredients designed to benefit the health and hydration of the skin, leaving skin with an even, airbrushed, supple appearance.

Stick Foundation

Stick foundation is a molded, compact foundation (in a container similar to lipstick but larger); it can be used on all skin types, provides excellent coverage, and serves as both a foundation and a concealer. Stick foundation can also provide a quick highlight or contour.

Stick foundations are **emollient based**, which means they are water-in-oil or oil-in-water blends of ingredients that soften and smooth the skin. Many stick foundations are considered a cream-to-powder foundation. For lighter coverage and a smooth, silky matte finish, stick foundation can be applied with a sponge.

Application Techniques

Because foundation is the base for the entire makeup application, foundation color, foundation type, and foundation application must all be precise.

Once you have determined the proper type of foundation, based on your client's skin type and the purpose of the makeup application, you must choose the proper shade of foundation. There are several techniques that makeup artists use to choose foundation shades.

Matching and Blending

To match a foundation to a skin tone takes a trained eye. Often a few products are tested on the client's face before a perfect match is identified. When testing and applying foundation, you can use clean fingers or single-use sponges. Single-use sponges are the best choice in order to prevent **cross-contamination**, the spread of bacteria from one place, person, or product to another.

Matching Technique 1

Choose two to three shades and apply a 2-inch (5 centimeter) line from the lower cheek down the jawline (**Figure 7–2**). View the application from

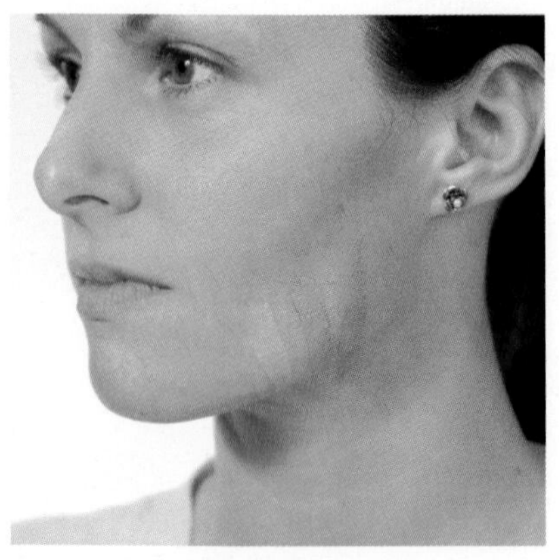

▲ Figure 7–2 **Three-line foundation matching technique.**

various angles to determine which shade blends the face to the neck. You always want to avoid a **line of demarcation**, a line that displays a distinct change in color. If you see such a line, that color is a poor choice. As your experience with skin tone, foundation shades, and your makeup kit grows, you will more quickly be able to choose the perfect foundation colors for each client.

Matching Technique 2

With this technique, you choose a foundation color that matches not only the face and neck, but also the chest. Again, choose two or three shades and apply a 2-inch (5 centimeter) line, but this time run the line from the lower cheek, down the jawline, and onto the chest (**Figure 7–3**). In many cases the chest is darker than the face. By choosing a slightly darker shade of foundation, the entire face, neck, and chest blend beautifully.

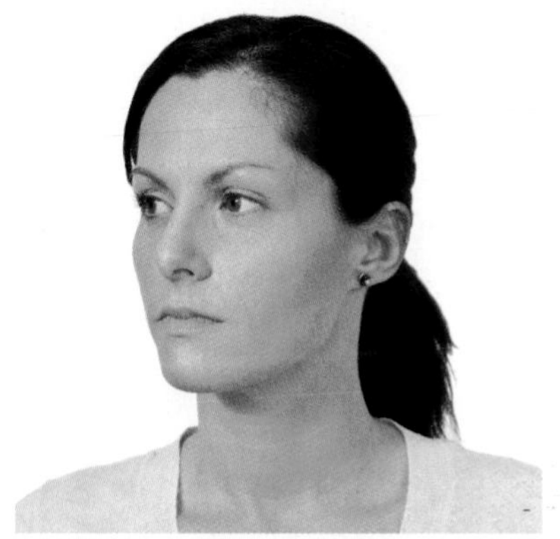

▲ Figure 7–3 **Foundation blended from face to neck and chest.**

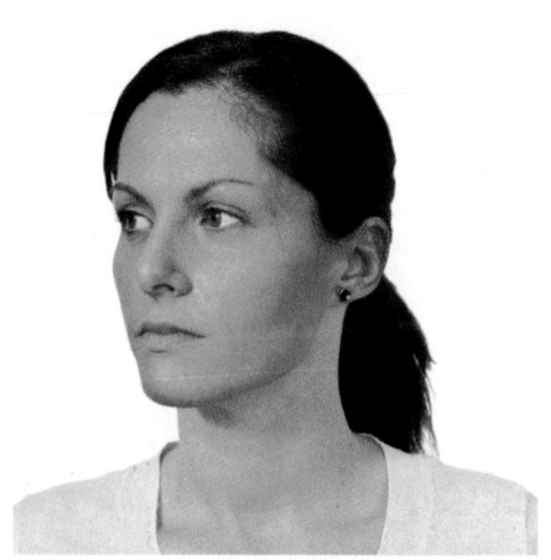

▲ Figure 7–4 **Foundation that is not matched and blended with the neck and chest.**

▲ Figure 7–5 **Foundation matching the face and neck, but not the chest.**

The objective with foundation is to create a flawless, natural-looking canvas. When the face does not match the neck (**Figure 7–4**), or when the face or neck do not blend with the chest (**Figure 7–5**), the look of the makeup is very unnatural. Remember that most clients want to wear makeup without looking like they are wearing makeup.

Highlighting and Contouring Using Foundation

Foundation can be used to change the appearance of a face shape by drawing attention to or away from specific facial features. Two techniques are involved: highlighting and contouring. A **highlight** is used to bring out, increase in apparent size, or draw attention to a feature. A **contour** is used to recede, minimize in apparent size, or draw attention away from a feature. For both techniques, two to three shades of foundation are necessary. The first shade will be the foundation that matches the skin tone and blends the face and neck to the chest. Foundation one shade lighter is used to highlight features, bringing them out and making them appear larger or wider (**Figure 7–6**). Foundation a shade darker

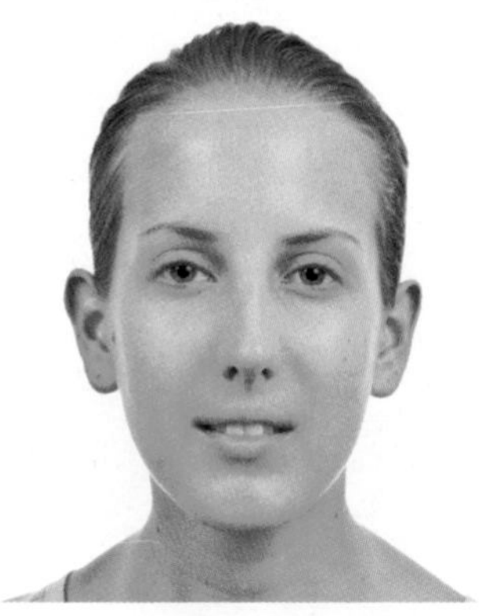

▲ Figure 7–6 **A narrow nose made to appear wider with highlight.**

will be used to contour features, making them recede and appear smaller or more narrow (**Figure 7–7**).

▲ **Figure 7–7 A wide nose made to appear narrower with contour.**

Covering Imperfections

In many cases it is a wise choice to use a foundation to conceal minor imperfections in the skin. Cream, mineral, and stick foundations provide heavier coverage and blend with the rest of the face. These work especially well for covering small blemishes, light discoloration, and mild redness. These foundation choices offer coverage without the use of additional concealer or heavy makeup. ☑ LO1

CONCEALER

Concealer is thicker and heavier than foundations; it is used to even discolored skin tone and to cover blemishes, scars, small veins, dark circles, and other prominent imperfections on the skin. Concealers are available in various shades to match all skin tones, and they conceal a range of imperfections. The proper concealer shade is slightly lighter (usually one shade lighter) than the foundation shade.

Concealer can be used alone in place of (rather than along with) foundation. When you use concelaer alone, make sure the shade of the concealer matches the skin tone.

Concealer wheels (**Figure 7–8**) include lavender, green, and yellow for use for in covering and concealing prominent discoloration such as bruises, diffused redness, and scars.

▲ **Figure 7–8 A concealer wheel.**

Types of Concealers

Many types and consistencies of concealer are available (**Figure 7–9**). Choose the best consistency depending upon the client's skin type and the purpose for which you are using the concealer.

▼ **Figure 7–9 Various types of concealer.**

Liquid Concealer

Liquid concealer is excellent for all skin types. It can be applied easily with a sponge or concealer brush. It provides lighter coverage than many other forms of concealer, but it is lightweight, smooth to apply, and easy to blend. Liquid concealer provides complete, flawless coverage to the entire face or to large areas in need of evening skin tone.

Cream Concealer

Cream concealer is similar to a liquid concealer, but it has a slightly richer consistency and offers more coverage. It is excellent for drier skin types. Cream concealer is best applied with a sponge or concealer brush. Cream concealer can also be used in place of foundation for an all-over flawless look; just be sure to match the skin tone and blend well.

Stick, Tube, and Pot Concealer

Stick, tube, and pot concealers provide maximum coverage for discoloration and imperfections. They can be applied with either a sponge or concealer brush, but for blending, a brush is the tool of choice.

Application Techniques

As you develop your skills as a makeup artist, you will also develop your own unique application styles and techniques. If you are using liquid or cream foundation, concealer should be applied over the top of the foundation. In many cases, foundation will cover slight imperfections that appeared more obvious on clean skin; by applying foundation first, you will even out the skin tone and be better able to see where concealer is really needed. If a powder or liquid-to-powder foundation is being used, then the concealer should be applied first so that it does not smear or cake the foundation.

A concealer that is too light can have an adverse effect around the eye area. Rather than having raccoon eyes, a client can look as if she wore sunglasses while tanning.

Matching and Blending

When choosing a foundation, matching the foundation color to the skin tone is critical. With an ideal match, blending will be easy. Choosing concealer color and shade is more complex. You must consider not only the skin tone and foundation color, but also the color of the imperfection that is being concealed. Concealer should usually be one to three shades lighter than the chosen foundation, depending upon the degree of color variation from the natural skin tone as well as the time of day. For most applications, one shade lighter is easiest to blend; however, in cases of more prominent discoloration an even lighter shade may be necessary. It is important to be able to properly blend the concealed area with the surrounding skin tone and makeup.

PROCEDURE **7-3** **THE FACIAL CANVAS** SEE PAGE 151

Highlighting and Contouring Using Concealer

Like foundation, concealer can be used for highlighting and contouring. Making the right choice in concealer and type is important in order to prevent the makeup application from looking heavy or thick. Even for high-definition (HD) photography and video, only so much makeup can be applied before it looks excessive.

Covering Imperfections

The main purpose of concealer is to disguise imperfections. Once you choose the proper shade of concealer, apply it with a concealer brush directly to the area of imperfection—over blemishes, under-eye circles, bruises, scars, or

▲ Figure 7–10 **Covered blemishes before and after concealer is applied.**

whatever is to be concealed (**Figure 7–10**). Then blend it into the surrounding area. ☑ LO2

POWDER

Powder adds the final touch to the entire facial canvas. While powder has many functions, its biggest role is to set the foundation and concealer, creating a flawless matte canvas with elegant contour and definition on which to apply blush and other color.

HERE'S A TIP

For a beautiful translucent powder finish, use a loose powder made of corn-silk powder.

Types of Powder

For the many purposes that a powder serves, they are available in several types. Make the best choice, considering the client's skin type and the purpose for which you are using powder. As a professional makeup artist, you will establish your favorite types of powders for creating different looks to an ideal canvas for each client. Except for bronzers, powders are not designed to add color to the face, but rather to enhance the natural skin tone.

Loose Powder

Loose powder contains few, if any, binding agents to keep it together. It usually comes in a container with a perforated top, like a salt shaker. Loose powder is the most effective powder to set foundation or to set the final makeup application. Loose powders come in a variety of colors in order to match a variety of skin tones. You can also buy powder that is **translucent**, having no color. And you can also buy powdered bronzers and shimmer powders.

Pressed Powder

Pressed powder comes in a compact in a cake form. Pressed powder is used to set foundation, and it is an excellent cosmetic for a quick makeup refresher throughout the day. It absorbs excess oil, removes shine, and leaves the face with a refreshed, matte appearance. Pressed powder comes in a variety of colors from translucent to the darkest of skin tones and bronzers.

Mineral Powder

Mineral powders are loose mineral-based powders that vary in color from translucent, through various skin tones, to bronzers and shimmer (**Figure 7–11**). The mineral properties are inert and nonbacterial, making them excellent choices for all skin types and for clients with sensitive skin and skin allergies. Mineral powders are also an excellent choice following a facial treatment of any kind to provide the skin with an even skin tone without disrupting the benefits of a skin treatment.

Application Techniques

Powders can be applied with either a powder fluff brush or a sponge. First, load powder onto a palette by shaking loose powder or scraping pressed powder with a spatula. Then, if you are using a brush, gently dab the brush into the powder, tap off any excess, and apply powder to the face using downward and outward strokes.

If you are using a sponge, press the sponge firmly into the powder and tap off any excess. Press the sponge firmly onto the skin and use a rolling motion to press the powder on. The sponge application provides complete coverage and a very matte finish.

▲ Figure 7–11 **Various powder colors.**

Matching and Blending

Powder is used to create a matte finish on the facial canvas. Translucent powder has no color and is often the powder of choice for the finishing product. Powders that contain color should be the same shade as the foundation or one shade lighter. To perfectly blend, apply a light powder application over the entire face and lightly onto the neck.

Note that if powder darker than the foundation is used and then reapplied to refresh throughout the day, the face will gradually take on a darker appearance, resulting in a clearly visible line of demarcation between the face and the neck and chest.

Highlighting and Contouring Using Powder

Like foundation and concealer, powder can be used to highlight and contour. Lighter shades of powder highlight, making features appear more prominent or larger. For example, lighter powder can be used to widen a jawline, chin, or nose. Darker shades of powder contour, making prominent features appear smaller. For instance, darker shades can be used in minimizing and narrowing a jawline, chin, or nose. ☑ LO3

HERE'S A TIP

Cream blush should not be applied over powder, so if you are using a cream blush a light powder can be applied at the very end of the makeup application to set the canvas.

BLUSH

The final step in creating the canvas is the application of cheek color, also known as blush. Blush is used to create a healthy, natural-looking, youthful glow. If used incorrectly, however, blush can age the appearance of the face or create a clown-like look.

Types of Blush

Blush products come in a wide variety of consistencies and colors. Your choices will depend upon your client's skin type, the foundation and powder products that you used, and the desired finished look.

Powder Blush

Powder blush comes in a compact, and it is available in a wide variety of colors, from the palest of pinks to the richest of browns. It is the perfect product for quick touch-ups and instantly provides the face with an uplifted, healthy, youthful look.

Mineral Blush

Mineral blush is exactly like mineral powder, except that it contains different pigments. Mineral blush is heavily pigmented, so very little is needed. Due to the mineral properties, mineral blush is excellent choice for clients with sensitive skin, allergies, or acne. Because mineral powder is in a loose powder form, only a very small amount needs to be applied using a blush brush.

Cream Blush

Cream blushes come in compacts, sticks, jars, and tubes. They are highly pigmented, and they are often a cream-to-powder product. Cream blush is long-lasting and often a nice choice for dry skin. Cream blush should be applied directly over a cream foundation. If it is applied over a powder-finish foundation, it may smear and cake the powder into the blush pigment.

HERE'S A TIP

Powder blush should be applied over the top of a liquid foundation. Apply a light translucent powder first to prevent streaking, caking, and uneven product application.

Application Techniques

As styles and cosmetic trends change, so too the methods of achieving the desired looks. The application process is the means to that end. Mineral and powder blush are best applied with a powder brush. The best size for the brush depends upon the desired look and the size of the client's face. Cream blush can also be applied with a short-bristled blush brush, but it is best applied with a single-use cosmetic sponge.

Blush applications are intended to look natural and to enhance the natural cheek area. To best accomplish this look, blush should be applied in a diagonal line that begins two fingers away from the corner of the nose between the corner of the nose and the corner of the mouth and that extends back to the outermost corner of the eye and the top of the ear (**Figure 7–12**).

Matching and Blending

Blush color choices depend on the skin tone of the individual client. First determine if the client's skin tone is warm or cool. Then determine the shade that best suits the natural skin color so that the blush enhances the natural cheek area and does not look like streaks or circles of color painted onto a face.

HERE'S A TIP

When choosing powder and blush products, remember the golden rule: Powder on powder; cream on cream.

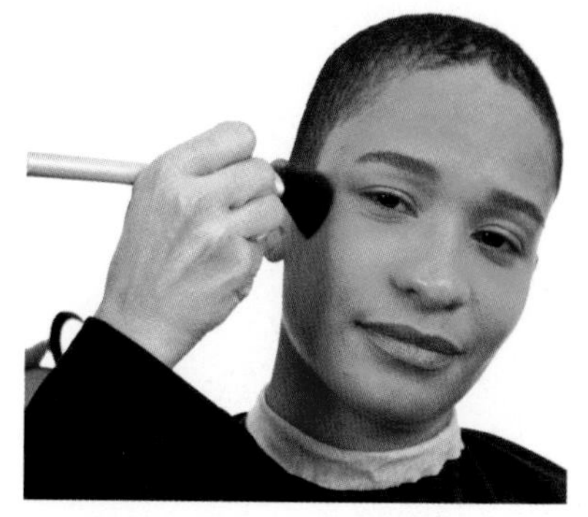

▲ Figure 7–12 **Measuring the placement of blush application.**

After blush color has been chosen and applied, it needs to be properly blended into the surrounding cheek area. This can be done with an additional light application of powder and a large fluff brush. The rule of thumb is to make sure that there are not any clear lines of demarcation where the blush begins and ends. It should be a gradual transition to create a natural-looking cheek.

▲ Figure 7–13a **Woman without blush**

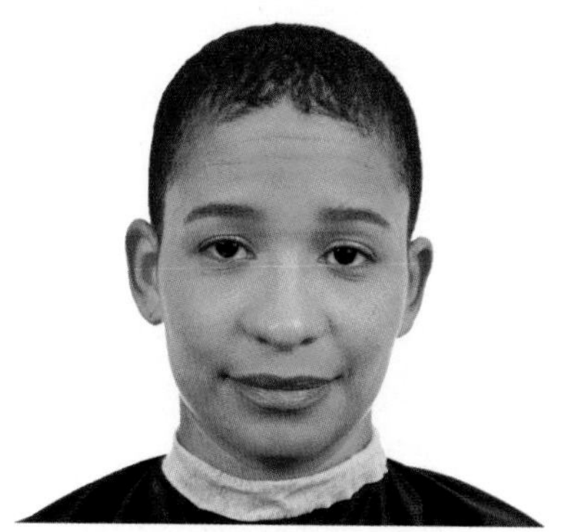

▲ Figure 7–13b **Woman with blush**

▲ Figure 7–13c **Woman with blush and highlight.**

Highlighting and Contouring Using Blush

Blush gives the skin a youthful, healthy glow, and it is the most important product for creating a defined cheekbone and cheek area. Recall that highlighting brings forward; contouring recedes. Remember that any time you emphasize one feature, you automatically deemphasize others. The placement of blush can completely change the look and the apparent structure of the face by seeming to change the location of the cheekbone (**Figure 7–13a and b**).

For a perfectly enhanced cheek area, apply a blush several shades lighter just above the original blush color (**Figure 7–13c**). This will further accent the cheekbone and structure of the face. ☑ LO4

HERE'S A TIP

For the most natural blush application, do not apply blush solely to the apples of the cheeks, or while your client is smiling. These techniques create an artificial "apple look" that is very aging.

SPECIAL CONSIDERATIONS

Before beginning to prepare your canvas, special consideration must be given to the client's skin type, any allergies or sensitivities, and the overall purpose of the makeup application. All of this information is covered in the client consultation process and on the consultation form in Chapter 6, Client Consultation. In all situations except theater or fantasy, the final canvas should appear natural and provide the perfect foundation for products that will enhance specific, unique facial features.

For many years new makeup artists would strive to create the perfectly proportioned face, regardless of individual variations. Professional makeup artists today strive to create overall proportion within each face and to emphasize facial features for individuality and uniqueness.

FACIAL SHAPES

The objective when working with any face shape is to create a more symmetrical, oval appearance. Historically speaking, the oval face shape has been considered the most desirable, because it provides a background for the precise proportion of the other facial features—a background that does not overly emphasize or deemphasize any feature. However, other facial shapes are just as attractive.

One of the greatest benefits of recognizing various facial shapes is that each client's basic face shape serves as a guide for highlighting, contouring, and blush application.

PROCEDURE 7-4 **CREATING PROPORTION TO A ROUND FACE AND WIDE NOSE** SEE PAGE 156

The Oval Face Shape

For many decades the oval face shape was long considered to be the "perfect" shape (**Figures 7–14** to **7–16**). As professionals in today's modern world, we are well aware that there is no such thing as the "perfect" face. All clients are perfect in their own way.

With that in mind, it is still possible to understand the concept of the perfect face shape. This concept came from the proportion and symmetry of the oval face, which can be divided evenly into thirds. The first third is from the hairline to the top of the eyebrows. The second third measures from the top of the eyebrows to the tip of the nose. The last third is measured from the tip of the nose to the chin.

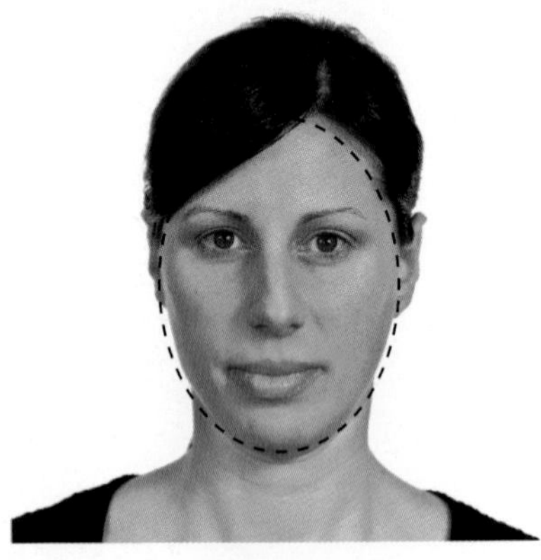

▲ Figure 7–14 Image of an oval face.

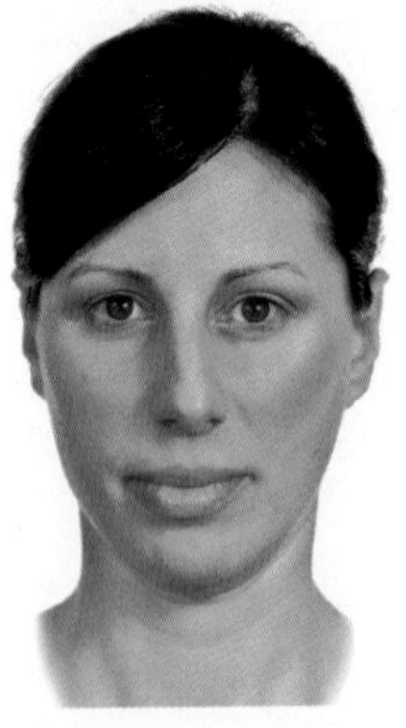

▲ Figure 7–15 Placement of foundation and blush for an oval face.

▲ Figure 7–16 Image of an oval face with blended foundation and blush.

The perfectly proportioned oval face is approximately three-fourths as wide as it is long, and the distance between the eyes is equal to the width of one eye. Overall, the oval face is considered to be the perfectly proportioned face.

Celebrities with Oval Face Shapes

Jennifer Aniston, Julia Roberts, Courtney Cox, Cameron Diaz, Mariah Carey, Cindy Crawford, Sharon Stone, and Tyra Banks.

The Oval Shape and Cheeks

The application of foundation and powder to the oval face simply requires choosing the proper shade to match and blend with the individual skin tone (**Figures 7–14, 7–15,** and **7–16**). When applying blush to the oval face, begin at the apple of the cheek, moving in circular motions and creating a smooth arc (**Figures 7–15** and **7–16**). This will create a gradual fading of blush color toward the top of the ear and place a slight emphasis on a perfectly plump inner cheek.

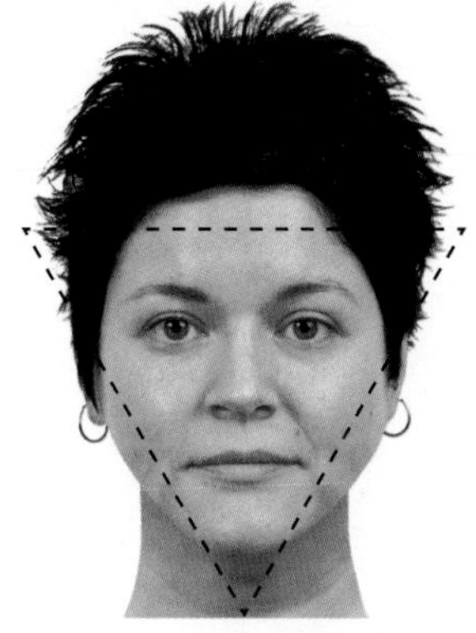

▲ Figure 7–17 **Image of a heart face.**

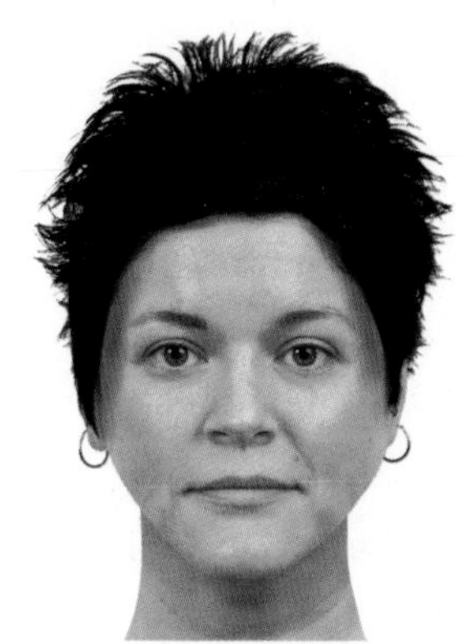

▲ Figure 7–18 **Placement of foundation and blush for a heart face shape.**

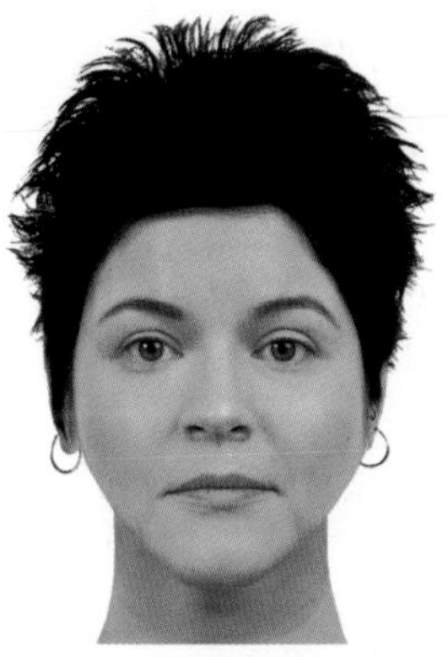

▲ Figure 7–19 **Image of a heart face with blended foundation and blush.**

Heart Face Shape

The "heart" face shape has more width at the forehead and the cheek area and gradually narrows at the chin (**Figures 7–17** to **7–19**). In the opposite case, where the chin area is wider than the forehead, it is often referred to as a pear-shaped face.

In many instances with a heart face shape, the eyes tend to become a focal point of the face, shifting the focus upward from the narrow jawline.

Celebrities with Heart Face Shapes

Eva Longoria, Michelle Pfeiffer, Lisa Kudrow, Naomi Campbell, Jennifer Love Hewitt, Avril Lavigne, and Mary Kate Olsen.

The Heart Shape and Cheeks

The objective with the heart-shaped face is to contour narrow areas, creating the appearance that they are wider while at the same time making wider areas appear more narrow. To accomplish this, choose foundation and pressed powder that are up to one shade darker than the client's skin tone. This color will be applied along the outside of the widest areas of the forehead, temple, and upper cheeks (**Figure 7–18**).

Choosing the appropriate blush color will help to ensure that you bring out the natural contour of the jawline, without overwhelming the center of the face with excessive width. For this technique, two shades of blush are used. The slightly darker blush color is applied in a slight vertical sweep toward the ear. The lighter color is applied in a circular motion on the apple of the cheek to draw attention to the center of the face and to the plump inner cheek (**Figures 7–18** and **7–19**).

The Oblong Face Shape

The oblong face is long and narrow, with greater length in proportion to its width (**Figures 7–20** to **7–22**). A usual goal with an oblong facial shape is to create the appearance of greater width, along with definition to the cheek line.

The Oblong Face and Cheeks

In some instances, using a slightly darker liquid foundation will help you to create this contour. The darker base helps reduce the length of the face, while adding a bit more width (**Figures 7–21** and **7–22**).

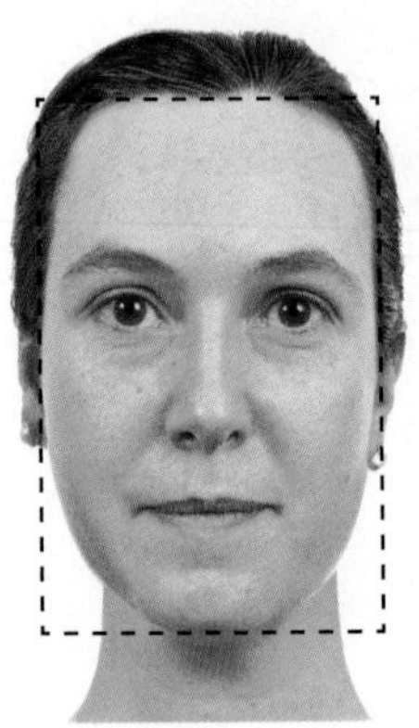

▲ Figure 7–20 **Image of an oblong face.**

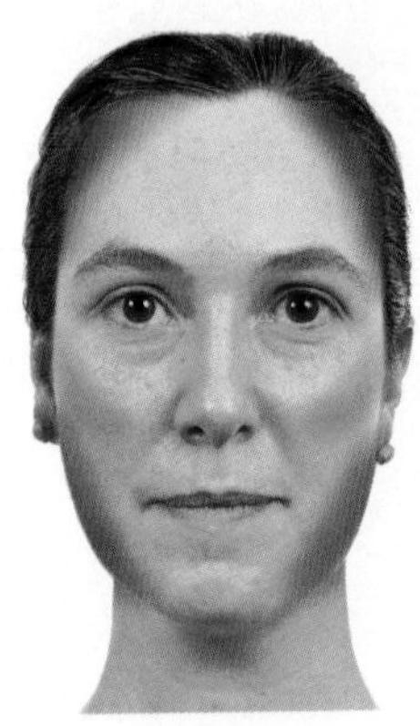

▲ Figure 7–21 **Placement of foundation and blush for an oblong face.**

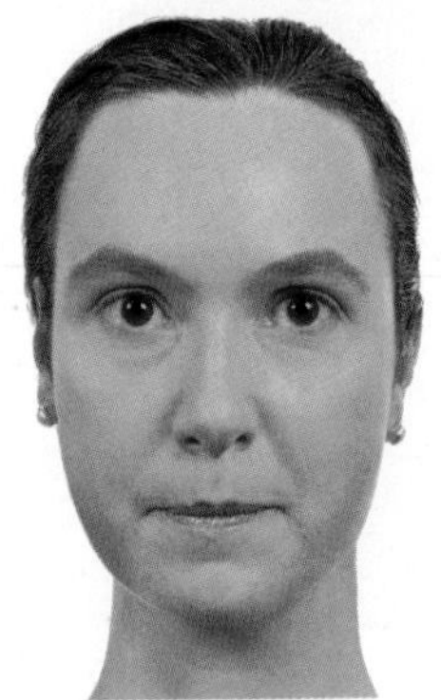

▲ Figure 7–22 **Image of an oblong face with blended foundation and blush.**

With an oblong face, contour the cheekbones in a natural manner. To achieve this look, apply a neutral-toned blush in a vertical, not horizontal, manner across the cheek line. This will allow you to create the appearance of a wider face, compared with the elongated natural shape. These areas can actually be contoured by using a blush that is a shade darker than the foundation and pressed powder.

To make a narrow face appear wider and more proportionate, the application of blush should begin at the outer edges of the face, working inward toward the nose and stopping just at the outside edge of each eyeball (**Figures 7–21** and **7–22**). If the blush is applied too far toward the inner cheek, it actually accents the narrowness of the face, making it appear even narrower.

Celebrities with Oblong Face Shapes

Iman, Kirstie Alley, Angelina Jolie, Niki Taylor, Sarah Jessica Parker, and Gwyneth Paltrow.

The Round Face Shape

The round face shape does not have any dominant or strong angle, and it is clearly widest at the cheekbones (**Figures 7–23** and **7–25**). In comparison to the oval and oblong face shapes, the round face shape is broader in proportion to its length, and it is distinctly round at the chin and the

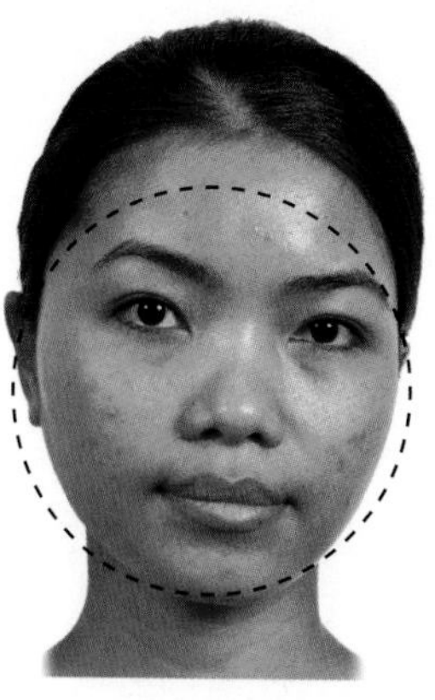

▲ Figure 7–23 **Image of a round face.**

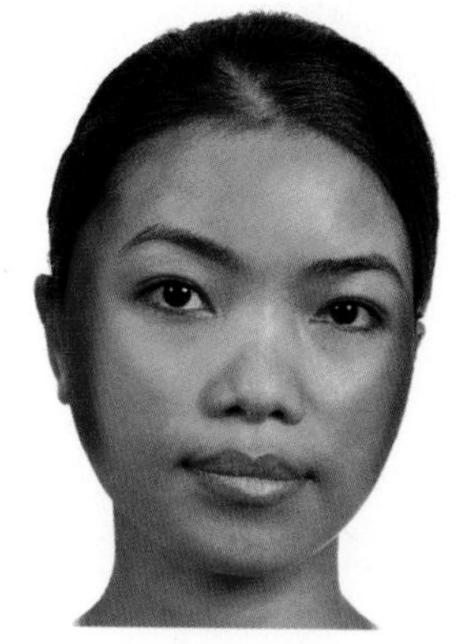

▲ Figure 7–24 **Placement of foundation and blush for a round face.**

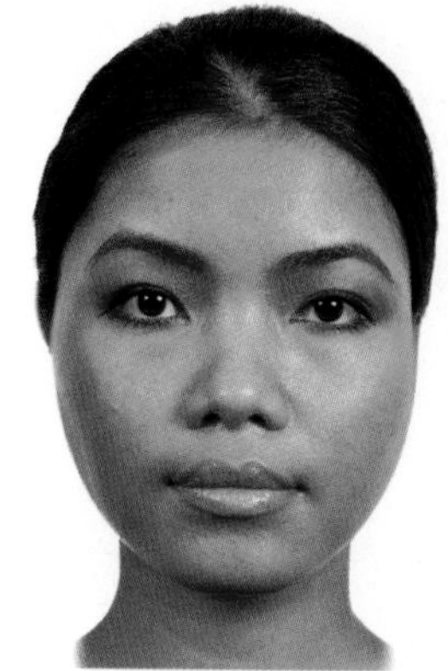

▲ Figure 7–25 **Image of a round face with blended foundation and blush.**

hairline. The makeup objective with a round face is to minimize the fullness through the midsection and create a more elongated appearance.

The Round Shape and The Cheeks

Contouring specific areas can alter the appearance of the round face and create a thinner, longer appearance. Highlighting will be required in certain areas such as the forehead, upper cheeks, and sides of the lower jaw. Contouring with darker colors will be necessary for placing emphasis on specific facial features. Dark colors will be used to draw the attention away from the sides of the face, to place emphasis on the inside features of the face (i.e., the eyes, lips, and nose), and to add height to the face (**Figures 7–24** and **7–25**).

The application of blush to the round face is unique. Blush is placed in a circle, slightly below the cheekbone with a gentle upward sweep (**Figures 7–24** and **7–25**). This application technique will draw attention to the center of the face.

Celebrities with Round Face Shapes.

Fergie, Paula Abdul, Drew Barrymore, Natalie Merchant, Carrie Underwood, and Christina Ricci.

The Square Face Shape

The square face shape is unique and is composed of relatively straight lines on all sides; the widest areas are the forehead, the jaw, and the cheeks (**Figures 7–26** to **7–28**). In an attempt to create a softer, more proportionate appearance, the makeup objective for the square face is to soften the angles and to create the appearance of a narrower forehead and jawline.

The Square Shape and Cheeks

When applying foundation to the square-shaped face, highlights should be used to emphasize the center of the face, especially around the nose, under the eyes, in the center of the forehead, and in the center of the chin. This highlighting will draw attention away from the outer angles of the face. Slightly darker foundation is applied to the lower outer cheek and jowl area; it can also be used at the sides of the forehead if they are visible (**Figures 7–27** and **7–28**).

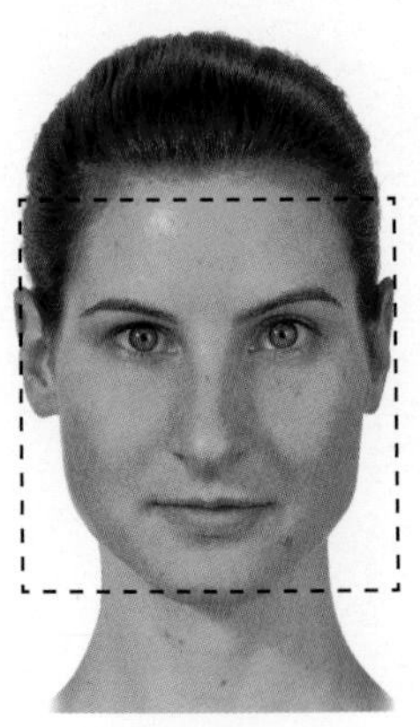

▲ Figure 7–26 Image of a square face.

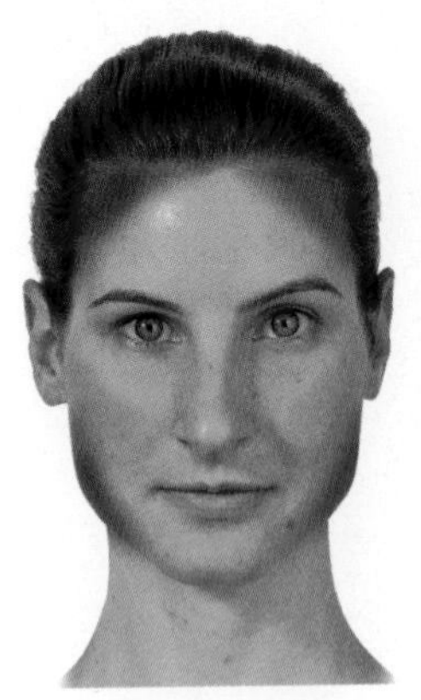

▲ Figure 7–27 Placement of foundation and blush for a square face.

▲ Figure 7–28 Image of a square face with blended foundation and blush.

Celebrities with Square Face Shapes

Jessica Simpson, Jackie Kennedy Onassis, Janet Jackson, Calista Flockhart, Ashley Judd, and Hilary Swank.

A lighter shade of blush is applied in the center of the face, in a sweeping, upward and outward motion to make the face appear longer, not wider (**Figures** 7–27 and 7–28).

The Diamond Face Shape

The diamond face shape has a narrow forehead and a narrow chin. It is widest across the cheekbones (**Figures** 7–29 to 7–31). The objective of the makeup application with the diamond face shape is to minimize the width of the face at the cheek area.

The Diamond Shape and Cheeks

To create the appearance of a more proportional look and minimize the width of the center of the face, two foundation shades can be used. The slightly darker foundation is applied to the center of the face, to the cheeks, and to the sides of the face in front of the ears; a slightly lighter shade is applied and blended across the forehead and the chin (**Figures** 7–29 and 7–30).

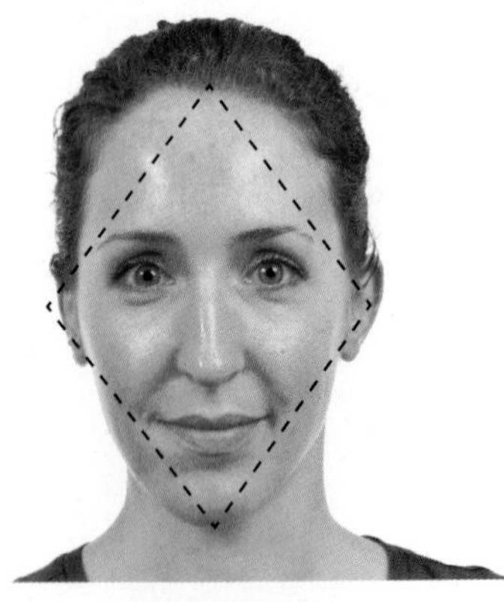

▲ Figure 7–29 Image of a diamond face.

▲ Figure 7–30 Placement of foundation and blush for a diamond face.

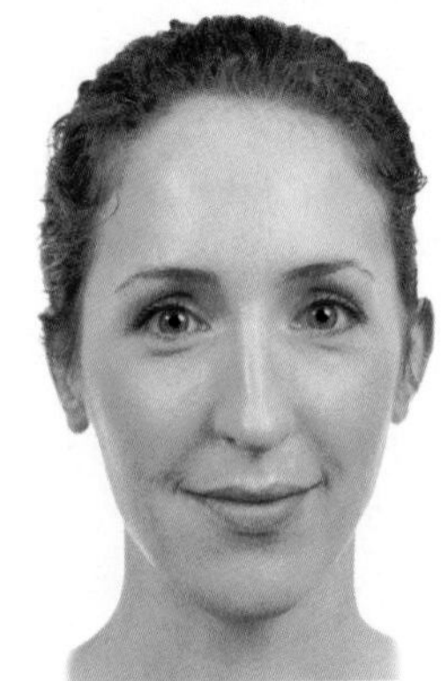

▲ Figure 7–31 Image of a diamond face with blended foundation and blush.

Choose a slightly darker blush in a neutral shade or earth tone. Apply in a circular motion at the apple of the cheek, in a light sweep outward and upward (**Figures 7–30** and **7–31**).

Although the canvas is only the beginning of a successful makeup application, it is the foundation upon which the entire look will be built. As such, it requires that you consider many options and pay great attention to detail. Practice and a creative eye will fine-tune the skills needed to create a perfect canvas every time. ☑ **LO5**

Celebrities with Diamond Face Shapes

Nicole Kidman, Kate Bosworth, and Elizabeth Hurley.

THE THREE-PART PROCEDURE

By breaking your makeup procedures into three parts, you will find it easier to keep track of what you are doing, to remain organized, and to give consistent service. The Three-Part Procedure consists of: 1) pre-service, 2) actual service, and 3) post-service.

Part One: Pre-Service Procedure

The pre-service procedure is an organized step-by-step plan for the cleaning and disinfecting of your tools, implements, and materials; for setting up your makeup station; and for meeting, greeting, and escorting your client to your service area. Draping is part of the pre-service protocol. The draping procedure is important to protect the client's clothing and hair. Depending upon the length, style, and occasion, you may not be able to place a headband on the client. If this is the case, simply push the hair out of the way so that the style is not altered.

PROCEDURE 7-1 **PRE-SERVICE PROCEDURE** SEE PAGE 144

Part Two: Service Procedure

The service procedure is an organized, step-by-step plan for accomplishing the actual service the client has requested, such as an everyday makeup application, eyelash application, or a special-event makeup application.

Part Three: Post-Service Procedure

The post-service procedure is an organized step-by-step plan for caring for your client after the procedure has been completed. It guides you as you help your client through the rescheduling and payment process, and it provides information about how to prepare for the next client. ☑ **LO6**

PROCEDURE 7-2 **POST-SERVICE PROCEDURE** SEE PAGE 148

Procedure 7-1

Pre-Service Procedure

A. Preparing the Makeup Work Area

1 Put on a fresh pair of gloves to clean and disinfect your work area and client chair before your client arrives.

2 Throw away all used single-use items.

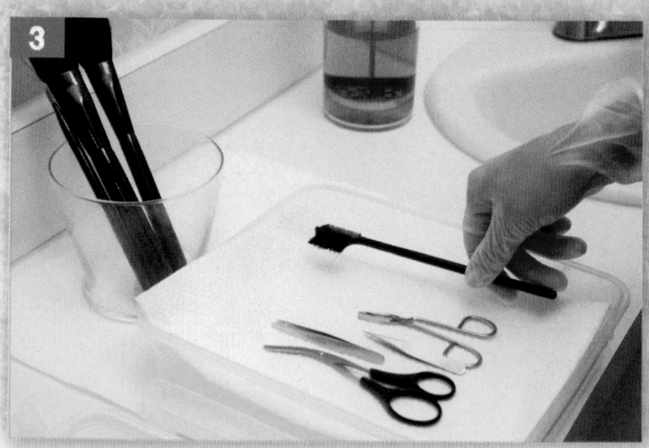

3 Clean and disinfect any used implements. Let brushes dry in the upright position or lying flat on a clean towel. Metal implements such as tweezers, scissors, and spatulas should be cleaned and disinfected per state regulations.

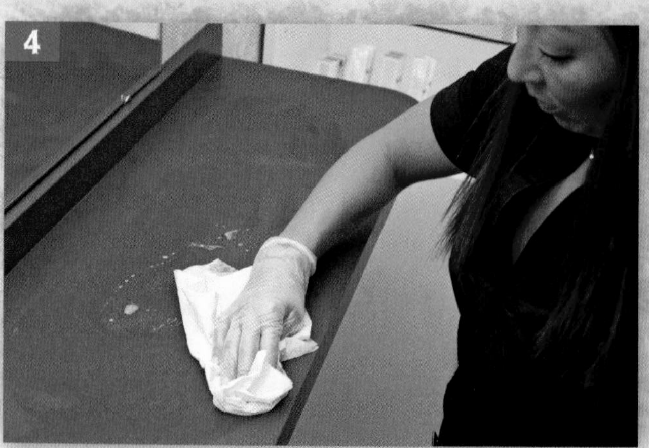

4 Clean and disinfect the makeup counters and tables.

5 Put away all makeup into clean, closed containers.

6 Restock any disposable implements, such as gloves, cotton pads, sponges for cleansing and makeup, spatulas, palettes, cotton swabs, facial tissue, and disposable makeup applicators (e.g., mascara wands, lip brushes, other brushes).

7 Review your client schedule for the day and decide which products you are likely to need for each service. Make sure you have enough supplies for the procedures you will be performing. This is also a good time to refresh your mind about each client you will be seeing and the reason for each visit. If you have returning clients, review the colors and techniques that were used and recorded during previous visits.

8 Your work area should be ready to go from the previous night's thorough cleaning and disinfecting. (See "At the End of the Day" in Post-Service Procedure 7–2.)

B. Preparing for the Client

9 Retrieve the client's intake form or service record card and review it. If the appointment is for a new client, let the receptionist know that the client will need an intake form.

10 Organize yourself by taking care of your personal needs before the client arrives—use the restroom, get a drink of water, return a personal call—so that when your client arrives, you can place your full attention on her needs.

Procedure 7-1 *(continued)*

Remember: Do not clean and disinfect tools at your workstation. An area near a sink should be set aside for cleaning and disinfecting tools.

11 Turn off your cell phone or PDA. Eliminate every possible distraction so that you can focus on your client.

12 Take a moment to clear your head of all your personal concerns and issues. Take a couple of deep breaths and remind yourself that you are committed to providing your clients with fantastic service and your full attention.

13 Wash your hands following Procedure 2–2, Proper Hand Washing, before going to greet your client.

C. Greet Client

14 Greet your client in the reception area with a warm smile and in a professional manner. Introduce yourself if you've never met and shake hands. The handshake is the first acceptance by the client of your touch, so be sure your handshake is firm and sincere. If the client is new, ask her for the intake form she filled out in the reception area.

15 Escort the client to the makeup area. Make sure you tell her where to securely place her personal items.

16 Ask the client to remove glasses and any jewelry that may interfere with the makeup service, such as dangling earrings, so that you do not have to stop the service for her to remove the items later. Place the client's belongings in a safe place.

17 Invite your client to take a seat in the makeup chair.

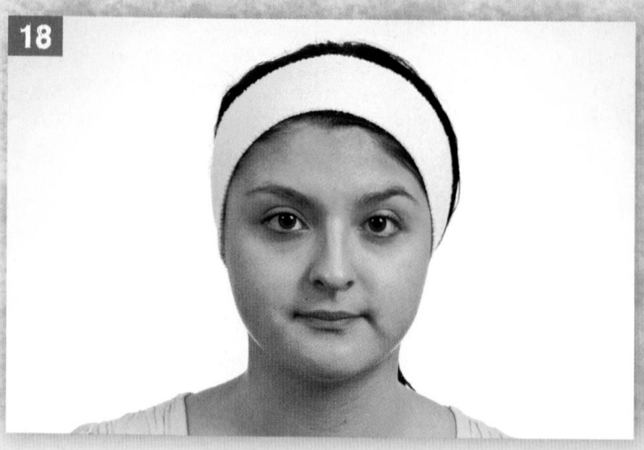

18 Drape the client properly and use either a headband or hair clip to secure her hair back away from her face. If their hair is already styled for a special event, you can avoid using the headband.

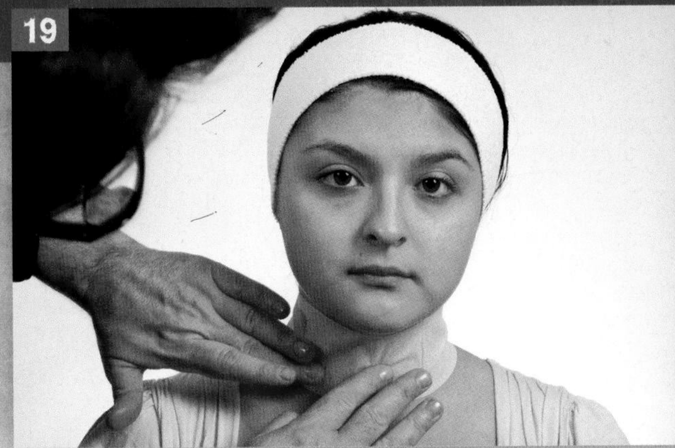

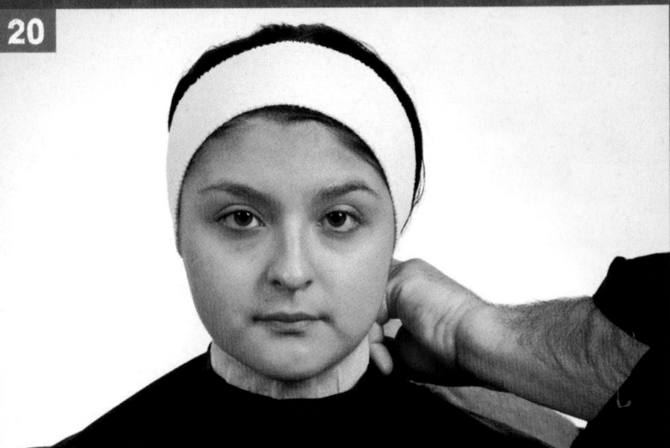

19 Place a neck strip or clean towel around the client's neck.

20 Secure a makeup cape around the paper neck strip or towel to avoid getting makeup on the client's clothes. If a cape is not available, you may use disposable towels to place over the client's clothing, tucking them in and around the collar of the client's shirt. The latter method may be preferred by men.

---

21 Make sure the client is comfortable before beginning the service. Remember, the client is not just another makeup service, but a person with whom you want to build a relationship. By showing clients respect, you will begin to gain their trust in you as a professional. Openness, honesty, and sincerity are always the most successful approach in winning clients' trust, respect, and, ultimately, their loyalty.

22 Perform a consultation before beginning the service. If you are servicing a returning client, ask how her skin has been since her last treatment. If the client is new, discuss the information on the intake form, and ask any questions you have regarding the reason for the visit, the condition of her skin, or any conditions listed on the form. Determine a course of action for the makeup application, and briefly explain your plan to the client. This will ensure that you and your client have the same objectives in mind.

23 Wash your hands again before getting started. Keep hand sanitizer within reach for use during the service if needed.

24 Lay makeup out in order of use. This makes it easier to find the products you need during the application procedure.

Procedure 7-2

Post-Service Procedure

A. Advise Clients and Promote Products

1 When the makeup service is complete, remove the towel or makeup cape and the headband or hair clip from the client.

2 Before your client leaves your makeup area, ask her opinion about the final makeup look and if she enjoyed the service. Explain the condition of her skin and your ideas about how to improve it. Be sure to ask if she has any questions or anything else she wishes to discuss. Be receptive and listen. Never be defensive. Determine a plan for future visits. Give the client ideas to consider before her next visit.

3 Advise client about proper home skin care and explain how the recommended professional products will help to improve any skin conditions that are present.

You can improve your retail sales by having a price list and highlighter pen on hand. As you apply each product, highlight it on the price list and show the client the actual product. This makes it easy for clients to select and purchase products, knowing in advance how much each item costs. Ask your client to check off the products she would like to take home with her today, and hand her the price list and a pen.

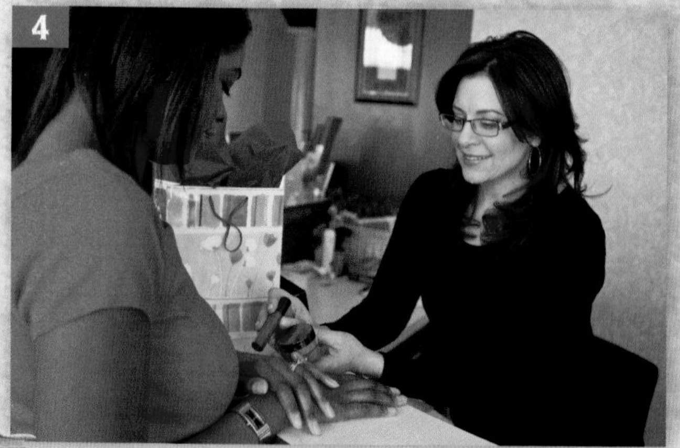

4 This is the time to discuss your retail product recommendations. Explain that these products are important and explain how they should be used.

B. Schedule Next Appointment and Thank the Client

5 Escort the client to the reception desk and write up a service ticket for the client that includes the service provided, the recommended home-care, and the next visit/service that needs to be scheduled. Place all recommended home-care products on the counter for the client. Review the service ticket and the product recommendations with your client.

6 After the client has paid for her service and her home-care products, ask if you can schedule her next appointment. Set up the date, time, and type of service for the new appointment, write the information on your business card, and give the card to the client.

7 Thank the client for the opportunity to work with her. Express an interest in working with her in the future. Invite her to contact you should she have any questions or concerns about the service provided. If the client seems apprehensive, offer to call her in a day or two in order to check in. Genuinely shake her hand and wish her a great day.

8 Be sure to record service information, observations, and product recommendations on the service record card, and be sure you return it to the proper place for filing.

Procedure 7-2 *(continued)*

C. At the End of the Day

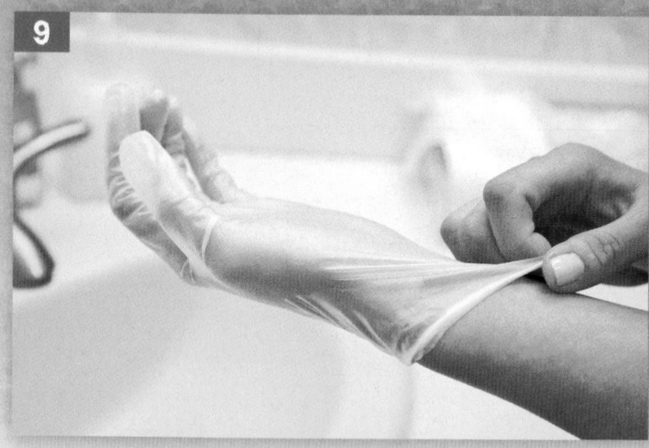

9 Put on a fresh pair of gloves to protect yourself from contact with soiled towels and implements.

10 Remove all dirty laundry from the hamper. Spray the hamper with a disinfectant aerosol spray or wipe it down with disinfectant. Mildew grows easily in hampers.

11 Remove all dirty spatulas, used brushes, and other utensils. Most of these should have been removed between clients during the day.

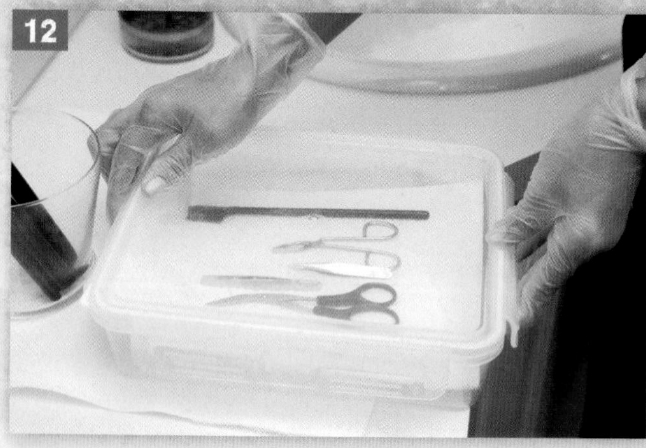

12 Thoroughly clean and disinfect all multiuse brushes and implements.

13 Clean and then disinfect all counters, the makeup chair, and any other furniture with disinfectant. If you use a magnifying lamp, this should be cleaned and disinfected on both sides.

14 Replenish the room with fresh towels, spatulas, utensils, and other supplies so that it is ready for the next day.

15 Change disinfection solution.

16 Check the room for dirt, smudges, or dust on the walls, on the baseboards, in corners, or on air vents. Vacuum and mop the room with a disinfectant.

Procedure 7–3

The Facial Canvas

Implements and Materials

You will need all of the following implements, materials, and supplies:

- **Brushes**

- [ ] Blush brush
- [ ] Foundation brush
- [ ] Concealer brush
- [ ] Powder brush

- **Utensils**

- [ ] Brush cleaner
- [ ] Hand sanitizer
- [ ] Headband or hair clip
- [ ] Makeup cape
- [ ] Makeup palette
- [ ] Neck strip or clean towel for draping

Brushes

Although the basic brushes are all that an artist really needs, as your experience and expertise grows you will acquire a personal preference for certain brush types. As extensive as your checklist of supplies may be, your list of favorite brushes may be even more extensive!

This makeup application will be performed on a Caucasian female. Note the oblong facial shape, narrow nose, and dark circles beneath the eyes.

Single-use Items

The following items are mandatory disposables that are a part of every makeup artist's kit, should never be reused, and are to be discarded immediately after use. They are inexpensive items that can be purchased in large quantities so that there is never a need to consider reusing them.

- Cotton pads or puffs
- Cotton swabs
- Tissues
- Sponge wedges
- Wooden sticks or spatulas

Products

An expert makeup artist will know that the largest mandatory product selection is foundation, since you may never know what skin tone you will be working with. It is critical to the success of the makeup application that you are able to match your client's skin tone with an appropriate foundation color and harmonious concealer, powder, and blush.

- Blushes
- Concealers
- Eye makeup remover
- Facial moisturizer (lotions are best for oily skin, and heavier creams are recommended for dry or mature skin types)
- Foundations
- Mild facial cleanser (although clients should always be instructed to arrive with a clean and moisturized face)
- Translucent powders

Preparation

- Perform

PROCEDURE 7-1 PRE-SERVICE SEE PAGE 144

Note: During the consultation note that this client has an oblong face, narrow nose, and dark circles under her eyes.

Procedure

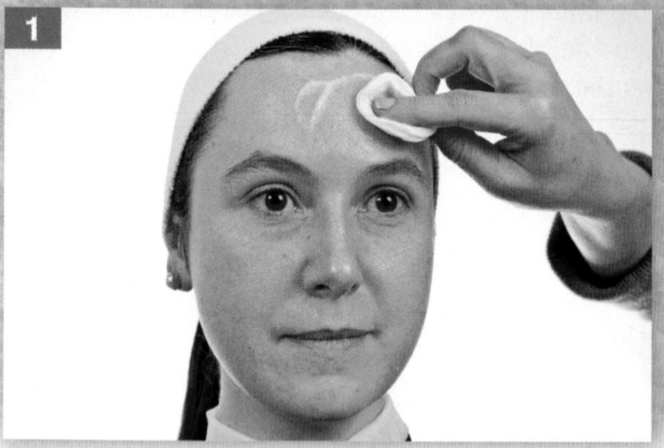

1 Optional: Depending on your state regulations and your license, apply cleanser to the client's face. This step can be avoided if your client is instructed to arrive with a clean face. Spread cleanser in upward and outward motion being sure to include all areas of the face and neck.

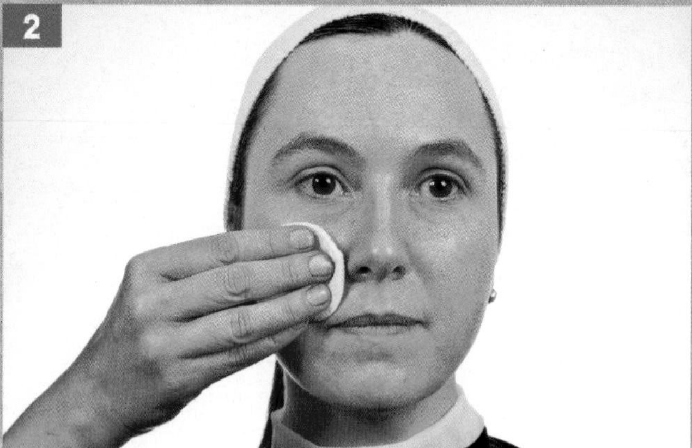

2 Optional: Remove cleanser with damp cotton pads.

3 Optional: Follow cleansing with an application of toner on a cotton pad. Pat the cotton pad around the entire face, the neck, and even the décolleté. This will remove any excess cleansing product and will balance the skin for application of a moisturizer.

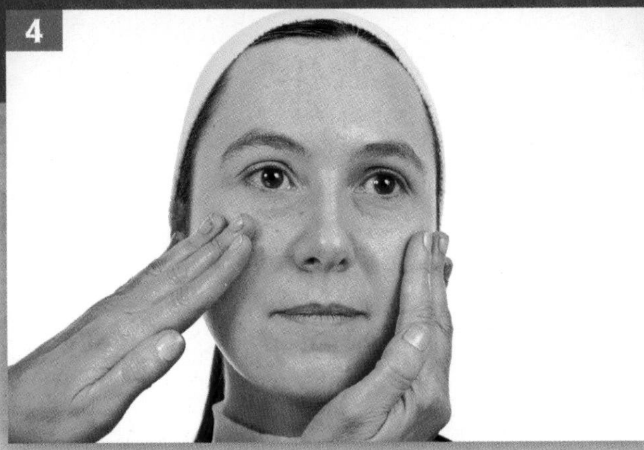

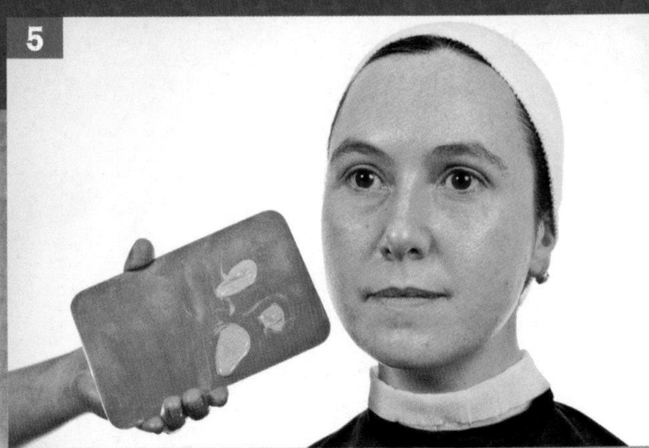

4 Apply skin-specific moisturizer and spread in upward and outward motions.

5 Choose the foundation color and type best suited for your client's skin. Try several color choices to determine which one will best match and blend with the client's natural skin tone.

---

6 Remove foundation from container with a disposable spatula and place it on a clean palette.

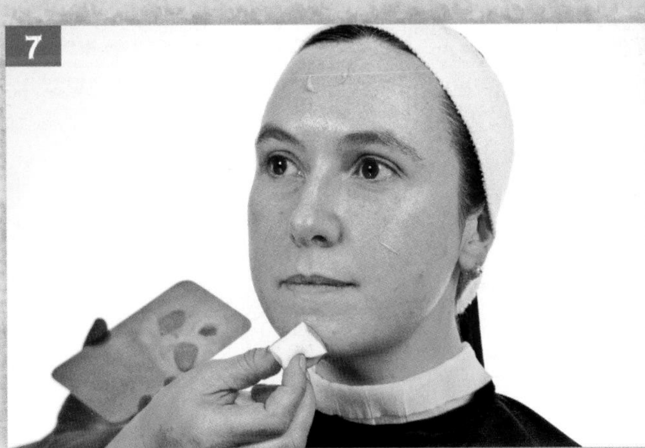

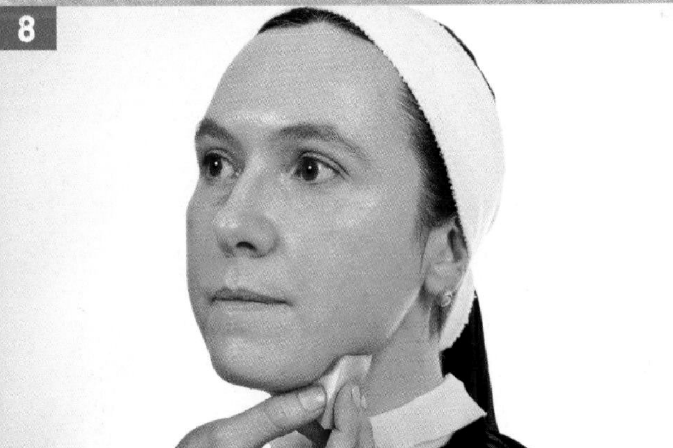

7 For a simple application technique, apply a dot of foundation to the forehead, cheeks, and chin. Blend in an upward and outward motion. Blend quickly and evenly to prevent foundation from drying out and becoming difficult to spread.

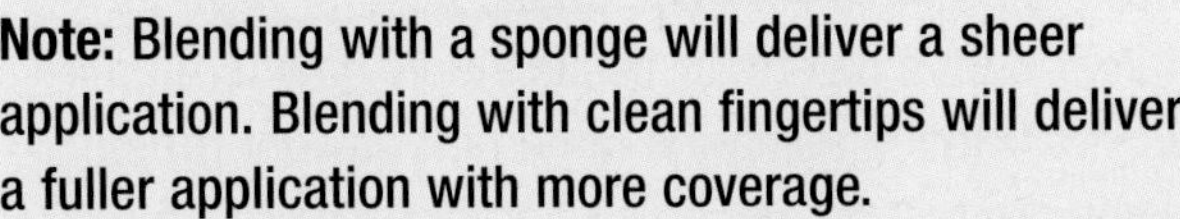

Note: Blending with a sponge will deliver a sheer application. Blending with clean fingertips will deliver a fuller application with more coverage.

Note: Using a disposable sponge, foundation can also be applied to particular areas of the face, one area at a time (rather than applying dots across the entire face). Begin at the forehead and work from the center of the face outward over each side. As you work and reach new areas of the face, apply more product to the sponge.

8 The proper foundation will blend from the jawline to the neck, and even to the chest.

Procedure 7-3 *(continued)*

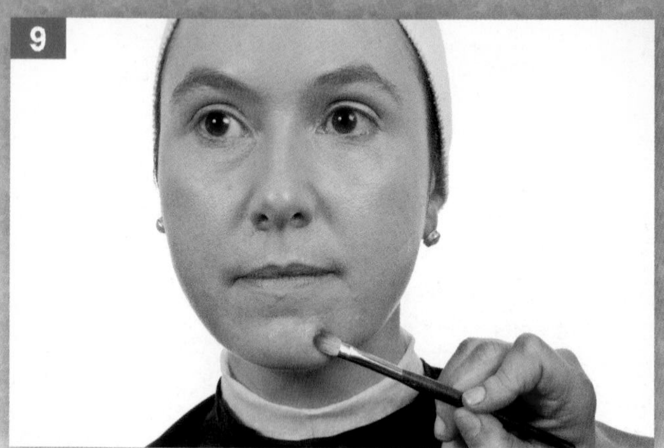

9 To create a slightly fuller look to a narrow face, apply a small amount of foundation, one shade lighter, to the outside of the face; from the mid-ear to the middle of the jawline. Blend well with natural foundation.

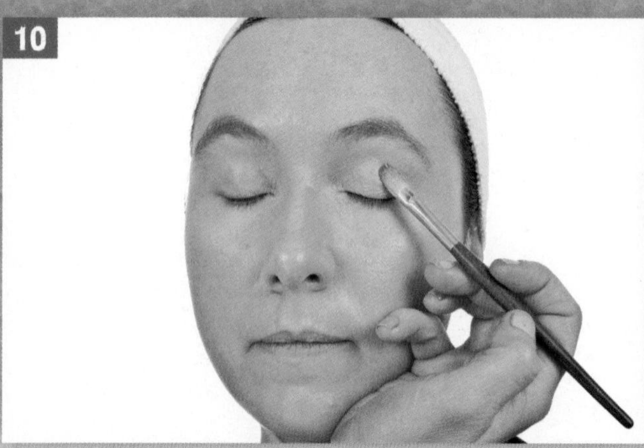

10 Select the concealer type and color appropriate for the client's skin. Remove a small amount of concealer from the container with a disposable spatula. Apply with a concealer brush on the upper eyelid and beneath the eyes to minimize dark circles and cause the eye area to match the contour of the face, rather than recede into it.

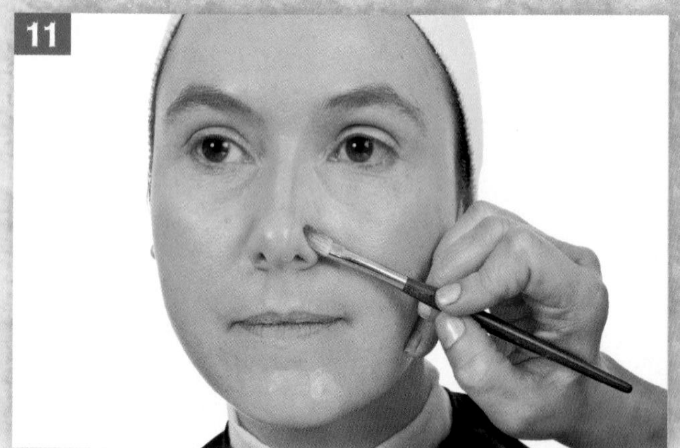

11 Apply a small amount of concealer with a concealer brush along the sides of the nose to create a wider appearance.

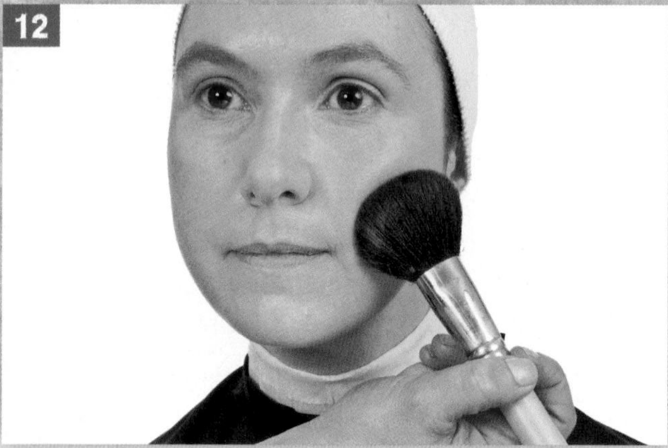

12 Apply translucent powder. Translucent powder is an excellent choice to set the foundation since the client's skin tone is very fair. Shake powder from its container onto a palette or tissue. Apply powder in a downward motion using the large fluff powder brush. A downward motion will brush fine facial hairs downward to make them disappear.

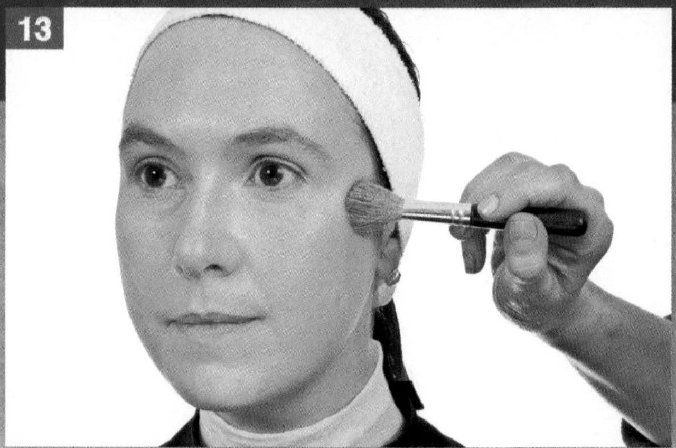

13 Choose an appropriate blush shade based on skin tone. Using a blush brush, apply blush in a "C" shape from the cheeks to the temple. Begin at the cheek, and continue in small, upward circular motions.

14 Complete the blush application by blending with a small amount of powder on a powder fluff brush.

15 The completed canvas.

Post-Service

- Complete PROCEDURE 7-2 POST-SERVICE SEE PAGE 148

Procedure 7–4

Creating Proportion to a Round Face and Wide Nose

Implements and Materials

You will need all of the following implements, materials, and supplies:

- **Brushes**
  - ☐ Blush brush
  - ☐ Concealer brush
  - ☐ Foundation brush
  - ☐ Powder brush
- **Utensils**
  - ☐ Brush cleaner
  - ☐ Hand sanitizer
  - ☐ Headband or hair clip
  - ☐ Makeup cape
  - ☐ Makeup palette
- **Single-use Items**
  - ☐ Cotton pads or puffs
  - ☐ Cotton swabs
  - ☐ Tissues
  - ☐ Wooden sticks or spatulas
  - ☐ Sponge wedges
- **Products**
  - ☐ Blushes
  - ☐ Concealers
  - ☐ Eye makeup remover
  - ☐ Facial moisturizer
  - ☐ Foundations
  - ☐ Mild facial cleanser
  - ☐ Translucent powders

This makeup application will be performed on an Asian female. Note the techniques for the roundness of her face and the wide nose.

Preparation

- Perform

PROCEDURE 7–1 PRE-SERVICE SEE PAGE 144

- Refer to optional steps 1 through 4 in Procedure 7–3 for skin preparation prior to beginning the service.

Note: These optional skin-preparation steps should always be considered before performing any makeup application service. These optional steps will not be referenced in subsequent procedures contained in the text.

Procedure

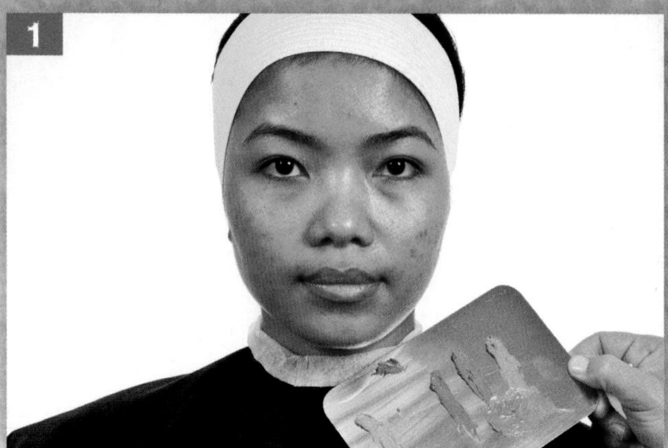

1 Choose the foundation color and type best suited for your client's skin. Try several color choices to determine which will best match and blend with your client's natural skin tone.

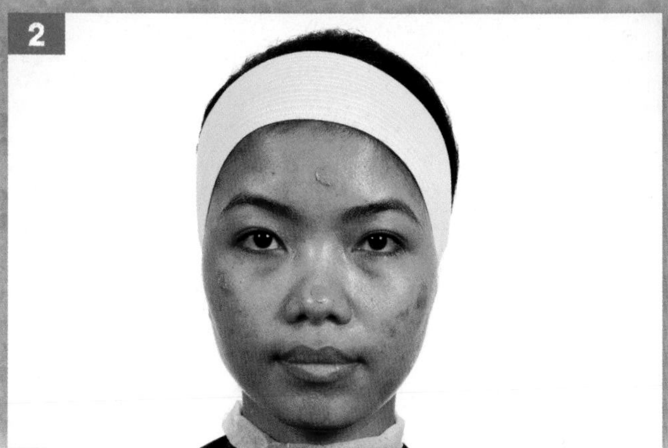

2 Remove foundation from container and place on a palette. Apply a dot of foundation to the forehead, cheeks, and chin; or apply it to one specific part of the face at a time.

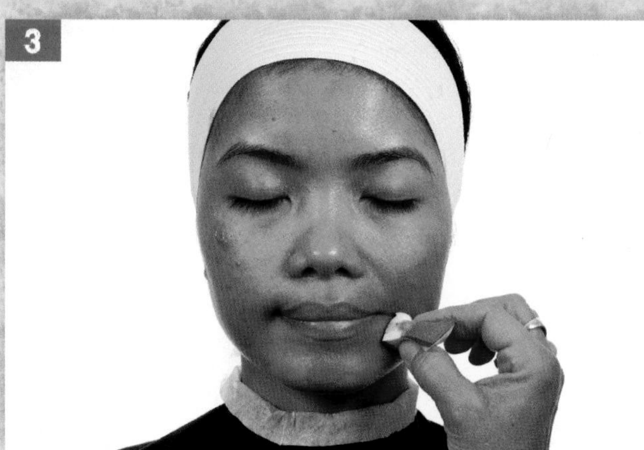

3 Blend in an upward and outward motion.

Note: Blending with a sponge will deliver a sheer application. Blending with clean fingertips will deliver a fuller application with more coverage.

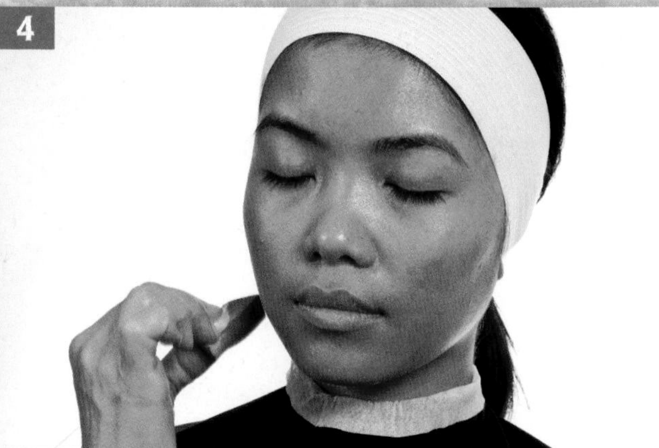

4 The proper foundation will blend from the jawline to the neck and chest.

Procedure 7-4 *(continued)*

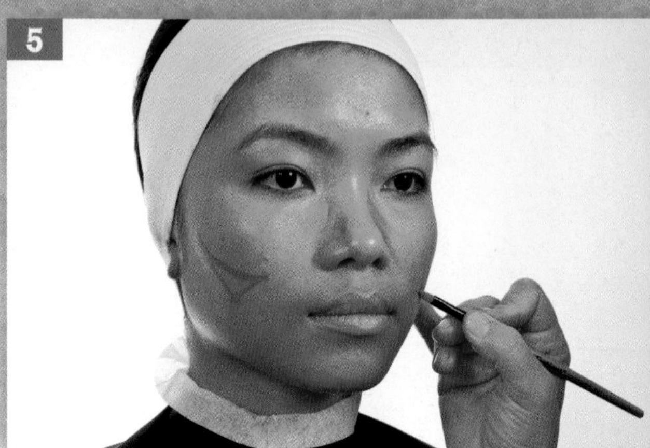

5 To create an oval appearance to a round face, apply a small amount of foundation, one shade darker than the overall foundation, to the outside of the face, from the mid-ear to the middle of the jawline. Blend well with natural foundation.

6 Select the concealer type and color appropriate for the client's skin. To minimize the width of the nose, choose a concealer color one to two shades darker than the foundation color. Remove a small amount of concealer from the container with a disposable spatula. Apply it with a concealer brush along sides of the nose.

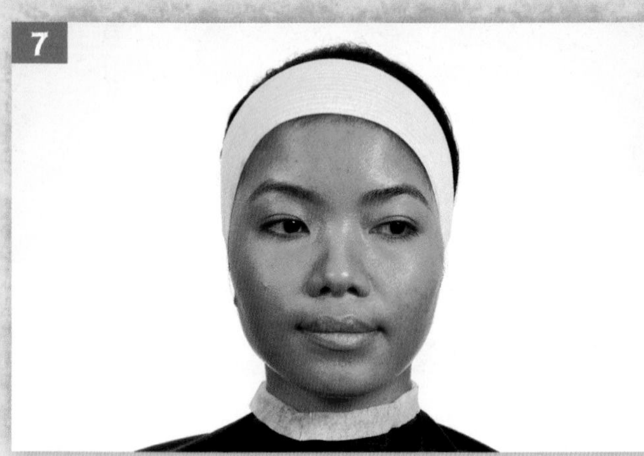

7 Blend well with foundation.

8 Apply powder. Choose powder best suited for your client's skin tone. Loose or pressed powder is acceptable. Scrape powder from its container onto a palette or tissue. Apply powder in a downward motion using the large fluff powder brush. A downward motion will brush fine facial hairs downward to make them disappear.

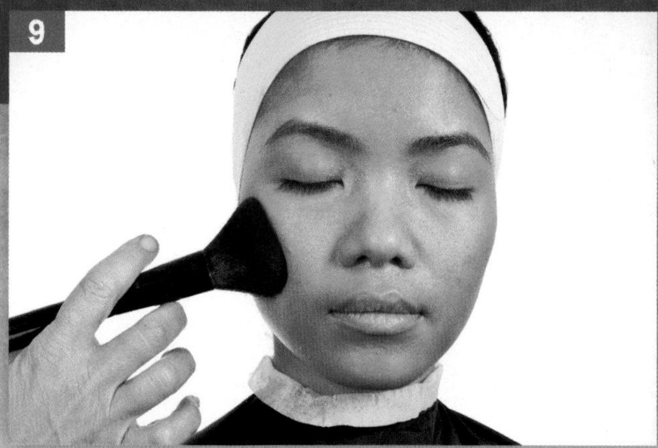

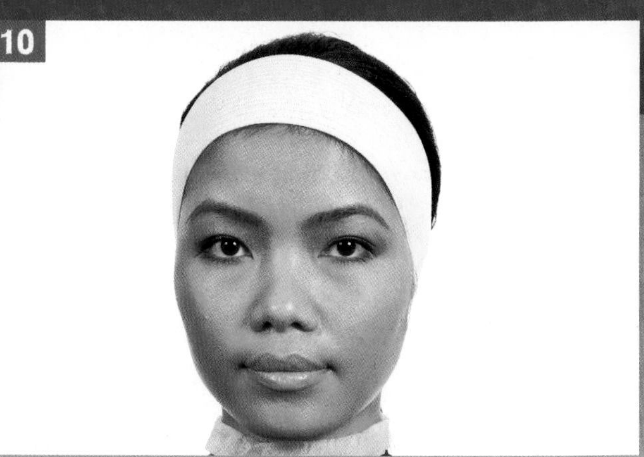

9 Choose appropriate blush shade based on skin tone. Using a blush brush, apply blush in a "C" shape from the cheek to the temple. Begin at the cheek, and continue in small, upward circular motions. Complete the blush application by blending with a small amount of powder on a powder fluff brush.

10 The finished look.

Post-Service

- Complete

PROCEDURE 7-2 **POST-SERVICE** SEE PAGE 148

Review Questions

1. Explain the condition that the skin should be in before beginning a makeup application.
2. What four types of products are necessary to create the ideal canvas?
3. What is the purpose of foundation?
4. Which type of foundation is a good choice for almost any skin type?
5. What is unique about mineral products?
6. What type of foundation can be both a foundation and a concealer?
7. What will a line of demarcation tell you about a foundation choice?
8. What effect will using a darker shade to contour have?
9. What is the purpose of concealer?
10. What colors are found in a typical concealer wheel?
11. List two forms of powder.
12. What is the purpose of blush?
13. Which type of blush should not be applied over a powder finish foundation?
14. Which face shape is considered perfectly proportioned?
15. Which face shape has more width at the forehead and the cheek area and gradually narrows at the chin?
16. What is the main objective with a diamond shape face when creating the canvas?

Chapter Glossary

concealer	Thicker and heavier than foundations; it is used to even discolored skin tone and to cover blemishes, scars, small veins, dark circles, and other prominent imperfections on the skin.
contour	To recede, minimize in apparent size, or draw attention away from a feature.
cream foundations	Foundations that can be either water-based or oil-based; they are thicker in consistency than a liquid foundation and provide overall coverage with a smooth texture and deep tone.
cross-contamination	The spread of bacteria from one place, person, or product to another.
emollient based	Water-in-oil or oil-in-water blends of ingredients that soften and smooth the skin.
foundation	A makeup product designed to even out skin tone and mild imperfections and provide a base for the makeup application.

Chapter Glossary *(continued)*

highlight	To bring out, increase in apparent size, or draw attention to a feature.
inert substances	Ingredients that cannot sustain bacterial growth and have no properties to which someone could be allergic.
line of demarcation	A line that displays a distinct change in color.
liquid foundation	A foundation suited for just about any skin type and provides a sheer, light, natural coverage; it can be oil-based, water-based, or mineral-based.
mineral makeup	Contains nonbacterial, finely ground particles from the earth; contains fewer chemicals and dyes than most traditional makeup; most are talc-free and less likely to cause allergic reactions.
mousse foundation	A liquid product that comes in an aerosol or spray can, boosted by air (like whipped cream); it is light, easy to apply, and an excellent choice for any skin type.
oil-based foundation	A foundation that contains more oil than water; best suited for dry or mature skin types.
parabens	Ingredients used as preservatives in cosmetics.
skin tone	Degree of warm color tone or cold color tone in the skin.
stick foundation	A molded, compact foundation (in a container similar to lipstick, but larger); it can be used on all skin types, provide excellent coverage, and serve as both a foundation and a concealer.
toner	Skin care product designed to complete the cleansing process by removing any remaining dirt, oil, or debris from the face while also balancing the pH of the skin.
translucent	Having no color.
water-based foundation	A foundation that contains more water than oil; it is better suited for oily skin, blemished skin, and is still a fine choice for combination to dry skin.

Chapter 8 Facial Features

Chapter Outline

Learning Objectives

After completing this chapter, you will be able to:

- ☑ **LO1** Identify various eye shapes and ways to alter their appearance.
- ☑ **LO2** List different eye makeup products and their uses.
- ☑ **LO3** Create a perfectly shaped eyebrow.
- ☑ **LO4** Identify techniques used to enhance eyelashes.
- ☑ **LO5** List types of lip products and their uses.
- ☑ **LO6** Identify various lip shapes and ways to change the shape of a lip.

Key Terms

Page number indicates where in the chapter the term is used.

brow cream
pg. 180

brow gel
pg. 180

brow pencils
pg. 180

brow shadows (brow powders)
pg. 180

brow stencils
pg. 180

close-set eyes
pg. 167

cream shadows
pg. 174

cream-to-powder shadows
pg. 174

deep-set eyes
pg. 166

even-set eyes
pg. 166

eye shadow primer
pg. 173

eyeliner
pg. 174

lip color (lipstick)
pg. 183

lip exfoliants
pg. 182

lip gloss
pg. 183

lip liner
pg. 182

lip primer
pg. 182

liquid eyeliner
pg. 175

mascara
pg. 175

pencil eyeliner
pg. 174

polymers
pg. 173

powder shadow
pg. 174

round eyes
pg. 167

silicones
pg. 173

small eyes
pg. 173

stick shadows
pg. 174

threading (banding)
pg. 179

white eyeliner
pg. 174

wide-set eyes
pg. 166

Career Profile

Cayo Lanza's calling for the art of makeup has led him to the high-end fashion industry. He uses his talent and natural affinity for beauty and fashion to create looks for major fashion events such as Mercedes-Benz fashion week and for clients such as model Gisele Bündchen. He is a contemporary artist constantly making sure his work is fresh and helping to maintain forward movement within the industry. Today, he is still heavily involved in the fashion industry, displaying innovation and technique in each show.

"Within every story there are various obstacles, but you have to be strong and believe in yourself and in your potential. For me, particularly, it was an early start and I had to prove the whole time that I was able to create beautiful work. I always seemed to be ahead in my visions, so it was difficult to make people see and understand one of my new concepts in makeup.

"My career in makeup began with drawing and painting. Today, I work as a makeup artist at Studio W, in Brazil, a salon that launches trends in the hair and makeup field. I specialize in the new technology of makeup for HDTV, where I search for the perfection, naturalness, and the feminine effect that this new technology can offer. I perform in an arena that mostly demands social and party makeup, along with updated and specialized interpretations for brides.

"In order to be in touch with the world I always look for the new trends in great magazines. The future of makeup will be even more artistic but will always work side by side with technology.

"One truly remarkable event in my life was signing The Fashion Week look for a brand's 30th anniversary. All the top models from the period were present, and I had exclusivity for one of them: Gisele Bündchen. It was incredible to participate in the event and to be in contact with such great names from the fashion world.

"I am proud of all my works. In each and every one of them I gave myself completely as an artist that has the freedom to create with colors, textures, and stories."

How often have you heard someone say "the eyes are the window to the soul"? That statement could not be more true. Our eyes depict emotion, physical wellness, exhaustion, and even personal character traits. Have you ever looked at someone and thought "they have such kind eyes"?

Our eyes are used to express emotion, interest, confidence, and honesty. Our eyes and our eye contact speak louder than words.

The eyes are often the first facial feature that a person is drawn to when looking at a face. Eyes have been touted by many as the most powerful feature of the face. Such power and influence makes the eyes a major focal point for the creative makeup artist and for clients.

As a general guideline, proportion and symmetry are guides for defining beauty. The face can be divided into thirds, and for many cultures, balanced symmetrical areas are criteria for defining a beautiful face. Creating the illusion of symmetry in individual facial features allows the makeup artist to create the balance and harmony of beauty.

WHY STUDY FACIAL FEATURES?

Makeup artists should study and have a thorough understanding of facial features because:

- Analyzing facial features is important to understand the role that they will play in the overall look of any makeup application.
- Studying facial features will provide the makeup artist with the ability to both minimize and accentuate defining features of any client's face.
- A complete understanding of facial features will make it easy to choose proper makeup colors and types for each individual client.

EYE SHAPES

As the focal point for the entire face, the eyes and their shape can influence the rest of the face and the makeup application. There are numerous eye shapes, and depending upon the shape of the face, a particular eye shape may be made to appear magnified or minimized. Your job will be to take the big picture into account and to work your magic to create an individual masterpiece. As with every chapter, keep in mind that this chapter contains guidelines and fundamentals of theory that will point you in certain directions for techniques of application as well as color choices. However, in the world of makeup, the sky is the limit when your creative and artistic abilities flourish. With time, practice, and experience, your makeup skills will never stop growing.

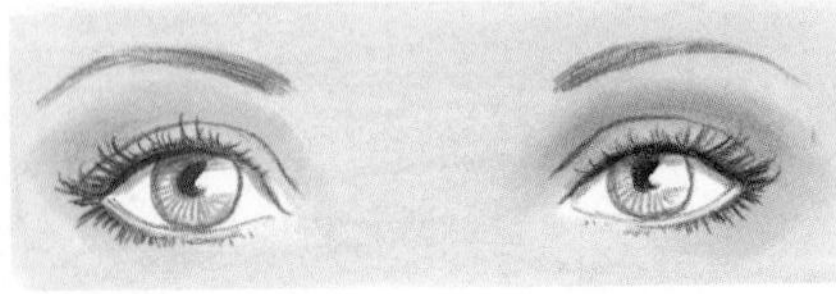

▲ Figure 8–1 Example of even-set eyes.

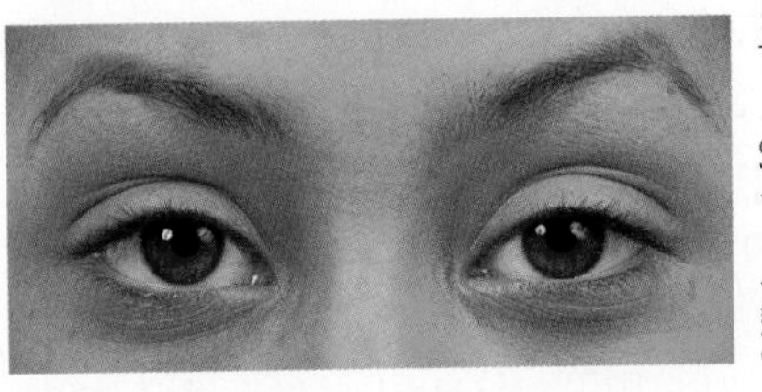

▲ Figure 8–2 Even-set eyes.

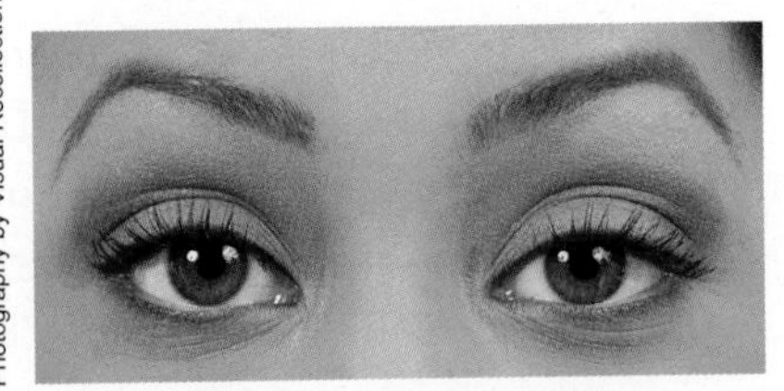

▲ Figure 8–3 Even-set eyes with makeup.

Even-Set Eyes

Even-set eyes are perfectly balanced and are the ideal eye shape for any face shape (**Figure 8–1**). Even-set eyes are the width of one eye apart from each other and require no corrective techniques. As a result, the makeup artist can use virtually any makeup technique on even-set eyes (**Figures 8–2** and **8–3**). Even-set eyes add symmetry to a face, regardless of other features or the shape of the face itself.

▲ Figure 8–4 Example of wide-set eyes.

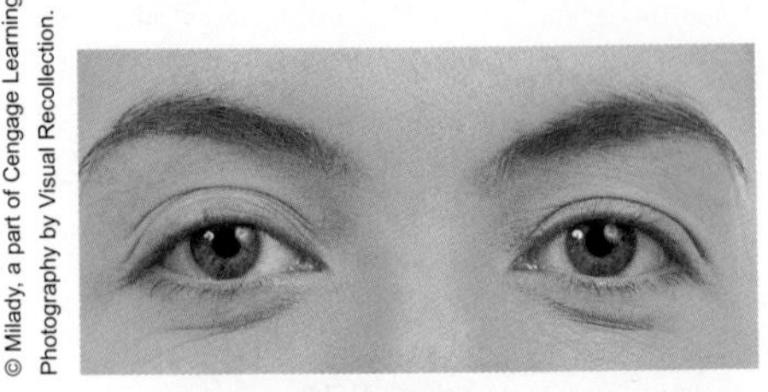

▲ Figure 8–5 Wide-set eyes.

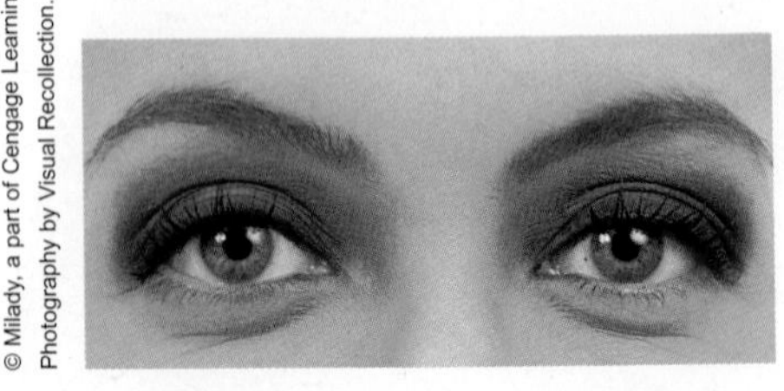

▲ Figure 8–6 Wide-set eyes with makeup.

Wide-Set Eyes

Wide-set eyes are further than one eye width apart (**Figures 8–4** and **8–5**). Wide-set eyes are a rare occurrence and are most often seen on striking runway models and high-fashion photo models. They are the perfect eye for dramatic makeup application and creative techniques because there is truly room to play and still end up with a relatively natural look. To bring wide-set eyes closer together, apply a darker color shadow toward the corner of the eyelid and be careful to blend carefully (**Figure 8–6**).

Deep-Set Eyes

Deep-set eyes are recessed deeper into the eye socket, creating a sunken-in appearance (**Figures 8–7** and **8–8**). The goal is to bring these eyes closer to the surface and pop them forward. This goal is achieved by using basic highlighting skills, lighter colors, minimal medium shades in the crease, and no dark shades. It is best to avoid eyeliner on the upper lid; using a medium eyeliner shade on the outer lower lid will accentuate without further receding the eye. With the deep-set eye, less is more (**Figure 8–9**).

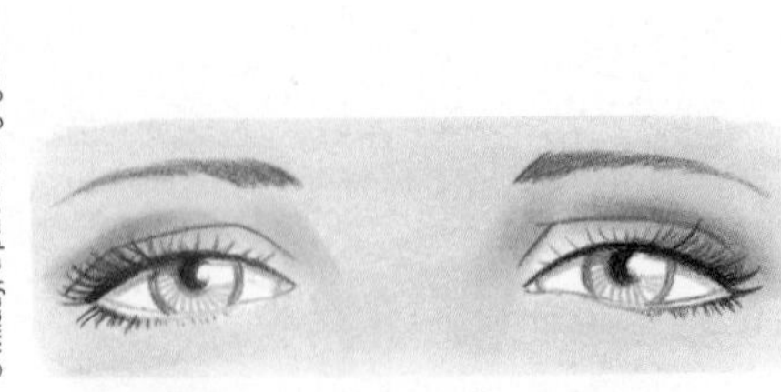

▲ Figure 8–7 Example of deep-set eyes.

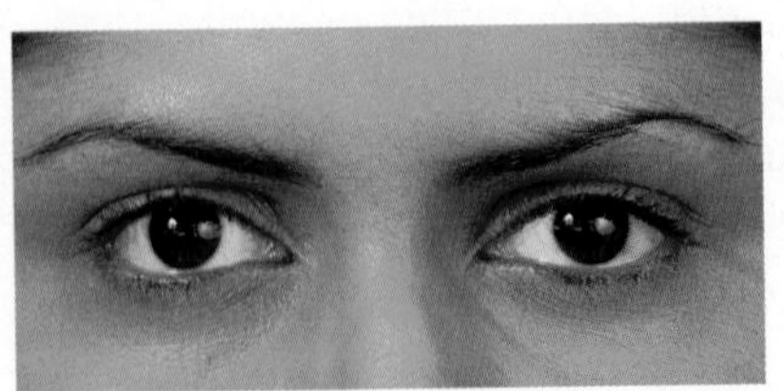

▲ Figure 8–8 Deep-set eyes.

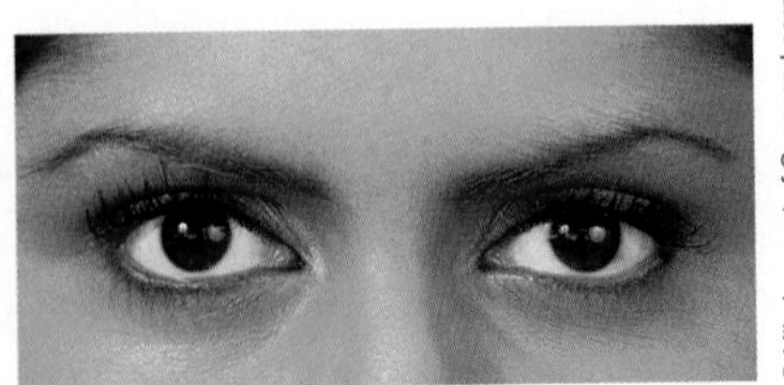

▲ Figure 8–9 Deep-set eyes with makeup.

Close-Set Eyes

Close-set eyes are separated from one another by less than one eye width. Close-set eyes are a common feature (**Figures 8–10** and **8–11**). Depending upon how close they are, close-set eyes can almost create the illusion that the eyes are crossed. Once again you will refer to your knowledge on highlighting and contouring discussed in Chapter 7, Creating the Canvas. To widen close-set eyes, you need to lighten the inner corners by applying a lighter shade of shadow and avoid bringing eyeliner across the eye into the inner corners.

For close-set eyes, darker colors for shading should be kept to the outer third of the eye (**Figure 8–12**).

HERE'S A TIP

False lashes should not be applied to the inner lash lines on close-set eyes. If they are, the eyes will appear closer together.

▲ Figure 8–10 **Example of close-set eyes.**

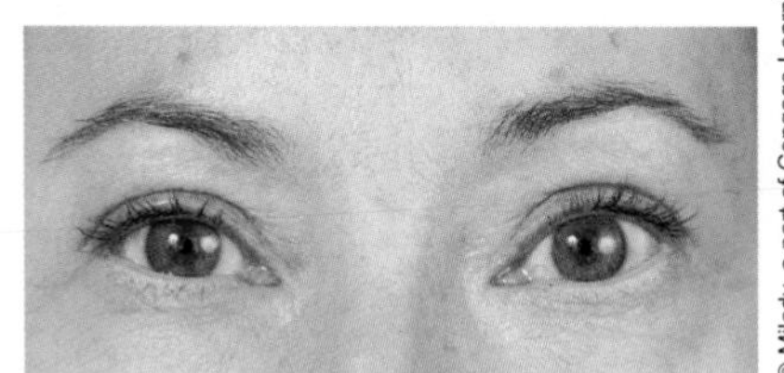

▲ Figure 8–11 **Close-set eyes.**

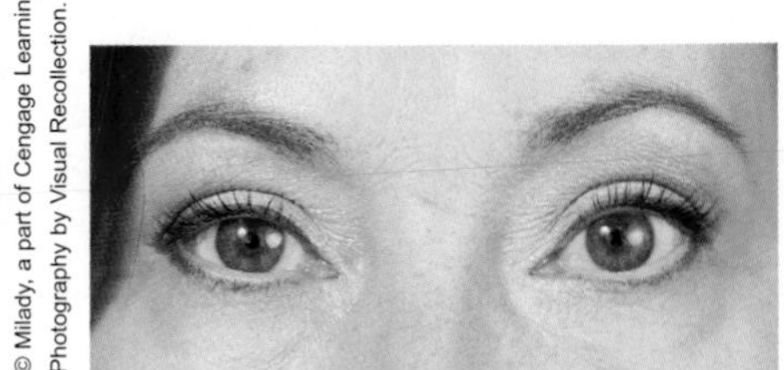

▲ Figure 8–12 **Close-set eyes with makeup.**

Round Eyes

Round eyes are lovely large circles; they are also classified as protruding or bulging eyes (**Figures 8–13** and **8–14**). The objective is to minimize the height and widen their appearance. Round eyes can handle any shadow color. Just avoid using light color directly above the pupil area, this would create an even rounder eye ball. A medium shadow can be applied to the lid, and a darker shadow can be applied in the crease, extending upward and out from the corner of the eye (**Figure 8–15**). Round eyes can be given a fabulous cat-like appearance by applying a dark eyeliner on the outer rim of the eye and/or by extending a dark eyeliner beyond the outer corner of the eye.

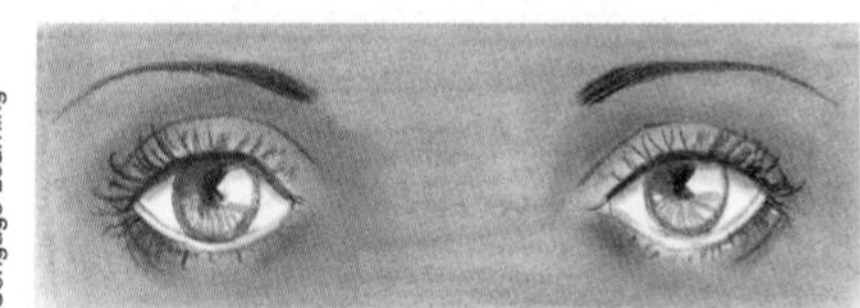

▲ Figure 8–13 **Example of round eyes.**

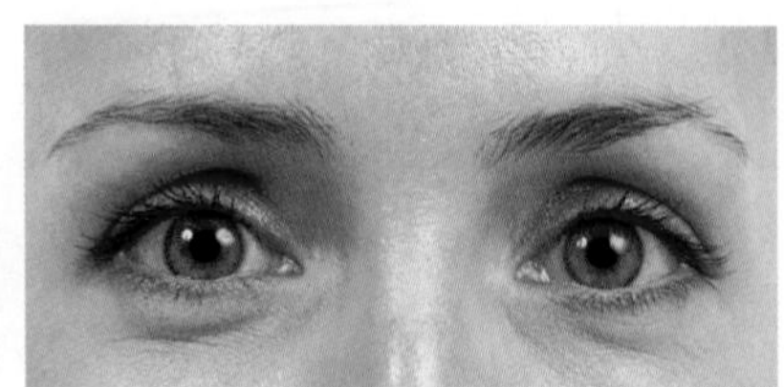

▲ Figure 8–14 **Round eyes.**

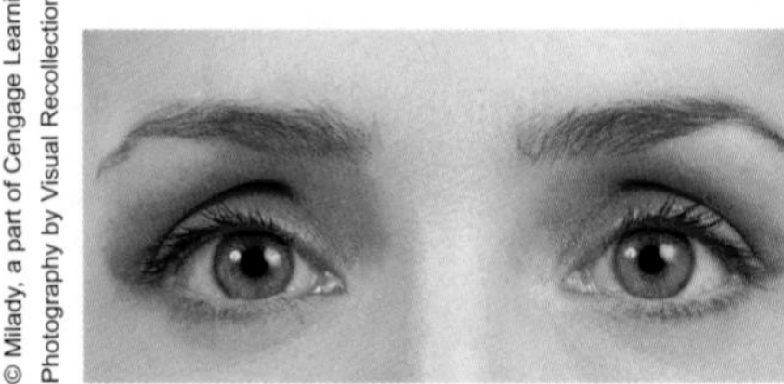

▲ Figure 8–15 **Round eyes with makeup.**

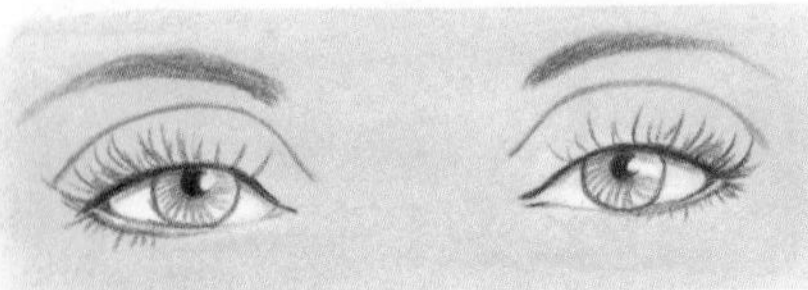

▲ Figure 8–16 **Example of heavy/drooping lids.**

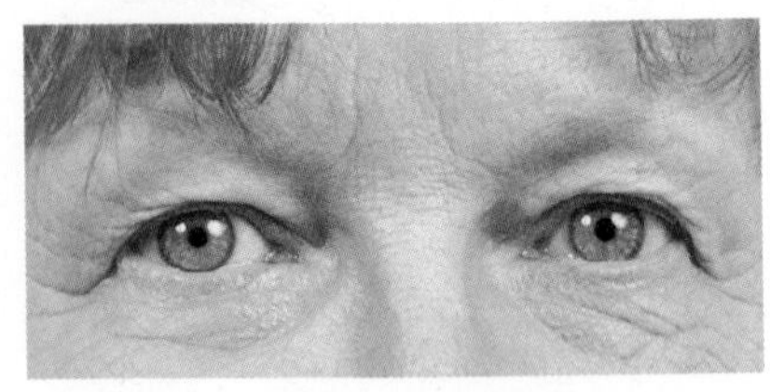

▲ Figure 8–17 **Heavy/drooping lids.**

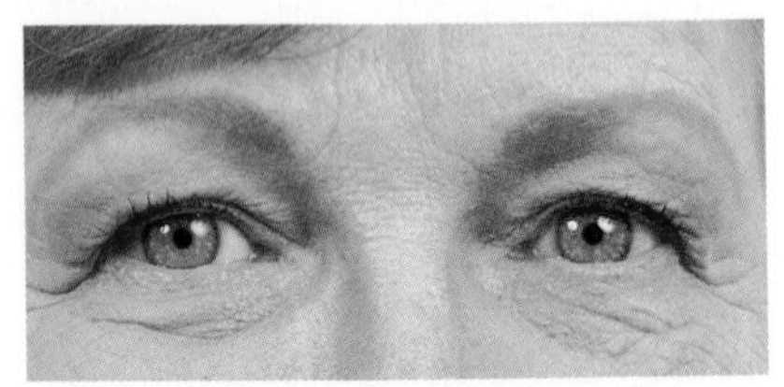

▲ Figure 15–18 **Heavy/drooping lids with makeup.**

Heavy/Drooping Lids

Heavy or drooping lids create the appearance of a small, tired eye (**Figures 8–16** and **8–17**). They often cause the misinterpretation of dark under-eye circles, so be sure to perform a careful analysis on a makeup-free face. For heavy/drooping lids, the first and most important step is to apply a neutral base or foundation over the entire eye area. Apply a lighter shadow directly on the lid above the upper lash line. Shadow evenly and lightly with a medium shade from the outer third of the lash line to the crease and brow (**Figure 8–18**). Be sure to blend well. Eyeliner is generally not recommended for heavy/drooping lids because it will make the eye itself appear to be smaller and taken over by the eyelid.

Asian Eyes

Asian eyes are completely different from a typical Western eye and astonishingly unique in shape. Although the eye shape is small and the main goal is to make it appear larger, the Asian eye is the ideal canvas for vibrant bold colors and eyeliner. Many Asian eyes have no clear definition between the eyelid, the crease area, and above; the entire area can appear to be one surface. This allows the makeup artist to create definition. Shadow is used to create a desired crease and add definition to the eye area.

Just as there are many Western eye shapes, there are many different Asian eye shapes. With various shapes comes a need for slightly different techniques based upon the specific details of individual eye-shape variation. Below you will find three mini-procedures to address three distinctly different-shaped Asian eyes.

HERE'S A TIP

Artificial lashes are a simple way to open and accent an Asian eye shape.

Mini Procedure

The Round Asian Eye

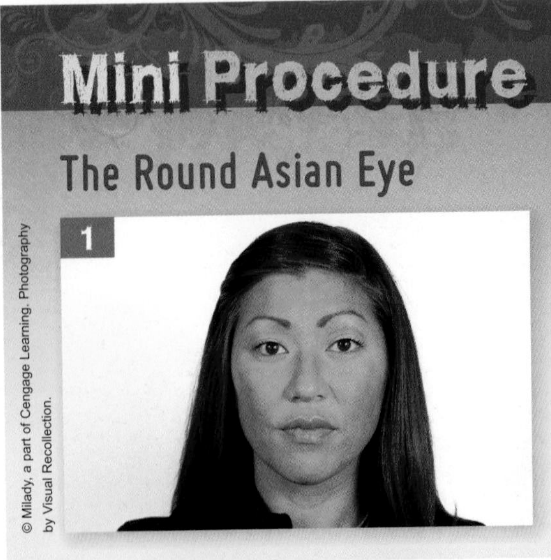

1 The makeup application for a full, round Asian eye does not require as much focus on creating the appearance of an eyelid as do many other shapes of Asian eyes.

(Continued)

Mini Procedure

The Round Asian Eye *(Continued)*

2 After a lighter shadow color is applied to the entire eye area, from the lid to the brow, a darker shadow is applied from the entire crease line, wrapping around the outer corner of the eye.

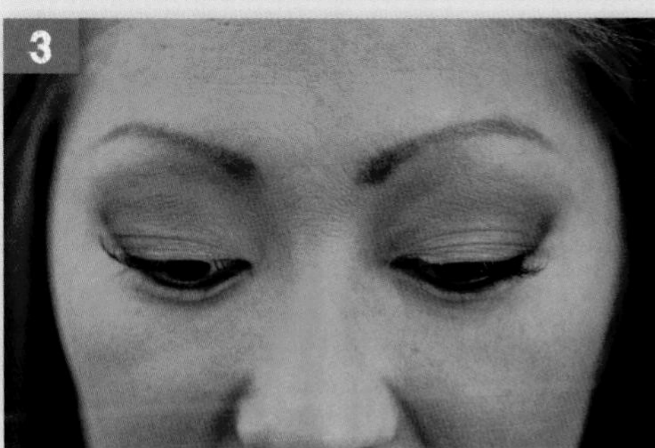

3 This technique creates the illusion of a very defined eyelid.

4 Eye shadow is applied as eyeliner along the lower lash line to create a softer eyeliner application.

5 This technique creates a lovely open eye with a distinct eyelid.

SERVICE TIP

Characteristic of Asian eyes, the eyelashes often grow straight out or downward. To open the eyes and enhance the lash line, curl the eyelashes before applying mascara.

Mini Procedure

A Partial-Lid Asian Eye

1 The technique for a partial lid requires a bit more focus on the creation of a clearly identifiable eyelid and on opening the eye.

2 Apply a base to the entire lid area.

3 Apply a darker shade of eye shadow where the crease would be and then blend the shadow very well. The trick is careful and precise blending so that you do not create a harsh line where you are creating the appearance of a crease.

4 Apply a light eye shadow color as a highlight at the bottom of the eyebrow.

(Continued)

Mini Procedure

A Partial-Lid Asian Eye *(Continued)*

5 Apply shadow with a brush as eyeliner beneath the entire lower lash line and blend well. This creates a soft eyeliner look.

6 This technique enhances the lid and opens the entire eye.

Mini Procedure

The Classic Asian Eye

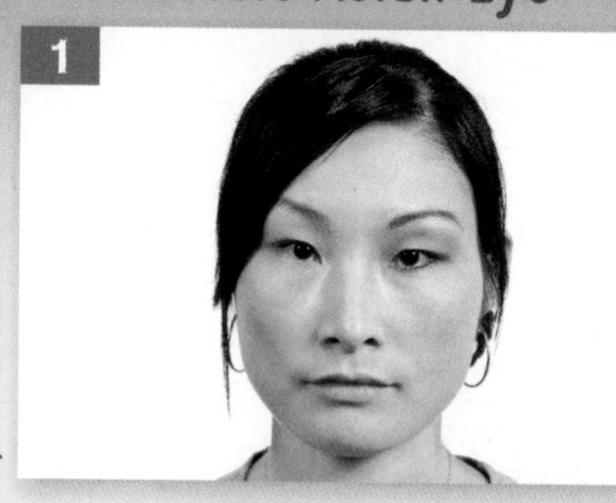

1 The technique for this classic Asian eye requires the complete creation of the appearance of an eyelid in order to open the eye.

2 After applying a neutral shadow beneath the eyebrow, a medium shadow is applied to create definition of the crease and the eyelid.

(Continued)

CAUTION

According to the American Medical Association, eye pencils should not be used to color the inner rim of the eyes because this can lead to infection of the tear duct, causing tearing, blurring of vision, and permanent pigmentation of the mucous membrane lining the inside of the eye.

Mini Procedure

The Classic Asian Eye *(Continued)*

3 Eyebrow shadow is applied to the eyebrows to darken them and to form a distinct arch shape. This creates a frame for the eye.

4 A light shadow color is placed directly in the center of the lid, approximately where the eyelid falls over the pupil of the eye. This technique draws the center of the eye outward, creating dimension to the entire eye area.

Note: Placing a dot of light shadow to highlight the center of the lid draws the lid outward, while at the same time creating the appearance of a more open eye.

5 Use a soft pencil to line the lower lash line. Gently smudge the liner with a sponge or brush to create a soft look.

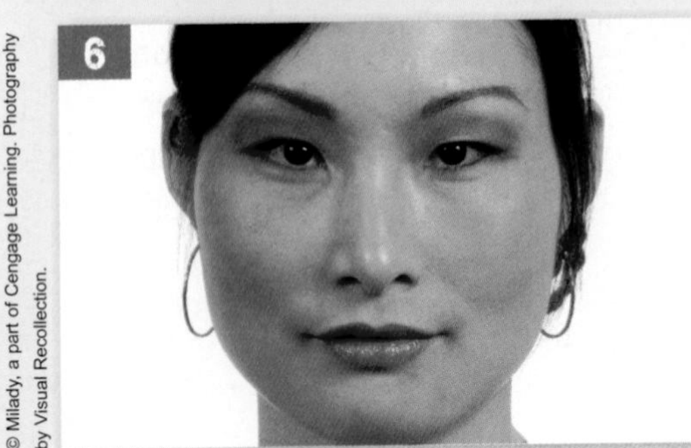

6 This technique will create definition and open the eye area.

Small Eyes

Small eyes can easily be made to look larger. Lighter colors make features look larger. To increase the size of small eyes, use plenty of highlight and light shades. This is one eye shape that will look smaller if you create depth in the crease. Medium-shade eyeliner is an excellent choice, especially when a white eye pencil is used to line the lid on both the upper and lower lash lines. Be sure to apply the eyeliner outside the lash line to avoid infection or injury. ☑ LO1

EYE COLORS

Just as there are many skin tones, there are many eye colors. It is easy to categorize eyes into blue, green, brown, and hazel; however, as any makeup artist knows, each of these colors has many variations. Individual eye color helps you as a makeup artist choose eye shadow colors, depending upon whether you are trying to enhance the natural color or to make it "pop" with a contrasting color. This topic will be covered in depth in the next few paragraphs when shadow color is discussed.

EYE PRODUCTS

Eye product colors and choices are endless. Try them all, use them all, and decide for yourself which you prefer and which are best suited for various clients, techniques, and looks. Your makeup kit can easily be overflowing with eye product in a very short time.

Eye Shadow Primer

Eye shadow primer is a product applied beneath eye shadow to create a smooth application base and extend wearability. It holds eye shadow in place and prevents creasing, smudging, and caking of eye shadow. Most eye shadow primers are a polymer or silicone base, and are best applied over a completely makeup-free eyelid. **Polymers** are chemical compounds formed by combining a number of small molecules (monomers) into long chain-like structures; they are used to deliver ingredients and hold products together. **Silicones** are synthetic compounds used in cosmetics as adhesives and lubricants. Silicones are oil that is chemically combined with silicon and oxygen and leaves a noncomedogenic, protective film on the surface of the skin.

Another alternative to shadow primer is concealer and/or foundation. The eyelid is known for discoloration due to its shape and thinness. It often appears darker, blue, or redder than the natural skin tone. Using a concealer or foundation as an eye shadow base evens the skin color, aids in a smooth shadow application, and extends the wearability of the product.

Eye Shadow

Eye shadows alone come in several different forms and a multitude of colors.

Powder Shadows

Powder shadow is either pressed or loose powder that is packed with pigment. Powder shadows can be found in sheer colors, shimmers, rich pigments, and matte black. Both pressed and loose shadow powders can also be used as eyeliner, and most can be used dry or wet.

Pressed shadows come in small palettes or compacts. Loose powders come in small jars and require a little practice for skilled use. They do not contain any binding agents to hold the powder together, making them a bit tricky when it comes to determining the amount to apply. However, if you use a high-quality brand and the right type of high-quality brush, your skills will quickly improve.

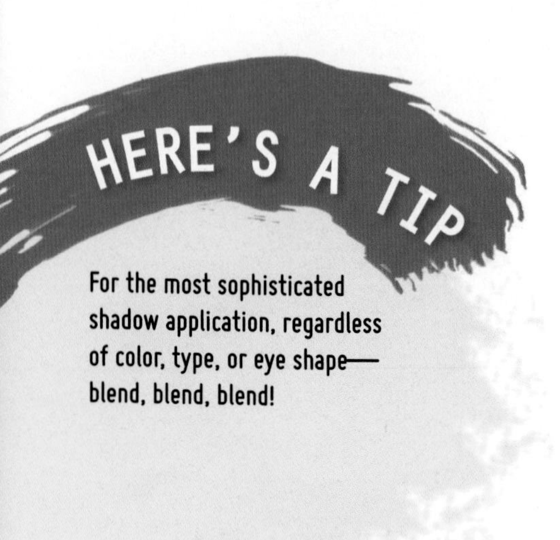

For the most sophisticated shadow application, regardless of color, type, or eye shape—blend, blend, blend!

Cream-to-Powder Shadows

Cream-to-powder shadows begin as a smoothly blending cream that dries as a light powder. They are excellent for a light or sheer application and are less likely to crease. Cream-to-powder shadows are excellent for all skin types but work especially well for clients with oily skin and eyelids.

Stick Shadows

Stick shadows are cream shadows in a stick form. Much like stick foundations, they have a heavy consistency, offering more coverage and easy application. Stick shadows often last longer than powder shadows.

Cream Shadows

Cream shadows are lighter than stick shadows and do not dry to a powder. Due to their consistency, they tend to smudge and crease very easily. They are available in consistencies from very sheer to opaque and come in pots, tubes, and sponge-wand applicators.

Eyeliner

Regarded as one of the most difficult makeup products to use, **eyeliner** is applied directly around the lash line and can completely alter the appearance of any eye. Eyeliner comes in only a few different forms but in limitless amounts of colors.

Pencil Liners

Pencil liners are the most traditional eyeliner. **Pencil eyeliner** is a firm or soft pencil used to draw an even line around the eye. The best pencil liners are not hard or waxy and go on smoothly and evenly. They can create a variety of looks, depending upon their sharpness, and they are easy to smudge into a soft or smoky look. Pencil liners come in every color from white to black, and they are available in shimmer and metallic.

White eyeliner is used to line the lash area to define the eye and increase the size of the eyeball itself. For a more natural look, many cosmetic companies produce beige and nude eyeliner pencils as well. There is much controversy regarding the use of white eye liner since it is often applied along the inner lash line. This technique can lead to eye irritation or possible infection if the eye pencil is not sharpened and cleaned between each eye, and between each client. However, it is a makeup artists favorite trick for creating a larger eye. Check your local state regulations to be safe.

Liquid Eyeliner

Liquid eyeliner is a fluid liquid makeup, comes in a tube much like a mascara container, and is applied with a very fine-tip brush. It is available in a variety of colors and requires a steady hand and a bit of practice to master.

HERE'S A TIP

To steady your hand when applying liquid eyeliner, gently rest the base of your hand on a tissue against the cheek of your client. Many makeup artists use their opposite hand to hold their own wrist.

Mascara

Mascara comes in a tube and is applied with a wand that has a spiral brush attached to the end; it instantly enhances the lashes by making them appear darker, longer, and thicker. Mascara alone can make a complete change to any eye by framing and accenting the eye itself, and it is available in a wide variety of colors: black, black-brown, brown, violet, and blue.

Depending on the type and purpose of the mascara, the brush may be curved or straight, with a variety of different shaped brush hairs. Mascara comes in waterproof, water resistant, and regular formulations. Your choice will depend upon the client's needs and the purpose of the makeup application. For clients that participate in a lot of outdoor sports, swimming, or cardiovascular activity, waterproof mascara is an excellent choice because it will stay in place during activity and perspiration. ☑ LO2

COLOR SELECTION

One reminder is frequently repeated throughout this textbook: The world of makeup has very few "musts." There are many guidelines to help the makeup artist choose proper products and colors, but very rarely are such guidelines the only options. The whole idea behind makeup artistry is the development of the artist's creativity and artistic abilities, along with the ability to apply such creativity to each individual client. With creativity and color selection, your options are unlimited.

Eye makeup comes in limitless quantities of colors, and fortunately there are guidelines for colors and families of colors best suited for a particular eye color. These choices either emphasize eye color or contrast with it to make the eye pop! These choices link directly back to the fundamentals of color theory and warm colors versus cool colors discussed in Chapter 5, Color Theory.

To make the best color choices for your clients and for the purpose of the makeup application, first determine eye color; next determine if the color is warm or cool; then determine if your intent is to emphasize the natural color or to intensify it with contrast.

HERE'S A TIP

To determine colors that will complement a particular eye color, look closely at the color in the iris to see if your client has small flecks of a different color within the iris. All of these small inflections determine overall eye color appearance and will help you choose makeup colors depending on your goals.

© Subbotina Anna/www.Shutterstock.com

▲ Figure 8–19 Warm-blue eye.

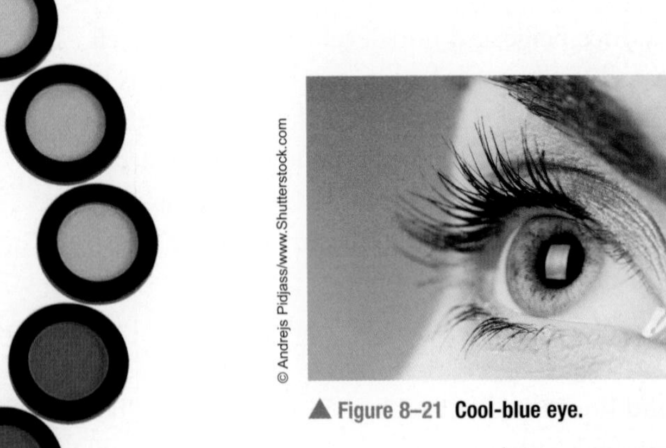

© Milady, a part of Cengage Learning

▶ Figure 8–20 Selection of blue-green shadow.

© Andrejs Pidjass/www.Shutterstock.com

▲ Figure 8–21 Cool-blue eye.

© Milady, a part of Cengage Learning

▶ Figure 8–22 Cool-blue shadow.

Blue Eyes

Nothing is more striking than a vibrant set of blue eyes. A group of individuals with blue eyes most likely all have different colors of blue. Warm-blue eyes are a blue-green color (**Figure 8–19**) and are best enhanced by blue-green shadow colors (**Figure 8–20**).Warm eyes sometimes have small flecks of light green or yellow in the iris.

Cool-blue eyes are a brilliant blue (**Figure 8–21**) and are enhanced by blue shadows that are clearly blue in color (**Figure 8–22**). Cool eyes will sometimes have small flecks of white in the iris. All blue eyes can be intensified with colors that are complementary on the color wheel, the oranges and corals.

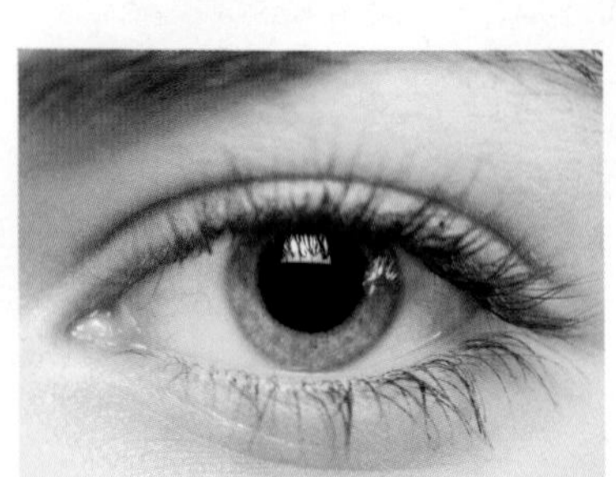

© Bo Valentino/www.Shutterstock.com

▲ Figure 8–23 Warm-green eyes.

© Milady, a part of Cengage Learning

▶ Figure 8–24 Selection of warm-green shadow colors.

Green Eyes

Green eyes are just as striking as brilliant blue eyes, and with the right shadow choices green eyes can grab an onlooker's attention in a heartbeat. Warm-green eyes have slightly more yellow in them (**Figure 8–23**) and are enhanced by green shadows with a yellow, chartreuse color (**Figure 8–24**). Cool-green eyes have more blue or brown in them (**Figure 8–25**) and are enhanced by green shadows that contain more blue or brown (**Figure 8–26**). All green eyes are intensified with contrasting pinks.

© tommiphoto/www.Shutterstock.com

▲ Figure 8–25 Cool-green eye.

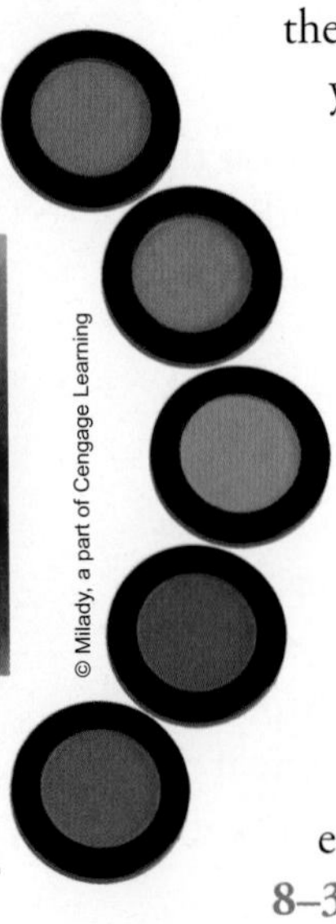

© Milady, a part of Cengage Learning

▶ Figure 8–26 Selection of cool-green shadow colors.

Brown Eyes

The most common eye color is deep dark brown, and eyes this color are soft, seductive, and sexy. Warm-brown eyes are lighter in color with a slight amount of yellow (**Figure 8–27**) and are enhanced by brown shadow colors that are lighter (**Figure 8–28**). Cool-brown eyes appear to have more red, black, or even a mahogany (**Figure 8–29**) and are enhanced by brown shadows that are deeper and darker (**Figure 8–30**). All brown eyes are beautifully intensified with contrasting colors such as blue and slate.

Hazel Eyes

The beauty of hazel eyes is the amazing combination of brown, green, and gold (**Figure 8–31**). These eyes are fabulous to work on and clearly change color with the client's clothing color. Hazel eyes are best enhanced by shadow colors that are yellow-green or brown-green (**Figure 8–32**). Warm-hazel eyes contain a larger amount of yellow (**Figure 8–33**) and are equally enhanced by shadow colors that are gold to almost a pink-brown (**Figure 8–34**). All hazel eyes are intensified with plum shadow colors.

This chapter provides wonderful guidelines for enhancing and accentuating eye color. However, there are literally hundreds of eye shadow colors, each with their own shade and degree of warmth and coolness. As you become more experienced, your artistic eye will guide you in choosing an array of colors to create breathtaking eyes for every eye color and for every client.

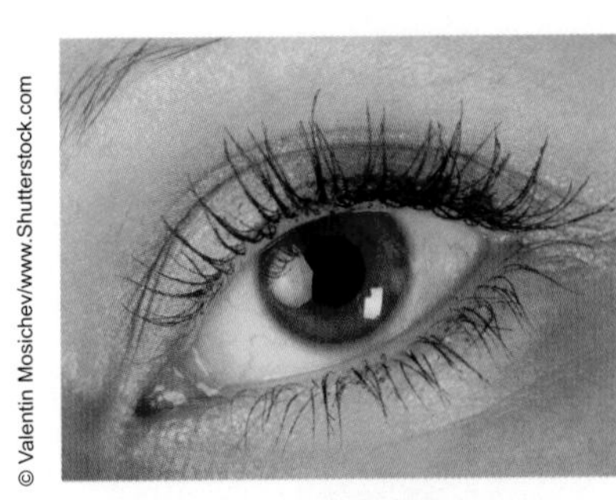

▲ Figure 8–27 **Warm-brown eye.**

▶ Figure 8–28 **Selection of warm-brown shadow colors.**

EYEBROWS

The eyes may be the "window to the soul," but in some ways eyebrows are even more important. When shaped properly, eyebrows not only alter the appearance of the eye, but also the look of the entire face. Overgrown brows can cast a shadow on the brow bone or between the eyes. Over-tweezed eyebrows can make the face appear puffy or protruding and create a surprised look. A well-groomed eyebrow is fundamental to any professional makeup application.

▲ Figure 8–29 **Cool-brown eye.**

▶ Figure 8–30 **Selection of cool-brown shadow colors.**

▲ Figure 8–31 **Hazel eye.**

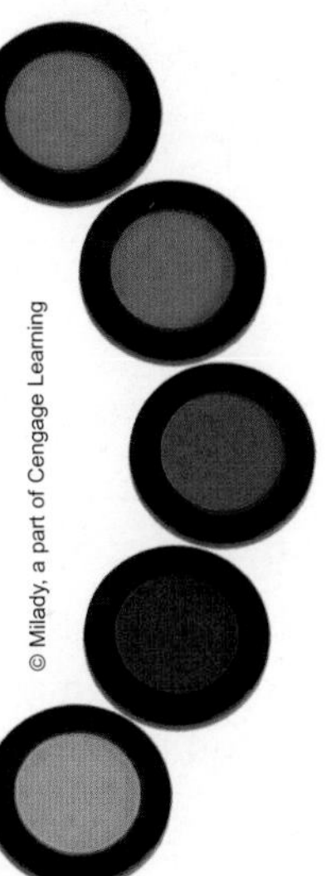

▶ Figure 8–32 **Selection of shadow colors to enhance a hazel eye.**

▲ Figure 8–33 **Warm hazel eye.**

▶ Figure 8–34 **Selection of golden-hazel shadow colors.**

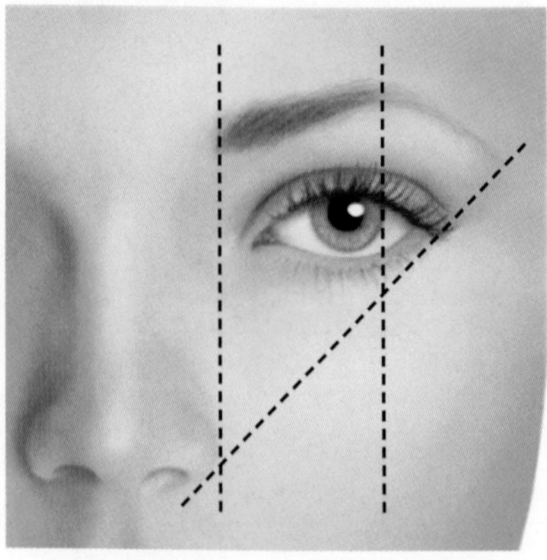

▲ Figure 8–35 Measuring the perfect brow.

▲ Figure 8–36 Low brow arch for a low forehead.

The Ideal Eyebrow Shape

The perfect eyebrow shape will depend upon the eye shape, as well as the face shape and nose (**Figure 8–35**). It takes a careful analysis of the entire face to determine how to best shape the eyebrows so that the entire face appears brighter.

Three simple lines will help you to determine the perfect brow shape for any eye. Using a brush or brow pencil establish three lines of distinction. Be sure the client is looking straight ahead, and has both eyes open.

Line 1. A vertical line from the inner corner of the eye upward. This is where the eyebrow should begin.
Line 2. A line drawn at an angle from the outer corner of the nose to the outer corner of the eye. This is where the eyebrow should end.
Line 3. A vertical line from the outer circle of the iris upward. Be sure the client is looking straight ahead as you determine this line. This is where the highest part of the arch would ideally be.

Creating Brows for Unique Features

The above guidelines are an excellent tool, but not all eye, nose, and face shapes are easily categorized. The following tricks will help you balance other facial features instantly by reshaping the eyebrows.

- **Low forehead.** A low arch gives more height to a low forehead. Keep the arch to a minimum and avoid being too drastic in the height of the arch (**Figure 8–36**).
- **Wide-set eyes.** The eyes can be made to appear closer together by extending the eyebrow lines to the inside corners of the eyes. Just be careful not to get the eyebrows too close, or your client will have the appearance of a permanent frown (**Figure 8–37**).

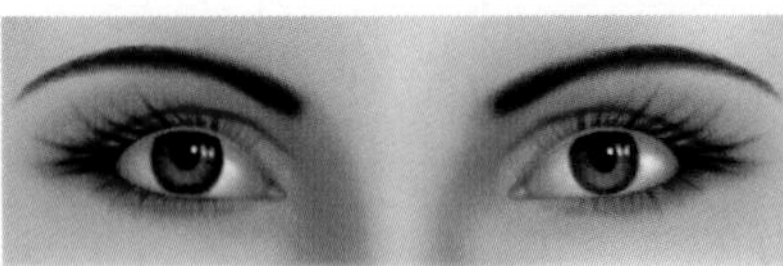

▲ Figure 8–37 An example of an extended brow arch.

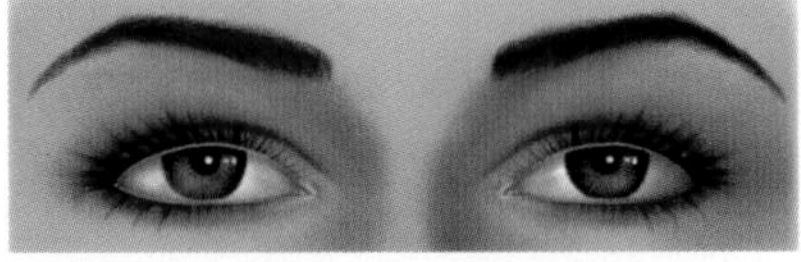

▲ Figure 8–38 Brows set farther apart.

▲ Figure 8–39 Brows with a high arch.

- **Close-set eyes.** The eyes can be made to appear farther apart by widening the distance between the eyebrows and extending them slightly beyond the outer corner of the eye (**Figure 8–38**).
- **Round face.** Arch the eyebrows high to make the face appear narrower. Begin the arch on a line directly above the inside corner of the eye and extend to the end of the cheekbone (**Figure 8–39**).
- **Long face.** To make the face appear shorter and wider, create a minimal arch. Do not extend the eyebrows farther than the outside corners of the eyes (**Figure 8–40**).

▲ Figure 8–40 **A minimal brow arch.**

▲ Figure 8–41 **A brow arch with slightly higher ends.**

- **Square face.** The face will appear more oval if there is a high arch on the ends of the eyebrows. Begin the lines directly above the corners of the eyes and extend them outward (Figure 8–41).

Creating perfect brows is a talent you will develop over time, with a trained eye and much practice. The ability to shape the perfect brow is a necessity because of the amazing impact that perfect brows have on the entire look of the face. ✓ LO3

Brow Shaping Techniques

The shape of the eyebrows can completely change the appearence of the eyes. To create perfectly shaped brows, you can use several different methods. In many cases, multiple methods will be required to achieve the desired results.

Tweezing Using tweezers, brows can be shaped and individual stray hairs can quickly and efficiently be removed. Tweeze above and below the brow area (Figure 8–42). Tweezers are available with slanted tips and pointed tips. Determine which type works best for you, and keep several pairs in your makeup tool kit. Usually during a makeup application there is limited time and a basic clean-up of stray hairs is all that is needed. In this case, tweezers will become the makeup artist's best friend.

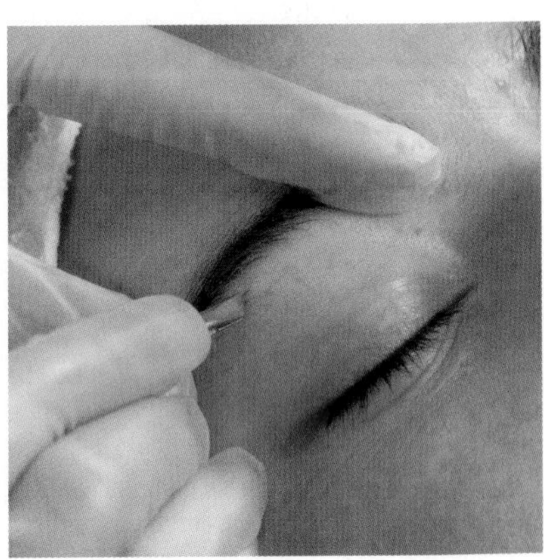

▲ Figure 8–42 **Tweezing eyebrow hairs.**

Trimming The best-shaped brows still need to be perfectly groomed. A small pair of brow scissors is a simple answer to long stray brow hairs, bushy brows, and unruly brows. Using a brow comb, brush the eyebrows straight upward toward the hairline and snip hairs that extend beyond the top of the desired brow (Figure 8–43).

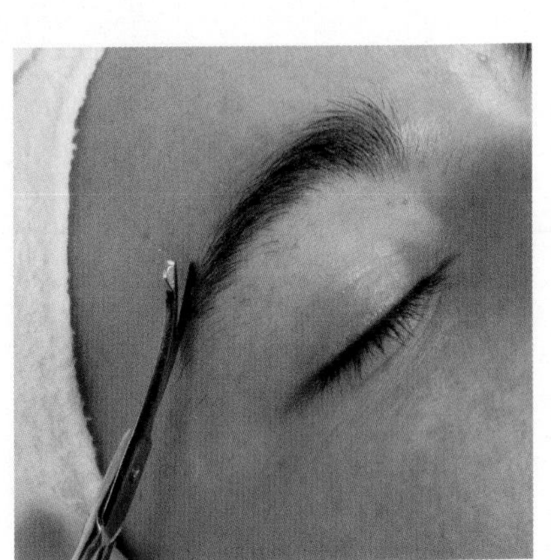

▲ Figure 8–43 **Trimming eyebrow hairs.**

Waxing Waxing is a quick and easy way to both shape the brows and remove unwanted stray hairs. Waxing can be performed with strip wax or a hard wax. Please be sure to check your state licensing requirements to make sure waxing falls within your professional scope of practice.

Threading Threading, also known as **banding**, is a Middle Eastern hair removal technique that is performed with cotton threads that are twisted and rolled along the surface of the skin, entwining the hair in the thread and lifting it out of the follicle.

All hair removal techniques require a certain amount of practice and skill. Waxing and threading take a bit of time and may leave the skin slightly red. These techniques should be booked to allow for adequate time and performed a few days prior to a makeup application intended for a special event, a photo session, or a TV appearance.

Eyebrow Products

There are many forms of products specifically designed for enhancing, defining, and creating beautiful eyebrows. Each one has a different consistency, feel, look, and application technique. You will probably develop a preference for one over another, or you may fill your kit with each type of product in order to suit the specific needs of your client and the various looks you are trying to achieve. To perfect your professional makeup skills, practice with each type to explore the differences and the results.

Brow Pencils

Brow pencils are similar to eyeliner pencils and are used to fill in sparse areas, define the brow, or completely re-create a brow. Brow pencils have long wearability and are easy to apply. They come in a variety of colors ranging from black and dark brown to brown taupe and gray. They are easy to disinfect between uses by sharpening.

Brow Shadow

Brow shadows, also known as **brow powders**, are used to create a soft-looking eyebrow; they are applied with an angled brow brush. Brow shadows come in a variety of colors to deliver the desired look. Eye shadow can be used as eyebrow color as well.

Brow Cream

Brow cream is a thick, colored cream used for very sparse eyebrows in need of heavier coverage. Applied with a small angled brush, brow cream can create the appearance of a full, thick brow.

Brow Stencils

Many eyebrow kits will come with a variety of brow stencils. **Brow stencils** are cut outs of various eyebrow shapes to guide the shaping of eyebrows, the removal of stray hairs, and application of product.

Brow Gel

Brow gel is a makeup product specifically designed to work like a hair gel; it holds the brows in position and provides them with a beautiful, long-lasting, finished look.

Brow Brush

Brow brushes are shaped similar to a toothbrush head with about half as many brush hairs and (often) with a comb on the opposite side. Some brushes are in the shape of a spiral, similar to a mascara wand, making disposable mascara wands a safer and cleaner alternative to a brow brush. Brow brushes are perfect for grooming the brows and will help you determine whether brow trimming is necessary.

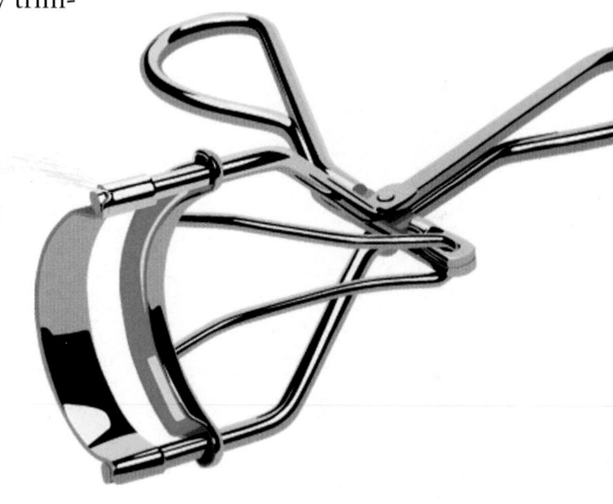

EYELASHES

Eyebrows frame the face, but eyelashes frame the eyes. Every client desires long, luscious lashes. Eyelashes accent the eyes and add elegance and sophistication to every makeup application.

Products for Eyelashes

Simply enhancing the eyelashes will instantly enhance any eye. Your kit will quickly fill with several different lash products.

Eyelash Curler

Eyelash curlers add instant shape, curve, and length to the lashes. They are best used prior to the application of mascara to prevent breaking or damaging the lashes. Place the lash curler at the base of the lash line without pinching the upper eyelid. Gently squeeze to turn the base of the lash line upward. Have your client look downward. Continue with gentle squeezing motions as you move the eyelash curler toward the tip of the lashes.

Mascara

Mascara is available in multiple colors and for many different purposes. Mascara can lengthen, strengthen, curl, thicken, and separate the lashes. The ultimate objective is to enhance the lashes to their fullest. Every makeup kit should contain several choices of mascara, including brown and black. With experience, you will find which type of mascara and which type of wand applicator works best for you.

Tinting Lashes

Vegetable dyes and hair dyes can be used to darken the lashes for several weeks. Tinted lashes will provide the client with a lovely dark lash, even without mascara. See Chapter 17, All About Lashes, for full eyelash tinting procedures.

Artificial Lashes

The perfect way to enhance every eye is to add a few extra lashes. Lash extensions are no longer used only for special occasions; they have become increasingly popular for daily wear. A well-applied set of lashes eliminates the need for mascara and can last several weeks to months with only a fill every few weeks. See Chapter 17, All About Lashes, for full artificial lash application procedures. ☑ LO4

HERE'S A TIP

Minking with mascara! Coat the lashes in brown, and then apply black mascara to the tips. The lashes instantly look longer!

Sherry Weizchowski

Licensed Esthetician, Makeup Artist, Business Owner; NY

LIPS

Every client wants beautiful, luscious, natural-looking lips. As with clothing, hairstyles, and other makeup colors and techniques, trends come and go, but a simple application of lipstick will instantly brighten the face, even making an otherwise makeup-free face look finished.

Choose lipstick shades that match skin tone. For cool skin tone, choose cool lipstick shades; for warm skin tone, choose warm lipstick shades!

Lip Shades

Lipstick colors are almost unlimited. Although there are no set rules for choosing lipstick color, many factors should be taken into account: individual skin tone, other makeup colors, purpose of the makeup application, lighting, day wear vs. night wear, seasons, outfits . . . the list goes on.

Lips that are well cared for wear lipstick better and longer than neglected lips. The lips shed skin more quickly than any other part of the body, making it necessary to gently exfoliate them and regularly hydrate them. Dry, cracked lips look even worse with lipstick.

Lip Products

There is a wide range of amazing lip products to create and enhance luscious, beautiful lips. From the most natural, to the most outlandish lips, your creativity and skill with lip products can completely change an entire look in just minutes.

Lip Exfoliant

For kissable, soft, smooth lips a lip exfoliant is the answer. **Lip exfoliants** are cream or gel-based products that contain mild exfoliating agents such as salt, sugar, or microbeads to gently slough off the superficial surface of dead skin cells on the lips.

Lip Primer

Lip primer is foundation for the lips; it is designed to fill in small cracks, add moisture, and create a smooth, full appearance prior to the application of lip color and other lip products. Lip primer is typically clear, matte, and unnoticeable on the lips. Its primary role is to aid in a longer-lasting wear time for lipstick and other lip products. Many primers also contain an SPF to protect the lips from UV rays.

HERE'S A TIP

Avoid using lip liner that is a completely different color than the lip color. When the lip color fades, your client will be left only with a lip line!

Lip Liner

Lip liner is a makeup product intended to fill uneven areas on the outer edges of the lips to define their shape. It is the ideal product for altering the shape of lips that are uneven, too small, too large, or lacking in definition. Lip liner is also used to outline the lips and keep lipstick inside the lip area, preventing the lip color from bleeding. Lip liner is most often found in a pencil form, but consistencies vary from a firm, waxy pencil to a softer, creamy pencil. The best choice depends upon your preference, technique, and the client's skin type. Lip liner colors are available in the same broad range as lip colors, allowing you to properly match the lip liner to the chosen lip color shade.

Lip Color

Lip color, also known as **lipstick**, is a well known and favorite makeup product that contains pigment, oils, emollients, and waxes to provide color and enhancement to every set of lips. It is available in a tube, pot, stick, and even a palette. Available colors cover the entire spectrum of the color wheel. As noted above, the only important rule when choosing lip color is to choose one that is the same as your skin tone: warm if your skin tone is warm, and cool if your skin tone is cool. Your task as a makeup artist is to provide your clients with many options. Most clients are creatures of habit and will wear the same lipstick, daily, for years. Consider reminding your clients that, although it may take a little getting used to, a change in lip color can alter the brightness of the face and even accent other facial features.

Lip color formulations are plentiful: moisturizing, flavored, plumping, sheer, matte, cream, and long-lasting. Your preferences will grow with experience, client needs, and application requirements.

Lip Gloss

Lip gloss is a product that provides the lips with moisture, shine, and color; it can be worn alone or over lip color. Lip gloss is perfect to place over the top of lip color to give it a glossy finish and help it to wear longer. Lip gloss is available in colors ranging from completely clear to the darkest of chocolate browns. Lip gloss is available in a pot, a tube with a wand applicator, or in a squeeze tube. ☑ LO5

Creating Lip Shapes

Rarely is a client happy with the shape of her lips; it seems that everyone wants something other than what they have. Luckily, changing lip shape and definition is a simple task. As times and trends change, the desired lip shape also changes—one thing that remains is the desire for slightly plump, luscious lips!

Lips are usually proportioned so that the peaks of the upper lip fall directly in line with the nostrils. Lips can be full, thin, uneven, or lack shape. Fortunately, any shape has a quick fix.

A thin lower lip can be enlarged by placing lip liner below the bottom lip line (**Figure 8–44**).

A thin upper lip can be enlarged by placing lip liner outside of the upper lip line and creating higher lip peaks (**Figure 8–45**).

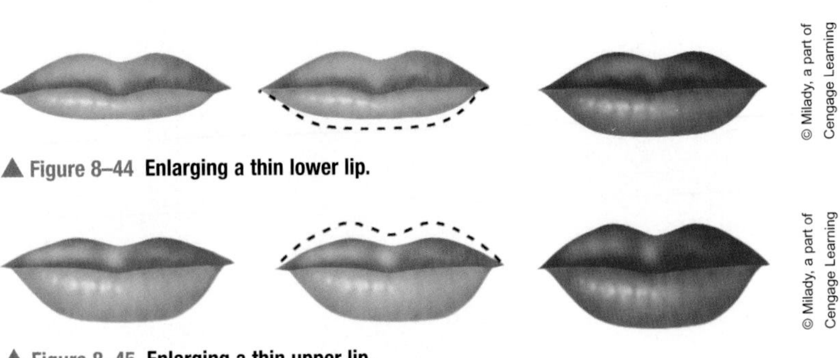

▲ Figure 8–44 **Enlarging a thin lower lip.**

▲ Figure 8–45 **Enlarging a thin upper lip.**

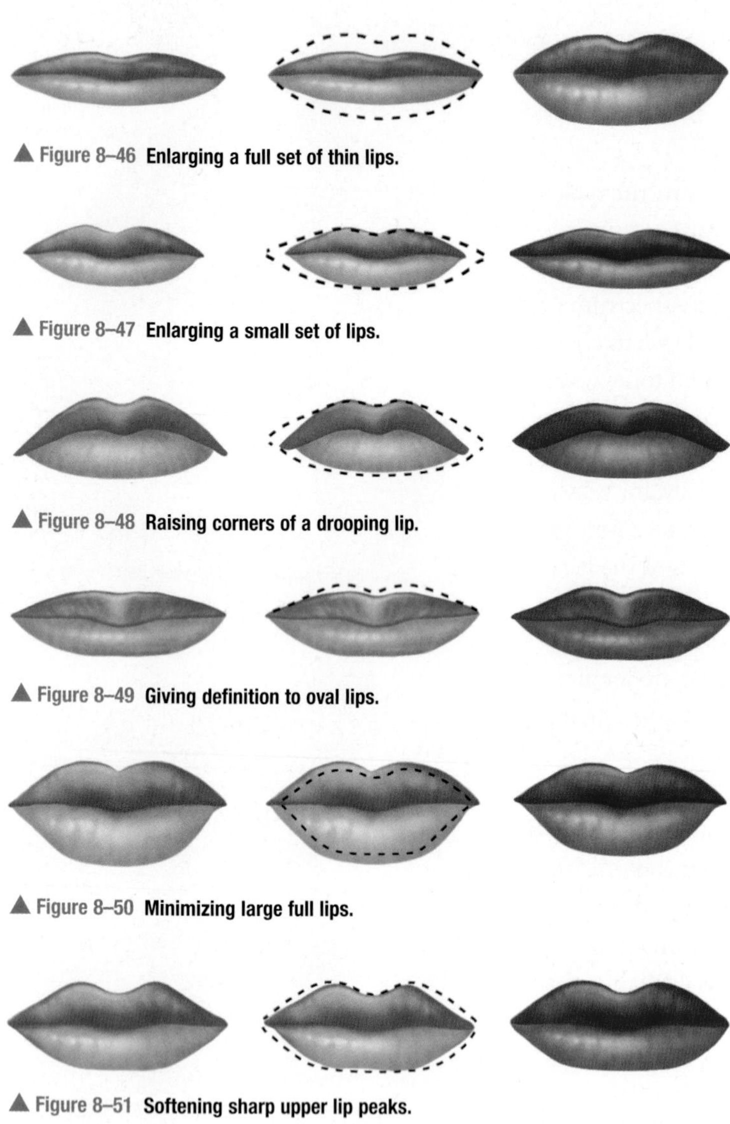

▲ Figure 8–46 Enlarging a full set of thin lips.

▲ Figure 8–47 Enlarging a small set of lips.

▲ Figure 8–48 Raising corners of a drooping lip.

▲ Figure 8–49 Giving definition to oval lips.

▲ Figure 8–50 Minimizing large full lips.

▲ Figure 8–51 Softening sharp upper lip peaks.

▲ Figure 8–52 Evening uneven lips.

A full set of thin lips can be made to appear larger and fuller by lining the entire lip area outside of the natural lip line and creating a full and shapely lip (**Figure 8–46**).

A small set of lips can be made larger by lining the outside of the lip area as needed in order to enlarge or balance the size of the lip (**Figure 8–47**).

To create an upward appearance where the lip corner droops, apply lip liner above the outer corner of the upper lip line and inside the lower inner corner of the bottom lip (**Figure 8–48**).

Oval lips can be easily defined by lining the outer corners of the lip with liner that extends slightly beyond the natural lip line (**Figure 8–49**).

Large lips can be made to appear smaller by applying lip liner inside of the natural lip line (**Figure 8–50**).

High upper lip peaks can be rounded or minimized by applying lip liner just below the peak in a smooth round application (**Figure 8–51**).

Uneven lips can be made to appear perfectly even by applying lip liner in an even technique to both sides, regardless of the natural lip line (**Figure 8–52**).

☑ **LO6**

People's uniqueness lies within their individual facial features. As a professional makeup artist, you are given the privilege and the gift to re-create, enhance, and perfect these amazing facial features. Study each face like you would study for a test in school. Analyze, memorize, and apply your knowledge and creativity to offer your clients cosmetic options that they had never before considered or envisioned.

Review Questions

1. Describe the difference between even-set, wide-set, and close-set eyes.
2. What is the basic objective when working with Asian eyes?
3. What is the best color choice to make a natural eye color "pop"?
4. Eye shadows that begin as a smoothly blending cream that dries as a light powder are known as what?
5. What is the purpose of white eyeliner?
6. What type of mascara is best suited for clients who participate in outdoor sports?
7. Explain the difference between a warm-blue eye and a cool-blue eye.
8. What is a possible result from over-tweezing eyebrows?
9. How many lines are needed to determine the ideal brow shape?
10. When determining a perfect brow shape, where does the first line begin and end?
11. How should brows be shaped in order to make close eyes appear farther apart?
12. What tool is used to remove individual stray hairs around the brows?
13. What is the purpose of an eyebrow stencil?
14. What is the purpose of brow gel?
15. What products are generally used to tint eyelashes?
16. Why is it important to use a lip exfoliant?
17. What is the best shade of lip color for an individual?
18. What type of lip product best changes the shape of a lip?

Chapter Glossary

brow cream	A thick, colored cream used for very sparse eyebrows in need of heavier coverage.
brow gel	A makeup product specifically designed to work like a hair gel; it holds the brows in position and provides them with a beautiful, long-lasting, finished look.
brow pencils	Similar to an eyeliner pencil and are used to fill in sparse areas, define the brow, or completely re-create a brow.
brow shadows	Also known as *brow powders*; used for creating a soft-looking eyebrow; they are applied with an angled brow brush.
brow stencils	Cut outs of various eyebrow shapes to guide the shaping of eyebrows, the removal of stray hairs, and the application of product.
close-set eyes	Eyes that are separated from one another by less than one eye width.

Chapter Glossary *(continued)*

cream shadows	Shadows that are lighter than stick shadows and do not dry to a powder.
cream-to-powder shadows	Shadows that begin as a smoothly blending cream and then dry as a light powder.
deep-set eyes	Eyes that are recessed deep into the eye socket, creating a sunken-in appearance.
even-set eyes	Eyes that are perfectly balanced; the ideal eye shape for any face shape.
eye shadow primer	A product applied beneath eye shadow to create a smooth application base and extend wearability.
eyeliner	A product that is applied directly around the lash line and can completely alter the appearance of any eye.
lip color	Also known as *lipstick*; makeup product that contains pigment, oils, emollients, and waxes to provide color and enhance every set of lips.
lip exfoliants	Cream or gel-based products that contain mild exfoliating agents such as salt, sugar, or microbeads to gently slough off the superficial surface of dead skin cells on the lips.
lip gloss	A lip product that provides the lips with moisture, shine, and even color; it can be worn alone or over lipstick.
lip liner	A makeup product intended to fill uneven areas on the outer edges of the lips to define their shape.
lip primer	Foundation for the lips; it is designed to fill in small cracks, add moisture, and create a smooth, full appearance prior to the application of lip color and other lip products.
liquid eyeliner	A fluid liquid makeup that comes in a tube much like a mascara container and that is applied with a very fine-tip brush.
mascara	Product that comes in a tube and is applied with a wand that has a spiral brush attached to the end; it will instantly enhance the lashes by making them appear darker, longer, and thicker.
pencil eyeliner	A firm or soft pencil used to draw an even line around the eye.
polymers	Chemical compounds formed by combining a number of small molecules (monomers) into long chain-like structures; they are used to deliver ingredients and hold products together.
powder shadow	Either pressed or loose powder that is packed with pigment.
round eyes	Lovely large circles; they are also classified as protruding or bulging eyes.
silicones	Synthetic compounds used in cosmetics as adhesives and lubricants. Oil that is chemically combined with silicon and oxygen and leaves a noncomedogenic, protective film on the surface of the skin.

Chapter Glossary *(continued)*

small eyes	Eyes that should be made to look larger.
stick shadows	Cream shadows in a stick form.
threading	Also known as *banding*; a Middle Eastern hair removal technique using cotton thread that is twisted and rolled along the surface of the skin, entwining hair in the thread and lifting it out of the follicle.
white eyeliner	A product used to line the lash area in order to define the eye and increase the size of the eyeball itself.
wide-set eyes	Eyes set farther than one eye width apart.

Chapter 9 The Everyday Application

Chapter Outline

Learning Objectives

After completing this chapter, you will be able to:

- ✓ **LO1** List all tools and products needed for a basic everyday makeup application.
- ✓ **LO2** List alternative tools and products that may be used for an everyday application.
- ✓ **LO3** Perform an everyday makeup application.

Key Terms

Page number indicates where in the chapter the term is used.

concealer wheels
pg. 195

harmonize
pg. 200

nasolabial folds
pg. 199

Career Profile

Peggy Sue Ruelke is a cosmetologist, RN, makeup artist, fashion photographer, educator, and owner of www.perspectivephotography.com. Her work and her many accomplishments have earned her the title of a true transformational artist.

The world of beauty is forever changing, and Peggy Sue continually finds herself at the forefront of the industry. Whether she is behind the scenes applying makeup or behind the camera transforming her clients, makeup remains her passion. She strives to give her clients a unique experience and to open up a whole new world for them.

"In the beginning of my career, I made sure every client, even those who were just there for a haircut, had makeup on before she left. Ironically, I developed a loyal clientele fairly quickly because my clients were attracted to my passion for transformational work.

"My love for learning has helped me integrate my cosmetology knowledge with a holistic approach. I was inspired to pursue a career as a registered nurse in the mental health field, as well as working with laser technology in a medi-spa. Ultimately, I was able to connect with people and create a look that empowered individuals to bring forth their personal beauty.

"I live on the beautiful Big Island of Hawaii with my husband Rick, and I am also a director for Focus International Model & Talent Agency where I do portfolios for aspiring models and actors and train potential makeup artists working in the fashion industry. Makeup is and will continue to be part of my practice in achieving a total look.

"I believe that opportunities arise around every corner. In the beginning of my career, I worked countless hours in the fashion industry for free to build relationships and master my skills. Some of the fundamental characteristics needed are passion, creativity, flexibility, efficiency, and timing. Being open and receptive to what life offers will open many wonderful and exciting doors to a variety of careers in the beauty industry.

This is the first of several chapters that direct you to use the information about color theory, tools, facial shapes and features, concealer, and foundation that you have learned in Chapters 1 through 8. It is time to place your book to the side and begin your first work of art.

The Professional Everyday Makeup Application is a basic, simple makeup application suited for every age, skin type, and individual. The aim is to create a perfectly crafted look using minimal tools, products, and time. The everyday application is the makeup artist's quick fix for every face.

One of the greatest challenges to mastering makeup artistry is the absence of unbreakable rules. With every makeup client, the makeup artist must think in an original and creative way, using core knowledge and applying it to the individual situation. In other words, use your knowledge of color theory, your tools, and facial shapes to create your masterpiece on the canvas that you are given. Every client will be different, and no two makeup applications will ever be exactly the same. Keep this in mind as you proceed through this chapter.

The procedure that appears at the end of this chapter addresses every aspect of a daily, basic makeup application; however, you can use other methods to get similar results. With practice, you will use your growing creative abilities to develop a personal style for the everyday application.

WHY STUDY EVERYDAY APPLICATION?

Makeup artists should study and have a thorough understanding of the everyday makeup application because:

- An everyday makeup application will serve as a foundation for all other makeup applications.
- Everyday makeup applications are the most frequently requested makeup services.
- Having confidence and skill with the everyday application will improve your confidence and creativity during other types of applications.

TOOL CHECKLIST

Before you begin, you will need to be completely prepared with all necessary tools and supplies. As you are aware from previous chapters, the list of makeup supplies is extensive. The objective of the everyday application is to keep it simple; therefore, the following tool checklist is as simple as it can be.

© iStockphoto/Daniel Bendjy

Brushes

As your experience and expertise grow, you will acquire a personal preference for certain brush types. Over time, your collection of brushes is likely to grow to an impressive number.

For this application, seven essential brushes are needed.

- Concealer brush
- Blush brush
- Powder brush
- Eye fluff brush
- Eye contour brush
- Eye blender brush (larger eye fluff brush)
- Eyebrow brush (you can substitute a disposable mascara wand)

Utensils

This utensils list consists of those items that are needed to help you do your job in a clean, efficient, and effective manner.

- Eyelash curler
- Pencil sharpener
- Cape
- Neck strip or clean towel for draping
- Headband or hair clip
- Tweezers
- Brush cleaner
- Hand sanitizer

Single-Use Items

The following disposables are mandatory for every makeup artist's kit. These items should never be reused and are to be discarded immediately after use. They are inexpensive items that can be purchased in large quantities so that there is never a need to consider reusing them.

- Disposable lip brush (minimum of two)
- Disposable mascara wands (minimum of three)
- Sponges
- Tissues
- Cotton pads for cleansing

PRODUCT CHECKLIST

Your product collection will expand very quickly. The list below is a basic list. For the everyday application, it can consist of core neutral colors that are suitable for any skin color, eye color, and age.

Foundation. An expert makeup artist knows that the area requiring the largest product selection is foundation because you never know what skin tone you will be working with. For a successful makeup application, it is critical to match your client's skin tone with an appropriate foundation color.

Eye color. The second category of makeup that can require a wide array of choices is eye color. Neutral tones—brown, beige, and champagne—are the best and easiest choice for a beginning makeup artist. The desire for sophisticated individuality, even in a basic everyday makeup look, is the norm for today's clients.

Your professional eye makeup selection, even a basic beginning kit, should also include a small palette of browns, blues, greens, and plums. An everyday look does not always need to be neutral. Although many clients will be looking for a simple, natural look, they might also want a bit of added color to bring attention to their brightest feature: their eyes. Times change, styles change, seasons change, and people change; *natural* does not always mean *neutral.*

Take a moment right now and look at the women in your classroom or workplace. How many different shadow colors do you see? A professional makeup artist is flexible and open-minded. Communicate with your client to determine her desired look and her individual flare. Use your creative abilities even in an application for a simple everyday look.

The beauty profession has boomed to such an extent that what was once considered the "natural" look has progressed from a no-color or minimal-color makeup application to a healthy, minimal color application with a splash of color to accent the individual client's features (**Figure 9–1**). A splash of color is most easily accomplished by accenting the natural color of the eyes. This is done either by enhancing the natural eye color or by intensifying the natural eye color. Enhancing eye color means choosing a shadow color that is analogous to (i.e., similar to) the client's eye color (**Figure 9–2**). Intensifying eye color means choosing a shadow color that is complementary to (i.e., opposite to) the client's eye color (**Figure 9–3**). ✓ LO1

▲ Figure 9–1 **Natural makeup application.**

▲ Figure 9–2 **Enhancing the natural eye color and makeup application.**

▲ Figure 9–3 **Intensifying eye color using colors that are complementary to the client's eye color.**

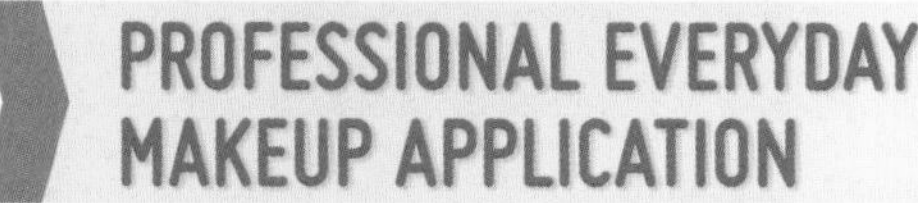

SEE PAGE 197

ALERNATIVES FOR THE EVERYDAY APPLICATION

As mentioned above, there are always alternative ways to perform basic makeup techniques. The technique you use is completely dependent upon your personal preferences and your client's individual features.

As you recall from Chapter 5, Color Theory, analogous colors are located directly next to each other on the color wheel. Complementary colors are located directly across from each other on the color wheel.

Brush Alternatives

The essential tools of the trade are your brushes. The everyday application uses seven basic brushes. The brush hair, ferrule, and handle vary from one brush to the next. Your choices will depend on you, and will very likely change as your skill and experience changes (**Figure 9–4**).

© ingret/www.Shutterstock.com

▲ Figure 9–4 **The essential tools of the trade are your brushes.**

The eye fluff brush comes in different types, with slight variations in the length of the brush hairs and how compact they are. Some makeup artists prefer a short hair, firm-bristled fluff; others prefer slightly longer hairs, which are less firm, softer, and fluffier.

If you choose to use dark shadow color as eyeliner, you will need to add an eyeliner brush to your tools as well (**Figure 9–5**).

© Milady, a part of Cengage Learning. Photograpy by Visual Recollection.

▲ Figure 9–5 **Eyeliner brush.**

Single-Use Alternatives

Single-use tools are the easiest way to keep the work environment clean and to prevent the spread of bacteria between clients and between products (**Figure 9–6**). Application techniques and the end result may differ from brush application, but single-use tools eliminate the need to worry about cross-contamination, the spreading of germs from one person or product to another.

© Milady, a part of Cengage Learning. Photograpy by Visual Recollection.

▲ Figure 9–6 **Various disposable applicators.**

Single-Use Sponges

Single-use sponges are excellent for applying and spreading foundation. They deliver a smooth, sheer application, and they can also be used to apply concealer and powder.

For the application of concealer, remove product with a spatula and place the product onto a palette. Tap the sponge into the product and apply it to the necessary areas (**Figure 9–7**).

For the application of powder, sprinkle or scrape powder onto a palette. Press the sponge into the powder and tap off any excess. Press the sponge onto the face using a firm, rolling motion. Use a clean powder fluff brush in a downward motion to remove excess product and create a polished, matte appearance.

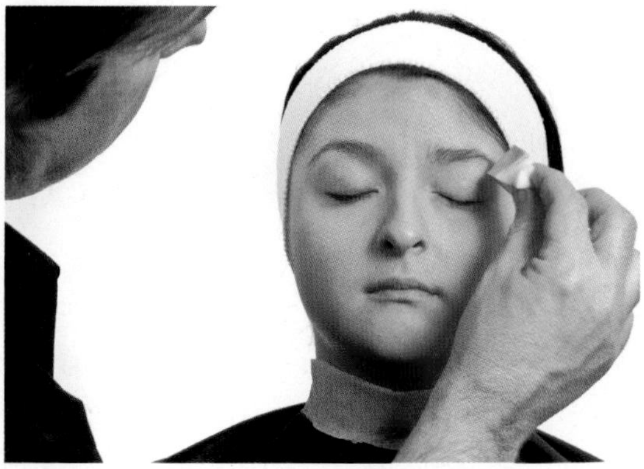

▲ Figure 9–7 **Application of concealer with a disposable sponge.**

Single-Use Eye Shadow Applicators

Single-use or disposable shadow applicators can be used for the application of eye shadow and for blending (**Figure 9–8**). They can also be used to apply lipstick.

▲ Figure 9–8 **Various disposable eye shadow applicators.**

Product Alternatives

The everyday application described in Procedure 9–1 provides makeup professionals with a a guideline pertaining to products. In many cases there are alternatives that can also be used.

Foundation

Liquid foundation is the most versatile foundation and is suited for all skin types. Cream foundation provides heavier coverage and added moisture for drier skin types. Both types should be a staple in your toolbox.

Concealer

Concealer is not always necessary for an everyday application, but some women will not leave the house without it. The objective for these clients is still a natural, basic makeup application. Concealer can be applied after the foundation, to target small problem areas.

Concealer wheels contain violet, green, and yellow concealer choices. Each one is effective for concealing specific problem areas such as blemishes, dark circles, mild scars, spots, and diffused redness.

Eyeliner

Use the darker shadow as eyeliner as an alternative to eyeliner pencil. This guarantees that your color choices are harmonious and replaces the need for an eyeliner pencil. Just be sure to use an eyeliner brush for application. Scrape a small amount of product onto a palette. Begin the application at the inner area of the eye and work toward the outer corner (**Figure 9–9**). LO2

SPECIAL CONSIDERATIONS

Regardless of clients' age, skin color, skin type, or ethnicity, the purpose of the everyday application is to create a fresh, natural appearance with an individual flare. No two people look exactly alike, and no two makeup applications should be exactly alike. Nevertheless, the overall objective still remains the same.

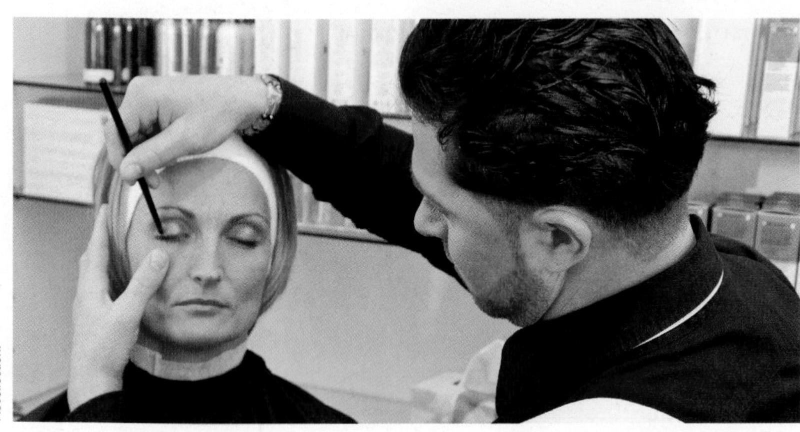

Figure 9–9 Using dark eye shadow as eyeliner.

Special consideration needs to be given to clients with blemishes, pigmentation conditions, scars, or permanent, diffused redness. These clients require simple steps to cover, conceal, or even skin tone. You can refer to Chapter 7, Creating the Canvas, for more specific details.

A quick application of an appropriate concealer is the perfect fix for blemishes and scars on any area of the face. Pigmentation variation can be evened with concealer and/or a heavier foundation. Mild, diffused redness is easily evened with a slightly heavier cream foundation. For more prominent redness, especially in the case of rosacea, a light application of green concealer will neutralize the redness.

Other factors that affect a makeup application are the client's daily activities and place of employment. (This information is obtained during the consultation.) For example, a client who works in a retail store will most likely be comfortable wearing more makeup than a client who is a personal trainer and spends her day in a health club.

Everyday means just that: everyday. The everyday makeup application is a basic application that is quick and simple and gives your client a healthy, natural look. Remember, the word natural does not necessarily mean neutral. In fact, the word *natural* can have different meanings for different people. A thorough consultation with your client will allow you to determine *her* definition of the word natural.

You are the artist. Your artistic abilities, your knowledge of color and facial features, and your expertise will guide you in creating basic everyday applications that are unique to each client. The everyday application might also be a look that your clients want to re-create each day at home.

Procedure 9-1 The Professional Everyday Makeup Application

Implements and Materials

You will need all of the following implements, materials, and supplies:

Brushes

- ☐ Blush brush
- ☐ Concealer brush
- ☐ Eye blender brush (larger eye fluff brush)
- ☐ Eyebrow brush
- ☐ Eye contour brush
- ☐ Eye fluff brush
- ☐ Powder brush

Utensils

- ☐ Eyelash curler
- ☐ Headband or hair clip
- ☐ Makeup cape
- ☐ Makeup chair
- ☐ Makeup palette
- ☐ Neck strip or clean towel for draping
- ☐ Pencil sharpener

Single-use Items

- ☐ Cotton pads for cleansing (optional)
- ☐ Cotton swabs
- ☐ Lip brushes (minimum of two)
- ☐ Mascara wands (minimum of three)
- ☐ Shadow applicators
- ☐ Spatulas
- ☐ Sponge wedges
- ☐ Tissues

Products

- ☐ Blush/cheek colors
- ☐ Brush cleaner
- ☐ Concealers
- ☐ Eyebrow pencils
- ☐ Eyeliner pencils
- ☐ Eye shadow colors
- ☐ Facial moisturizer foundations
- ☐ Hand sanitizer
- ☐ Lip pencils/lip liners
- ☐ Lip colors
- ☐ Mascara
- ☐ Mild facial cleanser
- ☐ Powders
- ☐ Toner for drier skin

Preparation

- Perform

PROCEDURE 7-1 PRE-SERVICE SEE PAGE 144

Procedure

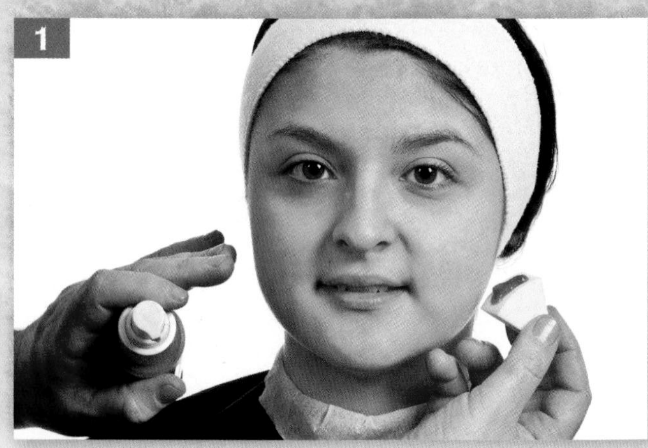

1 Apply cleanser to the client's face. This step can be avoided if your client is instructed to arrive with a clean face.

Procedure 9-1 *(continued)*

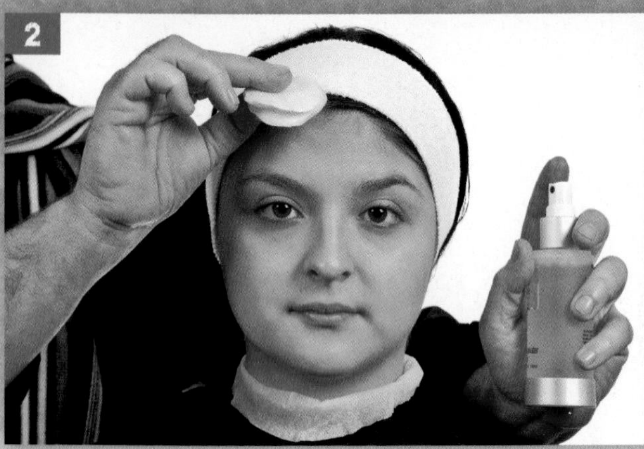

2 Remove cleanser with damp cotton pads. Follow cleansing with an application of toner on a cotton pad. Pat the cotton pad around the entire face, the neck, and even the décolleté if exposed. This removes any excess cleansing product and balances the skin for application of a moisturizer.

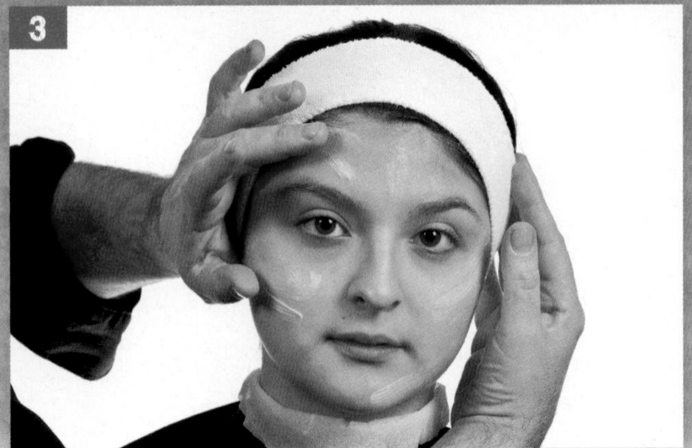

3 Apply skin-specific moisturizer and spread it in upward and outward motions.

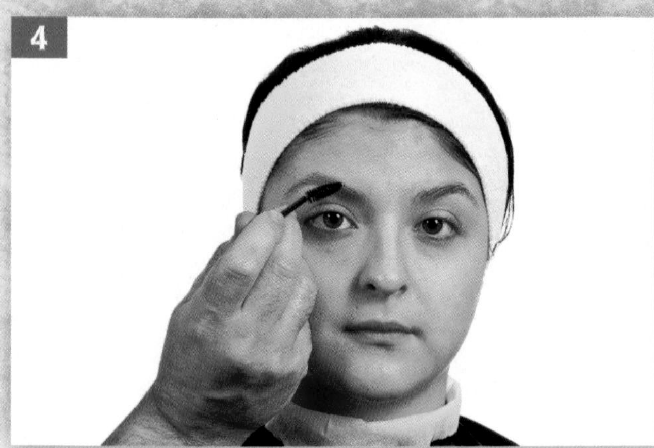

4 Groom eyebrows. Eyebrow shaping and tweezing is discussed in Chapter 8, Facial Features. Use an eyebrow brush or disposable mascara wand to brush the eyebrows into a groomed shape. Remove any stray hairs with tweezers.

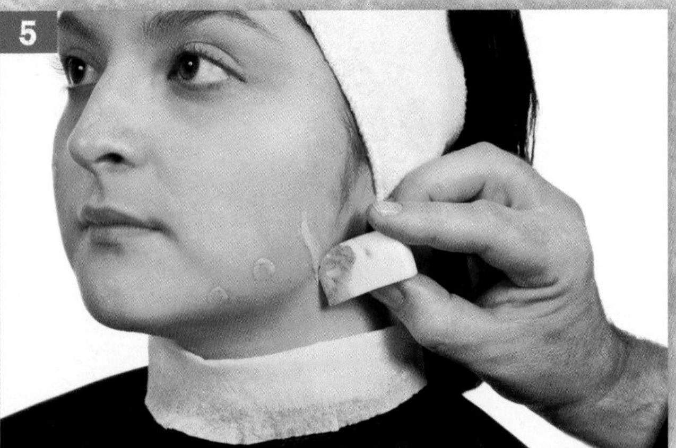

5 Apply foundation. Choose the foundation color and type best suited for your client's skin. The proper foundation will blend from the jawline to the neck.

6 Remove foundation from its container and place it on a palette. Apply a dot of foundation to the forehead, cheeks, and chin.

7 Blend in an upward and outward motion.

SERVICE TIP

Blending with a sponge delivers a sheer application. Blending with clean fingertips delivers a fuller application and more coverage.

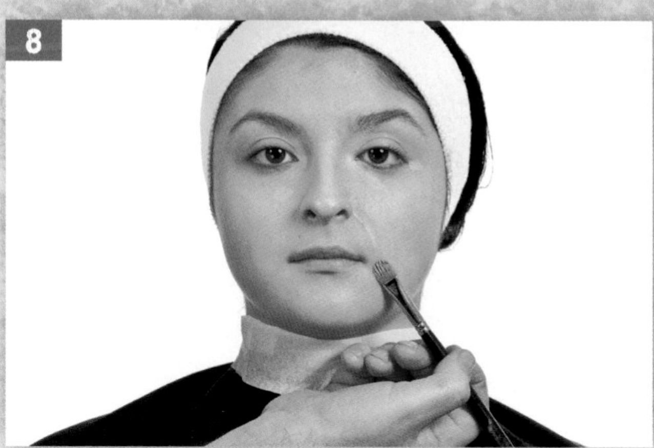

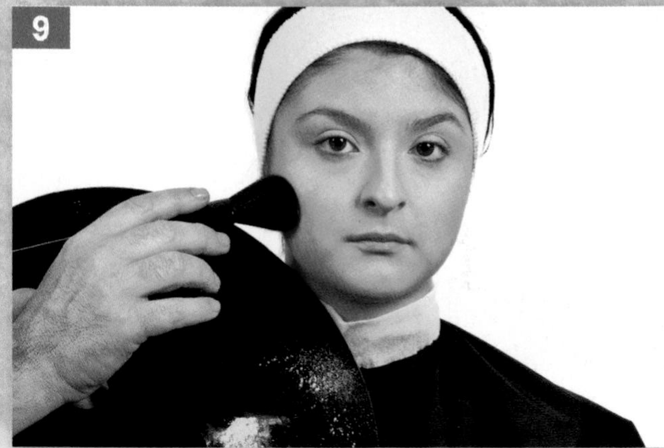

8 Apply concealer. (For a basic everyday application, concealer may not be necessary.) Select the concealer type and color appropriate for the client's skin. Remove a small amount of concealer from the container with a disposable spatula. Using a concealer brush, apply a small amount of concealer to areas of concern, such as under-eye circles, blemishes, pigmented spots, areas of redness, and nasolabial folds, the lines between the corners of the nose and the mouth. Blend well.

9 Apply powder. Powder can be shaken or scraped from its container onto a palette or tissue. Apply powder in a downward motion using the large fluff powder brush. A downward motion will brush fine facial hairs downward and make them disappear.

SERVICE TIP

As a rule of thumb, concealer should not be applied to more than 20 percent of the face.

Procedure 9-1 *(continued)*

10 Apply eye shadow color. For a basic everyday application, two shadow colors can be sufficient. Choose two complementary colors, one lighter than the other.

11 Using a brow fluff brush, apply the lighter color of eye shadow from the lash line to the brow, creating an even wash of highlight.

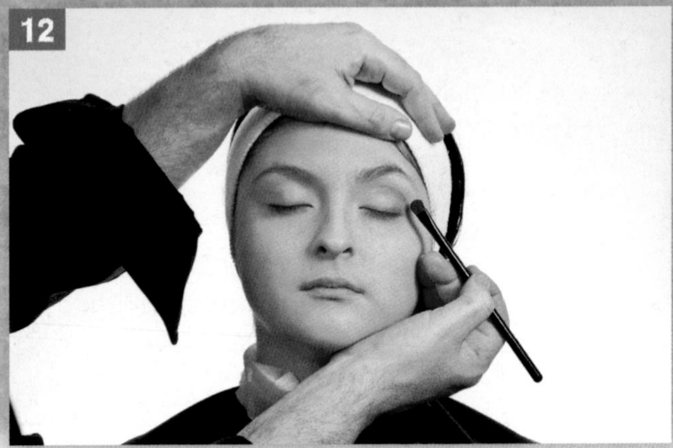

12 Using the eye contour brush, apply the darker of the two eye shadow colors in a sideways "V" shape, three-quarters of the way across the crease line and half-way across the lower lid.

13 Use a larger eye shadow fluff brush to blend the colors.

SERVICE TIP

Blend, blend, and blend. Think of a rainbow. No matter how hard you look, you can never see where one color stops and another one starts. This same visual experience should apply to all makeup applications. Colors should **harmonize**, which is to gently blend from one to another without a line of demarcation.

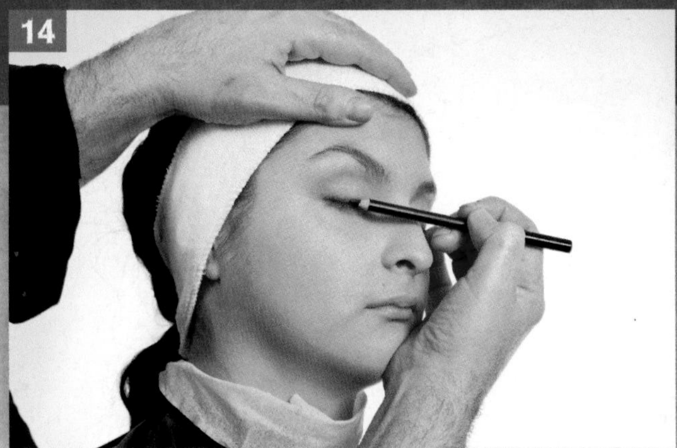

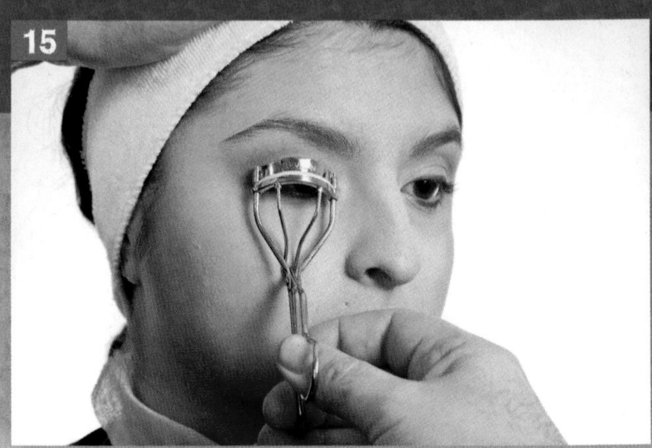

14 Apply eyeliner. Choose an eye pencil color that harmonizes with the chosen shadow colors. Be sure to sharpen it prior to each use. Hold the eyelid taut. Begin at the outer corner of the eye and apply the eyeliner in short, feather-like strokes across the upper lash line. Use the same technique to apply eyeliner across the outer half of the lower lash line.

15 Curl eyelashes. Use a clean lash curler and gently grasp lashes as close to the lash line as possible. Crimp the lashes two to three times as you work from the lash line to the ends of the lashes to create a natural bend.

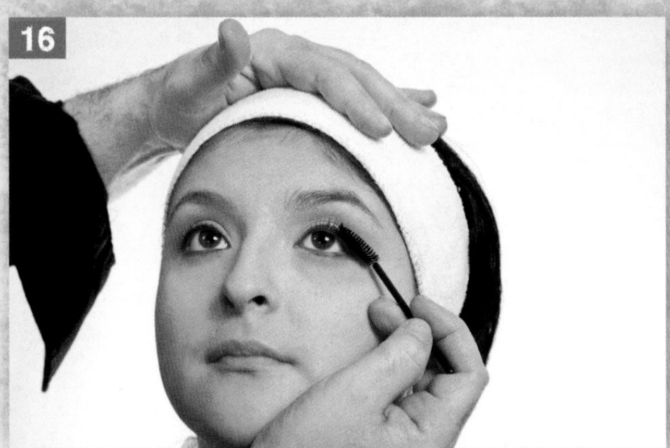

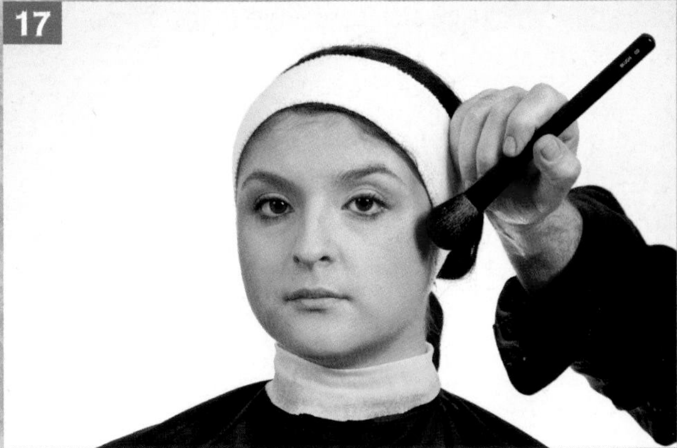

16 Apply mascara. Insert a disposable mascara wand into a tube of mascara. Wipe excess product from the tip and edges of the wand. Starting beneath the lash line, apply mascara to the upper lashes, gently rocking from side to side and rolling the wand upward to separate the lashes. If more product is needed, dispose of the wand and use a new one.

17 Apply blush. Using a blush brush, apply powder in a "C" shape from the temples to the cheek. Begin at the temple and continue in a small, downward circular motions. Complete the blush application by blending with a small amount of powder on a powder fluff brush.

Procedure 9-1 *(continued)*

18 Apply lip liner. Choose a lip pencil that closely resembles the color of the lipstick being used. For a basic everyday look, the lip liner and lipstick should match. Sharpen the pencil for a clean tip. Begin by drawing a small line along the edge, in the middle of the bottom lip.

Did You Know?

Blush wears away first from the area of lightest application. If you start a blush application closest to the nose and work outward to the cheeks, by the end of the day all that will remain are two rosy apples!

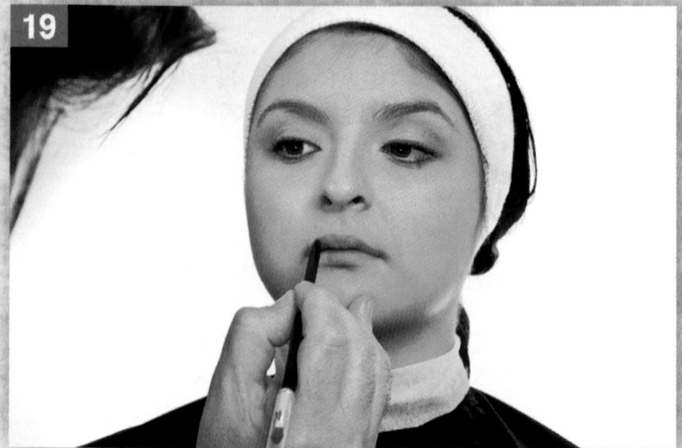

19 Draw a bow along the outside edge of the upper lip. Using short strokes connect the center lines to the corners of the mouth on the top and then the bottom.

SERVICE TIP

There should be a minimum of two finger-widths distance between the side of the nose and the blush application, and the blush should not extend lower than the bottom of the nose line.

SERVICE TIP

Fill in the entire lip with lip liner to keep lip color lasting for hours.

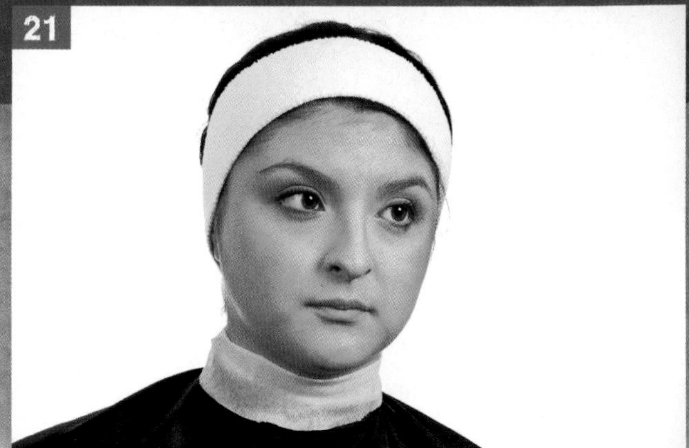

20 Apply lipstick. Choose a lip color appropriate to the client. Remove a small amount of lipstick from the tube with a spatula and place it on a palette. Using a lip brush, apply lipstick to the entire lip area.

21 The finished Everyday Application. ✓ LO3

SERVICE TIP

A perfectly "pouty" lip is quick and easy to create.

- Line the lips and fill in ONLY the upper lip with lip liner.
- Apply lipstick to entire lip area.
- Apply a light color or frosty lip gloss over the entire bottom lip ONLY.

Instant Perfect Pout!

Sherry Weizchowski, Licensed Esthetician, Makeup Artist, NY

Post-Service

- Complete

PROCEDURE **7-2** POST-SERVICE SEE PAGE 148

Review Questions

1. List the seven brushes needed for an everyday makeup application.
2. What eye-color palettes should be included in your makeup selection for an everyday look?
3. What is the objective of the everyday application?
4. List the necessary utensils for the everyday application.
5. Which product may not be necessary for a basic everyday application?
6. When do special considerations for the everyday application need to be given?
7. If extra mascara is needed during the application, how many times can mascara wands be reused?
8. For the everyday application, where should the application of blush begin?
9. To avoid cross-contamination of lip and eye pencils, what should you do prior to using one?
10. What is the purpose of applying powder in a downward motion?
11. To create a natural bend in eyelashes, how many times should the lashes be crimped with a lash curler?
12. What is the minimum number of eye shadow colors that can be used to create an everyday application?
13. Where is it recommended that the application of eyeliner begin?
14. For an everyday look, what is the best choice of color for a lip liner?

Chapter Glossary

concealer wheels	Compacts that contain violet, green, and yellow concealer choices, which are effective for concealing specific problem areas such as blemishes, dark circles, and diffused redness.
harmonize	To gently blend one color to another without a line of demarcation or dramatic contrast.
nasolabial folds	The lines extending from the nostrils to the corners of the mouth.

Part 3

Specialty Makeup

Chapter 10 Special Events

Chapter Outline

Learning Objectives

After completing this chapter, you will be able to:

- ☑ **LO1** List tips for photography makeup applications.
- ☑ **LO2** Learn techniques for special looks.
- ☑ **LO3** Identify different needs for brides at different times of day.
- ☑ **LO4** Create a smoky eye look.
- ☑ **LO5** Create a pouty lip.
- ☑ **LO6** Create a defined cheek and jawbone look.
- ☑ **LO7** Create a Candy Apple Glazed lip look.
- ☑ **LO8** Create a wedding makeup application.

Key Terms

Page number indicates where in the chapter the term is used.

afternoon bride
pg. 214

beach bride
pg. 215

candy apple glaze
pg. 212

chiseled cheek
pg. 212

evening bride
pg. 215

morning bride
pg. 214

special occasions
pg. 210

wedding consultation
pg. 213

Career Profile

Catherine Lavoie

Over the course of her career, Catherine Lavoie has created a film portfolio that is virtually unsurpassed. Working on dozens of A-List films, she has developed a true understanding of the way makeup and film work together to create innovation. One of Catherine's aspirations is to elevate makeup artistry to the level of other art forms. She continues to work on makeup for films, maintaining and furthering her own career as she participates in the film industry.

"I have been working as a makeup artist for more than 15 years in the Montreal area. I started out doing makeup for a small independent theatrical company as a sideline while I finished my film studies at Concordia University. After graduating, I realized that mixing the two art forms, makeup and cinema, would be the perfect road to follow. After 8 years of hard work, I finally had my big break. I landed a makeup position on the movie *The Whole Nine Yards* where I worked with Key Makeup Artists Clair Blondel and Gerald Quist. I was assigned to do makeup for Mathew Perry, Kevin Pollack, and Michael Clark Duncan.

"This officially marked the start of my career in the movie and TV-series business. I now have more than 40 Movies and TV series under my belt, both Canadian and American. Other memorable projects I have worked on include, *The Greatest Game Ever Played*, *The Fountain*, *The Aviator*, *300*, *See Jane Date*, and *St. Urbain's Horseman*.

"In the past few years, I have also started to make my mark in the editorial world and have had my work published in magazines such as *FHM Magazine* (UK), *Make-Up Artist Magazine*, *Canadian Hairdresser Magazine*, *Plaid Magazine*, *LOULOU*, and *Summum*.

"When I began my career, the Internet was just taking hold, and there were not a lot of makeup schools or books. What was available to me at the time was very expensive. So I had to be street-savvy and resourceful.

"Makeup artistry is ever-changing, and you are only as good as your last job. Creating and maintaining good business relationships is very important and will determine your future in the fashion world and the film business. Don't forget that hundreds of young aspiring makeup artists are graduating and starting to build their careers, so keep your strengths in mind and build on them."

Each of the techniques in this chapter will guide you to create individual looks for clients who want something different and unique for their special occasions. The easy part is that each technique is easy and repeatable; the exciting part is that each technique can be altered, tweaked, and personalized by both you and your client. These are only a few of the many different special techniques and makeup looks that exist. This chapter contains several of the most common and most sought-after looks, each of which can serve as a basis upon which to build other looks.

As your skills and experience grow, your ability to create and perfect amazing, unique looks will become part of your professional reputation. In the world of makeup, there is no one way to create a particular look; successful makeup artists take advantage of this fact and use their creativity to master many unique looks for every type of occasion, all with a unique flair of style and finesse.

WHY STUDY SPECIAL EVENTS?

Makeup artists should study and have a thorough understanding of special events because:

- Once they are mastered, special-event techniques can be altered, tweaked, and personalized by you and your clients to fit any special event.
- Your ability to create and perfect amazing and unique looks for every client will become part of your professional reputation and further your career in makeup artistry.
- Special events can be a fast and fun way to showcase your talent.

PHOTOGRAPHY TIPS

Makeup applications for photography will depend on a number of factors that vary from one event to the next: the time of day the event will be held; whether the event will be held indoors or outdoors; the lighting available at the event venue; and the colors that will be worn by people attending the event. It will take time, experience, and practice to completely grasp every element of special-event makeup; however, a few tips apply to every makeup application that will be photographed.

Light plays an enormous role in an individual's appearance, especially when it comes to makeup. The brighter the light, the more washed-out a makeup application will appear. In such situations, the makeup artist should use more color.

Many cosmetic companies make primers and complete makeup product-lines specifically for photography makeup applications. These products take into account the necessary degree of coverage and pigment.

Matte colors are best suited for high definition (HD) photography and for avoiding reflection from the camera lens and flash. This is true for every cosmetic product used in the application; foundation, powder, shadow, and blush should all be matte. A touch of shimmer in eye shadow is acceptable, but shimmer should not be used for the entire eye application or applied to the entire lid area. (Refer to Chapter 11, The Exciting World of High Fashion and High Definition, for more information about HD.)

Another consideration is that light or pale makeup colors will make an individual appear washed-out in photos. Choose a concealer that is two to three shades lighter than the foundation to create more contrast. Once the foundation is applied, be very sure that all highlights and contours are well blended because the camera will pick up the smallest details. Check that foundation is blended to the neck and chest and is blotted prior to the application of powder to avoid creasing or caking with facial movements.

White eyeliner or cream-color eye pencil can be added on the inner eyelid to help to brighten the eye and accentuate the eye color.

To fully understand the effects of lighting on your product choices for photograph-ready applications, you will need training, experience, practice, and a well-developed understanding of the color wheel. Your skills will develop over time; eventually, you will be able to prepare for and perform makeup applications for photography. ✓ **LO1**

SPECIAL LOOKS FOR SPECIAL OCCASIONS

Any occasion can be considered a special occasion, depending upon its meaning to the individual. **Special occasions** include birthdays, anniversaries, reunions, parties, weddings, and even a night out without the kids—any occasion that holds importance to an individual. All such occasions can start with a fabulous makeup look.

This chapter includes step-by-step procedures and suggestions for creating special looks. The looks focus on specific features and can be accomplished quickly, making the overall application appear more special, dramatic, and unique. Each procedure acts as a solid instructional map to guide you from start to finish. Once you perfect the simple steps, you can add creativity and individuality, making each of these procedures your own.

Be sure to follow pre-service and post-service procedures with each application. Proper infection control procedures must be followed for every makeup application, even those that are quick and easy.

This chapter will guide you through technical makeup applications for a dark, smoky eye; the perfect pouty lip; defined, high, chiseled cheekbones; luscious, red candy-apple lips; and various bridal looks. Remember, each procedure is meant to act as a guideline; use your creative talents to turn each look into an individual work of art, and each technique into one of your very own.

Smoky Eyes

The smoky eye is a soft, sultry, sexy makeup application. To avoid creating a raccoon-look, the smoky eye requires attention to detail and careful selection of color. The smoky eye can be paired with natural, flesh-colored lipstick or intensified with deep-red or plum-brown lip shades. There are many variations of a smoky eye, and the look can be subtle or dramatic, depending upon your color choices and the degree of pigment you use.

The smoky eye is requested in varying degrees of intensity and by clients of all ages. It is a very common eye makeup application for evening as well as for runway modeling and high-fashion photography. Prestige cosmetic lines, clothing lines, and accessory companies often seek a sophisticated, sultry look to represent their brand in advertisements. The smoky eye is the perfect solution.

In makeup education, eye makeup classes are very well attended, and the smoky eye is the number one sought-after technique.

HERE'S A TIP

Smoky eyes can be made more subtle by using less pigment or by choosing a dark-brown or medium-brown pigment as opposed to a black pigment.

PROCEDURE **10–1** **SMOKY EYES** SEE PAGE 217

The Perfect Pout

The eyes and the lips are the most unique and identifying factors of an individual face. They are the first two characteristics that people notice when looking at each other, and they are the features that best communicate with the world.

Women often say either that their lips are their favorite facial feature or that they are their least favorite facial feature. Plump, kissable, attractive lips are one of the reasons lipstick was invented. One of the best ways to accentuate the mouth and lips is to create a full, pouty, sultry lip. Many women possess full, plump lips; for those who do not, the illusion of a perfect pout can be created. As a makeup artist, you are likely to find that the perfect pout is desired not only for special events but also, in subtler forms, for everyday wear

Photographs from early times to modern day (especially those taken in the early- to mid-twentieth century) show that the lips have consistently been a featured attraction. In fact, the lips often command the center of attention.

Full, plump lips can belong to any client, at any time, for any occasion, even for everyday. Procedure 10–2, The Perfect Pout, will help you to create attractive, full lips on any client.

PROCEDURE **10–2** **THE PERFECT POUT** SEE PAGE 220

The Defined Cheek

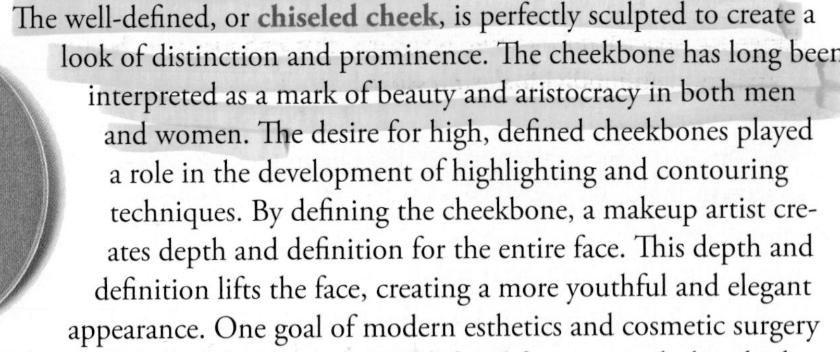

The well-defined, or **chiseled cheek**, is perfectly sculpted to create a look of distinction and prominence. The cheekbone has long been interpreted as a mark of beauty and aristocracy in both men and women. The desire for high, defined cheekbones played a role in the development of highlighting and contouring techniques. By defining the cheekbone, a makeup artist creates depth and definition for the entire face. This depth and definition lifts the face, creating a more youthful and elegant appearance. One goal of modern esthetics and cosmetic surgery is to help clients maintain youthful facial features, including high, defined cheekbones and firm, young-looking skin.

The makeup artist's ability to provide the look of high, defined cheekbones is in high demand for events such as weddings, parties, and reunions; it is in even higher demand for video and photography. Many clients will want to learn to perform this technique for their everyday makeup application so that they, too, can create and sustain a youthful look.

By using the right product to contour and highlight, you can create perfectly defined, chiseled cheekbones on any face. Defined cheeks also add a lift to the entire face and draw attention to the lips and eyes. This technique will help you and your clients create a natural, beautiful look.

PROCEDURE **10-3** **THE DEFINED CHEEK** SEE PAGE 223

Candy Apple Glazed Lips

Again the lips take center-stage. Once you learn to produce a plump, perfect pout, you will now have yet another technique for dramatizing and accentuating a set of lips. **Candy Apple Glaze**, a makeup application that creates the image of a hardened red, large, glossy look, represents an age-old technique that has never lost popularity. The color red has long been a mark of distinction in the makeup profession. It represents power, class, sophistication, authority, confidence, seduction, and drama. Luscious red lips are appropriate for evening events and elegant gatherings, but they can also be created, in a more subtle way, for day wear. They are quite commonly linked to high fashion, photography, marketing of prestige brands of clothing, accessories, and cosmetics, as well as magazines and advertisements.

Shades of red vary from cool to warm and can be made to harmonize with any complexion, clothing, or coloring. Regardless of the occasion or event, many clients want shiny, red, candy-apple lips—with just a few quick steps, any client can have this look. The trick is finding the perfect red for each client. ☑ **LO2**

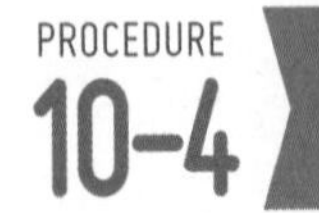

PROCEDURE **10-4** **CANDY APPLE GLAZED LIPS** SEE PAGE 226

WEDDINGS

Weddings are special and exciting occasions that enhance true beauty, self-confidence, and individual expression. Every woman is beautiful in her own way; your job is to use your skills and abilities to magnify that beauty.

You should meet with your wedding clients well in advance of the wedding day. A practice application is necessary (two or three may be better). Try to schedule the first **wedding consultation**, a makeup consultation that focuses on all of the details of the wedding event and reception (including before and after photos, colors, location, time of day, and specific requests of the bride) at least 2 to 3 months in advance of the wedding date. This will guarantee that your client is happy with the colors and techniques you use—and ultimately happy with the entire look. It is very important that the bride be completely satisfied and comfortable with her look on the day of her wedding, the last thing she needs to worry about is her makeup; she has far more important things to think about.

Before you consider specific makeup colors or techniques, a complete consultation with the bride, and even the entire bridal party, is critical. Complete a consultation form and take notes regarding important facts and desires that the bride shares. During the consultation or the trial makeup application, be sure to document all color choices and makeup types that were used in order to ensure a duplicate application on the wedding day. Also during the consultation, instruct the bride to have her brows tweezed and/or waxed for shaping prior to the wedding day.

Since your job is to create the picture-perfect bride, you must be well informed about every aspect of the event. Below is a list of questions you should ask in order to gather the information you need to accomplish your job:

- What overall "look" does the bride want for the event—classic, sophisticated, or glamorous?
- During which season will the wedding take place?
- What time of day will the wedding take place?
- What time of day will the reception take place?
- Is the wedding indoors or outdoors?
- What is the location for formal photos?
- Where will the wedding be held? The reception?
- How big is the room where the wedding will take place?
- How many people are in the bridal party?
- How many guests have been invited to the wedding?
- What colors will the wedding party be wearing? (Consider the color of the bride's gown, the bridesmaids' dresses, the groom's tuxedo, and the groomsmen's tuxedos.)
- What color are the flowers and decoration?

When you are hired to do makeup for an entire bridal party, you can recommend a practice application in advance of the wedding day. However, this is not always possible. To perform last-minute, high-stakes makeup applications, it is important for you to understand different eye shapes, facial features, and color schemes.

All of these factors play a role in the overall look and feel of the entire wedding. Remember that there is a reason the bride chose her gown, her bridesmaids' dresses, her flowers, decorations, location, and time of day. Your job is to take it all into account and make her the perfect centerpiece of the entire event.

Regardless of the details of the wedding itself, remember that the bride not only needs to be beautiful; she also needs to look like herself. You do not want to change her look to such an extent that people do not recognize her, and the bride should not have trouble recognizing herself in photos.

STATE REGULATORY ALERT

If your state allows you to wax or tweeze eyebrows, perform a brow shaping treatment during the bride's initial consultation or trial makeup application. Otherwise, instruct the bride to have her brows groomed well in advance of the wedding day to avoid any lingering redness or irritation on the day of the wedding.

Time of Day

The time of day that the wedding is held will influence the look of the makeup application, especially if the wedding and photography session are outdoors. As the sunlight changes throughout the day, so will the appearance of the makeup application. Even within a few hours, the movement of the sun can alter makeup colors, create shadows, and either enhance color or wash it out. These factors should be taken into consideration during the initial consultation so that they are easily managed throughout the wedding event.

Did You Know?

The way the sunlight changes throughout the day will influence the way that your makeup application appears in photos.

The Morning Bride

Morning weddings call for a soft, fresh, natural look (**Figure 10–1**), and the **Morning Bride**, a bride with a wedding ceremony schedule in the morning hours prior to noon, requires attention to the details of the early-day setting and lighting. The idea is to create the illusion of a well-rested, bright-eyed, refreshed bride. Foundation should be light and sheen, even if full coverage is necessary to even skin tone or cover flaws. Choose natural, warm shades that blend with the bride's skin tone, eye shadows, and lip colors. Choose light eyeliner, preferably a shadow, and accentuate the lash line with dark mascara. Add a few artificial lashes to enhance the eyes without applying a more pigmented liner or shadow.

▲ **Figure 10–1 A morning bride.**

The Afternoon Bride

During the afternoon, the sun is at its peak, where it will cast natural shadows across every face. In addition, afternoon light has an unforgiving blue tinge. The **Afternoon Bride**, a bride with a scheduled wedding ceremony set in the midday hours of noon until 4 p.m., requires attention to the details of the midday hours.

© Stephen Coburn/www.Shutterstock.com

◀ Figure 10–2 **An afternoon Bride.**

© Konrad Bak/www.Shutterstock.com

▲ Figure 10–3 **A dramatic evening bride.**

For this time of day, avoid makeup choices that contain sparkles or sheen, which will reflect natural sunlight. Instead, choose foundation, powder, and blush with a matte finish (**Figure 10–2**).

In harsh afternoon light, dark eye shadow can deepen the look of natural shadows around the eyes. Better choices are a shadow highlight with a slight shimmer (not a frost), along with a contour shade that is matte. Together these two textures will create a bright, accentuated eye without any dark shadows. Use eyeliner with medium color depth, and add a few artificial lashes to further open and accentuate the eyes.

The Evening Bride

The **Evening Bride**, a bride with a wedding ceremony scheduled from late afternoon through the evening hours, from 4 p.m. and later, can more easily pull-off a dramatic makeup application that includes vibrant color choices (**Figure 10–3**). The lighting is lower, and evening warrants a darker, more dramatic look. Flash will most likely be used for photographs, so be sure to focus on definition of the facial features: the cheekbones, eyes, and lips.

Shimmer shadows photograph nicely and are a great choice for evening weddings. Choose rich lip colors with a hint of gloss to create the look of colored glass on the lips. Add bronzer to the neck and décolleté to warm exposed skin. To further dramatize the eyes and create an elegant look, apply several artificial lashes or even a full strip. ☑ **LO3**

Beach Bridal Makeup

The **Beach Bride** is one that has a wedding ceremony scheduled on the sands of a beach near or in close proximity to the water. This wedding with all of the details of its coastal setting—from wind to moisture, sun exposure, and changes of the tide—allows for many acts of nature to play a role in every aspect of the event.

The following are a few makeup tips for beach weddings:

- Choose a lightweight, liquid foundation or airbrush foundation for longer-lasting, very sheer coverage.
- Apply a light application of translucent powder.

- Stick to light colors such as pink, peach, lavender, and sky blue.
- Avoid eyeliner, or use eye shadow to line the eyes for a soft, natural look.
- For clients who are seeking an edgier beach-look, shades of gold, silver, and even varying shades of green and purple are excellent choices.

▲ **Figure 10–4 A beach bride.**

The beach wedding offers the ultimate stress-free escape to warm breezes, maximum sunshine, and sand between the toes. Makeup selections must be based on weather conditions, which are usually quite warm and humid. Choose a lightweight foundation and translucent powder. (If translucent powder is not appropriate for the client's skin tone, choose a color that is a natural match.) Soft browns, peaches, and bronze colors work well for warmer skin tones; lavender, taupe, and pink work well for cool skin tones (**Figure 10–4**). Use a natural, light eyeliner color or use shadow as eyeliner for a delicate, soft eyeliner look.

PROCEDURE 10–5 **BASIC BRIDAL MAKEUP APPLICATION** SEE PAGE 229

Every bride is unique; therefore, every bridal makeup application is unique. However, many of the tips and theories stay the same. Know what your bride wants, but also remember that you are the professional and that you were hired for your skill, advice, and ability to create the beautiful look needed for this truly special occasion. Regardless of all extenuating factors—time of day, lighting, location, or dress colors—every makeup application should be beautiful and timeless, showcasing the bride's natural beauty.

Multiple factors must be considered for each client, occasion, and application. This textbook will help you develop the knowledge, skills, and creativity to meet each client's individual needs and desires. With a trained eye, you will begin to develop your own flare and unique techniques.

Each opportunity to help make a client's occasion unforgettable is a gift; as a makeup artist your profession is full of bountiful gifts.

Procedure 10-1

SMOKY EYES

Implements and Materials

You will need all of the following implements, materials, and supplies:

- **Brushes**
  - ☐ Eyeliner smudge brush
  - ☐ Eye shadow contour brush
  - ☐ Small eye fluff brush
  - ☐ Small, short shadow brush
- **Utensils**
  - ☐ Brush cleaner
  - ☐ Pencil sharpener
  - ☐ Headband or hair clip
  - ☐ Makeup cape
  - ☐ Makeup palette
  - ☐ Neck strip or clean towel for draping
- **Single-use Items**
  - ☐ Shadow applicators
- **Products**
  - ☐ Black eye shadow
  - ☐ Black eyeliner (for a softer look, gray or blue eyeliner can be used)
  - ☐ Black mascara
  - ☐ Brow pencil/powder
  - ☐ Hand sanitizer
  - ☐ Medium-gray eye shadow
  - ☐ Soft gray-blue eye shadow
  - ☐ White or cream eye shadow

Preparation

- Perform

PROCEDURE 7-1 PRE-SERVICE SEE PAGE 144

Procedure

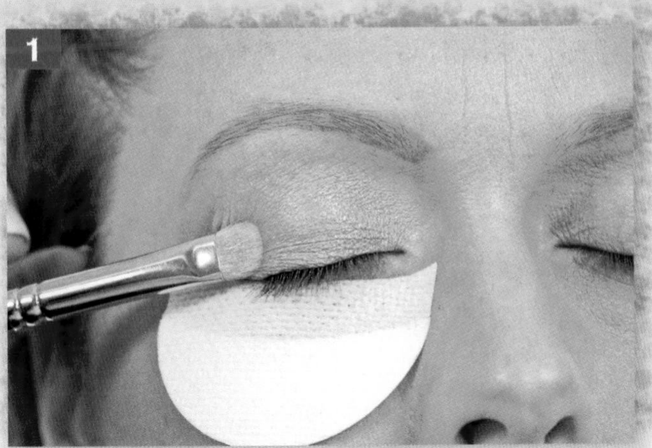

1 Apply white shadow to the base of the eyelid. If you're working with a darker skin tone, you can ensure that colors will remain intense by applying a primer instead.

Procedure 10-1 *(continued)*

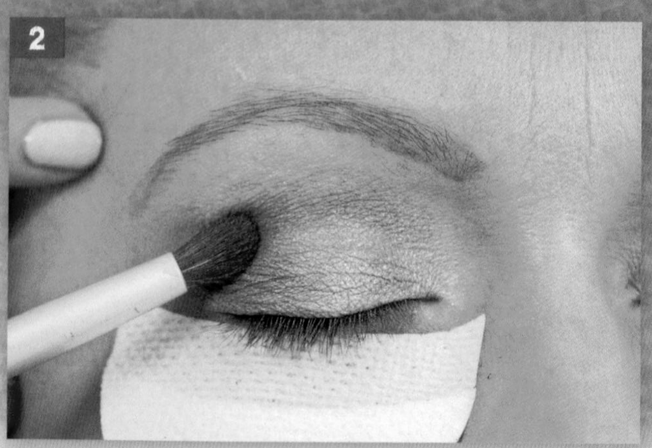

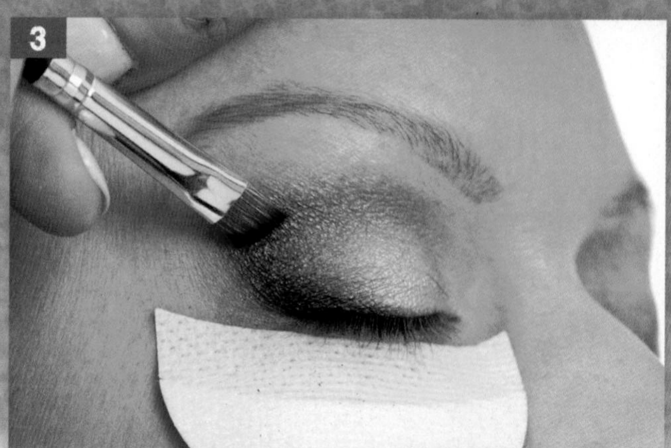

2 Apply soft, blue-gray shadow along crease to the outer corner of the lid, extending slightly beyond the outer corner of the eye.

3 Add black eye shadow to the crease and outer corner of the eye.

4 Sharpen the eyeliner.

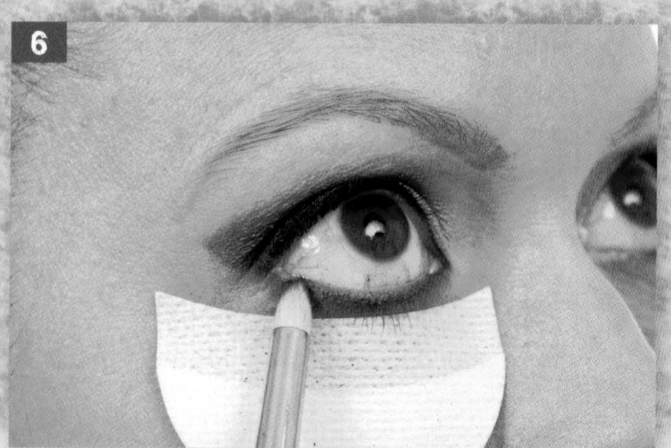

5 Apply black eyeliner in a thin line along the upper lash line. Gently smudge with a brush.

6 Apply soft blue-gray eye shadow along the lower lash line.

7 Apply black eye shadow along the outer corner of the lower lash line.

8 Sharpen the eyeliner.

9 Apply white shadow at the entire inner corner of the eye.

10 Apply white shadow beneath the brow.

11 Be sure that colors are blended well.

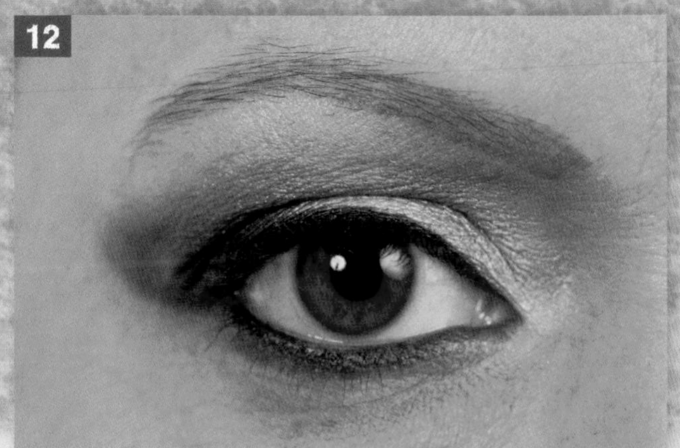

12 The completed smoky eye.

Post-Service ☑ LO4

- Complete

PROCEDURE 7-2 POST-SERVICE SEE PAGE 148

Procedure 10-2
The Perfect Pout

Implements and Materials

You will need all of the following implements, materials, and supplies:

- **Brushes**
  - ☐ See single-use items
- **Utensils**
  - ☐ Headband or hair clip
  - ☐ Makeup cape
  - ☐ Makeup palette
  - ☐ Neck strip or clean towel for draping
  - ☐ Pencil sharpener
- **Single-use Items**
  - ☐ Lip brushes
  - ☐ Cotton pads or cotton puffs
- **Products**
  - ☐ Brush cleaner
  - ☐ Hand sanitizer
  - ☐ Lip exfoliant
  - ☐ Light-colored, frosty lip gloss
  - ☐ Natural-tone, pink/brown lip liners
  - ☐ Natural-tone, pink/brown lip color

Preparation

- Perform

PROCEDURE 7-1 PRE-SERVICE SEE PAGE 144

Procedure

1

1 Apply lip exfoliant and remove with damp cotton.

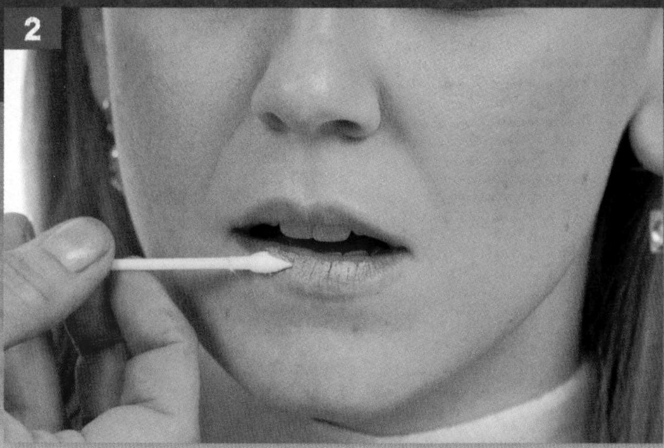

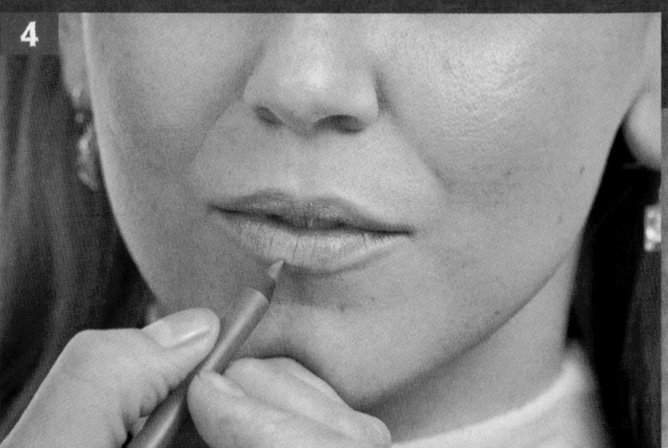

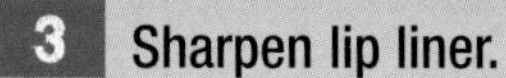

2 Apply lip moisturizer with a disposable applicator.

3 Sharpen lip liner.

4 Draw a small line on the outer edge of the center of the lower lip, and a bow at the outer edge of the top of the upper lip.

5 Connect the lines by carefully lining the entire lips with lip liner.

6 Fill in the upper lip with lip liner.

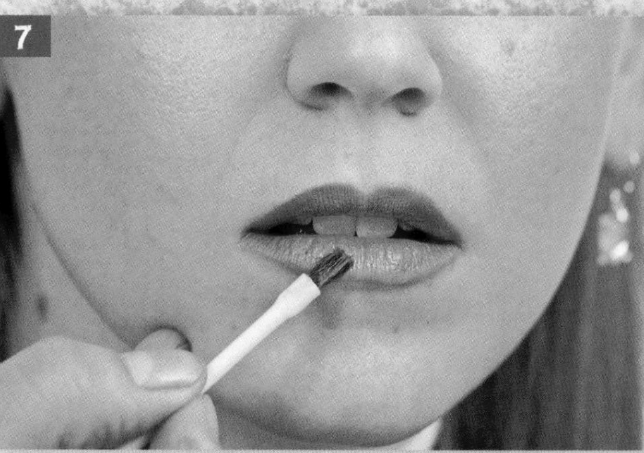

7 Apply lipstick to upper and lower lips with a disposable lip brush.

8 Apply frosted lip gloss to bottom lip only with a disposable lip brush.

Procedure 10-2 *(continued)*

9 The completed perfect pout.

Post-Service ☑ LO5

- Complete

PROCEDURE 7-2 POST-SERVICE SEE PAGE 148

Procedure 10-3 The Defined Cheek

Implements and Materials

You will need all of the following implements, materials, and supplies:

Brushes

- ☐ Blush powder brush
- ☐ Foundation brush
- ☐ Large powder brush/ kabuki brush

Utensils

- ☐ Brush cleaner
- ☐ Headband or hair clip
- ☐ Makeup cape
- ☐ Makeup palette
- ☐ Neck strip or clean towel for draping
- ☐ Pencil sharpener

Single-use Items

- ☐ Sponge wedges

Products

- ☐ Bronzer
- ☐ Foundations
- ☐ Hand sanitizer
- ☐ One shade lighter foundation or concealer
- ☐ Powder two shades darker than foundation
- ☐ Two cheek colors

Preparation

- Perform

PROCEDURE 7-1 PRE-SERVICE SEE PAGE 144

Procedure

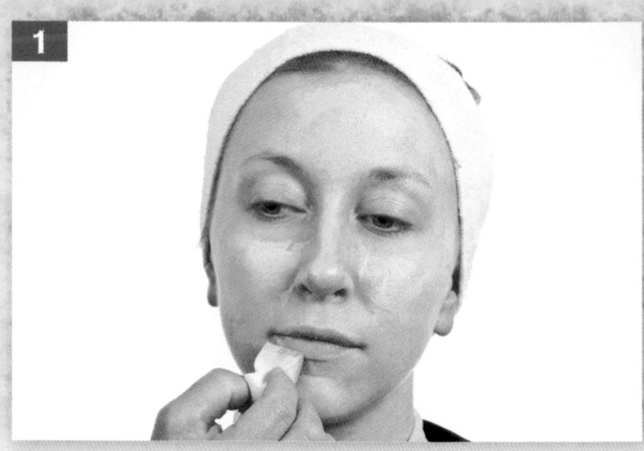

1 Apply appropriate foundation to a clean, moisturized face using a facial sponge.

Procedure 10-3 *(continued)*

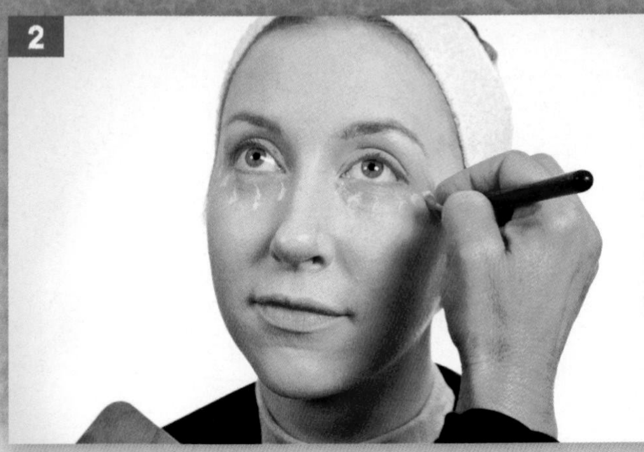

2 Apply foundation or concealer one shade lighter beneath the eyes using a concealer brush.

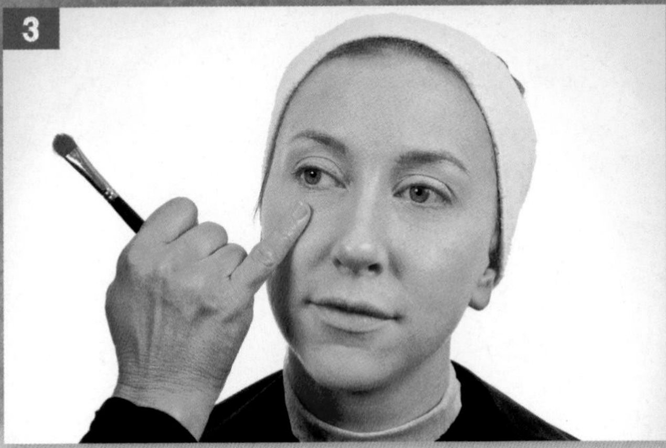

3 Extend and blend highlighter down toward the top of the cheek area.

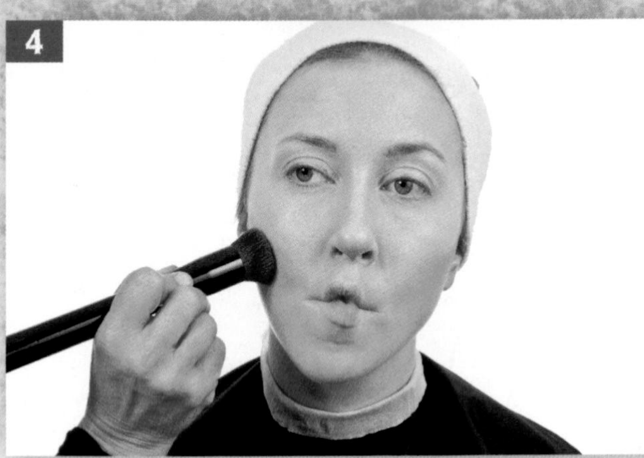

4 Have the client suck her cheeks in. Apply bronzer to the hollow of the cheek with a blush brush.

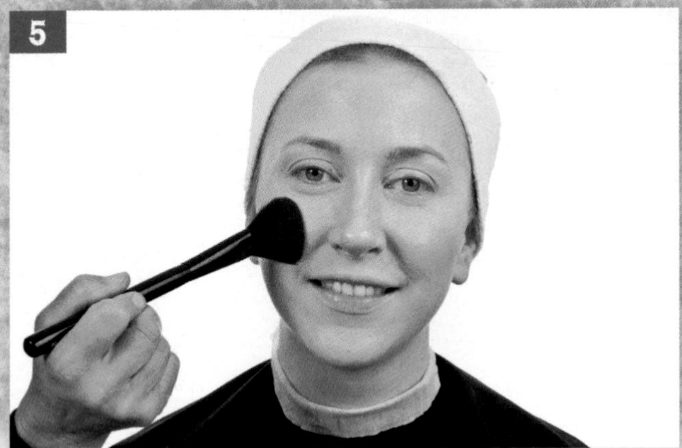

5 Apply cheek color to the apple of the cheek with a blush brush.

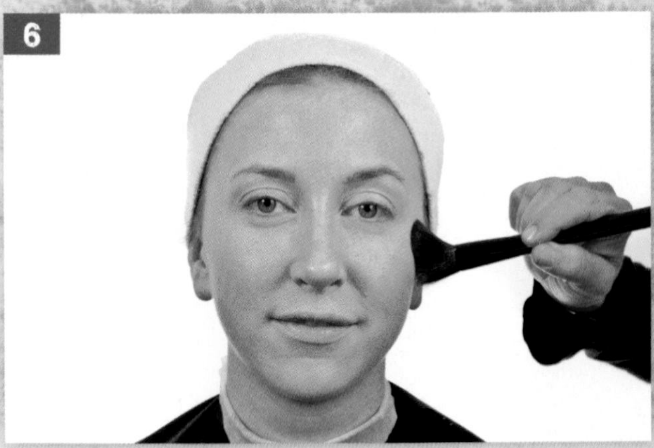

6 Apply highlight cheek color just above the apple of the cheek and sweep outward toward the temple with a blush brush.

7 Apply darker shaded powder under the chin and along the underside of the jawline to create the appearance of a more structured jawbone. Use a large powder brush or a kabuki brush.

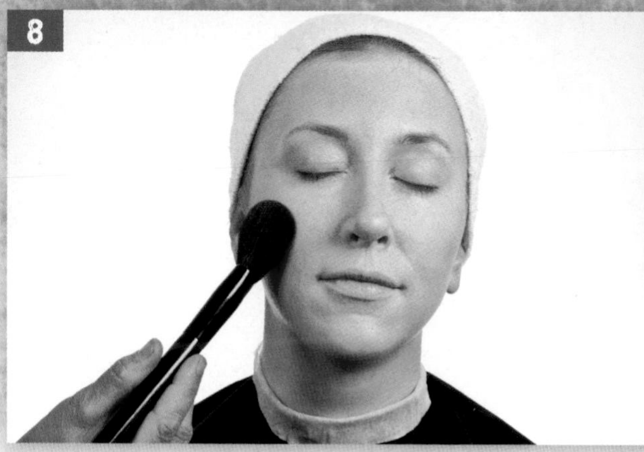

8 Use large powder brush to blend.

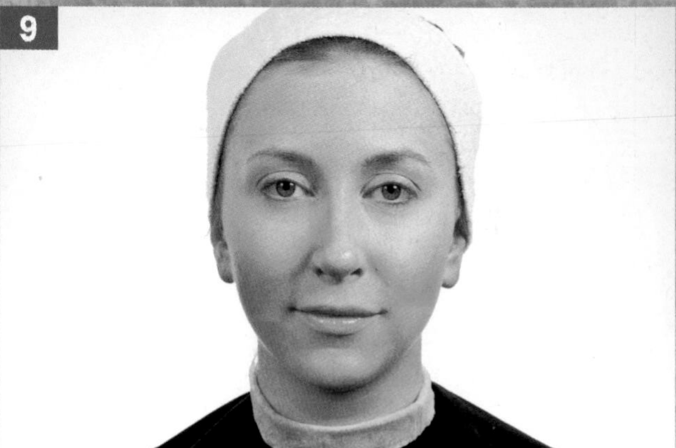

9 The completed defined cheek look.

Post-Service ☑ LO6

- Complete PROCEDURE 7-2 POST-SERVICE SEE PAGE 148

Procedure 10-4
Candy Apple Glazed Lips

Implements and Materials

You will need all of the following implements, materials, and supplies:

Brushes

- ☐ Short-haired, firm lip brush

Utensils

- ☐ Brush cleaner
- ☐ Pencil sharpener
- ☐ Headband or hair clip
- ☐ Makeup cape
- ☐ Makeup palette
- ☐ Neck strip or clean towel for draping

Single-use Items

- ☐ Lip brushes

Products

- ☐ Candy-apple red lip color
- ☐ Candy-apple red lip gloss
- ☐ Candy-apple red lip liner
- ☐ Clear lip lacquer
- ☐ Hand sanitizer
- ☐ Lip primer

Preparation

- Perform

PROCEDURE 7-1 PRE-SERVICE SEE PAGE 144

Procedure

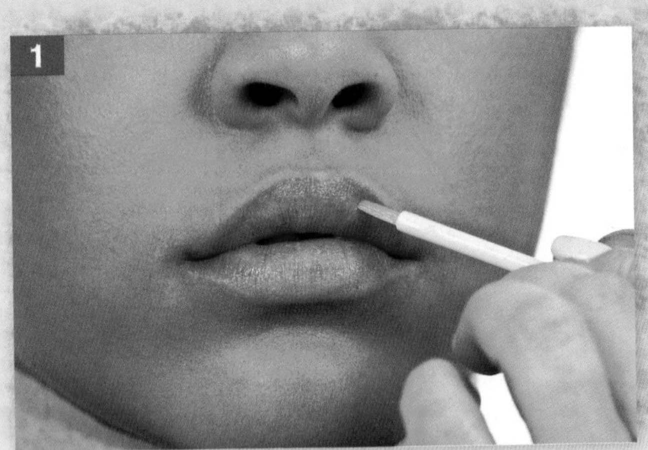

1 Apply lip primer to the entire lip area.

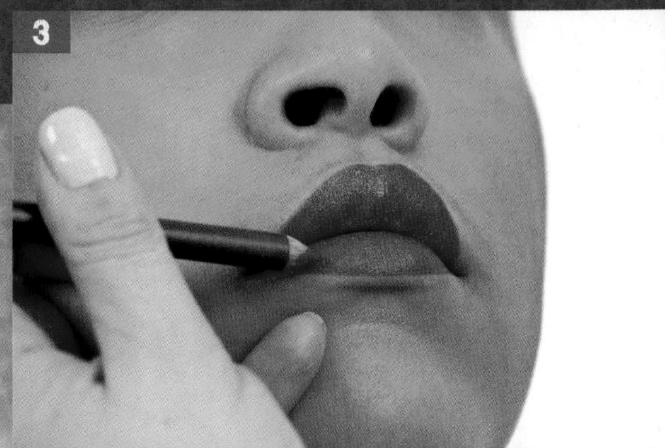

2 Stain the lips. To do this, first, line the lips with candy-apple red liner.

3 Fill in the entire lip area with a heavy application of lip liner.

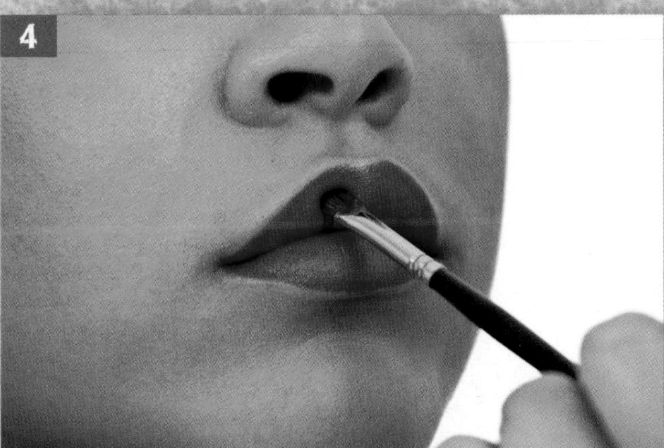

4 Using a small-bristle lip brush, firmly press the lip liner color into the lips in a pressing/rolling motion.

5 Apply lipstick with a disposable lip brush.

6 Apply a light layer of lip gloss the same color as the lipstick.

7 Reapply lipstick.

Procedure 10-4 *(continued)*

8 Apply a layer of clear lip lacquer. The completed Candy Apple Glazed lips.

SERVICE TIP

For a pouty lip, dab a frosted lip gloss right in the center of the lips.

Post-Service ☑ LO7

• Complete PROCEDURE 7-2 POST-SERVICE SEE PAGE 148

Procedure 10-5

Basic Bridal Makeup Application

Implements and Materials

You will need all of the following implements, materials, and supplies:

Brushes

- ☐ Full brush kit

Utensils

- ☐ Brush cleaner
- ☐ Eyelash curler
- ☐ Hair clips
- ☐ Headband (optional: most brides will have makeup done after hair is finished)
- ☐ Makeup cape
- ☐ Makeup palette
- ☐ Neck strip or clean towel for draping
- ☐ Pencil sharpener
- ☐ Tweezers

Single-use Items

- ☐ Cotton pads for cleansing (optional)
- ☐ Cotton swabs
- ☐ Mascara wands
- ☐ Lip brushes
- ☐ Shadow applicators
- ☐ Spatulas
- ☐ Sponge wedges
- ☐ Tissues

Products

- ☐ Artificial lashes
- ☐ Bronzer
- ☐ Cheek color (at least three shades)
- ☐ Concealer (at least two shades)
- ☐ Eyebrow pencils
- ☐ Eyeliner pencils
- ☐ Eye shadow (multiple colors and shades)
- ☐ Facial moisturizer
- ☐ Foundations (at least three shades)
- ☐ Hand sanitizer
- ☐ Lip gloss
- ☐ Lip liners (at least three shades)
- ☐ Lip color (at least three shades)
- ☐ Mascara
- ☐ Mild facial cleanser
- ☐ Primers for lips, eyes, and face
- ☐ Translucent powder

Preparation

- Perform

PROCEDURE 7-1 **PRE-SERVICE** SEE PAGE 144

Procedure

1. Apply cleanser in an upward and outward motion.
2. Remove cleanser with damp cotton pads.
3. Apply appropriate moisturizer.
4. Groom eyebrows and tweeze any stray hairs.

5 Apply primer with a foundation brush.

Procedure 10-5 *(continued)*

6 Using a concealer brush or sponge, apply concealer beneath eye and to any imperfections on the face. Include the lips.

a. For dark circles, choose a concealer the same color as or slightly lighter than the foundation. It needs to be moist, but not too moist. If it is too moist, it will travel from where it is placed; if it is too dry, it will create creases and wrinkles beneath the eye.
b. For redness, choose a red color corrector or green concealer and apply *only* to the areas in need of concealing.
c. To cover blemishes, scars, or other marks choose a concealer exactly the same color as the skin.

7 Choose an appropriate foundation. Take into consideration skin tone of the neck and chest. If necessary, choose a slightly darker shade of foundation so that all areas blend well.

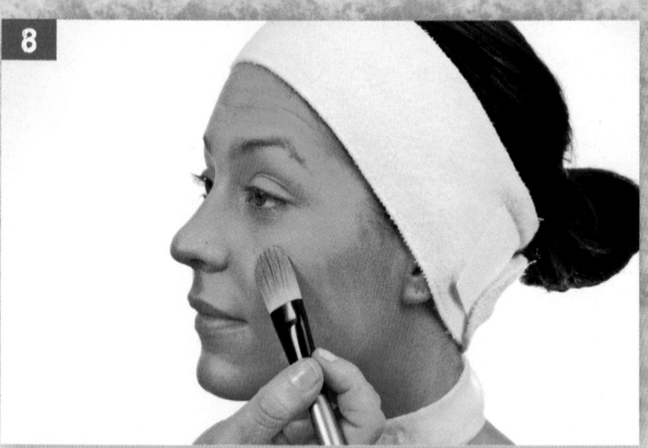

8 Apply foundation with a foundation brush. Begin at the center of the face and blend outward and down onto the neck. Be sure to include the lips.

SERVICE TIP

Blot the face after the application of foundation and prior to the powder. This will lengthen the staying power of foundation and allow more time before a touch-up is necessary.

9 Apply translucent powder over the foundation with powder brush. Be sure that the translucent powder does not contain any shimmer. Pressed powder can be kept on hand for touch-ups throughout the day.

10 Choose a brow pencil or powder the same color as the brows or a shade slightly lighter. Sharpen the brow pencil and apply in short strokes in the direction of the existing brows.

11 Using a small, stiff, angled brow brush, apply brow shadow in short strokes to the entire brow area.

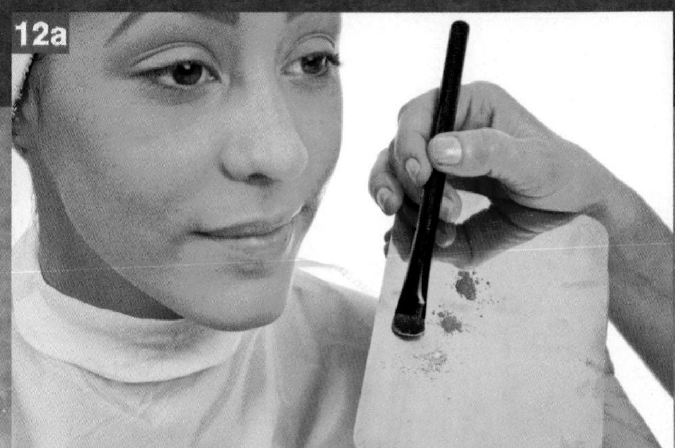

12a Choose three shades of eye shadow. For example, use the following colors for the brunette bride with hazel eyes:

- Shimmering flesh color for the highlight
- Shimmering golden brown for the crease
- Matte taupe for the lid color

Apply concealer and loose powder to eyelids using a small concealer brush or a short, firm shadow brush.

12b Apply highlight from the crease to the brow.

12c Apply matte taupe to the eyelid with a shadow brush.

12d Apply golden-brown shimmer to the crease with angled shadow brush. Use a large, clean blending brush to gently blend.

SERVICE TIP

- Deep set eyes: Use more highlight and lighter shades to make the eye "pop."
- Hooded eyes: Apply the crease color above the hood.
- Bulging eyes: Use highlight at the brow bone and apply crease color (or a shade just lighter) on the lid to the lash line.

Procedure 10-5 *(continued)*

13a Choose a color and type of eyeliner. For this model, choose a rich brown pencil and similar powder.

Sharpen the eye pencil. Then, beginning at the inner corner of the eye, apply a thin line of eyeliner, using small, feather-like strokes that slightly increase in width as the line extends to the outer corner.

13b Using a small, angled shadow brush, apply shadow to the lower lash line.

SERVICE TIP

For dramatic and long-lasting liner, choose a liquid, cake, or cream eyeliner.

SERVICE TIP

For morning brides and soft, natural looks, eyeliner may not be used at all.

14 Curl the lashes with a lash curler. Beginning at the base of the lashes and moving toward the tips, gently crimp three to four times.

15 Apply several coats of waterproof mascara with a disposable mascara wand. Never dip a used mascara wand back into the tube. If you need more product, use a new disposable mascara wand.

SERVICE TIP

Apply waterproof mascara as the final coat to prevent smearing and running. Remember, brides often shed tears of joy!

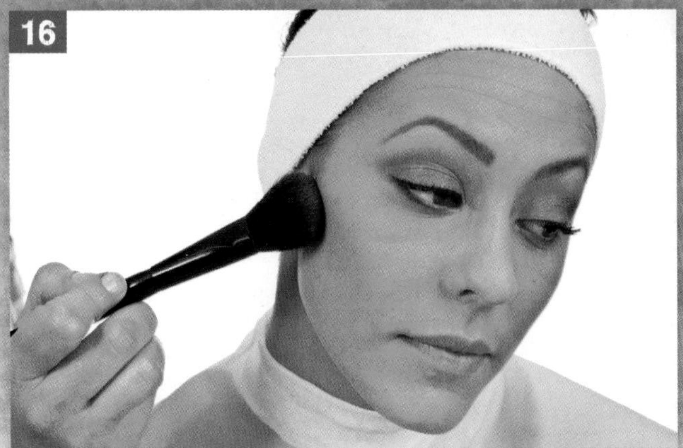

16 Apply bronzer to the cheekbone. Use a powder blush brush and begin at the back of the cheekbone, sweeping forward.

17 Choose an appropriate cheek color. For this model a honey-pink shade is best. Apply blush to the cheekbone. Use a powder blush brush and begin at the back of the cheekbone sweeping forward, *over* the bronzer.

SERVICE TIP

If lip color and eye color are intense, cheek color should be applied very lightly. If lips are sheer, a bit more cheek color is needed.

18 Be sure that lips have had concealer and foundation applied. For this client and the desired look, choose a lip liner and lip color in a rich-pink flesh color.

19 Apply lip liner to the outer edges of the lips. Then fill in the entire lip area.

20 Apply lipstick with a lip brush.

SERVICE TIP

Dark-colored lipstick does not photograph as well as softer shades. Unless the bride wears fire-engine red on a daily basis, recommend a soft, neutral shade.

Procedure 10-5 *(continued)*

21 Finish lips with a few dabs of lip gloss in the center of each lip.

22 The completed bridal look.

Post-Service ☑ LO8

- Complete

PROCEDURE 7-2 POST-SERVICE SEE PAGE 148

Review Questions

1. How do lighting and flash affect the look of a makeup application?
2. For looks that will be photographed, it is necessary to blot foundation before applying powder. Why?
3. What can be done to soften the look of a smoky eye?
4. What techniques are required to create perfect, chiseled cheeks?
5. How many products are needed to create a pouty lip?
6. Name one factor to consider for an afternoon makeup application.
7. Identify one technique for an evening bridal makeup application.
8. When should the first wedding makeup application be performed?
9. What questions should be asked in order to make special considerations for a wedding makeup application?

Chapter Glossary

afternoon bride	A bride with a wedding ceremony set in the midday hours of noon until 4 p.m.
beach bride	A bride who has a wedding ceremony scheduled on the sands of a beach in close proximity to the water.
candy apple glaze	A lip color application that creates the image of a hardened red, large, glossy look.
chiseled cheek	Perfectly sculpted to create a look of distinction and prominence.
evening bride	A bride with a wedding ceremony scheduled from late afternoon through the evening hours, from 4 p.m. and later.
morning bride	A bride with a wedding ceremony scheduled in the morning hours, prior to noon.
special occasions	Any occasion that holds importance to an individual such as birthdays, anniversaries, reunions, parties, weddings, or even a night out without the kids.
wedding consultation	A makeup consultation that focuses on all of the details of the wedding event and reception; includes before and after photos, colors, location, time of day, and specific requests of the bride.

Chapter 11 The Exciting World of High Fashion and High-Definition

Chapter Outline

Learning Objectives

After completing this chapter, you will be able to:

- ☑ **LO1** Describe the four different makeup styles.
- ☑ **LO2** Identify how a makeup artist keeps abreast of what is happening in the fashion scene to stay current.
- ☑ **LO3** Explain what the event coordinators and production managers do for the fashion production.
- ☑ **LO4** Explain the difference between a tear sheet and a model comp card.
- ☑ **LO5** Explain what a production schedule is and why it is so important.
- ☑ **LO6** Explain what a makeup artist is required to do at the production meeting.
- ☑ **LO7** Describe the paper palette and explain what the primary purpose of it is.
- ☑ **LO8** Explain what a makeup artist who wants to work in the exciting world of fashion needs to do to build a portfolio.
- ☑ **LO9** Describe high-definition technology.
- ☑ **LO10** Identify the challenges of working with High-Definition Makeup.
- ☑ **LO11** Differentiate between the traditional makeup application practices and high-definition makeup techniques.
- ☑ **LO12** Identify what colors HD camera is sensitive to and what happens to those colors.

Key Terms

Page number indicates where in the chapter the term is used.

avant-garde style
pg. 240

catwalk
pg. 241

contemporary style
pg. 240

couture style
pg. 240

high-definition television (HDTV)
pg. 249

luminous iridescent makeup
pg. 247

model comp cards
pg. 242

modern glamour style
pg. 240

oil blotting papers
pg. 252

paper palette
pg. 247

pixel
pg. 249

primers
pg. 252

production schedule
pg. 243

standard definition television (SDTV)
pg. 249

tear sheets
pg. 242

Courtesy of Jake Galvez

Career Profile

With years of experience in the fashion and beauty industry, Jake Galvez has built an impressive portfolio that includes numerous commercial and editorial bookings. He is accredited as one of the L'Oreal Professionel's Techni-Artists, Chief Make-up Artist of Kryolan Professional Make-up, a beauty columnist of *Manila Bulletin Newspaper*, and he is also the creative director of the Tony Galvez School of Cosmetology.

Trained by competent coiffeurs and expert aestheticians in the Philippines, including Tony Galvez himself, Jake began his extraordinary career several years ago. He has since been acclaimed across the country for his creative makeup artistry and styling. Now known in Manila for his memorable brushwork and transformations featured in magazines, on runways, on TV, and in advertising, Jake remains true to the vision he has for the profession: to raise it to international acclaim.

"I always believed that the passion for beauty is inherent in every person. In my case, I felt the inclination toward the arts through a propensity to dabble in any activity that entailed a squeeze of creative juice. I was fascinated with crafts, décors, fashion, theater arts, and everything artsy in-between. Growing up in a salon environment, where art and technique are essential prerequisites, paved the way for the evolution of my artistic passions. My uncle, Tony Galvez, was one of those well-meaning individuals who encouraged me to blaze a trail in the field of beauty, styling, and cosmetology. We traveled extensively for trade shows and beauty conventions worldwide since I was 14 years old. These experiences shaped my decision to take up Interior Design in college.

"However, because of my family's prodding, I half-heartedly took business administration classes at Thames International School and eventually earned my degree. I then took over the management of one of our family's businesses, The Tony Galvez School of Cosmetology. Immersed in the business, I eventually realized that my professional calling was to the beauty and cosmetology industry. Since then, I started studying trends and techniques in cosmetology schools abroad and began a profession which was long overdue. I've come full circle, I must say, and every twist and turn in my journey was an invaluable experience. Finally coming to terms with my calling is worth the wait.

"Being a makeup artist is a humbling experience. My service is not confined just to putting eye shadow on the lids or putting colors on the lips and cheeks; it transcends the physical level. My services are more about helping somebody improve his or her appearance and through that, making them feel better. Some stylists tend to overdo things, and their clients often end up looking fake. Makeup is just a simple understanding of the basics: facial structure and cosmetics placement. Once you've come to master these elements, you'll never go wrong.

"The industry is big for any new artist, and I am grateful that the industry has been kind to me, a new kid on the beauty block. I would like to end by saying that glamour is not in the money but in the hands that work beautifully."

Courtesy of Jake Galvez.

This chapter will help you see how your skills and talents can become part of high fashion and high-definition. If fashion—with its glamour and magic—appeals to you, you might find a home backstage, preparing models with the next great "look." Fashion is the launch of a look, creatively entwined with makeup and hair. If you have an interest in photography and high-definition (HD) technology, you may find a calling in the extremely technical application of HD makeup. HD makeup is becoming a necessity for people who work in front of TV and movie cameras, and it is increasingly popular for brides, runway models, working mothers, college students, and women with mature skin who want to look flawless in any light.

Shape, balance, color, and proportion all play a role in the art of hair, makeup, and fashion. Fabulous hair and elegant makeup accentuate the vision of the fashion designer. Top makeup artists complement fashion and create flawless looks for TV and film. A career in makeup artistry can open doors to the glamorous worlds of film, fashion, print, and commercial work.

This chapter will first orient you to the Faces of Fashion: What are the timeless looks? What are the seasonal trends? What does a makeup artist need to know in order to feel at home in the fashion industry? Next, the chapter will look behind the scenes at fashion shows—at the preparation and planning that help create the illusion, along with the specific types of makeup and makeup techniques makeup artists must consider as they plan their own work. Last but not least, the chapter looks at the world of HD. This exciting new world creates many concerns—and many opportunities!—for the makeup artist.

WHY STUDY HIGH FASHION MAKEUP AND HIGH-DEFINITION MAKEUP?

Makeup artists should study and have a thorough understanding of high fashion and HD makeup because:

- As a makeup artist you will have opportunities in film, fashion, and print. You should understand the differences among these specialties.
- HD makeup is used in television and film, as well as for brides, runway models, working mothers, college students, or women with mature skin who want to look flawless in any light. You need a working knowledge of HD techniques to provide your clients with cutting-edge makeup applications.
- Heavy-handed makeup application is unforgiving, and in the new world of HD Television (HDTV) it is critical that a makeup artist know that less is more.

THE FACES OF FASHION: TIMELESS LOOKS AND SEASONAL TRENDS

Like every industry, fashion has its own history, its own language, and its own culture. In order to function well in the world of fashion, it is important for you to understand the multiple levels and facets that are responsible for creating each look and trend.

Timeless Looks

Imagine that an event coordinator describes the theme of the fashion show as "Glamour." What comes to your mind? Is it images of red lips, flawless skin, and an upper-lined, pale eye with sweeping lashes? When you understand the different styles and trends of makeup, you will understand the look that your colleagues are talking about when they use key words such as *glamour*.

- The **modern glamour style** makeup enhances the individuals features with a timeless quality of beauty and always looks modern; this look includes red lips, pale eye shadow, and a defined upper eyelid (**Figure 11–1**).
- The **avant-garde style** represents pushing the boundaries, resulting in a very edgy, high-voltage look (**Figure 11–2**).
- The **contemporary style** represents a fresh, clean look with an edgy avant-garde feel featuring current ideas in style, fashion, and design (**Figure 11–3**).
- **Couture style** breathes the beauty of Hollywood glamour and mystique with eye-catching elegant, yet subtle, trend-setting fashions (**Figure 11–4**). ✓ **LO1**

© Luba V Nel/www.Shutterstock.com

▲ **Figure 11–2 Avant-garde style makeup.**

© Valua Vitaly/www.Shutterstock.com.

▼ **Figure 11–1 Modern glamour style has a timeless quality.**

Seasonal Trends

In addition to understanding the "lingo" of fashion as it applies to timeless trends, the makeup artist needs to understand seasonal trends—how they evolve and how to create those looks. To bring these looks to life, the artist needs basic skills such as the ability to analyze, understand, and enhance a model's facial structure. With such skills, the makeup artist can create elegance and beauty that can take your breath away.

Makeup artists who work in high fashion focus on trendy looks and the color palette for each season's fashion collection. The spring/summer season is usually expected to have light- to vibrant-neon colors. The fall/winter season is expected to have the drama of deep, dark tones.

High-fashion makeup artists must also keep abreast of the latest in cosmetic products and fashion trends to stay on the leading edge of makeup styles, colors, and techniques. Fashion magazines and Web sites, trend forecasters, designer/runway television shows, and seasonal fashion color palettes will give you the insight you need into what is hot and happening in the fashion scene. Top cosmetic companies forecast their color palette for each season in advance by considering the colors that are impacting the fashion industry. A makeup artist who pays attention to all of this information will be able to see the colors and makeup styles for the next season's trends.

Professional makeup artists must stay up-to-date on ever-evolving fashion, and they must also stay up-to-date on ever-evolving makeup techniques, colors, products, and applications.

- When working within a color palette, the makeup artist must ensure that the makeup is current, original, and within the venue's theme. Fashion designers are displaying one-of-a-kind creations for the runway, so the models' makeup must coordinate with the designs. An example of a very specific fashion show could be a bridal show where the makeup artist is expected to follow to the tiniest detail a particular makeup style for each bridal gown.
- With runway fashion, the possibilities are endless. Brows or lips can take center stage. Brows can take a contemporary shape or an avant-garde shape or anything in between. Eyeliner can convey a variety of personalities, attitudes, or styles depending on the shape, color, thickness, and texture of the line. ☑ LO2

▲ Figure 11–3 **Contemporary style makeup.**

▲ Figure 11–4 **Couture style makeup.**

BEHIND THE BEAUTY—BACKSTAGE

Until you have experienced it for yourself, the chaos, heat, and noise backstage at a fashion show is like nothing you have ever imagined. Seemingly multi-armed hairdressers and makeup artists line the workroom, while semi-dressed models rush to get into the next designer's collection. It is an exciting, exhilarating atmosphere where countless people work tirelessly to bring forth the beauty of the industry.

You have probably watched enough red carpet premieres in your lifetime to know that the glamour and dazzle of fashion is a planned production. The most creative artists have come together to achieve the look on the runway. This show begins backstage, and every second counts.

Each fashion event has an overall concept or theme. Event coordinators and production managers orchestrate a visual mood that permeates every detail of the production. Whether you are working in the fashion capital of the world or at a local event, it all comes down to perfectly coordinated details.

There are two types of fashion shows: runway shows and fashion presentations. In a runway show, the models walk down the **catwalk,** or runway, and show the designer's collections. In fashion presentations, the models pose on platforms or podiums for the entire duration of the show.

None of the million-dollar looks would be possible without the makeup artist. Imagine a model strutting down the runway in perfectly tailored clothes and with perfectly styled hair… and no makeup! The coordination of hair, makeup, and fashion gives the look needed to set trends. LO3

Creative Direction and Collaboration

Fashion is collaboration. The producers, the event coordinator, the designers, and the crew must all work together for a show to be a success. Nowadays, fashion shows go way beyond a still or static look by presenting full runway productions, complete with actors, models, choreographers, directors, producers, stylists, set designers, and dressers. A technical crew handles light, music, and audio. Teamwork is the key to producing a successful event.

You are part of a team that is bringing to life the fashion designer's vision, and there are various ways that the designer communicates that vision to others on the team—such as you, the makeup artist. Some fashion designers sort through magazines to collect photos of the hair and makeup styles they want for their signature, branded looks. The result is a stack of tear sheets. **Tear sheets** are photos from fashion magazines of hair and makeup styles, and these tear sheets can be shown to the hair and makeup teams to communicate the designer's ideas and inspiration.

Another way to prepare and acquire knowledge in advance of the show is through model comp cards. Agency **model comp cards** include photos and a given model's measurements and height; they also provide useful visual information that you can use as you develop a plan for creating the overall look and makeup application for each model. LO4

The most important way that ideas are communicated with the team is through meetings. Fashion shows are choreographed productions, so plan to attend several meetings and perhaps even a rehearsal before the big event. Your specific expectations and directions will come from the makeup production head, the event co-coordinator, or the designers themselves. In some instances the co-coordinators meet with the designers and then require the makeup artist to come to a production meeting to review makeup for the event. Sometimes there is a makeup and hair "test" before the show. Your individual ability to take direction on a production level will be a key element in your success. Each style—from contemporary to couture—has a look that represents the designer's collection.

The organizers of fashion events have many responsibilities, including casting the models, pulling the talent and crew together, and arranging delivery of runway platforms and stage equipment. Most co-coordinators have production managers who each head-up a different section of the backstage crew. In such cases, the makeup production manager will be your contact for guidance and instructions.

Although model comp cards are still used, most of this information, along with the model's portfolio, are now on-line. Most agencies send out a link rather than a card.

The Production Meeting

The production meeting is where the theme, color scheme, and planning of the event will be presented to the makeup artists and the rest of the backstage crew. Event coordinators and sometimes event sponsors have decided on how the fashion show will be presented to the audience. No details—however minor—are overlooked during the planning of a choreographed fashion production. The creative aspects of fashion makeup are limitless; however, *you* must have a plan because each designer demands a specific look that reflects an overall theme.

At the production meeting, you will be given a **production schedule**, which provides written information concerning the event; it will list call times, along with the names of designers, models, and backstage crew.

Schedules will include specific dates and timelines, along with each individual's involvement and scheduled responsibilities. Refer to the example production schedule shown in **Figure 11–5**. The production schedule will tell you who you will be working with, where you will be working, and when you will be working. Make a plan according to this information, but remember that your duties can change at a moment's notice; you must remain professional, organized, and flexible even during unforeseen situations. ☑ **LO5**

PRODUCTION SCHEDULE			
Core Fashion Productions			
Fashion on the Edge Designer: GEGI — *www.gegifashion.com* — Location: 54321 Main			
ATTENTION MODELS Models will work with Choreographer Lela Tate on 9/20: 7:00 pm rehearsal.			
SETUPS, SCHEDULE, AND REHEARSALS			
COMPANY	DATE	CONTACT	CALL TIMES
Stage/Runway	9/20	Bill James	1:00 pm
Lighting Technicians	9/20	Steve Simms	3:00 pm
Audio/Music	9/20	Neo	3:00 pm
Table, Chair, Linen Designs	9/20	Cecelia Duke	1:00 pm
Floral Designs	9/20	Su Ze	4:00 pm
Choreographer	9/20	Lela Tate	7:00 pm MODEL CALL REHEARSAL

▲ **Figure 11–5 The production schedule will inform the makeup artist of the scheduled working team, location, times, and dates.**

continued

PRODUCTION MANAGERS/DEPARTMENT HEADS					
DEPARTMENT	**CONTACT**				
Back Stage	Kelli Hall	Marco Mills			
Makeup	Jan Zoe				
Hairstyling	Tony Trey				
Dressers for Designer	Blaire Alison				
PRODUCTION CREW					
DEPARTMENT	**CREW**				
Makeup	Sandy	Katie	Steve	Guy	Denis
Hairstyling	Rusty	Carmen	Kit	Randy	Trey
Dressers	Kyle	Dani	Carly	Mindy	Faith
MODEL MANAGEMENT AGENCY	**CONTACT**				
Haute Model Management	Greg Wede				

MODELS (14)					
Olga	Ashley	Brodie	Courtney	Madeline	Brit
Nikolina	Graciela	Shelby	Danielle	Carly	Lu Lu
Eva		Riley			

9/21 Backstage Setup 1:00 pm. Check with the Production Manager listed above for your assigned work station.
Start time at 2:00 pm for Hair and Makeup / 7:00 pm for Wardrobe.
Fashion Show start 8:00 pm

▲ Figure 11–5 continued

At the production meeting, you will also be given instructions about your required duties and information on what to expect the day of the event. During this meeting, it is very important that you take detailed notes. A fashion show's behind-the-scenes crew can be made up of 50 or more people, and because the production depends on strong teamwork, your ability to listen carefully and take direction is incredibly important.

By the end of the production meeting, you will clearly understand what the designers expect because they have shared their wishes and given their expectations to the hair and makeup teams. The color palette and the particular style of makeup and hair for each designer's collection has been discussed and explained in detail. However, if you still have any questions about what is expected of you, the production meeting is the time to ask for clarification.

Although tear sheets will give you ideas about the desired looks and model comp cards will give you visuals of the models involved, you still must take detailed notes. Furthermore, it is your personal responsibility to get clarity on any concerns or questions. You may not walk away with any tear sheets or model comp cards, so your notes and your own understanding of expectations are very important. If you are working with/for more than one designer, you should make a separate section in your notebook for each designer.

Sometimes, as a makeup artist, you will be requested to attend a dress rehearsal where you will get a sneak-peek at the designer's collection and the models. This is a great advantage, and you will again have the opportunity to take notes about what is expected of you at the live show. ☑ LO6

Prepping Your Supplies

After the production meeting, you will have a clear idea of the desired looks for the fashion event. This is the time to gather all the equipment, implements, and materials that you will need to bring with you on the day of the event. In some cases, you may be required to bring your own makeup chair because there is not enough equipment being supplied by the venue. Creating a checklist in advance of the event is essential for organization and success.

Fashion Makeup Checklist

As previously discussed, high-fashion makeup artists must stay abreast of the latest in trendy looks and every new season's palette. Trends and products are ever-evolving, and keeping up-to-date with the latest in makeup products, colors, and techniques will give you an edge. On the other hand, there are some makeup application techniques that are timeless fashion favorites; whatever the makeup style, whatever the era, these fundamentals always apply, so it is very important that you understand them completely.

- **Highlight and contour.** A simple way to remember what needs to be highlighted is that everything you highlight comes forward, noticeably enhancing it. Highlight is a shade or two lighter than the foundation. Contour is the opposite, recessing and pushing back the depth in the areas where it is applied. Contour is a shade or two darker than the foundation.

Imagine a narrow forehead with a large jaw. The objective is to create an oval appearance. If you highlight around the hairline and temple area and finish the forehead with a shade lighter foundation, the forehead area will appear wider. The jaw can appear smaller if you contour the jawbone at the side of the face under the ear, stopping before the ball of the chin, then finish with a darker foundation from the nose down. This corrects the facial structure and creates a balanced oval look, the most desirable face shape.

Did You Know?

If your client has under-eye circles that are purple or bluish in appearance, beware! Using blue or purple eye shadow or eyeliner can make them stand out—or even reappear after you've concealed them.

- **Eyelashes.** False eyelashes are available in strips, individual flares, and single strands. There are many trendy, dramatic, and fashionable false eyelash lines that offer many different colors. Some even have gems on the band; before you use these, make sure the theme of the show allows it. False eyelashes can be intimidating to beginning makeup artists, but they are actually easy to use. Flares and single strands can be added to the lashes to add volume and length. Refer to Chapter 17, All About Lashes, for a step-by-step procedure for applying eyelashes.
- **Products for accentuating eye color.** The first step in accentuating any eye is to curl the eyelashes. This makes the eye appear more open. By choosing the right colors of shadow and eyeliner, you can brighten the eyes and make their color "pop" or stand out. Understand you are not matching shadows and liners with the eye color. Instead, you are bringing the eye color forward by pairing two opposite colors. In other words, you will use a complementary color to the eye color. This will intensify the appearance of the eye color.

  For example, blue eyes brighten with gold, warm browns, and taupe. Green eyes brighten with coppers, purples, and warm browns. This proven color theory will make the eyes center stage. Do not let shadow colors and lashes detract from or compete with the natural eye color. You need to know what colors in combination work well with the entire face. All of your makeup colors should always complement each other.

Multicultural CONSIDERATIONS

Spray the face with a fine mist of water or add a moisturizer to foundation to make matte makeup appear like natural skin.

- **Face perks.** Certain techniques of a makeup applications can give the face a lift. A lifted appearance can make a significant difference in the final makeup look. Eyes can get a fresh, open, and awake look by curling the lashes. Using mascara to sweep the lash toward the outer corner of the eye can create a fuller, more noticeable lash. Brow shapes with an upward horizontal stroke can lift the eye.

  On the other hand, remember that any line executed in a downward motion can pull the face down and make the face appear sad or older. The direction of your application stroke will affect the overall appearance of your finished product, so keep the "lifting" goal in mind.

PROCEDURE 11-1 **LUMINOUS 3-D COUTURE MAKEUP** SEE PAGE 255

Matte Glamour Makeup

Matte makeup has a lackluster or dull appearance. The application of matte colors on a woman's face and neck can create a more natural look. The use of luminous makeup will add a pearly sheen and iridescence that can attract attention to the fine lines and wrinkles. This makes matte makeup a good option for women with aging skin. Luminous makeup can also produce an undesired effect to large pores. Matte colors give the face a more balanced color palette. Free from reflection and shine, strong facial features, such as the nose, appear flatter, smaller, and less defined. To achieve this more natural look refer to Procedure 11–2, Matte Glamour Makeup.

PROCEDURE **11-2** **MATTE GLAMOUR MAKEUP** SEE PAGE 259

Luminous Iridescent Makeup

Luminous iridescent makeup gives the skin a radiant all-over glow and is available in paste, powder, and liquid form. It can bring youth to a washed-out complexion. A luminous product can be used as a highlighter to bring features to the forefront, enhancing areas where it is applied. Luminous makeup works best when applied to accentuate just one or two features such as the eyes, cheekbones, shoulders, or cleavage. For step-by-step directions on how to achieve an iridescent glow, refer to Procedure 11–1, Luminous 3-D Couture Makeup.

Multicultural CONSIDERATIONS

Shiny, iridescent, glittery, metallic, and shimmer are all reflective. Using them highlights small features, making them look larger.

CREATING THE LOOK—SHOWTIME

The day of the fashion show has arrived; you must be prepared for anything! After attending the production meetings and perhaps a rehearsal, you now have all your notes. You know which models you will be working on. You know the direction and theme of each designer's collection. You know the color palette. You have your makeup products, equipment, and implements according to the checklist. It is time to set up your backstage work station.

Using Paper Palettes

When working with a single client, you will usually use a reusable palette. However, when you are working with groups of people, paper palettes can be very useful. A **paper palette** is made of disposable waterproof parchment paper or artist paper; it holds all the different products that you will use on an individual model (**Figure 11–6**). The paper palette is an extremely useful tool that allows the makeup artist to employ a unique technique to be very organized and efficient when working with a lot of different models.

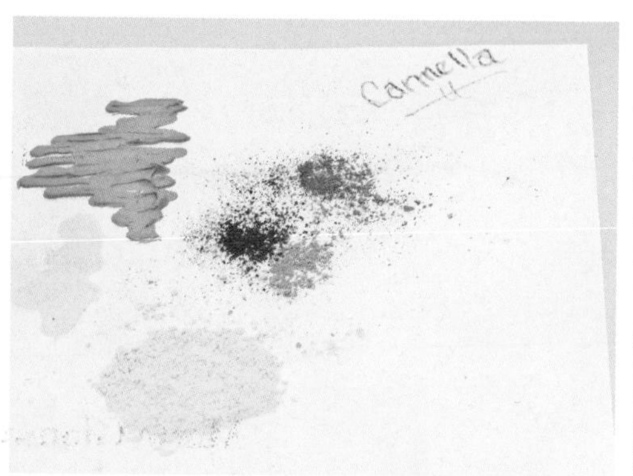

▲ **Figure 11–6** **Paper palettes are disposable parchment paper used to organize products for individual models.**

Mini Procedure

Paper Palettes

© Milady, a part of Cengage Learning. Photography by Visual Recollection.

1 Place all of the products to be used for a given model, along with colors from the fashion designers selected palette, on disposable waterproof parchment or artist paper. Always keep in mind the theme of the event and the application style for the makeup.

© Milady, a part of Cengage Learning. Photography by Visual Recollection.

2 With your spatula, remove product from its container and place it on your paper palette. Include all products: foundation, primer, contour, highlighter, blush, eye shadow, lipstick, and gloss. Use your product sparingly; a small dot of color will go a long way.

© Milady, a part of Cengage Learning. Photography by Visual Recollection.

3 To keep track of each model's color palette, write the model's name at the top of the paper.

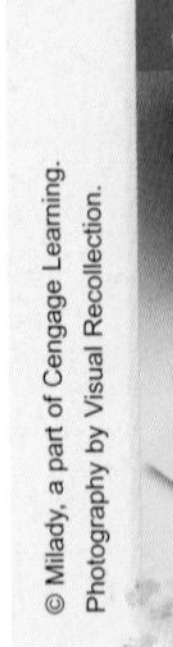

© Milady, a part of Cengage Learning. Photography by Visual Recollection.

4 Fold the parchment paper, paperclip the sides of the palette, and set it aside.

(Continued)

HERE'S A TIP

Paper palettes can also be used for large bridal parties.

© Jakub Pavlinec/www.Shutterstock.com

Mini Procedure

Paper Palettes *(Continued)*

5 Continue stacking the individualized, labeled paper palettes. If you are asked to touch-up the model's makeup, you can refer to the personal paper palette and there will be no question on the color.

The paper palette technique works well in fashion shows when working with several models. The technique keeps you organized and cuts down on time and the confusion that could otherwise be spent searching for a product or color. ✓ LO7

BREAKING INTO FASHION

There are several ways to break into the world of fashion. Begin by researching what is happening in your your local fashion scene. Attend productions and introduce yourself to people who work in the industry.

You will need to enhance your portfolio. Start by gathering images of your work in both a digital format and a print format. Digital images can be e-mailed to clients or used for on-line portfolios. Print images can be presented in person.

Try to find work behind the scenes as an apprentice to a more experienced makeup artist. This will allow you to learn to take direction and become a team player. As a fashion makeup artist's assistant, be observant and mindful and learn all you can. Your passion, your interpersonal skills, your makeup skills and techniques, your understanding of color and product knowledge—all of these will take your career down the catwalk to the exciting world of Fashion. ✓ LO8

STATE REGULATORY ALERT

It is your responsibility when working on multiple models to follow health and safety measures as regulated by your state. Keep your hands clean, and wash your hands when you switch from one model to the next. Be prepared with numerous disposable lip brushes, mascara wands, and gloves to be changed between each model. Have a bag to dispose of the soiled disposables and have your hand sanitizer and makeup-brush sanitizer at your work station.

FASHION PHOTOGRAPHY: HIGH-DEFINITION MAKEUP

Whether you are hired for a runway event, a photoshoot, or on a television or film set; you need to be familiar with the application of high-definition (HD) makeup. Fashion events can be televised, and photographers line up to shoot the models and the fashion designs, so fashion shows (not only film sets) require flawless, camera-ready HD makeup.

HD makeup has been created in response to the latest photographic technology. **High-definition television (HDTV)** has greatly increased display or visual resolution. HD, which is digital, has one or two million pixels per frame, roughly six times that of traditional analog television systems known as **standard definition television (SDTV)**. A **pixel** is the smallest single element of a digital image or display unit. Because of the increase in pixels, the image becomes sharper, brighter, and more realistic. The Federal Communications Commission (FCC) required that all television stations switch from analog to digital by the end of 2008, which means that HDTV will soon completely replace traditional TV.

▲ **Figure 11–7 HD cameras can see 6X the human eye causing images to be sharper and more realistic.**

HD cameras can see 6X sharper (with more clarity) than the human eye, which means actors, models, and newscasters must look flawless on camera (**Figure 11–7**). HD is also becoming the industry standard among all camera/camcorder equipment, including those purchased for home use. As a result, makeup artists and everyday women need to be ready for a close-up at any given moment. Perfected resolution calls for perfected makeup application.

Makeup companies have had to meet the demands of technology by offering specialized products designed to give an airbrush finish, and makeup artists have had to adopt new application techniques to conceal, camouflage, smooth, and perfect while still preserving a completely natural look (**Figure 11–8**).

▲ **Figure 11–8 HD makeup must smooth, perfect, and camouflage imperfections yet look natural under the spotlight.**

HD makeup suits people of any ethnicity working in television and film, as well as brides, runway models, working mothers, college students, or women with mature skin who want to look flawless in any light.

✓ **LO9**

Challenges of HD Makeup

HD technology poses many challenges to the makeup artist. Some of these include: magnified pores, emphasized lines and wrinkles, amplified blemishes, pink tones turning orange, noticeable brush strokes, mismatched foundation, and an overall unnatural "mask" appearance (**Figure 11–9**).

HD makeup formulas have been created to meet the challenges of this latest technology. These formulas use super-fine microbead pigments that blend effortlessly into the skin while photochromic pigments react with different lighting to diffuse any imperfections. The light ultimately becomes a cosmetic to create a natural picture-perfect complexion for the 6X magnification of the HD lens. HD makeup is used to even skin tone, camouflage imperfections, conceal dark circles or blemishes, and reflect natural and artificial light.

SDTV required makeup artists to create layer after layer of makeup to hide imperfections. In low resolution, this was advantageous; in fact, with SDTV, even prosthetics and wig lace fronts seemed unnoticeable. Studios in the past used strong overhead track lights which in turn required strong products to bounce

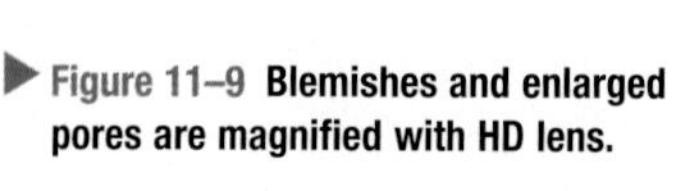

▶ **Figure 11–9 Blemishes and enlarged pores are magnified with HD lens.**

the light. These techniques are not compatible with HD. With HD makeup, less is more and heavy-handed application is obvious and unattractive. The use of specialized, high-quality makeup products as well as new techniques are allowing the makeup artist to deal with the rapid pace of advancing technology. To be successful in the world of High-Definition, makeup artists have to pay great attention to detail, carefully select color choices, and continually blend the makeup. ☑ L10

Get a mirror with 6X magnification. First look on the standard side; then, turn it over to the high-definition side. Notice the appearance of pores, fine lines, and blemishes. This is an example of how an HD camera will replicate its subject.

PROCEDURE **11-3** **H-D MAKEUP APPLICATION** SEE PAGE 264

Prepping the Skin Before an HD Photoshoot

The following simple steps will prepare the face for HD makeup application and minimize any imperfections:

1. Hair removal is highly important for HD filming as unruly eyebrows and lip-area peach fuzz will be magnified. Wax, tweeze, or thread the day before a photoshoot to allow redness and swelling to calm before the shoot.
2. The night before the photoshoot, gently exfoliate the face and neck area with a gentle exfoliant to remove dead skin cells.
3. Steam the face after exfoliation to help soften fine lines and help to increase circulation for a natural, luminous glow. Follow with a moisturizer appropriate for skin type.

Supply List for HD Makeup

The following supplies should be used in HD makeup preparation and application:

- Makeup-brush cleaner should be used on all tools prior to use and in-between uses.
- Use a cape to protect clothing from makeup spills.
- Pull hair back with butterfly clips or a terry headband so that makeup can be blended into the hairline.
- Concealer brushes are best for hard-to-reach areas in the corners of the eye. Invest in high-quality brushes for optimal results.
- Foundation brushes work best for seamless application. Make sure your kit has at least two of each brush for multiple clients.
- A kabuki brush is a makeup brush with a short, flat head and a short stem. The head has a curved edge and is ideal for applying finely milled powders.
- Eyeliner brush, small contour brush, medium contour brush, and large blending brushes are necessary for precise eye makeup application.

Courtesy of Jake Galvez.

▲ Figure 11–10 **The proper supplies for high-definition makeup ensures the best results.**

- An eyelash curler should be used to open up the eye area and add curl.
- An eyelash/eyebrow comb is vital to make sure lashes are free of clumps and brows are neatly shaped.
- Tweezers are a must for last-minute hair removal.
- A double pencil sharpener works for skinny pencils and thicker pencils to help give a smooth, precise edge and to clean the pencils between eyes and between clients.
- Disposable lip brushes should be used to dip into lipstick or gloss. Do not double dip.
- Disposable mascara wands should be used when applying mascara. Get a new one in-between each application.
- Spatulas are excellent tools to scoop out foundations, creams, concealers, or lipstick from containers.
- A metal artist palette works well to customize foundation and lipstick colors.
- Touch up excessive shine with **oil blotting papers**, silky sheets which help to absorb oil without compromising the makeup.
- Most important, you will need an HD camera to check how the makeup is interpreted. Good makeup application involves trial and error, so checking on makeup midway prevents having to start over.

▲ **Figure 11–11 HD makeup products are sold in kits.**

Product Checklist for HD Makeup

HD makeup is often sold in kits (**Figure 11–11**). Whether you use a makeup kit, create your own, or use a variety of separate products, the following makeup items will be needed for a HD photoshoot:

- **Primers** are silicone formulas that are clear or colored for correction of skin tones; they help to fill in fine lines, blur imperfections, and allow makeup to glide effortlessly across the skin and last longer. Primers are a new must-have makeup category when it comes to HD application. Although some color correctors appear to have color, they will not be seen on the skin. Green primers cancel redness. Purple primers cancel yellow or sallow tones (**Figure 11–12**). Peach combats blue tones under the eyes. Quality primers will

▲ **Figure 11–12 Primers, a new category of makeup for HD filming, are available in clear or color correctors.**

contain nourishing ingredients to soften and protect the skin.

- **HD concealers** contain a higher density of pigments to hide stubborn discolorations or dark circles. They also have a higher melting point to prevent the formula from breaking down or creasing under the eyes. Concealers should only be one to two shades lighter than skin tone. Traditional makeup required yellowish or white colors to cover dark circles. However, HD captures these products as grayish, causing the circles to be more noticeable. Instead, use a salmon color—directly opposite blue on the color wheel—in order to cancel out dark tones.
- **HD liquid foundation** uses fine micronized optical correctors that sit on the skin rather than settling into lines and crevices. HD foundations are oil-free liquid. Some HD foundations contain SPF, but these formulations are not recommended because they tend to be thicker and cause a chalky appearance. Foundations are used to even skin tone, cover redness and blemishes, and minimize pores. Finding a perfect match can be tricky, but for most people blending two colors helps to get a truer skin tone. It is best to err on the lighter side rather than darker, because dark tones cause the skin to appear harsh and aged.
- **HD liquid highlighter** is used to accentuate areas of the face and provide a natural glow. HD highlighters are also referred to as *illuminizers*. These formulations should not be confused with traditional iridescent highlighters. Iridescent products typically use a thicker shimmer pigment that reflects color and can age mature skin. HD highlighters have micro-fine colorless photo pigments that diffuse light to optically blur any imperfections.

Having the right balance of matte and dewiness for HD cameras will effect the entire makeup look. Makeup that is too dewy will cause too much shine and look awkward and distracting; makeup that is too matte gives an aged appearance while amplifying imperfections. Highlighters can be used on the brow bones, the upper cheekbones, the bridge of nose, the temples, and in the bow of the lip. Highlighters can be used after foundation, before powder, or mixed in with foundation for sheer, tinted coverage.

- **HD cream blush** creates the prefect replica of a natural blushing beauty. Blush is used to accentuate the cheeks and bring a flush of energy to the face. Blush can be applied to the apples of the cheeks for a youthful glow or on the cheekbones for a more sophisticated look. Cream blushes appear more natural and three-dimensional. Powder blushes can have an intense texture that looks like the color is sitting on the skin.
- **HD setting powder** is required to set the foundation. HD powders are finely milled and very light. Most formulas contain silica which prevents dryness caused by loose powders. Translucent is the best choice because it matches all skin tones and provides a

Mix concealer and/or foundation on the inside of the back of your hand to warm the formula and help it to melt into the skin more naturally. Make sure your hands are clean. Check that this technique complies with your state regulations.

HERE'S A TIP

Apply a small dab of highlighter to the bow of the lip to give a precise, pouty appearance of a fuller upper lip.

CAUTION

Contouring is an important traditional makeup technique that is extremely difficult to achieve naturally in HD because it tends to make the face look dirty. Contouring was heavily used in SDTV because faces appeared one-dimensional and required contouring to create the appearance of depth. With the three-dimensional technology of HD, less contouring is required. It is important to experiment to find the right shade and to use a much lighter touch with contouring for HD.

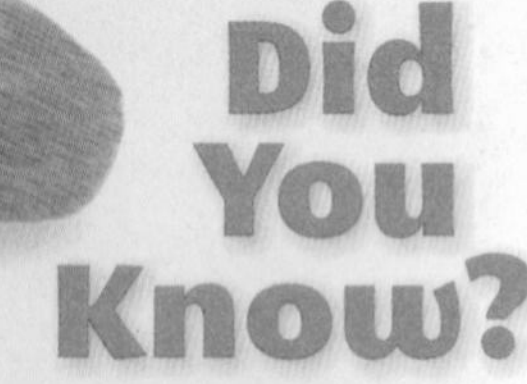

Did You Know?

HD cameras are highly sensitive to reds and pinks. Pinks tend to turn orange. The tone of cool reds can be intensified. It is best to use warm shades of red or corals rather than cool reds and pinks for blush and lip colors.

fresh, natural look. Be sure to choose a light, fluffy formula; some translucent powders can appear chalky. Setting powders can be used over the foundation or alone. Powder can be applied after highlighter and blush to help soften the effect.

- **Eyeliner** is used to intensify and emphasize the eyes. Like shadow, it can play a major role in creating illusions for corrective application. While colored liners are creative, for HD photography, black, charcoal, and dark brown work best with most shadows colors. If you choose colored eyeliner, avoid using colored shadows; otherwise, the eye area will appear too busy.
- **Eye shadow** is used to accentuate the eyes and make the color of the iris "pop." Proper use of color can create the illusion of increased size, or it can alter the shape of the eye. Emphasis should be on color selection and well-blended application. Color choice should be limited to two or three shades, and heavy shimmer should be avoided. Matte and pearl finishes work best. The highlighting color can be a bit more pearlescent, but the lid color should be matte. Use matte shadows to fill in the eyebrows.
- **Mascara** is used to enhance and define the eye area. In HD, it is important to use mascara with a separating brush that will lengthen, thicken, and separate each lash. Black or dark brown mascara colors work best in HD. Mascara should be used after the eyelash curler. Applying too much mascara on the lower lash line can cause shadows and raccoon eyes.
- **Lip liner** defines the lip line and can be used in corrective application techniques. Lip liners also prevent lipstick or gloss from feathering by creating a boundary that other products are unlikely to cross. Pick a color one shade darker than the client's natural lip color. Avoid anything other than a nude tone to prevent a clownish appearance.
- **Lipstick** can be used to give lips a fuller look and to clearly define and shape the lips. Lips should not be too matte or too shiny. Do not allow the lip color to compete with eye color. Lipstick should bring the look together.
- **Lip gloss** is the final step needed to give a three-dimensional, youthful, fuller appearance to lips. Avoid heavily sparkled gloss. Opt for a lightly tinted shimmer gloss on the center of the bottom lip only.

☑ LO11 ☑ LO12

Procedure 11-1

Luminous 3-D Couture Makeup

Implements and Materials

You will need all of the following implements, materials, and supplies:

Brushes

- ☐ Cosmetic brushes

Utensils

- ☐ Artist palette or paper (place your product on palette to avoid cross-contamination)
- ☐ Breath mints
- ☐ Brow scissors
- ☐ Brush cleanser
- ☐ Cleanser and or makeup remover pads
- ☐ Container or bag for your soiled disposables
- ☐ Eyelash curler
- ☐ Hand sanitizer
- ☐ Headband or hair clip
- ☐ Makeup cape
- ☐ Makeup chair
- ☐ Makeup palette
- ☐ Neck strip or clean towel for draping
- ☐ Pencil sharpener
- ☐ Shears (optional)
- ☐ Tweezers

Single-use Items

- ☐ Eyelash wands
- ☐ Lipstick wands
- ☐ Spatulas
- ☐ Sponge wedges

Products

- ☐ Adhesive for lashes
- ☐ Artificial eyelashes
- ☐ Bronzers
- ☐ Concealers
- ☐ Eye shadows
- ☐ Eyebrow comb
- ☐ Eyebrow gels
- ☐ Eyebrow pencils
- ☐ Eyebrow powder
- ☐ Foundations
- ☐ Light, nonoily moisturizer
- ☐ Lip colors
- ☐ Lip conditioner
- ☐ Lip liners
- ☐ Liquid and pencil eyeliners in various colors
- ☐ Luminous iridescent paste/powder/liquid
- ☐ Makeup primer
- ☐ Matte foundation
- ☐ Powders (setting and translucent)

Preparation

- Perform

PROCEDURE 7-1  PRE-SERVICE SEE PAGE 144

Procedure

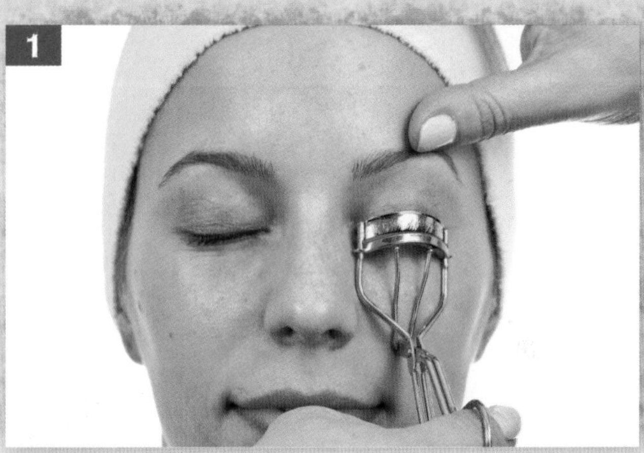

1 Wash hands. Groom the client's eyebrows, if needed, by removing any stray hairs, tweezing the hair in the same direction in which it grows. Curl the lashes to open the eye area.

Procedure 11-1 *(continued)*

2 Apply eye and face primer to prepare the skin for the makeup.

3 Analyze the face shape and highlight and contour the skeletal structure to create the shape you desire. With your foundation brush, highlight the areas of the face you want to bring forth, then contour to create recesses and dimensional depth of the makeup.

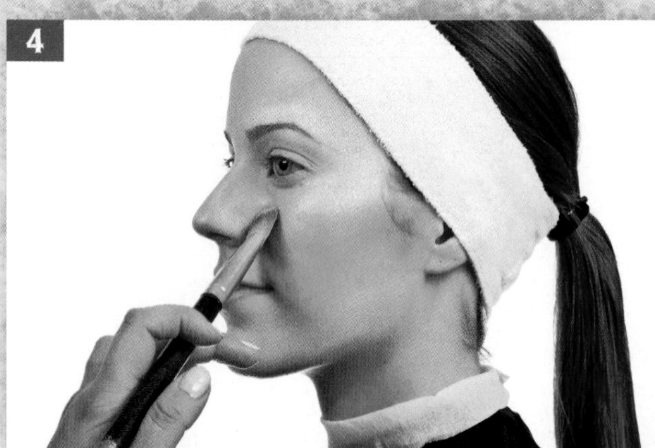

4 Apply your luminous iridescent product on top of the highlighted areas. This will create the glow from beneath the skin. With your foundation brush, apply the matte foundation. The foundation is applied on top of all areas of the face that have been highlighted or contoured along with the areas that have had the luminous iridescent applied. Continue applying the foundation to all areas and blend from the face into the neck and hairline. Blend all edges to a flawless finish.

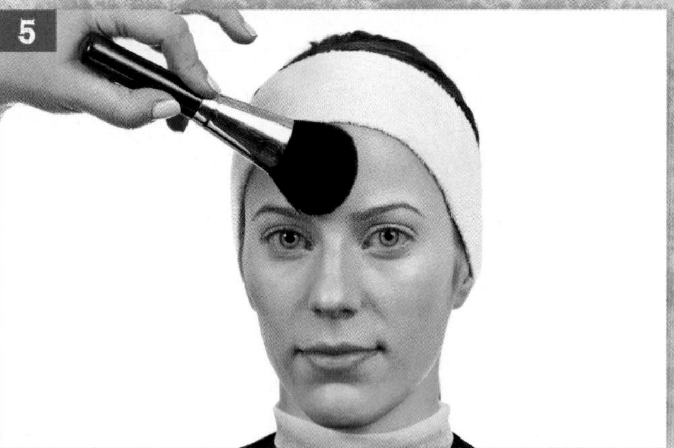

5 Apply loose powder with a powder makeup brush to set the foundation. Press it into the skin in a rolling motion and buff any excess powder with your powder brush.

SERVICE TIP

Luminous iridescence can be applied before or after foundation.

6 Iridescent or shimmer eye shadow will define the luminous look in style. Start with your mid-tone eye shadow and apply from lash to the crease of the eye. Use the contour to create depth with the darkest of the three shadows. Finish with your lightest shadow below the brow. Use a clean eye shadow blending brush to blend and soften the contour shadows.

7 Define the eye with eyeliner at the top lash line and the bottom lash line. Using your darker contour eye shadow, smudge the shadow into the eyeliner. This technique will soften the look of the eyeliner.

8 If false eyelashes are requested, re-curl the lashes and place lash adhesive on the strip lash band. Wait for the glue to set (about 1 minute) and apply lash strip at base of top lashes. Place in the same area on both eyes to create an even appearance. Lash strips may need to be cut or shortened before applying.

9 Use black powder shadow or eyeliner to connect the strip lash band to the eye. Apply the shadow and liner on the inner corner of the eye near the tear duct.

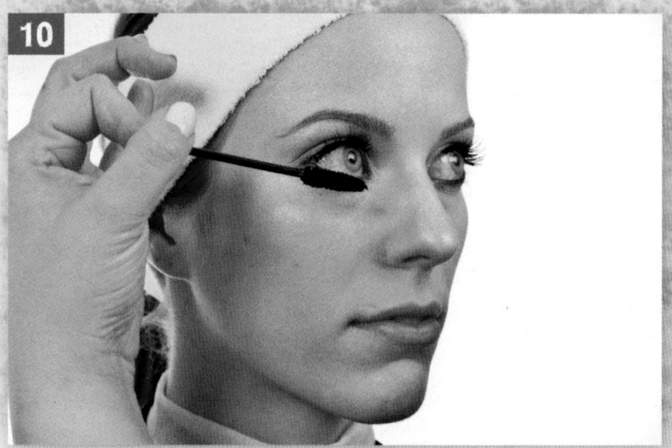

10 With mascara blend the natural lashes into the false lashes on the upper lid and create a balance by adding mascara to the bottom natural lash.

Procedure 11-1 *(continued)*

11 Determine the mouth shape and apply a lip concealer around the edge of the lips. Line the lips with lip liner.

12 With a lip brush fill the lip areas with luminous lip color. For shimmer, shine, and to create a fuller lip be very aware where lip gloss is placed.

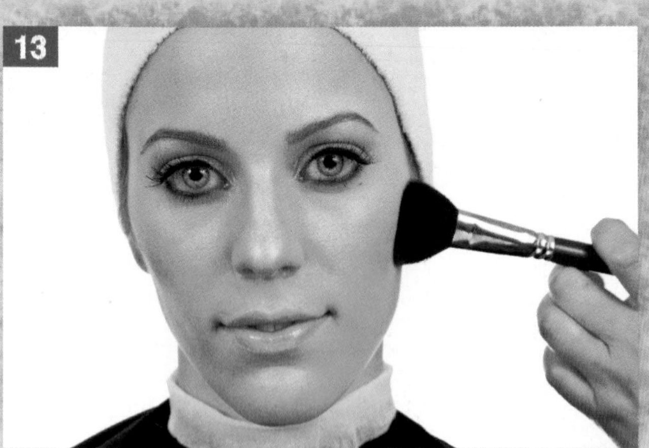

13 Finish with luminous blush color to create a healthy, even appearance. The application and the execution of the stroke need to pull the face upward. Blush application pulls all the makeup colors of the face together. Apply on cheeks, forehead, and nose.

14 The completed Luminous 3-D Couture Makeup Look.

Post-Service

- Complete

PROCEDURE 7-2 POST-SERVICE SEE PAGE 148

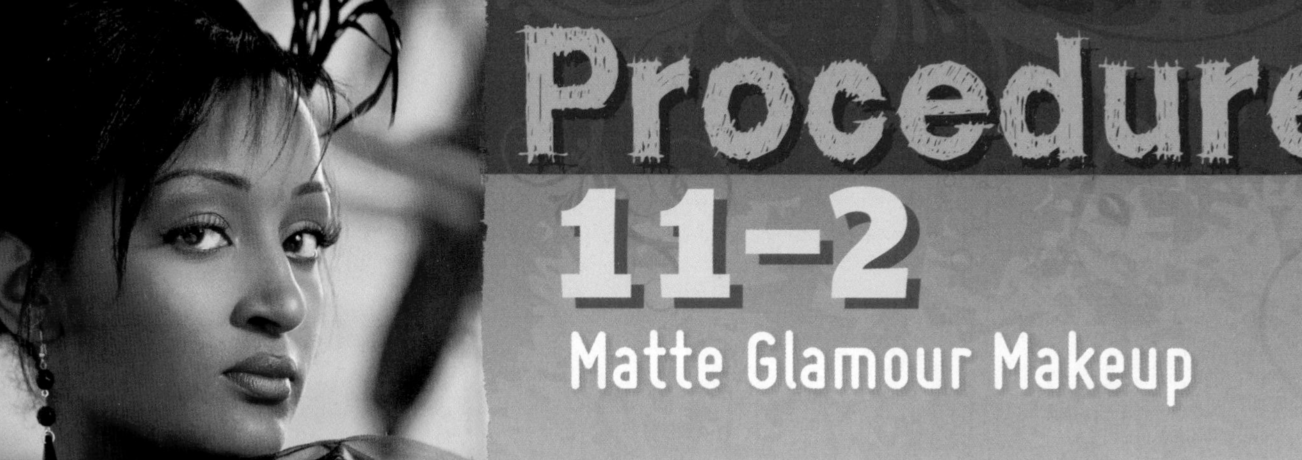

Procedure 11-2
Matte Glamour Makeup

Implements and Materials

You will need all of the following implements, materials, and supplies:

Brushes

- ☐ Cosmetic brushes

Utensils

- ☐ Brush cleaner
- ☐ Electric liners or trimmers (licensed stylist only)
- ☐ Hand sanitizer
- ☐ Headband or hair clip
- ☐ Makeup cape
- ☐ Makeup chair
- ☐ Makeup palette
- ☐ Neck strip or clean towel for draping
- ☐ Pencil sharpener
- ☐ Shears (optional)
- ☐ Tweezers

Single-use Items

- ☐ Cotton pads for cleansing (optional)
- ☐ Cotton swabs
- ☐ Lip brushes
- ☐ Mascara wands
- ☐ Razor (optional)
- ☐ Shadow applicators
- ☐ Spatulas
- ☐ Sponge wedges
- ☐ Tissues

Products

- ☐ Adhesive for lashes
- ☐ Artificial eyelashes
- ☐ Eye shadows (pale matte tones)
- ☐ Eyelash curler
- ☐ Foundations
- ☐ Light, nonoily moisturizer
- ☐ Lip colors
- ☐ Lip conditioner
- ☐ Lip liners
- ☐ Liquid and pencil eyeliners in various colors
- ☐ Matte foundation
- ☐ Powders
- ☐ Primer

Preparation

- Perform

PROCEDURE 7-1 PRE-SERVICE SEE PAGE 144

Procedure

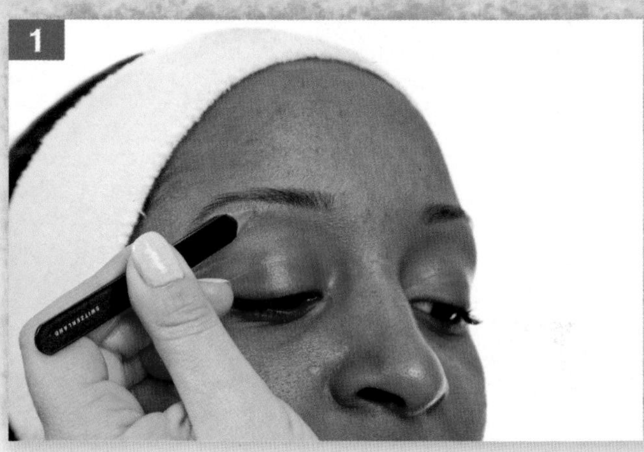

1 Wash hands. Condition the lips with a lip moisturizer and groom the eyebrows by removing any stray hairs, tweezing the hair in the same direction in which it grows.

Procedure 11-2 *(continued)*

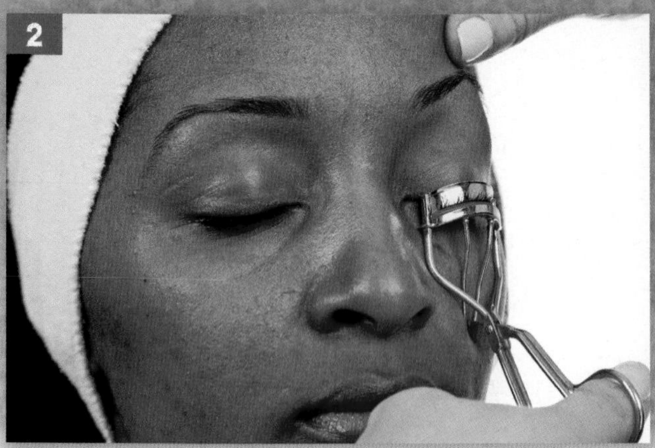

2 Curl the lashes with a clean eyelash curler to open the eye area.

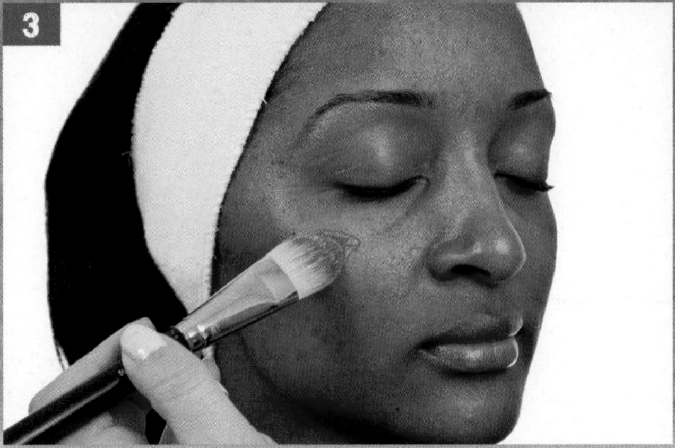

3 Apply eye and face primer in a matte formula with a foundation brush, which prepares the skin for the foundation makeup.

4 Analyze and determine the model's face shape. With your foundation brush, highlight the areas of the face you want to bring forward and contour to create recesses and the depth and dimension of the makeup.

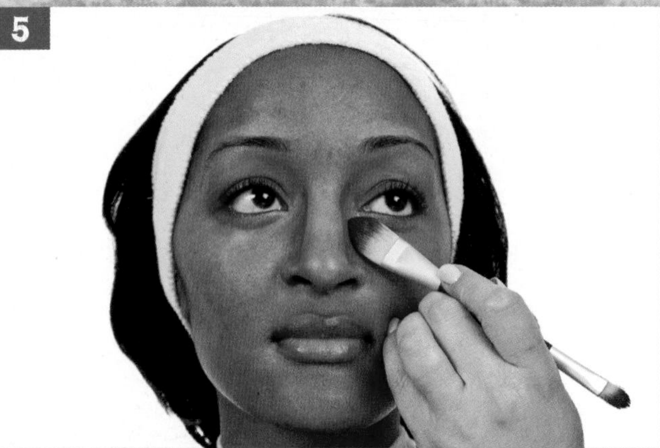

5 With your foundation brush apply the matte foundation. Apply foundation on all areas that have been highlighted and contoured. Continue applying the foundation to all areas and blend from the face into the neck and hairline. Blend all edges to a flawless finish.

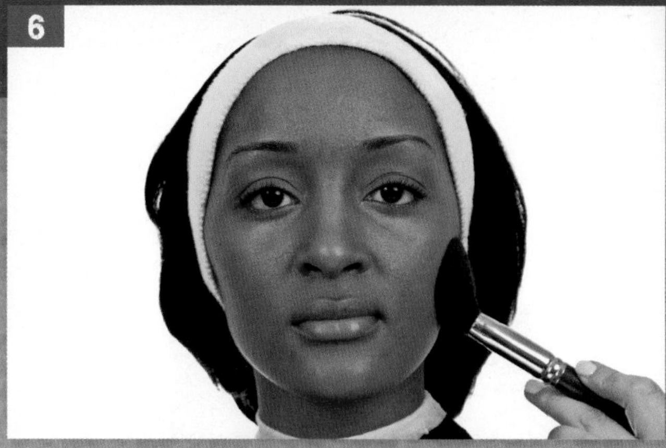

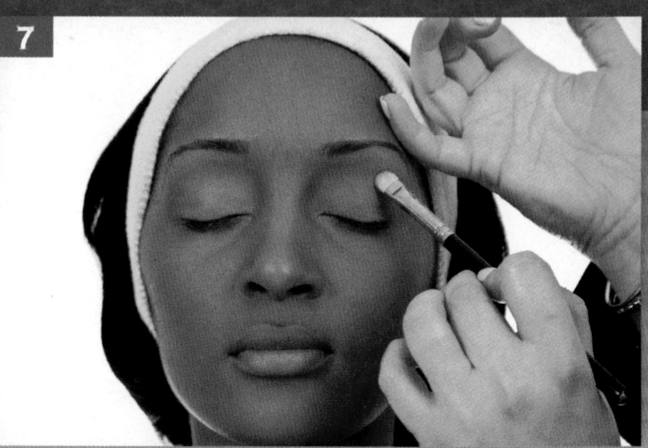

6 Apply loose powder with a powder makeup brush to set the foundation. Press it into the skin in a rolling motion and buff any excess powder with your powder brush.

7 Matte eye shadow will define the style of the matte glamour look. Start with your palest-cream or white-color eye shadow and apply from lash to brow. Use the mid-tone contour in the crease of the eye to create depth with one of the two eye shadows. Use a clean eye shadow blending brush to blend and soften the contour shadow.

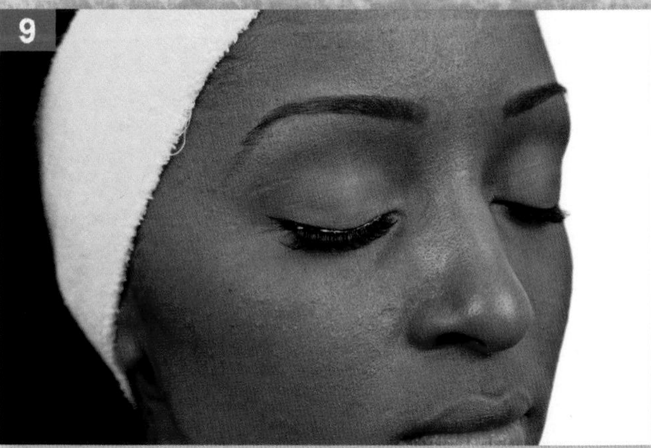

8 Define the eye by lining it with eyeliner at the top lash line and the bottom lash line. Use your darker, mid-tone contour eye shadow and apply the shadow over the eyeliner. With your liquid eyeliner, create a thicker line on the top of the eyelashes ending in a swept point.

9 Re-curl the lashes and place lash adhesive on the lash strip. Wait for the glue to set (about 1 minute) and apply lash strip at base of top lashes. Place in the same area on both eyes to create an even appearance. Lash strips my need to be cut or shortened before applying.

Procedure 11-2 *(continued)*

10 Use black powder shadow or eyeliner to connect the strip lash band to the eye. Apply the shadow and liner on the inner corner of the eye near the tear duct.

11 Apply mascara with a disposable mascara wand, which will blend the natural lashes into the false lashes on the upper lid and create a balance by adding mascara to the bottom natural lash.

12 Apply a lip concealer around the edges of the lips. You can define the lip shape and create a full, voluptuous lip by lining the lip's outer edge with red matte lip liner.

13 With a lip brush, fill in the lip area with matte red lip color.

14 Finish with matte blush color to create a healthy, even appearance. The application and the execution of the stroke need to pull the face upward, and the blush will pull all the makeup colors of the face together. Apply on cheeks, forehead, and nose.

15 The finished Matte Glamour Makeup Look.

Post-Service

- Complete PROCEDURE 7-2 POST-SERVICE SEE PAGE 148

Procedure 11-3

HD Makeup Application

Implements and Materials

You will need all of the following implements, materials, and supplies:

Brushes

- ☐ Concealer brushes
- ☐ Contour brush (medium)
- ☐ Contour brush (small)
- ☐ Eyelash/eyebrow comb
- ☐ Eyeliner brush
- ☐ Foundation brushes
- ☐ Kabuki brush
- ☐ Large blending brushes

Utensils

- ☐ Brush cleaner
- ☐ Double pencil sharpener
- ☐ Hand sanitizer
- ☐ Headband or hair clip
- ☐ Makeup cape
- ☐ Makeup chair
- ☐ Makeup palette
- ☐ Neck strip or clean towel for draping
- ☐ Tweezers
- ☐ HD camera

Single-use Items

- ☐ Lip brushes (minimum of two)
- ☐ Mascara wands (minimum of three)
- ☐ Cotton pads for cleansing (optional)
- ☐ Cotton swabs
- ☐ Mascara wands
- ☐ Oil blotting papers
- ☐ Shadow applicators
- ☐ Spatulas
- ☐ Sponge wedges
- ☐ Tissues

Products

- ☐ HD concealers
- ☐ HD cream Blush
- ☐ HD liquid foundation
- ☐ HD liquid highlighter
- ☐ HD setting powder
- ☐ Lip gloss
- ☐ Lip liner
- ☐ Lip colors
- ☐ Mascara
- ☐ Primers

Preparation

- Perform

PROCEDURE 7-1 PRE-SERVICE SEE PAGE 144

Procedure

1 Wash hands. Cleanse the client's skin only if there is makeup or skin appears oily.

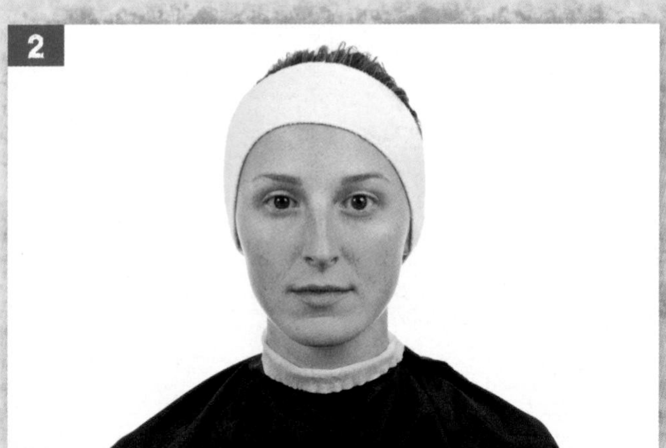

2 To exfoliate, use a light scrub and facecloth to gently exfoliate any dead skin cells on lips. This will help to make lips appear fuller and smoother.

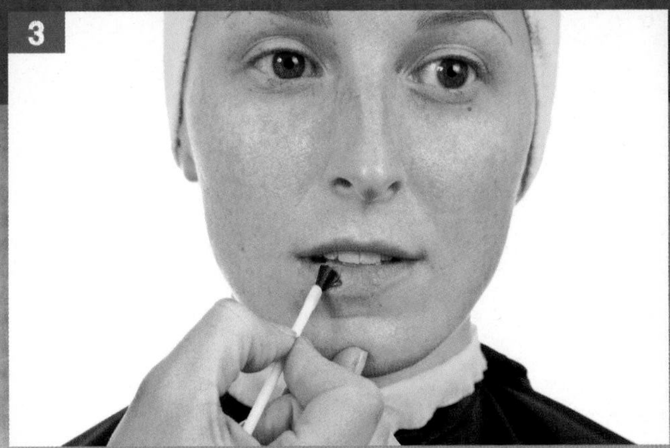

3 To moisturize, apply facial moisturizer and lip balm.

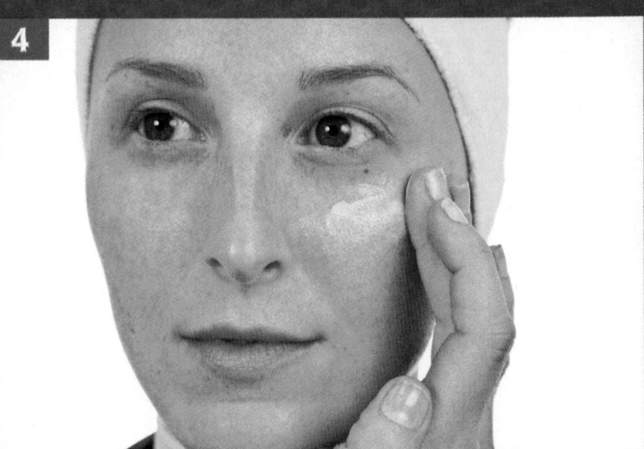

4 Using fingertips or a foundation brush, use two pumps of primer to fill in lines and pores. Pay special attention to forehead lines, frown lines, and under-eye lines.

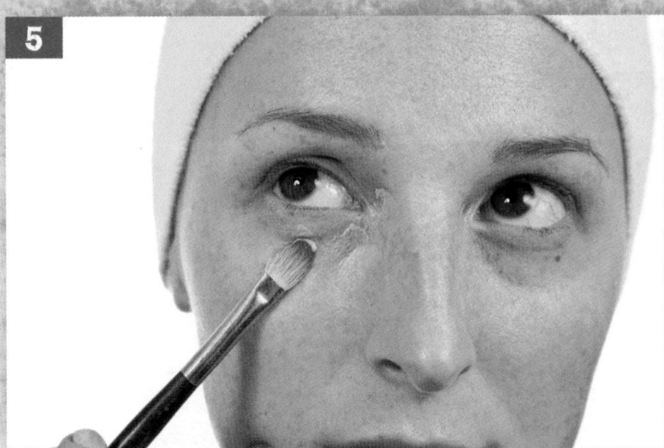

5 Apply concealer using a concealer brush. Choose a tone one or two shades lighter than natural skin color. To cancel blue tones, opt for salmon over yellow tones. Focus concealer on the inner corner of eyes rather than the outer corner where makeup settles in lines.

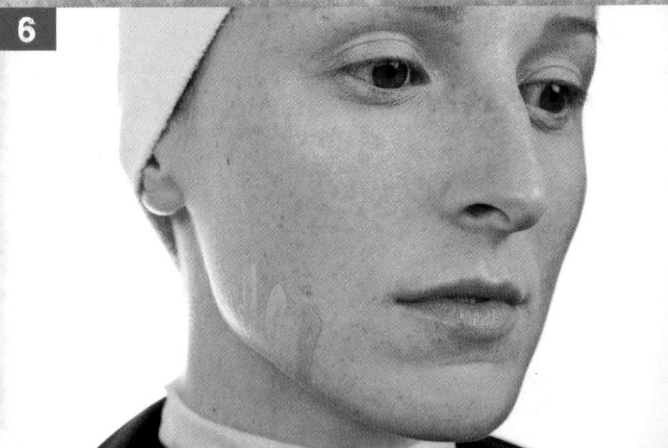

6 Using a foundation brush or fingertips, apply foundation directly on jawline to see if the color is a match. The color should disappear into the skin. Typically, two shades will need to be mixed for a true match.

Procedure 11-3 *(continued)*

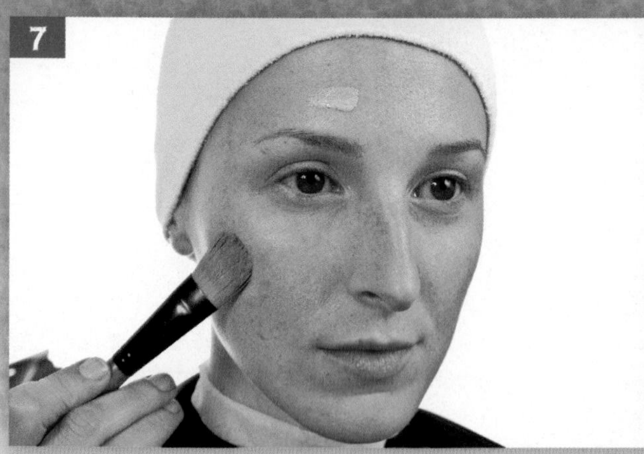

7 Start with the center of the face and work your way outward. Make sure to apply using downward small strokes to go with the grain of facial hair. Pay special attention to blend gently into the hairline and jawbone so that you do not see where the color ends and the color begins. Continue to blend with dabbing motions rather than swiping motions.

8 Using an HD camera, check the monitor to see that the skin tone appears natural. Before proceeding to other steps, use this moment to check for flaws and prevent further errors.

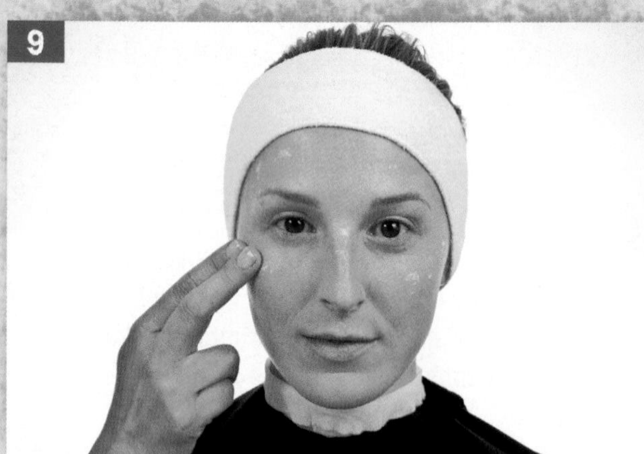

9 Accentuate areas of the face and help to diffuse light and blur imperfections. Using your fingertips, apply highlighter in a dabbing motion on upper cheekbones, temples, the bridge of nose, and the bow of the lip.

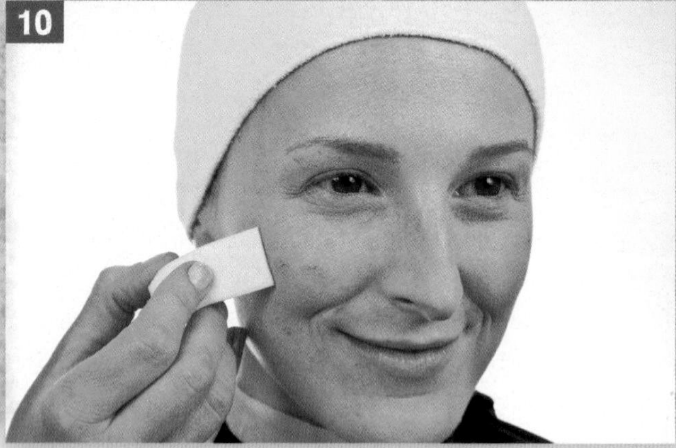

10 Opt for a warm blush shade because it will appear more natural. Using a cream blush gives a more youthful and subtle look. Apply blush directly to the apples of the cheeks. Avoid applying blush to the highlighted area or too close to the nose so that the area does not appear red. Do not apply too much blush or the face will appear to be enlarged.

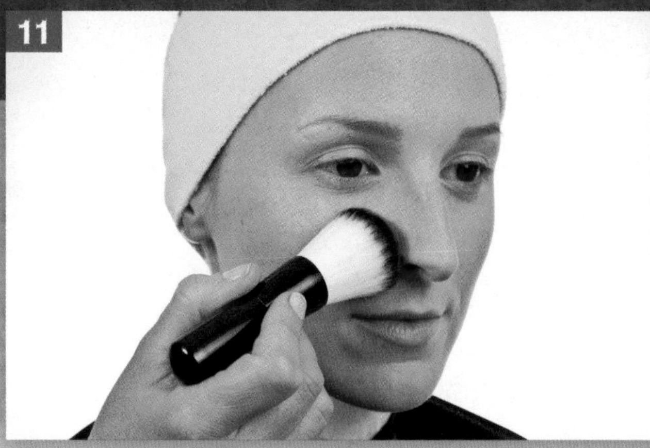

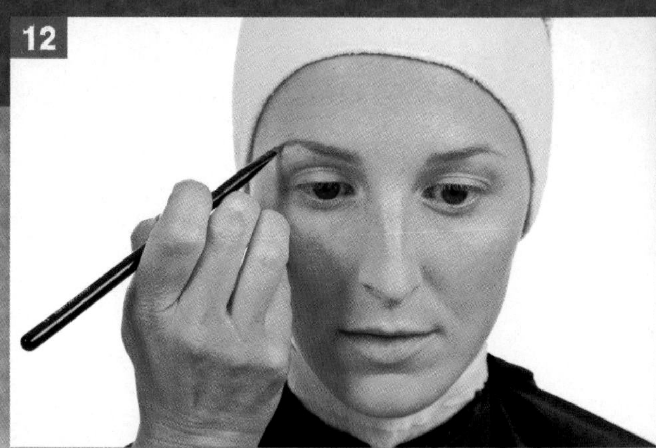

11 Pour powder onto the palette. Using a kabuki brush, gently swirl powder on the ends of brush. Tap off excess powder. Start at the center of the face using small circular motions to blend the powder. Then finish with downward strokes to set the foundation. Avoid heavy application on highlighted areas to keep the natural glow.

12 Using a brow comb, lightly smooth the eyebrows. Apply eye shadow using an angled brush in small dabbing motions. Use a shade that is one or two shades lighter if the client is a brunette or one or two shades darker for a blond. If the client is a redhead, use dark blond shades because red brows will appear saturated and unnatural.

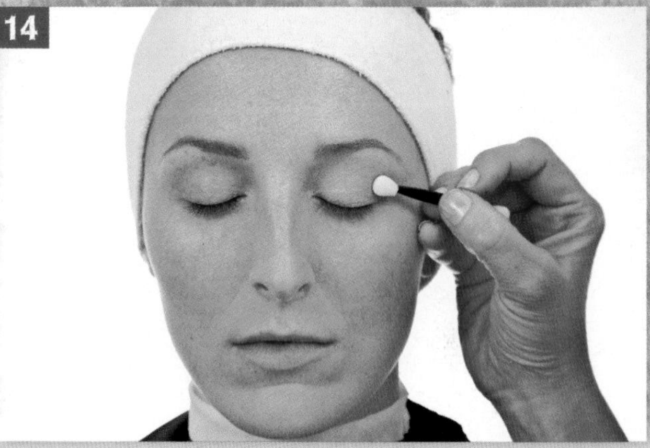

13 Sharpen pencil for a smooth precise end. With the client's eyes closed apply small, dotted lines on lash line. Then color in between the lines. Avoid coloring the entire lash line. Instead, end just before the inner corner of the eye. You can use a wet shadow or gel liner for a smudged effect. Liquid liner gives a more retro appearance but only use if you have a steady hand. Avoid a heavy wing and choose among black, charcoal, or dark chocolate. Then have client look up and to the side to apply the liner under the eyes.

14 Choose colors close in value. Two to three shades work best. Apply lighter shade to entire eyelid from lash line to brow bone. Apply darker shade to crease and outer edge of eye. To make eyes appear wider apart, emphasize the outer corners of the eye with color. To make eyes appear closer together, emphasize the inner corner of the eye.

SERVICE TIP

Some makeup artists prefer to apply eye shadow before eyeliner. There is no wrong or right way.

Procedure 11-3 *(continued)*

15 Brush the eye shadow to the crease of the lid.

16 Apply a pearlescent shade on the brow bone for an illuminating effect.

17 After curling lashes with the eyelash curler, use a disposable mascara wand to apply mascara. Have the client look down and gently wiggle the wand at the base of the lashes. Then dab the tips of the lashes. Allow the lashes to slightly dry for 30 seconds. Then run a comb through the lashes to take off any flakes or clumps. Apply a second layer, then follow with comb. Avoid mascara on the lower lashes.

18 After sharpening the lip liner, use a nude tone or a tone slightly darker-than-natural lip color. Line just on the outer edge of the lip line. Do not use liner as lipstick as this will cause settling in fine lines. Pay special attention to defining the bows of the lips.

19 Use a spatula to remove lipstick from the container. Apply it using a lip brush for a precise application. Have the client part her lips and smile to get into every small crevice. Avoid blotting with tissue as this will cause an uneven texture. You may use a clean disposable sponge to blot the lips to remove any excess lipstick.

20 Using a lip brush, dab a slightly shimmer lip gloss on the center of the lower lip to add more dimension. Do not add gloss to the entire lip area.

21 Using the HD camera again, check the eye, cheek, and lip tones to make sure they appear flawless before the final shoot. Make any necessary adjustments. Use blotting paper if an area appears too shiny. Share the look with the client and list all items used to achieve the look.

Post-Service

- Complete PROCEDURE 7-2 POST-SERVICE SEE PAGE 148

Review Questions

1. What are the four different classic makeup styles reviewed in the chapter and how do they differ?
2. Why is it important for makeup artists to stay abreast of trends and techniques? How can this be done?
3. Explain what a tear sheet is and why a tear sheet is so important.
4. Who gives makeup artists direction for fashion show assignments?
5. What information does a production schedule supply?
6. What two colors of eye shadow or eyeliner could create a problem if the client has dark circles under the eyes?
7. What is HD technology and how does it affect makeup artists?
8. List four challenges of HD makeup.
9. Why are primers so important in high fashion makeup?
10. Give examples of the differences between traditional makeup application and HD makeup application.

Chapter Glossary

avant-garde style	A look that represents pushing the boundaries, resulting in a very edgy, high-voltage look.
catwalk	The runway that models walk down as they show the individual designer's collections in a fashion show.
contemporary style	Represents a fresh, clean look with an edgy avant-garde feel featuring current ideas in style, fashion, and design.
couture style	Breathes the beauty of Hollywood glamour and mystique with eye-catching elegant, yet subtle, trend-setting fashions.
high-definition television	Abbreviated HDTV; an increase in display or visual resolution.
luminous iridescent makeup	Makeup products that give the skin a radiant all-over glow and are available in paste, powder, and liquid form.
model comp cards	Cards that provide information including a given model's measurements and height; they also provide useful visual information that makeup artists can use as they develop a plan for creating each model's overall look and makeup application.
modern glamour style	Makeup that enhances the individual's features with a timeless quality of beauty and always looks modern; red lips, pale eye shadow, and a defined upper eyelid.
oil blotting papers	Silky sheets that help to absorb oil without compromising the makeup.

Chapter Glossary *(continued)*

paper palette	A palette made of disposable waterproof parchment paper or artist paper; it holds all the different products that you will use on an individual model.
pixel	The smallest single element of a digital image.
primers	Silicone formulas that are usually clear or colored for correction of skin tones; help to fill in fine lines, blur imperfections, and allow the makeup to glide effortlessly and last longer.
production schedule	A document that provides information concerning the event; it lists call times, along with the names of the designers, models, and the backstage crew.
standard definition television	Abbreviated SDTV; traditional analogue transmission with lower resolution.
tear sheets	Photos from the fashion magazines of hair and makeup styles that can be shown to the hair and makeup teams to communicate the designer's ideas and inspiration.

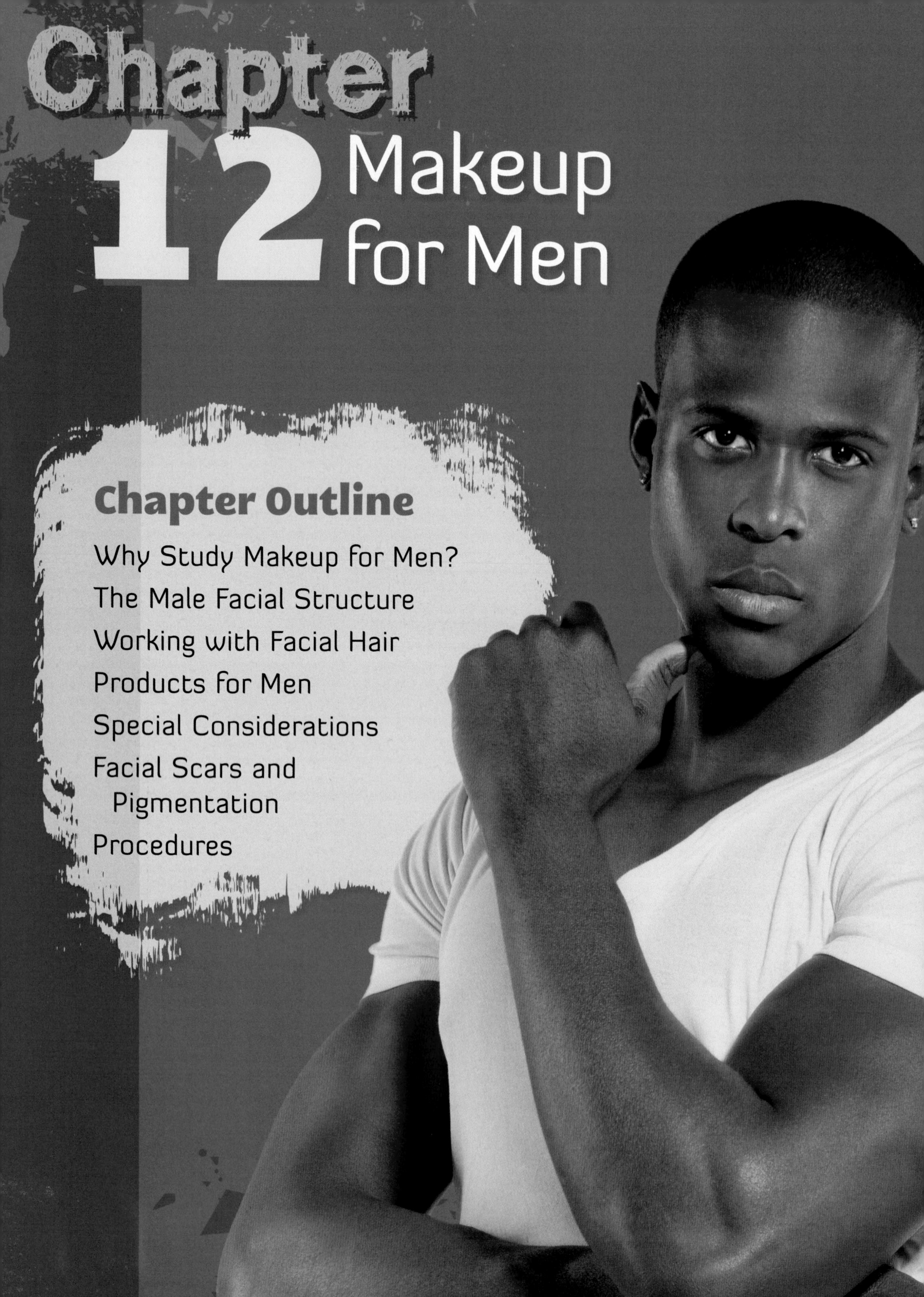

Chapter 12 Makeup for Men

Chapter Outline

Learning Objectives

After completing this chapter, you will be able to:

- ✓ **LO1** Identify the 10 areas of the anatomy of the head that are important to know when applying makeup for men.
- ✓ **LO2** Identify 11 male features that may be challenging for makeup application.
- ✓ **LO3** Identify a product you can use to groom facial hair.
- ✓ **LO4** Identify the four basic areas for men's facial hair.
- ✓ **LO5** Identify four remedies for ingrown hairs.
- ✓ **LO6** Identify the five makeup products that are most likely to interest men.
- ✓ **LO7** Explain how you would solve pigmentation problems for men.
- ✓ **LO8** Perform a basic makeup application procedure for men.

Key Terms

Page number indicates where in the chapter the term is used.

chin curtain
pg. 277

"five-o'clock shadow"
pg. 279

friendly mutton chops
pg. 278

Fu Manchu moustache
pg. 278

full beard
pg. 278

goatee
pg. 278

goatee with the moustache
pg. 278

grooming cream
pg. 277

handlebar moustache
pg. 278

ingrown hairs
pg. 279

mutton chops
pg. 278

salicylic acid
pg. 279

soul patch
pg. 278

Career Profile

Photographed by Joseph Schuyler.

Thom Cammer was first introduced to the concept of makeup artistry through theatre arts education at The New York State Theatre Institute. An actor as well, Thom made the connection between human appearance, how it could be drastically altered or enhanced by the proper use of makeup, and the ways that makeup can be used as a tool for communication. Makeup could take an ordinary man and turn him into Mr. Toad or make the beautiful features of the human face even more striking.

Today, Thom is a freelance makeup artist, using his skills mostly for media purposes. He is a member of the Make-Up Artists And Hair Stylists Guild, I.A.T.S.E. Local 706. He holds cosmetology licenses in both New York state and in California.

Courtesy of Chris Brinker.

"I have had a broad range of wonderful experiences as a makeup artist. My job has taken me many places, such as shooting films at breathtaking locations, shooting editorial fashion on the streets of London, and shooting for commercial print jobs in elegant New York studios.

"When I was the Makeup Department Head on a well-known feature film, I stepped out of the makeup trailer after an exhausting day. I was struck by the golden light of the setting sun illuminating the Hollywood sign in the hills above. Then and there I realized that, for good or bad, I had achieved one of my life's largest aspirations: working in the motion picture industry.

"Since many makeup artists will work on a freelance basis from time to time, I highly recommend that all students take an entrepreneurial management class. There, they can learn to value and organize their makeup artistry in abusinesslike way. Makeup artists can often be undervalued in a business setting, especially in the beginning of their careers. Knowing how to value yourself in the workforce and knowing how to have your contractual agreements and other details in order before you begin a job is one key to a successful career.

"Through a career as a makeup artist, you will encounter all varieties of personality types. One's own ego or the egos of other people can wreak havoc in industries like fashion, beauty, and film. People skills and a basic familiarity with human psychology are good tools to help you diffuse negative situations in the workplace. I suggest that artists always try to remain humble, be grateful for their work, and as they say, 'Keep Calm and Carry On.'"

Courtesy of Eric Raptosh Photography.

Men's makeup and skin care has evolved, and cosmetic products now exist exclusively for use by men. It is no longer unusual or taboo for men to want to improve their appearance; they are just unsure about how to do so. Skin care is not always something men practice, so their skin can appear rough and in need of attention. Preparing male skin by cleansing and moisturizing is important to achieve the best makeup application. Share with your male clients the importance of basic home-care for their skin as this is important in order for the application of makeup to look natural.

Many men struggle with dark circles, scars, or pigmentation problems that can easily be disguised with appropriate products such as primer, concealer, foundation, and powder. This chapter will explore the challenges posed by male clients, including their unique facial shapes and facial hair.

As discussed in Chapter 11, The Exciting World of High Fashion and High-Definition, makeup is a necessity when working in film, television, photography, and fashion. Makeup techniques can produce dramatic and immediate changes in clients' appearance. For men, makeup can improve the skin tone by correcting blotchy skin, uneven areas, and other imperfections. Perfecting the skin tone and appearance with the correct products provides a finished, groomed look. Makeup artists need to pay attention to men's facial hair because it can create an unkempt look if it is not groomed properly.

WHY STUDY MAKEUP FOR MEN?

Makeup artists should study and have a thorough understanding of makeup for men because:

- Makeup for men is becoming very popular.
- The segment of the market that is devoted to men's makeup is growing.
- Male models and actors require makeup for photoshoots, television, film, theater, and fashion.
- Men often need professional photos for business purposes, and makeup will ensure high-quality photos.

▲ Figure 12–1 **Determine your client's face shape and facial features.**

THE MALE FACIAL STRUCTURE

Men's facial structures vary, and they pose different challenges for the makeup artist than female facial structures do. It is very important when working with a male client to take time to assess the face shape and proportions so that you can determine how to best enhance the client's unique facial features (**Figure 12–1**). During the assessment process, you will decide which areas and/or features you will emphasize. Take into consideration the features of the anatomy of the head when you decide which features to emphasize and the techniques you will use to emphasize them:

- Hairline
- Brow
- Tapered wedge of the nose
- Cheekbones
- Eye sockets
- Barrel of the mouth
- Box of the chin
- Angle of the lower jaw, or jawline
- Side of the cheekbone
- Shell of the ear ☑ LO1

▲ **Figure 12–2 The oval face shape.**

Once you have assessed those areas, be aware that most faces differ from side to side. That is to say, most faces are not perfectly symmetrical. Some examples could be:

- One eyebrow with a higher arch than the other
- One eye that appears more open than the other
- One nostril that is more flared than the other
- One side of the lip that is fuller
- One side of the lip line that is more down-turned

▲ **Figure 12–3 The square face shape.**

Being aware of what you are working with gives you the ability to conceptualize the results you want to achieve. Using the highlighting and contouring techniques of corrective makeup will allow you to create a formal or symmetrical balance, which means equal distribution. Since male facial features are usually strong, you will encounter clients with various features that can be challenging when applying men's makeup such as receding hairlines, protruding brows, chiseled jawlines, large noses, thin lips, various styles of facial hair, fine lines, prominent Adam's apples, scars, blotchy skin, and blemishes. This chapter will discuss how you can use makeup to minimize imperfections to create a more harmonious and balanced look. ☑ LO2

PROCEDURE 12-1 NATURAL MAKEUP FOR MEN SEE PAGE 284

▲ **Figure 12–4 The round face shape.**

Although the facial type of every male is determined by the individual position and overall prominence of their facial bones, there are eight basic facial types. Classic face shapes include:

- Oval (**Figure 12–2**)
- Square (most men) (**Figure 12–3**)
- Round (**Figure 12–4**)

▲ Figure 12–5 The triangular face shape.

▲ Figure 12–6 The heart (inverted triangle) face shape.

▲ Figure 12–7 The oblong face shape.

- Triangular (**Figure 12–5**)
- Heart (inverted triangle) (**Figure 12–6**)
- Oblong (**Figure 12–7**)
- Diamond (**Figure 12–8**)
- Combination of shapes (**Figure 12–9**)

The majority of human faces do not fall into one particular category or shape, and face shapes change with fluctuations in weight and maturation. Men and women have different hormonal compositions and bone structures which can result in women having softer features, and men generally having more pronounced or stronger features.

▲ Figure 12–8 The diamond face shape.

WORKING WITH FACIAL HAIR

Male facial hair is often course in texture and dry in appearance, creating challenges for facial grooming. Grooming cream or paste can be used to control and add moisture to facial hair, including the brows, beard, mustache, goatee, and sideburn. **Grooming cream** is a hair product for men that adds flexibility to the facial hair, making it more pliable. ☑ LO3

Men's facial hair is usually concentrated in the upper lip, the chin, the sideburns, and the sides of the face. The way it is trimmed can enhance or diminish particular structural features of the face. Trimming techniques are variations of basic themes. The basic styles and their descriptions appear in the list below: ☑ LO4

- The **chin curtain** style is marked by facial hair growth only along the lower portion of the face at the chin and along the jawline (**Figure 12–10**).

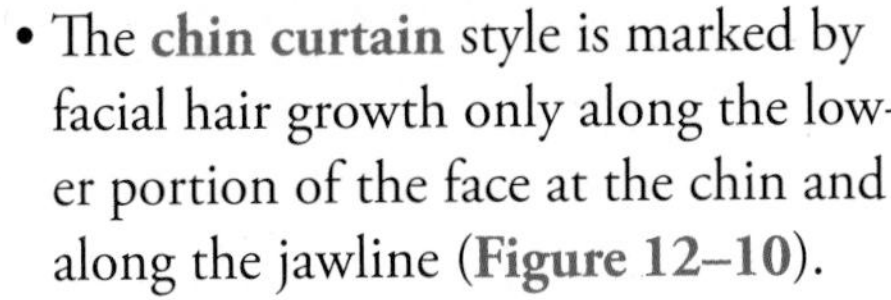

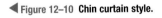

◀ Figure 12–10 Chin curtain style.

▲ Figure 12–9 Combination of face shapes on a male client.

▲ **Figure 12–11 Goatee.**

- The **goatee** style, which has been popular throughout history, is facial hair confined to the chin area. There are a number of variations; goatees can be close-trimmed, long and full, or even combed into geometric shapes (**Figure 12–11**).
- The **goatee with the moustache** is achieved by adding the moustache (facial hair under the nose area) to the goatee. The look can be square or round depending on what best suits the individual's face shape (**Figure 12–12**).
- The **soul patch** is achieved by confinement of the facial hair just below the lower lip. This style was very popular among the beatniks and jazz artists of the 1950s and 1960s (**Figure 12–13**).

▲ **Figure 12–12 Goatee with the moustache.**

▲ **Figure 12–13 Soul patch.**

▲ **Figure 12–14 Handlebar moustache.**

- The **handlebar moustache** is area moustache that is long enough to curl the ends; the look is usually achieved and maintained by using a specialized styling wax (**Figure 12–14**).
- The **Fu Manchu moustache** is created by facial hair that grows over the lip and extends down each side of the mouth to the jaw area (**Figure 12–15**).

▲ **Figure 12–15 Fu Manchu moustache.**

- **Mutton chops** are characterized by wide swaths of sideburns growing down the sides of the face, almost to the corners of the mouth. The mutton-chop style was popularized in the 1970s by Elvis Presley (**Figure 12–16**).
- **Friendly mutton chops** are a combination of mutton chops and a moustache to create one continuous line of facial hair (**Figure 12–17**).
- The **full beard** is created by covering all the basic areas of the face: the upper lip, the chin, the sideburns, and the sides of the face. This style is typically groomed at the neck area, at the lip line, and at the sides (**Figure 12–18**).

▲ **Figure 12–16 Mutton chops.**

© iStockphoto/SensorSpot

▲ Figure 12–17 **Friendly mutton chops.**

© AYAKOVLEV.COM/www.Shutterstock.com

▲ Figure 12–18 **Full beard.**

© CURAphotography/www.Shutterstock.com

▲ Figure 12–19 **The "five-o'clock shadow" is popular among men.**

- The **five-o'clock shadow** is created by not shaving for a day or two and is currently a popular fashion look (**Figure 12–19**).

Ingrown Hairs

Some men experience frequent ingrown hairs on the face and neck. **Ingrown hairs** are the result of hair that has broken off inside the follicle and irritates the follicle wall; these ingrown hairs can cause bumps and even eventual scarring (**Figure 12–20**). Typical causes of ingrown hairs include:

- Dry skin
- Stiff beard hair
- Coarse curly hair
- Oil embedded in the hair follicle
- Build-up of dead skin cells in the pores on the skin's surface
- Irritation to the hair follicle caused by hair removal techniques such as shaving, waxing, and tweezing
- A shave that is too close

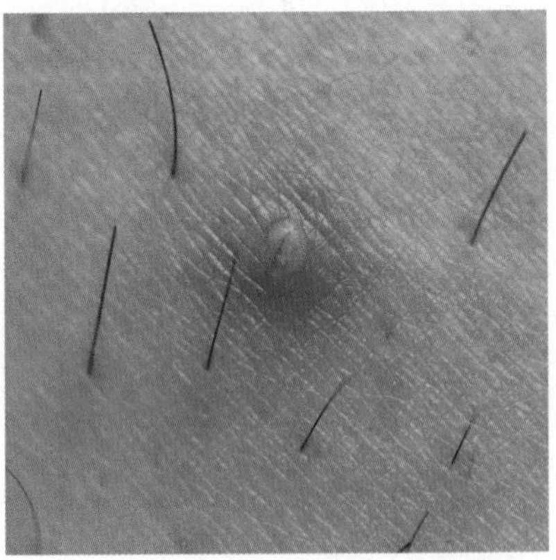

© F.C.G. /www.Shutterstock.com

▲ Figure 12–20 **Ingrown hairs are commonly found on the face and neck of male clients.**

Some remedies for ingrown hairs are as follows:

- Products and treatments that include salicylic acid. This can be acquired from an esthetician or a dermatologist and is an excellent ingredient to minimize the occurrence of ingrown hairs. **Salicylic acid** is a beta hydroxy acid ingredient that exfoliates, prevents bacterial growth, cleanses the pores, and helps prevent infection.

Activity

Practice creating a portfolio or look-book using photographs or drawings. Find 4 photos that show how faces typically differ from one side to the other. Find 10 photos of the different types of facial hair styles.

STATE REGULATORY

ALERT

Check with your state's regulatory agencies on laws regarding extraction and removal of ingrown hairs. Most states prohibit removing ingrown hair unless you are a licensed esthetician or physician.

- Shaving cream that is formulated for sensitive skin will help the skin maintain moisture. Choose a product with lubricating agents, rather than one containing alcohol.
- A skin exfoliation routine which removes dead epidermal skin cells will assist in managing ingrown hairs.
- A shaving routine that does not include pulling the skin or applying pressure to the razor to get a closer shave will help men avoid ingrown hairs. (The shave might not be as close, but there will be fewer ingrown hairs.)

Removal of ingrown hairs can only be performed by a licensed esthetician. As a makeup artist, you can camouflage an ingrown hair by using a matte concealer and a matte foundation. The process for removing ingrown hairs is to create an opening in the bump and then carefully lift the ingrown hair out of the follicle with disinfected tweezers. Do not pluck the hair. Using allantoin, azulene, or witch hazel will help in reducing the redness and swelling. ☑ LO5

▲ Figure 12–21 Facial hair can be trimmed by licensed cosmetologists.

Trimming Men's Facial Hair

Licensed cosmetologists can trim a client's facial hair (**Figure 12–21**). The shear-over-comb technique works best, allows more control, and helps the stylist avoid cutting the hair too short. It is only necessary to trim the unwanted stray hairs. Electric trimmers can also be used to line the sideburns, beard, and moustache or to clean-up the neck area. Be sure to check whether the client needs to have his eyebrows trimmed or stray hair in his ears cut as well.

PRODUCTS FOR MEN

Cosmetics for men have become very popular, and several new men's lines are being manufactured (**Figure 12–22**). Men's skin is different from women's, so it makes sense to have different products for the two markets. Such differences include the following:

- Men's skin is 20 to 30 percent thicker than women's.
- Men have more hair follicles on the face than women.
- Daily shaving helps to exfoliate men's skin and bring the new skin cells to the surface.
- Men often have oiler skin than women.
- Most men are concerned with their appearance; they are likely to be interested in skin care products, but they are also likely to have less patience for the process. The trick is to explain and demonstrate products quickly—usually in less than 10 minutes.
- Some men want to keep their use of skin care products (and especially makeup) private. Maintaining confidentiality for male clients is very important.

▲ Figure 12–22 Products for men.

Client Consultation

Once you have analyzed your male client's face, consider recommending the following skin care products:

- Cleanser
- Toner
- Moisturizer
- Exfoliator
- Mask
- Antiaging serum, if needed

Some men may be interested in the following makeup products:

- Primer
- Oil-free foundation
- Concealer
- Matte powder
- Lip moisturizer ☑ LO6

Mineral makeup is an alternative product that men may wish to consider. Mineral powder foundation acts as foundation, concealer, and powder all-in-one product. Also, it looks natural—an important consideration for men who do not want to look like they are wearing makeup.

SPECIAL CONSIDERATIONS

The male makeup client will likely have concerns and issues that are very different from those of your female clients. Evaluating these issues in the initial assessment will help you create perfect results.

- Bald heads and receding hairlines require special consideration. The makeup used on the head needs to match the facial makeup and blend with the overall look. The top of the head can shine when light strikes it, so use makeup and powder on that area. When working with bald men or men with a receding hairline, apply powder in a blotting motion to get the best anti-shine effect (**Figure 12–23 a–d**).
- For clients who have a receding hairline, do not get makeup in the hair. Pull the product from a thicker application to a minimal application as you move toward the hairline (**Figure 12–24a and b**). Start with minimal makeup; if you need more product, it can always be added.

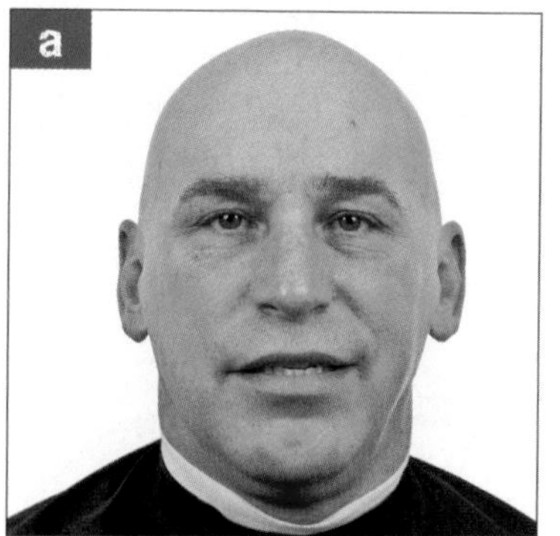

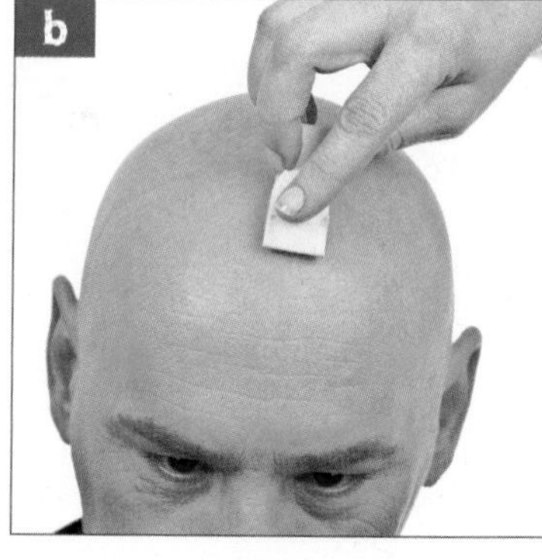

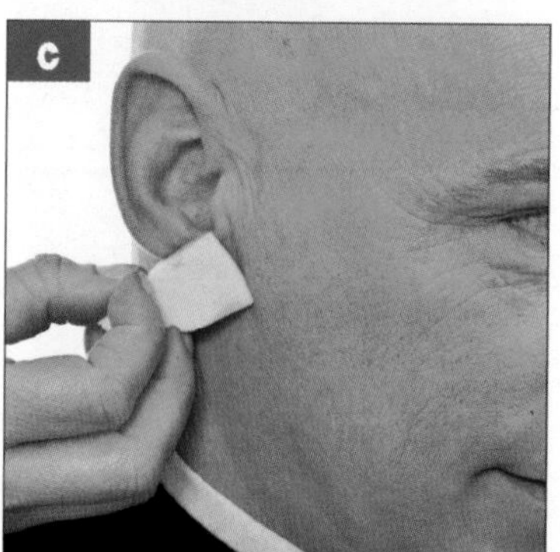

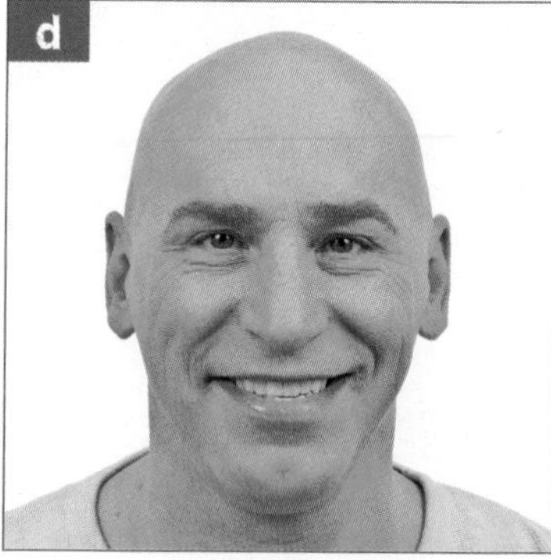

▲ Figure 12–23 a-d **Blotting makeup is the best technique on a bald head.**

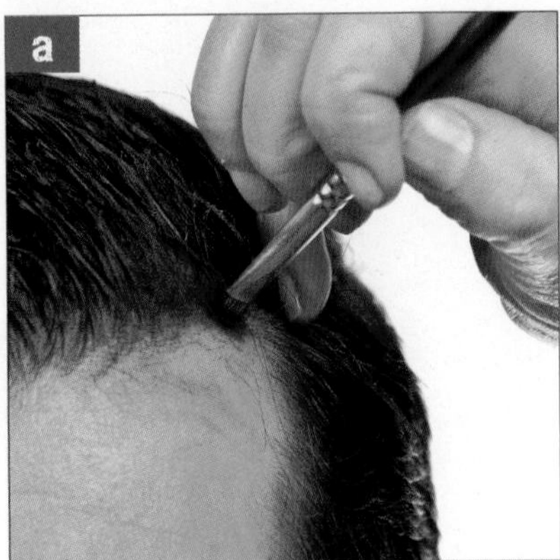

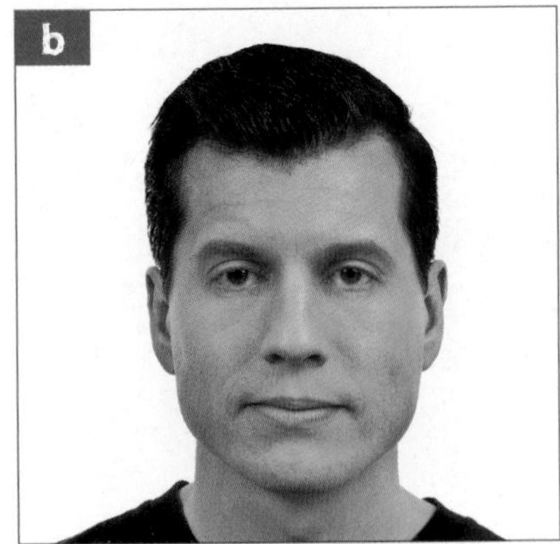

▲ Figure 12–24 a-b **Applying makeup to a client with a receding hairline.**

To ensure that men's makeup is even less noticeable, match the hands to the face. A bit of bronzer on the finger tips usually does the trick.

- Circles under the eyes can be corrected with a concealer that matches the natural skin tone. Feather, or blend, the product very gently (**Figure 12–25a and b**).
- If the eyebrows are very light and you want to add more definition, you can softly run the tip of a brow pencil over the eyebrow to add color. Another option is to softly brush a brow powder into the eyebrow to achieve definition without a strong line.
- When working with a protruding Adam's apple, apply matte contour to the Adam's apple using a foundation brush to create a dark recess. Then apply matte highlighter around the Adam's apple on the neck. Blend well. Using a sponge, apply and blend the foundation, making sure to match the natural skin tone of the neck and the face (**Figure 12–26a and b**).
- Primer can be used to create a more uniform skin surface if the client has fine lines or skin imperfections.

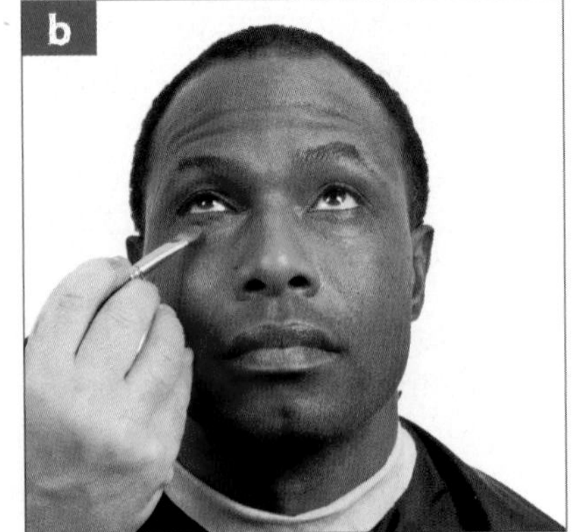

▲ Figure 12–25 a-b **Concealing dark circles under the eyes.**

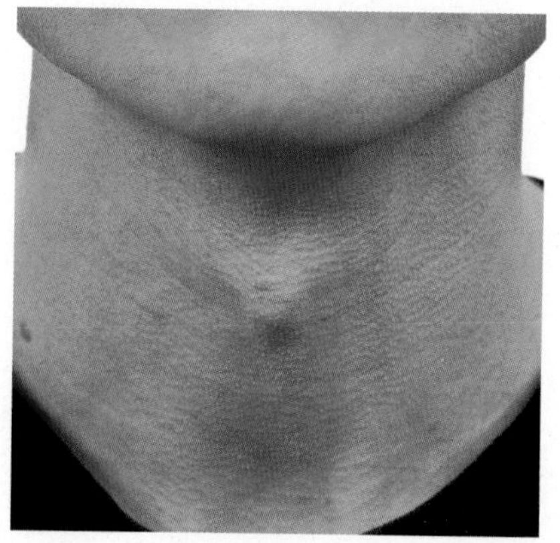
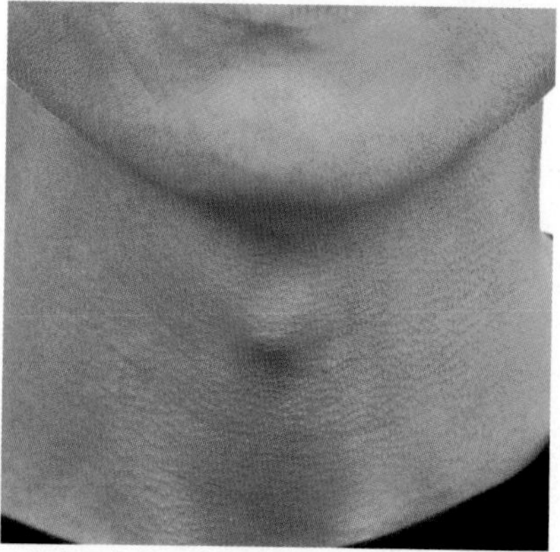

▲ Figure 12–26 a-b **Concealing an Adam's apple by applying matte contour makeup.**

FACIAL SCARS AND PIGMENTATION

Take special care when applying makeup to scars. Scars do not contain sweat glands or hair follicles, so product may not adhere well. Try layering the product and using a very well-matched concealer. Use a small brush to feather the edges, blending the product into the natural skin. Finish with a setting powder and then apply foundation all over the face.

Both light and dark pigmentation problems can be solved by matching concealer to the natural skin color. To start, pick a small area to test your product; get as close as you can to the natural color of the face. If makeup is to be applied over a large area to be corrected, applying dusting powder will make the product adhere better.

You do not want to conceal pigmentation, you want to minimize it and cover it with the correct color. Concealer might work in a small area, but if the problem covers a larger area, concealer may not give you a natural look. Mixing and blending foundation and concealers may be necessary to achieve the right color, consistency, and coverage. Concealing product is denser than foundation and sometimes concealer applied over a large area looks like paste. Some makeup artists prefer to use stick foundation when covering pigmentation problems because stick foundation is a little heavier than other types of foundation and not as dense as a concealer. ☑ LO7

Makeup artistry and skin care for the male client is a very exciting, evolving, and growing market. Many doors will be open to makeup artists who understand the special considerations of this market segment. To become a makeup artist skilled with male clients, take all the information in this chapter and combine it with your practical experience.

Demonstrate the application of men's runway makeup. Take photographs of the client before and after the makeup application for your portfolio or look-book.

PROCEDURE **12-2** **MEN'S RUNWAY MAKEUP** SEE PAGE 289

Procedure 12-1

Natural Makeup for Men

Implements and Materials

You will need all of the following implements, materials, and supplies:

- **Brushes**
  - ☐ Assorted cosmetic brushes

- **Utensils**
  - ☐ Cleansing wipes
  - ☐ Cutting shears
  - ☐ Electric or cordless trimmers 000
  - ☐ Shaving gel

Note: Depending upon your state regulations, you will most likely need to be a licensed stylist to use shears and trimmers.

- **Single-use Items**
  - ☐ Cotton swabs
  - ☐ Razor (optional)
  - ☐ Spatulas
  - ☐ Sponge wedges
  - ☐ Makeup remover wipes

- **Products**
  - ☐ Bronzer
  - ☐ Concealer
  - ☐ Facial moisturizer
  - ☐ Foundation
  - ☐ Hair grooming cream
  - ☐ Lip conditioner
  - ☐ Matte powder

Preparation

- Perform

PROCEDURE 7-1 PRE-SERVICE SEE PAGE 144

Procedure

1 Analyze the face shape and proportions so you know which features you will enhance and which you will diminish.

2 Check the face for areas of facial hair that need to be groomed. You may need to ask the client to shave before application. Always have disposable razors and shaving gels available.

Your goal on the natural male face is to create even natural color without creating the appearance of makeup. Matte product choices are the solution to the natural look. Always choose matte products in a men's makeup applications unless specifically asked to use a product with a different finish—such as a luminous iridescent product for a runway application.

---

3 Assess the face for skin imperfections: blemishes, scars, blotchy skin, facial hair, large Adam's apple, receding hairline, dark circles, and pigmentation problems.

4 Cleanse and tone the face to remove any surface debris. Use only cloth or cosmetic remover wipes, sponges, and cosmetic brushes. Do not use cotton or facial tissues on a male face because stubble will shred the cotton or tissue and the debris will stick to the face.

5 Moisturize the skin to improve its appearance. Use a moisturizer that is appropriate to the client's skin type.

6 Using a disposable lip wand, apply a lip moisturizer to soften, smooth, and condition the lips.

7 Using a sponge, test the foundation on the client's jawline before applying to the entire face. This is the time to test various colors of concealer for highlighting and contouring; choose the colors best suited for the client's skin tone.

SERVICE TIP

If your client has facial hair that stops at the jawline, match the foundation from the top of the neck to where the jawline starts.

8a With a concealer brush and matte concealer, conceal dark circles, broken blood vessels, and scars or pigmentation problems.

To conceal a blemish. Using a matte concealer that is close to the client's skin tone, apply a small amount of concealer to a very fine, disposable makeup concealer brush and then dab the product on the center of the blemish. Move to the outer edge with a gentle circular motion. Then blend the concealer into the skin.

8b **To conceal dark circles.** Apply matte concealer with a concealer brush. To soften the appearance of the concealer use a disposable sponge to very gently and lightly blend the concealer under the eye, working it from the inner corner the outer corner until the concealer is totally blended. Remember to counterbalance the most prominent undertone when you choose the concealer color.

8c **To conceal broken blood vessels.** A matte concealer can be used to counterbalance the redness of broken blood vessels. Using a disposable sponge, gently tap the matte concealer in the areas of the broken blood vessels and then blend in with gentle strokes.

Note: Depending on the scars and pigmentation challenges, use one of the techniques described previously and the matte concealer to camouflage the scar and/or pigmentation issue (see "Facial Scars and Pigmentation," page 283).

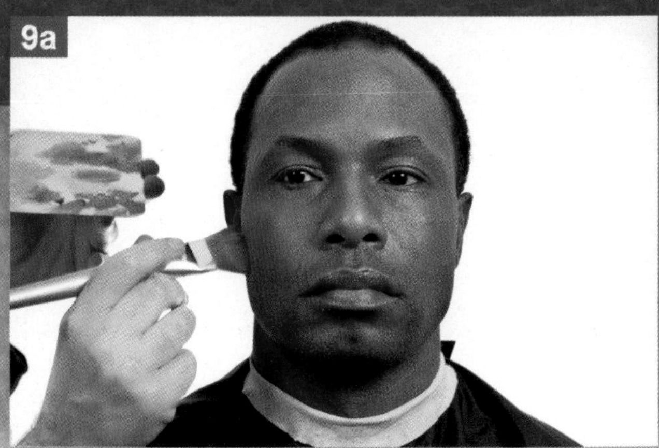

9 To emphasize facial features, highlight and contour the recesses of the face. Contour pushes features back and adds depth. Highlighting brings features forward and accentuates them. When highlighting the male face always use matte products to avoid a hue or a shine. The typical male facial structure will have recesses in the cheek area, under the chin area, and possibly around the eye area (where you would apply highlighter). Highlight can be applied to enhance the overall facial structure.

9a Choose a matte foundation that is closest to the client's skin tone. Remove the foundation from its container with a disposable spatula.

SERVICE TIP

With a larger nose, you may want to contour by applying a stroke of the contour product at the tip of the nose. To narrow the nose, you can apply the contour down each side of the nose. Blend the contour with a sponge by gently feathering in a vertical movement.

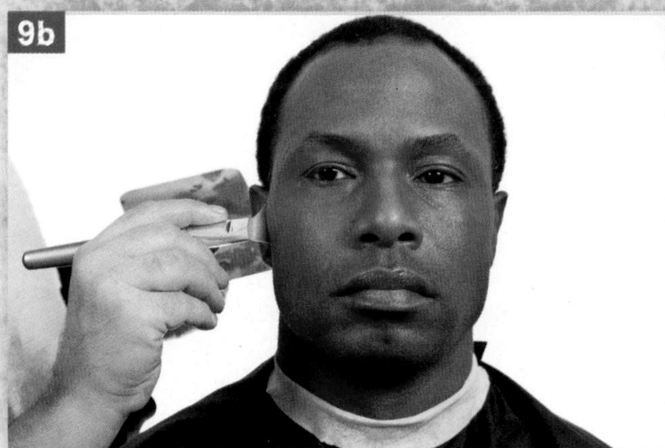

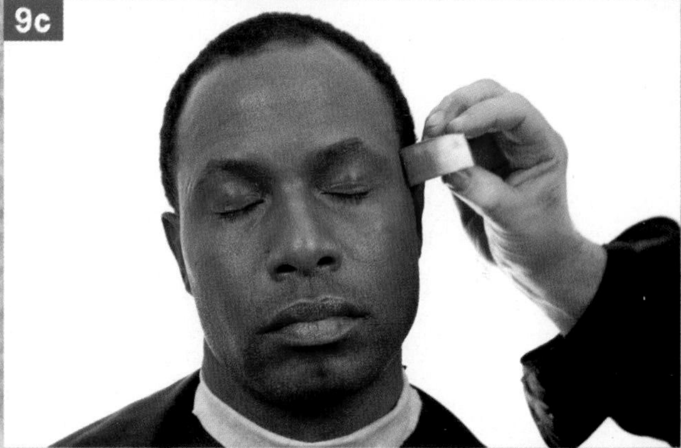

9b Apply your matte foundation over the concealed and contoured areas by blending and stretching the foundation in the focus areas of the forehead, chin, nose, and cheek.

9c With your sponge, blend the foundation from the forehead into the hairline. You are stretching the product from a light application to a minimal application. Keep your foundation away from the hairline and facial hair, especially if the client has a mustache, beard, or goatee.

Procedure 12-1 *(continued)*

10 For male clients with a lighter skin tone, use bronzer/blush that is slightly darker to add color to the face and create an all-over healthy glow. With a blush brush sweep the bronzer over the forehead, nose, and contours of the face.

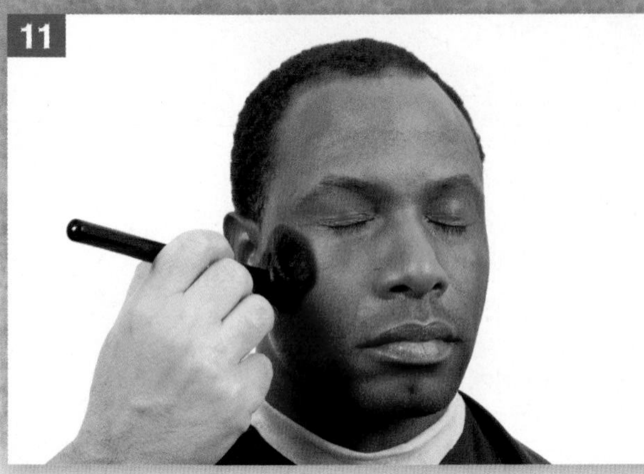

11 Set the foundation and bronzer with a matte powder. You can dip the tip of the powder brush into the matte powder and dust lightly over the forehead and face.

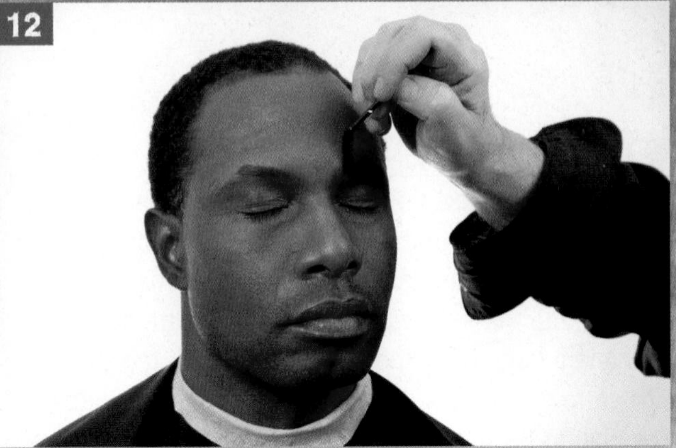

12 Using a brow brush, gently comb through the eyebrows.

13 The finished look.

SERVICE TIP

Bending the disposable eyebrow brush before use is one way to prevent injury to a client's eye.

Post-Service ☑ LO8

- Complete

PROCEDURE 7-2 POST-SERVICE SEE PAGE 148

Procedure 12-2

Men's Runway Makeup

Implements and Materials

You will need the following implements, materials, and supplies:

Brushes

- ☐ Assorted cosmetic brushes

Utensils

- ☐ Brush cleaner
- ☐ Cutting shears
- ☐ Electric or cordless trimmers 000
- ☐ Makeup remover
- ☐ Shaving gel

Note: Depending upon your state regulations, you will most likely need to be a licensed stylist to use shears and trimmers.

Single-use Items

- ☐ Cotton swabs
- ☐ Razor (optional)
- ☐ Spatulas
- ☐ Sponge wedges
- ☐ Makeup remover wipes

Products

- ☐ Black eyeliner
- ☐ Bronzer
- ☐ Concealers
- ☐ Facial moisturizer
- ☐ Foundations
- ☐ Hair grooming cream
- ☐ Highlighter
- ☐ Lip conditioner
- ☐ Luminous iridescent powder/paste/cream
- ☐ Matte powders
- ☐ Shaving gel

Preparation

- Perform

PROCEDURE 7-1 PRE-SERVICE SEE PAGE 144

Procedure

1 Analyze the face shape and proportions so you know which features you will enhance and which you will contour.

Procedure 12-2 *(continued)*

2 Check for facial hair that needs to be groomed. You may need to ask the client to shave before the makeup application. Always have disposable razors and shaving gels available.

3 Assess the client's face for imperfections such as blemishes, scars, blotchy skin, unruly facial hair, a large Adam's apple, a receding hairline, dark circles, broken blood vessels, and pigmentation problems.

4 Cleanse, tone, and lightly apply moisturizer that is appropriate to the client's skin type.

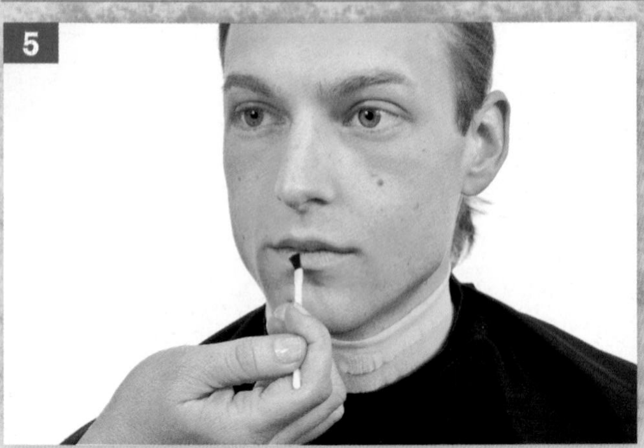

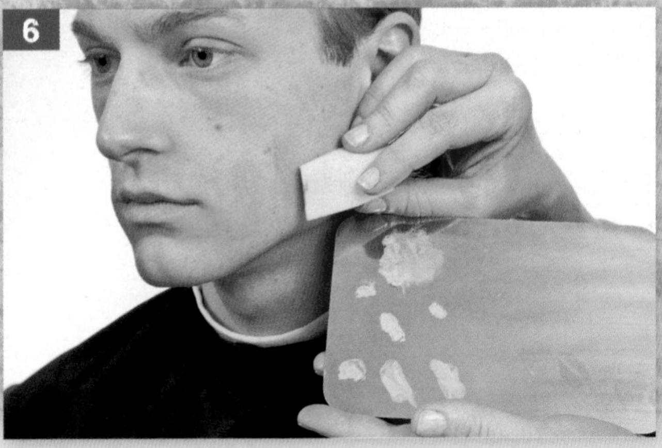

5 Using a disposable lip wand, apply lip moisturizer to condition, soften, and smooth the lips.

6 Using a sponge, test foundation colors and concealer colors (for highlighting and contouring) on the jawline before application.

7 With a concealer brush—and using matte concealer—cover dark circles, broken blood vessels, scars, and uneven pigmentation. The sections below provide more tips about how to apply concealer effectively to color blemishes, dark circles, and broken blood vessels. Depending on the types of scars and pigmentation challenges your client has, you will likely find one of these techniques to be useful as well (see also "Special Considerations," page281).

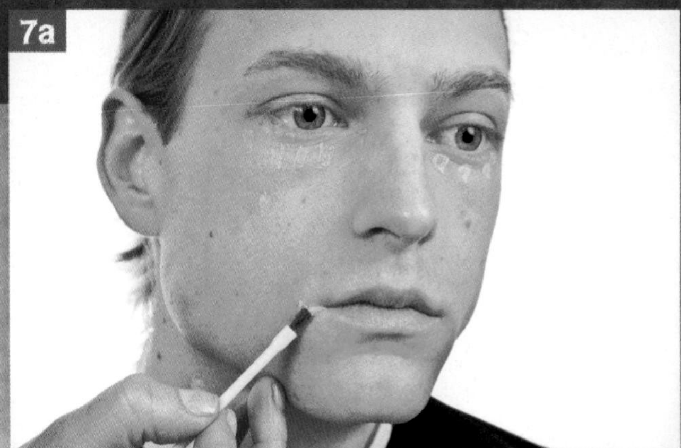

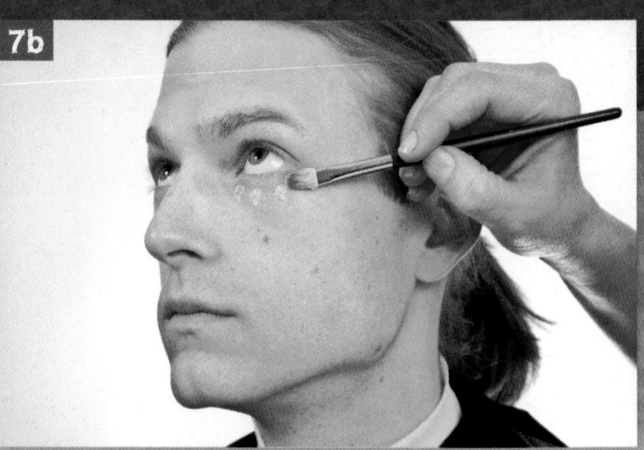

7a **To conceal a blemish.** Using matte concealer that is close to the client's skin tone, apply concealer with a very fine disposable concealer brush and dab the product on the center of the blemish. Move toward the outer edge with a gentle circular motion. Then blend concealer into the skin.

7b **To conceal dark circles.** When working with dark circles under the eyes, remember to choose a concealer color that will counterbalance the most prominent undertone of the dark circles. Apply the matte concealer with a concealer brush. To soften the appearance of the concealer, very gently and lightly blend it under the eye by working from the inner corner to the outside corner until the concealer is totally blended into the skin.

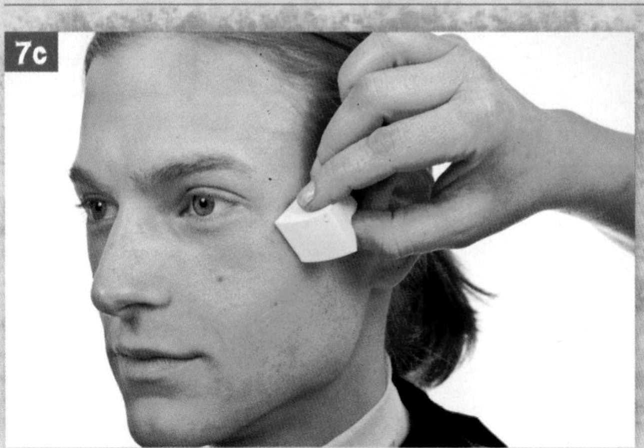

7c **To conceal broken blood vessels.** A matte concealer for broken blood vessels can be used to counterbalance redness. Using a disposable sponge, gently tap the matte concealer in the areas of the broken blood vessels. Blend using gentle strokes.

8 To emphasize specific facial features, highlight and contour the recesses of the face using a powder brush.

9 Add your luminous iridescent powder/paste/cream with a sponge to the highlighted areas of the face. When highlighting the male face you are creating a luminous hue.

10 With a foundation brush, apply foundation over the concealed, contoured, and luminous areas. Continue to cover all areas of the face, keeping your foundation away from the hairline and facial hair.

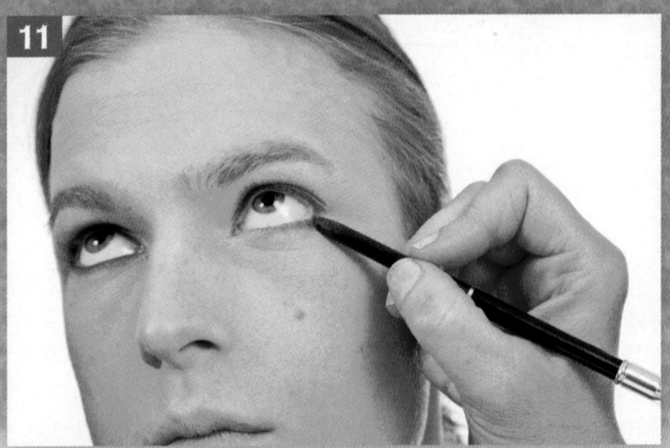

11 Cleanse and disinfect the eyeliner pencil by spraying disinfectant on the tip, sharpening the pencil, and disinfecting it again. Apply eyeliner at the lash line to make the eyes appear more noticeable and defined on the runway. Lining the eye will give the client a dark, mysterious look. As mentioned several times throughout this text, lining the inner rim of the eye may lead to irritation and the possible spread of bacteria causing an eye infection. Follow proper cleansing and disinfection of the eyeliner before application, between each eye, and upon completion.

12 You can soften the eyeliner by placing a lighter eye shadow over the eyeliner or by smudging the eyeliner with an angled shadow brush.

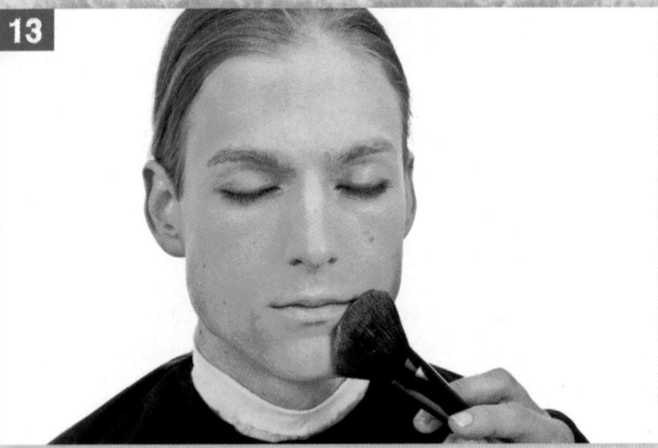

13 Set the face with a matte powder. Dip the tip of the powder brush into the matte powder, tap to remove excess powder, and then lightly dust the forehead and face.

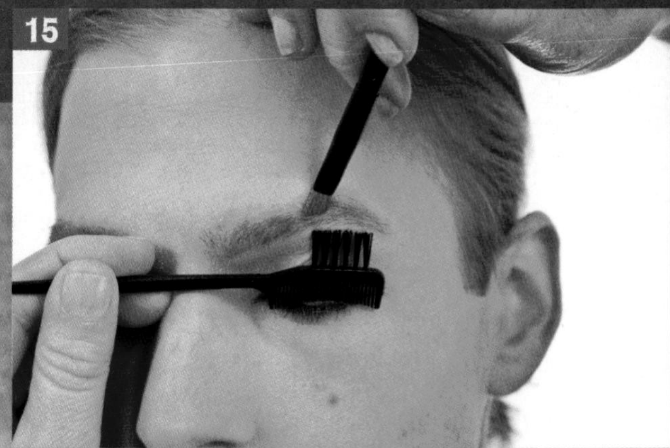

14 Use bronzer that is slightly darker than the foundation to add color to the face and create an all-over healthy glow. With a blush brush, sweep the bronzer over the forehead, nose, and contours of the face.

15 Using a brow brush, gently comb through the eyebrows and any facial hair.

16 The finished look.

SERVICE TIP

If the eyebrows are very light and you want to add more definition, you can place the comb under the eyebrow and using a brow pencil softly run the tip of the pencil over the eyebrow to add light color and definition without a real strong line to finish off the look.

Post-Service

- Complete

PROCEDURE 7-2 POST-SERVICE SEE PAGE 148

Review Questions

1. Why is it important to assess the male face before proceeding with the makeup application?
2. What are the two major differences between men and women that result in women having softer features and men having more pronounced features?
3. What product can be used to groom men's facial hair, and what does this product do?
4. Name five factors that cause ingrown hairs.
5. What procedure can be used to correct dark circles under the eyes?
6. How do you diminish the appearance of the Adam's apple?
7. Why do you want to minimize pigmentation differences rather than conceal them?
8. What is the difference between contour and highlighting?
9. How do you apply makeup in order to minimize a large nose?
10. What is the consistency of the luminous iridescent product used in the men's runway application?

Chapter Glossary

chin curtain	A style marked by facial hair growth only along the lower portion of the face at the chin and following the jawline.
"five-o'clock shadow"	A style created by not shaving for a day; currently a popular fashion look.
friendly mutton chops	A combination of mutton chops and a moustache to create one continuous line of facial hair.
Fu Manchu moustache	A style created by facial hair that grows over the lip and extends down each side of the mouth to the jaw area.
full beard	A style in which hair covers all three basic areas: the upper lip, the chin, and the sides of the face. This style is typically trimmed at the neck area, at the lip line, and sides.
goatee	A style that has been popular throughout history; facial hair growth is confined to the chin area.
goatee with the moustache	A style achieved by adding the moustache (facial hair under the nose area) to the goatee.
grooming cream	A hair product for men that adds flexibility to the facial hair, making it more pliable.
handlebar moustache	A moustache that is long enough so that the ends can be curled; the look is usually achieved and maintained by using a specialized styling wax.

Chapter Glossary *(continued)*

mutton chops	A style characterized by wide swaths of sideburns growing down the sides of the face, almost touching the corners of the mouth. The mutton chop style was popularized in the 1970s by Elvis Presley.
salicylic acid	A beta hydroxy acid ingredient that exfoliates, prevents bacterial growth, cleanses the pores, and helps prevent infection.
soul patch	A style achieved by confinement of the facial hair just below the lower lip; this style was very popular among the beatniks and jazz artists of the 1950s and 1960s.

Chapter 13 Makeup for Teens

Chapter Outline

Why Study Makeup for Teens?

Consulting with a Teenage Client

Skin Care Basics for Teens

Makeup Basics for Teens

Makeup for Blemished Skin

Prom Makeup

Procedures

Learning Objectives

After completing this chapter, you will be able to:

- ✓ **LO1** Understand the importance of a client consultation with teenagers.
- ✓ **LO2** Recognize and comprehend the do's and do not's when working with teenagers.
- ✓ **LO3** Comprehend basic skin nutrition for teens.
- ✓ **LO4** Perform three makeup applications for teenage (teen) clients: basic, blemished skin, and prom.

Key Terms

Page number indicates where in the chapter the term is used.

mineral makeup
pg. 303

stipple
pg. 304

undertone
pg. 304

skin nutrition
pg. 301

Career Profile

Lydia Milars

With a portfolio that includes major films such as *A Cinderella Story, Cheaper by the Dozen, Seabiscuit,* and *Dude, Where's My Car?,* Lydia Milars has plenty of advice to offer up-and-coming makeup artists. Her professional achievements come from the emphasis she places on proper education, professionalism, and forward thinking. Currently, she works to educate students about makeup artistry, while still holding positions as department head with major film and entertainment productions.

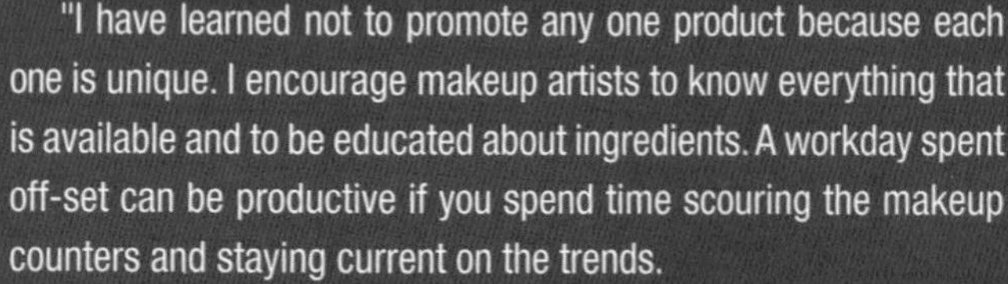

"Over the past 30 years I have worked in almost every capacity as a makeup artist and esthetician. The only path I did not take was to work a cosmetics counter; I did, however, work with the public in a salon. In many ways, that time in my life was the most gratifying of all. There is no better feeling than seeing the joy on someone's face as you reveal her beauty.

"I have learned not to promote any one product because each one is unique. I encourage makeup artists to know everything that is available and to be educated about ingredients. A workday spent off-set can be productive if you spend time scouring the makeup counters and staying current on the trends.

"As a teacher and a neat freak, the things I can't stress enough are cleanliness and sanitation. Professional manners and appearances, especially for women, make a huge impact on how you are perceived in those first 5 minutes with a new client or employer. In a medi-spa, you should appear kind and compassionate. In print, film, or television, you should appear enthusiastic and collaborative. A 'diva' will not make it on these sets. Success hinges on realizing that the makeup department is no more important than other aspects of the production. There is no time on-set for an ego, and word will travel fast if clients have bad experiences with you.

"Know what you want from this profession. It offers a lot of flexibility, so think about what you want for your life. If your goal is to be a star who is constantly in demand, then you may be on location for 8 months of the year. That can be a great life, unless you want a life that includes kids, a house, and a garden.

"There is tremendous competition in this industry, and having goals will keep you moving in the right direction. I point out to every class that there are 50 students in this class, 50 more in the room next door, 50 more upstairs, and so on. Perseverance is the key. Build a loyal clientele, a good portfolio, and a presence on the Internet. If you need a cosmetology license or a bachelor's degree go out there and get one. Many jobs now require these types of education.

"Test your work with photographers every chance you get, and be fearless! Listen to what everyone is telling you. Make sure you are not so highfaluting that you can't hear potential employers telling you to 'come back when you have more.' They mean it, so make sure you do go back."

In order to feel confident and beautiful, teenagers need to be educated about the importance of good skin care, good nutrition, and appropriate makeup. Teenage skin can be unpredictable; some teens have flawless skin, while others are dealing with oily, acneic skin and conditions that may seem out of control. Makeup artists can put teenagers at ease by helping them understand that we have all experienced awkward periods in life, and that celebrating our own unique beauty has been the key to self-confidence (**Figure 13–1**). An important factor in working with teenage clients is to help them understand that less is more.

© Palmer Kane LLC/www.Shutterstock.com

▲ Figure 13–1 **Teenage girls with an everyday makeup look.**

WHY STUDY MAKEUP FOR TEENS?

Makeup artists should study and have a thorough understanding of makeup for teens because:

- As a makeup artist, your primary job responsibility is promoting skin health and beauty. To be successful you will need to work well with clients of all ages.
- Makeup artists work with different age groups. Understanding their differences—interests, lifestyles, and skin health—will help you have positive interactions with clients of every age.
- Makeup artists can educate teenagers and young consumers on best practices for skin care and makeup application.
- Makeup artists can teach teens that their makeup should be fun, clean, and simple (**Figure 13–2**).

© Monkey Business Images/www.Shutterstock.com

▲ Figure 13–2 **Everyday makeup applications for teens should take no more than 5 minutes.**

CONSULTING WITH A TEENAGE CLIENT

Makeup consultations and applications—including those with teenagers—should be suited to the individual client. Ask questions about your client's lifestyle. Is she extremely active and involved with sports? Does she love makeup, or does she wear minimal makeup? Does she like to try each new color and funky trend? Is her skin clear or prone to acne? The answers to those questions will affect your work with individual teen clients, but the focus will always be clean, healthy skin and simplified beauty. Teenage makeup techniques are completely different from those appropriate for mature skin. Heavy foundation, concealer, and eyeliner is too harsh for teenagers' youthful appearance. ☑ **LO1**

The goal of the teen makeup application is to bring out the best features of the individual and to promote her self-confidence. Focus on the feature she loves most about her face, whether it is her eyes, lips, or cheekbones. Offer solutions for your client's problems and concerns. For example, when a teenager is self-conscious about acne or a particular facial feature, let her know there are ways to correct the problem so she can feel beautiful.

HERE'S A TIP

When you work with teens, it is important to respect the wishes of the parent or guardian. Usually this will mean keeping the makeup looking light and playful, not overly sophisticated or heavy.

▲ **Figure 13–3 A confident and beautiful teenage girl.**

Makeup is a powerful tool. We can disguise acne with concealer, narrow a wide nose or a strong jaw with contour, and lift a drooping eye with shadow. As a makeup artist you have the magic to instantly change how someone looks and feels about herself (**Figure 13–3**). Even a 5-minute makeup application can transform someone's life. Makeup artistry is that powerful.

Do's and Do Not's for Working with Teens

Teen clients offer many special opportunities for makeup artists. You have the opportunity to influence a lifetime of skin care and to make a life-long client. With this in mind, you want to pay particular attention to the special needs of teen clients. Here are some Do's and Do Not's to support you in your work with teens.

- **Do** determine the client's needs and what she expects from the application.
- **Do** use the proper formulation of foundation. A clean, natural look is very important.
- **Do** choose an appropriate color of eye shadow.
- **Do** blend the eyeliner so that there are no hard lines.
- **Do not** draw a heavy line on the brow.
- **Do not** line the inside rim of eye with eyeliner.
- **Do not** cover entire face with bronzing powder.
- **Do not** use a noticeably darker lip liner than lip color if you choose to line lips.

HERE'S A TIP

A great way to promote yourself is to offer teens classes in skin care and makeup application. Even mother–daughter classes are a hit!

The goal with teen makeup is to emphasize individual, natural beauty. As a makeup artist, you will probably have the influence necessary to convince your teen clients not to cover up their features, but rather to enhance them. You can also subtly make clients aware of which features to emphasize and which ones to deemphasize. Be cautious, though; you do not want to imply that a teen client needs a lot of corrective work. Teenagers can be very sensitive and impressionable. ☑ **LO2**

SKIN CARE BASICS FOR TEENS

A critical factor in any makeup application is healthy skin. Overactive hormones, participation in sports, and very active lifestyles wreak havoc on skin and leave many teens battling with acne, blemishes, and a mass of oil production. However, with proper hygiene these issues can be improved. Guiding teenagers on how to adopt an appropriate skin care regimen is imperative for healthy skin throughout life (**Figure 13–4**).

▲ **Figure 13–4 Establishing a skin care regimen during the teen years is essential for long-lasting healthy skin.**

Teen Skin Care Do's

It is never too soon to begin healthy, basic skin care. Adopting a skin care regimen while they are young will help your teenage clients maintain healthy, youthful skin as they age. Try to impress upon your young clients the importance of the following "do's" for proper skin care.

- **Do** remove all makeup and debris morning and night with an appropriate cleanser.
- **Do** use only noncomedogenic products (products that do not clog pores).
- **Do** wash your hands before touching your face.
- **Do** cleanse skin after sweating.
- **Do** eat a healthy diet that includes fruits and vegetables.
- **Do** use sunscreen daily.

HERE'S A TIP

Remind teenage clients to keep phones, computer keyboards, and pillowcases clean. These items are usually teeming with bacteria, which then migrate to users' faces. If pillowcases are not cleaned properly, they collect debris and bacteria; every night when the client rests her head, she will further irritate any oily, irritated, or acneic conditions.

Teen Skin Care Do Not's

The things that teens should not be doing usually pose more of a challenge for young clients. Breaking bad habits, or preventing them from ever starting, helps prevent damage, permanent scarring, and uneven pigmentation. Communicate the following "do not's" to your clients:

- **Do not** pick acne.
- **Do not** try to extract blackheads yourself.
- **Do not** use products that dry and irritate the skin.
- **Do not** over-cleanse, over-exfoliate, or over-stimulate the skin.

HERE'S A TIP

Help teens think about their future. A lifetime of sunscreen use will save them from dealing with premature aging, uneven pigmentation, and maybe even skin cancer.

Nutrition as Skin Care

Teenage skin can be unpredictable; hormones, diet, improper skin regimens, and sports can send skin out of control. More than any other food choices, dairy and sugar products wreak havoc on teen skin. There is nothing more gratifying then helping teenagers manage their skin health through this daunting time. Let your clients know that what they are eating and how their body processes those foods affects their skin. **Skin nutrition** is the health of the skin based upon the health of the body, diet, and exercise. Develop an understanding of how to maintain skin health and body health. Then share that understanding with your clients—especially teens. The information will benefit them for a lifetime.

Hormones, Steroids, Antibiotics, and Other Food Additives

Many animals that are raised for food are given added doses of hormones, steroids, and antibiotics. Research has shown that these additives are linked to acne flare-ups and inflammation. In addition, clinical nutritionists Dr. Andre Weil and Dr. George Georgiou believe that the human body cannot properly digest dairy products, and that they are

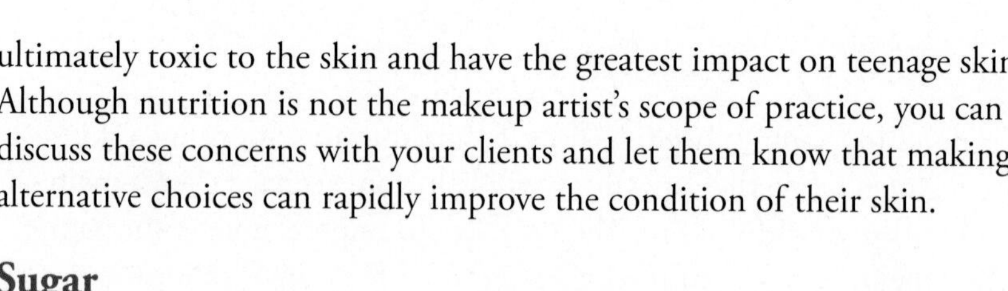

ultimately toxic to the skin and have the greatest impact on teenage skin. Although nutrition is not the makeup artist's scope of practice, you can discuss these concerns with your clients and let them know that making alternative choices can rapidly improve the condition of their skin.

fyi

Most grocery stores offer a wide variety of hormone-free and antibiotic-free dairy. They also offer numerous alternatives to dairy such as soy milk, almond milk, hemp milk, and rice milk. Most of these alternatives have the same calcium levels as milk. Check your labels and make good choices to support the health of your skin.

Sugar

Another poor nutrition choice is sugar. High sugar consumption elevates blood-sugar levels, which can trigger a rise in cellular inflammation. Sugar creates a burst of inflammation in the skin. This inflammation produces an enzyme that causes a breakdown in collagen, resulting in premature aging and the aggravation of acneic conditions.

Proper Diet and Teen Skin

Helping teenagers understand the importance of a healthy diet will benefit them tremendously, protecting them from a wide range of problems now and as they age. Healthy nutrition begins with drinking water and eating a balanced diet that includes protein, good carbohydrates, and fats (**Figure 13–5**). It is also a good idea to load up on fruit and vegetables, which are full of age- and disease-fighting antioxidants. Eating a healthy diet is an important step toward healthier, more beautiful skin.

© Dmitriy Shironosov/www.Shutterstock.com

▲ **Figure 13–5 Proper diets and water intake can improve overall health and skin conditions.**

Remember you are not a nutritionist. You cannot legally change a client's diet. Recommend that clients see their physician or a licensed nutritionist for proper nutrition guidelines. This recommendation will help create the beautiful canvas upon which they will apply makeup for many years to come. ☑ **LO3**

MAKEUP BASICS FOR TEENS

▼ **Figure 13–6 Teenage makeup should be fun, clean, and simple.**

© Brian Chase/www.Shutterstock.com

Teenage skin is youthful and radiant, so when it comes to makeup for teenage skin, less is more. Teenagers' makeup applications should take no longer than 5 minutes and the techniques should be simple. As a makeup artist, you are in a position to advise young women about how to make the most of their personal beauty while at the same time concealing or deemphasizing what they view as flaws. The main thing is to keep the application simple and keep the consultation fun. (**Figure 13–6**).

Color Theory for Teens

After studying Chapter 5, Color Theory, you know that with any makeup application, basic color theory always applies. To help teenage clients understand color theory and how it can help them select makeup, it is a great idea to have a color wheel on hand. Suggest to your teenage clients that they invest in a color wheel to guide them in making proper color choices. Take a few minutes with your teenage client and explain the basic principles of color theory and how to use the color wheel in makeup applications.

Mineral Makeup for Teens

Mineral makeup is very popular among teenage girls. As you recall from previous chapters, **mineral makeup** contains nonbacterial, finely ground particles from the earth and fewer chemicals and dyes than other types of makeup. Mineral makeup comes in a wide variety of formulations and color choices; it is not just limited to foundations. In addition, mineral makeup is lightweight and long-lasting.

Most mineral makeup contains either titanium dioxide or zinc oxide. These ingredients are known to be anti-inflammatory and oil-absorbent, which makes mineral makeup ideal for oily or acneic teenage skin. Zinc oxide and titanium dioxide are also two natural sources of sunscreen that have a sun protection factor (SPF) of 15. It is important for teenagers to understand the damaging effects that the sun can have on skin. Discuss these conditions and disorders with your young clients. Help them understand how the use of mineral makeup can help control acneic disorders and prevent damage from overexposure to the sun.

Remind all clients to use a sunscreen with an SPF of at least 15. (The higher the SPF, the more sun protection the product offers.)

Mica

Teenagers often enjoy shimmering and shining makeup—especially for special occasions. Mica is an ingredient added to cosmetics, including some mineral makeup, to provide these qualities. For most clients, mica will be fine; however, for sensitive or allergy-prone skin, mica is a known irritant that can cause redness, irritation, and itching. Advise clients with sensitive or allergy-prone skin to avoid products containing mica. Keep in mind that not all mineral makeup contains mica; mineral makeup that does not contain mica is a fine choice for sensitive skin.

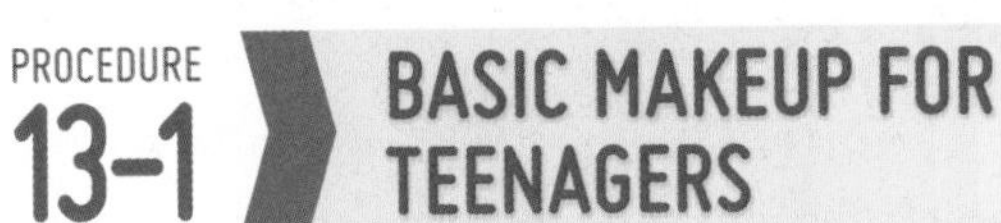

SEE PAGE 305

At-Home Tips for Teen Makeup

A discussion of teen makeup basics could not be complete without a discussion of home-care. Consistent care is essential for improving problem skin and maintaining healthy skin. Recommend the following tips to teenage clients:

- Cleanse the skin two times per day.
- Always remove makeup and cleanse face before bedtime.
- Wash makeup brushes after each use.
- Wash your hands before touching your face and/or cosmetics.
- Never use oil-based cosmetics on young skin.

- Never share makeup with anyone. This can spread bacteria and disease.
- Replace makeup on a regular basis. Mascara should be replaced every few months, and all powder products on a yearly basis.

MAKEUP FOR BLEMISHED SKIN

▲ Figure 13–7 Cover blemishes with the appropriate shade of concealer.

Young skin—even skin that is blemished—should never be covered with a thick layer of makeup. Spot-treating affected areas is a better strategy than covering the entire face with a weighted foundation. Layers of product will worsen the condition of the skin, accentuate the appearance of the acne, and make the face look uneven, unattractive, and older. Oily skin presents a similar problem; clients might be inclined to layer powder over the skin in an effort to absorb oil, but multiple layers of powder will only make the skin look like a layered mask.

The key to properly covering blemishes is to choose an appropriate shade of concealer or creamy stick foundation (**Figure 13–7**). To do this, you must first identify the skin's undertone. **Undertone** is the predominant color in the skin; this color can be either warm or cool. If blemished areas have warm red undertones, neutralize the redness with a green-yellow based concealer or foundation stick. If the blemished area is hyperpigmented, choose a flesh-toned concealer and/or foundation. When applying concealer or foundation stick be sure to **stipple**, or gently pat, the area to prevent over-blending.

HERE'S A TIP

Never cover a blemish with a concealer or foundation stick that is lighter than the skin or base foundation; doing so will highlight the blemish, making it appear more prominent.

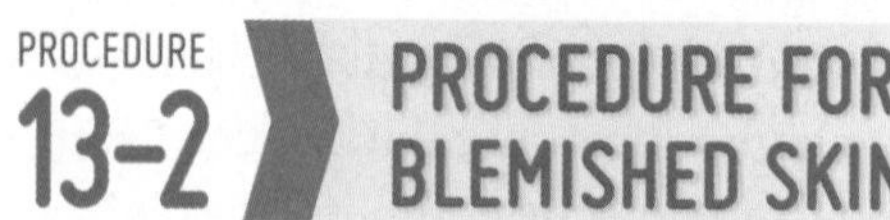

SEE PAGE 310

PROM MAKEUP

There is nothing more exciting for teenage girls than the prom (**Figure 13–8**). This is their chance to shine, and they are relying on you

▶ Figure 13–8 Prom is the perfect occasion for makeup services.

to help them do that. Wearing a gorgeous dress, having their hair styled beautifully, and showing off an amazing, glamorous makeup look is a dream come true for most young girls. Usually, prom makeup will be fun, flirty, and fantastic, but remember that each teenager is unique and has her own style. As a makeup artist, you must create a look that reflects the client's individual beauty.

Even for glamorous occasions, makeup applications should emphasize only one feature. If you play-up the eyes with a smoky look, then choose a soft, neutral lip color. Trying to emphasize the eyes *and* the lips will be too much. Also remember that the event will be photographed; with this in mind, choose a classic look that does not obviously date the photos.

HERE'S A TIP

For photographed events such as prom, avoid "trendy" looks such as colored mascara, colored/sparkled shadows, or gemstones on the face or in the lashes.

Artificial Lashes

One way to emphasize the eyes in a timeless, subtle way is to apply artificial lashes or lash extensions. For teenagers, these are a perfect choice for special occasions. Artificial lashes are fun, easy to apply, typically last 1 to 2 days, and can be easily removed. Refer to Chapter 17, All About Lashes, for more information on lash choices and application techniques.

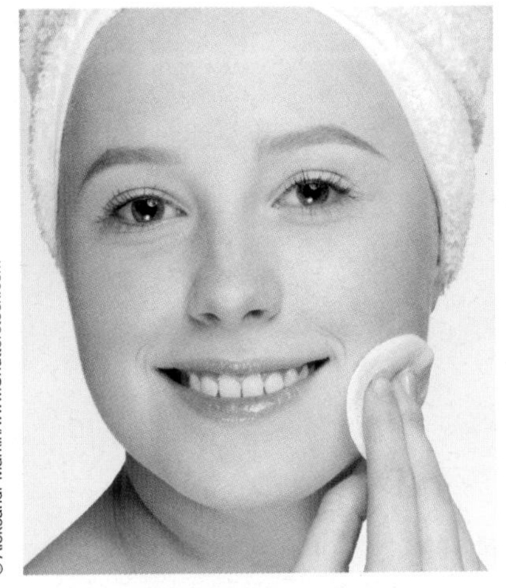

▲ **Figure 13–9 Skin care should start before prom to ensure optimal results.**

Tanning

Many teenagers will choose to tan before a prom, which can change the condition and the tone of their skin. A consultation form should include a question on the tanning history of the client. If you perform the consultation several days in advance of prom, be sure to ask your client whether she intends to tan before the final application. If so, you will know to expect that the skin may be dryer, dehydrated, and more pigmented (**Figure 13–9**).

HERE'S A TIP

Discourage clients from using tanning beds. Encourage them instead to opt for spray-on tans or self-tanning products that do not wreak havoc on the skin.

PROCEDURE 13-3 PROM MAKEUP PROCEDURE SEE PAGE 314

Makeup for teens can be a very lucrative and rewarding part of your profession. Many teens attempt to duplicate makeup techniques and styles that they see in magazines, in movies, or in television shows. Guiding your teen clients through the process of looking beautiful and natural by eating well, properly caring for their skin, and knowing how to select and apply their makeup will start a lifetime trend toward health and beauty.

Procedure 13-1

Basic Makeup for Teenagers

Implements and Materials

You will need all of the following implements, materials, and supplies:

- **Brushes**
  - ☐ Blush brush
  - ☐ Concealer brush
  - ☐ Eye blender brush (larger eye fluff brush)
  - ☐ Eyebrow brush
  - ☐ Eye contour brush
  - ☐ Powder brush
- **Utensils**
  - ☐ Brush cleaner
  - ☐ Eyelash curler
  - ☐ Hand sanitizer
  - ☐ Headband or hair clip
  - ☐ Makeup cape
  - ☐ Makeup chair
  - ☐ Makeup palette
  - ☐ Neck strip or clean towel for draping
  - ☐ Pencil sharpener
  - ☐ Tweezers
- **Single-use Items**
  - ☐ Cotton pads for cleansing (optional)
  - ☐ Cotton swabs
  - ☐ Lip brushes (minimum of two)
  - ☐ Mascara wands (minimum of three)
  - ☐ Shadow applicators
  - ☐ Spatulas
  - ☐ Sponge wedges
  - ☐ Tissues
- **Products**
  - ☐ Blush/cheek colors
  - ☐ Concealers
  - ☐ Eyebrow gel
  - ☐ Eyebrow pencils
  - ☐ Eyeliner pencils
  - ☐ Eye shadow colors (two to three shades)
  - ☐ Facial moisturizer
  - ☐ Foundation
  - ☐ Gentle cleanser
  - ☐ Lip pencils (liners)
  - ☐ Lip colors
  - ☐ Lip gloss
  - ☐ Mascara
  - ☐ Mild facial cleanser
  - ☐ Powders
  - ☐ Toner for drier skin

Preparation

- Perform

PROCEDURE 7-1 PRE-SERVICE SEE PAGE 144

Procedure

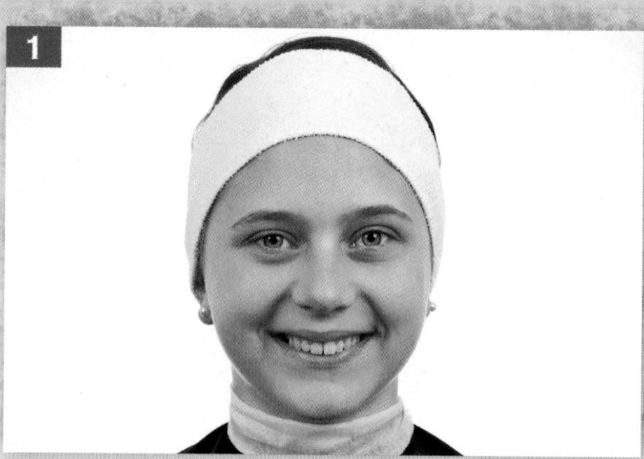

1 If necessary, apply cleanser in upward and outward motion. Remove with damp cotton pads.

2 Apply moisturizer to the client's face, if needed.

3 A face primer can be applied to even out skin tone or ensure that the makeup is long-lasting.

STATE REGULATORY ALERT

Be sure to check with the appropriate state regulatory agency to be sure you are legally allowed to apply and remove cleansing products.

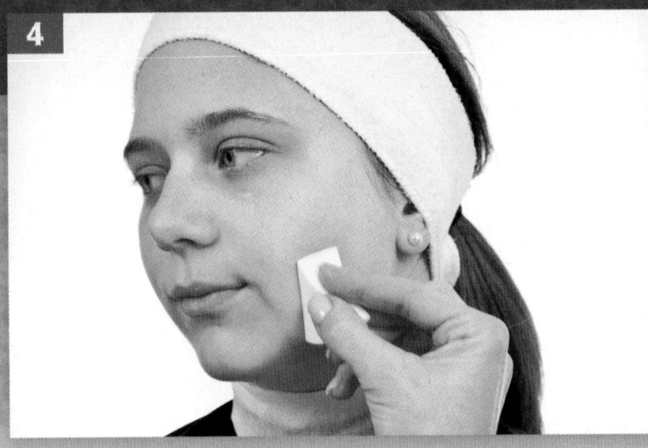

4 Choose a light-weight liquid foundation, mineral foundation, or tinted moisturizer depending on the client's skin type. Apply the foundation with a disposable sponge, or with a kabuki brush if using mineral foundation.

5 Use an appropriate concealer only if needed. Most teenagers will not need concealer unless they have acne. Refer to Procedure 13–2, Procedure for Blemished Skin, when working with blemished skin.

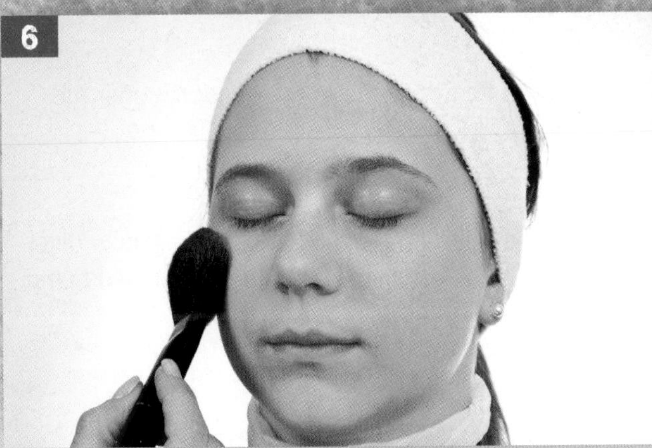

6 Apply a light application of powder with a powder brush.

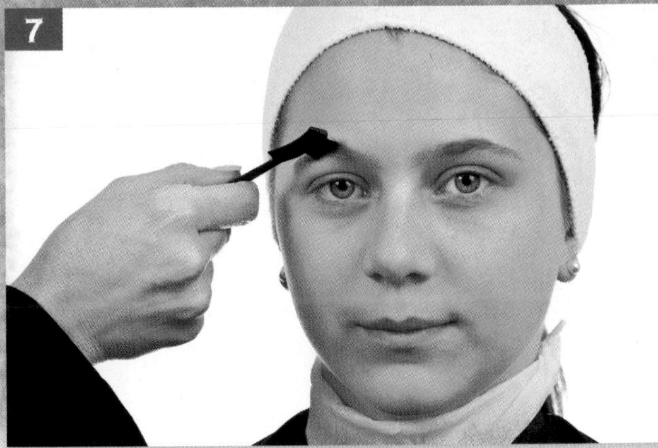

7 Groom the eyebrows by brushing the hair up.

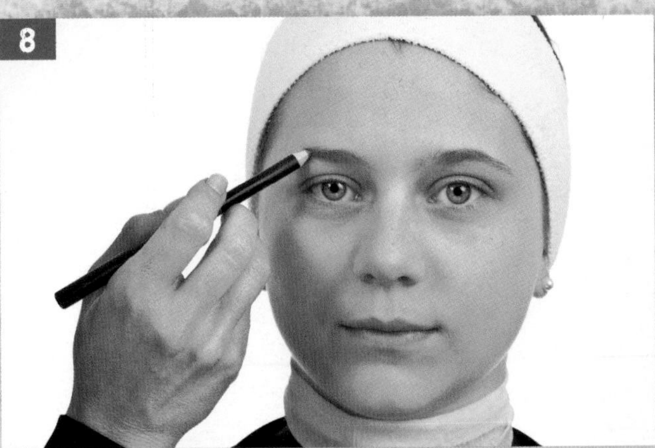

8 Fill in the brow area (if any areas are sparse) with brow pencil or powder. Avoid drawing a heavy brow; the look is too dramatic for teenagers. Then set with eye gel.

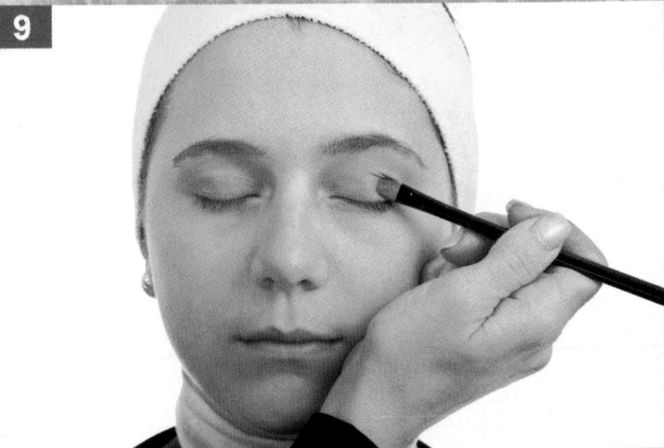

9 Choose a flattering eye shadow color that is appropriate for your client. Color-wash the entire eye with a neutral color from the lash line to the brow.

Procedure 13-1 *(continued)*

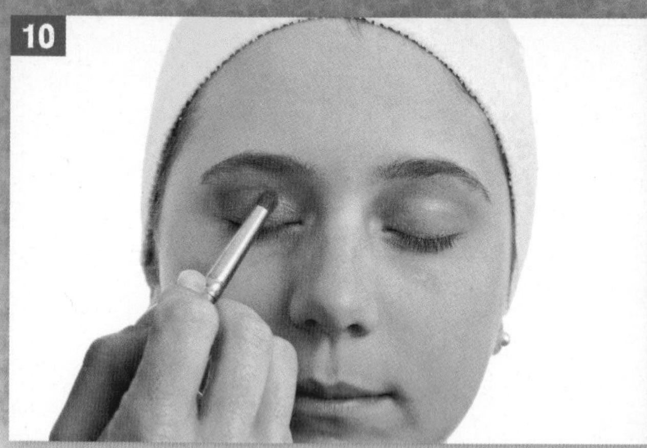

10 Apply a mid-depth color to the crease.

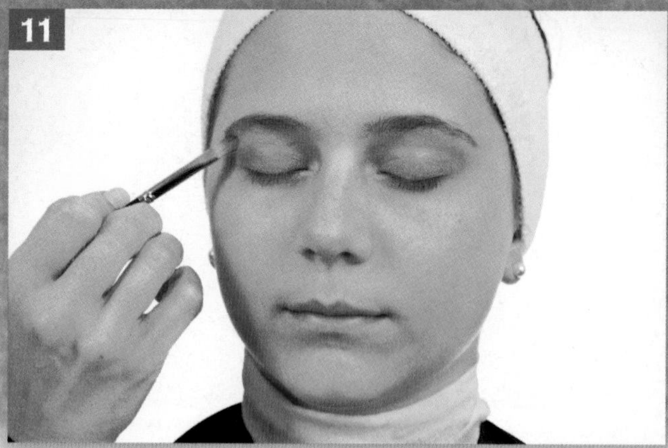

11 Apply a lighter shade of eye shadow under the brow bone.

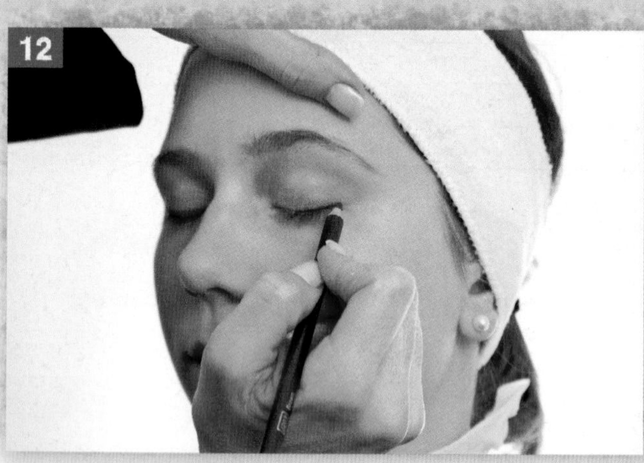

12 Apply a mid-depth pencil or darker shadow color to the lash line as eyeliner. Use a liner brush and blend to avoid creating a hard line.

SERVICE TIP

Explain to teen girls not to use eyeliner on the inside of the eye. This technique visually closes the eye and can cause eye irritation and infection.

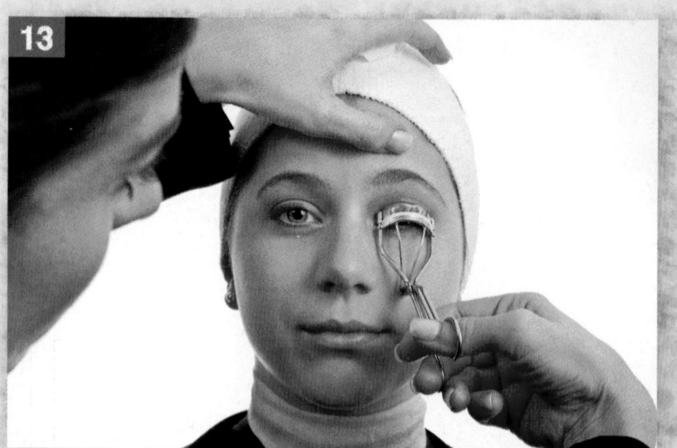

13 Gently curl eyelashes with an eyelash curler.

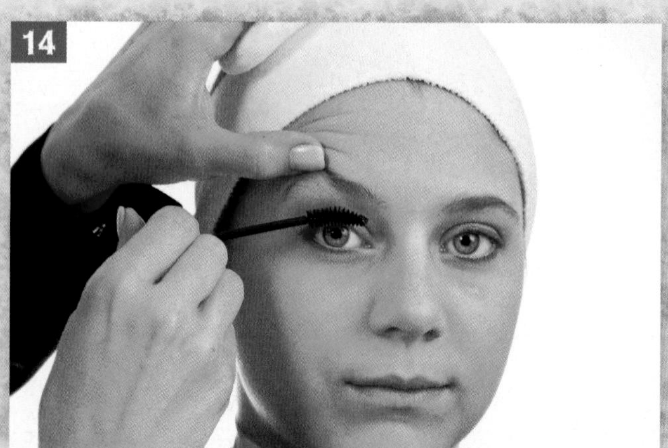

14 Apply one or two coats of mascara with a disposable mascara wand.

15 Find the apple of the cheek and apply a natural fresh color to that area, continuing with a gentle stroke toward the hairline at the center of the ear. Be sure to keep the look soft (with no hard angles) and to follow the client's natural bone structure.

SERVICE TIP

If client desires a sun-kissed look, apply a hint of bronzer to where the sun would naturally hit the face. Do not cover the entire face with bronzer or it will look like a mask.

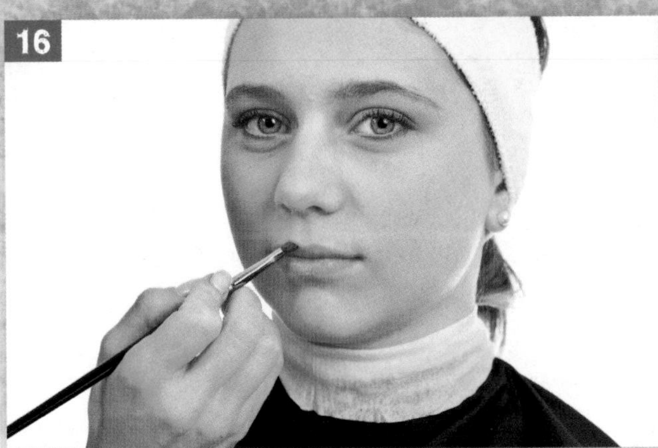

16 Choose a shade of lip gloss. Lip glosses are more appropriate and flattering to teenage skin than a heavier lipstick. Apply the gloss with a disposable lip brush.

Note: Never use a lip liner that is noticeably darker than the lip color.

17 Show the client the finished look.

Post-Service

- Complete

PROCEDURE 7-2 **POST-SERVICE** SEE PAGE 148

Procedure 13-2

Procedure for Blemished Skin

Implements and Materials

You will need all of the following implements, materials, and supplies:

Brushes

- ☐ Blush brush
- ☐ Concealer brush
- ☐ Eye contour brush
- ☐ Powder brush

Utensils

- ☐ Brush cleaner
- ☐ Eyelash curler
- ☐ Hand sanitizer
- ☐ Headband or hair clip
- ☐ Makeup cape
- ☐ Makeup chair
- ☐ Makeup palette
- ☐ Neck strip or clean towel for draping
- ☐ Pencil sharpener
- ☐ Tweezers

Single-use Items

- ☐ Cotton pads for cleansing (optional)
- ☐ Cotton swabs
- ☐ Lip brushes (minimum of two)
- ☐ Mascara wands (minimum of three)
- ☐ Shadow applicators
- ☐ Spatulas
- ☐ Sponge wedges
- ☐ Tissues

Products

- ☐ Blush/cheek colors
- ☐ Concealers
- ☐ Eyebrow gel
- ☐ Eyebrow pencils
- ☐ Eyeliner pencils
- ☐ Eye shadow colors (two to three shades)
- ☐ Facial moisturizer
- ☐ Foundation
- ☐ Gentle cleanser
- ☐ Lip pencils (liners)
- ☐ Lip colors
- ☐ Lip gloss
- ☐ Mascara
- ☐ Mild facial cleanser
- ☐ Powders
- ☐ Toner for drier skin

Preparation

- Perform

PROCEDURE 7-1 PRE-SERVICE SEE PAGE 144

Procedure

1 Apply oil-free moisturizer if needed.

2 Stipple or gently pat a color corrector or veil for sheer application into red areas.

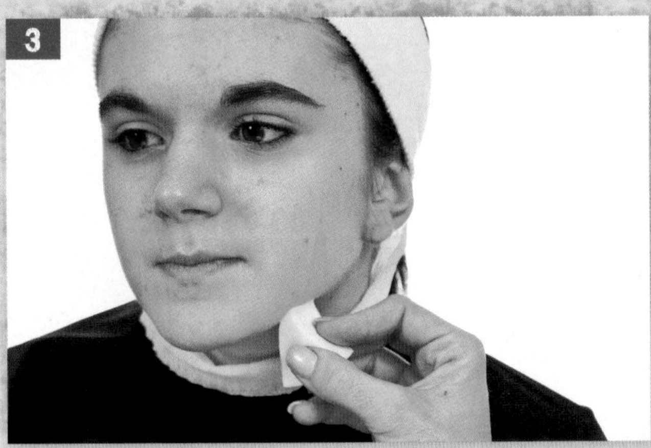

3 Choose a light-weight, oil-free liquid foundation or mineral foundation. Apply the foundation with a disposable sponge, or with a kabuki brush if using mineral foundation.

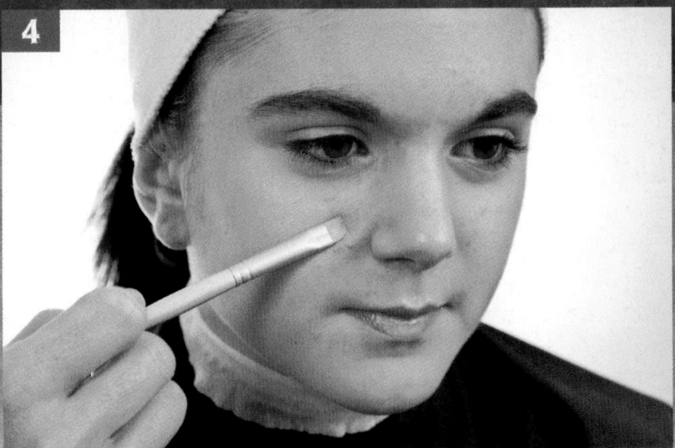

4 Apply concealer or foundation stick and stipple blemished areas. Be sure to layer the blemished area only with a small brush until desired area is covered.

5 Apply a light application of powder over the entire face.

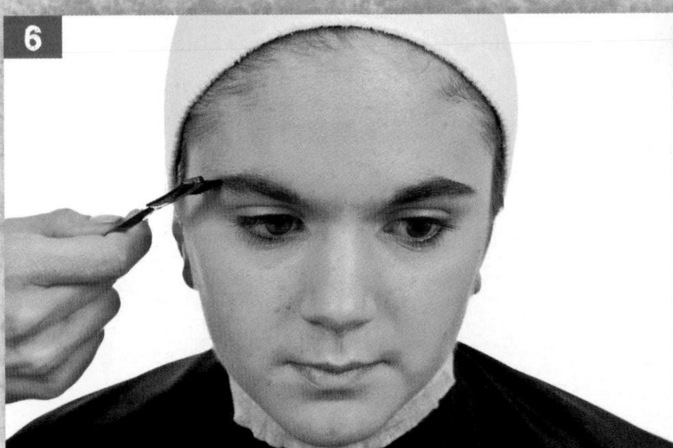

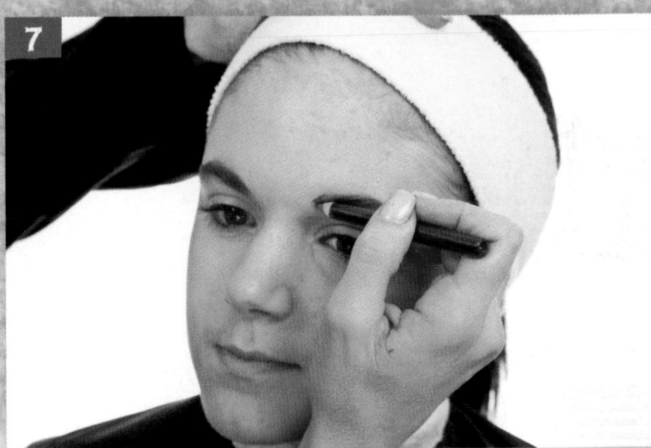

6 Groom the eyebrows by brushing up the eyebrow hair.

7 If any areas of the eyebrows are sparse, fill in the brow area with brow pencil. Avoid drawing a heavy brow; this look is too much for teenage faces. Then set with eye gel.

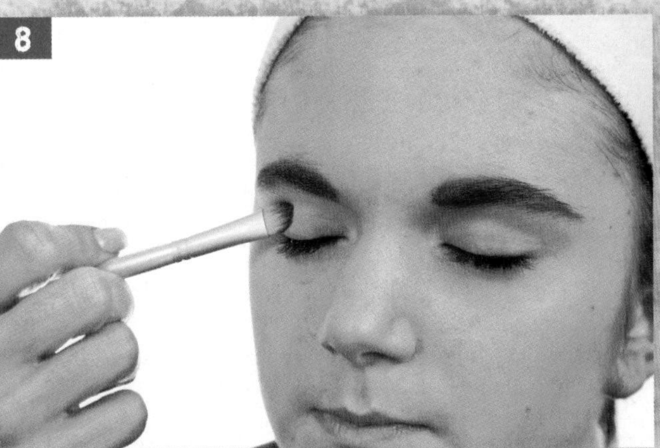

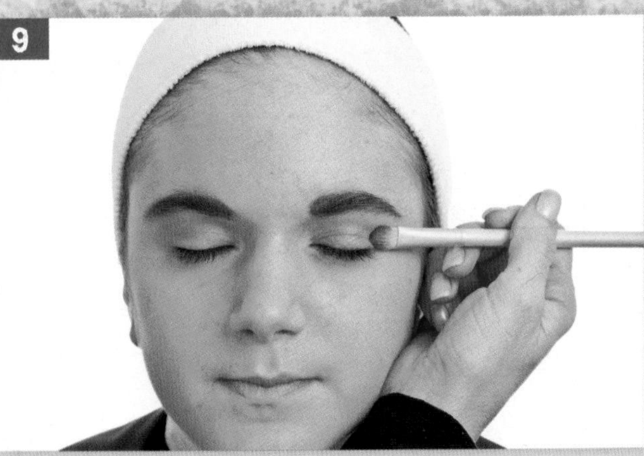

8 Choose an eye shadow color that is appropriate for your client. Color-wash the entire eye with a neutral color from lash line to brow.

9 Apply a mid-depth eye shadow color to the eyelid crease.

Procedure 13-2 *(continued)*

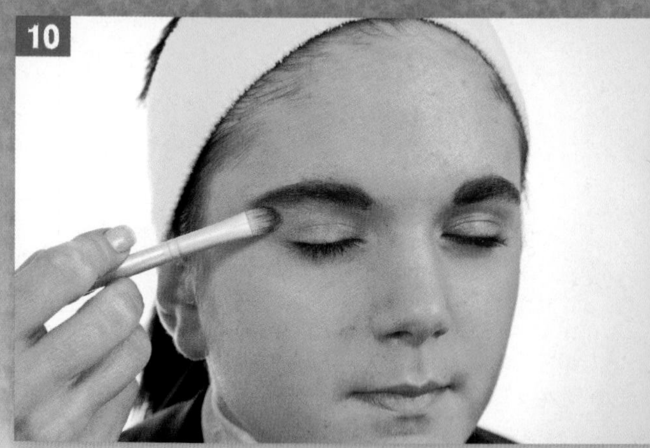

10 Apply a lighter eye shadow color under the brow line.

11 Apply a mid-depth or darker shadow color to the lash line as eyeliner. Use a liner brush and blend to avoid creating a hard line.

12 Gently curl eyelashes with an eyelash curler.

13 Apply one or two coats of mascara with a disposable mascara wand.

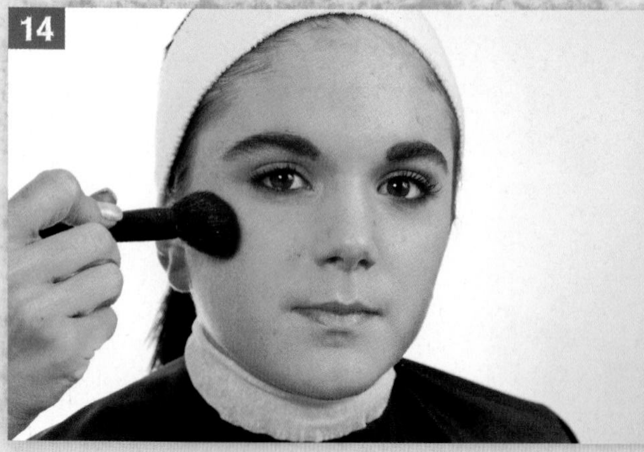

14 Find the apple of the cheek and apply a natural fresh color to that area, continuing with a gentle stroke toward the hairline at the center of the ear. Be sure to keep the look soft (with no hard angles) and to follow the client's natural bone structure.

Note: For this model, we did not apply mascara to the bottom lashes to avoid darkening the eye.

SERVICE TIP

Bronzers are an excellent choice for sun-kissed areas of the face. It brings attention away from blemished areas and evens the skin tone.

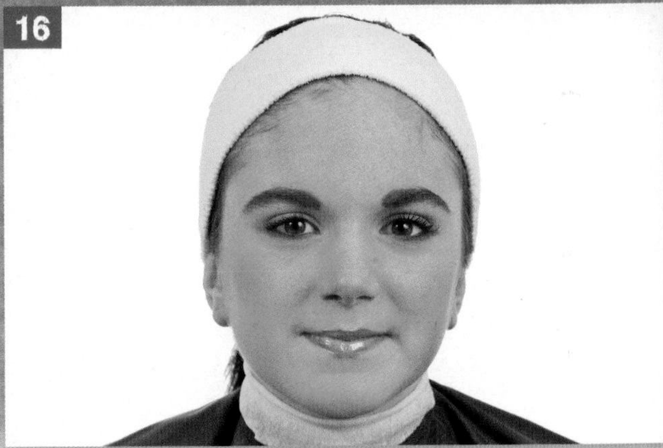

15 Choose a shade of lip gloss. Lip glosses are more appropriate and flattering for teenagers than heavy lipsticks. Apply lip gloss with a disposable lip brush.

16 Show the client the finished look.

Post-Service

- Complete

PROCEDURE 7-2 POST-SERVICE SEE PAGE 148

Procedure 13-3
Prom Makeup Procedure

Implements and Materials

You will need all of the following implements, materials, and supplies:

- **Brushes**
  - ☐ Blush brush
  - ☐ Concealer brush
  - ☐ Eye contour brush
  - ☐ Powder brush
- **Utensils**
  - ☐ Brush cleaner
  - ☐ Eyelash curler
  - ☐ Hand sanitizer
  - ☐ Headband or hair clip
  - ☐ Makeup cape
  - ☐ Makeup chair
  - ☐ Makeup palette
  - ☐ Neck strip or clean towel for draping
  - ☐ Pencil sharpener
  - ☐ Tweezers
- **Single-use Items**
  - ☐ Lip brushes (minimum of two)
  - ☐ Mascara wands (minimum of three)
  - ☐ Cotton pads for cleansing (optional)
  - ☐ Cotton swabs
  - ☐ Mascara wands
  - ☐ Shadow applicators
  - ☐ Spatulas
  - ☐ Sponge wedges
  - ☐ Tissues
- **Products**
  - ☐ Blush/cheek colors
  - ☐ Concealers
  - ☐ Eyebrow gel
  - ☐ Eyebrow pencils
  - ☐ Eyeliner pencils
  - ☐ Eye shadow colors (two to three shades)
  - ☐ Facial moisturizer
  - ☐ Foundation
  - ☐ Gentle cleanser
  - ☐ Lip pencils (liners)
  - ☐ Lip colors
  - ☐ Lip gloss
  - ☐ Mascara
  - ☐ Mild facial cleanser
  - ☐ Powders
  - ☐ Toner for drier skin
  - ☐ Glitter (optional)
  - ☐ Eyelash enhancements (optional)

Preparation

- Perform

PROCEDURE 7-1 PRE-SERVICE SEE PAGE 144

Procedure

1 Apply moisturizer if needed.

SERVICE TIP

The neck should match the face and the décolleté when applying foundation. Pay special attention to the differences in skin color that may be present if your teen client has been tanning and her face is lighter than the rest of her body.

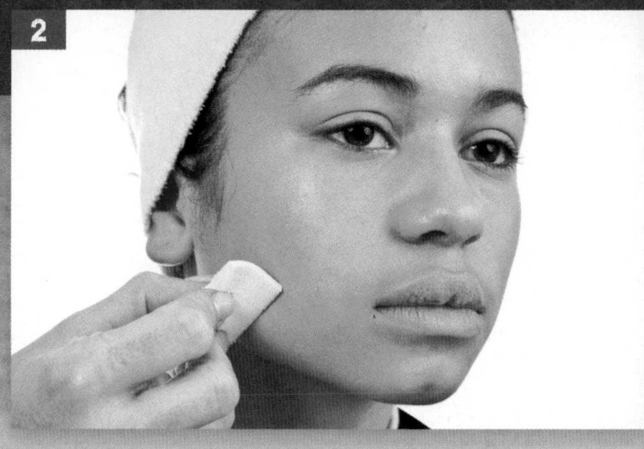

2 Choose a liquid foundation or a mineral foundation. Apply the foundation with a disposable sponge, or with a kabuki brush if using mineral foundation. The prom foundation application will be slightly heavier than an everyday application to allow for better coverage that will last throughout the evening. Use enough product to cover blemishes and imperfections but not so much that the natural skin is concealed.

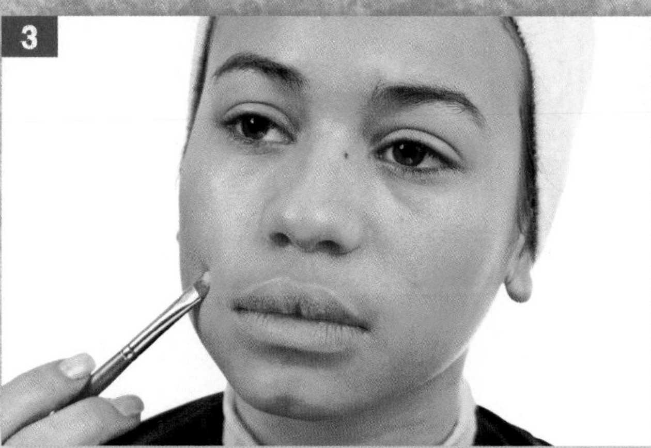

3 Cover any remaining imperfections with concealer using a sponge or brush. Blend well.

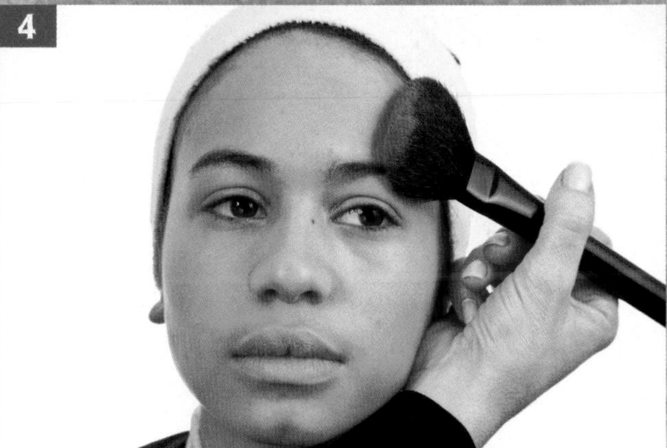

4 Apply powder over the entire face with a powder brush.

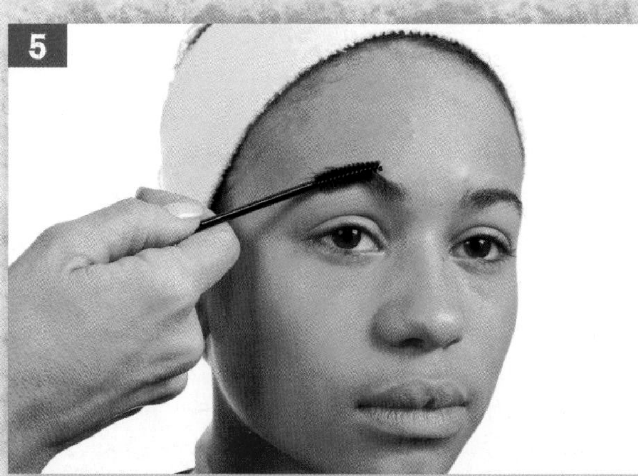

5 Groom the eyebrows. Brush the eyebrow hair upward.

6 Fill any sparse areas of the brow with brow pencil. Avoid drawing a heavy brow. Then set with an eye gel.

Procedure 13-3 *(continued)*

7 Choose eye shadow colors that are appropriate for your client's young skin and that accent the prom attire. Color-wash the entire eye with a base color, from the lash line to brow. Use a smaller, round fluff brush to avoid hard lines.

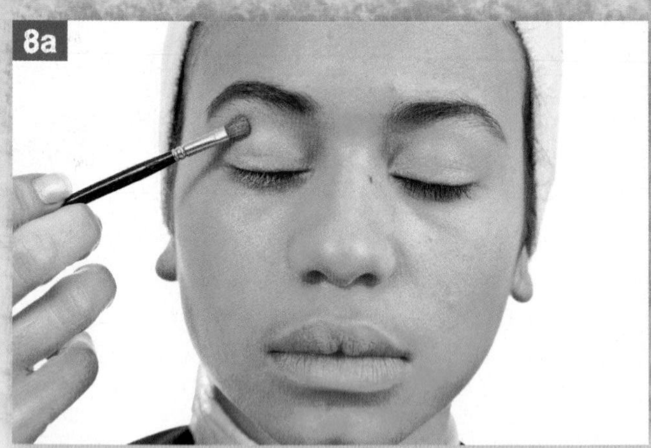

8 Apply a mid-depth tone to the crease of the eye to give more depth to the look.

9 Apply eyeliner to the upper and lower lash line. Pencil liner or a darker shadow color can be used. Be sure to blend the eyeliner to avoid the look of a hard line. Glitter can be applied on top of the eyeliner for a fun look.

SERVICE TIP

Do not use pencil eyeliner across the entire eye as it will visually close the eye. When you are applying eyeliner, make sure client does not look straight into the light; doing so causes tearing.

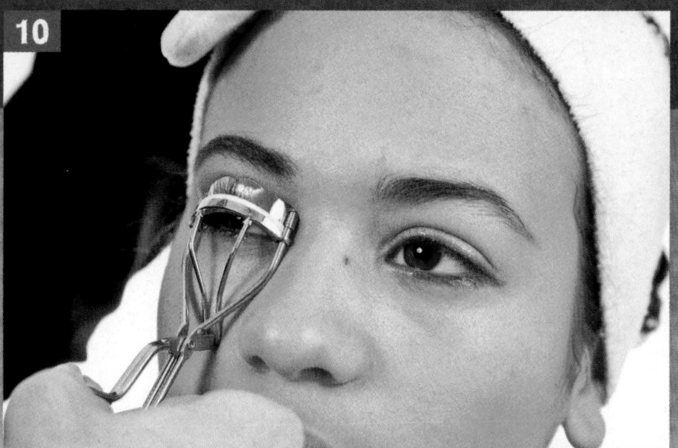

10 Gently curl eyelashes with an eyelash curler.

11 Apply two coats of mascara with a disposable mascara wand. The bottom eyelashes are coated first before moving on to the top lashes.

12 Find the apple of the cheek and apply a blush color to that area, continuing with a gentle stroke toward the hairline at the center of the ear; apply slightly more than you would use for a daytime application.

SERVICE TIP

Blush balances the face, so be sure to choose blush from the same color family as the lip color and eye color you are using. This helps to avoid a look that does not flow. For example, coral lipstick with a pink blush creates a jarring, unnatural look.

SERVICE TIP

Choose an appropriate lip shade. Apply lipstick with a lip brush. Then follow with lip gloss.

13 Choose an appropriate lipstick and lip gloss. To make lip gloss last longer use lip primer and fill in the entire lip with the same colored lipstick or lip liner. Pat the lipstick or lip liner into the lips, then apply lip gloss. Be sure not to choose a darker liner than lipstick.

Procedure 13-3 *(continued)*

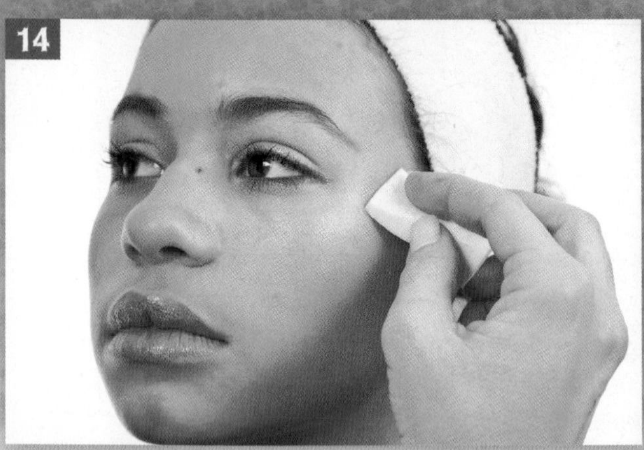

14 Highlight if needed. Use a mineral highlight, cream highlighter, or lighter shadow. Apply the product to one or more areas of the face, particularly the apples of the cheeks or the top of the cheekbones.

15 Highlight the bow of the mouth.

16 Contour the face if needed.

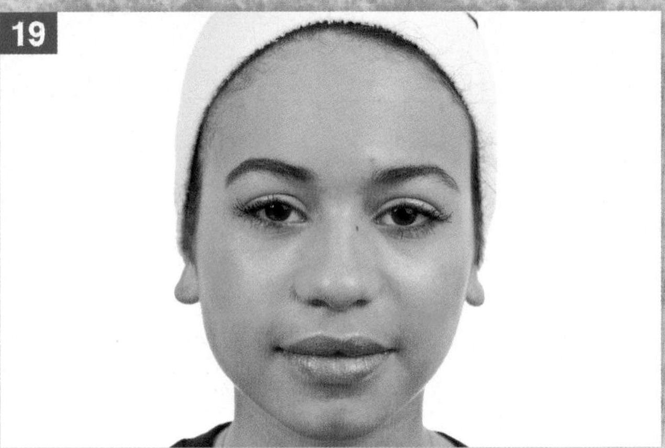

17 Optional: Add a few artificial lashes or strip lashes to complete the eyes.

18 Add a touch of bronzer to bare shoulders, neck, or décolleté for a sun-kissed look.

19 Show the client the finished prom look.

Post-Service  LO4

- Complete

PROCEDURE 7-2 POST-SERVICE SEE PAGE 148

Review Questions

1. What is the main objective of a teenage makeup application?
2. Why are teenage consultations so important?
3. What are some Do's and Do not's when you are working with teens?
4. What are the two main food choices that can wreak havoc on teenage skin? Why?
5. How long should a teenager take to apply her makeup?
6. What is the best method for covering a blemish?
7. What are the two types of artificial lashes?
8. Why is it important to avoid using heavy foundation on teen skin?
9. How does tanning affect teenage skin?

Chapter Glossary

mineral makeup	Contains nonbacterial, finely ground particles from the earth; contains fewer chemicals and dyes than most traditional makeup; most are talc-free and less likely to cause allergic reactions.
skin nutrition	Health of the skin based upon the health of the body, diet, and exercise.
stipple	Gentle patting motion used to prevent over-blending during makeup application.
undertone	Predominant color in the skin; undertone can be either warm or cool.

Chapter 14 Makeup for Aging Skin

Chapter Outline

Learning Objectives

After completing this chapter, you will be able to:

- ☑ **LO1** Understand why makeup application is different for aging skin.
- ☑ **LO2** Determine correct skin types.
- ☑ **LO3** Recognize the characteristics of each stage of aging skin.
- ☑ **LO4** Understand the key items needed for mature makeup application.
- ☑ **LO5** Choose appropriate colors based on skin tone and depth.
- ☑ **LO6** Perform a professional aging-skin makeup application.

Key Terms

Page number indicates where in the chapter the term is used.

Botox®
pg. 326

capillaries
pg. 324

dimethicone
pg. 328

hyaluronic acid
pg. 328

pigment discoloration
pg. 324

resting phase
pg. 326

skin color intensity
pg. 331

skin undertone
pg. 331

Career Profile

Tony Galvez has made a name in the beauty industry by providing high-quality service using only products that are widely known for superior results. He is one of the most respected people in the Hair and Beauty Industry in the Philippines. He stays abreast of the latest trends and hones his expertise by attending trainings and seminars abroad. He is noted for his pioneering efforts in the beauty industry, for conceptualizing and organizing the international standards of cosmetology in the Philippines, and for introducing students to the global beauty industry and encouraging their active participation in it.

He is the president and director of the Tony Galvez School of Beauty. The school exposes practitioners and beauty students to international hairdressing and beauty-care standards. The beauty school offers advanced courses on hairdressing and beauty care.

"I was born in Malabon, Metro Manila, the Philippines. I began my studies looking to receive a Bachelor's degree, but I didn't complete it because of my growing interest in the hairstyling and beauty profession. Instead, I enrolled in a 2-year vocational course in hairstyling and beauty culture. I started in the hairdressing profession during my teens in the 1970s, when hairstyling and makeup were trending. I was inspired to study and attend seminars in different countries to expand my professional makeup expertise and skills.

"Today, I keep traveling abroad to stay current with the latest technology for makeup applications. I provide professional services as a hair and beauty-care consultant and help my clients to look and feel beautiful. Being a professional makeup artist, consultant, and mentor, I believe higher education is the key to a successful career.

"Every time I attend seminars, workshops, and studies, I learn from every artist, and they impart to me various makeup techniques. I use this education to hone my techniques and create a basis for my own style of makeup.

"One of my favorite experiences is the radical transformation of dry and aging skin into a fresh, radiant, and glowing makeup performance. Through the latest makeup techniques I learned abroad, I have been able to satisfy my clients' needs. It is very rewarding to see my clients happy and fulfilled with my work, especially when they return again for another service and tell me of all the compliments they have received since their last visit.

"The Tony Galvez Centrum in the Philippines was built with my own hard-earned money that I made as a hairstylist and makeup artist. It is my mission in the Philippines to see cosmetology as a licensed profession comparable to international practice. The Technical Education and Skills Development Authority has started to acknowledge my undertaking and includes me in the Technical and Vocational Schools Association of the Philippines, as a Public Relations Officer and as a Board Member, so that I can share my expertise on how education in the Philippines became globally competitive.

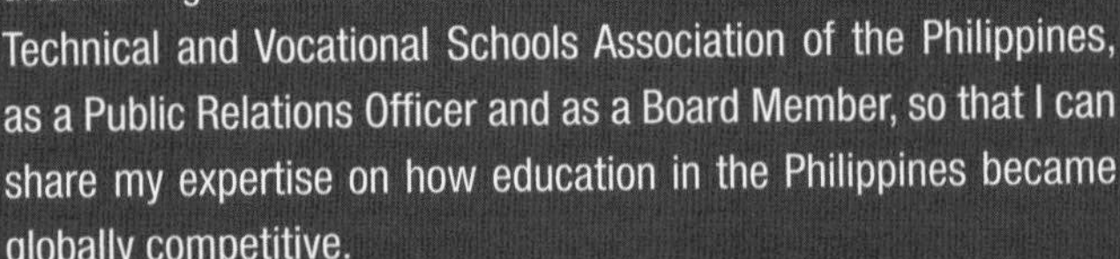

"In my long career as a makeup artist, I am proud of all my work. From party makeup and wedding makeup to photoshoot makeup and stage makeup, I have tried my best to make all of my work a masterpiece."

Courtesy of Tony Galvez.

Makeup applications for aging skin are a challenge, even for the best makeup artists. However, this area of practice can be one of the most rewarding aspects of a professional's career. The right technique can instantly take years off a client's appearance and immediately improve their self-esteem.

As skin ages, several factors affect the appearance of makeup on the skin: loss of firmness, skin discolorations, fine lines, wrinkles, and loss of color intensity. Ideally, makeup for mature skin helps clients look younger and more vibrant. However, when done incorrectly, makeup can actually age mature clients, making them look older and generally unhealthy.

Correct skin care is vitally important for aging skin, and it is necessary in order for makeup to look good on mature skin. Teaching clients the basics of appropriate skin care is part of the makeup artist's job. Prepping the skin with the appropriate products provides a smooth canvas for better application. By understanding how to take care of the skin, a makeup artist can advise clients on proper home-care and refer them to a licensed esthetician for further treatments.

Older clients also face challenges applying their own makeup. These challenges can range from a reduction in eyesight to joint mobility issues from arthritis. A professional makeup artist should not only be concerned with application but also with teaching clients to duplicate the makeup application at home. Many clients try to use makeup to cover the effects of aging on the skin, but often make it look worse. Tailoring techniques for each client is an important part of makeup for aging skin. ✓ LO1

STATE REGULATORY ALERT

Make sure to check with your state's rules and regulations before working on any client as a makeup artist. Esthetic procedures such as chemical exfoliation and facials require an esthetician's license, and medical procedures such as Botox® can only be performed by licensed medical personnel.

WHY STUDY MAKEUP FOR AGING SKIN?

Makeup artists should study and have a thorough understanding of makeup for aging skin because:

- The over-50 age group is the fastest-growing segment of the population. As a result, it may comprise a large portion of a makeup artist's clientele.
- A makeup application is different for aging skin due to skin health, tone, color intensity, and texture.
- Color choices and makeup formulations are different for aging skin.
- Makeup artists can help mature clients look years younger by using the proper application tools and techniques.
- If makeup is applied to mature skin incorrectly, it can add years to the face and give the client a generally unhealthy appearance.

CHALLENGES OF AGING SKIN

Understanding the challenges of aging skin is the first step in learning makeup application techniques that will work well for this segment of your clientele. Prepping the skin prior to makeup application is essential, and an effective daily home skin care routine, along with monthly facial treatments, is part of this process.

Thorough consultation and appropriate skin analysis is critical before the application of makeup to mature skin. To make proper product choices for mature makeup applications, you must determine the client's specific skin type and product usage. ✓ LO2

Did You Know?

Clients with aging skin will often refer to their skin as "losing the glow" or looking very "dull." This is a common result of the declining rate of cellular turnover.

Determing Stages of Aging Skin

Determining the correct skin type is important in order to prep the skin and choose appropriate makeup formulations. It is also important to understand the stages that aging skin goes through and to determine where the client is in the aging process. Although it is simple to categorize stages of aging skin based upon a client's age, it is important to know that environmental factors, lifestyle, and genetics all play an important role. Different ages can easily fall into different stages. Each stage requires unique application techniques to minimize the appearance of aging.

Stage 1: Fine Wrinkles/Mild Loss of Firmness/Mild Pigment Discolorations

The first visual signs of aging are (**Figure 14–1**):

- Lines (appearing with facial movement) at the sides of the eyes and at the upper lip.
- Mild **pigment discoloration**, or uneven skin color, that appears in two types:
  - Hyperpigmentation—dark spots caused by sun damage and hormonal changes.
  - Hypopigmentation—light spots caused by a loss of pigment.
- Mild smile-line depth.
- Fine visible **capillaries**, or small blood vessels.
- Rough skin texture, increased fine wrinkles, and dark circles under the eyes.
- General dull skin color.
- Fading hair or eyebrow color.

▶ Figure 14–1 Stage 1 aging can start as early as 35.

Communication

Makeup artists should always perform a complete consultation with mature clients prior to each makeup application. (See Chapter 6, Client Consultation, for more information on performing effective consultations.) Active listening is one of the most important skills to develop in this process. To practice active listening try this activity:

In a group of two or more people, have one person describe the skin concern that bothers her the most.

1. Without precisely repeating the speaker's statement, have the listeners state their names and then describe the speaker's concern.
2. Have the speaker repeat the names of the listeners.
3. Evaluate the active listening skills of the speaker and the listeners. Discuss how to improve listening skills.

This stage of aging is usually found in the late-30s to late-40s. Lifestyle choices including smoking and UV exposure are starting to show their effects. Chronic stress is also a major contributor to skin aging.

Makeup Application Tips for Stage 1 Aging Skin

For clients at Stage 1, use makeup formulations from the matte (non-shiny) to satin range. Choose colors from a shade family that enhances the clients' skin without looking too dramatic. Eyebrows and eyelashes are the focus for this client; a well-designed brow will give the eyes an immediate, lifted look. Use contour and highlighting techniques, even for a daytime look, and blend well.

Good skin care is essential for this client; keeping the skin well hydrated will help makeup applications last longer.

PROCEDURE 14-1

SEE PAGE 333

Multicultural CONSIDERATIONS

Darker skin shows the signs of aging slower.

Stage 2: Moderate Wrinkles /Moderate Loss of Firmness/Early to Moderate Pigment Discoloration

Signs that indicate the client's skin has reached Stage 2 include (**Figure 14–2**):

- Wrinkles.
- Soft, sagging jawline.
- Folds of skin above the eyes.
- Double chin.
- Sunken cheeks.
- Fat pillows under the eyes.
- Moderate pigment discoloration across the entire face (uneven skin color and patches of dark spots).
- Dull yellow/gray overall skin tone.
- Graying hair and/or eyebrows.
- Possible thinning hair on eyebrows and scalp.

▲ Figure 14–2 **Stage 2 is usually seen early 50s to late-60s.**

This stage of aging is usually found in the early 50s to late-60s, depending on lifestyle choices. The effects of accumulated sun damage, smoking, chronic stress, and a sedentary (inactive) lifestyle is evident.

Makeup Application Tips for Stage 2 Aging Skin

At this stage, the skin is going through many changes. General dullness and uneven texture are more prominent now than in Stage 1. Correct skin care is essential, and a general knowledge of skin care concepts is very helpful when working with this client. Monthly skin treatments are essential at this time, and many clients may be receiving cosmetic treatments for improving these signs, such as Botox injections. **Botox®** is a prescription medicine created using the botulin toxin; it is used to treat lines and wrinkles by paralyzing the muscles located at the site of injection. It is often used to temporarily improve the look of moderate to severe frown lines between the eyebrows (glabellar lines), across the forehead, and around the eyes. Be sure to check the client consultation form that is completed prior to the makeup service to find out whether the client is receiving Botox, other injectables, or cosmetic aging treatments.

Makeup formulations used for Stage 2 clients should provide a satin, luminous finish. Matte products begin to settle into lines at this stage; primer can reduce this settling. Colors need to be less intense and well blended. Pick one feature to focus on when designing a daily makeup look.

HERE'S A TIP

Do not manipulate the skin immediately after Botox® injections. It takes at least 12 hours for the Botox to settle into the targeted muscles and up to 2 weeks to see the full effects of the drug. A general rule for safety is to wait 72 hours before massaging or manipulating the areas of injection. This means that makeup application immediately after an injection should be avoided.

PROCEDURE 14-2 MAKEUP FOR STAGE 2 AGING SKIN: DAYTIME LOOK SEE PAGE 338

Stage 3: Moderate to Deep Wrinkles/Severe Loss of Firmness/Severe Pigment Discoloration

Stage 3 is the most challenging for the makeup artist, simply because loss of firmness and visible wrinkles are evident even when the skin is in a resting phase. The **resting phase** is when the face is not moving. Visual signs of aging that can be observed in this stage are (**Figure 14–3**):

- Deep wrinkles, present even without facial movement.
- Soft, sagging jawline.
- Folds of skin above the eyes.
- Double chin.
- Sunken cheeks.
- Fat pillows under the eyes.
- Distinct pigment discoloration.
- Dry, rough texture.
- Thin, hollow-looking cheeks.
- Gray hair.
- Thinning hair on eyebrows and scalp.
- General loss of color on lips and cheeks.

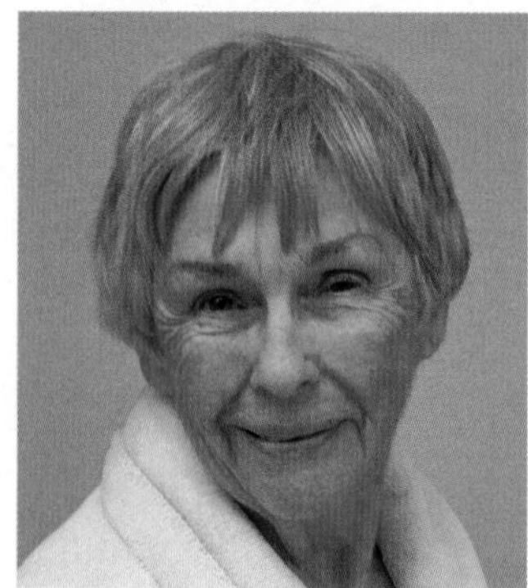

▲ Figure 14–3 Stage 3 aging is usually found from the late-60s and upward.

This stage of aging can show up in the mid-50s but is most often seen in the late-60s and beyond. Lifestyle choices add to the intrinsic (internal) aging caused by genetic factors.

HERE'S A TIP

Always check the clients skin type before choosing formulas. Aging skin can still have oil production which would indicate a matte finish product in order to minimize the oily shine.

Makeup Application Tips for Stage 3 Aging Skin

Makeup application for clients at Stage 3 should focus on the client's best features. If this is the lips, for example, a brighter lip color should be used. Keep colors in a light- to medium-depth range and use highlighting and contouring techniques. Avoid matte products as they tend to settle into deep lines and wrinkles. Use a cream concealer for discolorations and broken veins. **Table 14–1**, Stages of Aging: Application Techniques and Tools, shows the stages of aging and the techniques and tools to use for each stage. ☑ **LO3**.

PROCEDURE 14-2 MAKEUP FOR STAGE 2 AGING SKIN: DAYTIME LOOK SEE PAGE 338

TABLE 14–1 STAGES OF AGING: APPLICATION TECHNIQUES AND TOOLS

STAGE OF AGING	APPLICATION TECHNIQUES	TOOLS NEEDED
STAGE 1	Mild contouring, soft-focus eyes, bright lip color, bronzer for glow, well-defined brows, soft matte-finish foundation, eye-line definition	Contour brushes, large fluff brush, angle wedge brush, lash enhancements, brow color, lash curler, liquid eyeliner, makeup primer
STAGE 2	Moderate contouring, well-defined brows, bright or sheer blush, muted lips, soft satin-finish foundation, eye-line definition	Contour brushes, large fluff brush, small eyeliner brush, lip brush, angle wedge brush, lash enhancement, lash curler, brow color, makeup primer
STAGE 3	Heavy contouring, well-defined brows, focus on a single feature using bright clear color, bright blush, dewey-finish foundation, eye-line definition, soft muted eye shadow	Contour brushes, large fluff brush, small eyeliner brush, lip brush, angle wedge brush, lash enhancement, lash curler, brow color, makeup primer, foundation sponge

▲ Table 14–1 **Stages of Aging: Application Techniques and Tools.**

TOOLS AND PRODUCTS FOR MATURE SKIN

Certain tools and product formulas are key assets in makeup applications for mature skin.

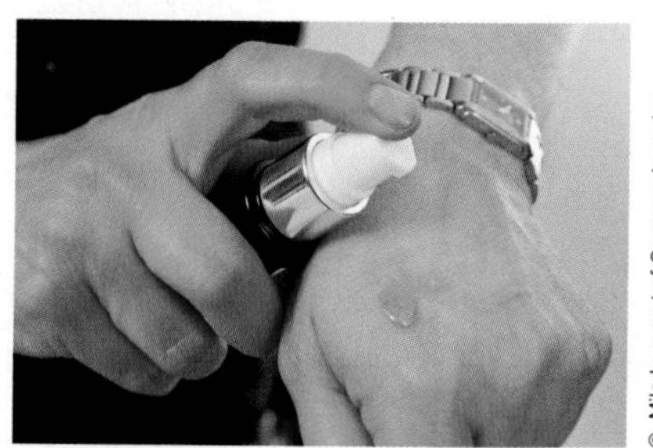

▲ Figure 14–4 **Makeup primer is used to smooth the surface of the skin.**

Makeup Primer

Makeup primer is important for improving the appearance of aging skin and improving the wear time and appearance of makeup (**Figure 14–4**).

Purpose

Primer is used to smooth the surface of the skin by creating a cushion of hydration or light-reflective properties. Some primers also provide a temporary tightening effect.

Multicultural CONSIDERATIONS

Use concealer instead of foundation around the mouth for mature women. This keeps lip color in place and away from fine lines around the lips. Always be sure the concealer blends seamlessly and matches the natural skin tone of the face.

Choices

Primers come in various formulations with most creating a barrier over the skin that helps the foundation adhere well. There are different formulations for each skin type. People with oily skin should avoid oils, such as cholesterol and vitamin E as well as **dimethicone**, a cosmetic ingredient that is derived from silicon polymers and that is used to create slip and seal in hydration. All skin types can benefit from **hyaluronic acid,** a humectant ingredient that improves skin hydration and influences biological processes that promote healthy skin function. Moisturizer is not generally used as a primer since the right formulation of moisturizer will penetrate the stratum corneum, causing the moisturizer to lose its long-term effect on the surface of the skin, altering the makeup application.

Application Tips

Apply primer to clean, moisturized skin. It can be applied all over or only in areas where aging is most evident, such as around the lips and under the eyes. Let the primer dry before applying concealer or foundation.

Concealer

Concealer is essential for minimizing skin imperfections (**Figure 14–5**).

▲ Figure 14–5 **Concealor is essential for minimizing imperfections.**

Purpose

Concealer is used to camouflage imperfections such as blemishes, dark under-eye circles, pigment discolorations, and scarring.

Choices

Many concealer formulations and colors are available. Compared with foundation, concealer has a thicker texture and is drier. The thickest concealer texture is used for camouflage makeup. Mature skin should use a creamier consistency so that the product will not settle into fine lines. Yellow-based concealer is best for a lighter skin, and golden-orange concealer is best for darker skin.

Application Tips

Using a concealer brush, apply concealer very lightly over areas of discoloration; if necessary, mix the concealer with moisturizer to thin the texture (**Figure 14–6**).

To cover pigment discolorations and broken veins, apply cream concealer directly on the problem area before applying foundation. Do not apply concealer outside the area being covered. Use your finger to stipple (gently pat) the edges around the area being covered. Apply foundation in stipple fashion in order to not remove concealer. Then apply powder to set. If you are using mineral makeup, use a large soft brush and gently blend.

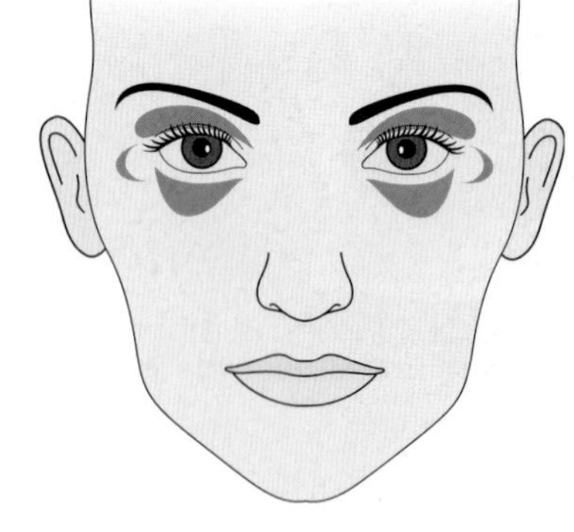

▲ Figure 14–6 **Apply concealer with a brush to minimize areas of discoloration.**

Foundation

Foundation is essential for creating the appearance of youthful skin. It covers discolorations and provides a flawless finish (**Figure 14–7**).

▲ **Figure 14–7 Foundation is essential for providing a flawless finish.**

Purpose

Foundation is used to create a flawless look and to provide a canvas for color.

Choices

Foundation comes in many shades and formulations. The goal is to find the appropriate finish for the client's skin type. Formulation types include:

- Matte, which is oil-absorbing with little light reflection.
- Luminous or satin, which is mildly moisturizing and has gentle light reflection.
- Dewey, which is highly moisturizing and has intense light reflection.

These formulations can also be found in cheek-color and lip-color products.

To determine the correct undertone in skin of any color, put a bright white piece of paper up against clean makeup-free skin. Undertones such as yellow, red (pink), olive (green), or blue (brown) will appear obvious.

Application Tips

Foundation should be applied in an even, thin layer with a sponge, a foundation brush, or the fingertips. Begin at the center of the face and blend outward. Foundation can be applied over the lips. Airbrush application can also be used.

Eyelash Curler

Eyelash curlers are an important tool for creating youthful-looking eyes (**Figure 14–8**).

Purpose

Curling the eyelashes draws attention to the eyes by creating the illusion of thicker lashes and by opening the eye area.

Choices

Eyelash curlers come in three types. The most commonly used curler is the crimp eyelash curler. The second type, the heated eyelash curler, uses a mild heating tip. The third type of eyelash curler is the detailed eyelash curler; it looks like small tweezers with a flat head.

▲ **Figure 14–8 An eyelash curler is an essential tool for youthful-looking eyes.**

Application Tips

All curlers except for the heated curler should be used before mascara application. Detailed curlers are very effective for curling closer to the lash root and in tight areas such as the inner and outer eye. The heated lash curler uses mascara as the heating catalyst, and is used after mascara is applied.

Multicultural CONSIDERATIONS

Dark-skinned clients tend to sink before they sag. Avoid over-contouring mature clients.

Sculpting Shades

Sculpting shades are cosmetic products and shades that are used to highlight and contour. They help to sculpt the face and create the illusion of youthfulness (**Figure 14–9**).

Purpose

Contour shades are used for minimizing facial features and for reducing the appearance of wrinkles and loss of firmness. Highlighting shades are used to bring attention to certain areas of the face as well as to lessen the appearance of facial wrinkles.

▲ Figure 14–9 **Multiple sculpting shades are important for correct contour of the face.**

Choices

Contour and highlighting shades come in powder or cream form, and many are the same formulation as eye shadow and blush. Choose a level darker than the client's skin tone for contouring and a level lighter than the skin tone for highlighting. Brushes and/or sponges should be used for application. ✓ **LO4**

APPLICATION TIPS FOR MATURE SKIN

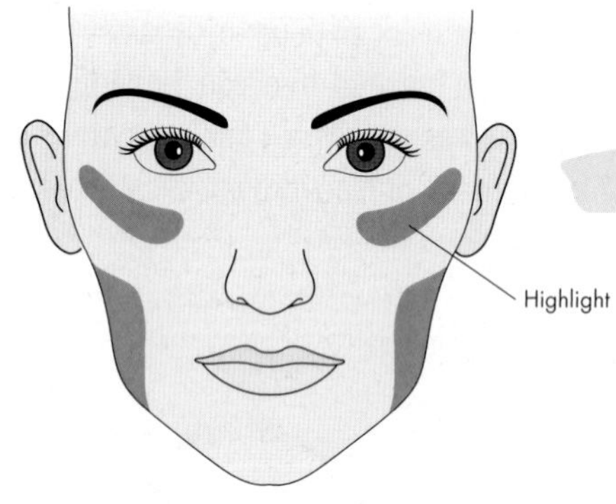

▲ Figure 14–10 **To make a face look thinner, use a powder contour.**

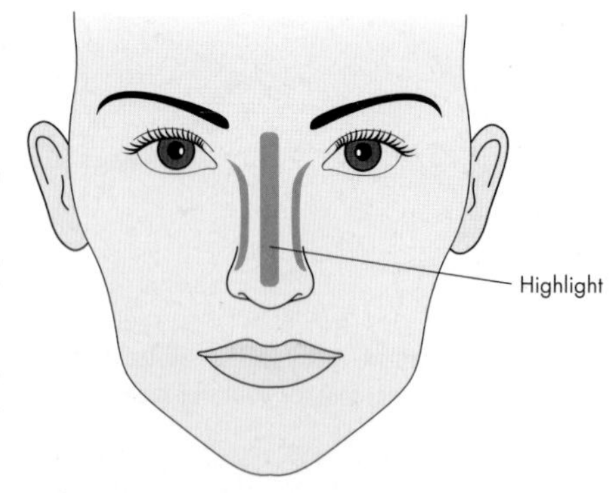

▲ Figure 14–11 **Apply highlight and contour to thin the nose.**

Use the following tips to turn back the hands of time.

- ***To make the face look thinner***, use a powder contour color two or three shades darker than the skin tone. Apply the powder contour color after foundation application. Blend well at the jawline and under the cheekbones. Use a highlight color at the upper part of cheekbones (**Figure 14–10**).
- ***To reduce the appearance of wrinkles,*** apply a primer and follow it with liquid foundation for a dewy or soft finish. Set with a translucent matte powder. Then use a small face brush to place a matte highlight color, one or two shades lighter than the skin tone, inside of the wrinkle or naso-labial fold. Gently blend. Set with a translucent matte powder. Avoid using a highly reflective shimmer product as it draws attention.
- ***To thin the nose,*** first apply foundation. Then apply contour powder one shade darker along the outer portion of the nose and a lighter highlight color to the bridge of nose and the inner corner of eyes (**Figure 14–11**).
- ***To reduce a double chin,*** first apply foundation. Then apply contour powder from the edge of the jawline and back under the chin. Blend well. Apply highlight color that has a matte finish to the center of the chin (**Figure 14–12**).

COLOR CHOICES FOR MATURE SKIN

Mature skin presents particular challenges when it comes to the application of color. Colors that the client wore 20 years ago will most likely look too dramatic 20 years later and can enhance the appearance of aged skin. Skin tone and texture also change. Choosing colors based on a client's undertone and skin color intensity is important for mature makeup.

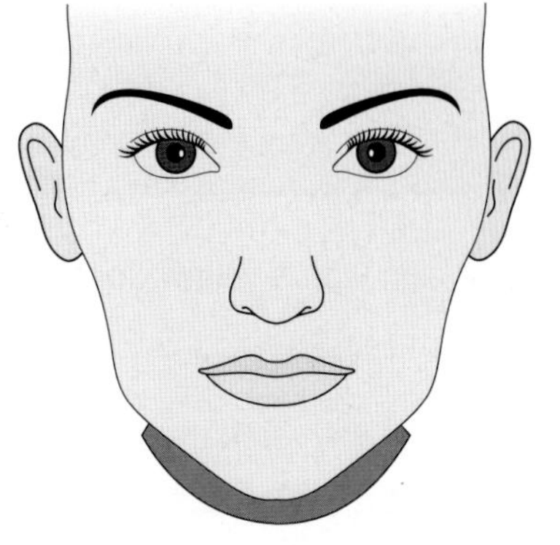

▲ Figure 14–12 To reduce a double chin, use a contour under the jaw.

Skin Undertone

Skin undertone is the color that is most predominant in the skin. To determine the client's undertone, use the neck or forearm. If the client has a large amount of sun damage use the neck as the primary indicator of skin undertone. In natural light, place a white piece of paper or cloth next to clean skin and determine the color that is most apparent. Look for yellow, red (pink), green (olive), or blue (brown) undertones.

Skin Color Intensity

Skin color intensity is the depth of color in the skin. Light skin has a light intensity and dark skin has a dark intensity. Skin color intensity will help determine the type of color to use, while undertone will help determine the correct shade. For example, skin with light intensity and a yellow undertone will do well with peach, bronze, and brown in formulas that are sheer or luminous. Refer to **Table 14–2,** on page 332, Color Use for Skin Tone, for other examples of color choices.

HERE'S A TIP

Brow ptosis is the drooping of the brow. To improve the appearance of sagging eyebrows, reshape the eyebrow arch to give a lifted appearance and use shading techniques to minimize sagging areas. Remember dark colors recede or push back, light colors bring forward.

SPECIAL CONSIDERATIONS

A few easy tips can quickly turn back the signs of aging and address the special concerns presented by mature skin. Paying attention to detail and using a few simple tricks can take years off of the client's appearance.

Dark Skin

Different skin colors require special techniques to minimize the signs of aging. Dark skin shows the signs of aging at a slower rate, but discoloration is common. In addition, dark skin can have a mottled (blotchy) appearance, especially around the lip and jaw due to sun damage or distribution of melanocytes to name a few reasons. Undertones in dark skin can range from golden-yellow to red-blue. Skin color intensity can range from medium to dark.

Match the foundation to the skin tone and use a lighter tone of foundation through the center of the face to create a gentle glow. A highlight color should be used on the cheekbones, the inner corner of the eyes, and under the brows (on the brow bone). Lip color should be bright and based on the undertone of the skin. ☑ LO5

As we age, the skin's pigment changes. This can appear as an overall lightening of the skin as well as a mottling of the skin tone (blotches of color). Brighter or sheer colors with less intensity help the skin look youthful.

SKIN COLOR	COLORS TO USE
Light skin with a yellow undertones	Warm colors: peach, light pink, bronze, yellow-brown, light blue, taupe, gold, cream
Light skin with pink undertones	Cool colors: pink, cream, dark brown, white, dark purple
Medium skin with yellow undertones	Warm colors: dark brown, bronze, peach, warm red, taupe
Medium skin with pink undertones	Cool colors: rich pink, dark brown, purple, cool bronze, silver, navy
Dark skin with yellow undertones	Warm colors: peach, creamy white, blue, warm red, light yellow
Dark skin with pink undertones	Cool colors: vibrant pink, cool red, navy, silver, cool taupe, cool cream

▲ Table 14–2 Color Use for Skin Tone.

HERE'S A TIP

Colors to Avoid

Colors to avoid on aging skin are based on texture and luminosity. For example, a client with mature skin should avoid shimmers, glitter, and overly dark foundation. Many aging clients use foundation with a pink undertone thinking that it will add a glow to the skin, but it actually makes them look older. Always use sculpting shades and matte bronzer—not foundation—to enhance the skin's glow.

If the client has the skin tone for a brighter color, use it on the client's most prominent feature such as eyes or lips, but not both. Always blend shades well and use the correct makeup brushes for a professional finish.

Lash Extensions

Lash extensions are synthetic lash fibers that are adhered to individual lashes. Reapplication is done as the natural lash falls out. Chapter 17, All About Lashes, covers in detail the process of artificial eyelash extensions. A few additional lashes can open the eyes, accentuate the eye shape and color, and draw attention to one of the face's most appealing features. Artificial lashes will also accent the eyes in the absence of other makeup, so they are a great trick for quick, on-the-go, youthful appeal.

Permanent Makeup

Permanent makeup can add color to fading lips and enhance the lash line. A form of tattooing, permanent makeup is an enhancement that offers a polished look without effort. It requires specialized training, a steady hand, and a keenly artistic eye. Excellent permanent makeup artists are in high demand.

Create a "color look-book" by gathering pictures of mature models with a variety of skin colors and makeup applications. These can be found in magazines marketed to an older clientele and on the Internet. Use this book as you consult with mature clients.

Procedure 14-1

Makeup for Stage 1 Aging Skin: Daytime Look

Implements and Materials

You will need all of the following implements, materials, and supplies:

Brushes

- ☐ Chisel cheek brush
- ☐ Eye contour brush
- ☐ Fan brush
- ☐ Large powder brush
- ☐ Soft, square eye shadow brush

Utensils

- ☐ Brush cleaner
- ☐ Eyelash curler
- ☐ Hand sanitizer
- ☐ Headband or hair clip
- ☐ Makeup cape
- ☐ Makeup chair
- ☐ Makeup palette
- ☐ Neck strip or clean towel for draping
- ☐ Pencil sharpener

Single-use Items

- ☐ Cotton pads for cleansing (optional)
- ☐ Cotton swabs
- ☐ Lip brushes
- ☐ Mascara wands
- ☐ Shadow applicators
- ☐ Spatulas
- ☐ Sponge wedges
- ☐ Tissues

Products

- ☐ Eyebrow pencil/powder
- ☐ Brow gel
- ☐ Matte cheek color
- ☐ Matte bronzer
- ☐ Cleanser/toner (appropriate for skin type)
- ☐ Concealer (appropriate for skin type and color)
- ☐ Eye shadow (highlight, mid-tone, and contour shades)
- ☐ Black mascara
- ☐ Foundations (luminous, matte, or satin as appropriate for skin type)
- ☐ Lip liner (match natural lips)
- ☐ Lip color (pale and bright); for example: peach with a blue undertone or mild shimmer
- ☐ Moisturizer with sunscreen (appropriate formulation for skin type)
- ☐ Primer (hyaluronic acid-based serum or specific makeup primer)

Preparation

- Perform

PROCEDURE 7-1 PRE-SERVICE SEE PAGE 144

Procedure

SERVICE TIP

Put on tight-fitting, non latex disposable gloves for protection.

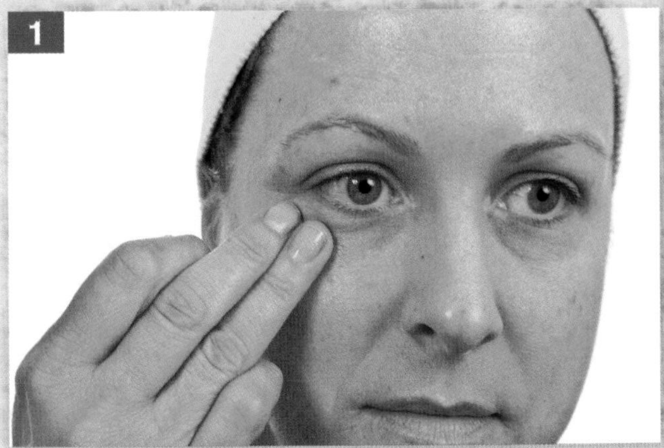

1 Apply a serum with hyaluronic acid to the face, including under the eyes and over the lips.

Procedure 14-1 *(continued)*

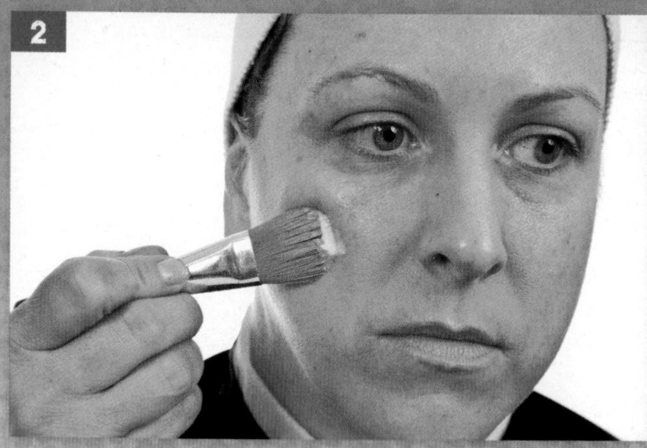

2 Apply moisturizer that contains sunscreen and that is appropriate for the client's skin type.

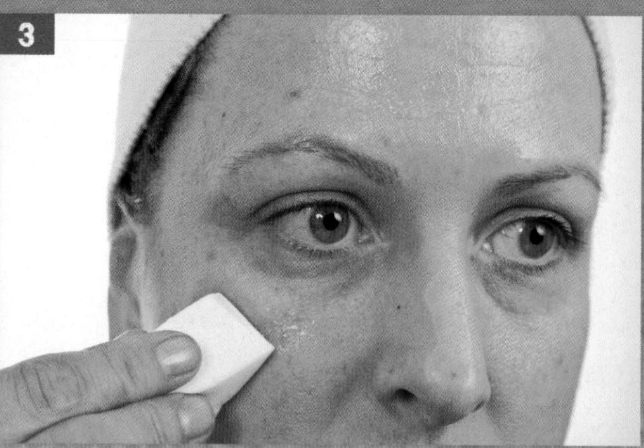

3 Apply makeup primer as directed by the manufacturer.

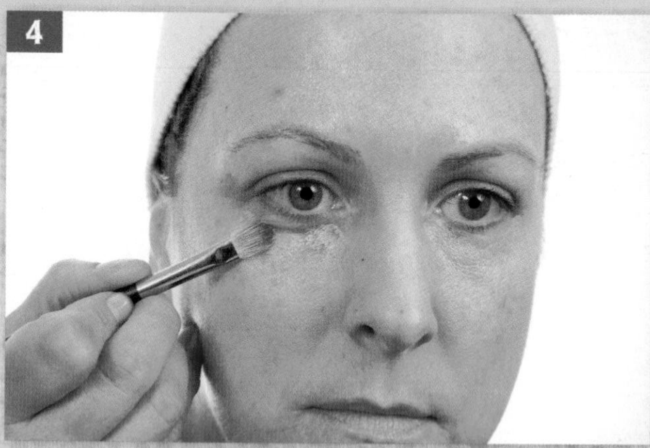

4 Using a concealer brush, apply a yellow-toned cream concealer around the eyes and over blemishes. Keep color only on the areas of discoloration and blend well using a stipple technique.

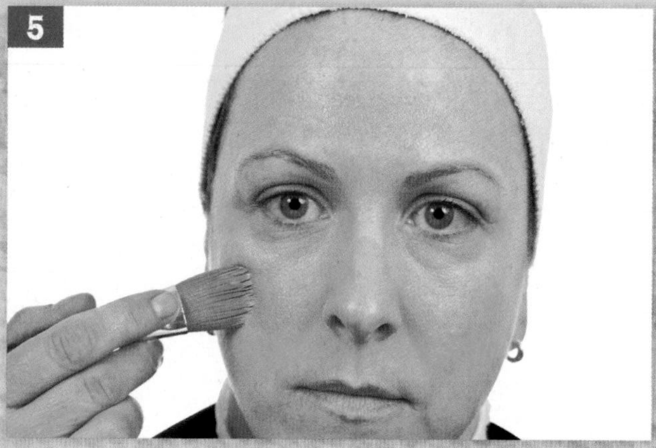

5 Using a foundation brush or airbrush, apply a matte (nonshiny) liquid foundation appropriate for the client's skin type.

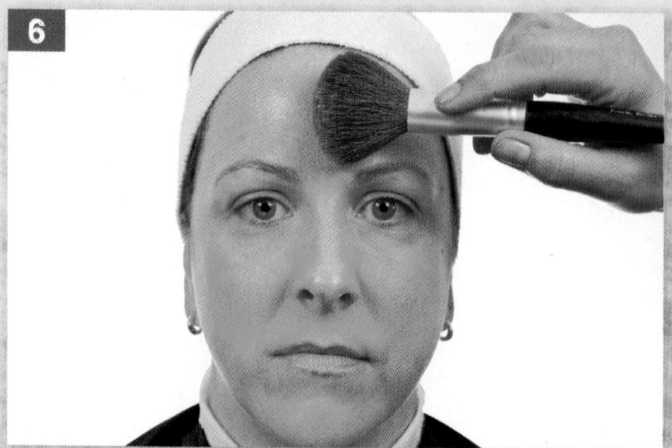

6 Using a large fluff brush, set the foundation with a *small amount* of translucent setting powder.

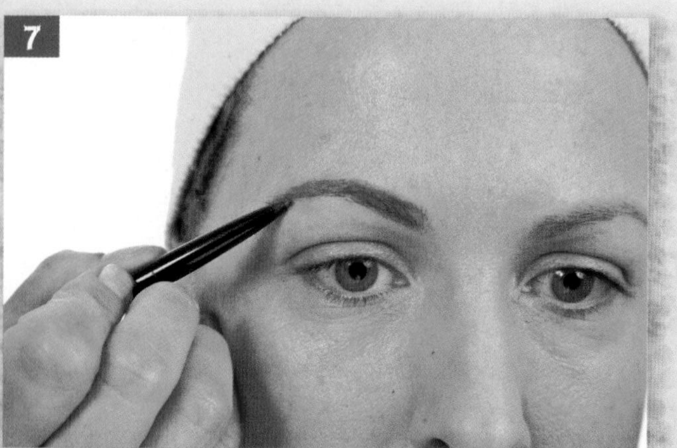

7 Fill in the brows with a brow pencil, using light strokes and following the direction of hair growth.

8 Use a disposable spiral mascara wand or brow brush to soften the brow pencil.

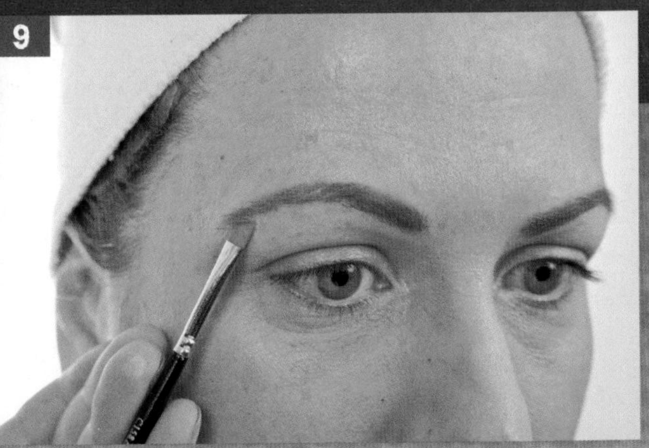

9 Apply brow powder with a stiff angle brush over the softened brow pencil to set.

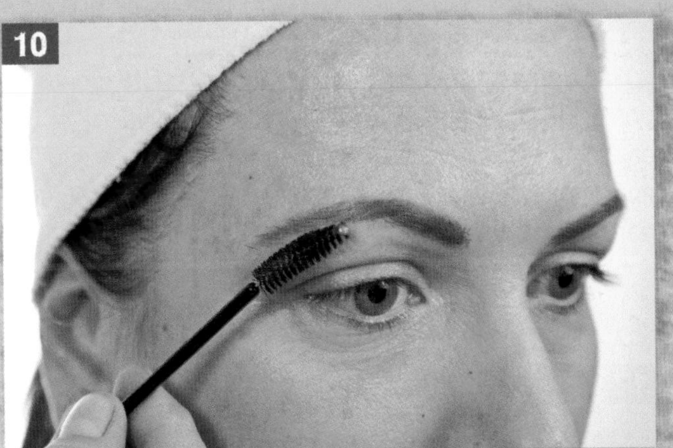

10 Apply clear brow gel over the eyebrows.

11 Using a soft, square eye shadow brush, apply a highlight eye shadow from lash to brow.

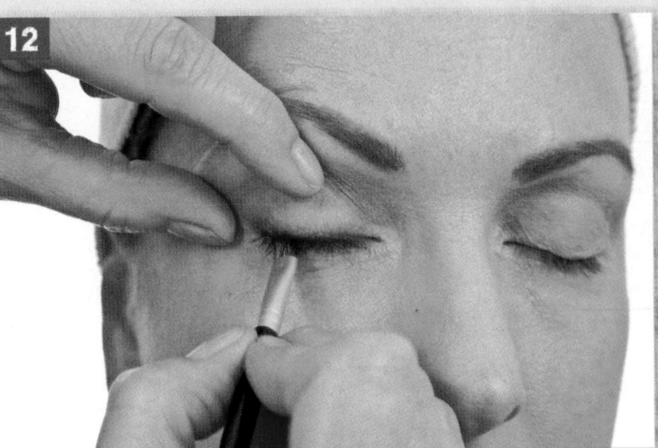

12 Apply a black or brown cream or powder eye shadow to the root of lashes with a small stiff eye brush. Follow along the entire lash line to give the illusion of full lashes.

13 Apply a cream, liquid, or pencil eyeliner from the outer corner of the eyes three-quarters of the way across the eyelid. Make the line slightly thicker on the outer part of the eye to provide an uplifted look.

Procedure 14-1 *(continued)*

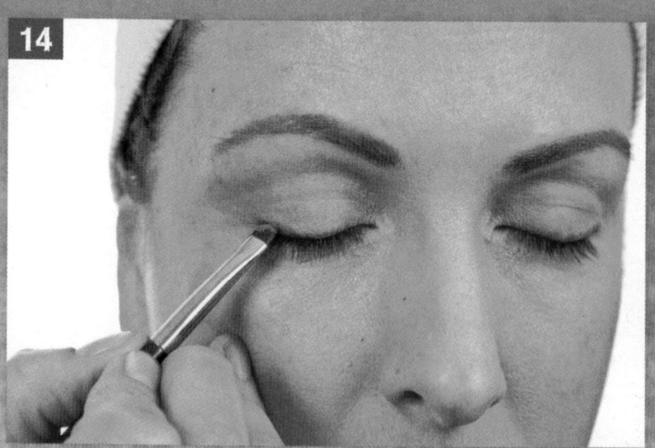

14 Using a small wedge brush, apply a contour color from the outer part of the eye and over the top of the eyeliner to soften and set the color. Use the guidelines in Chapter 8, Facial Features, to determine which application to use for specific eye shapes. Blend well with the soft, square eye shadow brush.

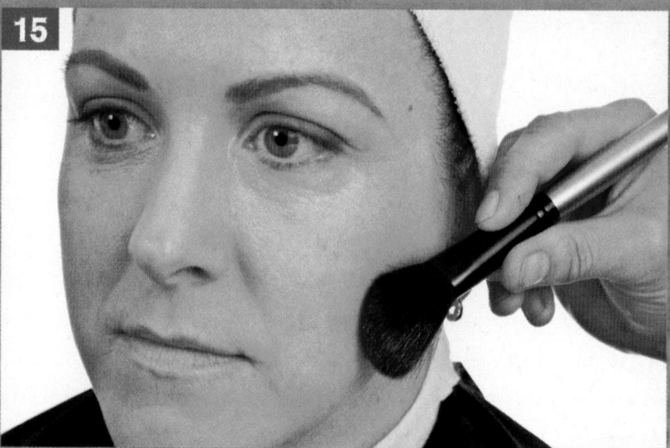

15 With a chisel cheek brush, apply a matte bronzer under the cheekbones. Refer to sculpting shades application tips discussed in this chapter to determine the appropriate application for the client's features. Remember dark colors minimize and light colors accentuate.

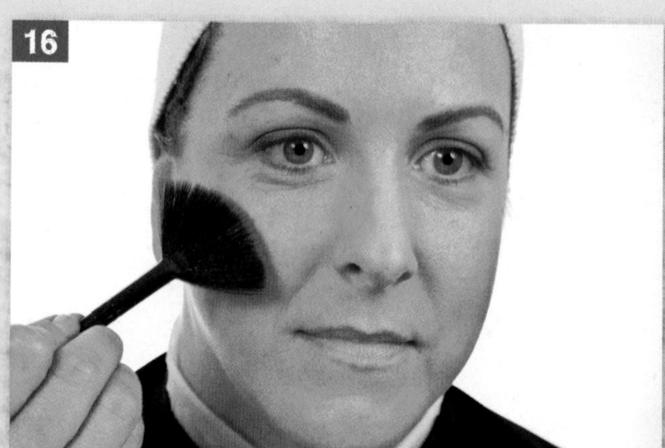

16 Using a fan brush, apply a matte cheek color to the apples of the cheeks and back toward the hairline.

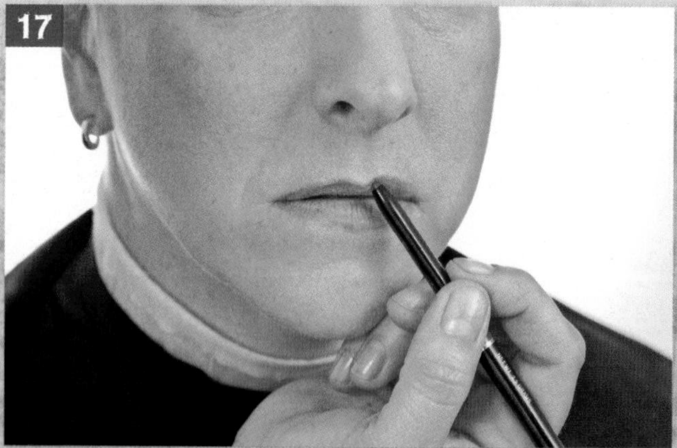

17 Line the lips with a pencil lip liner in a color that closely matches the client's lips. Follow the natural lip line. Fill in the lip with the lip liner.

18 Using a lip brush, apply lip color that is appropriate for the client's skin tone.

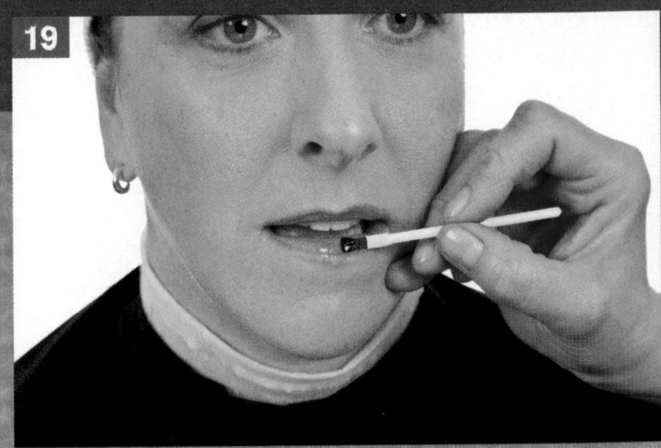

19 Using a lip brush, apply a clear gloss over top of the lip color.

20 Apply two coats of mascara.

21 The finished daytime look.

Post-Service

- Complete PROCEDURE 7-2 POST-SERVICE SEE PAGE 148

An evening look can be created by:

- Adding a mid-tone color shade appropriate for a client's eye color and shape, (See Chapter 8, Facial Features, for reference.). Refer to Table 14–2, Color Use for Skin Tone, for suggestions.
- Applying false lashes. Refer to Chapter 17, All About Lashes, for specific information.
- Applying a shimmer highlight on the top of the cheekbones and at the inner corner of eyes.
- Applying a darker eyeliner color.

Procedure 14-2 Makeup for Stage 2 Aging Skin: Daytime Look

Implements and Materials

You will need all of the following implements, materials, and supplies:

Brushes

- ☐ Chisel cheek brush
- ☐ Eye contour brush
- ☐ Fan brush
- ☐ Large powder brush
- ☐ Soft, square eye shadow brush

Utensils

- ☐ Brush cleaner
- ☐ Eyelash curler
- ☐ Hand sanitizer
- ☐ Headband or hair clip
- ☐ Makeup cape
- ☐ Makeup chair
- ☐ Makeup palette
- ☐ Neck strip or clean towel for draping
- ☐ Pencil sharpener

Single-use Items

- ☐ Cotton pads for cleansing (optional)
- ☐ Cotton swabs
- ☐ Lip brushes
- ☐ Mascara wands
- ☐ Shadow applicators
- ☐ Spatulas
- ☐ Sponge wedges
- ☐ Tissues

Products

- ☐ Brow gel
- ☐ Brow pencil and powder
- ☐ Cleanser/toner (as appropriate for skin type)
- ☐ Concealer (cream)
- ☐ Cheek color (satin)
- ☐ Contour color (mid-tone)
- ☐ Eye shadows (highlight, mid-tone, and contour shades)
- ☐ Finishing powder (matte)
- ☐ Foundations (luminous, matte, or satin as appropriate for skin type)
- ☐ Lip liner (match client's natural lip color)
- ☐ Lip colors (pale and bright)
- ☐ Mascara (black)
- ☐ Moisturizer with sunscreen
- ☐ Primer
- ☐ Serum (formulated to firm and tighten the skin)
- ☐ Setting powder (translucent)

Preparation

- Perform

PROCEDURE 7-1 PRE-SERVICE SEE PAGE 144

Procedure

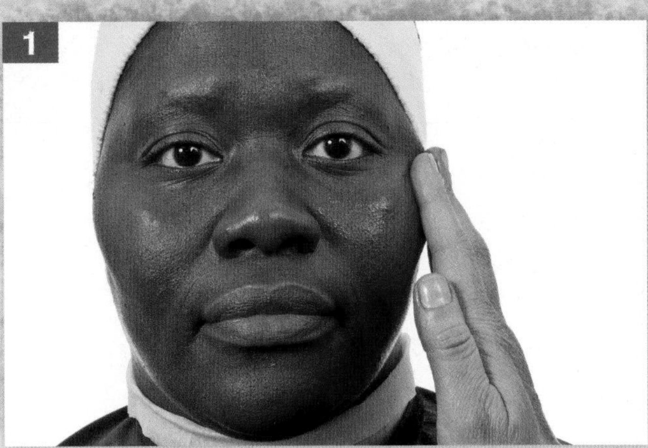

1 Apply a firming and tightening serum. Include the eye area. Be careful to avoid getting product in the client's eyes.

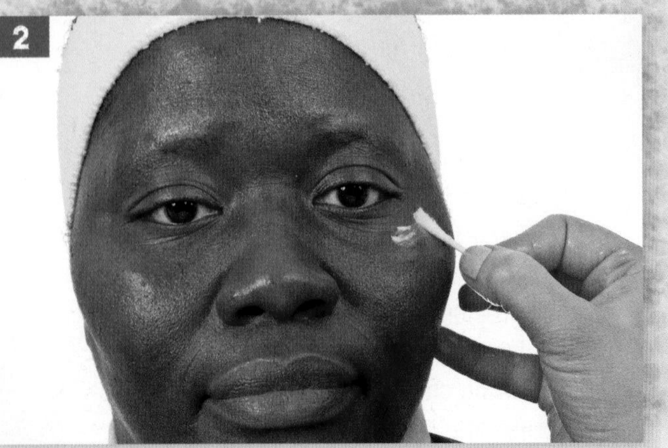

2 Apply eye cream around the eye, excluding the eyelid.

3 Apply moisturizer that contains sunscreen. Use a formulation that is appropriate for the client's skin type.

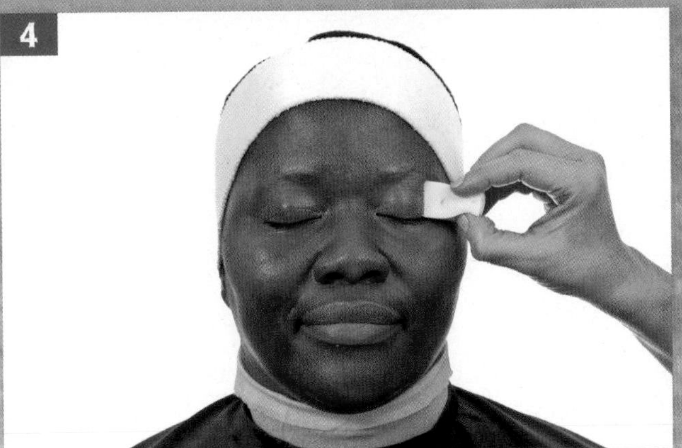

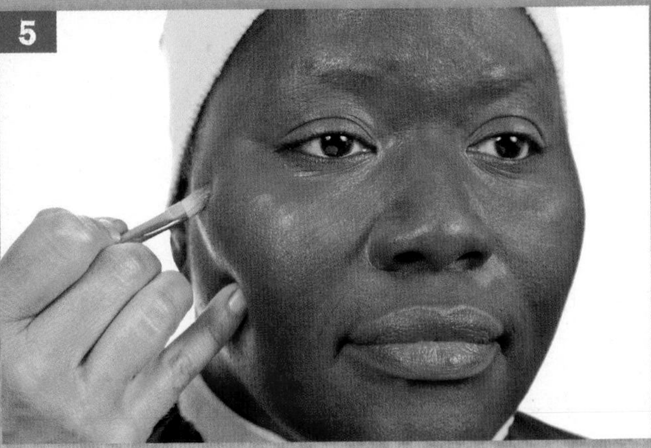

4 Apply makeup primer, eye shadow primer, and lip primer as directed by the manufacturer.

5 Using a concealer brush, apply cream concealer around the eyes and over blemishes. Apply color only to the areas of discoloration. Blend well using a stipple technique.

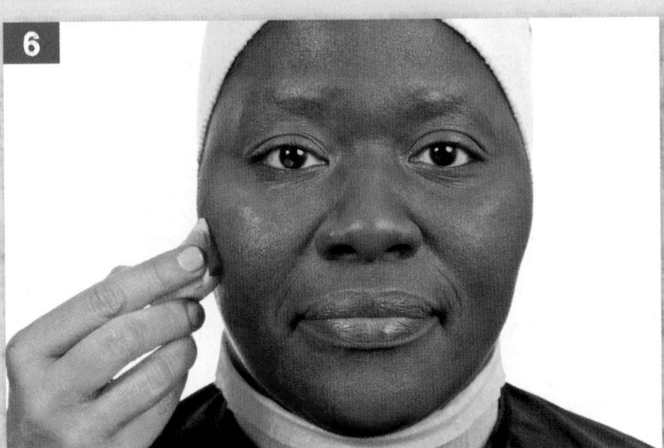

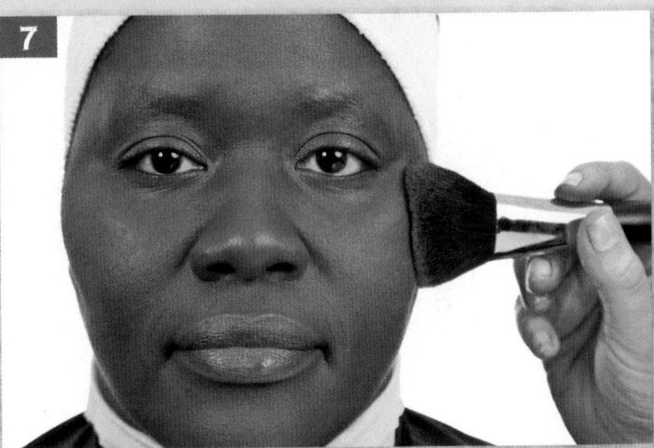

6 Using a foundation brush, airbrush, or sponge, apply a matte to satin liquid foundation that is appropriate for the client's skin type.

7 Using a large fluff brush, set the foundation with a small amount of translucent setting powder.

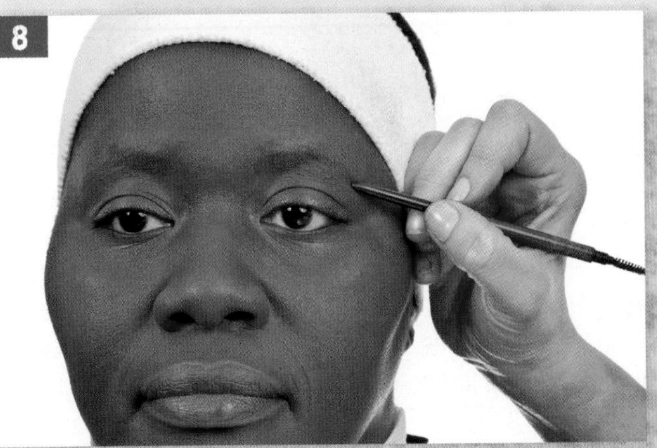

8 With a brow pencil, fill in the brows using light strokes and following the direction of hair growth.

Procedure 14-2 *(continued)*

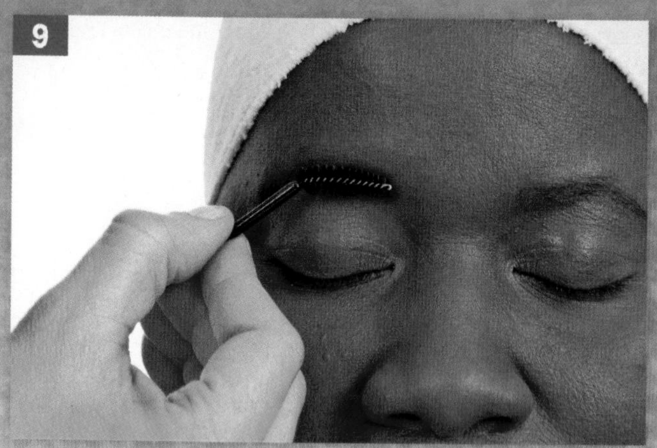

9 Use a spiral mascara wand or brow brush to soften the brow pencil.

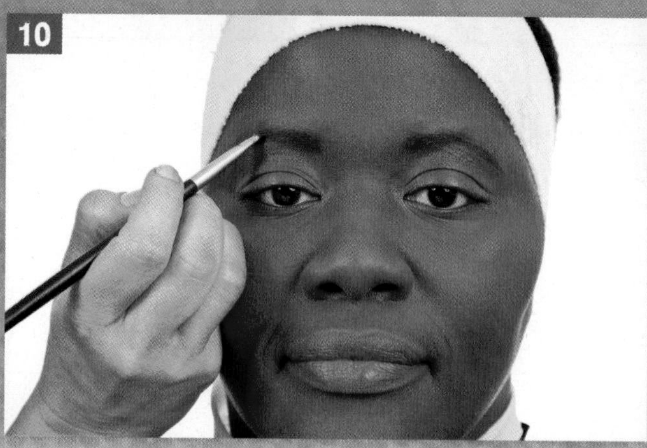

10 Apply brow powder with a stiff angle brush over the softened brow pencil to set.

11 Apply clear brow gel over the eyebrows.

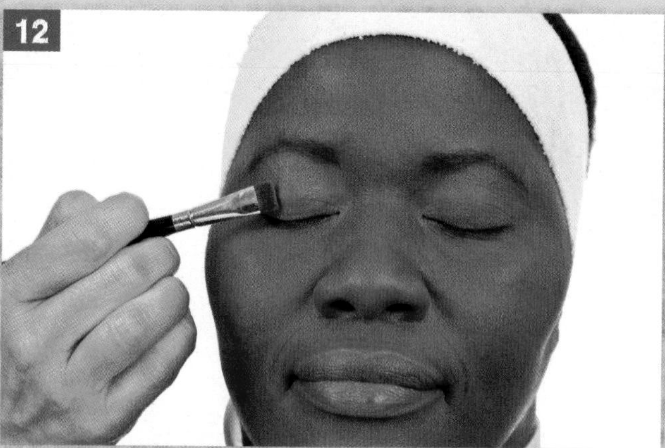

12 Using a soft, square eye shadow brush, apply a highlight eye shadow from lash to brow. Use a color that matches the client's skin tone.

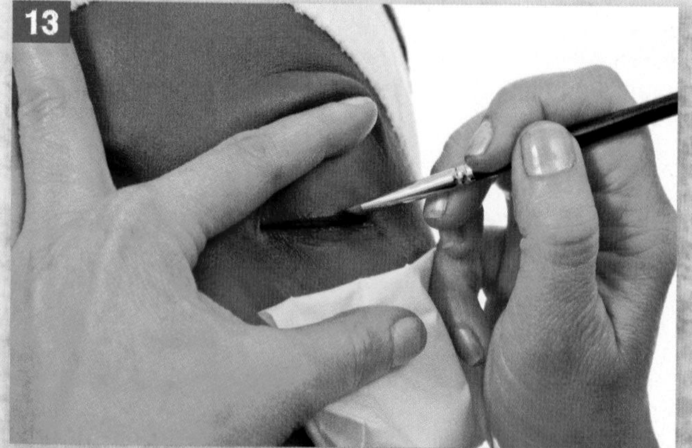

13 Use your index finger to pull up on the brow, lifting the eyelid.

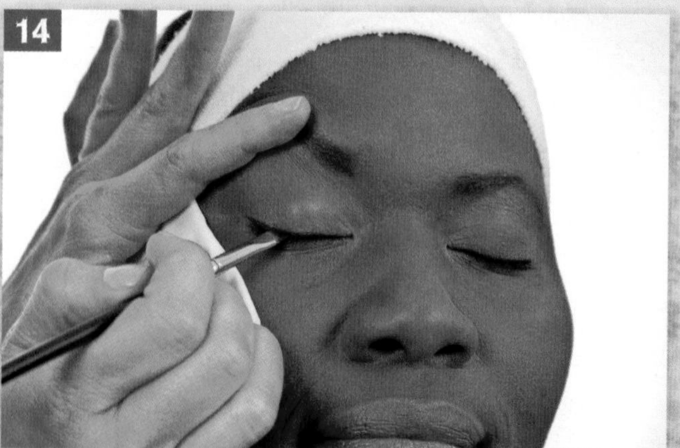

14 Apply a black or brown cream or powder eye shadow to the root of lashes with a small, stiff brush. Follow along the entire lash line to give the illusion of full lashes.

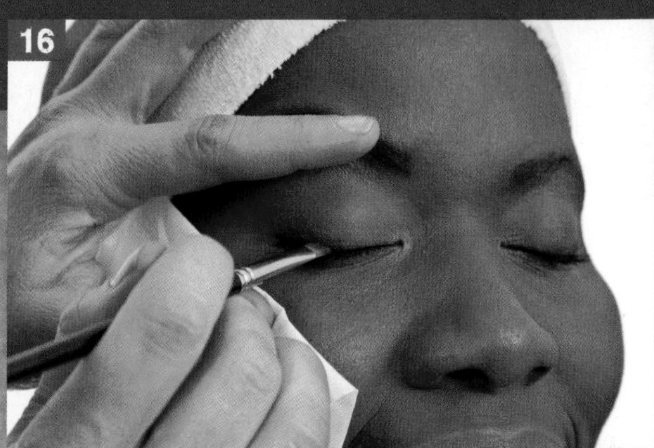

15 Apply a cream, liquid, or pencil eyeliner from the outer corner of the eyes three-quarters of the way across the eyelid.

16 Using a small wedge brush, apply a contour color from the outer part of the eye and over the top of the eyeliner to soften and set the color. Use the guidelines in Chapter 8, Facial Features, to determine which application techniques to use for specific eye shapes. Blend well with the soft, square eye shadow brush.

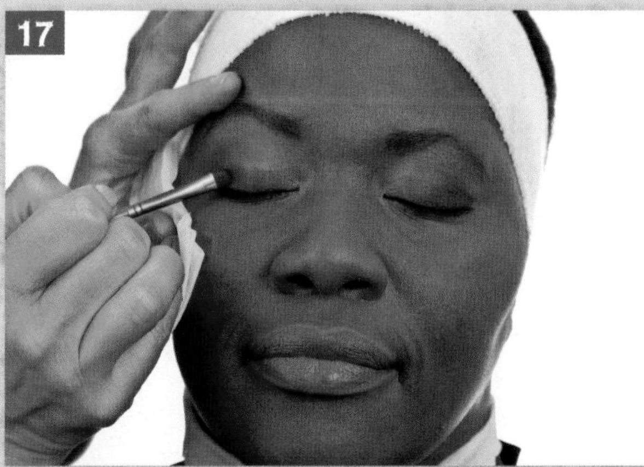

17 Apply a mid-tone eye color as appropriate for the client's eye shape as discussed in Chapter 8. Blend well.

18 With a chisel cheek brush, apply a mid-tone color under the cheekbones, under the jawline, and along the forehead.

19 Using a small fan brush, apply a flesh-toned (muted or non-glossy) highlight color to the inner corner of the eyes, on top of the nose, above the lips, inside the smile lines, on top of the cheekbones, and on the outer part of the eye socket.

Note: If deep lines are apparent, use a small brush to apply a light color to the inside of the line.

Procedure 14-2 *(continued)*

20 Using a fan brush, apply a satin or sheer cheek color to the apples of the cheeks and extending toward the hairline.

21 Using a pencil lip liner, line the lips following the natural lip line.

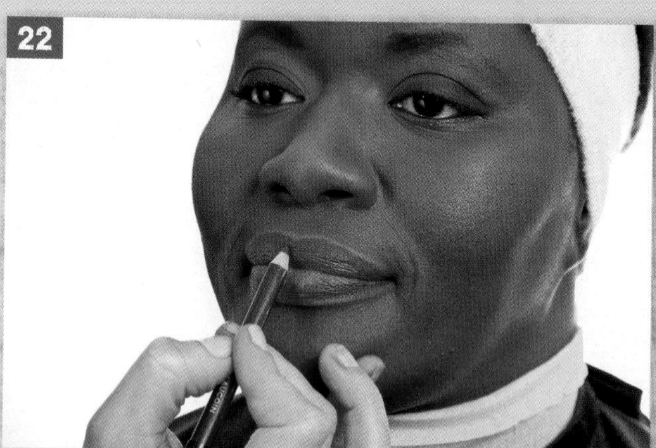

22 Fill in the lips with the lip liner.

23 Using a lip brush, apply a lip color that is appropriate for the client's skin tone.

24 Optional: Use a lip brush to apply a clear gloss.

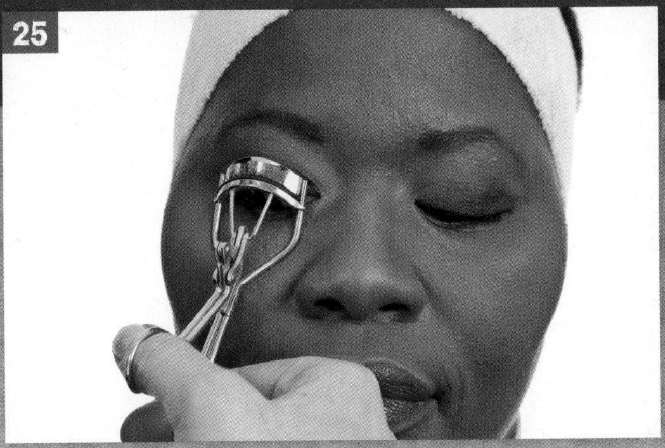

25 Curl the lashes with a lash curler. If you are using a heated curler, curl the lashes after mascara is applied.

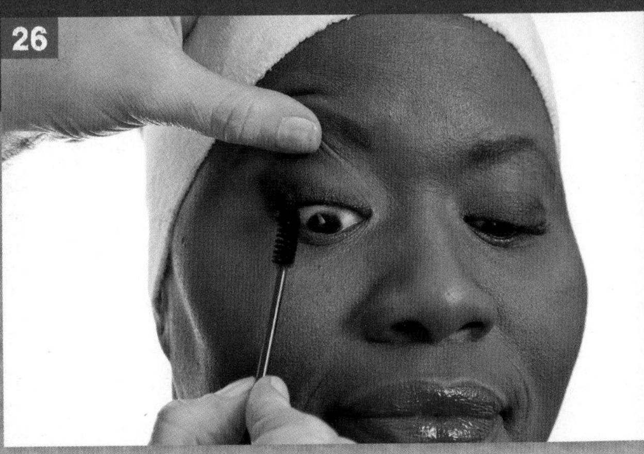

26 With a disposable mascara brush, apply lash primer and then mascara.

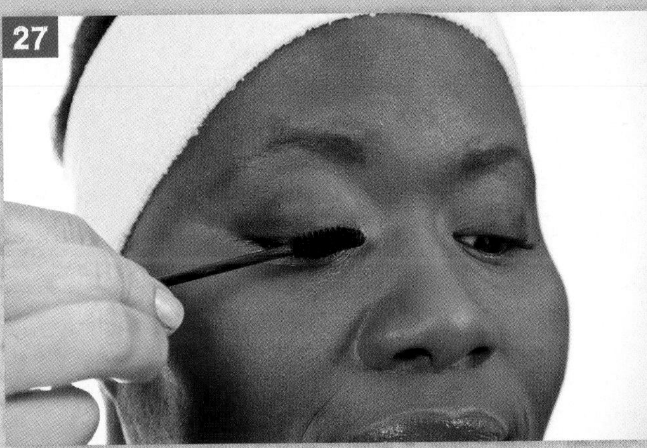

27 Apply two coats of mascara.

28 The finished daytime look.

Post-Service

- Complete PROCEDURE 7-2 POST-SERVICE SEE PAGE 148

An evening look can be created by:

- Adding a deeper mid-tone color shade that is appropriate for a client's eye color through the lash line and crease. Blend well. Refer to Table 14–2, Color Use for Skin Tone, for suggestions.
- Applying false lashes. Refer to Chapter 17, All About Lashes, for directions.
- Applying a shimmer highlight on the top of the cheekbones and at the inner corner of the eyes.
- Applying a more intense lip color.

Procedure 14-3

Makeup for Stage 3 Aging Skin: Daytime Look

Implements and Materials

You will need all of the following implements, materials, and supplies:

Brushes

- ☐ Chisel cheek brush
- ☐ Eye contour brush
- ☐ Fan brush
- ☐ Large powder brush
- ☐ Soft, square eye shadow brush
- ☐ Angled shadow brush

Utensils

- ☐ Brush cleaner
- ☐ Eyelash curler
- ☐ Hand sanitizer
- ☐ Headband or hair clip
- ☐ Makeup cape
- ☐ Makeup chair
- ☐ Makeup palette
- ☐ Neck strip or clean towel for draping
- ☐ Pencil sharpener

Single-use Items

- ☐ Cotton pads for cleansing (optional)
- ☐ Cotton swabs
- ☐ Lip brushes
- ☐ Mascara wands
- ☐ Shadow applicators
- ☐ Spatulas
- ☐ Sponge wedges
- ☐ Tissues

Products

- ☐ Eyebrow pencil/powder
- ☐ Brow gel
- ☐ Cheek colors (cream or powder; bright and luminous)
- ☐ Contour color (powder formulation; mid-tone)
- ☐ Cleanser/toner (appropriate for skin type)
- ☐ Lash primer
- ☐ Lip colors (pale, bright)
- ☐ Lip liner (match client's natural lip color)
- ☐ Moisturizer with sunscreen (appropriate for skin type)
- ☐ Concealer (cream texture)
- ☐ Eye cream
- ☐ Eye shadows (highlight, mid-tone, and contour shade; matte formulation, muted shades)
- ☐ Mascara (black)
- ☐ Foundations (appropriate for skin type; luminous or satin—NO matte finish)
- ☐ Setting powder (translucent color; matte finish)
- ☐ Primer (also for line filler)
- ☐ Serum (formulated to firm and tighten the skin)

Preparation

- Perform

PROCEDURE 7-1 PRE-SERVICE SEE PAGE 144

Procedure

1 Apply a hydrating and firming serum. Include the eye area, if the product is appropriate for the delicate eye tissue. Be careful to avoid getting the product in the client's eyes.

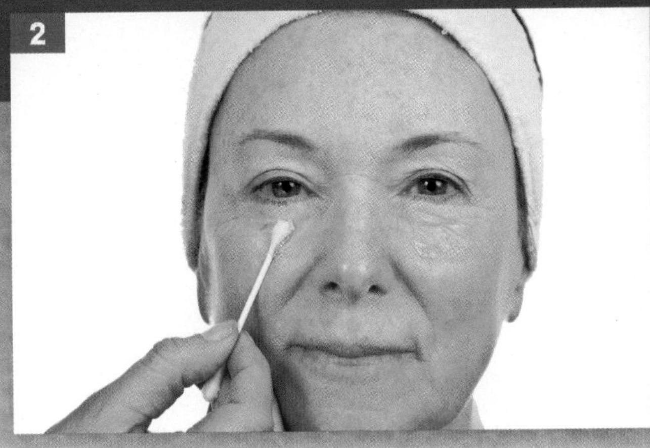

2 Apply eye cream around the eyes, excluding the eyelid.

3 Apply moisturizer that contains sunscreen. Use a formulation that is appropriate for the client's skin type.

4 Apply makeup primer, eye shadow primer, and lip primer as directed by the manufacturer.

5 With a concealer brush, apply cream concealer around the eyes and over blemishes. Keep color only on the areas of discoloration. Blend well using a stipple technique.

6 With a foundation brush, airbrush, or sponge, apply a satin luminous liquid foundation that is appropriate for the client's skin type.

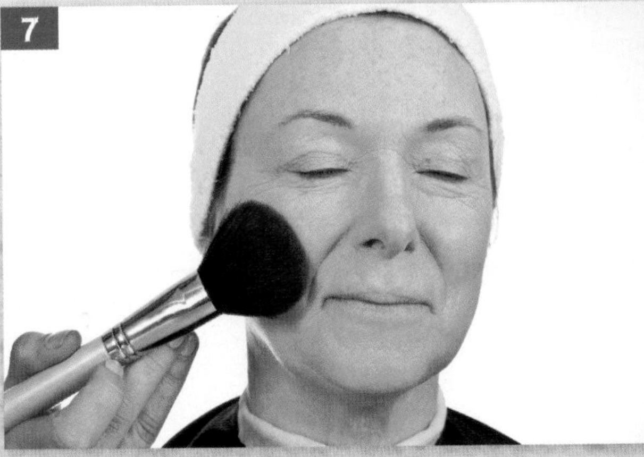

7 Using a large fluff brush, apply a small amount of translucent setting powder.

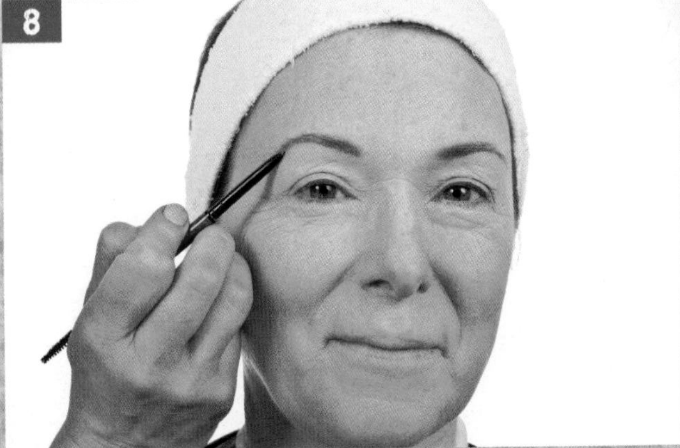

8 With a brow pencil, fill in the eyebrows using light strokes and following the direction of hair growth.

Procedure 14-3 *(continued)*

9 Use a spiral mascara/brow brush to soften.

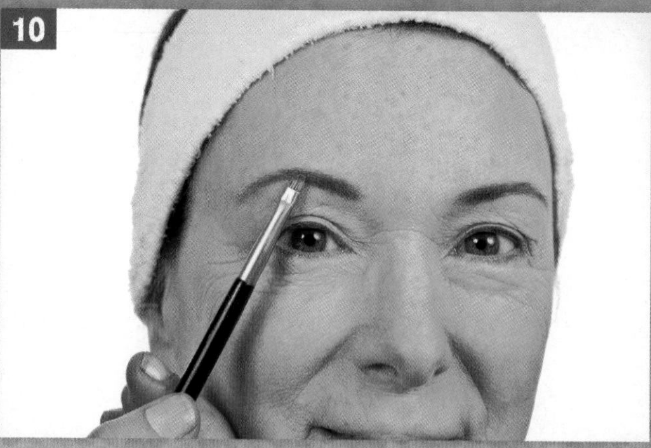

10 Apply brow powder with a stiff angle brush over softened brow pencil to set.

11 Apply clear brow gel over the eyebrows.

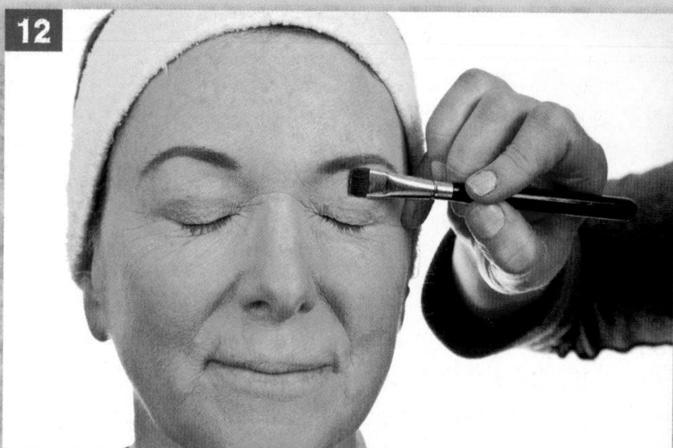

12 Using a soft, square eye shadow brush, apply a highlight eye shadow from lash to brow. The shadow color should match the client's skin tone.

13 Use your index finger to pull up on the brow, lifting the eyelid. Apply a black or brown cream eye shadow or eyeliner to the root of lashes with a small stiff brush. Follow along the entire lash line to give the illusion of full lashes.

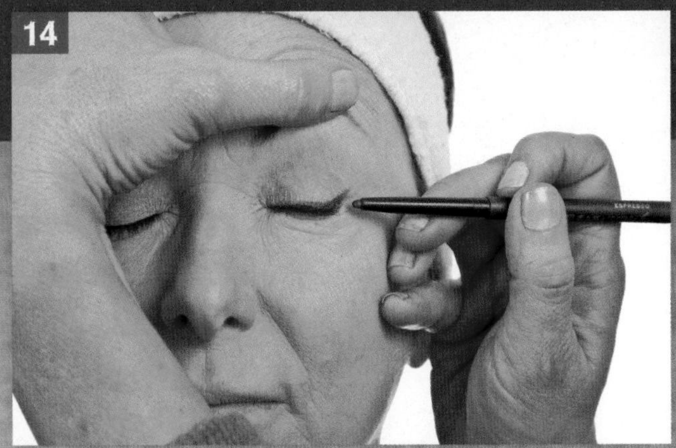

14 Apply a gel, liquid, or pencil eyeliner from the outer corner of the eyes three-quarters of the way across the eyelid and extending slightly up from the corner of the eye.

15 Using a small angled brush, apply a darker contour color from the outer part of the eye and over the top of the eyeliner to soften. Use the guidelines for appropriate application on specific eye shapes. Blend well with a soft, square eye shadow brush.

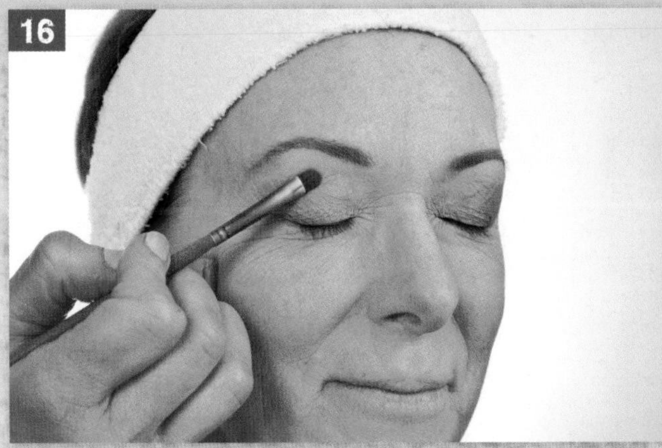

16 Apply a mid-tone eye color as appropriate for the client's eye shape as discussed in Chapter 8, Facial Features. Blend well.

17 With a chisel cheek brush apply a mid-tone color under the cheekbones, under the jawline, and along the forehead.

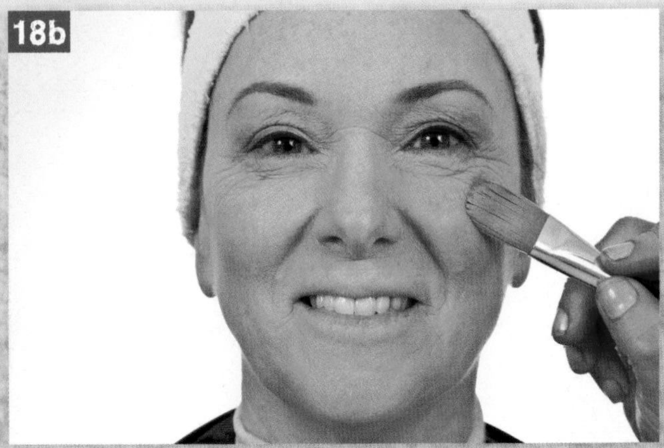

18 Using a brush, apply a flesh-toned cream or gel highlight color to the inner corner of the eyes, on the top or sides of nose, above the lips, inside the smile lines, on top of the cheekbones, and on the outer corner of the eye to conceal redness.

Note: If deep lines are apparent use a small brush to apply a light color to the inside of the line.

Procedure 14-3 *(continued)*

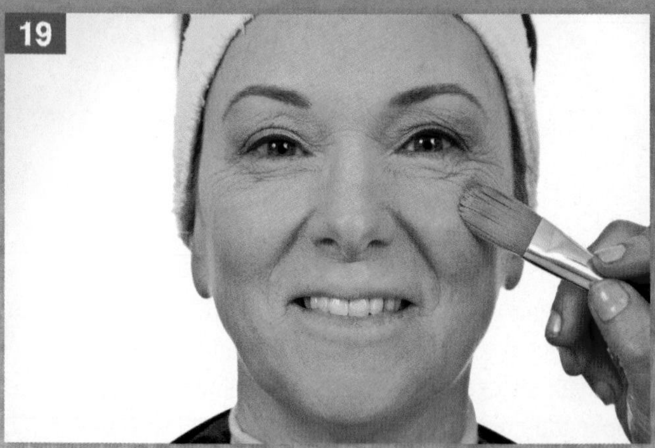

19 Using a fan brush, apply a bright, light-intensity cheek color to the apples of the cheeks and extending back toward the hairline. (Gel blush is another option.)

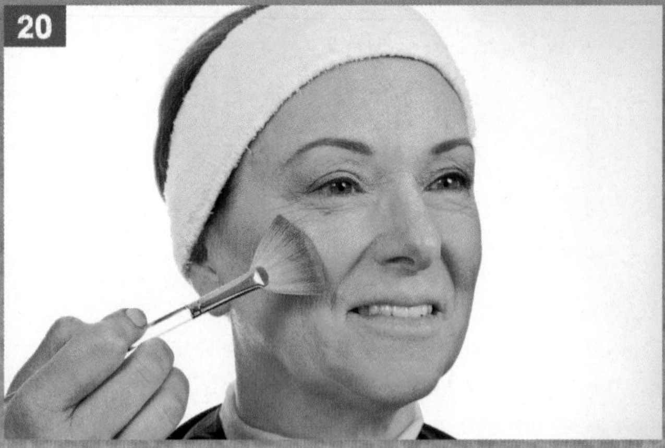

20 Using a pencil lip liner, line the lips following the natural lip line.

21 Fill in the lip with the lip liner.

22 Using a lip brush, apply lip color that is appropriate for the client's skin tone.

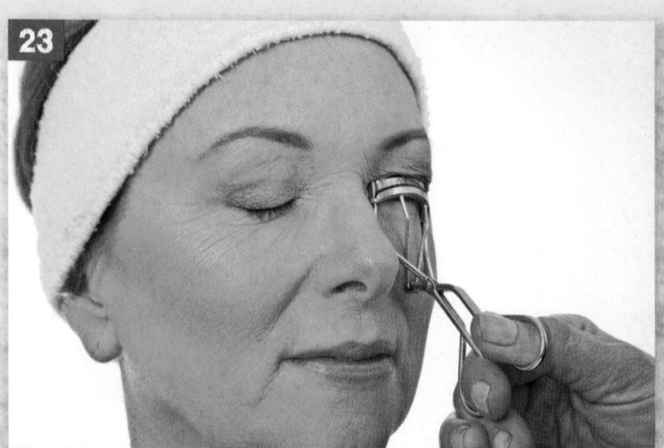

23 Curl lashes with a lash curler. If you are using a heated curler, curl the lashes after mascara is applied.

24 With a disposable mascara brush, apply lash primer.

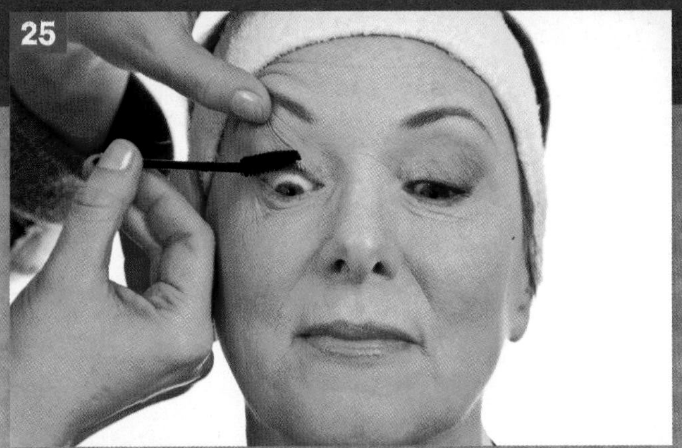

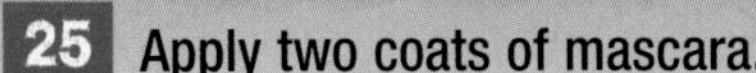

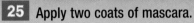

25 Apply two coats of mascara.

26 The finished daytime look.

Post-Service ☑ LO6

- Complete

PROCEDURE 7-2 POST-SERVICE SEE PAGE 148

An evening look can be created by:

- Adding a deeper mid-tone color appropriate for the client's eye color and shape. Refer to Table 14–2, Color Use for Skin Tone, for suggestions.
- Applying false lashes. Refer to Chapter 17, All About Lashes, for directions.
- Applying a shimmer highlight on the top of the cheekbones and at the inner corner of the eyes.
- Applying a more intense lip color.

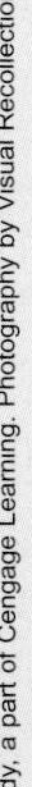

Review Questions

1. Why is makeup application different for aging skin?
2. Why is proper skin assessment important for mature makeup application?
3. What are the characteristics of Stage 1 aging skin?
4. What are the characteristics of Stage 2 aging skin?
5. What are the characteristics of Stage 3 aging skin?
6. What are three key items needed for mature makeup application?
7. What is the purpose of using light colors for highlighting? What is the purpose of using dark colors for shading?
8. How do you determine skin undertone and depth?

Chapter Glossary

Botox®	A prescription medicine created using botulin toxin; it is used to treat lines and wrinkles by paralyzing the muscles located at the site of injection.
capillaries	Small blood vessels.
dimethicone	Cosmetic ingredient that is derived from silicon polymers; creates slip and seals in hydration.
hyaluronic acid	A humectant that improves skin hydration and promotes biological reactions that improve skin health including collagen synthesis and increase of retinoic acid.
pigment discoloration	Uneven skin color that appears in two types: hyperpigmentation and hypopigmentation.
resting phase	When the face is not moving.
skin color intensity	The depth of color in the skin.
skin undertone	The color that is predominant in the skin.

Part 4

Advanced Makeup

Chapter 15 Camouflage Makeup

Chapter Outline

Learning Objectives

After completing this chapter, you will be able to:

- ✓ **LO1** Understand basic formulations of camouflage makeup.
- ✓ **LO2** Properly apply each formula.
- ✓ **LO3** Identify skin conditions needing camouflaging.
- ✓ **LO4** Identify the client's concerns.
- ✓ **LO5** Recommend retail take-home products and use.

Key Terms

Page number indicates where in the chapter the term is used.

camouflage makeup
pg. 355

dyspigmentation
pg. 355

hypertrophic
pg. 359

hypopigmented
pg. 359

iron oxides
pg. 357

paramedical makeup
pg. 355

postinflammatory hyperpigmentation
pg. 355

skin grafts
pg. 359

titanium dioxide
pg. 356

turgor
pg. 361

zinc
pg. 357

Career Profile

David Michaud's passion for makeup stemmed from the esthetics of fashion. Understanding the beauty of the whole picture led him to the love of makeup and what it can do to accentuate that picture. He has been able to base an entire career on freelancing, using his skills on several different types of people all around the world. Today, David continues to freelance, traveling around to different cities, continuing to explore the potential of makeup artistry.

"In 1978 I was 22 years old and had recently moved to San Francisco to work as a window dresser for a couture-fashion specialty store. There I learned that a successful window presentation was the result of several key elements working together. Done correctly, the result was so exquisite that it somehow appeared to be greater than the sum of its parts.

"After 3 years of window dressing, I ascertained that it was the makeup that truly made everything magical for me. I decided to become a makeup artist for fashion photoshoots. I had no formal training but was friends with one of the best makeup artists in the city. At that time there were perhaps eight working artists in San Francisco, and if you wanted to stay busy you had to know how to style hair as well. Models were often expected to do their own hair and makeup. Having artists on the set was a novelty. I paid for one lesson from my friend, who later became my mentor. Then I simply practiced, pushing my own boundaries each time. Within 3 years I was able to make a living solely from doing what I loved to do. I was fortunate that the need for makeup artists was growing in the fashion industry. Finding work was easy if you were talented and dependable.

"Over the next 28 years, I moved to New York, South Beach, Miami, and Los Angeles to experience the different kinds of work being done in each place. It was exciting, but I had to start from the beginning every time I moved. The transition from a job with a steady income into the freelance world was the hardest move and the biggest leap of faith I ever made. On the flip-side, being able to pack up my kit and move wherever I want to go has been one of the best parts of being freelance.

"Each generation has its unique challenges to conquer. I do not think there was ever a time when so many well-trained artists, armed with excellent skills and technical knowledge, have entered the job market. Sometimes it is much better to be a big fish in a small pond. I have learned more about makeup working on the average person than on a beauty model. My favorite part of being a makeup artist is the instant gratification. If it ceases to be fun, stop and ask yourself why. The solution may be as simple as signing up for an airbrush class to restore your passion."

David Michaud www.michaudbeauty.com

Makeup artists are trained to assist clients with a wide variety of beauty concerns. Uneven skin requires advanced makeup application techniques. **Camouflage makeup** is the strategic layering of various colors and textures to hide pigmentation issues. Mastering camouflage techniques allows you to conceal severe under-eye discoloration, acne scars, pigmentation issues that occur as the result of severe trauma, and a darkening of the skin following redness and irritation known as **postinflammatory hyperpigmentation.** **Dyspigmentation** is hypopigmentation or hyperpigmentation and can be caused by trauma, illness, medications, or hormonal imbalance.

The appearance of these issues is improved with the use of camouflaging. Camouflaging techniques are even used to hide tattoos that may not be appropriate for formal occasions like weddings. While makeup is only a temporary solution, it can really boost the client's self-esteem. A skilled makeup artist can provide a channel through which clients begin to see themselves as whole and complete.

Paramedical makeup is a special branch of makeup artistry that routinely utilizes camouflaging techniques. Paramedical makeup artists are concerned with hiding severe skin trauma. This rewarding field allows makeup artists to work with plastic surgeons or dermatologists who perform ablative resurfacing and re-pigmenting procedures.

WHY STUDY CAMOUFLAGE MAKEUP?

Makeup artists should study and have a thorough understanding of camouflage makeup techniques because:

- You will be expected to hide various skin issues.
- You must learn how various products can be layered to achieve an even canvas.
- You will be expected to cover the tattoos of clients attending up-scale events.

fyi

Paramedical Makeup

Para is a Greek prefix meaning beside or along with. Paramedical makeup artists work with medical professionals to help patients achieve their aesthetic goals. Clients may be recovering from laser resurfacing or from reconstructive surgery after an accident. Paramedical makeup artists are adept at blending a variety of colors to create realistic flesh tones. This field also requires a thorough understanding of anatomy, histology, and biology. Cosmetic surgery patients often worry whether they will have a favorable outcome. They rely on paramedical makeup artists to create a plan for each stage of the healing process. The paramedical makeup artist is able to determine if a particular type of makeup is contraindicated by a skin condition. Paramedical makeup artists are also well informed on the psychological aspects of injury or cosmetic procedures.

CORRECTIVE TECHNIQUES

Corrective techniques are used in camouflage makeup applications to conceal and disguise any number of skin imperfections and markings. Several makeup products in the form of creams, pastes, liquids, and powders are applied to temporarily create the appearance of even skin. Corrective techniques generally fall into the following three categories:

- **Conceal discoloration.** This corrective makeup technique utilizes pastes and creams to even out skin tone and texture.
- **Balancing pigmentation.** This corrective makeup technique employs color theory to select the ideal color corrector for the discolored area.

Did You Know?

Working in concert with a physician, estheticians and nurses who are certified in permanent makeup can use tattooing techniques to re-pigment burn scars with flesh-toned ink.

HERE'S A TIP

Conducting a consultation before a camouflage makeup application allows the makeup artist to discover the client's primary concerns. The degree of your client's dyspigmentation will determine which products are used.

- **Spot correction.** The goal of this corrective makeup technique is to target small areas of discoloration, balancing skin tone through the use of pastes, creams, and color correctors.

TYPES OF MAKEUP

Selecting the appropriate formulation is the key to natural-looking camouflage makeup. Different pigmentation issues require different foundation consistencies. Modern makeup tends to be sheer and perfectly mimics healthy skin. Layering and blending a variety of formulations may be necessary to achieve realistic results.

Pastes and Creams

The original camouflage makeup is in the form of a heavy paste (**Figure 15–1**). Its tacky consistency creates maximum waterproof coverage that stays in place. Coverage lasts through a strenuous workout as well as while swimming. Camouflage paste erases all surface abnormalities to create a smooth, even canvas. The mineral **titanium dioxide** is a key ingredient that creates opacity and allows paste makeup to stay in place. Since titanium is a white pigment, camouflage paste has a limited color range. As makeup evolved, cream foundations became more popular. Cream formulations require skill to apply (**Figure 15–2**). They can be blended to a sheer finish by using a damp non latex sponge. Cream foundations can also be applied with a synthetic concealer brush and then layered intermittently with a light layer of powder for maximum coverage. Paste and cream formulations can be applied together when covering bruises, birthmarks, vitiligo, and tattoos.

▲ Figure 15–1 The original camouflage makeup comes in the form of a heavy paste.

▲ Figure 15–2 Cream formulations require skill to apply.

Liquid Foundations

While liquid makeup generally does not provide dense coverage, it can be used in conjunction with heavier formulations (**Figure 15–3**). The mineral silica is featured in many modern liquids. Silicone-derived oils like dimethicone are added to these formulations to create slip and glide. Dimethicone's water-proofing properties give liquid foundations more staying power. Oil-based pastes and creams can be stippled over these types of liquid foundations.

▲ Figure 15–3 Liquid makeup generally does not provide dense coverage.

HERE'S A TIP

Set up your workspace with a water source, an atomizer that emits a fine mist, and/or a squirt bottle to saturate sponges.

Color Correctors

Mild discoloration can be balanced with the use of color correctors. For example, orange neutralizes blue pigment, the color that determines the depth of brown in hyperpigmentation marks (**Figure 15–4**). Clients recovering from plastic surgery may need a green corrector to neutralize redness.

▲ Figure 15–4 **Color correctors neutralize discoloration.**

Color correctors come in cream and liquid formulations. They are applied directly to the problem area and should be applied before foundation. As with all spot correctors, the edges must be blended to create an even finish.

Airbrush

Airbrushing releases tiny droplets of makeup onto the skin to provide a natural finish. Like conventional makeup, airbrush makeup can be layered to camouflage pigmentation issues. By concentrating color in one area the dot application technique can be used to create the illusion of even skin. (Refer to Chapter 16, Airbrush Makeup, for more information.)

Mineral Makeup

Mineral makeup is a type of powder foundation (**Figure 15–5**). Like all foundations, the pigments are derived from mineral ingredients; however, they do not have a liquid carrier. Since powders are inert, mineral makeup does not need preservatives, which can be irritating to newly healed skin. Mineral makeup is usually applied with a brush for a natural-looking finish. However, coverage can be intensified by applying this foundation with a damp sponge.

The main element in this type of foundation is **zinc**, a base ingredient that contains titanium and a white pigment. **Iron oxides** are brown, red, yellow, and green minerals that are added to cosmetics to create realistic flesh tones. However, iron oxides are unstable and generally need a carrier to prevent oxidation.

Because of the healing power of zinc, one of its key ingredients, mineral makeup is often suggested for burn survivors. Mineral makeup is available in a limited shade-range and is not well suited for darker skin tones. To avoid a mask-like finish, a warmer

▲ Figure 15–5 **Mineral makeup is a type of powder foundation.**

HERE'S A TIP

Oily makeup removers are great at dissolving heavy foundation; however, they should not be used for touch-ups or corrections. These removers leave behind a film that make it difficult to add a new layer of foundation. They also break down latex glue used for false eyelashes. Use a nonoily makeup remover to correct minor errors.

HERE'S A TIP

Use a dry non latex sponge or synthetic brush to stipple the edges of heavy concealers and color correctors into liquid foundations.

shade should always be applied wherever the sun would normally tan the skin.

▲ **Figure 15–6 Setting powder helps makeup stay in place.**

Setting Powder

Use a setting powder to ensure that oil-based makeup stays in place (**Figure 15–6**). Lightweight powders in a pink shade interact with the light to hide early signs of aging. Sheer yellow powders accent warm skin tones. Translucent, silica-based powders create a colorless semi-matte finish that is well suited for all skin tones. Some powders are set in pans that are sized to fit compact containers. Powder can be applied with a brush for a light finish, a terry cloth powder puff for a medium finish, or a sponge to create a heavy, opaque layer.

Pigmentation is often uneven on the lips of women of color. Use a pencil close to the natural shade of the lip to even out the color.

Bronzer

Bronzers add a warm tone to the skin. Formulations for bronzers include loose powder, pressed-powder compacts, and iridescent creams sticks (**Figure 15–7**). They are often applied in the shape of the number "3" on either side of the face: along the hairline, over the temples, just below or across the cheekbones, and along the chin. These are the areas that would commonly show the most sun exposure.

▲ **Figure 15–7 Bronzers add warmth to the skin.**

Highlighter

Even heavy makeup can look natural if it properly reflects light. Highlighters re-create the glow of healthy skin (**Figure 15–8**). These products can be iridescent pigments in a light oil base or an illuminating cream, or they can be a liquid formulation. Highlighters are applied along the high planes of the face, down the upper bridge of the nose, along the brow bone, and across the upper cheekbone. Applying highlighter to the tip of the nose and chin will elongate the face. Tracing the bow of the lips makes them appear fuller. ☑ **LO1** ☑ **LO2**

▲ **Figure 15–8 Highlighters re-create the glow of healthy skin.**

SKIN CONDITIONS TO CAMOUFLAGE

Camouflage makeup is used to conceal a number of skin conditions. Certain conditions such as infections can be bacterial, fungal, or viral and should not be covered with makeup. Makeup artists must learn to recognize these diseases so as not to further harm the client or contract diseases themselves. Refer to Chapter 3, Facial Anatomy and Physiology, for an overview of skin disorders and diseases.

Burn Survivors

Skin grafts are a series of treatments used to repair severely burned skin. This is a painful process that occurs over several months. Pressure garments are worn to reduce inflammation and control scarring. Once a physician determines that the wounds have healed, clients can begin to apply makeup so that newly grafted skin appears more like the surrounding healthy skin. Burn scars are often **hypertrophic**, meaning very fibrous and raised (**Figure 15–9**). A combination of massage and microdermabrasion (a form of mechanical exfoliation that abrades the skin) is often the recommended spa treatment for burn survivors. A series of treatments can smooth scar tissue. Severely burned skin usually lacks hair follicles, making it difficult for makeup to adhere. Although burn scars can never be completely concealed with makeup, applying a green color corrector neutralizes redness for a more even appearance.

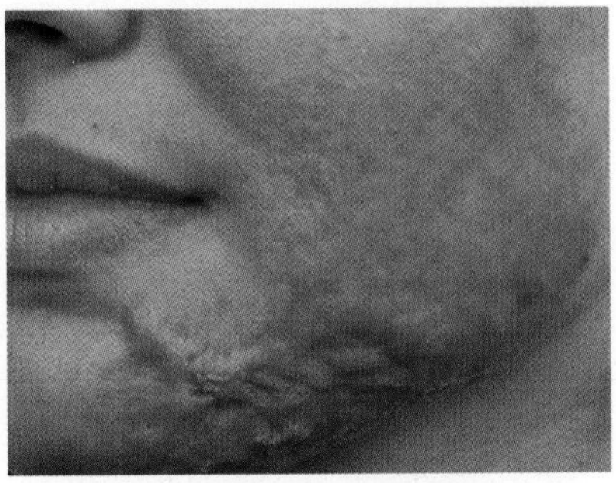

▲ **Figure 15–9 Hypertrophic scars can never be completely concealed.**

HERE'S A TIP

If you are applying makeup for a photoshoot or on a film set, you may be required to camouflage an infectious condition. In these cases, use disposable applicators so as not to risk contamination.

WEB RESOURCES

www.burnsurvivorsttw.org
www.phoenix-society.org

PROCEDURE **15-1** **MAKEUP APPLICATION FOR BURN SURVIVORS** SEE PAGE 362

Vitiligo

Vitiligo appears as depigmented patches of skin that often spread in a symmetrical pattern over large areas of the face and body (**Figure 15–10**). **Hypopigmented** skin is characterized by depigmented, white patches or areas; it can occur in all races but is most noticeable in clients with darker skin. Camouflage pastes form an opaque layer over uneven pigmentation. Other corrective makeup techniques are based on striking a balance between the light and dark patches. Skin-staining dyes will temporarily camouflage hypopigmented patches. Airbrushing layers of neutralizing shades using the dot technique creates a believable color balance.

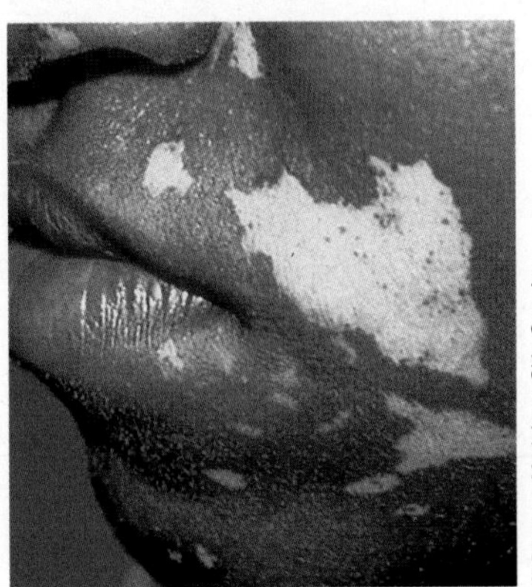

▲ **Figure 15–10 Vitiligo appears as depigmented patches of skin.**

HERE'S A TIP

Severe facial burns may make it impossible for eyebrows to grow. Using a stencil allows you to re-create a more symmetrical eyebrow than attempting to re-create the brows freehand.

PROCEDURE **15-2** **CONCEALING VITILIGO WITH MANUAL MAKEUP APPLICATION** SEE PAGE 365

Multicultural CONSIDERATIONS

Vitiligo takes on a more marked appearance for clients with dark skin and may be difficult to conceal.

Hyperpigmentation

Hyperpigmentation is a darkening of the skin that occurs after trauma or inflammation. It can be caused by something as simple as eczema or even acne. This is primarily a concern of clients with dark skin, which tends to have an extreme reaction to trama (**Figure 15–11**).

Zinc oxide, titanium dioxide, and aluminum are thickening agents used in many cosmetic preparations. These ingredients increase the density of camouflage makeup. Since they are white pigments very few camouflage pastes have the right color balance to re-create the appearance of healthy brown skin. The makeup artist will need to blend several products to customize the right shade. Mixing in an orange color corrector to the camouflage paste will help neutralize hyperpigmentation of clients with darkly pigmented skin.

▲ Figure 15–11 **Hyperpigmentation occurs after inflammation.**

PROCEDURE 15–3 **CAMOUFLAGING HYPERPIGMENTATION SCARS** SEE PAGE 367

Multicultural CONSIDERATIONS

Always apply an orange neutralizer to deep hyperpigmentation areas before attempting to conceal.

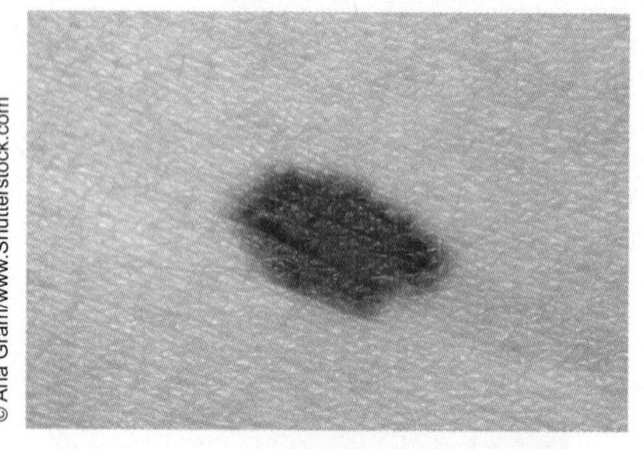

▲ Figure 15–12 **Birthmarks range from dark brown or tan, bluish-purple, pink, or red.**

Birthmarks

Birthmarks are abnormal pigmentation visible at the time of birth. Sometimes the discoloration disappears during infancy. Birthmarks can be dark brown, tan, bluish-purple, pink, or red (**Figure 15–12**). Port-wine stains are vascular irregularities arising from the veins. They are a dark red or purple pigment and are difficult to conceal. A brown pigment is visible when melanocytes, the pigment-producing cells, irregularly congregate in the upper layer of the skin known as the epidermis. These pigmented birthmarks often show through when covered with makeup. It is best to neutralize the pigment in birthmarks with a color corrector before using a flesh-tone concealer.

PROCEDURE 15–4 **CAMOUFLAGING BIRTHMARKS AND TATTOOS** SEE PAGE 370

Tattoos

Pastes are used to cover tattoos. No matter what formula you choose, you will need to blend a variety of color correctors with darker and lighter flesh tones to create a natural-looking shade. Several layers of paste and powder may be needed to hide dark tattoos. ☑ LO3

THE MAKEUP APPOINTMENT

Although each makeup appointment follows the same sequence, it may take a while to help trauma survivors expand their comfort zone before initiating service. Be sure to block out additional time for the consultation and application phase. The recommendation of home-care products is extremely important to camouflage clients.

Consultation

After greeting the client and making him or her comfortable in the makeup chair, conduct a short consultation to assess the client's primary concerns (**Figure 15–13**). Every client has a different communication style. Well-skilled makeup artists are able to tailor their approach to suit the client. During this phase of the appointment feel free to touch the skin to analyze its texture and **turgor**, which is the amount of elasticity in the skin. This will help you select the appropriate type of coverage. Explain the expected outcome and preview the directions you will be giving to the client throughout the process. Let clients know you will expect them to occasionally turn their head or look in a different direction to assist in the application. Prepare the skin for makeup application. ☑ LO4

▲ Figure 15–13 **Conduct a short consultation to assess client's primary concerns.**

Application

Communicate each step as you perform the makeup application. Makeup artists typically blend several colors to achieve a desired look. While some clients who suffer from disfiguring skin conditions may be receptive to layering products, most of them would prefer to minimize preparation time. Use a gentle touch when camouflaging an area that has undergone a traumatic injury.

Recommendation

When teaching clients to re-create your professional application techniques, be mindful of the number of products that you use and recommend—keep mixing to a minimum. Identify the features and benefits of each product, explaining how each one contributes to the finished look. End the service by reviewing each step, making certain that the client knows how to re-create their new look at home. ☑ LO5

Procedure 15-1 Makeup Application for Burn Survivors

Implements and Materials

You will need all of the following implements, materials, and supplies:

Brushes

- ☐ Concealer brushes
- ☐ Large powder brush

Utensils

- ☐ Brush cleaner
- ☐ Hand sanitizer
- ☐ Hand wipes
- ☐ Headband or hair clip
- ☐ Makeup cape
- ☐ Makeup chair
- ☐ Makeup palettes
- ☐ Neck strip or clean towel for draping

Single-use Items

- ☐ Cotton pads for cleansing (if necessary)
- ☐ Cotton swabs
- ☐ Eyebrow brush
- ☐ Mascara wands
- ☐ Terry cloth powder puff
- ☐ Tissues

Products

- ☐ Camouflage paste
- ☐ Foundation
- ☐ Facial moisturizer
- ☐ Mild facial cleanser
- ☐ Nonoily makeup remover
- ☐ Thin eyebrow pencils
- ☐ Translucent powder

Preparation

- Perform

PROCEDURE 7-1 PRE-SERVICE SEE PAGE 144

Procedure

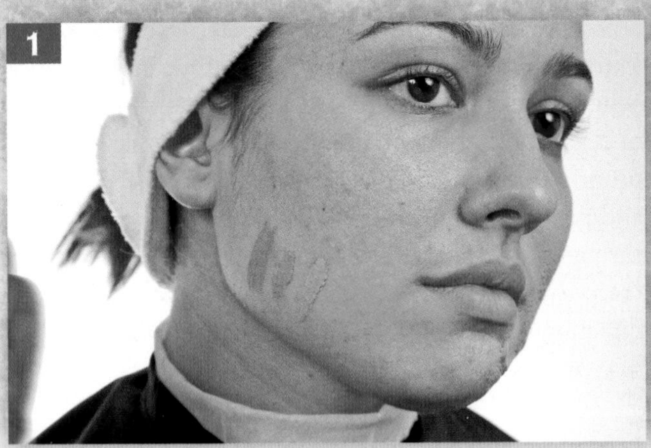

1 Perform a color-match test to select the appropriate foundation shade. Use a cotton swab to apply three shades of foundation at the client's jawline. The shade that seems to disappear is the correct shade.

2 Scoop out a tiny amount of color corrector and paste with a spatula. Place it on a palette.

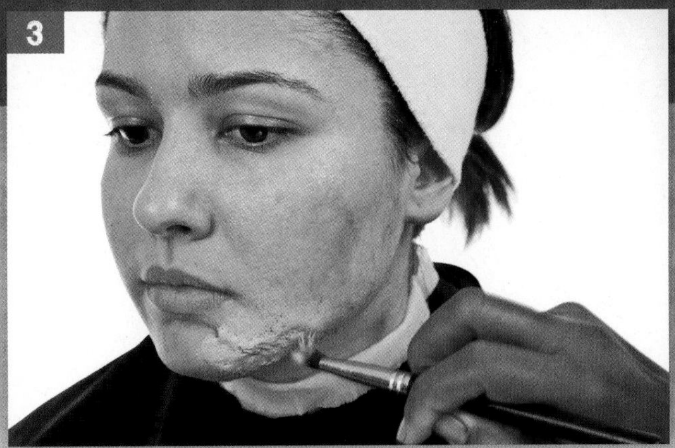

3 With a concealer brush, dot appropriate corrector onto discolored areas.

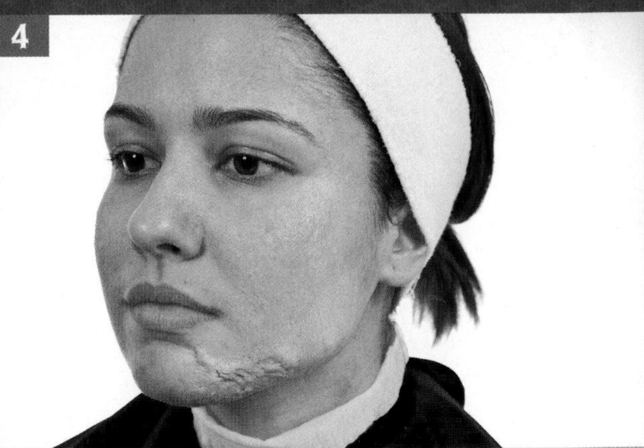

4 Blend by feathering out the edges with the concealer brush or use a stipple technique with a non latex sponge.

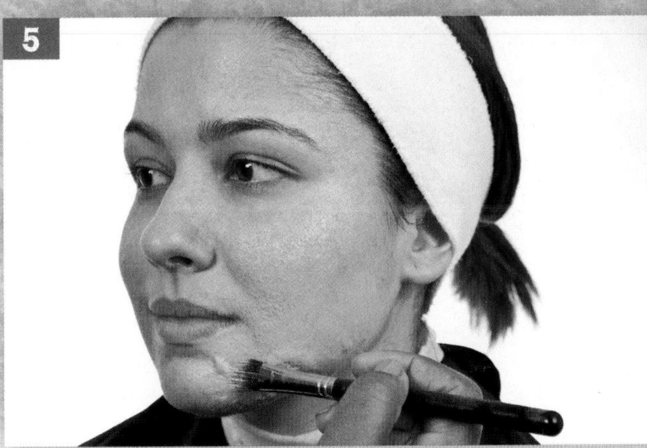

5 Use a dual-fiber brush to layer paste over corrector.

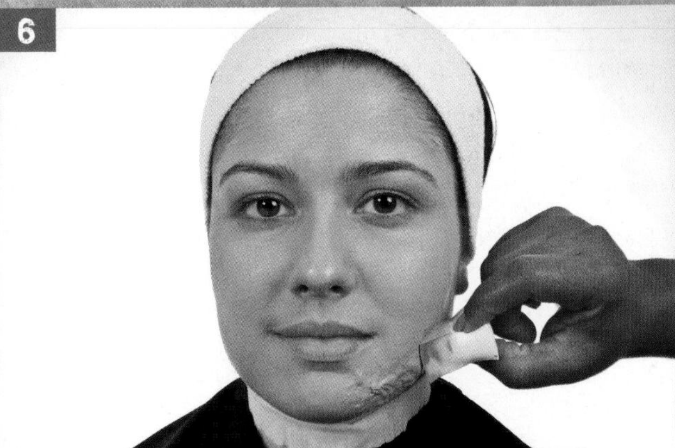

6 Use a non latex sponge to apply foundation in the appropriate color and consistency for client's skin.

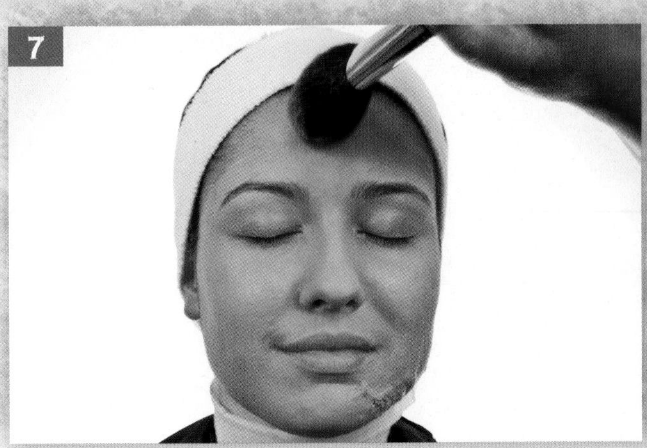

7 Ask client to close his or her eyes while you apply a light layer of translucent powder with a large powder brush.

8 Layer paste, foundation, and powder to create a heavier camouflage where needed. Repeat until the skin looks completely even.

Procedure 15-1 *(continued)*

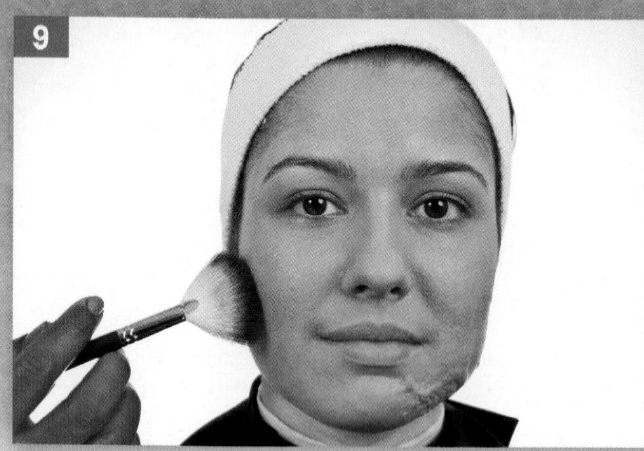

9 Use a fan brush to apply bronzer along the hairline, over the temples, just below or across the cheekbones, and along the chin.

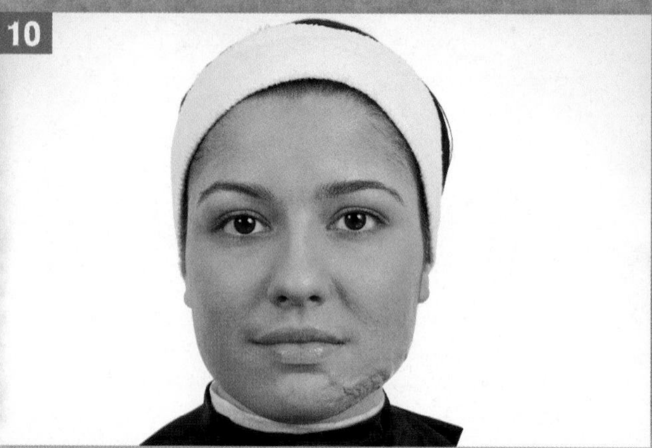

10 Complete basic makeup application based on the client's features.

SERVICE TIP

When hair follicles are damaged, foundation may not adhere well. Layer products over small areas to create heavier camouflage where needed.

Post-Service

- Complete PROCEDURE 7-2 POST-SERVICE SEE PAGE 148

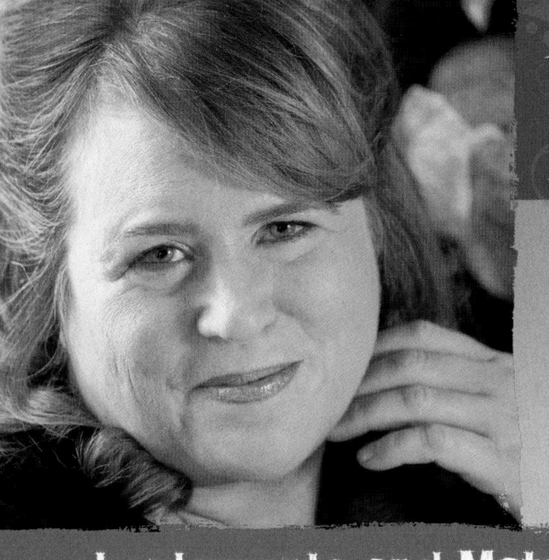

Procedure 15-2

Concealing Vitiligo with Manual Makeup Application

Implements and Materials

You will need all of the following implements, materials, and supplies:

Brushes

- ☐ Dual-fiber foundation brush
- ☐ Large powder brush
- ☐ Synthetic concealer brush

Utensils

- ☐ Brush cleaner
- ☐ Hand sanitizer
- ☐ Hand wipes
- ☐ Headband or hair clip
- ☐ Makeup cape
- ☐ Makeup chair
- ☐ Makeup palette
- ☐ Neck strip or clean towel for draping

Single-use Items

- ☐ Cotton pads for cleansing (if necessary)
- ☐ Cotton swabs
- ☐ Eyebrow brush
- ☐ Mascara wands
- ☐ Spatula
- ☐ Terry cloth powder puff
- ☐ Tissues

Products

- ☐ Camouflage paste
- ☐ Cream foundation
- ☐ Colored eyebrow gel
- ☐ Facial moisturizer
- ☐ Mild facial cleanser
- ☐ Nonoily makeup remover
- ☐ Thin eyebrow pencils
- ☐ Translucent powder

Preparation

- Perform

PROCEDURE 7-1 PRE-SERVICE SEE PAGE 144

Procedure

1 Scoop out a small amount of camouflage paste a shade darker than natural skin tone with a disposable spatula. Place it on a palette.

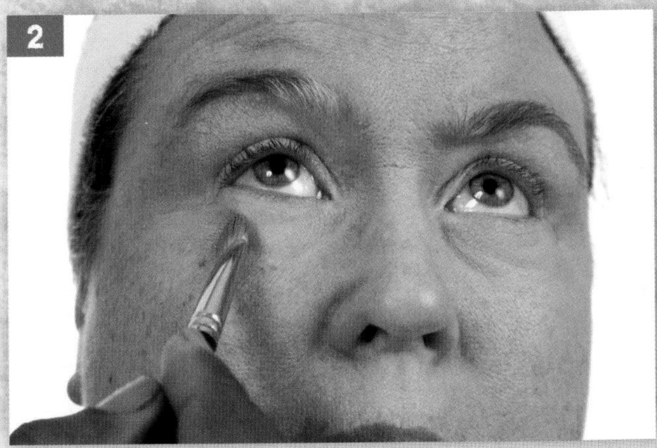

2 Blend cream paste onto depigmented areas with a synthetic concealer brush. Feather out the edges.

3 Select a foundation in the appropriate consistency that is a bit warmer than the client's skin tone. Place it on a palette.

Procedure 15-2 *(continued)*

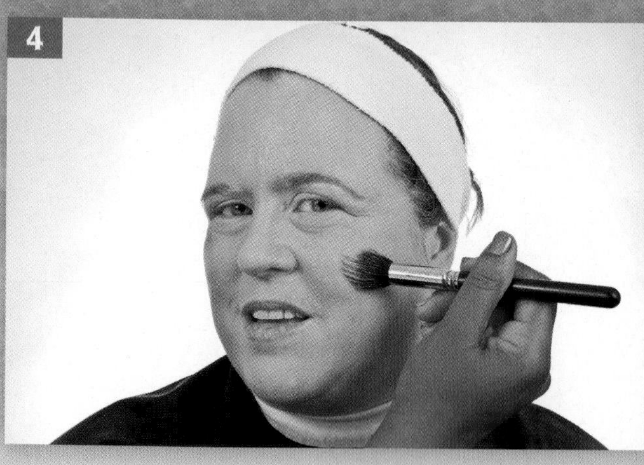

4 Apply foundation by moving a dual-fiber foundation brush in a circular motion over every part of the face, blending onto the ears and neck.

5 With a concealer brush, apply concealer to the concave area under the eyes.

SERVICE TIP

To re-create brows with a thin eyebrow pencil, draw short hair-like strokes through the eyebrows. Lighter shades form the majority of the brow with darker strokes used to accent the inner corner, arch, and tail-end. Brush through eyebrows with a disposable mascara wand to soften the pencil.

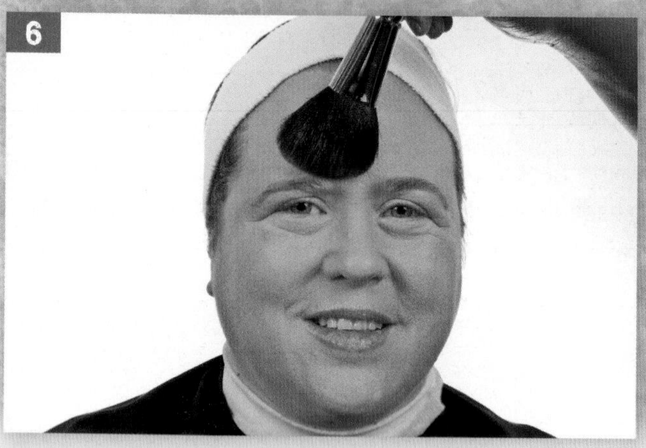

6 Shake a light setting powder from its container onto a palette or tissue. Apply the powder using a large powder brush.

7 Using a disposable mascara wand, fill in brow with tinted eyebrow gel.

8 Complete a basic makeup application based on the client's features.

Post-Service

- Complete PROCEDURE 7-2 POST-SERVICE SEE PAGE 148

Procedure 15-3

Camouflaging Hyperpigmentation Scars

Implements and Materials

You will need all of the following implements, materials, and supplies:

Brushes

- ☐ Blush brush
- ☐ Concealer brushes
- ☐ Powder brush

Utensils

- ☐ Brush cleaner
- ☐ Hand sanitizer
- ☐ Hand wipes
- ☐ Headband or hair clip
- ☐ Makeup cape
- ☐ Makeup chair
- ☐ Makeup palettes
- ☐ Neck strip or clean towel for draping
- ☐ Pencil sharpener

Single-use Items

- ☐ Cotton pads for cleansing (if necessary)
- ☐ Cotton swabs
- ☐ Mascara wands
- ☐ Eyebrow brush
- ☐ Spatulas
- ☐ Tissues

Products

- ☐ Blushes
- ☐ Concealers
- ☐ Corrective concealer
- ☐ Facial moisturizer
- ☐ Liquid foundation
- ☐ Mild facial cleanser
- ☐ Nonoily makeup remover
- ☐ Thin eyebrow pencils
- ☐ Terry cloth powder puff
- ☐ Translucent powders

Preparation

- Perform

PROCEDURE 7-1 PRE-SERVICE SEE PAGE 144

Procedure

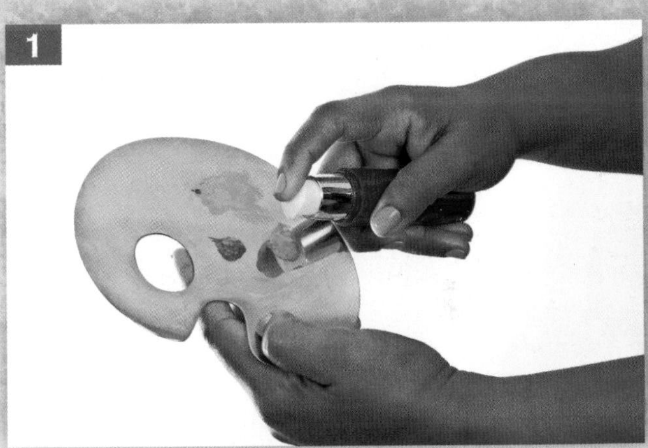

1 Scoop out a small amount of orange corrector and a flesh-toned concealer with a disposable spatula. Place the corrector and concealer on a palette. Choose the foundation color and formulation best suited for your client's skin type and skin tone. Place the foundation on the palette.

Procedure 15-3 *(continued)*

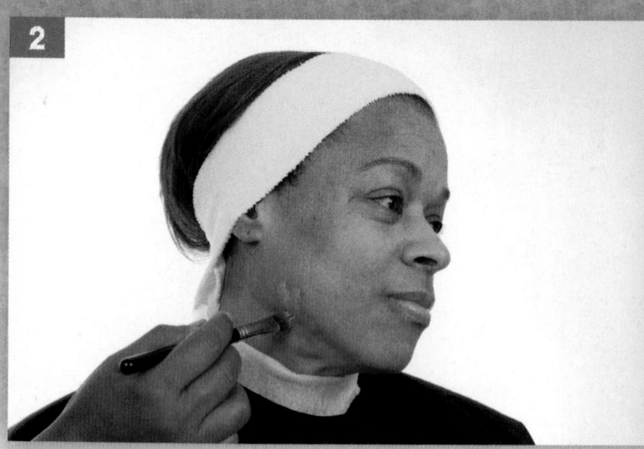

2 With a small synthetic brush, apply corrector to discolored areas to neutralize them.

Note: Orange color correctors can be adjusted for skin tone by blending with concealer or foundation.

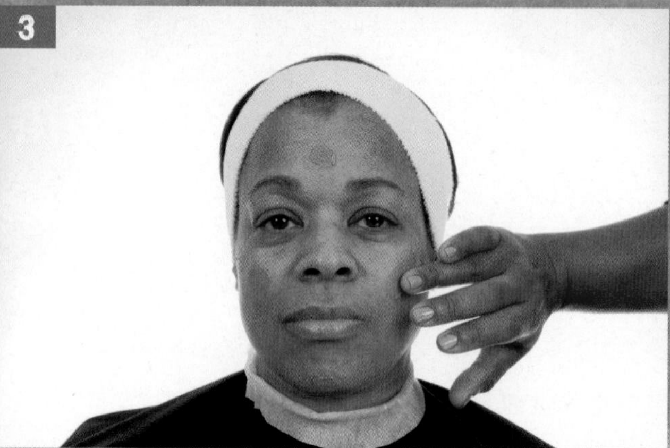

3 Apply a dot of liquid foundation on the forehead, cheeks, and chin.

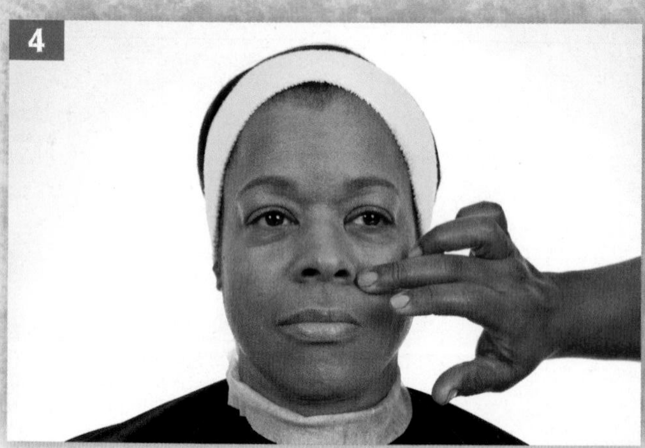

4 Use a clean pointer and middle finger to spread foundation over the entire face, blending onto the ears and neck.

SERVICE TIP

Blending foundation with a sponge will deliver a sheer application. Blending with clean fingertips or a foundation brush will deliver fuller coverage.

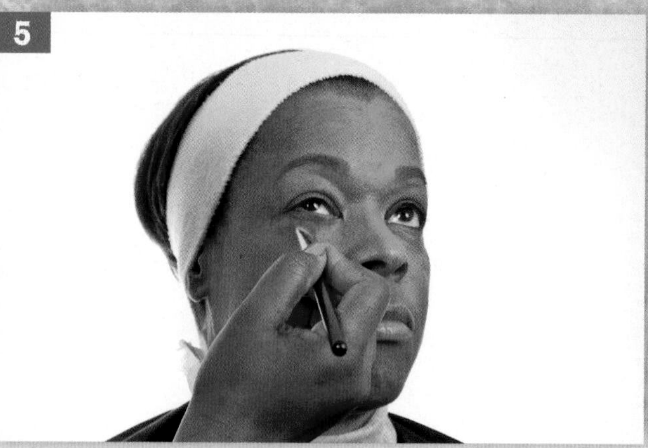

5 Apply concealer beneath the eyes with a synthetic brush.

SERVICE TIP

Contour by placing a small amount of dark concealer or powder along fuller areas to create a narrow appearance. For this client, we are contouring under the cheekbones and along the sides of the nose.

6 Shake powder from its container onto a palette or tissue. Apply a light layer of setting powder in a downward motion using a large fluff powder brush.

7 Proceed with a full makeup application.

Post-Service

- Complete PROCEDURE 7-2 POST-SERVICE SEE PAGE 148

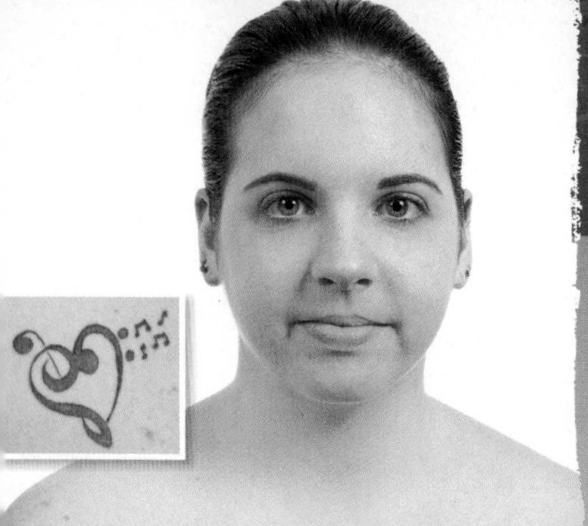

Procedure 15-4

Camouflaging Birthmarks and Tattoos

Implements and Materials

You will need all of the following implements, materials, and supplies:

- **Brushes**
  - ☐ Concealer brush
- **Utensils** (optional depending on area of birthmark or tattoo)
  - ☐ Brush cleaner
  - ☐ Cape
  - ☐ Hand sanitizer
  - ☐ Hand wipes
  - ☐ Headband or hair clip
  - ☐ Makeup cape
  - ☐ Makeup chair
  - ☐ Makeup palette
  - ☐ Neck strip or clean towel for draping
- **Single-use Items**
  - ☐ Cotton pads for cleansing (if necessary)
  - ☐ Cotton swabs
  - ☐ Spatulas
  - ☐ Terry cloth powder puff
  - ☐ Tissues
- **Products**
  - ☐ Camouflage paste
  - ☐ Cream foundation
  - ☐ Facial moisturizer
  - ☐ Mild facial cleanser
  - ☐ Oil-based makeup remover

Preparation

- Perform

PROCEDURE 7-1 PRE-SERVICE SEE PAGE 144

Procedure

1a

1b

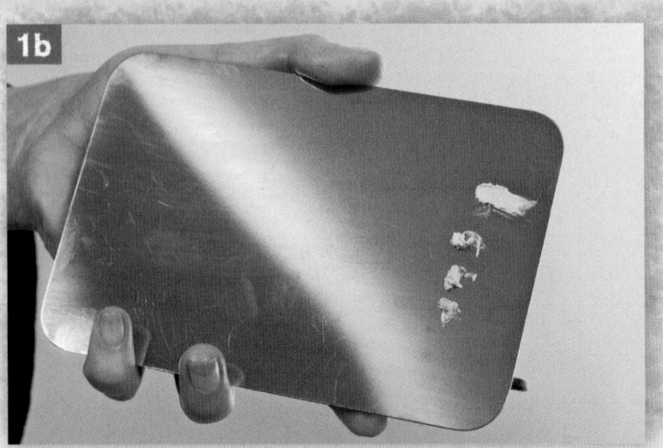

1 With a spatula, scoop out a small amount of the appropriate color corrector and paste. Place the cream on a palette.

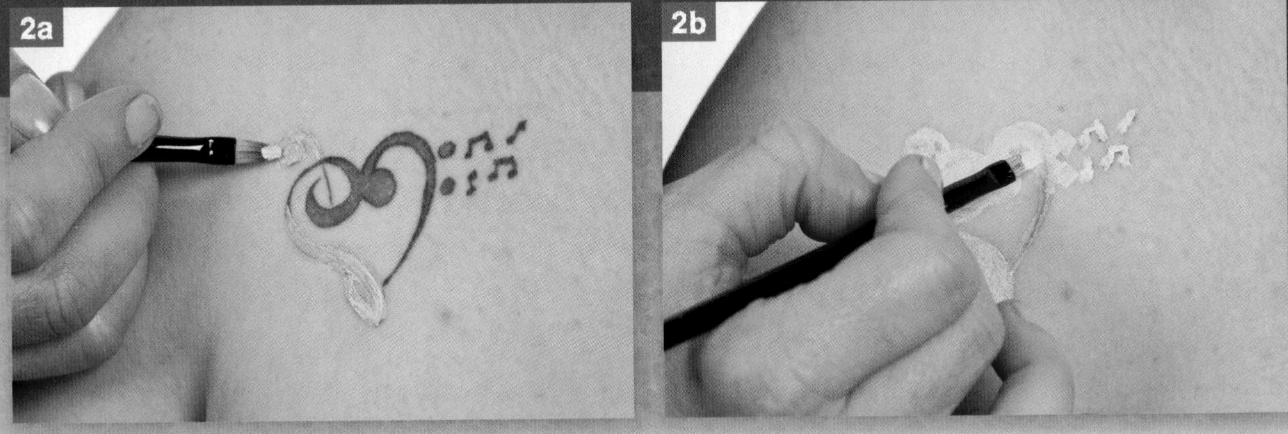

2 Apply corrector to discolored areas with a small synthetic brush.

3 Apply a light layer of translucent powder with a powder puff to set makeup.

SERVICE TIP

Open powder puff packages in front of clients. These can be given away at the end of the makeup service.

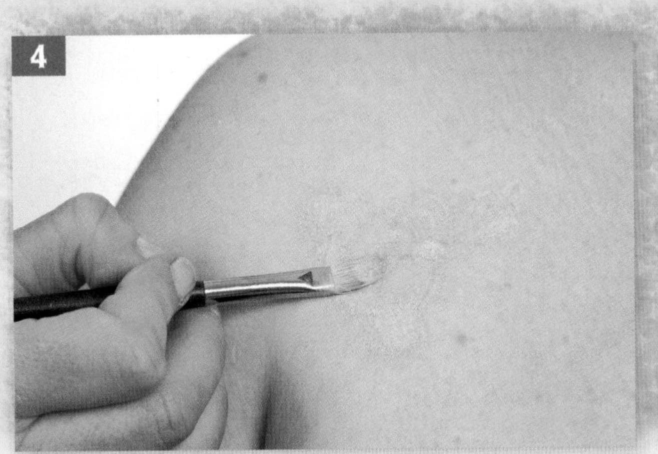

4 Cover tattoo or birthmark with a cream or paste that is closest to the client's skin tone.

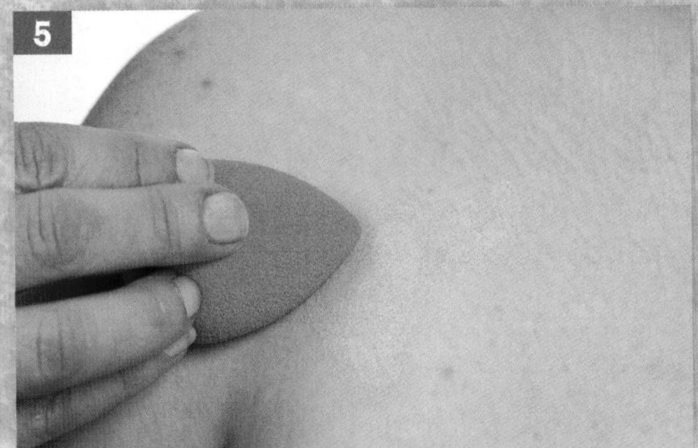

5 Blend by feathering out edges with a sponge.

Procedure 15-4 *(continued)*

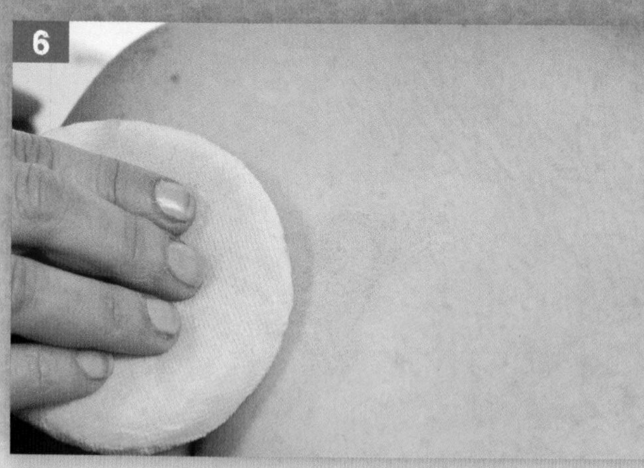

6 Apply a light layer of translucent powder with a powder puff to set makeup.

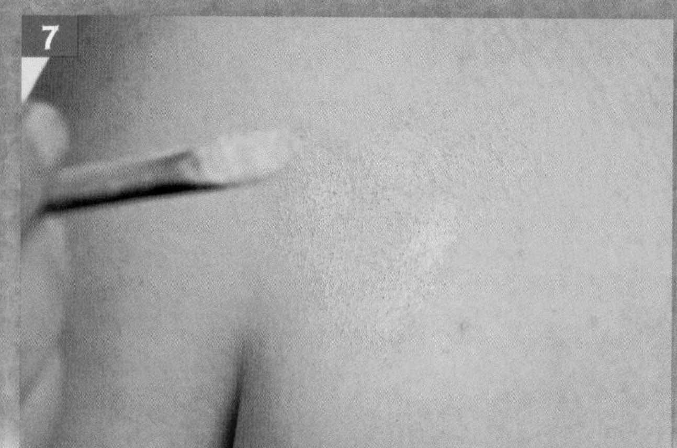

7 Continue layering powder and concealer until the tattoo or birthmark is no longer visible.

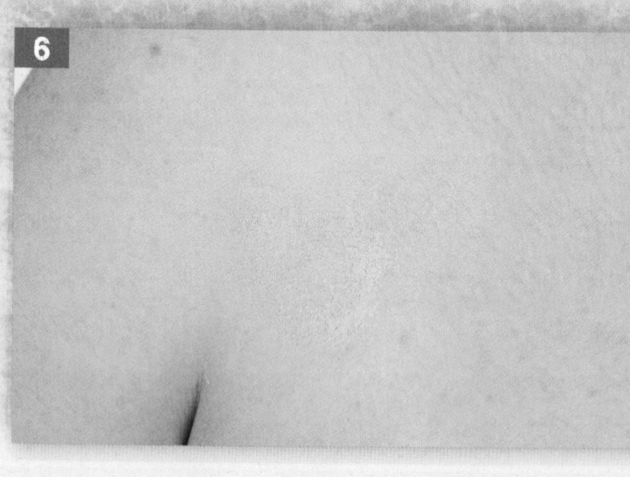

8 The finished look.

SERVICE TIP

You may need to add a few color correctors to neutralize tattoo colors.

Post-Service

- Complete

PROCEDURE  7-2 **POST-SERVICE** SEE PAGE 148

Review Questions

1. What is concealed using camouflage makeup techniques?
2. What special branch of makeup artistry is concerned with hiding severe skin trauma?
3. Which products are strategically layered when applying camouflage makeup?
4. Name the original camouflage makeup formula.
5. What gives paste its waterproof coverage?
6. Name the ingredient that gives modern liquid formulas their slip and glide.
7. Which product is placed wherever the sun would normally tan the skin?
8. What are the characteristics of a hypertrophic scar?
9. What is the autoimmune disorder that appears as hypopigmented patches of skin?
10. List makeup technique used to camouflage vitiligo.

Chapter Glossary

camouflage makeup	The strategic layering of various colors and textures to hide pigmentation issues.
dyspigmentation	Hypopigmentation or hyperpigmentation caused by trauma, illness, or hormonal imbalance.
hypertrophic	Fibrous and raised; often a quality of burn scars.
hypopigmented	Characterized by depigmented (or white) patches or areas; it can occur in all races but is most noticeable in clients with darker skin.
iron oxides	Brown, red, yellow, and green minerals that are added to cosmetics to create realistic flesh tones.
paramedical makeup	A special branch of makeup artistry that routinely utilizes camouflaging techniques.
postinflammatory hyperpigmentation	A darkening of skin caused by trauma to the skin; they can result from acne pimples and papules.
skin grafts	A series of treatments that repair severely burned skin.
titanium dioxide	Key mineral ingredient with a white pigment; it creates opacity and allows paste makeup to stay in place.
turgor	The amount of elasticity in the skin; it can be assessed by touch.
zinc	A base ingredient that contains titanium and a white pigment.

Chapter 16 Airbrush Makeup

Chapter Outline

Learning Objectives

After completing this chapter, you will be able to:

- ☑ **LO1** Identify products and equipment used for airbrush makeup.
- ☑ **LO2** Learn the techniques required to control an airbrush.
- ☑ **LO3** Understand the basics of airbrush maintenance.
- ☑ **LO4** Demonstrate a basic airbrush makeup application.
- ☑ **LO5** Understand how to cover a tattoo using maximum coverage airbrush techniques.

Key Terms

Page number indicates where in the chapter the term is used.

air compressor
pg. 378

airbrush
pg. 377

airbrush makeup
pg. 377

alcohol-based makeup (waterproof makeup)
pg. 380

back bubble
pg. 383

dash method
pg. 381

dot method
pg. 381

dual-action airbrush
pg. 378

frisket film
pg. 382

lever
pg. 378

needle
pg. 378

neutralization
pg. 386

nozzle
pg. 378

precise detail
pg. 382

single-action airbrush
pg. 378

soft focus
pg. 382

transformable airbrush
pg. 378

water-based makeup
pg. 379

Career Profile

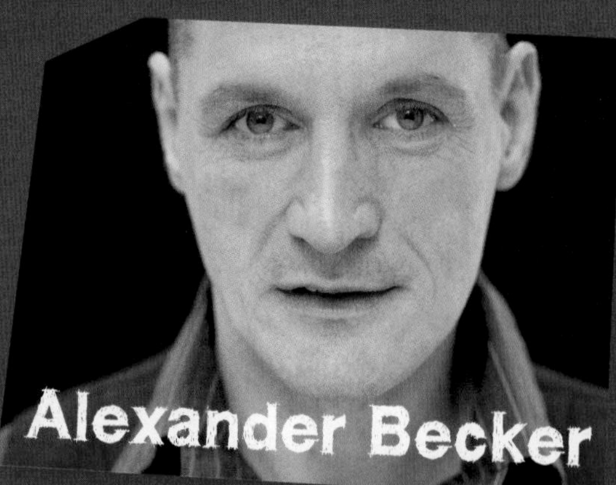

Alexander Becker has used his decades of experience in the makeup industry to innovate his own work and the industry as a whole. With improvements such as airbrushing, Alexander has made it his mission to change efficiencies in the industry. Through his years of experience—with top companies such as L'Oréal and Redken and with designers such as Calvin Klein—he understands the forward movement of the makeup world and has been a large part of its modernization and advancement.

"My career as a makeup artist began in Stuttgart, Germany in 1979. I was fortunate enough to obtain an internship and be trained in a hair salon. I then moved on to become an apprentice in a prestigious hair salon that was housed by a chic and exclusive department store whose high-end environment was ahead of its time.

"From there I became a hairdresser in a small, privately owned, and independently operated hairdressing school. During this time I was introduced to the world of photography. For 2 years I was an active model for Photographic Studios in Stuttgart, Germany. My involvement with the world of photography awakened my desire to explore options with fashion-industry makeup artistry and hairdressing.

"I began to expand my knowledge by acting as a Workshop Leader and teaching basic hairdressing and salon operations. I also traveled to trade and fashion shows for international companies such as Wella and L'Oréal. I began offering a makeup service to my salon customers, and through trial and error, I began my self-taught career as a makeup artist.

"As my new venture and career began to take off, I moved to many cities of the world in order to gain the international experience and knowledge that I desired. In the 1990s I lived in Madrid, Milan, Zurich, Miami, Los Angeles, Sydney, New York, Athens, and Berlin. During my travels, I worked for international magazines such as *Vogue, Marie Claire,* and *Elle.* I also worked on advertorial and editorial campaigns for Calvin Klein, Coca-Cola, Saks Fifth Avenue, Redken, Wella, and L'Oréal.

"In 2004 I shifted to the use of airbrush makeup and began a cross-marketing collaboration where I would exchange experience for feedback. The use of the airbrush made application at photoshoots and fashion shows simple and fast. A crisp look could be achieved in a short time.

"My airbrush colors were water-based, accommodating the market need for a light look and feel with complete coverage. This makeup offered a natural, fresh, and healthy look. Airbrush makeup photographs flawlessly, reducing the customary retouching time and cost—especially in regards to high definition (HD) television, where the visuals are not forgiving. Airbrush makeup is becoming an important instrument in beauty and hairdressing salons

"Currently, I am working on mobilizing manufacturers and gathering information to make airbrush makeup accessible for day-to-day personal use. I desire to activate and motivate people to make progress in the makeup industry."

www.alexanderbecker.com.

Twenty-first century makeup fuses traditional and modern airbrush techniques and offers precise, durable, and diverse applications ideal for every type of makeup (**Figure 16–1**).

By learning airbrush makeup techniques, you will become a more versatile makeup artist, whether you work on movie sets, in a photography studio, in a salon, or with brides. Enhancing your makeup abilities will prepare you for the rapid progress being made in the makeup world, and it will prepare you for the new opportunities emerging because of high-definition (HD) and digital technology.

© Kett Cosmetics. Makeup and photography by Sheila McKenna.

▲ Figure 16–1 **Airbrushing techniques provide a smooth look to clients' makeup.**

Airbrush makeup is a unique product specifically developed to be used with an airbrush device. When makeup is airbrushed onto the skin it lands in small microdroplets. This sheer, almost invisible, type of application is what creates the appearance of perfect skin. With each airbrush layer applied, makeup coverage is increased and imperfections disappear. Airbrush makeup represents the easiest way to neutralize unwanted discolorations and balance skin tones (**Figure 16–2**).

The airbrush/atomization process sprays ultra-sheer layers onto the skin. When the layers are applied consecutively, they produce sheer to maximum coverage. The result is a seamless, beautiful blend that can be completely customized to create endless options. From soft, natural makeup to graphic design, the airbrush can achieve a multitude of looks.

WHY STUDY AIRBRUSH MAKEUP?

Makeup artists should study airbrush makeup because:

- Airbrushing makeup will broaden your skill set, enabling you to achieve flawless coverage, even with the most challenging applications.
- Requests for skilled airbrush makeup artists are on the rise. By becoming an educated and skilled airbrush artist, you will expand your career opportunities.
- Airbrushing is the fastest way to achieve maximum results with a minimum amount of makeup. Faster makeup application equals time for more clients.

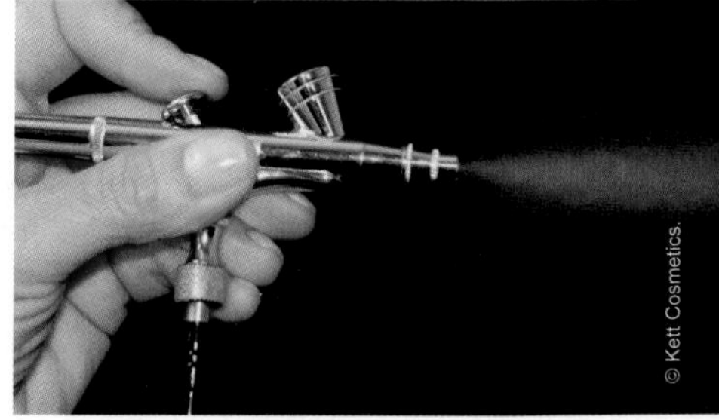

© Kett Cosmetics.

▲ Figure 16–2 **The airbrush sprays product in sheer layers onto the skin.**

AIRBRUSH EQUIPMENT

An **airbrush** is a tool used in conjunction with an air compressor to spray liquids (**Figure 16–3**). Together, the compressor and the airbrush produce different forms of art from delicate makeup designs on the face to extreme creations on the body. For airbrush makeup, a low-pressure compressor and airbrush are ideal. Both compressors and airbrushes vary in size, capacity, and weight. Below is a detailed description of the items that you will need to airbrush makeup.

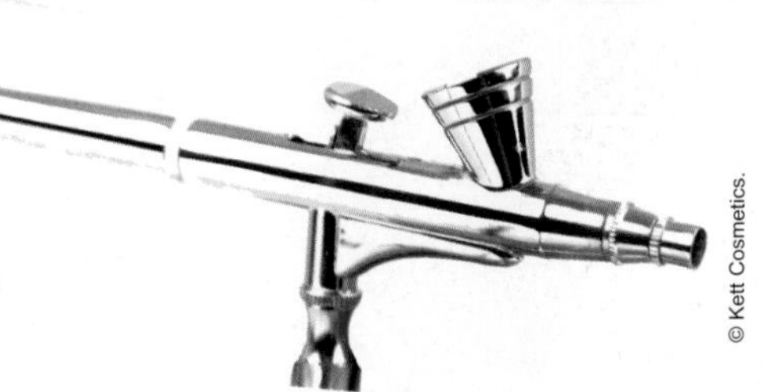

© Kett Cosmetics.

▲ Figure 16–3 **Airbrushes can provide a multitude of different looks.**

Airbrushes

Airbrushes come in a variety of models, ranging from low pressure to high pressure, with each model capable of creating various designs. The **nozzle** is one of the replaceable parts of the airbrush; it determines the size of the spray pattern (**Figure 16–4**). A low-pressure, 2.5 millimeter-sized nozzle is ideal for airbrushing makeup on the face and body. Larger 3mm, 3.5mm, or 5mm airbrushes will release more makeup than needed for beauty makeup and body corrections.

▲ Figure 16–4 **The nozzle determines the spray pattern.**

The **needle** is the part of the airbrush that controls the amount of makeup flowing through the nozzle. The needle is also a disposable part and must match the nozzle in size (**Figure 16–5**).

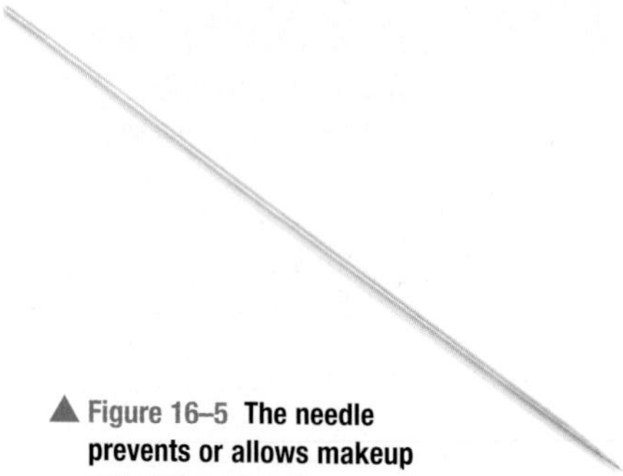

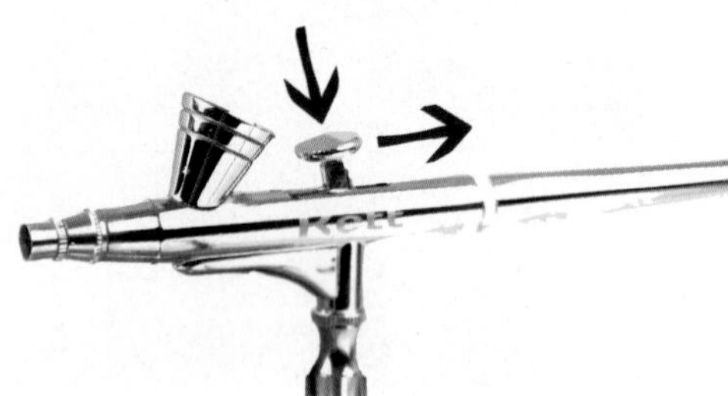

▲ Figure 16–5 **The needle prevents or allows makeup out of the airbrush.**

Airbrushes come in either a single-action or a dual-action design. Most are similar in appearance, so it is important to know which type of airbrush you are using.

On both models, the forefinger controls the airbrush **lever**, the part of the airbrush that controls the amount of product being sprayed out. The farther back you pull the lever, the more product is released. Both types of airbrushes can be used for applying makeup; they are different in the following ways:

- A **single-action airbrush** releases air and makeup simultaneously when the artist pulls back on the lever (**Figure 16–6**). The air is automatically active when you pull the lever.
- A **dual-action airbrush** has two stages: the first stage releases air when the artist presses down on the lever; the second stage allows makeup to be sprayed when the artist pulls back on the lever (**Figure 16–7**). The dual-action brush lets you create stippling techniques that are not attainable with a single-action airbrush.
- A **transformable airbrush** can function as two airbrushes in one; the design allows artists to switch from single-action to dual-action when needed.

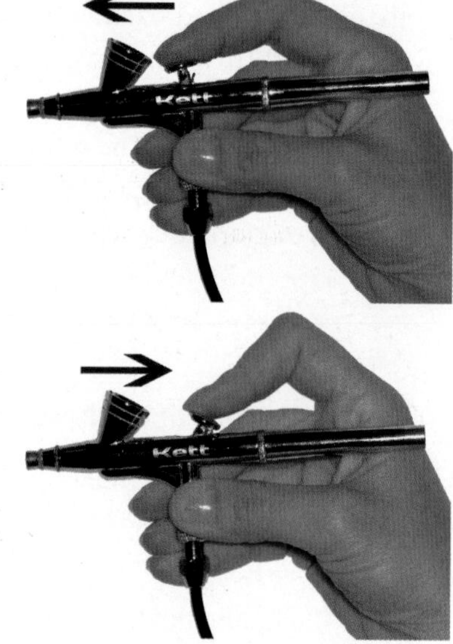

▲ Figure 16–6 **Single-action airbrush releases air and makeup together.**

▲ Figure 16–7 **Dual-action airbrush allows air and makeup to be released separately.**

Air Compressors

An air compressor is used in conjunction with an airbrush. An **air compressor** is a device that takes in atmospheric air and releases it through a hose connected to the airbrush. The most important feature of an air compressor is its air pressure or pounds per square inch (PSI) (**Figure 16–8**). For makeup, a lightweight, battery-optional compressor will give you the freedom to work at a makeup station or on location.

▲ Figure 16–8 **The air compressor determines the amount of product being released.**

Although many compressors have an adjustable airflow dial, the user will control the amount of product being released with the lever on the airbrush. Makeup will not spray through an airbrush if the airflow dial is set too low.

The PSI of a compressor is not as important as how the airflow feels on your skin. If your client feels as if they need to hold their breath during the application, the airflow is too high.

METHODS AND USAGE

Airbrush makeup techniques were designed to enhance traditional makeup techniques. Airbrushing makeup is faster than traditional makeup application and uses a minimum amount of product to achieve maximum results. It is often preferred because of its high-detail, high-precision accuracy. The objective is to create a three-dimensional look whether airbrushing on the face or a canvas (**Figure 16–9**).

Airbrush Foundation Formulations

Understanding airbrush makeup formulations is the key to a successful application when airbrushing makeup. Each formulation performs differently in the airbrush and on the skin. Choosing the correct product formulation is important for achieving the desired results. The formulation you choose will also determine the method used for cleaning—a key element in maintaining trouble-free makeup applications with the airbrush. There are two preferred airbrush formulations: water-based and alcohol-based. Both formulations are designed to look like perfect skin. The foundation should provide a range of coverage options from natural to opaque as well as have the ability to cover tattoos.

▲ Figure 16–9 **An example of a face chart.**

Water-Based Makeup

Water-based makeup is a liquid makeup comprised of primary ingredients such as water, humectants, vitamins, oil absorbers, and color pigments. It is also the most versatile of airbrush makeup formulations. It can be applied with a brush, a sponge, the fingertips, or an airbrush. Thus it offers the ultimate artistic flexibility (**Figure 16–10**). A water-based formulation is ideal during the learning process because it allows the artist to blend away any mistakes. This blendability is available not only with airbrush applications of water-based makeup but with traditional applications as well. After completing the makeup application use the appropriate powder to set water-based makeup for maximum durability. Translucent powder will not interfere with the color or texture of the makeup. Using a powder with pigment offers fuller coverage.

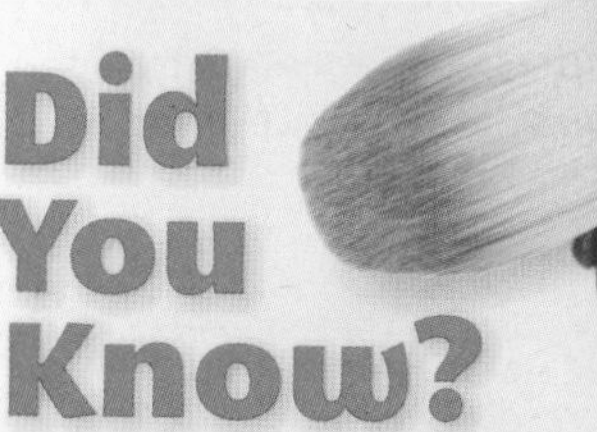

Did You Know?

Airbrush makeup is the safest method of applying makeup because the risk of infection and cross-contamination is much lower—plus you don't have to clean or disinfect your gun while using it to apply different makeup products as you do with pencils and brushes.

◀ Figure 16–10 **Water-based makeup allows for easy correction and blending of mistakes.**

Some powders contain mica which can appear shiny when photographed with HD equipment.

Alcohol-Based Makeup (Waterproof Makeup)

Alcohol-based makeup, also known as **waterproof makeup**, is a product in which the primary ingredient is alcohol, rendering it waterproof, smudge-proof, and completely nontransferable (**Figure 16–11**). Alcohol-based makeup will not come off until it is taken off; it meets the most demanding requirements of long, outdoor, and aquatic photoshoots. It withstands extended exposure to the elements and is ideal for underwater scenes, stage performances, and any environment where perspiration can be an issue.

Waterproof makeup is meant for use by the most experienced airbrush artists. In a waterproof formula, alcohol is the essential ingredient; when the alcohol combines with air, it evaporates rapidly, activating the other ingredients and binding them together to create an immovable, waterproof product. Only alcohol-based formulas offer this level of immovability and adhesion.

© Kett Cosmetics.

▲ Figure 16–11 **Alcohol-based makeup (waterproof makeup) is only used by professional airbrush makeup artists.**

© Kett Cosmetics. Makeup by Leah Dorane Fonal. Photographed by Steve Azzarra.

▲ Figure 16–12 **A model with water-based makeup for a photoshoot.**

© Kett Cosmetics. Makeup by Sheila McKenna. Photography by James C. McAward.

▲ Figure 16–13 **A model with alcohol-based makeup, perfect for underwater shoots.**

Choosing the Formula: Water-Based or Alcohol-Based Choosing the right formula is essential to achieving maximum results. Makeup used for beauty purposes—such as fashion, TV, print, and special occasions—need withstand only normal circumstances and should be easily removed, making water-based makeup an ideal choice (**Figure 16–12**). Alternatively, the demanding conditions of underwater shoots, stage performances, and tattoo coverage require alcohol-based (waterproof) makeup (**Figure 16–13**). ☑ **LO1**

CAUTION

Alcohol-based makeup dries quickly and must be cleaned out of the airbrush immediately after use. Water-based and alcohol-based makeup should never be mixed on the skin or in the airbrush.

AIRBRUSH TECHNIQUES

The most important feature of airbrushing is total control of the airbrush. The artist maintains this control with the index finger on the lever.

Precision and Control (Dot & Dash)

All spray patterns are based on distance from the skin, airflow, and the amount of makeup product being released. The closer the airbrush is to the client's skin, the narrower the spray pattern will be. This is when the least amount of makeup product should be released. The farther the airbrush is from the client, the wider the spray pattern will be and more makeup can be applied. Increase or decrease the distance between the airbrush and the skin to control the width of the spray pattern.

The Dot Method

The **dot method** is an airbrush application technique that creates a circular shape; it is produced by holding the airbrush stationary to create the dot. Use the following technique to create a diffuse (spread out) shape on lager areas, such as blush on the cheek or in order to conceal an imperfection, like a blemish.

Pressing down (for air) and then pulling back gently on the lever will release air and makeup on the skin. While maintaining a downward position, gently move the lever backward to produce a dot of makeup. Then, roll the lever back to the forward position to stop the flow of makeup. Increase or decrease the makeup flow gently, without lifting your finger off the lever.

When using a single or dual-action airbrush, aiming at close range to the skin will cause an indentation on the skin. This is a perfect indication of where the makeup will be applied when you release the makeup product (**Figure 16–14**).

© Kett Cosmetics. Makeup and photography by Sheila McKenna.

▲ Figure 16–14 **The dot method is used to determine where makeup will be applied by releasing air only.**

If a spatter of makeup is needed for creating a freckled effect, use a dual-action airbrush. For creating spatter, pull the lever back without pressing it down. Wait 2 seconds, release the lever, aim at the skin, and push down on the lever. The air will push out the droplet of makeup onto the skin, creating a spatter effect (**Figure 16–15**).

Cleaning the Airbrush After Use

To clean the airbrush properly, use the base ingredient from the makeup: Use water to cleanup after using water-based makeup, and use alcohol to cleanup after using alcohol-based makeup.

© Kett Cosmetics.

▲ Figure 16–15 **Use the dual-action airbrush to create the spatter effect.**

The Dash Method

The **dash method** is an airbrush stroke that is used to create an elongated spray pattern on the eyes, face, or body. This method is also used at a distance to blend and/or build opacity on large areas (**Figure 16–16**).

© Kett Cosmetics.

▲ Figure 16–16 **The dash method is done at a distance to create an elongated spray pattern.**

Dashes should have ends that fade away. The makeup application stroke created with an airbrush should be much the same as those created using traditional makeup brushes. However, an airbrush offers an added benefit: The user can adjust the distance from the skin and in doing so adjust the width of the spray pattern, which provides the same variation as if you were to use a wide variety of traditional brushes.

Moving your hand in a circular motion will create a donut shape on the skin preventing you from targeting the area you intend to conceal.

A single pass of the airbrush creates a veil of makeup. Use multiple passes to build opacity.

HERE'S A TIP

Practice doing dots and dashes on paper before practicing on yourself.

HERE'S A TIP

If you are using frisket film for artwork on canvas, the plastic should be separated from the paper and the sticky side adhered to the canvas. When using frisket film for beauty makeup or for creating freckles, the paper and plastic should remain together. This way you can use the stencil multiple times. Frisket film is readily available at any art supply store.

Spray Variance

Part of learning how to control the airbrush is learning how close to or far from the skin the airbrush should be in order to achieve the desired result—whether that result is a soft-focus blend, a precise detail, or somewhere in between.

Soft Focus **Soft focus** is an airbrush effect created by holding the airbrush 3 to 6 inches (7.5 to 15 centimeters) from the skin; color intensity and opacity can be enhanced by using consecutive passes. This method is used for the application of foundation, blush, contour, and highlight.

Precise Detail **Precise detail** is an airbrush effect created by holding the airbrush ¼ to 3 inches (.6 to 7.5 centimeters) from the skin; this method is used for fine detail work, such as spot-concealing of imperfections (using the dot method) and contouring of the eyes and nose.

Additional Supplies

As your skill level increases, so will your need to be creative and think outside the box. Airbrush makeup is new; however, airbrushing itself has been around for a very long time. An airbrush is not the first or the only product taken from the craft industry and used for applying makeup.

▲ Figure 16–17 Frisket film is used to create stencils.

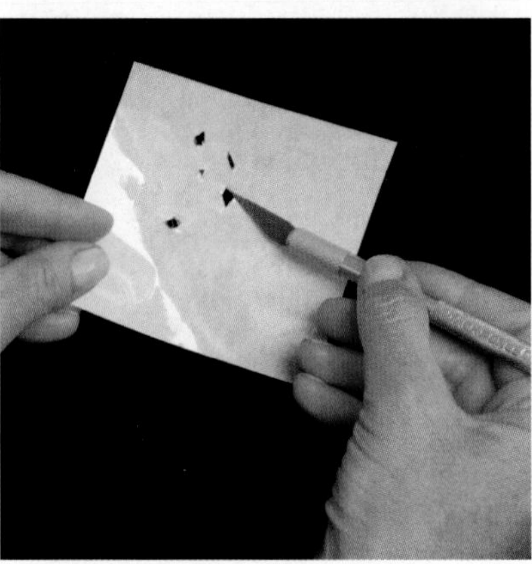

▲ Figure 16–18 Making freckles with frisket film.

© Kett Cosmetics.

Another such item is frisket film, a must-have item in all airbrush kits. **Frisket film** is an adhesive-backed paper and plastic combination that is used by airbrush artists to create templates (stencils) (**Figure 16–17**). Frisket film can be used for creating eyebrow and body art stencils and for creating freckles on the skin as seen in Procedure 16–2, Camouflaging Tattoos. The design is drawn on the paper side of the film and then precisely cut away with an exacto knife (**Figure 16–18**). ✓ LO2

AIRBRUSH MAINTENANCE

It is critical to clean the airbrush after every use. You also must clean the airbrush after using a color that might affect the next hue to be used. Artists often work with the lightest colors first and then graduate to deeper ones. However, at some point the airbrush must be cleaned to avoid unwanted color interference.

Back Bubble Cleaning Technique

The **back bubble** technique is used to clean the airbrush. Use the following process with the cleaning solution indicated by the manufacturer.

1. Fill the airbrush cup halfway with the appropriate cleaning fluid.
2. With your finger, use a tissue to cover the tip of the airbrush to prevent the air from escaping.
3. Pull the lever backward. This creates a back-bubble effect, which will flush the makeup into the cup.
4. Remove your finger from the tip and spray the tissue (**Figure 16–19**).
5. Pour the excess fluid onto the tissue and repeat this step until the fluid sprays clear.
6. Finish cleaning by using a clean cotton swab and tissue to remove any excess residue remaining in the cup.

Replacement Parts

The needle and the nozzle of the airbrush will need to be replaced due to normal wear and tear. With use, the nozzle will begin to stretch open, creating continuous makeup flow even when the needle is in the forward position. Because the needle must be perfectly straight in order for the makeup to flow in the desired direction, it must be replaced immediately if the tip is bent. Therefore, it is important to have a spare needle available. Some manufacturers provide a wrench that can be used to remove the nozzle; if your airbrush did not come with such a wrench, make sure you get one and keep it at hand along with your spare needles.

HERE'S A TIP

Remember, water cleans water-based formulations, and alcohol cleans alcohol-based formulas.

Multicultural CONSIDERATIONS

Back bubble to blend color seamlessly for any ethnicity.

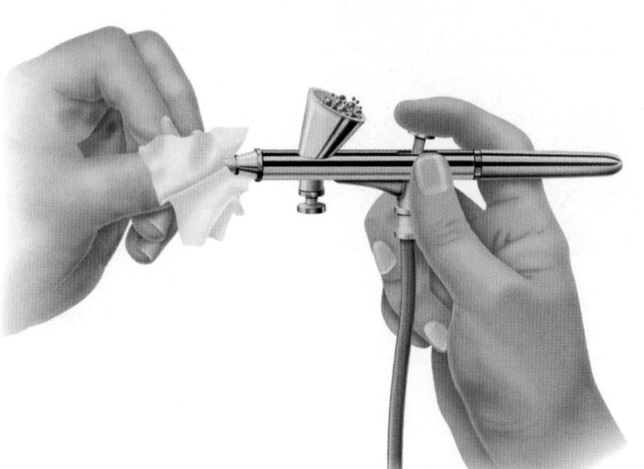

Figure 16–19 The back-bubble method is used to clean the airbrush after use.

CAUTION

Each part of an airbrush is delicate and cannot be forced into place. Part replacement should be performed or supervised by an experienced airbrush artist. The first time you replace parts, have your instructor supervise you.

Mini Procedure

Sample of how to replace the needle and nozzle parts of an airbrush.

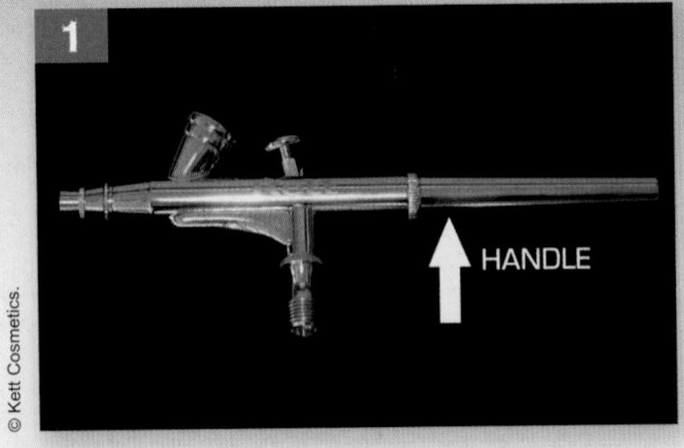

© Kett Cosmetics.

1 Remove the handle.

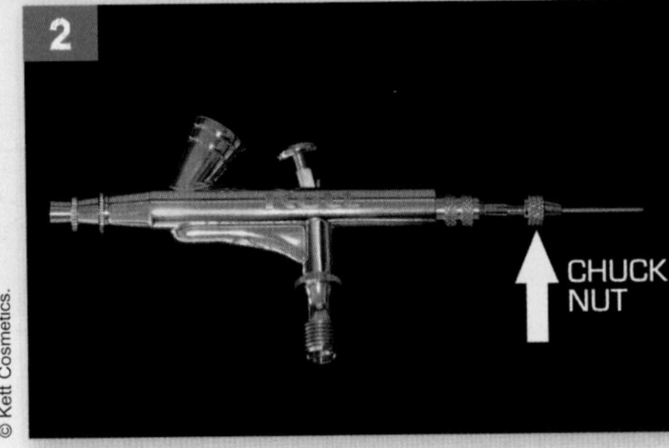

© Kett Cosmetics.

2 Remove the chuck nut.

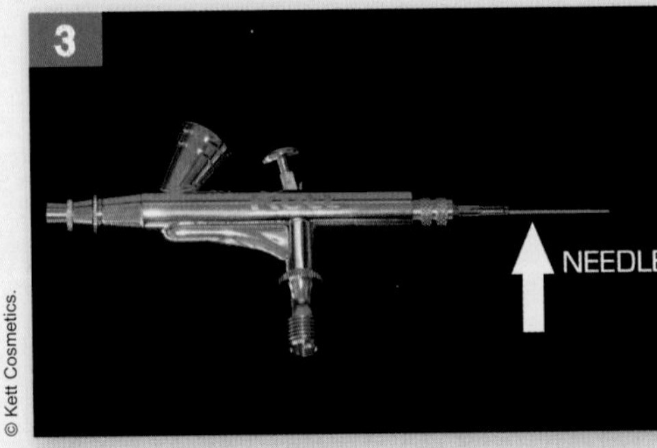

© Kett Cosmetics.

3 Pull out the needle.

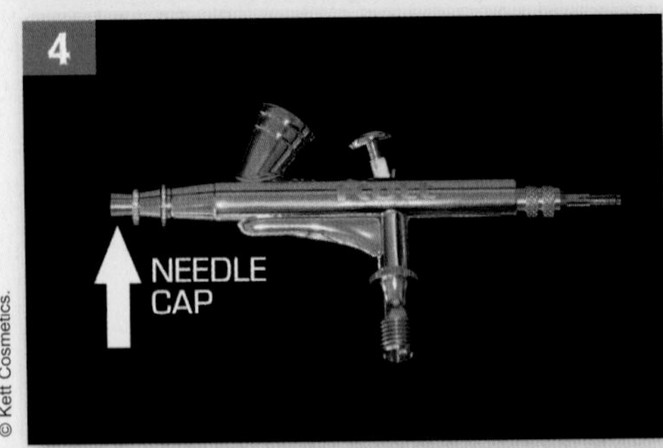

© Kett Cosmetics.

4 Remove the needle cap.

© Zhukov Oleg/www.Shutterstock.com

(Continued)

Mini Procedure

Replacement needle and nozzle *(Continued)*

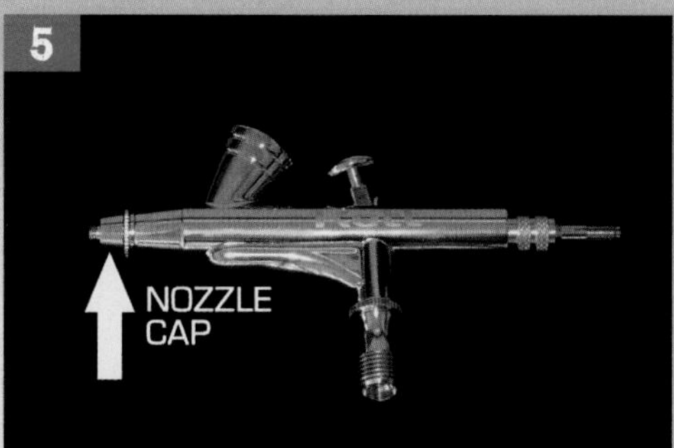

5 Remove the nozzle cap.

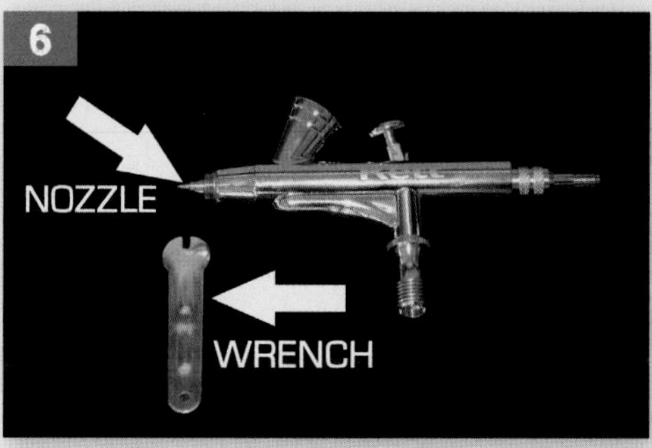

6 Unscrew the nozzle using the wrench provided.

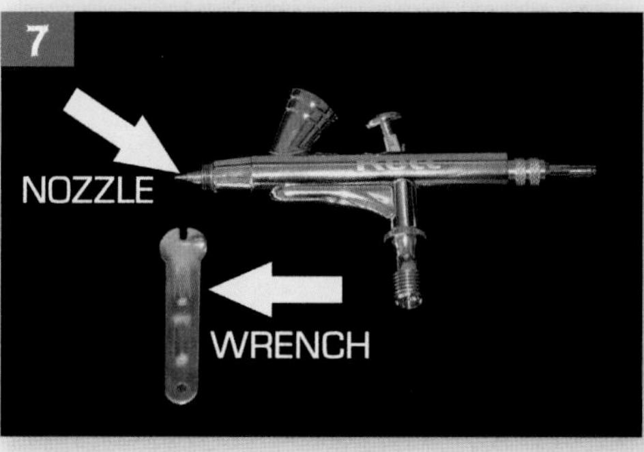

7 Replace the nozzle.
☑ LO3

Multicultural CONSIDERATIONS

When making color selections for women of color, choose shades that closely match those of the natural skin.

AIRBRUSH BEAUTY BREAKDOWN

All skin colors—light, medium, and deep—are enhanced in the same way, ideally using four makeup tones: one to match, one to highlight, one to contour, and one to color the complexion. The application routine includes makeup product for skin tone, contour, blush, and shading colorations. The objective is to produce three-dimensional makeup by correcting imperfections and by shading and sculpting the complexion. Choosing the correct shades is paramount. In addition to doing a jawline swatch, you should test the color on the forehead and nose. On some complexions, these areas of the face can be darker than the jawline. When airbrushing, it is simple to segue from one color to the next. Very few artists can perfectly match skin using just one color.

PROCEDURE 16–1 BASIC AIRBRUSH APPLICATION SEE PAGE 387

Cool colors neutralize warm colors. Warm colors neutralize cool colors.

For example, a warm/RED and cool/GREEN complement one another. When mixed together, RED and GREEN neutralize each other.

AIRBRUSHING CAMOUFLAGE MAKEUP

As a makeup artist, you will often be asked to cover undesired colorations on the face and body, including tattoos. **Neutralization** is the color-theory method of concealing unwanted or uneven color on the skin. It is the most effective method for concealing unwanted color. This process requires an understanding of color theory, which you studied in Chapter 5, Color Theory. Refer to that information and apply the same rules. Procedure 16–2, Camouflaging Tattoos, is an exercise in color-neutralization theory and in applying multiple layers of makeup.

If your client's skin is warm/red, neutralize the redness by choosing a makeup base that has a cool/olive tone. If your client's skin is cool or ashy, choose a neutralizing color that has warmth. When working with skin tones, the rules are very simple: Use a yellow-based/olive-based makeup to neutralize red/peach tones; use a red-based/peach-based makeup to neutralize yellow/olive tones. Some tattoos are a solid black design which will turn green when olive-based makeup is applied. Therefore, you should start with a red/peach color. As the coverage evolves, you will be able to see whether you need to switch and alternate the base tones.

PROCEDURE 16–2 CAMOUFLAGING TATTOOS SEE PAGE 394

As discussed in Chapter 15, Camouflage Makeup, camouflage makeup can be used to temporarily cover discoloration in the skin. Skin-staining dyes temporarily camouflage hypopigmented patches. Applying neutralizing shades using the airbrush dot technique creates a believable color balance. In Procedure 16–3, Covering Vitiligo on the Hands with Airbrush Makeup, you will see the step-by-step airbrush camouflage process for vitiligo on the hands. The end result shows a more balanced skin tone with the hypopigmented patches of skin concealed.

PROCEDURE 16–3 COVERING VITILIGO ON THE HANDS WITH AIRBRUSH MAKEUP SEE PAGE 397

Procedure 16-1
Basic Airbrush Application

Implements and Materials

You will need all of the following implements, materials, and supplies:

- **Brushes**
  - ☐ Assorted makeup brushes
- **Utensils**
  - ☐ Air compressor
  - ☐ Airbrush
  - ☐ Hand sanitizer
  - ☐ Headband or hair clip
  - ☐ Makeup cape
  - ☐ Makeup chair
  - ☐ Neck strip or clean towel for draping
- **Single-use Items**
  - ☐ Hand wipes
  - ☐ Makeup remover wipes
  - ☐ Tissues
- **Products**
  - ☐ Alcohol
  - ☐ Facial moisturizer
  - ☐ Liquid airbrush makeup
  - ☐ Setting powder
  - ☐ Traditional cream makeup
  - ☐ Traditional powder eye shadows
  - ☐ Water

Preparation

- Perform

PROCEDURE 7-1 PRE-SERVICE SEE PAGE 144

Procedure

1 Test the airbrush with makeup to see if it is working properly.

2 Review client's needs and desired makeup look.

3 Inform the client about the airbrush procedure and what to expect.

4 Wash and dry your hands.

5 Cleanse and moisturize the client's skin.

Procedure 16-1 *(continued)*

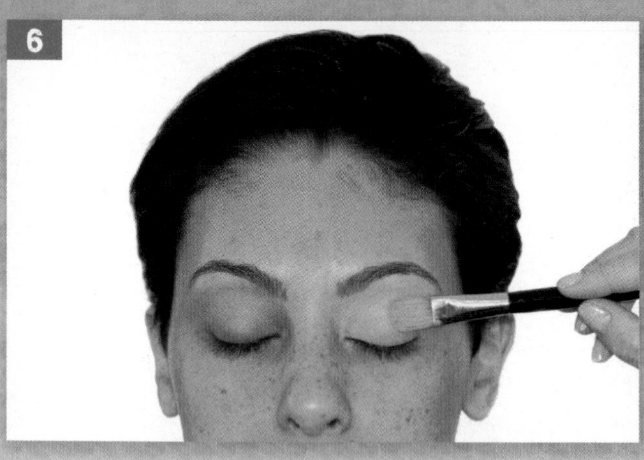

6 Conceal the eyelid and set with translucent powder to create a clean canvas.

Note: To apply eye shadow that looks as good to the naked eye as it does on camera, a layering process that alternates between traditional powders and airbrush makeup is necessary. This produces a well-saturated effect that will stand up to both natural and professional lighting. This process will create deeper pigmentation and a longer-lasting application.

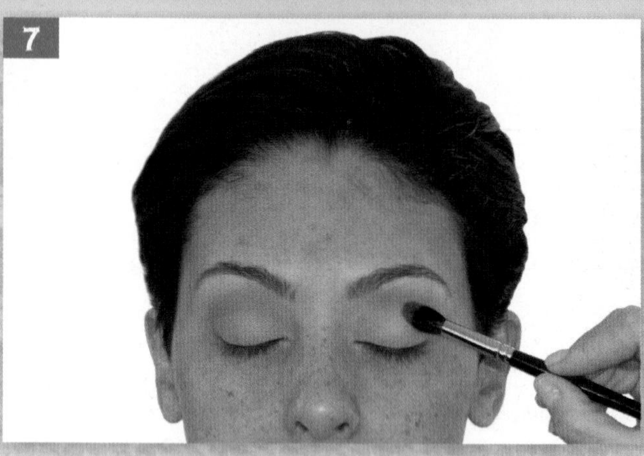

7 Start by applying shadow to the crease of the eye with a blending brush. This will enhance the eye socket.

SERVICE TIP

Mapping out your design with powder shadows first will make it easier to follow the design with the airbrush.

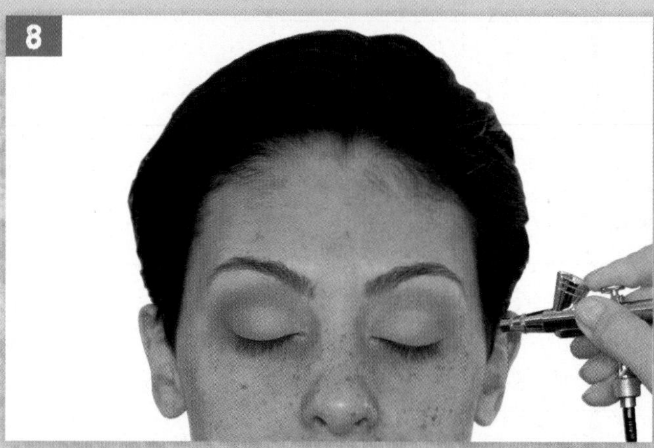

8 Using the dash method, follow the design with a layer of airbrush makeup in the crease to create more depth and dimension.

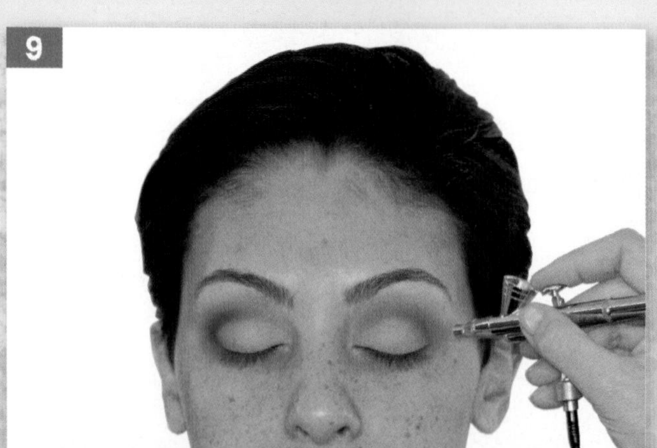

9 For a deeper socket, switch to a darker brown, move your hand closer to the skin, and release very little makeup onto the desired area.

SERVICE TIP

Be conservative. No more than two drops of makeup is needed to enhance the crease.

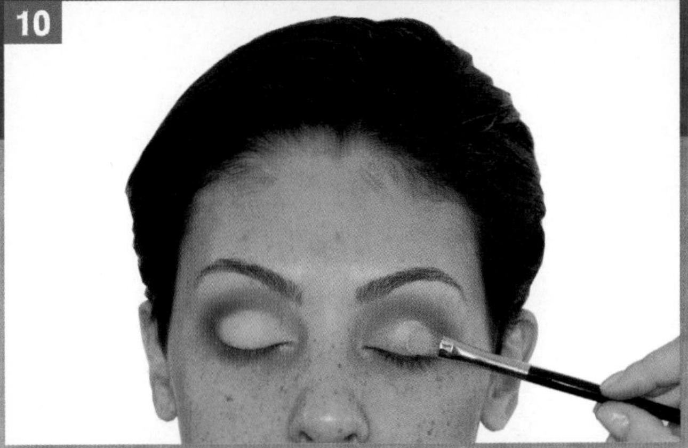

10 Choose a powder eye shadow to be applied traditionally on the eyelid with an eye shadow brush.

11 Use a light, iridescent color with an eye shadow brush or a small eye shadow brush to create a highlight on the inner corner of the eyelid.

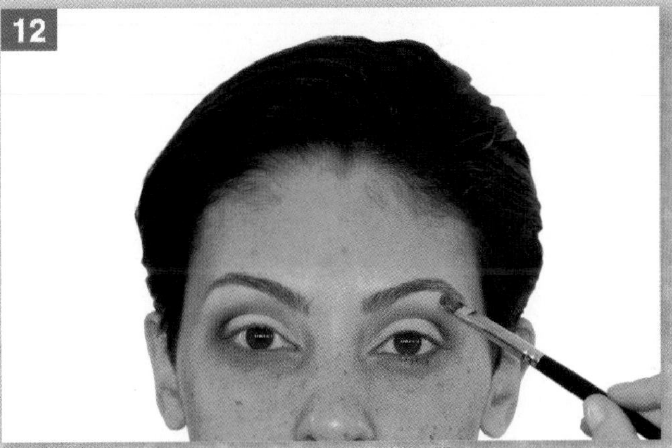

12 Use the same brush to highlight the brow bone.

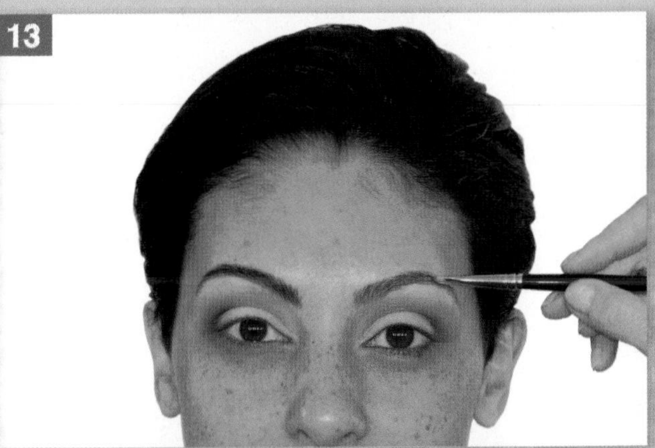

13 For a soft beauty effect, fill in the brows with the appropriate color using a flat angle brush.

SERVICE TIP

Brows can also be airbrushed for a dramatic, theatrical effect. Stencils can be created with frisket film or found on-line.

14 To enhance the lash line, use an angled brush with the appropriate shading color.

15 To create an angular-shaped eye, place the straight edge of a tissue under the eye and airbrush a dark color using the dash method.

Procedure 16-1 *(continued)*

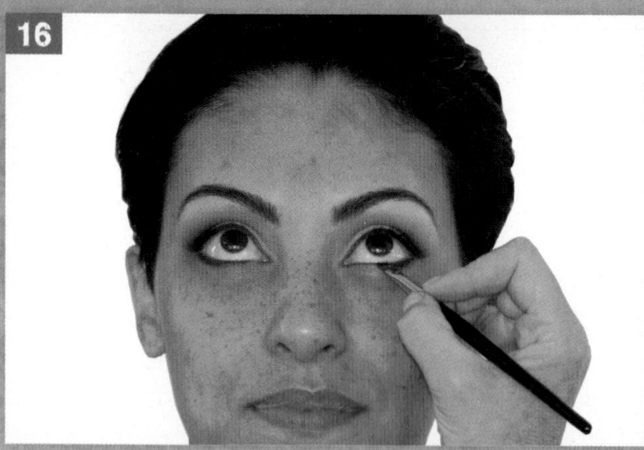

16 Shade the lower lash line with an angle brush, depositing color at the base of the lashes.

Never airbrush near eyes that are open.

17 Using a makeup-remover wipe, clean any overspray or powder fallout that may have landed under the eye or on the cheeks.

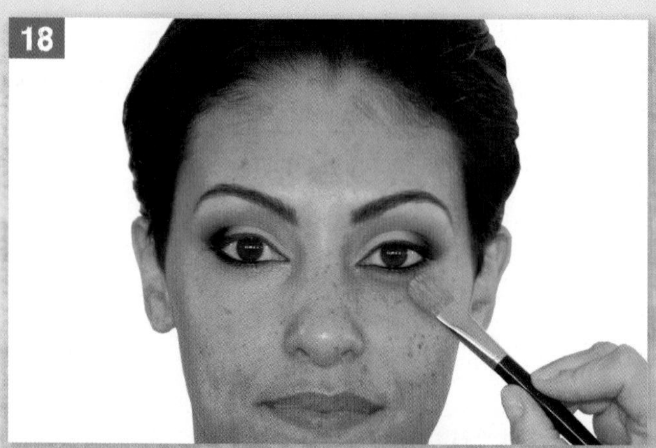

18 Start with a manual application of concealer under the eyes and around the nostrils. Use a concealer brush for this application.

SERVICE TIP

Always *lightly* set concealer immediately with powder to prevent creasing.

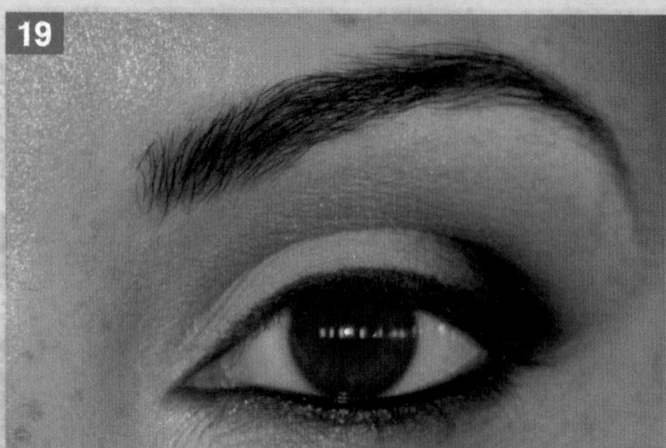

19 Check to be sure concealer application is not wrinkled or set in fine lines and creases.

CAUTION

Concealing darkness under the eyes must be done using traditional methods. Airbrushing too close to the under-eye area will cause a client to squint, enhancing the tiny lines around the eye.

20 To start the application, select the primary color that will be used on the majority of the face. For the illustrated application, a medium olive tone has been used.

Note: Airbrushing the face is the next step. First, neutralize any unwanted discolorations—such as scars, redness, or hyper/hypopigmented spots—using the dot and dash method. All airbrush makeup applications will vary depending on the level of coverage needed and the color-layering process required to produce the illusion of perfect skin. For the initial application of foundation, approximately six to eight drops of makeup is the appropriate amount for an average complexion. A complete makeup application can require three to four colors, which will produce a look that highlights, shades, and creates dimension. For maximum coverage on problematic skin, more drops of makeup should be added.

21 Utilize the dot method with the primary color. The dots will be used to target and cover imperfections.

SERVICE TIP

Highlights should be used to enhance and brighten features on the face and body. Once you have determined the primary skin tone, choose one or two shades lighter for the highlight. For a beautiful sparkle effect, a luminous iridescent color can be used after the application of highlight.

SERVICE TIP

Only two or three drops of makeup are necessary for delicately highlighting the face.

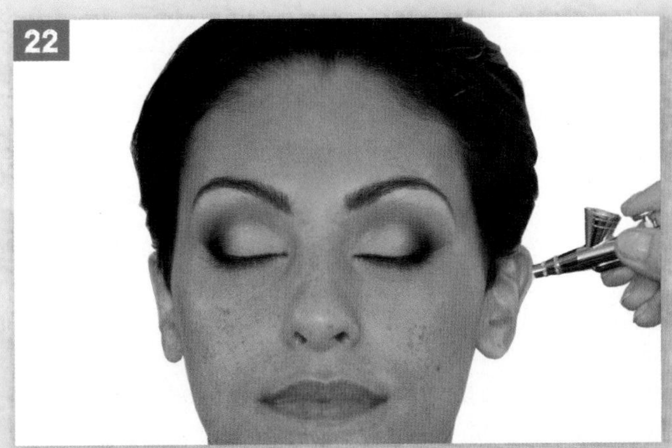

22 Use the dash method to blend and apply foundation to the rest of the face as needed. To build coverage, increase the number of passes on targeted areas.

Note: The most even application consists of a combination of dots and dashes. In the initial practice sessions, carefully monitor the distance between the airbrush and the skin. If the airbrush is too close to the skin surface, a line pattern may be produced. To avoid creating lines, increase the distance from the skin.

Procedure 16-1 *(continued)*

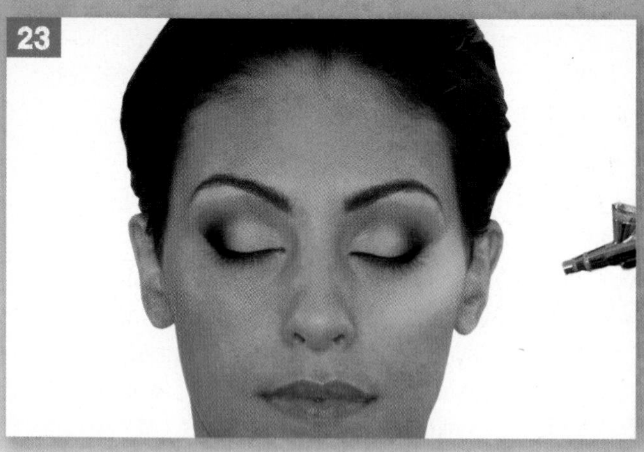

23 Using strategic placement of product and the utmost control of makeup flow, apply the highlight color to the targeted area, such as the upper cheekbones and/or the bridge of the nose.

SERVICE TIP

When using a blendable water-based foundation, lightly powder every two layers for the most durable, transfer-resistant finish.

24 For this step, the contour should look like a shadow on the face. Choose a neutral brown color that is two or three shades darker than the skin tone.

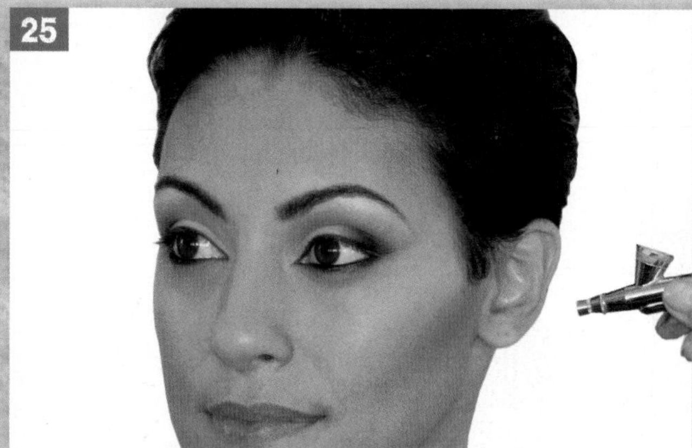

25 Using the dash method, start at the hairline just below the cheekbone, adding the contour color beneath the cheekbone and tapering off below the apple of the cheek. This will enhance the structure of the cheekbone.

26 Add a blush color with approximately two to three drops of makeup. In the illustrated example, a light-plum color was used.

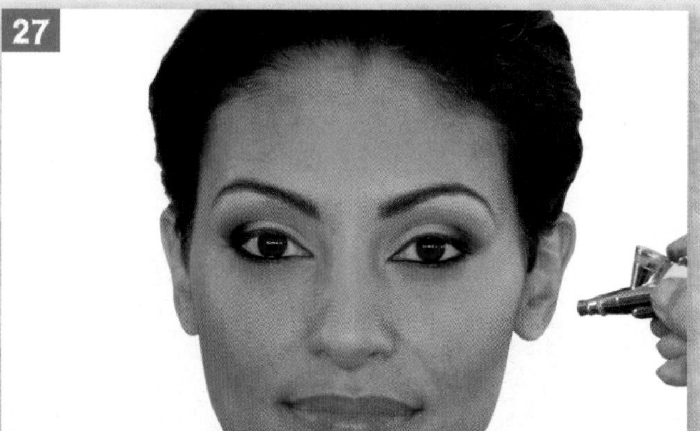

27 Start with a few large dots on the apple of the cheek and finish with a dash moving out toward the hairline. Repeat this action until the desired depth of color is achieved.

28

CAUTION

Be conservative with your dots and dashes when applying blush. More product can always be applied if needed.

28 Bronzer is not always needed, but it has been used in the illustrated example. Choose a warm bronzer color that is darker than the client's primary color.

29

30

29 Using the dash method, apply the bronzer to the upper forehead, close to the hairline. It can also be applied on the top of the cheeks, the bridge of nose, and the collar bone for a natural effect.

CAUTION

Be careful not to use circular motions when airbrushing; doing so will create a circular pattern on the face. The purpose of the airbrushing is to create a seamless, soft-focus effect that harmonizes with the structure of facial features.

30 Finish the application with mascara, artificial lashes, liquid eyeliner, and lip gloss.

Note: The secret to a successful airbrush application is to understand that the hand movements used with an airbrush are identical to the brush strokes used with a traditional makeup brush.

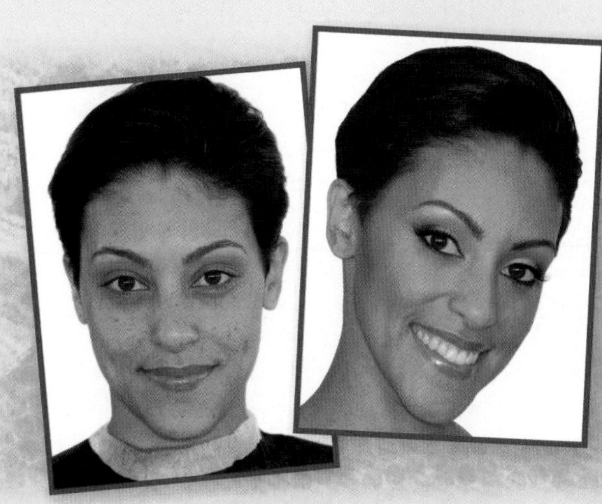

Post-Service ☑ LO4

- Complete

PROCEDURE 7-2 POST-SERVICE SEE PAGE 148

- If you are using a water-based product, advise the client to avoid rubbing the area.
- If you are using an alcohol-based foundation, provide the client with instructions for makeup removal.
- Clean the airbrush unit.

Procedure 16-2

Camouflaging Tattoos

Implements and Materials

You will need all of the following implements, materials, and supplies:

Brushes

- ☐ Makeup brush for applying powder

Utensils

- ☐ Airbrush equipment
- ☐ Brush cleaner
- ☐ Frisket film for freckle replication, if needed
- ☐ Hand sanitizer
- ☐ Headband or hair clip
- ☐ Makeup cape
- ☐ Makeup chair
- ☐ Neck strip or clean towel for draping

Single-use Items

- ☐ Disposable razor (optional)
- ☐ Hand wipes

Products

- ☐ Airbrush foundations
- ☐ Setting powder (translucent)
- ☐ Water or alcohol for cleaning the airbrush

SERVICE TIP

Use a yellow-based/olive-based makeup to neutralize red/peach tones; use a red-based/peach-based makeup to neutralize yellow/olive tones. Most tattoos contain solid black lines which will turn green when olive-based makeup is applied. Therefore, you should start with a red/peach color.

Preparation

- Perform

PROCEDURE 7-1 PRE-SERVICE SEE PAGE 144

Procedure

Note: To provide a smudge-proof and waterproof application, alcohol-based makeup was used for this procedure.

1 Be sure to test the airbrush with makeup to see if it is working properly.

2 Before the service, talk with the client about the airbrush procedure and what to expect.

3 Seat the client and cover surrounding clothing with tissue.

4 If covering a tattoo, shave the area, or have the client shave before they arrive.

5 Perform a patch test to determine the skin tone surrounding the tattoo. Keep this color handy to use for the final layer.

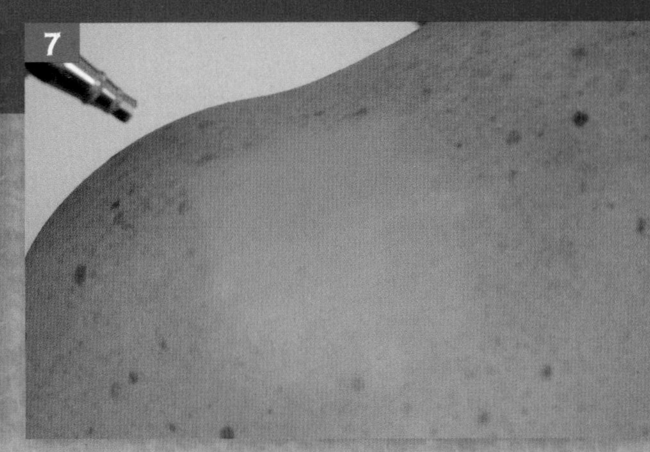

6 Using the neutralizing color, airbrush with a light touch, targeting the shape of the tattoo. Try not to go too far outside of the tattoo lines with the neutralizing color, but do cover the tattoo completely.

7 If the surrounding skin is darker on one side of the tattoo than on the other side, use a darker shade of neutralizing color for a natural-fade effect. In this image, the top of the shoulder is darker and required a deeper shade of makeup.

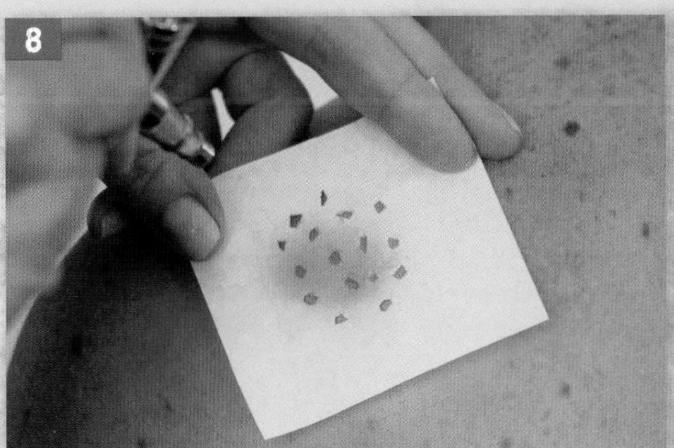

8 If freckles are needed, choose a color that matches the freckles and start placing them randomly, using a stencil made of frisket film. Freckles are not perfect or even.

9 Rotate the frisket film with each layer of freckles for an imperfect effect.

SERVICE TIP

If freckles are not needed, switch to the primary color and airbrush the final layer with broad sweeping dashes that extend outward onto the surrounding skin.

SERVICE TIP

Holding your frisket film slightly above the skin will soften the edges of the freckles, creating a natural appearance.

Procedure 16-2 *(continued)*

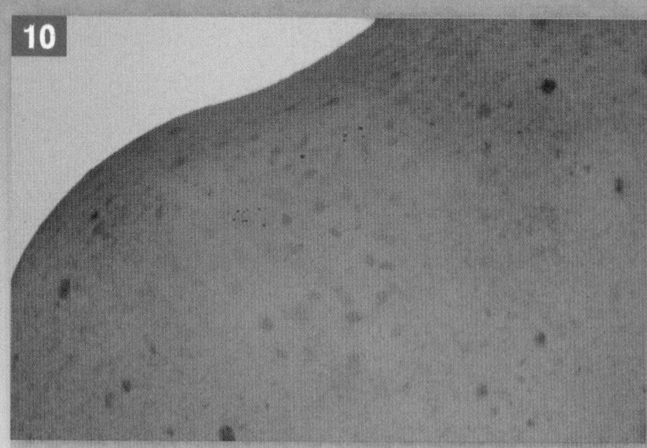

10 Switch the freckle colors accordingly.

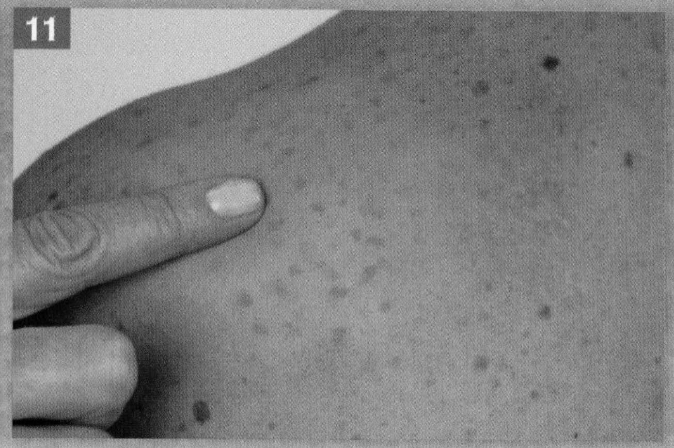

11 Create spatter and tap the color with your fingertip to soften the edge.

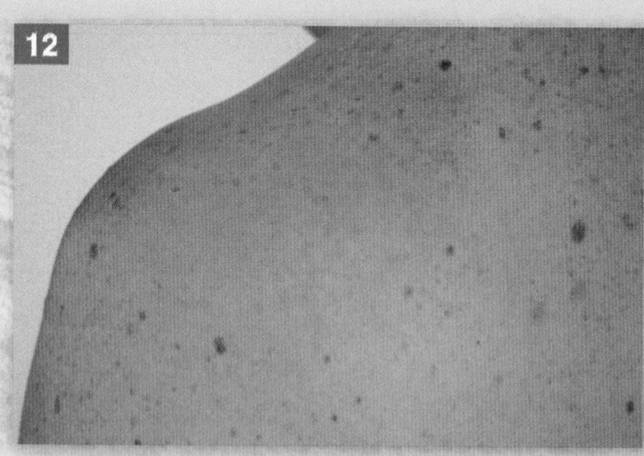

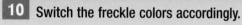

12 Repeat these steps until the tattoo is completely covered.

13 Finish with a light dusting of translucent powder.

SERVICE TIP

When using alcohol-based makeup, it is not necessary to powder between layers. However, you should powder when finished.

14 As you work, step back and view your results to check your progress. The application will look different from a distance than it does up close.

Post-Service ☑ LO5

- Complete

PROCEDURE 7-2 **POST-SERVICE** SEE PAGE 148

- If using a water-based product, advise the client to avoid rubbing the area.
- If using an alcohol-based foundation, provide the client with instructions for removal of makeup, as this is waterproof.
- Clean the airbrush unit.

Procedure 16-3

Covering Vitiligo on the Hands with Airbrush Makeup

Implements and Materials

You will need all of the following implements, materials, and supplies:

- **Brushes**
  - ☐ Makeup brush for applying powder
- **Utensils**
  - ☐ Airbrush compressor
  - ☐ Airbrush equipment
  - ☐ Airbrush cleaner or alcohol
  - ☐ Brush cleaner
  - ☐ Frisket film for freckle replication (if needed)
  - ☐ Hand sanitizer
  - ☐ Headband or hair clip
  - ☐ Makeup cape
  - ☐ Neck strip or clean towel for draping to protect garments
- **Single-use Items**
  - ☐ Hand wipes
- **Products**
  - ☐ Airbrush foundations
  - ☐ Oil or petrolatum product
  - ☐ Setting powder (translucent)
  - ☐ Water or alcohol for cleaning the airbrush

Preparation

- Perform

PROCEDURE 7-1 PRE-SERVICE SEE PAGE 144

- Make sure the client properly washes the hands before the service.

Procedure

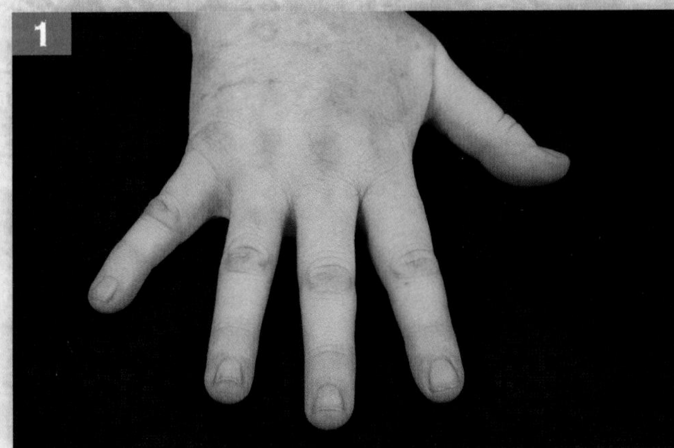

1

1 Coat nails with oil or petrolatum product to protect the nail bed.

2 Choose airbrush foundation that is one shade darker than the primary skin color. Place two to three drops into the cup.

Procedure 16-3 *(continued)*

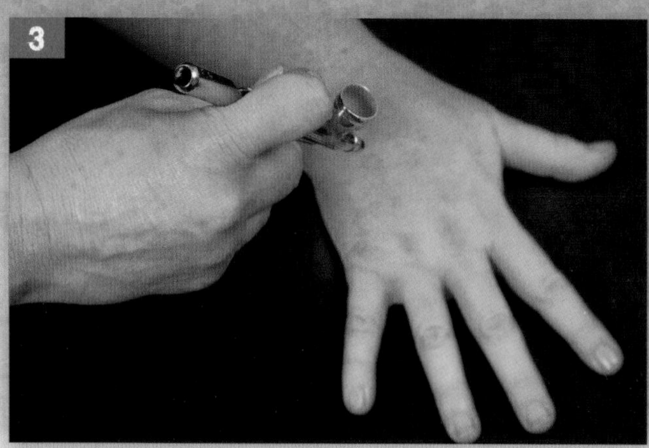

3 Press airbrush trigger button to engage the air, then turn on the compressor. Hold the nozzle close to the skin to identify where the product will be placed.

SERVICE TIP

The airbrush should be held at a constant 6 to 10 inches (15 to 25 centimeters) away from the skin.

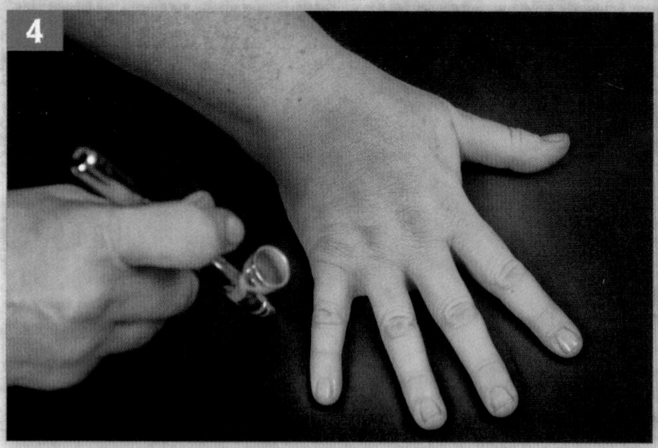

4 Pull back the lever to release the makeup from the airbrush. Use dots and dashes to apply the foundation to hypopigmented areas.

5 Use a dot method for more concentrated coverage in particular areas.

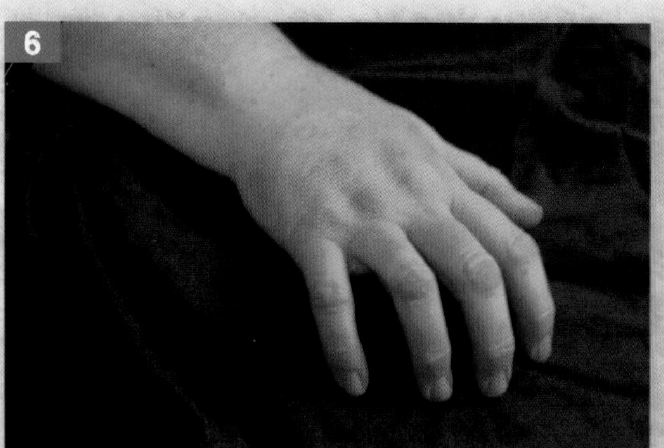

6 Slightly bend fingers to avoid dark finger tips.

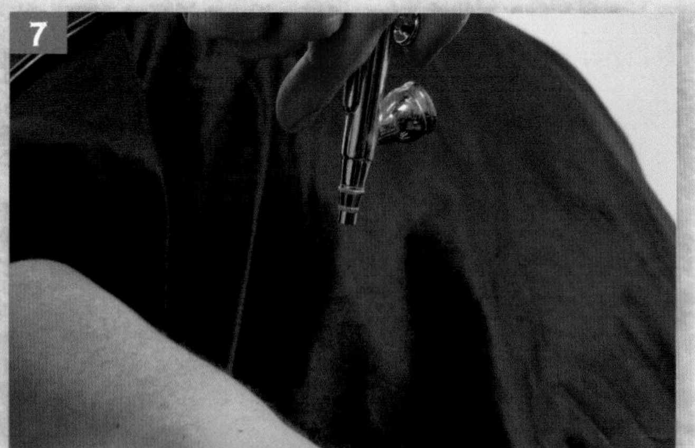

7 Pull airbrush to a farther distance, 10 to 12 inches (25 to 30 centimeters), over the knuckle area to avoid dark knuckles.

8 Select a skin-matching foundation shade.

9 Spray onto a tissue to clean between color selections and to test the accuracy of any new color.

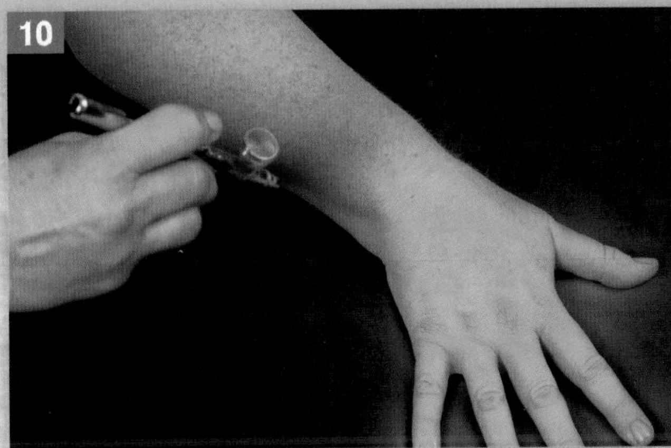

10 Hold airbrush nozzle away from the surface of the skin and blend the entire area with foundation that matches the client's skin tone.

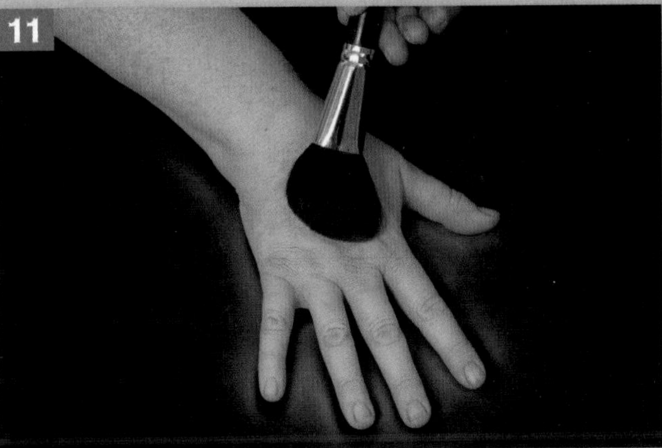

11 Apply translucent powder with a large powder fluff brush to set airbrush makeup.

Post-Service

- Complete

PROCEDURE 7-2 POST-SERVICE SEE PAGE 148

Review Questions

1. What is unique about the application and appearance of airbrush makeup?
2. Which part of the airbrush determines the size of the spray pattern?
3. Which part of the airbrush will be used to control the amount of product being sprayed?
4. Which part of the airbrush takes in atmospheric air and releases it through a hose connected to the airbrush?
5. Describe the difference between water-based and alcohol-based airbrush makeup.
6. What two factors influence all spray methods?
7. What two methods are used to determine precision and control?
8. Describe the difference between the two types of spray variance.
9. What is the best technique to apply eye shadow that looks as good to the naked eye as it does on camera?
10. How many drops of makeup are needed for an average initial foundation application?

Chapter Glossary

air compressor	Equipment that takes in atmospheric air and releases it through a hose.
airbrush	A tool used with an air compressor to spray liquids, such as makeup.
airbrush makeup	The process of applying makeup to the skin using an airbrush device.
alcohol-based makeup	Also known as *waterproof makeup;* a makeup product containing alcohol as its primary ingredient, rendering it waterproof, smudge-proof, and completely nontransferable.
back bubble	A technique that is used to clean an airbrush.
dash method	An airbrush application technique (a stroke) that is used to create an elongated spray pattern.
dot method	An airbrush application technique that creates a circular shape; produced by holding the airbrush stationary.
dual-action airbrush	An airbrush with two stages: it releases air when you press down on the lever, and it sprays makeup when you pull back on the lever.
frisket film	An adhesive-backed paper and plastic combination that is used by airbrush artists to create templates (stencils).
lever	The part of the airbrush used to control the amount of product being sprayed out.

Chapter Glossary *(continued)*

needle	The part of the airbrush that controls the amount of makeup flowing through the nozzle.
neutralization	The color-theory method of concealing unwanted or uneven color on the skin.
nozzle	One of the replaceable parts of the airbrush; it determines the size of the spray pattern.
precise detail	An airbrush application method created by holding the airbrush ¼ to 3 inches (.6 to 7.5 centimeters) from the skin; this method is used for fine detail work, such as spot-concealing of imperfections (using the dot method) and contouring of the eyes and nose.
single-action airbrush	An airbrush that releases air and makeup simultaneously when the artist pulls back on the lever.
soft focus	An airbrush application method created by holding the airbrush 3 to 6 inches (7.5 to 15 centimeters) from the skin; color intensity and opacity can be enhanced by using consecutive passes.
transformable airbrush	An airbrush that can function as a single-action airbrush or as a dual-action airbrush; the artist can switch back and forth as needed.
water-based makeup	A liquid makeup comprised of primary ingredients such as water, humectants, vitamins, oil absorbers, and color pigments.

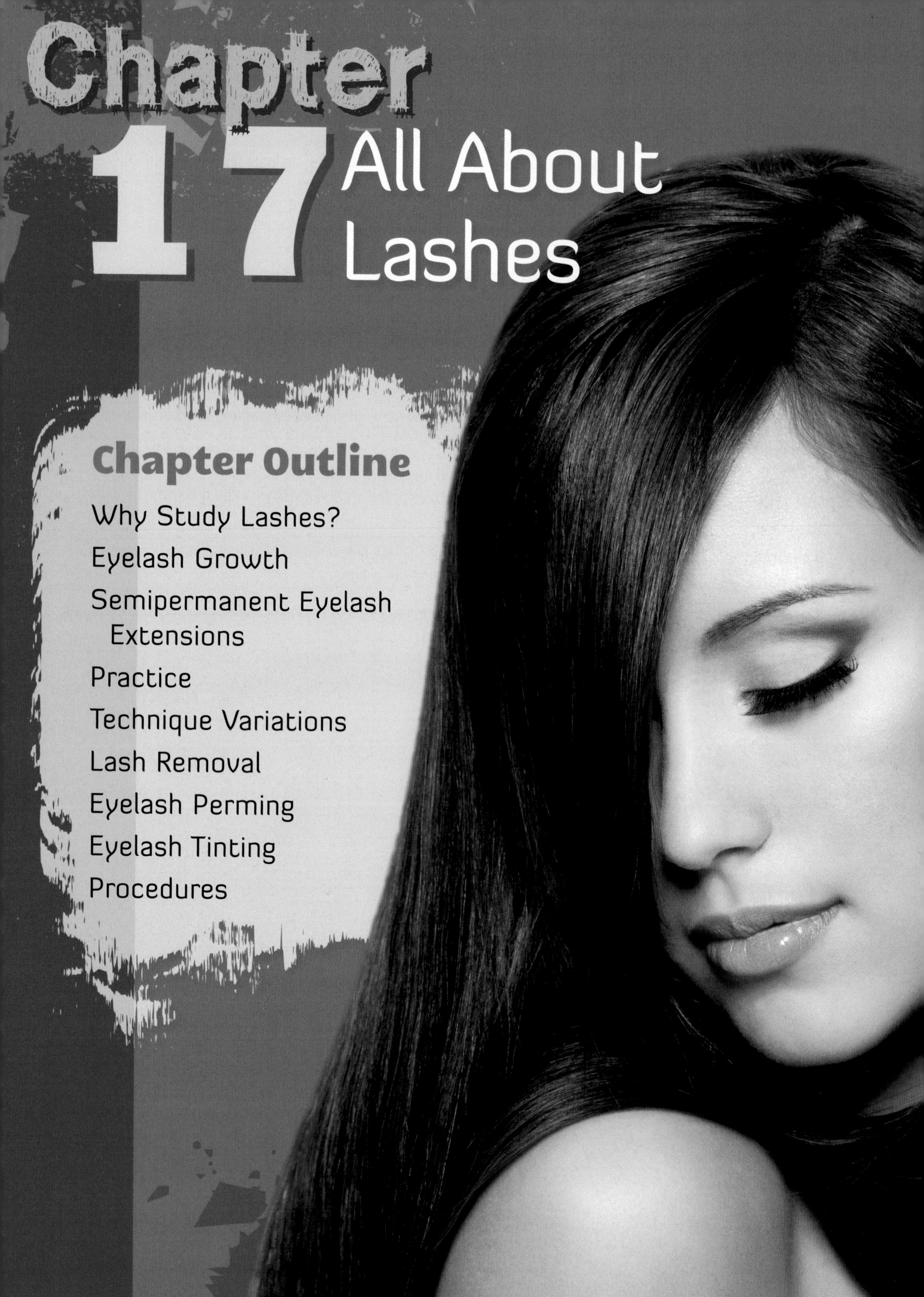

Chapter 17 All About Lashes

Chapter Outline

Learning Objectives

After completing this chapter, you will be able to:

- ✓ **LO1** List contraindications for lash extension application.
- ✓ **LO2** Identify tools and supplies needed for lash application.
- ✓ **LO3** List contraindications for lash perming.
- ✓ **LO4** Identify tools and supplies needed for eyelash perming.
- ✓ **LO5** Identify proper practices for performing eyelash perming with other eyelash and makeup services.
- ✓ **LO6** List contraindications for lash tinting.
- ✓ **LO7** Identify tools and supplies needed for eyelash tinting.
- ✓ **LO8** Perform a lash application procedure.
- ✓ **LO9** Perform an eyelash removal procedure.
- ✓ **LO10** Perform an eyelash perming procedure.
- ✓ **LO11** Perform an eyelash tinting procedure.

Key Terms

Page number indicates where in the chapter the term is used.

anagen
pg. 405

blepharitis
pg. 407

catagen
pg. 405

glaucoma
pg. 407

telogen
pg. 406

Career Profile

Megan Fields

In the short 7 years since she set out to accomplish her dream, Megan Fields has gone from retail makeup sales to working with renowned artists and photographers. Her passion to enlighten people about the artistry of makeup has given her the drive to get where she is today. As an African American woman herself, she focuses on women of color, helping them discover the makeup that suits their particular needs. Currently she manages a high-end cosmetic line, working toward the dream of creating her own line specific to women of color.

"I've always had an eye for fashion, especially when I was younger. I was fascinated that changing a couple things about a person would alter their appearance and that creating a new look for someone could change their life.

"At 15 years old I entered the world of beauty at its most basic level, working at the local beauty supply store. I learned to appreciate a variety of makeup lines and discovered what worked best with different skin types and skin tones. I learned that multiple product lines used together could create an incredible palette. People often love and wear only one specific makeup line, but when they do this, they are missing out on the magic that other lines offer.

"Being an African American woman, it is very hard for me to find foundation colors that match my skin tone and help with my oily skin. If I had not learned to love and embrace the best product from every makeup line, I would have struggled as a makeup artist and as a consumer. A great makeup artist educates the client about what is best for her skin and which tones, textures, and colors enhance her unique features.

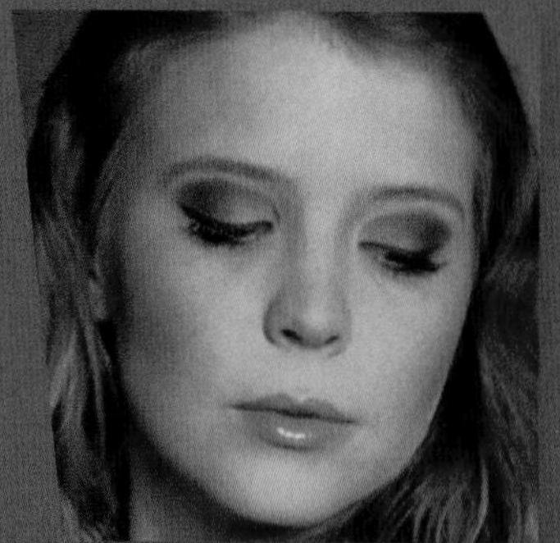

"After working as an assistant manager for a cosmetic line in a department store, my next adventure was into the world of the freelance artist. It's an amazing feeling, to be an artist and create masterpieces for every client, every time! During my time as a freelance artist, I learned that rules are made to be broken.

"After freelancing, I knew I wanted to continue my education, so I enrolled at the Make-Up Designory (MUD) institution in Burbank, California. Through this education, I found that I could do things that I never thought possible, and I saw creativity from different perspectives. It opened my eyes to the endless possibilities available in this field.

"Since my time in school, I've had the opportunity to work on photoshoots, fashion shows, infomercials, and product videos. I have even had the privilege of working with an Emmy award-winning video photographer and a world-renowned artist. It's been 7 years since that first job in the supply store, and today I am working for one of the top 10 cosmetic lines as a counter manager. My big dream is to eventually start my own makeup line for darker-skinned women. I think every makeup line has a story and a goal; I would love to lead the makeup industry to empower future makeup artists and women of color! I love that the beauty industry continues to grow, and I'm thankful each day that I get to be a part of that."

Courtesy of Megan Fields

As you have learned in this textbook, makeup artistry goes beyond the knowledge of skin tones, face shapes, and product application. The industry has undergone dramatic changes as new products and techniques flood the market and offer Hollywood-style enhancement to everyday clients. When it comes to lashes, women have moved from false, temporary eyelashes to semipermanent extensions, lash tinting, and lash perming. If the eyes are the window to the soul, then long, dark, luscious lashes provide an elegant entryway. Today's makeup artists must be knowledgeable about each of these techniques because the demand is tremendous.

WHY STUDY LASHES?

Makeup artists should study and have a thorough understanding of lashes because:

- The eyelashes accentuate the eyes, one of the most attractive features.
- Learning eyelash enhancement techniques allows you to offer instant alternatives to accentuate the eyes.
- Learning eyelash techniques gives the makeup artist the ability to further dramatize any makeup application.

STATE REGULATORY ALERT

State laws vary when it comes to lash enhancements. Be sure to check state regulations, especially as they pertain to lash tinting and perming.

EYELASH GROWTH

The main purpose of the eyelash and eyelid is to protect the eye from harmful substances and objects. Like other hair, the lashes follow a growth cycle. Knowing the stages of this cycle is important because this will allow you to select the best lashes for extension application, ensuring that the extensions last as long as possible (**Figure 17–1**).

The Anagen Stage

The **anagen** stage is when lashes are undergoing new growth. Application of extensions at this stage is not recommended because they tend to weigh down the natural lashes, which can result in premature detachment. Additionally, lashes applied during the anagen stage will look unnatural once the natural lashes reach full growth.

The Catagen Stage

The **catagen** stage is the transitional stage of hair growth (between anagen and telogen stages) and last for about 2 weeks. At this stage the lash has just finished growing. This is the ideal growth stage for extension placement. Artificial lashes applied at this stage will last longer and look more natural than extensions applied during other growth stages.

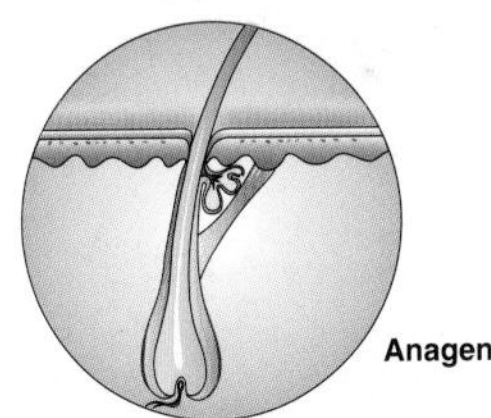

Anagen: The period of active hair growth

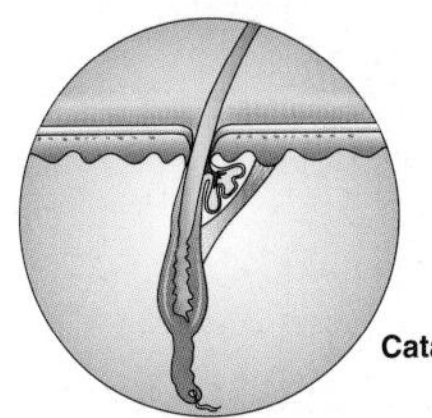

Catagen: A transient period marked by a cessation of growth of the hair follicle

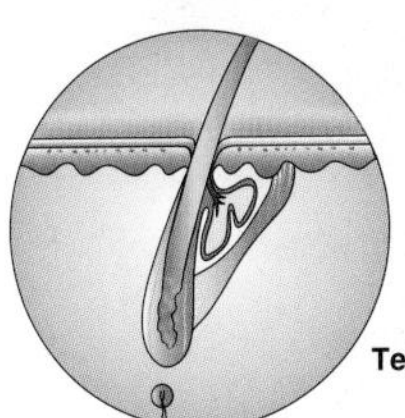

Telogen: A period of relative inactivity that occurs approximately every 60 to 90 days

▲ Figure 17–1 **Hair growth-cycle of eyelashes.**

The Telogen Stage

The **telogen** stage is the resting stage and can last for several weeks. This is an acceptable stage for lash placement, although lashes at this stage will be shed before those applied to lashes in the catagen stage.

SEMIPERMANENT EYELASH EXTENSIONS

Semipermanent eyelash extensions are different from traditional false eyelash strips, clusters, or individual lash tabbing. These recently invented synthetic eyelash extensions are single lashes applied one-by-one to natural lashes for longer, fuller, more natural-looking eyelashes (**Figure 17–2**). With the right combination of products, adhesive, and proper application, semipermanent lashes can last for up to 2 months. Clients can enjoy eyelash extensions year round by following simple maintenance and care instructions along with retouch applications every 2 to 4 weeks (**Figures 17–3** and **17–4**).

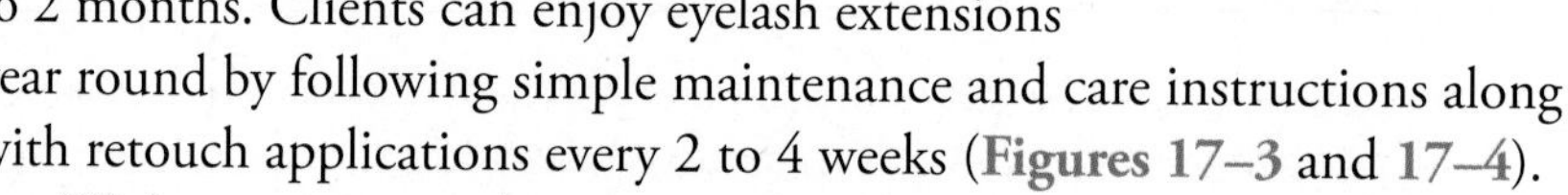

▲ Figure 17–2 **Single lashes for application.**

▲ Figure 17–3 **Client before eyelash extensions.**

▲ Figure 17–4 **Client after eyelash extensions.**

With growing popularity, semipermanent eyelash extensions are becoming a standard in the beauty industry and provide an amazing source of additional income for makeup professionals. There are even lash-extension boutiques that only offer lash-extension application services, and these boutiques are busy throughout the year.

Consultation

The eyes are one of the most delicate and sensitive areas of the face. They are also the first facial feature to react to sensitivities and allergies. Proper consultation is critical for a successful lash application. Have clients come in the day before their lash-application appointment for a 15-minute consultation to discuss what they should expect during the procedure. At this time have them complete a consultation form pertaining to eye conditions, sensitivities, product use, and expectations. Examine the eye area: If there is visible redness, swelling, itching, or crusting, the lash application should not be performed. The client should be referred to a physician or eye doctor to determine the cause. The condition should be cleared before you apply the lashes.

Some adhesives may have fumes that can cause a burning sensation to the eyes. During your consultation, you will be able to determine if sensitivity may be an issue for your client. If sensitivity seems likely, perform a test by applying one lash to each eye 24 hours before the application. At the application appointment, you can check for reaction.

The consultation is also the time to determine the client's desired outcome. This will help you determine the lash-extension length that will be necessary to achieve the desired look.

Contraindications

Due to the sensitivity of the eye area and the importance of healthy eyes, there are some situations in which eyelash extensions should not be applied. Never apply lash extensions to clients with the following conditions:

- Pregnancy
- Eye irritations
- Eye infections
- Eye allergies
- **Blepharitis**, an eye condition characterized by chronic inflammation of the eyelid
- **Glaucoma**, a disease in which the optic nerve is damaged and can lead to progressive, irreversible loss of vision
- Excessive tears
- Thyroid problems affecting lash growth or causing hair loss
- Asthma (Clients with asthma may be sensitive to the adhesive odor.) ☑ LO1

HERE'S A TIP

Clients who wear contact lenses should bring a pair of glasses to lash-application appointments. The eyes may be a bit irritated immediately following the procedure. Wearing glasses home will give the delicate eye area a chance to adjust to the luscious new lashes.

Preparation, Health, and Safety

Because this service is so close to the eye, safety is your number one priority. Follow all sterilization and disinfection guidelines for your equipment. In addition, incorporate as many single-use disposable products as possible. Wash your hands thoroughly before beginning the procedure.

Provide a comfortable place for your client to recline, and be sure the neck and head are adequately supported. This procedure can last up to 2 hours, and you want your client to be as comfortable as possible during that time.

- Have the client remove contact lenses before the procedure.
- Make sure you have a good light source, as this is important for proper application.
- Make sure saline or water is available close to your workstation in case you need to irrigate the eye for any reason. If adhesive gets in the eye, immediately flush with plenty of water and contact a physician. Adhesive should not come in contact with the skin. If this should occur, remove the adhesive immediately by gently using a small amount of adhesive remover. Then rinse thoroughly with water and pat dry.
- Clean and disinfect all tools before the procedure to ensure that you will not introduce bacteria into the client's eyes.
- Handle tweezers only by the handle, never the tip, and always have an extra pairs of tweezers available so you can disinfect one pair while you use the other pair on your next client.
- When removing lashes from their container, use clean tweezers rather than your fingers.
- Dispose of all leftover lash extensions. Never put potentially contaminated lashes back into the container with new ones.

CAUTION

The client should keep her eyes closed during the entire procedure and at no time should adhesive be allowed to enter the eye. If adhesive gets in the client's eye, follow emergency eye cleansing protocol: Flush with sterile eyewash solution and assist the client in washing her eyes with warm water for at least 15 minutes. Then seek medical attention immediately.

HERE'S A TIP

Before considering the use and placement of variations of lash lengths, become proficient in basic lash selection and application techniques!

Artificial Lashes

You can use lash extensions that are all one length, or for a softer look, you can use lashes that vary in length. Depending on the desired look and style, you may use from three to seven different lengths of lashes. Synthetic black lashes are the most common extensions used; however, many manufacturers carry lash extensions in a variety of colors for different occasions, events, and client requests.

Check the client's natural lash length and then select lashes based on the goal for the finished look.

- **Natural.** Select lashes slightly longer than the client's lashes. This makes the lashes appear fuller.
- **Feminine.** Select lashes about a third longer than the client's lashes. Increase the diameter to .20 mm for thickness and flair slightly longer at outside corners (**Figure 17–5**).
- **Dramatic/maximum.** Select lashes half again as long as the client's lashes. Use .20 to .25 mm diameter for thickness and effect (**Figure17–6**).

© Junial Enterprises/www.Shutterstock.com

▲ Figure 17–5 **Feminine lashes are one-third longer than the client's natural length.**

© claires/www.Shutterstock.com

▲ Figure 17–6 **Dramatic lashes are half again longer than the client's natural length.**

Types of Lashes

Artificial lashes not only come in a wide variety of lengths and diameters, they also can be found in strips and groups of lashes, referred to as *clusters* or *tabs*.

- Strip lashes are full strips that cover the length of the lash line and are applied as a full unit at one time (**Figure 17–7**).
- Tab lashes are groupings, or clusters, of lashes (2 to 5 in a group) that are applied using a similar technique as that used for individual lashes. Tab lashes create a fuller lash line in less time (**Figure 17–8**).

© Africa Studio/www.Shutterstock.com

▲ Figure 17–7 **Strip lashes take less time to apply.**

Tools

You will need a special toolkit for your lash extension procedures. For efficient treatments and preparation, it is recommended that you keep all supplies and tools together in one case or container.

Single-Use Supplies

For your protection, and the protection of your clients, use as many single-use items as possible. This will speed clean-up time, minimize the sterilization process, and promote consumer safety. Disposable supplies will include tissues, tape, eye pads, and cotton pads.

Prior to the start of every procedure, disinfect all nondisposable supplies and work areas. Some manufacturers recommend the use of a jade stone to hold the adhesive; if you use a jade stone, it must be disinfected between clients. Another option is to apply two strips of tape side by side on the jade stone or use a disposable adhesive holder and follow manufacturer's directions for its use.

Tweezers

Some manufacturers recommend only straight tweezers, while others recommend both straight and curved tweezers. Based on practice and experience you will find which type of tweezers you are most comfortable using. In any case, you will need two pair of tweezers for eyelash extension application, and the choice between straight and curved is all yours. Use the type of tweezers that is most comfortable for you (**Figure 17–9**).

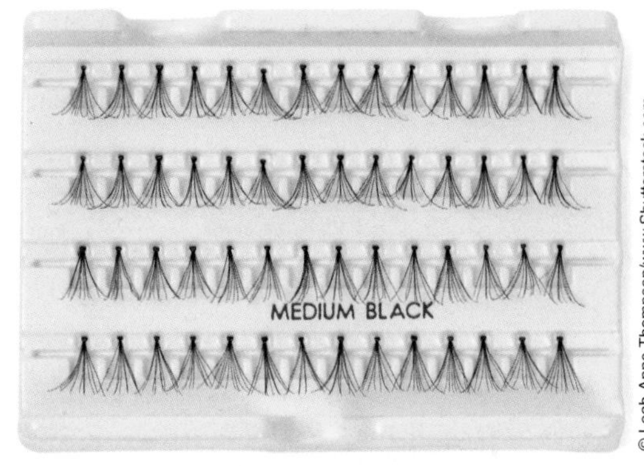

© Leah-Anne Thompson/www.Shutterstock.com

▲ Figure 17–8 **Tab lashes give a fuller, more natural look.**

Forced Hot Air

Forced warm or hot air is a great tool for speeding the drying time of lash adhesive. Always blow from the top of the lash down toward the nose. Be sure to keep in mind that this may not be a good idea for every client; blowing air into a client's eye may increase the risk of drying the cornea, increasing tearing, and irritate the eye.

© Milady, a part of Cengage Learning. Photography by Visual Recollection.

▲ Figure 17–9 **Use different types of tweezers when appropriate.**

Makeup Remover

For best results, the client should arrive to the appointment wearing no mascara or eye makeup. If your client is wearing makeup, it must be removed with an oil-free eye makeup remover. Oil-free makeup removers will minimize eye irritation and will not interfere with the lash adhesive.

Under-Eye Pads and Surgical Tape

Under-eye pads and surgical tape are used to tape the lower lash line and the upper lid in order to keep the eyelid in place and secure while you work. Gel under-eye pads are also available; they are often more comfortable than tape. Consider your own preferences and client safety as you select the technique you will employ.

Mini Procedure

Taping Technique

1. Trim the bottom quarter of the gel pad and set it aside.
2. Place the gel pad directly over the lower lashes, up to the lash line, but do not allow it to come into contact with the inner eye-rim.

(Continued)

CAUTION

Oil-free eye makeup remover is essential for properly cleansing the eye area before all eyelash procedures.

Mini Procedure

Taping Technique *(Continued)*

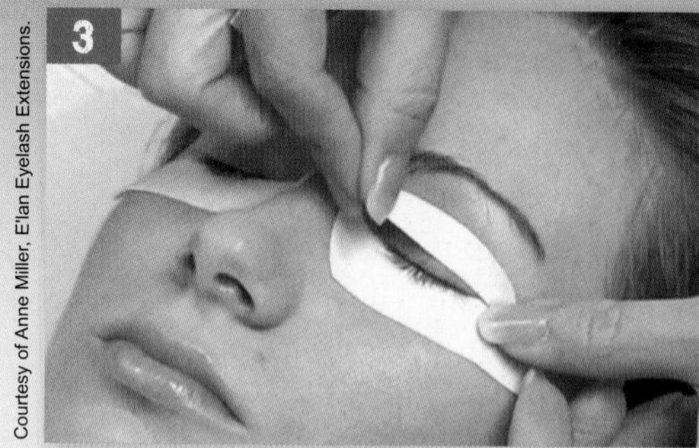

Courtesy of Anne Miller, E'lan Eyelash Extensions.

▲ Figure 17–10 Under-eye area with lower lashes taped to an eye pad.

3 Apply white surgical tape to cover any exposed lashes. The surface of the gel pad is made with a very fine-fibered fabric. The fibers near the upper curved line may become loose during the procedure, causing the upper lashes to stick to the fibers. Covering the upper edge of the pad with white surgical tape will prevent this from being an issue (Figure 17–10).

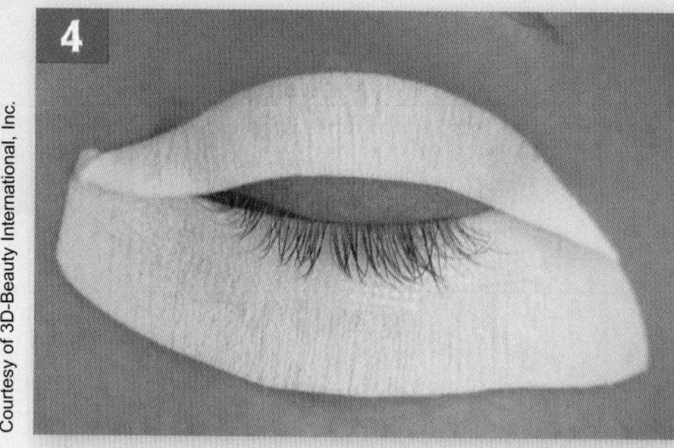

Courtesy of 3D-Beauty International, Inc.

▲ Figure 17–11 Eye secured with tape over and under the lashes.

4 Another option is to place the tape directly on the lower lashes and the skin, making an eye pad unnecessary. If you are not careful, removing the tape from the skin can cause skin irritation, even tearing of this delicate tissue, but this method does work effectively (Figure 17–11).

Adhesive

Lash adhesive comes with most lash extension kits, but it will need to be replenished frequently. Adhesives are available in a variety of different consistencies, ranging from gel to a more fluid liquid. Heavier gel adhesives are excellent for the beginner; they are easier to work with and take a longer time to dry and set. However, they do have a tendency to lump and clump at the application point. Fluid adhesives are a good choice for the expert lash technician since they dry very quickly and deliver a very natural look. Many manufacturers have excellent adhesive with a consistency between gel and liquid. Personal preference alone will determine your choice, and your preference will develop with practice (**Figure 17–12**). You will also need adhesive remover and an adhesive holder.

© Milady, a part of Cengage Learning. Photography by Visual Recollection.

▲ Figure 17–12 Lash adhesive is essential for the application of eyelash extensions.

Equipment

Keep in mind that your client will be lying down for as much as 1½ to 3 hours. For clients' optimal comfort, you will need a comfortable massage bed or a treatment chair with an adjustable headrest. You will also need a bedside table or cart to hold your supplies. ☑ LO2

PRACTICE

Before you attempt this service on a client, you must practice your technique. Experts recommend a minimum of 12 full applications prior to charging full price for lash application. One manufacturer has developed a very clever way to allow you to practice. You will need the following supplies:

- Plastic-type mannequin head
- Set of upper false eyelashes
- Set of lower false eyelashes and adhesive
- Colored electrical tape

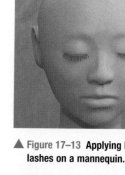

▲ Figure 17–13 Applying lower lashes on a mannequin.

Prepare your mannequin by applying the lower lashes to the lower rim of the mannequin eyelid (**Figure 17–13**). Next apply the eye gel pad as directed in Procedure 17–1, Applying Semipermanent Eyelash Extensions (**Figure 17–14**). Take the upper eyelash strip and set it on your mannequin along the brow bone. Carefully place a strip of colored electrical adhesive along the lash line of the false upper lashes (**Figure 17–15**). Pick up the strip adhered to the tape and reposition on the mannequin to simulate a client with closed eyes (**Figure 17–16**). You are now ready to practice lash extensions on a live subject (**Figure 17–17**).

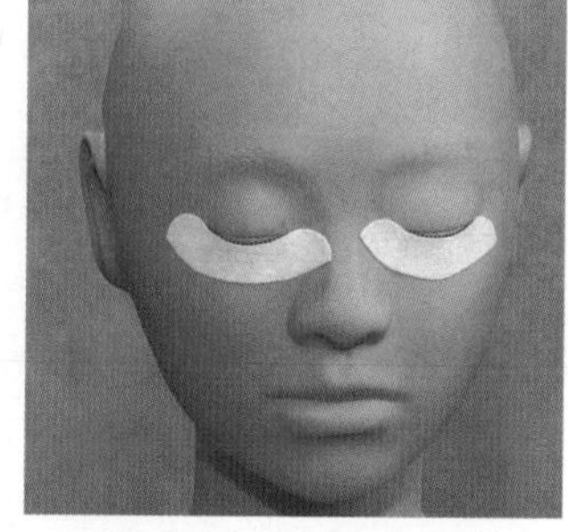

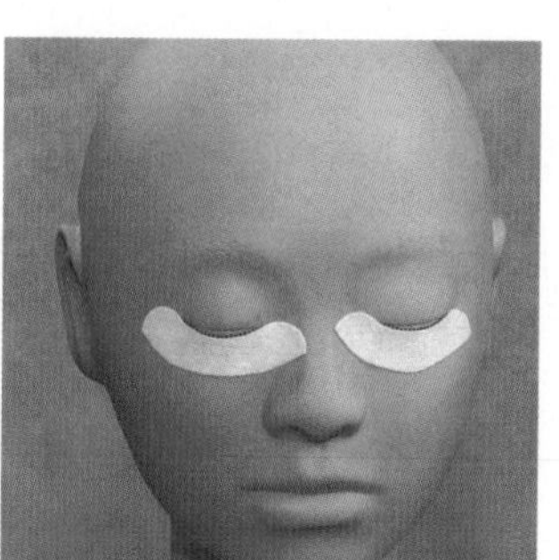

▲ Figure 17–14 Apply eye pad over lashes.

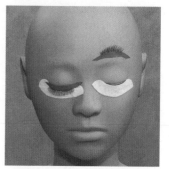

▲ Figure 17–15 Upper lashes adhered to tape.

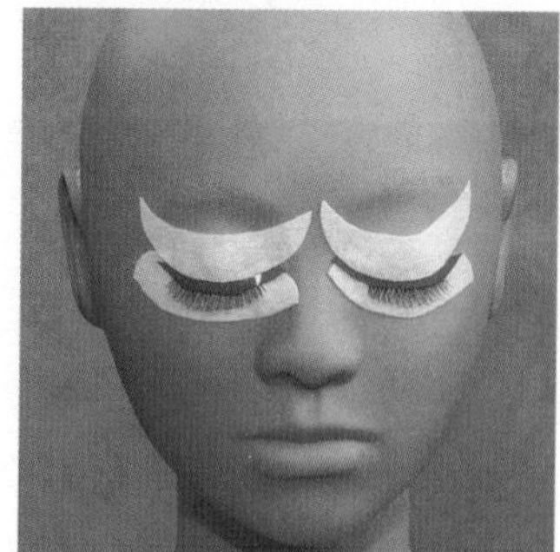

▲ Figure 17–16 Upper lashes adhered to simulate a closed eye.

PROCEDURE **17-1** APPLYING SEMIPERMANENT EYELASH EXTENSIONS SEE PAGE 417

TECHNIQUE VARIATIONS

Different lash lengths can be used to achieve a variety of different looks. Following are some suggestions for variations.

1. To make the eyes appear wider, apply three to five different lengths of eyelash extensions.
2. For an almond-shaped eye:
   a. Use the longest extension at the outside corner of the eye.
   b. Use the medium length to fill the center portion of the lashes.
   c. Use the shortest extensions at the inside of the eye. Example: 12 mm/11 mm/10 mm/9 mm.
3. For a larger, more open-eyed look:
   a. Use medium-length extensions at the outer portion of the eye.
   b. Use the longest extensions to fill in the center. Example: 8 mm/10 mm/12 mm/10 mm/8 mm.
   c. Use the shortest lash extensions at the inner corner.

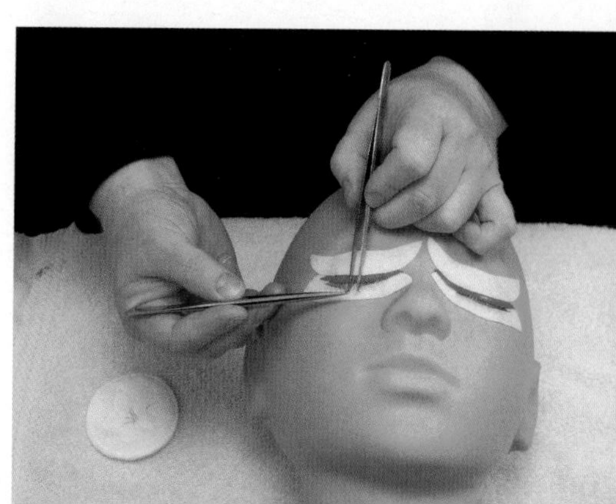

▲ Figure 17–17 A mannequin ready for practice.

4. To create a thick, lush, glamorous look (**Figure 17–18**):
   a. Apply long lash extensions evenly across the eye.
   b. Use a longer lash extension for every second or third lash. For example: alternate 12 mm/14 mm.

Lashes are available in 0.1 mm, 0.15 mm, 0.2 mm, and 0.25 mm thicknesses and lengths from 6 mm to 17 mm.

.1 mm is approximately 3/32 of an inch.

10 mm is approximately 13/32 of an inch.

Application Variations

Procedure 17–1, Applying Semipermanent Eyelash Extensions, describes how to apply lashes by alternating from one eye to the other and progressing from the outside in. The following method involves applying lashes to one eye at a time. This allows you to offer the client a break when you have completed one eye. No matter which technique is used, it is important that the lashes are applied evenly and in the proper direction.

Mini Procedure

Single Eyelash Application

When applying lashes to one eye at a time, follow these simple steps:

1. Start with the centermost lash application.
2. Next, proceed to the outermost lash. Then apply a lash halfway between the first two. Then apply a lash halfway between the center lash and the inner corner of the eye.
3. Once these are in place, go back to the center and start adding a lash next to each of those already in place, moving across the eyelash.
4. Repeat this step until you have applied all of the lashes.
5. Proceed to the other eye and repeat the process.

Courtesy of Anne Miller, E'lan Eyelash Extensions.

▲ Figure 17–18 A glamorous lash application.

After the Procedure: Home-Care Instructions

Artificial lashes will wear better and last longer if they are properly cared for at home. The following list provides general aftercare instructions for the client. Always be sure to follow the manufacturer's guidelines if they vary from this list, but these directives are a good starting point.

- You can maintain your regular cosmetics and cleansing routine; however, for 24 hours after the application, you should avoid contact with water, moisture, makeup, makeup removers, and so on.
- For 48 hours, avoid hot steam or swimming.
- Avoid using any product on the bonded area of your new lashes and avoid using oil-based products of any kind near the eyes, especially oil-based eye makeup remover.
- Do not rub your eyes or pick at the lashes.
- Do not use waterproof mascara. However, you can use water-based mascara on the tips of your lashes for a more dramatic look.

- Do not use mechanical eyelash curlers. These can damage lash extensions and break the bond of the adhesive.

Common Reasons Lash Extensions Fall Off

- Mascara residue compromises the contact between the eyelashes and the extensions.
- Product or oil residue on the eyelashes compromises the contact area between the eyelashes and the extensions.
- Actual eyelashes fall off due to the natural eyelash growth cycle.
- The technician used poor technique with inadequate lash bonding.
- Lashes come in contact with water too soon after application.

Correctly applied eyelashes will eliminate the need for mascara!

LASH REMOVAL

When removing the semipermanent lash extensions, take extra care to protect the eyes from the removal solution and to avoid taking natural lashes in the process. It is important to learn the proper removal procedure for semipermanent eyelash extensions because if an error occurs during application (e.g., with desired length), the makeup artist will need to remove and reapply the lashes.

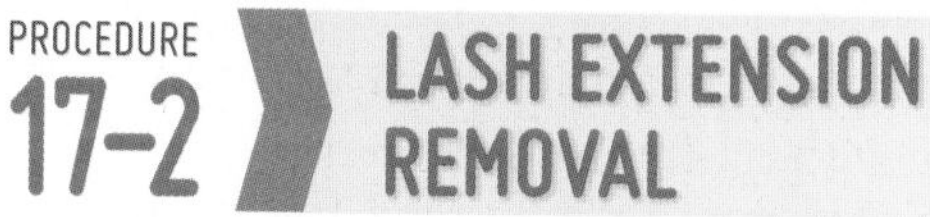

SEE PAGE 422

EYELASH PERMING

Permanent eyelash curling involves the use of specially formulated products that keep eyelashes curled for long periods of time without the use of eyelash curlers. Permanent eyelash curling can make the eyes appear more open, giving the lashes a longer, more youthful look that lasts for several weeks (**Figures 17–19** and **17–20**). When the permed lashes fall out, they are replaced by straight lashes and the effect of the perming disappears. Women are not the only clients for this procedure; men have caught on to the charming effect of curled eyelashes as well.

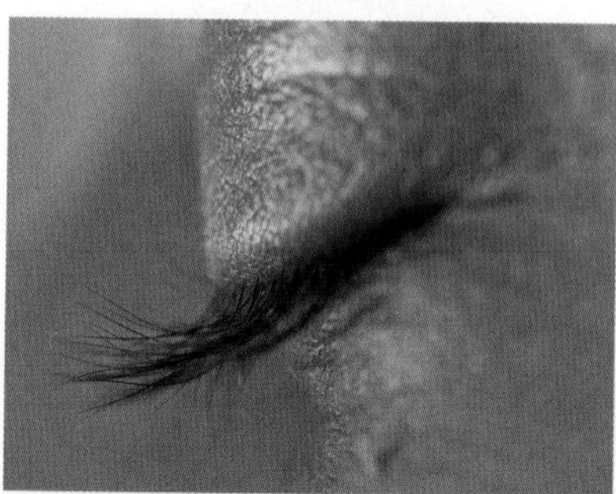

▲ Figure 17–19 **Eyelashes before a perming treatment.**

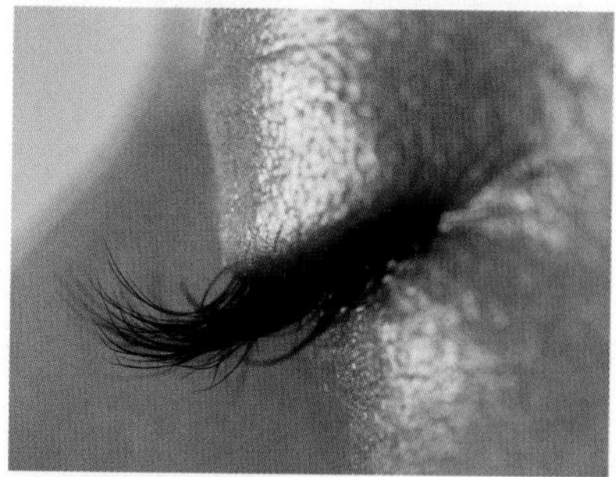

▲ Figure 17–20 **Eyelashes after a perming treatment.**

Consultation

Have the client come in for a 15-minute consultation 24 hours before the application appointment. Examine her eye area; if you see any redness, swelling, signs of conjunctivitis, or flaking, recommend that she be seen by her physician or eye doctor before you apply the lashes. Clients with glaucoma, sensitivity to perming solutions, or thyroid conditions that affect lash growth are not candidates for eyelash perming. Clients with recent vision-correction surgery should have clearance from their physician or wait until their eyes return to feeling normal.

To avoid an allergic reaction to the perming products, do a patch test. Follow the manufacturer's recommendations for this process and refer any reaction to the client's physician. Do not perm lashes that appear weak or brittle. As with any products that you use on or near the eyes, be sure to follow manufacturers' recommendations carefully. Failure to do so can result in ocular damage or blindness.

Contraindications

Clients with the following conditions should not seek lash perming:

- Pregnancy
- Eye irritations
- Eye infection
- Eye allergies
- Blepharitis
- Glaucoma
- Excessive tears
- Thyroid Conditions
- Asthma (Client with asthma may be sensitive to the perming-solution odor.) LO3

Preparation, Health, and Safety

Advise the client not to wear mascara or eye makeup to the appointment. Removing mascara right before perming can irritate the eye. Client's contact lenses should also be removed prior to the procedure. Wash your hands thoroughly before starting the procedure.

Place your client in a reclined position on a disinfected treatment chair or bed. Clean the lashes thoroughly with oil-free makeup remover and allow them to dry completely. This will ensure that the rods adhere to the lids.

Tools

Be sure that all equipment and supplies are prepared before beginning the service. Clean and disinfect your work area and utensils.

Single-Use Supplies

To prevent the spread of bacteria and viruses, disposable supplies are the best choice. You will need cotton pads, cotton swabs, eyelash rollers, applicator sticks, and toothpicks.

Small Scissors

Small delicate scissors are needed to cut cotton strips. Be sure that they are fully cleansed and disinfected between clients.

Makeup Remover

Oil-free makeup remover is the most effective product for thoroughly cleansing the lashes.

Lash Perming Products

Product used for eyelash perming have some similarities in function to regular hair perming products. Perming products first soften the hair follicle making it workable and easy to reshape. The products are designed so that the hair returns to its original firmness allowing it to retain the newly curled shape and conditioning it to maintain its health.

The following is a list of eyelash perming products:

- Perming Lotion
- Setting Lotion
- Conditioning Lotion
- Glue ☑ LO4

PROCEDURE 17-3 EYELASH PERMING SEE PAGE 424

STATE REGULATORY ALERT

Always check with your state licensing division to be sure that eyelash perming and eyelash tinting fall within your scope of practice.

Perming with Other Lash Procedures

In some cases, clients may want to combine other services—such as eyelash extensions or eyelash tinting—with eyelash perming. Unless otherwise indicated by a manufacturer, perform these procedures after you have permed the lashes according to the following guidelines.

- When adding semipermanent eyelash extensions, wait a minimum of 48 hours after perming the lashes to ensure that no residue from the perming solution remains on the lashes; be sure to use larger rollers to avoid over-curling. It is difficult to adhere lash extensions to tightly curled lashes.
- Eyelash tinting should be performed no sooner than 24 hours after eyelash perming. Clients who have had permanent eyeliner procedures should wait a minimum of 2 weeks before any other procedures; the eyes need to be completely healed to avoid loss of lashes, irritation, and heightened risk of infection. ☑ LO5

EYELASH TINTING

Eyelash tinting involves the use of vegetable dye, semipermanent dye, or permanent dye to darken the natural lashes, making them appear longer and thicker (**Figures 17–21** and **17–22**). The consistency of tinting products varies. Vegetable dyes are usually fluid, and hair dyes are a thicker cream. The cream consistency provides more thorough coverage and is easier to apply consistently and precisely. Most lash tints are formulated using the same ingredients as hair dyes and come in a wide variety of colors including black, blue-black, brown-black, brown, gray, blue, auburn, and chestnut.

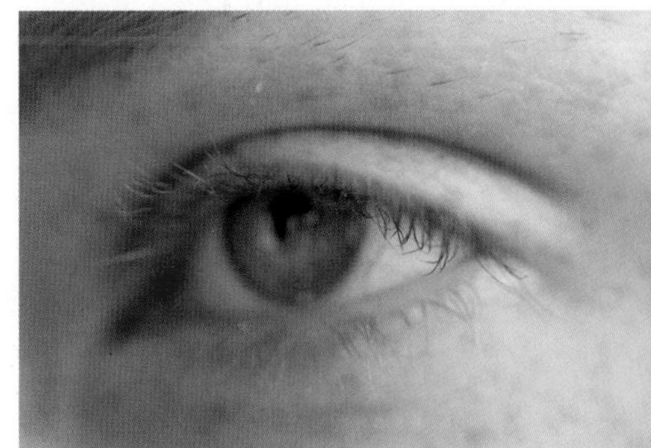

▲ Figure 17–21 **Eyelashes before tinting.**

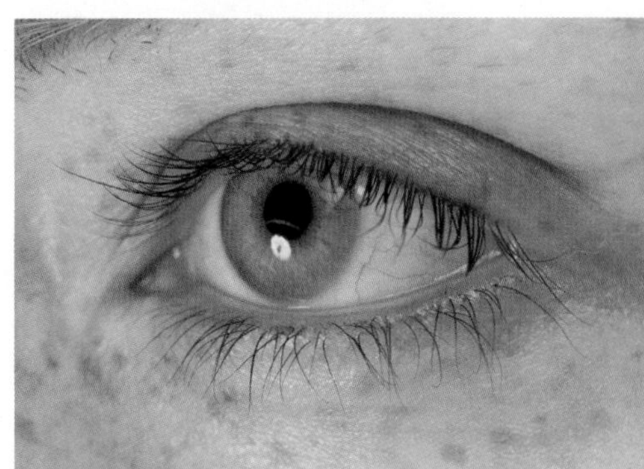

▲ Figure 17–22 **Eyelashes after tinting.**

Consultation

As with other eyelash treatments, a complete consultation is necessary prior to eyelash tinting services. When in doubt, a patch test is recommended 3 to 5 days before a full lash-tinting application. Be sure to review the type of product, likely results, and the procedure with the client.

Contraindications

Some situations indicate that eyelash tinting should not be performed. Clients with the following conditions should not have their lashes tinted:

- Pregnancy
- Eye irritations
- Eye infection
- Excessive tears ✓ LO6
- Eye allergies
- Blepharitis
- Glaucoma

STATE REGULATORY ALERT

In many states cream eyelash tint is prohibited for any tinting application, only the use of vegetable dyes are allowed. Check your local and state laws for specifications.

Preparation, Health, and Safety

Before performing an eyelash tinting procedure, complete a consultation with your client. If sensitivities seem likely, perform a patch test. Make sure your client is comfortable and seated so that her head can be slightly reclined.

Mix ¾ inch (2 centimeters) of tint cream with 2 to 4 drops of developer solution until the consistency is a creamy paste. Make sure that the consistency is not runny. Let the mixture set for at least 3 minutes while you prepare your client. For absolute accuracy follow the product manufacturers instructions.

CAUTION

Eyelash tinting requires attention to detail because if the tint gets into the eyes, it can cause severe eye irritation or blindness.

Tools

Be sure that all implements and supplies are clean, disinfected, prepared, and organized before beginning the service.

Single-Use Items

To prevent the spread of bacteria and viruses, disposable supplies are the best choice. You will need cotton pads or other protective pads, cotton swabs, cotton balls, birchwood sticks, and tissues.

Supplies

Supplies for the tinting application will include a small bowl or dampen dish, a tint brush, and petroleum jelly.

Products can include the following items:

- Auburn tint
- Blue-black tint
- Brown tint
- Deep black tint
- Graphite tint
- Tint developer
- Tint spot remover ✓ LO7

PROCEDURE 17-4 EYELASH TINTING SEE PAGE 428

Many amazing makeup techniques can be used to enhance your client's eyes. By accentuating the lashes with enhancements, perming, and tinting, you will improve the overall look of makeup applications. Each of these treatments will also provide your client with a striking, natural look, even without makeup. In addition, artificial eyelash treatments virtually guarantee return business.

Procedure 17-1

Applying Semipermanent Eyelash Extensions

Implements and Materials

You will need all of the following implements, materials, and supplies:

Utensils

- ☐ Bulb syringe or mini-fan (optional)
- ☐ Eye makeup remover (nonoil)
- ☐ Magnifying lamp or light
- ☐ Scissors
- ☐ Tweezers, curved (optional, but you need two pair of tweezers)
- ☐ Tweezers, straight pointed tip (must have)

Single-use Items

- ☐ Cotton swabs
- ☐ Micro swabs
- ☐ Paper towels
- ☐ Under-eye pads (single-use, disposable)

Products

- ☐ Surgical tape
- ☐ Adhesive (for professional use only)
- ☐ Adhesive holder (sterilized or disposable)
- ☐ Adhesive remover
- ☐ Assortment of individual synthetic eyelashes

Optional Supplies

- ☐ Heated eyelash curler (optional)
- ☐ Moisture-barrier lash coating

Preparation

- Perform

PROCEDURE 17-1 PRE-SERVICE SEE PAGE 144

1 Set up the facial lounge and treatment room. Most clients do not dress down for this procedure.

2 Gather supplies.

3 Review the client's history with her and have her read and sign a consent form.

4 Review the client's expectations and the procedure.

5 Confirm that the client has removed her contact lenses.

Procedure 17-1 *(continued)*

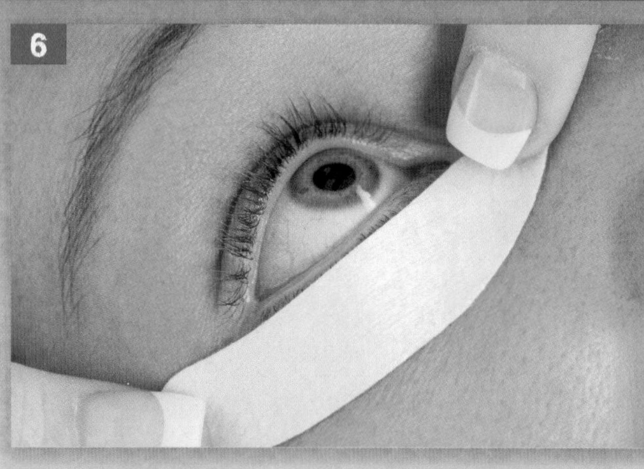

Procedure

6 Trim the lower quarter of the soothing eye pads, saving the extra pieces. Standing behind the client's head, have the client open her eyes and look upwards toward you. Remove the gel pads from their protective backing and position them under each eye, covering the lower lash line and being careful not to let the eye pad come into contact with the client's inner eye-rim. Check for comfort. Then apply surgical tape to cover any exposed lashes and fibers.

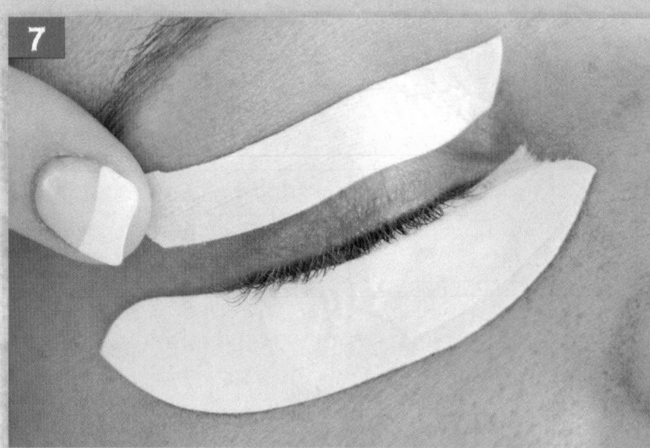

7 Have the client close her eyes. Apply the remaining section of the eye gel pad at the crease of the upper lid. This helps remind the client to keep her eyes closed during the procedure.

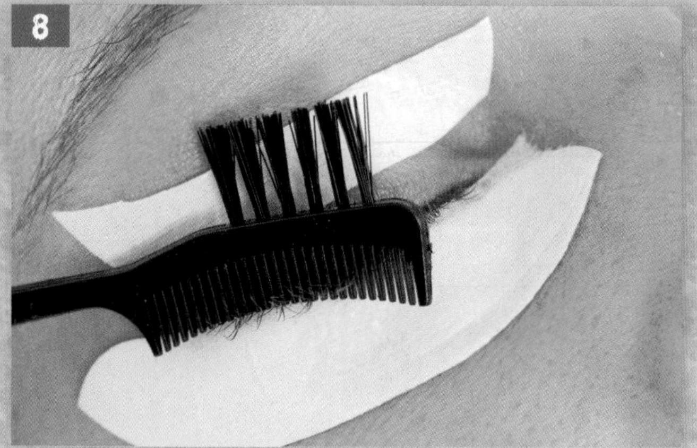

8 Optional: Gently comb through the lashes to straighten them and to remove any loose lashes.

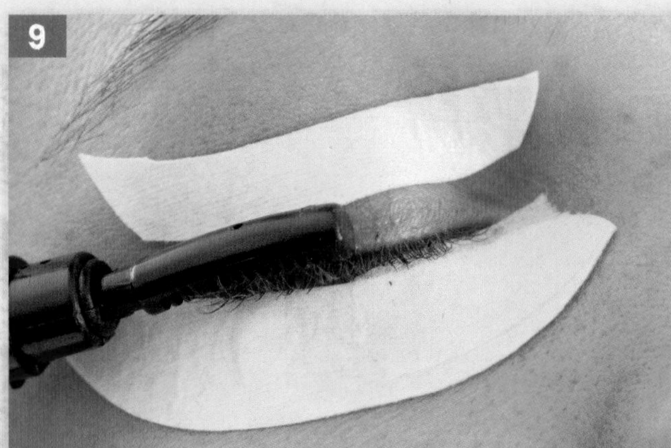

9 Optional: You may want to use a heated eyelash curler for straightening lashes that are curled or twisted. Keep in mind that this effect is only temporary and will not have an impact on the natural-lash growth pattern.

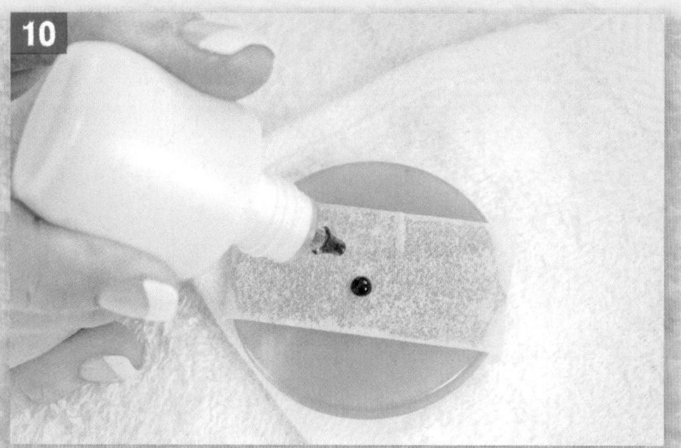

10 Place a drop of adhesive onto the taped and disinfected jade stone, tile, or a disposable container. Choose the lashes that suit your client best and place them onto the lash pad.

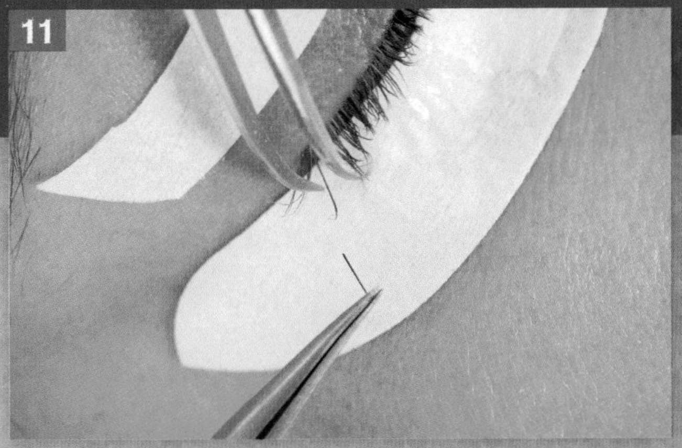

11 Isolate a single lash, beginning with the outside corner of the eye and using the curved or straight tweezers in your nondominant hand.

12 With a second set of tweezers in your dominant hand, pick up a lash extension by the tapered end of the lash. Gently swipe about $^2/_3$ of the thick end of the lash through the adhesive, blotting any excess adhesive off of the lash.

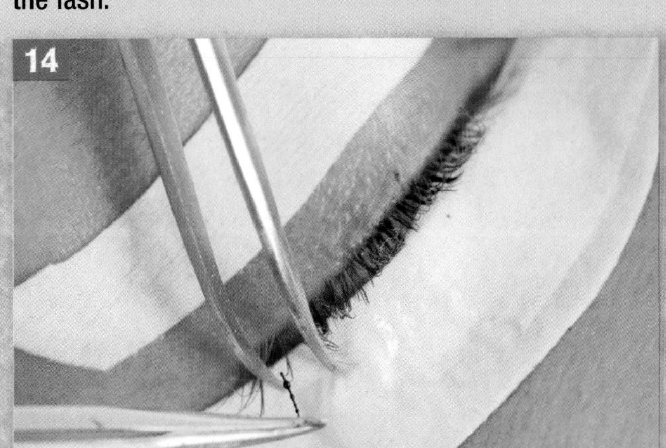

13 Leave enough adhesive so you can see tiny droplets along the length of the lash extension.

CAUTION

Keep the adhesive from coming into contact with the skin or the eye.

14 Apply the lash extension to the isolated lash. For best results, hold the lash and tweezers at a 45-degree angle. Place the extension on top of the lash roughly .05 mm to .1 mm from the base of the lash. Do not apply it at the base of the lash because this can cause skin irritation or breakage.

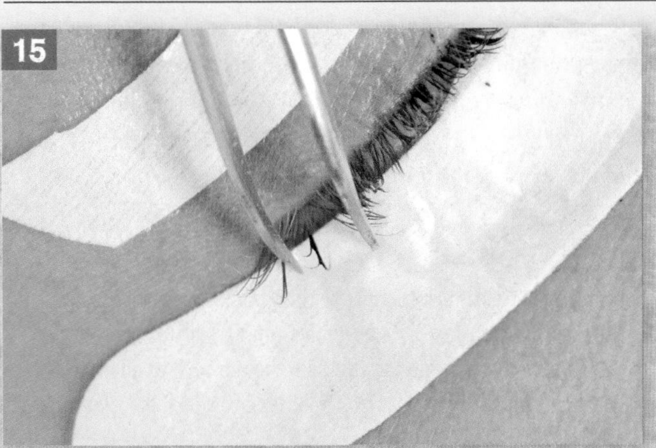

15 Using the backside of the tweezers, gently spread the adhesive and smooth out any excess droplets to ensure a natural, flawless appearance. The J curl (lashes curved in the shape of a J with the blunt end at the bottom and the tapered end at the top) should be curved in the direction of the natural lash. Allow 5 to 10 seconds for the adhesive to dry.

16 Optional: To prevent sticking to adjacent lashes or clumping, dry the lash with gentle puffs of air with a bulb syringe or a mini-fan while the lash is still isolated.

Procedure 17-1 *(continued)*

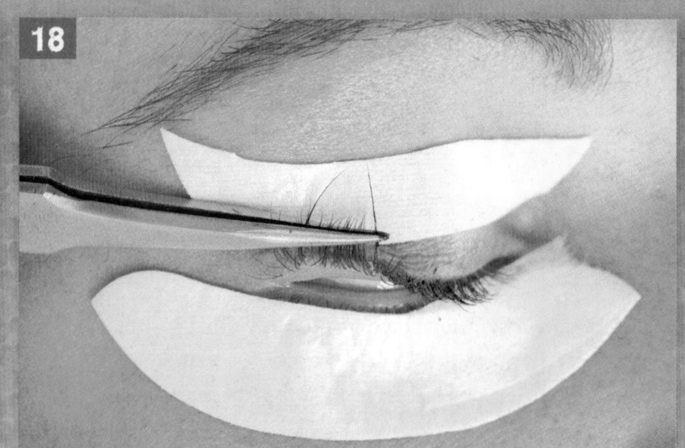

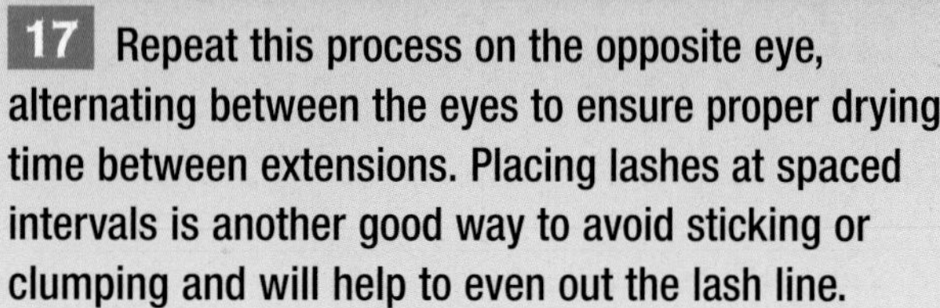

17 Repeat this process on the opposite eye, alternating between the eyes to ensure proper drying time between extensions. Placing lashes at spaced intervals is another good way to avoid sticking or clumping and will help to even out the lash line.

18 Check for sticking by grasping a group of lashes with the tweezers. Turn the lash line back just enough to expose the inside of the lash line. You should check for sticking several times during the procedure.

19 If a client's lashes are stuck together, use a clean micro swab or tweezers to gently separate them. You may need to use a small amount of lash-adhesive remover on the swab to break the bond. Alternatively, you can use your tweezers to gently pull stuck lashes apart, or you can remove them using the removal technique and then reapply.

CAUTION

Once the lashes are in place, perform any necessary trimming with great care. Place your client in a reclined position, and have her close her eyes. Trimming can be kept at a minimum by selecting the proper lash lengths before application.

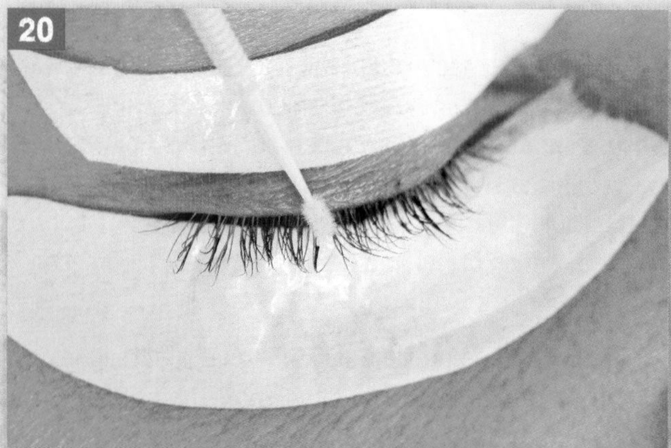

20 Once all lashes are in place, wait 10 minutes for the adhesive to completely set up and then apply a coat of protective coating solution with a disposable brush. Allow this to dry completely—at least 5 minutes—before moving to the next step.

SERVICE TIP

Many manufacturers suggest coating the lashes with a special solution that acts as a moisture barrier for the first 24 hours. Before applying this solution, be sure to allow the adhesive to set up at least 10 minutes after lash placement.

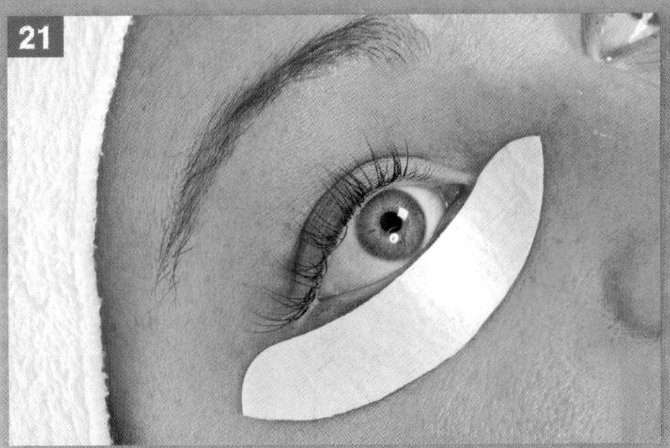

21 If you used the technique that tapes the lower lashes to the gel pad, remove the pad now.

22 Gently remove the gel pad, removing the strips of tape first and the gel pad last to avoid pulling out lower lashes that may be tucked between the pad and tape.

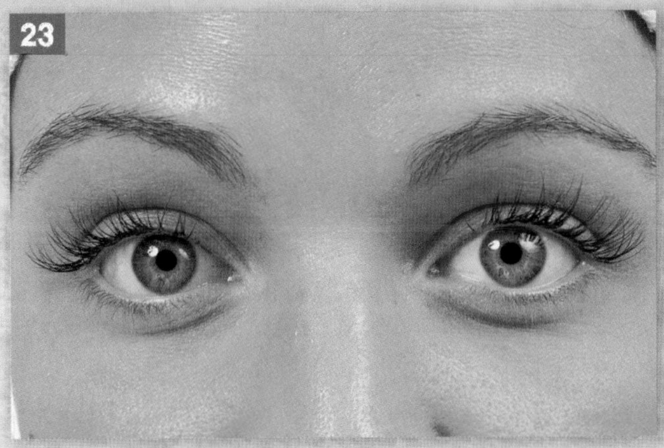

23 The completed eyelash extension look.

Post-Service ☑ LO8

• Complete PROCEDURE 7-2 POST-SERVICE SEE PAGE 148

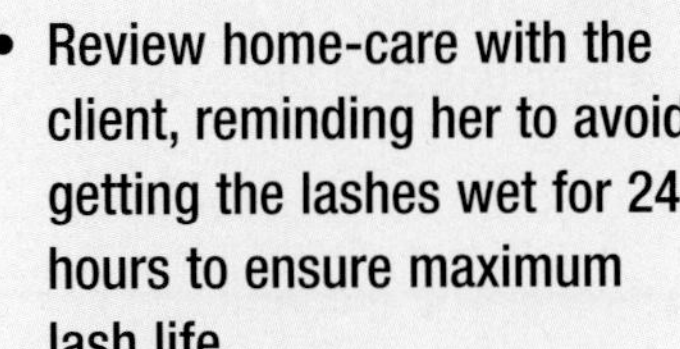

- Review home-care with the client, reminding her to avoid getting the lashes wet for 24 hours to ensure maximum lash life.
- Remind the client not to use waterproof mascara; removing it can result in loss of lashes.

Procedure 17-2

Lash Extension Removal

Implements and Materials

You will need all of the following implements, materials, and supplies:

- **Utensils**

- [ ] Headband or hair clip
- [ ] Magnifying lamp or light

- **Single-use Items**

- [ ] Cotton swabs
- [ ] Micro swabs
- [ ] Paper towels
- [ ] Under-eye pads (single-use, disposable)

- **Products**

- [ ] Clear surgical tape
- [ ] Adhesive holder (sterilized or disposable)
- [ ] Adhesive remover

Preparation

- Perform

PROCEDURE 7-1 PRE-SERVICE SEE PAGE 144W

1 Set up facial lounge and treatment room. Most clients do not dress down for this procedure.

2 Gather supplies.

3 Review the client's history with her and have her read and sign a consent form.

4 Review the client's expectations and the procedure.

5 Confirm that the client has removed her contact lenses.

Procedure

6 Ask your client to sit upright for the procedure to prevent adhesive remover from entering the eyes and so that you can clearly see the lash line and the extension.

7 Clip her hair back.

8 Protect the under-eye area with gel pads.

9 Saturate two large swabs with adhesive remover. Gel-type remover is preferred; if you are using liquid remover, blot off any excess liquid with a paper towel.

10 Gently hold the swabs on both sides of the lash for approximately 60 to 90 seconds. Then stroke the lash in a gentle outward motion until the lash is completely removed.

11 Repeat step 10 until the bond is dissolved and all eyelash extensions have been removed.

A. For single-lash removal:

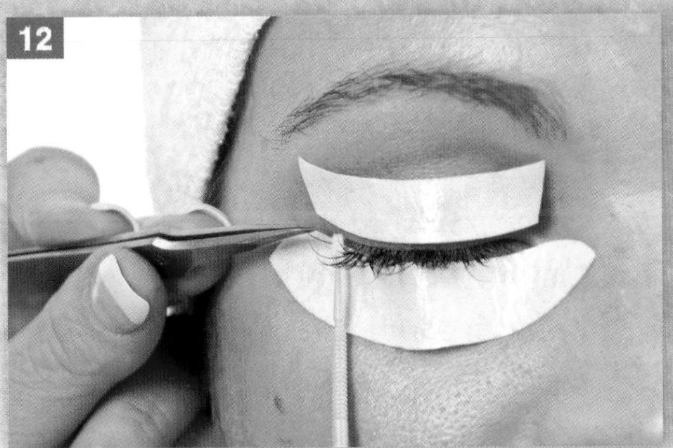

12 Grasp the eyelash extension at the tip with the tweezers.

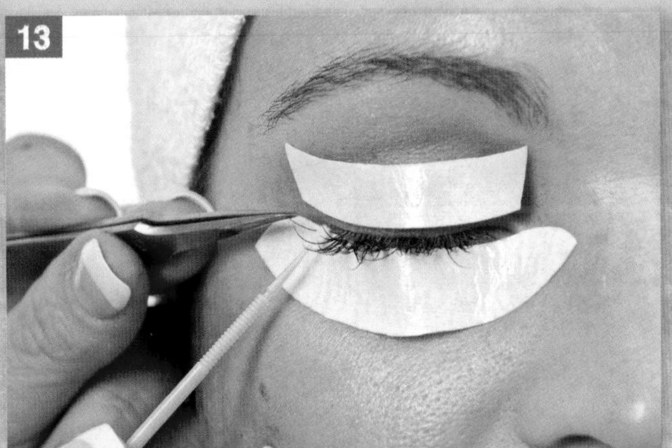

13 Pull the lash back gently.

14 Clean off any residue with gentle cleanser, lash toner, or a protein remover pad.

SERVICE TIP

You may need to clean the lashes with a fresh remover swab to remove any adhesive residue left on the lash.

CAUTION

If lower lashes are taped to the gel pad and you do not remove the tape before removing the gel pad, the client may lose lashes.

Post-Service ☑ LO9

- Complete PROCEDURE 7-2 POST-SERVICE SEE PAGE 148

Give the client any home-care instructions in writing.

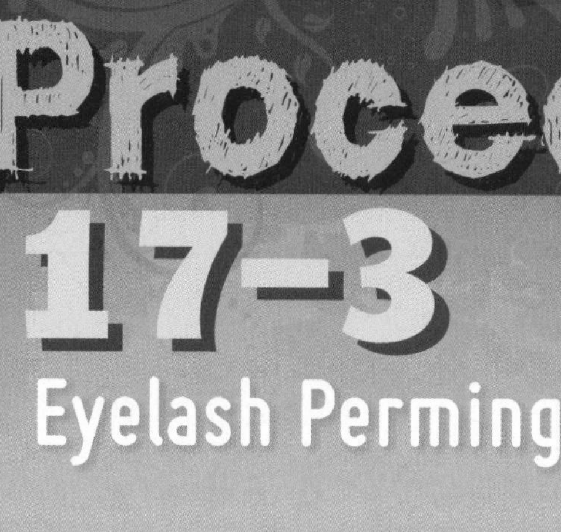

Procedure 17-3
Eyelash Perming

Implements and Materials

You will need all of the following implements, materials, and supplies:

Utensils

- ☐ Bowl of warm water
- ☐ Clean towels
- ☐ Hand mirror
- ☐ Oil-free makeup remover
- ☐ Pre-glued eyelash rollers
- ☐ Timer
- ☐ Toothpicks

Single-use Items

- ☐ Applicator sticks
- ☐ Cotton pads
- ☐ Cotton swabs

Products

- ☐ Cleanser
- ☐ Conditioning lotion
- ☐ Glue
- ☐ Perming lotion
- ☐ Setting lotion

SERVICE TIP

Pre-curl the lashes with a lash curler to help adhere lashes to the roller.

CAUTION

Do not use hair perming solution on or near the eyes, as this can cause blindness and damage to the skin.

Preparation

- Perform

PROCEDURE 7-1 PRE-SERVICE SEE PAGE 144

1 Set up facial lounge and treatment room. Most clients do not dress down for this procedure.

2 Gather supplies.

3 Review the client's history with her and have her read and sign a consent form.

4 Review the client's expectations and the procedure.

5 Confirm that she has removed her contact lenses.

Procedure

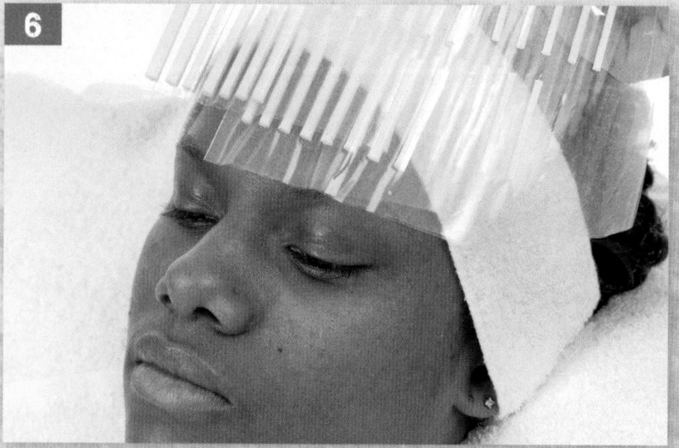
6

6 Use the following guidelines to select the roller size:

- Smaller rollers are best for shorter eyelashes or if a tighter curl is desired.
- Medium rollers are the most commonly used for a good all-around curl.
- Large rollers are best for longer lashes or a looser curl.

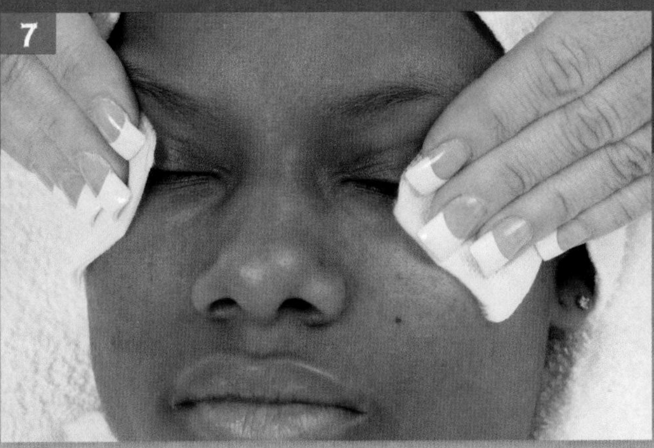

7 Cleanse the eyelashes, removing all eye makeup.

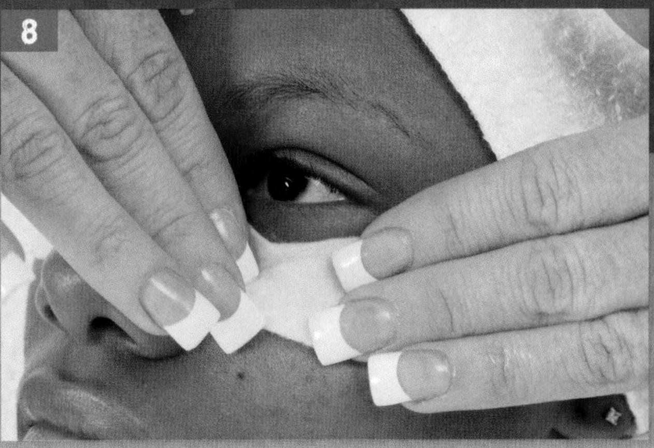

8 Place a damp cotton pad on the lower lid to prevent fumes from irritating the client's eyes.

SERVICE TIP

If you have a facial steamer, use it after step 7 to aid in creating heat, but keep it well away from the client.

SERVICE TIP

For very coarse lashes, apply perming solution to lashes for 3 to 5 minutes before starting the procedure. Rinse and remove. Then start the perming process.

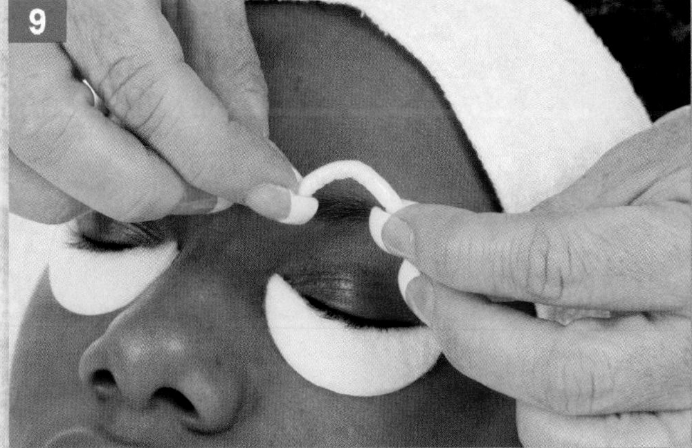

9 The rollers are self-adhesive so be careful to handle them only at the tips. Bend the roller slightly to fit the shape of the eyelid.

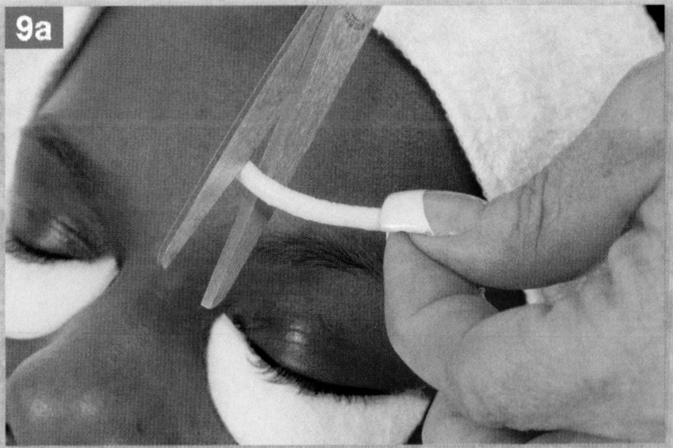

9a Trim the roller to the appropriate length of the eyelid.

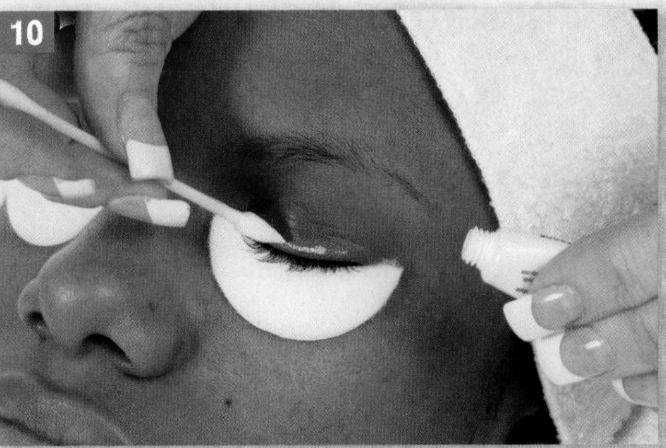

10 Apply eyelash perming glue in a line at the base of the lashes.

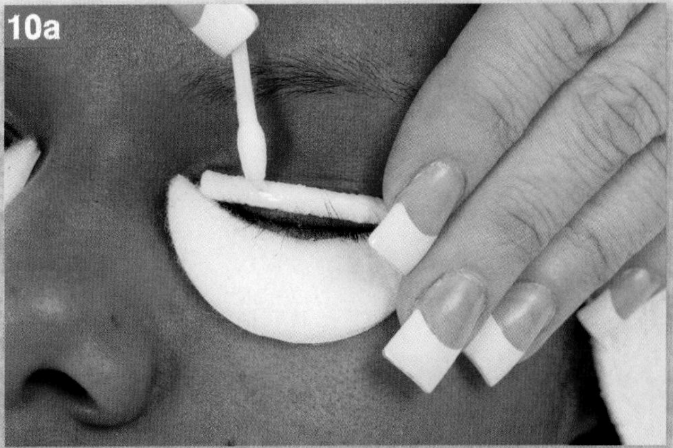

10a Position the roller as close as possible to the root of the lashes. After positioning the roller, add more glue on the top of the roller.

Procedure 17-3 *(continued)*

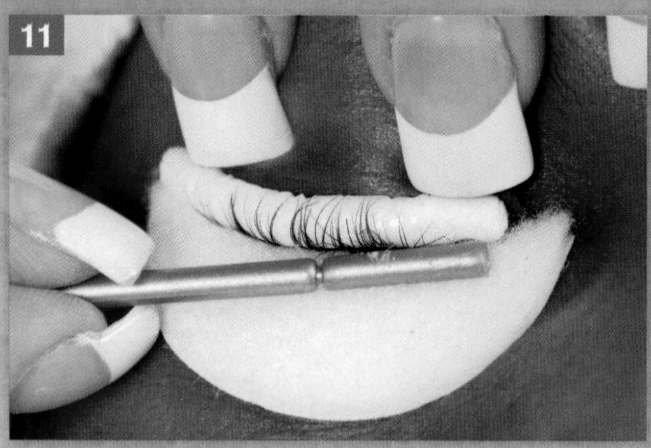

11 Using the applicator, carefully press the lashes on the roller one at a time to avoid overlapping or crossing of lashes.

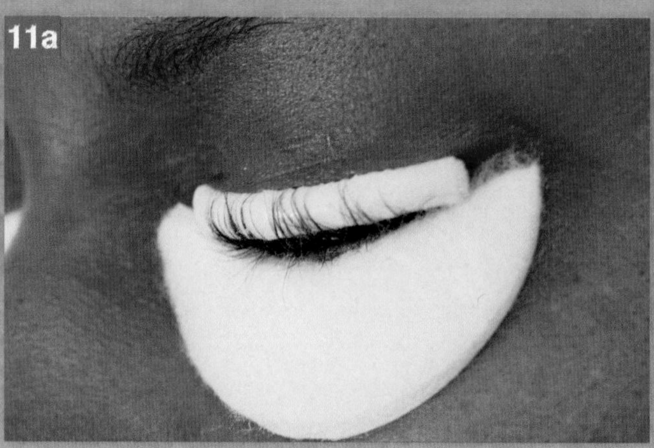

11a Make sure that the lower lashes are not curled onto the roller.

12 Apply perm solution with a cotton swab or manufacturer's applicator across the lashes that are adhered to the roller. Avoid contact with the skin. Carefully follow manufacturer's instructions for processing; depending on the kit, timing ranges anywhere from 8 to 15 minutes.

13 Check lashes by separating one or two from the roller with a toothpick. If you do not yet see the curl you are trying to achieve, leave the lashes on the roller for 2 to 3 minutes longer. Wipe off any excess perming lotion and rinse thoroughly following manufacturer's guidelines. Blot dry.

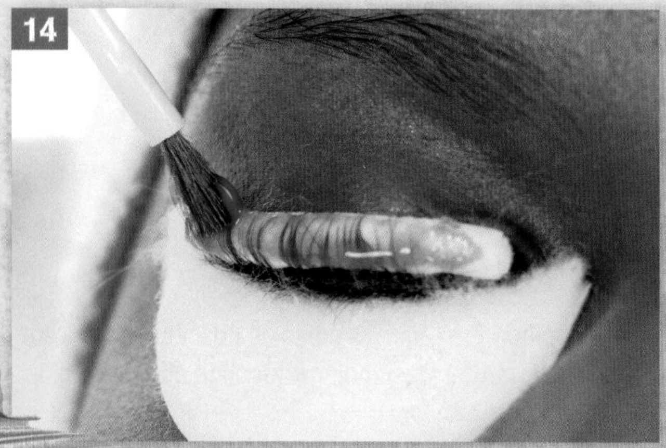

14 Apply setting or neutralizer lotion to the lashes with the application stick. Leave neutralizer on according to manufacturer's instructions, generally 5 to 10 minutes.

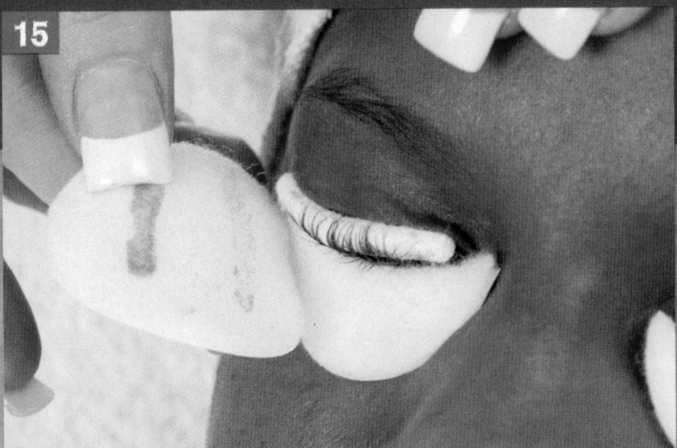

15 Remove setting lotion with wet cotton-tipped swabs or wet cotton rounds, rinsing thoroughly.

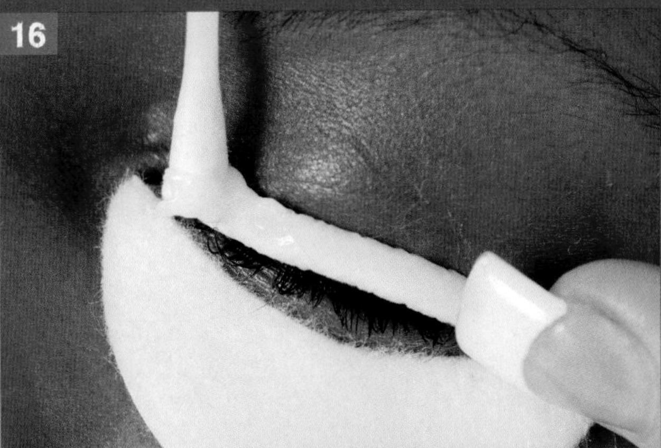

16 If the kit includes a post-treatment lotion, apply it now with an applicator stick or cotton swab. Let lotion set for 5 minutes or according to manufacturer's instructions.

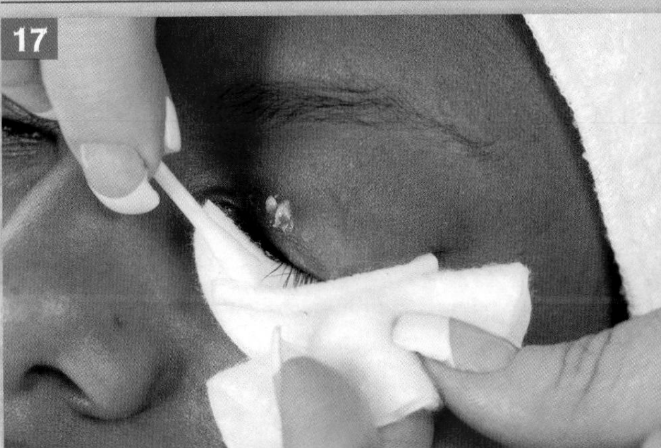

17 Use cleanser and gently swipe the upper part of the roller, touching the eyelid. Using a damp cotton-tipped swab, clean the eyelid from side to side. Slowly roll the roller downward with the cotton swab, freeing the lash from the roller.

CAUTION

Do not let any perming solution enter the client's eyes or touch her skin.

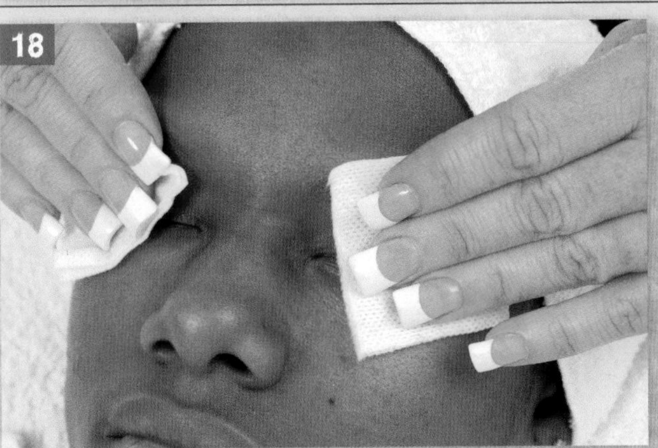

18 Clean lashes with warm, damp cotton or gauze pads.

19 The finished look.

Post-Service ☑ LO10

- Complete PROCEDURE 7-2 POST-SERVICE SEE PAGE 148
- Provide the client with home-care instructions. It is best to let the lashes rest for 24 hours prior to applying mascara.
- Be sure to dispose of perm rods.

Procedure 17-4
Eyelash Tinting

Implements and Materials

You will need all of the following implements, materials, and supplies:

- **Brushes**
  - ☐ Tint brush
- **Utensils**
  - ☐ Brush cleaner
  - ☐ Small bowl or dampen dish
- **Single-use Items**
  - ☐ Birchwood sticks
  - ☐ Cotton balls
  - ☐ Cotton pads or other protective pads
  - ☐ Cotton swabs
  - ☐ Tissues
- **Products**
  - ☐ Auburn tint
  - ☐ Blue-black tint
  - ☐ Brown tint
  - ☐ Deep black tint
  - ☐ Graphite tint
  - ☐ Petroleum jelly
  - ☐ Tint developer
  - ☐ Tint spot cleanser
  - ☐ Tint spot remover

Preparation

- Perform

PROCEDURE 7-1 PRE-SERVICE SEE PAGE 144

Procedure

1 Seat your client in a chair with her head slightly tilted. Mix ¾ inch (2 centimeters) of tint cream with 2 to 4 drops of developer solution until the consistency is a creamy paste. Make sure that the consistency is not runny. Let the mixture set for at least 3 minutes while you prepare your client. For absolute accuracy follow the product manufacturers instructions.

2 Put on gloves. Cleanse eyelashes and eyebrows thoroughly. Lashes and brows should be free of oil and makeup.

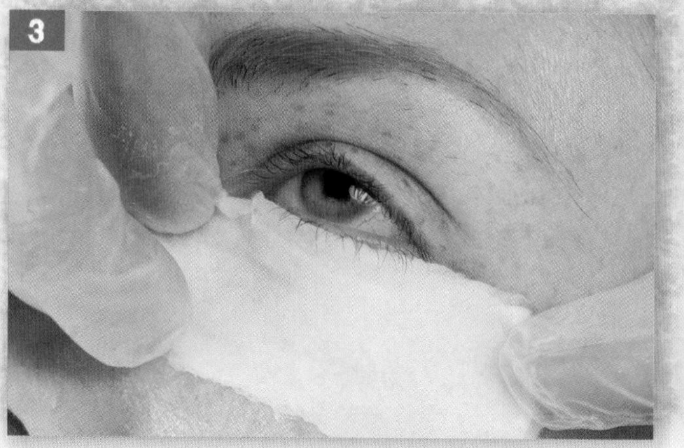

3 With your client looking upward, apply petroleum jelly under the lower eyelid and place protection pad under the lower lid. This will prevent the tint from staining the skin.

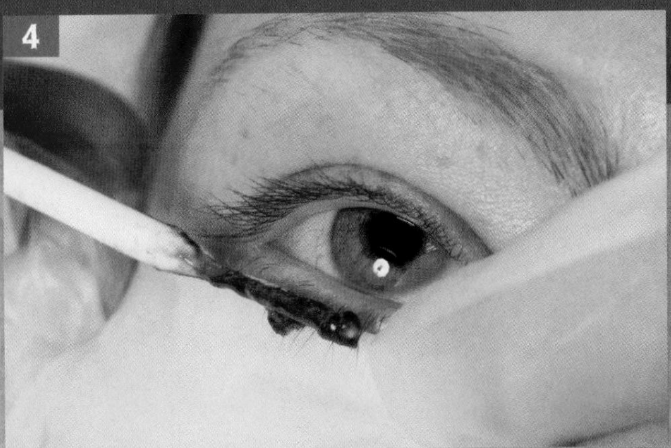

4 Using a tint brush or birchwood stick, apply cream tint to lower lashes on both eyes. Carefully apply tint from the lash base to the lash tip as well as on the small lashes at the corners of the eye. Instruct the client to close her eyes until the application and removal process is completed.

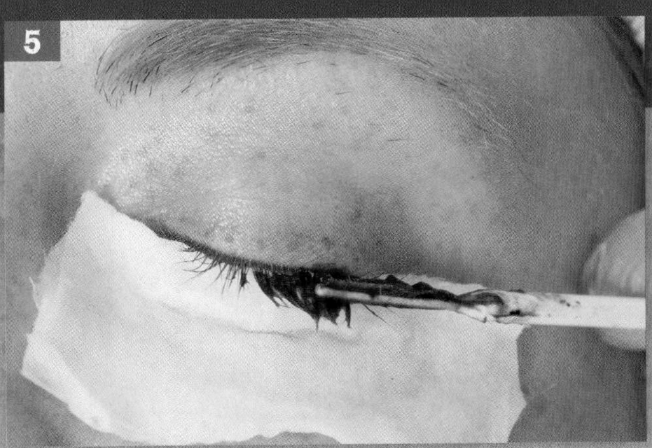

5 Instruct the client to close her eyes until the application and removal process is completed. Apply cream tint to the upper lashes from the base to the tip, making sure to include the small lashes in the corners of the eye.

6 Use a cotton swab with tint spot remover to remove any excess from the skin.

7 Allow the client to rest with her eyes closed while the color develops for approximately 10 minutes.

8 Remove protection pads from the under-eye area.

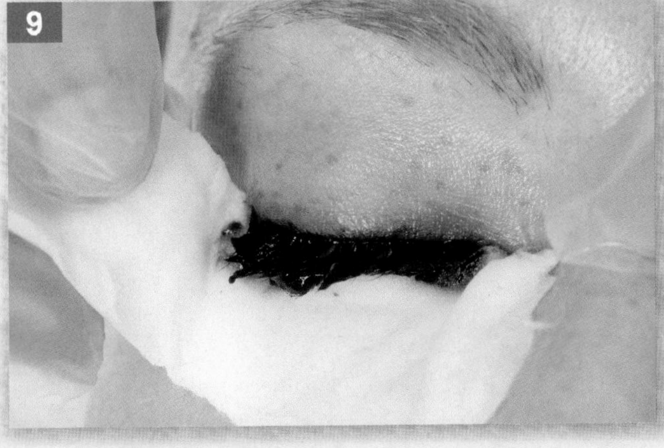

9 Use dampened cotton with warm water to remove product until no residue is visible. Make sure that your client keeps her eyes closed until the process is completed.

Procedure 17-4 *(continued)*

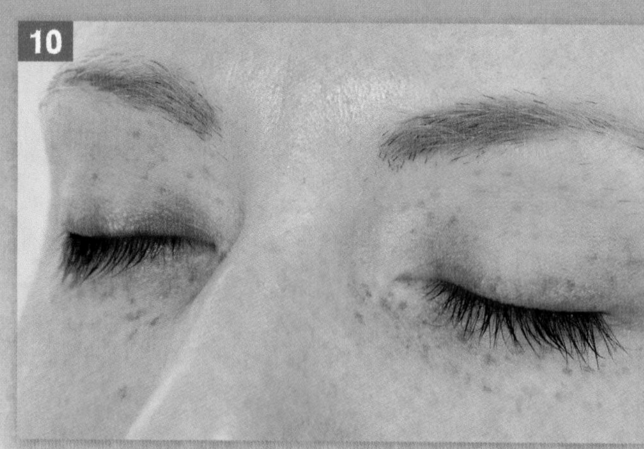

10 Lovely dark lashes will hold their color for about 6 weeks!

SERVICE TIP

Eyelash tint can also be used to darken eyebrows. Apply in a similar manner, one hair at a time. Allow only 3 to 4 minutes for processing.

Post-Service ☑ LO11

- Complete PROCEDURE 7-2 POST-SERVICE SEE PAGE 148

Review Questions

1. During which stage of hair growth are hairs actively growing?
2. Why is it important to perform a complete consultation before any eyelash service?
3. If there is any visible redness, swelling, itching, or crusted areas, when should the lash application be performed?
4. List contraindications for receiving eyelash enhancement treatments.
5. What action do you take if eyelash adhesive, perming, or tinting product enters the eye?
6. What type of eye makeup remover is required for properly cleansing the eye area before all eyelash procedures?
7. What technique is used to make eyes appear wider with eyelash extensions?
8. What is the result of artificial lashes coming in contact with water too soon after application?
9. How far in advance should a lash perming consultation be performed?
10. How soon after eyelash perming can an eyelash tinting treatment be performed?

Chapter Glossary

anagen	First stage of hair growth during which new hair is produced and actively growing.
blepharitis	Eye condition characterized by chronic inflammation of the eyelid.
catagen	The transitional stage of hair growth between active growth (anagen) and the resting stage (telogen); lasts for about 2 weeks.
glaucoma	Disease in which the optic nerve is damaged, leading to progressive, irreversible loss of vision.
telogen	Resting stage of hair growth.

Chapter 18 Advanced Makeup Techniques

Chapter Outline

Learning Objectives

After completing this chapter, you will be able to:

- ✓ **LO1** Recognize Avant-garde Makeup techniques, its special features, characteristics, and purposes.
- ✓ **LO2** Distinguish Fantasy Makeup techniques, its special features, characteristics, and purposes.
- ✓ **LO3** Identify Permanent Makeup techniques, its special features, characteristics, and purposes.
- ✓ **LO4** Understand Mortuary Makeup techniques, its special features, characteristics, and purposes.
- ✓ **LO5** Identify Special Effects Makeup techniques, its special features, characteristics, and purposes.
- ✓ **LO6** Identify Mendhi Makeup techniques, its special features, characteristics, and purposes.

Key Terms

Page number indicates where in the chapter the term is used.

areola
pg. 439

avant-garde
pg. 435

decedents
pg. 439

fantasy makeup
pg. 436

henna
pg. 442

Mendhi makeup
pg. 442

mortuary makeup
pg. 439

niches
pg. 435

non-thermogenic makeup
pg. 440

permanent makeup (permanent cosmetics, dermapigmentation, micropigmentation, cosmetic tattooing)
pg. 437

prosthetic makeup
pg. 441

special effects makeup
pg. 440

Courtesy of Jake Galvez.

Career Profile

Christian Mitchell created a career for himself with a relentless passion for makeup and the art of the industry. Christian began his career working as a Makeup artist for MAC. In his more current career, he has worked with people like Kembre Pfahler from Voluptuous Horror of Karen Black. As he worked his way from the ground on up, he learned through trial and error. Today, he continues to explore all the makeup industry has to offer.

"I studied Fine Arts and Display and Exhibit Design at the Fashion Institute of Technology, SUNY. It was the early 1990s and the club scene in New York was extremely colorful. I began experimenting more and more with makeup on my own face and heading out to clubs like the Pyramid, Disco 2000 at Limelight, and Adel Vice. After graduating from FIT, I found myself working in a display studio and feeling uninspired. I was buying my personal makeup at a small boutique. I started to talk to the artists there who encouraged me to apply as a makeup artist. I had no professional experience, but I was hired a few weeks later.

"I worked for several years as a makeup artist, eventually becoming the manager of a new concept store. After a few years, I wanted to try something different and moved to Miami as the Resident Trainer for my company and after a year there, managed the store in South Beach. It was only a year later that I was asked by the company to move back to New York to work in the Artist Relations Department and focus on Master Classes. It is now 10 years later and I am still working in the Artist Relations Department, with a much bigger team, focusing on our Membership Program globally. I ended my freelance career several years ago, but I continue to experiment on my own and learn from the masters in the industry.

"In my current career, I've had the pleasure of working with some of the best talents in the industry—many have become personal friends that continue to inspire me. One of the highlights of my career was working with Kembre Pfahler of the band Voluptuous Horror of Karen Black. In addition, working with the renowned French makeup artist Topolino inspired me to look at makeup artistry a little bit differently.

"I would encourage every artist out there to always push boundaries and not believe what you hear until you try it for yourself."

Courtesy of Christian Mitchell

When someone says the word *makeup*, certain images automatically come to mind: brushes, products, colors, eyes, lips, perfect skin tone, beauty, fashion, and perfection. These are just a few simple terms to describe a profession full of vibrancy, life, excitement, and unexpected changes and challenges. Becoming a successful professional makeup artist requires skill, talent, and an eye for true pizazz—the energy, vitality, and vigor—in color and design. Many makeup artists will become true masters of their profession; others will choose to master and fill specialized **niches**, or areas, in the makeup profession—for makeup artists these niches include avant-garde, fantasy, permanent, mortuary, special effects, and Mendhi makeup.

In any profession there are always a choice few that reach outside the limits and wander into the small, specialized niche areas. This chapter will introduce areas of the makeup profession that are advanced and specialized, offering yet another avenue to maximize your creative makeup abilities.

Many individuals enter the makeup profession knowing that these specialized areas are where they want to exercise their craft, while others' discover them as they become more educated and experienced. In either case, the world of makeup is never at a standstill and comes alive with new avenues of opportunity every day.

Working in the advanced makeup artistry field requires supplemental skills beyond those learned in a basic makeup course. There are many specialized courses and a number of schools that offer a concentration in areas such as camouflage, theater, special effects, prosthetic, and permanent makeup. The more experience and skill that you can acquire in any given area greatly increases your opportunities for employment. Volunteer and apprenticeship experience, even if unpaid, will be invaluable to your resume and career in the long term.

WHY STUDY ADVANCED MAKEUP TECHNIQUES?

Makeup artists should study and have a thorough understanding of advanced makeup techniques because:

- Advanced makeup techniques will broaden your skills and abilities.
- Studying advanced makeup techniques will expand your opportunities for employment.
- Learning advanced makeup techniques will allow you to create unique makeup applications based upon the foundational skills you mastered in basic makeup application.

AVANT-GARDE MAKEUP

Avant-garde is a French term meaning *advance guard*, and refers to things that are unique and new; experimental or

innovative in nature. It refers to pushing the boundaries or limits of what is socially accepted as the norm, or the status quo. Avant-garde is dramatic, artistic, and often extreme—the complete opposite of a natural or "everyday" look (**Figure 18–1**). It is often true, though, that trendy everyday looks evolve from a particular makeup artist's avant-garde creation.

▲ Figure 18–1 **Woman with fantasy-gold avant-garde makeup application.**

Avant-garde makeup-looks are typically seen on fashion models in a show or on the runway, in exclusive advertisements, special photoshoots in high-fashion and beauty magazines, and in makeup artists' portfolios as a representation of their unique talents, individual expression, and creativity (**Figure 18–2**).

▲ Figure 18–2 **High-fashion avant-garde makeup application using accessories.**

For the average woman, avant-garde cosmetic styles are certainly not the norm, but this cutting-edge look can be an exciting and impactful alternative for a special occasion or event.

Characteristics of Avant-Garde Makeup

Characteristics of avant-garde makeup include:

- Unusual or unique colors and techniques.
- Dramatic and stylized finishes.
- A specific theme in order to evoke a certain image.
- Heavy emphasis on a specific feature such as the eyes or lips (**Figure 18–3**).
- Use of additional accents beyond the basic makeup palette such as gems, feathers, or glitter.
- A significant time-investment to create the specialized look. ☑ LO1

▲ Figure 18–3 **Avant-garde eye makeup application.**

FANTASY MAKEUP

Fantasy makeup differs from avant-garde makeup in that it takes the imagination to places that are representative of iconic images, places, people, and characters that are not real but often hold an easily recognizable and clear vision or memory in people's minds (**Figure 18–4**). Both styles can represent anything—except what is considered by most to be the societal norm.

▲ Figure 18–4 **"Doll style" fantasy makeup application.**

Fantasy makeup is a popular technique for parties and theme-specific events (**Figure 18–5**). Fantasy applications are often re-creations of images or photos, or are new creations of images that have been left completely to the creative talent of the makeup artist's imagination (**Figure 18–6**).

© Brian Chase/www.Shutterstock.com

▲ Figure 18–5 **Fantasy makeup application: snow angel.**

Characteristics of Fantasy Makeup

Characteristics of fantasy makeup include:

- Creations of imaginary or mythological beings such as nymphs, angels, mermaids, vampires, and fairies.
- Re-creations of animals such as bears, monkeys, dogs, cats, and so forth.
- Re-creations of characters from cinematic productions that include iconic images such as Freddy Kruger, Norbit, or Woody from *Toy Story*.
- Re-creations of celebrities who are or were athletes, movie stars, musicians, or even politicians.
- The use of unusual or unique colors and techniques.
- Dramatic and stylized finishes.
- Following a specific theme meant to evoke a certain image or memory.
- The use of additional accent pieces beyond the basic makeup palette, such as gems, feathers, or glitter.
- A significant time-investment to plan, prepare, and create.
- The use of body paint and airbrush makeup applications.

© Kryvenok Anastasiia/www.Shutterstock.com

▲ Figure 18–6 **Fantasy makeup application: woman as a bird.**

The list can go on and on, but the premise underlying fantasy makeup is to create a look that belongs to another person, time, or place. ☑ LO2

Avant-garde and fantasy makeup techniques are advanced makeup applications in which the skills are acquired only after basic makeup techniques are mastered. There are many Advanced Makeup academies and schools that offer short- and long-term classes for specialized makeup techniques. Search "makeup artist schools" on the Internet for a sample of what is available. Before deciding on a school be sure to do your research: ask for details regarding the qualifications of the instructors and the career successes of former students, job placement programs, details of what tuition includes, and if possible tour the facility and meet the staff.

PERMANENT MAKEUP

Permanent makeup, commonly called **permanent cosmetics** and also known as **dermapigmentation**, **micropigmentation**, and **cosmetic tattooing**, is the introduction of permanent pigments, or dyes, into the dermal layer of the skin for enhancement of color. It is quite similar to tattooing and dates back as far as the Ancient Egyptians circa 3500 BC.

Procedures entail the deposit of selected pigments into the skin using needles of various sizes and shapes, depending upon the area being worked on. The most common uses for permanent makeup are enhancement and coloring of the lips, permanent eyeliner and permanent eyebrows for cosmetic purposes and in particular for people who have lost hair as a result of old age, diseases such as alopecia, or due to chemotherapy during cancer treatments. Permanent makeup is also used to disguise color abnormalities from scarring or diseases such as vitiligo and other pigmentation disorders.

Permanent makeup requires far more than artistic finesse with color selection; it requires skill and knowledge, a steady hand, the ability to create fine detail, and practice. A permanent makeup artist must be able to tolerate puncturing the skin of another individual.

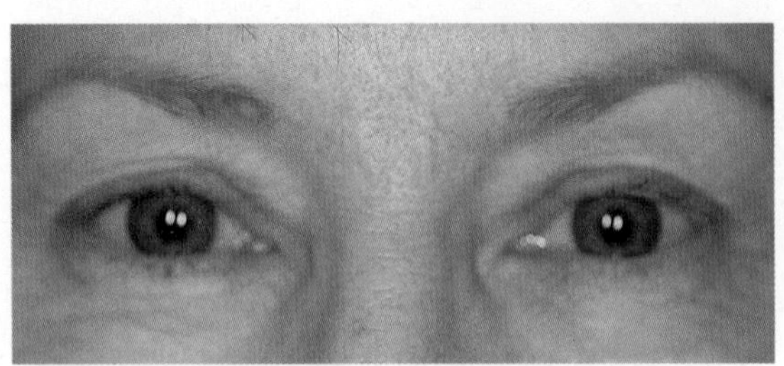

▲ Figure 18–7 **Before a permanent makeup application.**

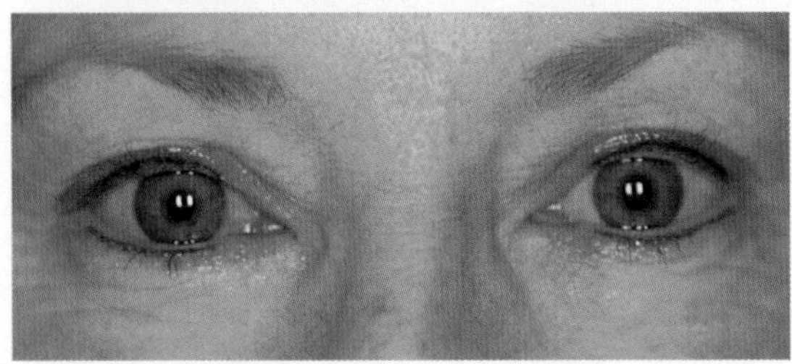

▲ Figure 18–8 **After a permanent makeup application.**

Permanent makeup application results can appear to look like topically applied cosmetics or can be minimal and almost unnoticeable, depending upon the purpose, design, and amount of pigment applied (**Figures 18–7** and **18–8**). Upon initial application, results can appear more intense than intended. This is due to a large amount of pigment remaining in the outermost layers of the epidermis. If this is the case, color will generally soften within a few days during the healing process as the upper layers of epidermis slough off and are replaced by new epidermal cells. Often, a re-touch may be required several weeks later, after the area has healed, as well as several years down the road as the skin ages.

Regulations

Permanent makeup regulations vary by state, province, county, and even city to city. In the United States most regulations guiding the practice of permanent makeup fall under the jurisdiction of the U.S. Department of Health and Human Services and have little or no association with state boards that regulate cosmetology, esthetics, or makeup. There are some locations across the United States in which it is mandatory to have either an esthetics or cosmetology license in order to perform permanent makeup procedures, while in other locations it is prohibited for estheticians and cosmetologists to practice permanent makeup procedures. In still other areas there is no license requirement or regulation at all!

Check state and local license and permit guidelines to make sure that you are operating within your scope of practice.

Licensing, local, and state regulations may also be in place regarding the location in which permanent makeup procedures can be performed, not just regarding the individual performing the procedures. Be sure to verify if a license or certificate of registration is required by your state or local regulating agency or Department of Health.

In many countries, including the United States, the many inks used in permanent makeup procedures are regulated by the FDA for safety and use.

Permanent Makeup Training and Practice

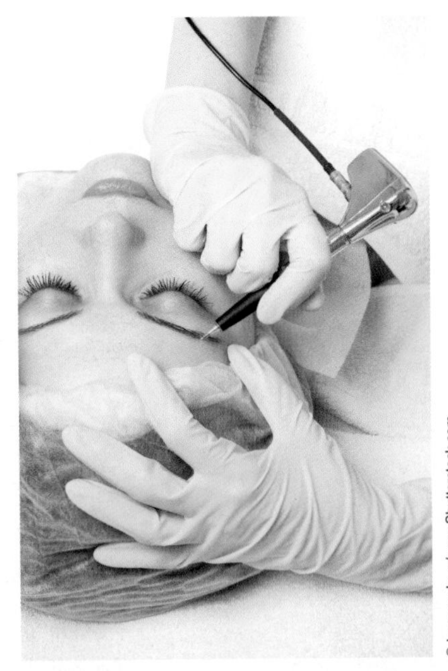
▲ Figure 18–9 A permanent makeup service.

© Ivanova Inga/www.Shutterstock.com

Permanent makeup requires training and practice to perfect (**Figure 18–9**). There are many reputable training facilities and practitioners throughout the country. As mentioned previously, before choosing a training facility do your homework. Talk to students, graduates, and to clients of the graduates to receive feedback and validate your selection. Confirm the experience and expertise of the instructor(s)—ask to view before and after photos of the work that the instructors have performed.

A permanent makeup artist must be well informed on technique, indications, contraindications, safety precautions, the use of Universal Precautions, needles, types of machines, and proper disposal practices (Refer to Chapter 2, Infection Control: Principles and Practices). Topping the list of client concerns is safety and infection control practices. Unclean permanent makeup procedures can result in infection and permanent tissue damage.

As an Advanced Permanent Makeup professional you may also find yourself working in specialized areas that treat individuals such as cancer patients who have lost all of their hair; women who need the replacement of the appearance of the **areola**, the circular area of darker pigmentation surrounding the breast nipple, after a mastectomy; and any number of other clients with disfigurements of the body. Excellent interpersonal communication skills are a must for the permanent makeup artist.

Characteristics of Permanent Makeup

Characteristics of permanent makeup include:

- Creating, enhancing, or re-creating eyebrows.
- Permanently lining the eyes.
- Lining or adding permanent color to the lips.
- Reshaping or enhancing the shape of the lips.
- Re-creating parts of the body due to illness, disease, or surgery (such as the areola of the breast). ☑ LO3

MORTUARY MAKEUP

Mortuary makeup is the application of makeup on persons that are deceased, who are generally referred to as **decedents**. Mortuary makeup is practiced and applied most frequently in preparing the decedent for a wake or funeral. It often consists of fixing the hair, manicuring the nails, dressing the body, and reconstructing minor disfigurements. In some cases the decedent's esophagus or Adam's apple may have to be reconstructed for a "lifelike" look.

Mortuary makeup specialists use a special non-thermogenic makeup specifically formulated for decedents. Thermogenic makeup is used for

STATE REGULATORY ALERT

Check with state and local agencies. Many states require that a Mortuary Makeup Artist have a cosmetology license.

live skin; it is broken down by body heat so that it can be easily and properly applied to the skin. **Non-thermogenic makeup** does not soak into the skin and is manufactured for application to skin that has no heat or normal body temperature. It can be applied in a light layer or as a heavy application to conceal imperfections, damage, bruises, scars, or other marks.

Mortuary makeup is not for everyone. It takes a special artist to be able to work with a deceased body and to re-create an individual's lifelike look. The satisfaction of this career choice comes from the appreciation and gratitude shown by the family and loved ones' of the deceased. Many times, the final visual memory someone may have of a loved one is from the viewing at the wake or funeral, and as a mortuary makeup artist, your skill and expertise will create that final memory.

There are several Mortuary Makeup schools across the Unites States. Search "mortuary schools.com" for additional information. Information can also be obtained by contacting local funeral homes.

© Sergey Lavrentev/www.Shutterstock.com

▲ Figure 18–10 **Special effects makeup of a wounded arm.**

Characteristics of Mortuary Makeup

Characteristics of mortuary makeup include:

- Applying makeup to create the individuals natural look while alive.
- Styling and coloring the hair to duplicate a picture or everyday look prior to passing away.
- Painting fingernails.
- Matching makeup to chosen clothing.
- Dressing the cadaver.
- Assisting in the selection of clothing, makeup, and hairstyle. ☑ LO4

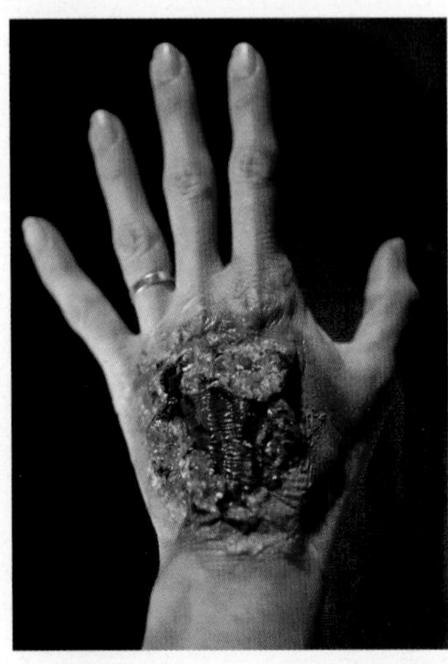

© Carlos Gutierrez/www.Shutterstock.com

▲ Figure 18–11 **Special effects makeup of a burned hand.**

SPECIAL EFFECTS MAKEUP

Special effects makeup is used to make a person look older; younger; injured; alien; or of a different gender, age, or race—in other words, different from normal (**Figures 18–10** and **18–11**). Special effects makeup is most commonly used in the production of plays and movies to increase the believability of the characters. Special effects makeup can be as subtle or dramatic as needed and is used in graphic creations of horror makeup designs, blood-and-gore concepts, science fiction creations, and extreme alterations detailing the transition from human to animal or alien and vice versa (**Figure 18–12**).

© Milady, a part of Cengage Learning. Photography by Visual Recollection.

▲ Figure 18–12 **Special effects makeup of a bloody cut on the head.**

© Harper/www.Shutterstock.com

▲ Figure 18–13 **Man with prosthetic face of a clown.**

Special effects face and body makeup include foundations, eye shadows, lipsticks, blushers, bronzers, mascaras, grease paints, gels, and adhesives. All the products carry similar names to everyday cosmetics, but entail completely different consistencies, formulations, amounts of pigment, and application techniques.

Special effects makeup also incoporates **prosthetic makeup**, the application of artificial parts that are created from a variety of material and includes products such as wax, latex, foam, gels, gypsum, silicone, and rubber (**Figure 18–13**). These artificial parts are then attached to the face and/or body with special adhesives or adhesive strips. Special effects makeup is applied over and around the edges of the prosthetic to create a seamless appearance, making it look as if it were a real part of the person.

Some prosthetic pieces are specially made and can be purchased from a professional makeup supplier.

Cornmeal or wheat germ can be used with latex to create a rough skin texture.

Blocking Out

Unique to special effects makeup is a technique known as *blocking out*, an application in which wax and makeup are used to "block out" facial hair, sideburns, eyebrows, and hairlines. Blocking out allows for a complete transformation of the appearance of the face.

Characteristics of Special Effects Makeup

The characteristics of special effect makeup are very different and very unique from other forms of advanced makeup. These characteristics are specific to their purpose and require great skill and practice to perfect their use. Characteristics of special effects makeup include:

- A tendency toward heavier application.
- High amounts of saturated, intense color.
- Waterproof and sweat-proof products.
- Special applicators for precise application.
- The use of adhesives and fixatives.

Most special effects makeup need to be purchased from specialized manufacturers and retailers. Special effects makeup products are not generally available through the majority of cosmetic suppliers.

Artificial Facial and Body Hair

Although hair may not seem to be a part of the makeup artist's job description, the application of artificial facial and body hair is definitely an important part of special effects makeup. Hair is used to create moustaches, beards, stubble, sideburns, chest hair, and even full-body coverage for animal characteristics (**Figure 18–14**). The most common materials for hair include crepe, yak, angora, horsehair, and human

© Reinhold Leitner/www.Shutterstock.com

▲ Figure 18–14 **Face after a moustache is applied for a Charlie Chaplin look.**

hair. These materials are available in a wide variety of lengths and colors and can be cut to create specific looks once applied to the skin. Artificial facial and body hair applications require a special adhesive and need to be removed with spirit gum or alcohol-based removers.

Pre-made hairpieces can be purchased from suppliers. These are made of either real or synthetic hair ventilated on a piece of lace, called a foundation. This form of hairpiece is the easiest to apply, and tends to be more comfortable to wear. In many cases, individual hair attachments are either necessary or needed for a more lifelike look. In these instances individual hairs are attached directly to the skin with a special adhesive.

Special effects makeup techniques are taught at specialized makeup classes and schools that offer programs specifically for theater, prosthetics, and special effects. Search the Internet for "advanced makeup academies and schools." As with any continuing education, check the references, background, and experience of instructors and the job placement of graduates. Also confirm the details of what is included in your tuition and kit. ☑ **LO5**

▲ Figure 18–15 **Henna on a pregnant woman's belly and hands.**

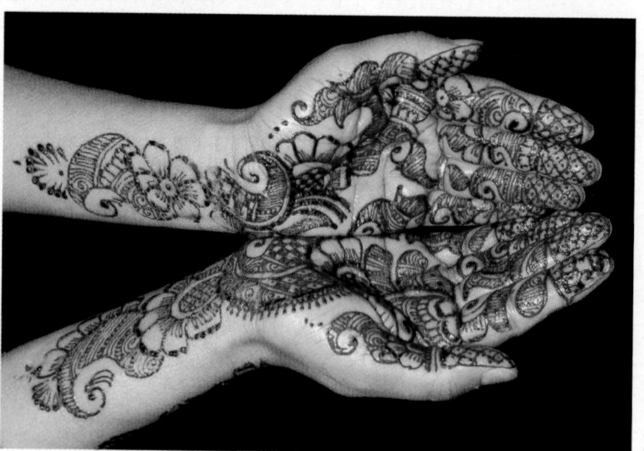

▲ Figure 18–16 **Henna on the palms of the hands and forearms.**

MENDHI MAKEUP

Mendhi makeup is the art of decorating the body with **henna**, a natural pigment derived from the mignonette tree. Mendhi is an ancient tradition of body painting originating in India, and its use dates back to over 5,000 years ago. Mendhi's roots are founded in its use for celebratory occasions such as weddings, pregnancies, births, and circumcisions as well as for displays of bravery, friendship, and luck (**Figure 18–15**). Today, temporary henna tattoos are used for special events, fashion displays, and as a means of self-expression. Mendhi makeup applications are finely detailed, beautiful forms of artistic work (**Figure 18–16**).

Henna

▲ Figure 18–17 ***Lawsonia inermis*, or henna leaves.**

Henna pigment is derived from the leaf of the flowering henna plant, *Lawsonia inermis* (also known as mignonette tree), native to tropical and subtropical regions of Africa and South Asia (**Figure 18–17**). It is a semipermanent dye that stains only the outer layer of the epidermis, as well as the hair and nails. When first applied it appears very dark and bold, but will quickly lighten depending upon the henna recipe, length of time it was left on the skin, condition of the skin, and temperature of the room in which it was applied. Vibrant colors of henna designs also come from a variety of pressed flowers and various pigmented plants (**Figure 18–18**).

Henna skin art can remain on the skin from several days to several weeks and can be applied to any area of the face or body. Mendhi skin decoration not only requires a steady hand and artistic skill, but also warrants a complete client consultation prior to application to avoid any adverse allergic reaction to the henna application.

Creating Mendhi and henna designs is an art, and one that is best learned from practitioners (and former apprentices—native or otherwise) native to India, Pakistan, and other Middle Eastern locales.

Characteristics of Mendhi Makeup

Characteristics of Mendhi makeup include:

- Creating artful imagery on any part of the body for cultural events such as birthdays or weddings.
- Creating temporary artful designs in place of permanent pigment application.
- Adding colorful works of art to display cultural beauty and significance for a short time. ☑ LO6

▲ Figure 18–18 **Red hibiscus flowers used in henna designs.**

The world of makeup is limitless, and every day new techniques and concepts are introduced into the profession. From working with the "girl next door" to fashion models, theater and film personnel, deceased bodies, and the creation of supernatural beings, makeup and advanced makeup techniques are in high demand. Your skill, passion, and desire to exceed the boundaries of everyday makeup techniques will thrust you into an exciting world of creativity and artistic design through which you will never stop growing and learning.

Review Questions

1. Define avant-garde.
2. In what type of events is Fantasy Makeup most widely used?
3. Name three other terms for permanent makeup.
4. Define the term decedent.
5. Describe the difference between thermogenic and non-thermogenic makeup.
6. What is a prosthetic? What materials are generally used to make prosthetics?
7. List the types of hair most commonly used in special effects makeup.
8. Define Mendhi.

Chapter Glossary

areola	The circular area of darker pigmentation surrounding the breast nipple.
avant-garde	French term meaning advance guard, and refers to things that are unique and new; experimental or innovative in nature.
decedents	Persons that are deceased.
fantasy makeup	Popular technique that takes the imagination to places that are representative of iconic images, places, people, and characters that are not real but often hold an easily recognizable and clear vision or memory in people's minds.
henna	Natural pigment derived from the mignonette tree (*Lawsonia inermis*); used as a reddish hair dye and in tattooing.
Mendhi makeup	The art of decorating the body with henna.
mortuary makeup	The application of makeup on individuals that are deceased.
niches	Specialized areas; in the makeup profession these are avant-garde, fantasy, permanent, mortuary, special effects, and Mendhi makeup.
non-thermogenic makeup	Does not soak into the skin and is specifically manufactured for application to skin that has no heat or normal body temperature; can be applied in a light layer or as a heavy application to conceal imperfections, damage, bruises, scars, or other marks.
permanent makeup	Commonly called *permanent cosmetics* and also known as *dermapigmentation*, *micropigmentation*, and *cosmetic tattooing*; the introduction of permanent pigments, or dyes, into the dermal layer of skin for the enhancement of color; similar to tattooing.
prosthetic makeup	The application of artificial parts that are created from a variety of material and includes products such as wax, latex, foam, gels, gypsum, silicone, and rubber.
special effects makeup	Makeup technique used to make a person look older; younger; injured; alien; or of a different gender, age, or race—in other words, different from normal; used in the production of plays and movies to increase the believability of the characters, or create something that is otherwise considered not normal.

Part 5

Business Skills

CHAPTER 19
YOUR PROFESSIONAL IMAGE

CHAPTER 20
BUSINESS OF MAKEUP

Chapter 19 Your Professional Image

Chapter Outline

Why Study Your Professional Image?

Shaping Your Professional Image

Creating Your Personal Portfolio

Your Professional Image and Your Attitude

Enhancing Your Professional Image with Continuing Education

Learning Objectives

After completing this chapter, you will be able to:

- ☑ **LO1** Understand the broad definition of professionalism and identify key qualities a professional makeup artist should display.
- ☑ **LO2** Understand the importance of developing an on-line portfolio and portfolio binder.
- ☑ **LO3** Have a clear understanding of how attitude affects success.
- ☑ **LO4** Learn about and utilize image enhancers that will maximize your professional image.
- ☑ **LO5** Identify continuing education resources that will keep you up-to-date on the latest trends and innovations in the makeup industry.

Key Terms

Page number indicates where in the chapter the term is used.

ethics
pg. 458

image enhancer
pg. 455

nonverbal communication
pg. 457

on-line portfolio
pg. 453

personal hygiene
pg. 463

professional image (professionalism)
pg. 451

toolbox
pg. 451

work ethic
pg. 458

Career Profile

Photography by Teri Lowery

Staci Broski has worked in Makeup Artistry for the past 16 years. She began as a canvas artist and quickly moved to makeup artistry after attending several photoshoots. Staci now runs her own company, 7th Row Productions, and makes it her top priority to provide excellent service and variety to her clients.

"I have been privileged to work for the past 16 years in the world of makeup and have been educated and influenced by the ever-changing, sometimes radical, progression of the industry. At my start, I took every art class I could, and in the late 1990s While working for a talent agency, I met a variety of photographers and artists. After observing several photo shoots, I realized the makeup artists were doing the same thing I was doing with my art, only on a live canvas.

before

James Ferris Photography © 2011.

"I began to study the art of makeup by attending sessions taught by professional makeup artists already established in film and television. I became involved as a freelance artist with MAC Cosmetics, and found that environment to be the best education I could ever give myself. The artists were diverse, each customer different, product knowledge was important, learning new brush techniques was exciting, and watching artists do little application tricks that provided a big result was amazing.

after

James Ferris Photography © 2011.

"It's so fun when working with a client and not only do they love what you've done, but they get so excited when taught the simplest trick that they can now use in their own makeup routine.

"My desire to freely explore the various facets of the industry has lead me to create and develop my own company, 7th Row Productions. I attribute the success of my company to slowly growing my business in fertile soil with an innovative perspective in which it could thrive.

before

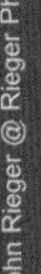
John Rieger @ Rieger Photo

"I pride myself and my team on the versatility we are able to provide for our clients, whether the task is to create a special look for a bridal client on one of the most memorable days of her life or working backstage with the Broadway cast of *The Lion King* while on tour in Kansas City. I have built my company based on my passion and drive for success in every aspect of my life.

after

John Rieger @ Rieger Photo

"Anyone can call themselves a 'makeup artist,' but what separates those who apply makeup from the true professional artist is knowledge, appearance, attitude, and their ongoing desire to make a difference."

You are now at the point where you are about to embark on your career as a professional Makeup Artist. You have spent the previous chapters learning what it takes to identify facial shapes, features, skin tone, color, tools, application techniques, and special skills. Now it is time to turn all of that creative energy and knowledge into a business—your business—and it all begins with you.

The makeup profession offers flexibility, immense creativity, and can be extremely lucrative. Like any profession, it is the dedication to your craft and the commitment to your client that will set you apart and earn you the success you deserve. Regardless of whether you work on brides, teens, and local clients or top fashion models and movie stars, you will be enhancing individual images, and, in many cases, creating an entirely new look for a client. Your skill, artistry, and knowledge combined with the right makeup application can positively affect the way someone sees their self—sometimes for a few short hours and often for a lifetime!

As varied as the tools, color choices, and techniques are in makeup application, career options are also just as diverse. You will be amazed to discover the multitude of opportunities available to you as a makeup artist, many of which you will discover yourself and create on your own.

The most important thing to remember is that the only doors that are closed to you are the ones that you do not open. Your success lies within your own abilities and ultimately depends upon your motivation, desires, and goals.

WHY STUDY YOUR PROFESSIONAL IMAGE?

Makeup artists should study and have a thorough understanding of your professional image because:

- In the business of makeup it is your knowledge, talent, and professional reputation that are your most valuable assets.
- It is your knowledge, talent, and professional reputation that define you as a professional and will keep you in demand.
- The most successful professionals stay informed, educated, up-to-date, and on the cutting-edge of what is new and trending in the makeup industry.

SHAPING YOUR PROFESSIONAL IMAGE

At this stage of your makeup career, you may know exactly what type of makeup "artist" you would like to be, and which particular area you would like to specialize or focus in; or you may not have any idea where you would like to apply your skills and creative talents at all. Regard-

less of where you are, each one can be a bonus. Whichever career path you choose will be a journey full of twists and turns filled with exciting opportunities. The important thing is to remain true to yourself while staying open to the many career options and opportunities available. The key is to be flexible, open, willing, and ready to work. There are certain qualities that will define your professional image and most of these are already a part of who you are. Successful makeup artists are representations of themselves and their beliefs; trying to be someone you are not will hinder your creativity and sway you from the individual beauty and uniqueness that defines you.

Activity

There are several key qualities that are representative of the true professional. Select 10 qualities from the list below that you think demonstrate professionalism. These qualities will become the template through which you begin to shape your career and your reputation. There are no right or wrong selections, your choices will simply help in guiding you to become the outstanding professional you are meant to be.

KEY QUALITIES	
• Specialized knowledge	• Appearance
• Expert in chosen field	• Prepared
• Confident	• Organized
• Communicates positively	• Creative
• Responsible	• Team player
• Accountable	• Works well under pressure
• Integrity	• Looks for solutions, not blame
• Respected	• Savvy business knowledge
• High standards	• Time management
• Ethical	• Current and up-to-date on trends, techniques, and products

The 10 professional qualities you have selected are unique to you and these will shape your reputation in the makeup industry. These are the qualities that you will bring to every job, every project, and every client you work with. Type these qualities into your smart phone or print them and keep a copy in your makeup kit. Review them often and, from time to time, ask yourself whether or not you are living up to your professional image. ✓ LO1

Your Professional Image

Your **professional image**, also known as **professionalism**, is the impression you project through your outward appearance and your conduct in the workplace. Your professional image is reflected in your appearance, communication skills, competence, and willingness. To rise to the top and succeed, skill and talent may get you there, but it is your professional image and reputation that will keep you there. We are not always able to control circumstances, but we are always able to control how we are perceived as a professional. A constant awareness and fine-tuning of the qualities that represent a professional makeup artist will set you apart and present a complete package to colleagues, coworkers, employers, and clients.

If you asked five different people to define *professionalism*, you would very likely get five completely different answers. What frequently gets us into trouble is that professionalism oftentimes is in the eye of the beholder; however, there are universal qualities that transcend all professionals from surfers and musicians to doctors and politicians (**Figure 19–1**). Simply put, your professional image is how clients, colleagues, and employers perceive you.

▲ Figure 19–1 **Always present yourself professionally.**

Creating a Toolbox That Reflects Your Professional Image

The key qualities you selected are intangible, meaning they are perceived subtly by the people around you. That being said, it is these qualities that will mold others' perceptions of you as a professional. Your **toolbox** is a makeup kit containing all the supplies, tools, and implements needed to perform a professional makeup application. Your toolbox is also a representation of who you are and the quality of work you do as a makeup artist. Keeping a well-stocked, organized, clean kit is essential to the comfort and safety of your clients and can also elevate or diminish your professional image (**Figure 19–2**). A good rule of thumb is: don't just be prepared, be over-prepared! You can rarely have too much when it comes to makeup. Chapter 4, Tools of the Trade, details specific tools, makeup products, implements, and supplies that should be included in a basic professional makeup toolkit.

▲ Figure 19–2 **Your makeup kit or toolbox should be organized and well stocked.**

Toolbox Basics at a Glance

Every toolbox should include the following items at a minimum. As your professional experience increases, you will quickly find yourself expanding the tools of the trade in your personal kit.

- Assorted brushes to achieve various desired looks
- Brush cleaner
- Makeup products for various applications, looks and skin types

HERE'S A TIP

If you don't live in Hollywood... order on-line.

Specific items will become a necessary part of your kit and reflect your preferences. These items will often be determined by the particular area of makeup artistry you work in, and as with so many things you say and do in the industry, your toolkit is a representation of your professional image and abilities. Preparation, organization, cleanliness, diversity, flexibility, and *supplies* are all key factors that help to develop and maintain your professional image.

- Utensils (tweezers, eyelash curlers, palettes, blotting paper, lash comb)
- Single-use items (cotton swabs, sponges, tissues; shadow, lip, and mascara applicators)
- Headband
- Cape
- Hand sanitizer

As you become more experienced and the variety of jobs that you perform widens and diversifies, your kit will grow quickly. You will come across particular items that you personally feel are necessary to your kit. The makeup artist is always the person that everyone turns to for items that are needed or were forgotten.

Toolbox Extras

The following is a list of items to help you begin compiling a well-stocked toolbox that will promote your professional image in a positive light as you embark on your career as a professional makeup artist.

WEB RESOURCES

www.Naimies.com, located in Burbank, CA, is a favorite of Hollywood's top makeup artists. Naimie's Beauty Center offers a variety of kit essentials at very reasonable prices.

www.Frends.com is an excellent source for on-line purchases. Frends Beauty Supply, located in North Hollywood, is another favorite among top makeup artists.

Both establishments cater to the professionals and offer products and tools with the makeup artist in mind.

TOOLBOX EXTRAS	
• Two-sided clothing tape	• Hand mirror
• Clothing lint-remover roll	• Mouthwash and dental floss
• Eyedrops	• Mints or breath spray
• Hairpins	• Tweezers
• Band-aids	• Nail polish remover
• Antibacterial ointment	• Nail file
• Hairspray	• Clear top coat
• Comb, pick, and brush	• Needle and thread
• Safety pins	• Quick fabric spot remover
• Alcohol wipes	

CREATING YOUR PERSONAL PORTFOLIO

The Internet is a world unto itself and the number of on-line users is increasing daily. There is a saying in marketing: "If you are not on the Web, then you don't exist." Your **on-line portfolio** or Web site will be a personal calling card where you display your talents and work for potential customers and employers to evaluate your professional skills. The Internet and your Web site is also where potential employers and clients will be able to find you. In the makeup profession, your on-line portfolio is just as important, and often times more important, than your resume, client list, and physical portfolio. Your on-line portfolio is a visual representation of your talent and skill and contributes as much to your professional image as your "toolbox" and the display of professional qualities you selected.

Think of a portfolio as an exhibit of your work on display for potential clients and employers that allows them to evaluate your professional skills and makeup artistry. Your portfolio should contain a wide range of photos and diverse makeup applications, as well as a list of clients and productions you have worked on (the bigger the better of course, but everyone has to start somewhere). Start an on-line portfolio right away, even while you are still in school. The progression of your skills and expertise will be clearly represented in a portfolio that originates with the beginning of your career. The important thing is to establish your presence in the industry as soon as you can.

Do your homework, research carefully, and think long-term—you, your portfolio, and Web address want to be around for years to come. Investigate and discover what top makeup artists are doing with their on-line portfolios by viewing the Web sites of the artists profiled throughout this book.

If creating a Web site is currently not in your budget, then create a "Fan Page" on Facebook to showcase your work. Remember: Your fan page is your business page and is not just a professional representation of your work, but it is also a representation of your professional image.

Portfolio Photos

When you are starting out as a makeup professional, compiling quality photos can be a challenge. Create your own design "dream team" for a photoshoot consisting of a photographer, hairdresser, clothing stylist/designer, and fledgling models. Contact cosmetology students, photography schools, fashion institutes, and modeling agencies as novices are always in need of great photos. Come together as a team and collaborate on the look and feel of each shot you will take in your photoshoot. This will not only help you acquire photos, but it will also teach you how to work on a team with other creative professionals in the industry.

By taking photos of your best work you will have a true representation of your talents, artistry, and skills. Your photo selection should be diverse;

WEB RESOURCES

The following is a list of "Portfolio Hosting Sites" to help get you started in establishing your on-line portfolio:

- www.bigblackbag.com
- www.viewbook.com
- www.getparade.com
- www.styleseat.com

*the*EDGE video (Metroluxe and Muse editions) by Milady, a part of Cengage Learning, deconstructs the creative process of design from concept to completion and will give you the tools and insights of what it takes to design a collection and produce a photoshoot. Find *the*EDGE at www.milady.cengage.com.

James Ferris Photography © 2011

▲ Figure 19–3a **Before makeup application.**

James Ferris Photography © 2011

▲ Figure 19–3b **After makeup application.**

this will show that you are capable of adapting to different clients, needs, environments, techniques, products, styles, designs, and colors. Include makeup applications on teens, brides, fashion or glamour models, camouflage subjects, men, fantasy makeup models, or any other unique makeup application that you perform. Before and after photos will clearly depict the details of your work (**Figure 19–3a** and **b**).

Portfolio Binder

If you are not in a position to create an on-line portfolio or Web site, you can begin with a portfolio binder. These binders can be purchased at any photography or office supply store. They are available in various sizes and colors. Choose a size that is easy to carry and show to potential employers and clients. Keep in mind that whichever size portfolio you choose, your photos should also be that size (**Figure 19–4**). For example, if your portfolio is 8" × 10" (20 × 25 centimeters) then all of the photos inside should be 8" × 10" (20 × 25 centimeters). The presentation and layout of your portfolio will be critiqued along with the photos that are in it. The organization of your portfolio is not only a representation of your personal organization skills and makeup artistry, but also a demonstration of your professional image.

On-Line and Binder Portfolio Guidelines

As you become more experienced you may want to consider investing in a professional portfolio that is developed using a professional photographer. This can be done in a day or two, depending on your skill and the timing. Arrange for eight to ten individuals with different facial features, skin tones, and characteristics to serve as your makeup models and schedule them accordingly. To create an appropriate professional image and display the breadth of your skills and makeup abilities:

- The photos should all be the same dimensions.
- The photos should be diverse showcasing a variety of features, models, and makeup applications.
- Include several before and after sets in an opposing view (before on the left, after on the right). ☑ LO2

▼ Figure 19–4 **Always have your portfolio binder to show off your work.**

© Kovalev Sergey/www.Shutterstock.com

YOUR PROFESSIONAL IMAGE AND YOUR ATTITUDE

Professional behavior, a strong on-line presence, and a well-stocked toolbox are essential as you begin to develop your professional image; however, these elements comprise only part of what helps a professional makeup artist become a successful makeup artist.

Your artistic abilities and creativity are a gift; your attitude is something you can improve, polish, and continually develop to help you in achieving success. Amazing talent will most certainly be a factor in propelling you on a fast track to opportunity and success in the makeup profession, but a negative attitude will just as quickly derail you. As a makeup artist it is your artistic talent, makeup skills, and the correct professional image that will generate the job referrals and job offers, but it is a positive attitude that keeps the job referrals and offers flowing.

In shaping your professional image, your attitude can be your biggest asset or greatest liability. Numerous employers and clients will often say "attitude and fit" are more important when hiring than "talent." Don't underestimate talent, it is extremely important; but talent alone will not get you the job. There are many talented makeup professionals in the industry competing for the same job you are interviewing for; it is your attitude that will propel you above the crowd.

Merriam Webster's (11th ed.) defines *attitude* as: a mental position with regard to a fact or state <a helpful *attitude*>; an organismic state of readiness to respond in a characteristic way to a stimulus (as an object, concept, or situation) <her *attitude* toward the designer's demands was hostile>

The demands of the makeup profession require a makeup artist's attitude to encompass multiple facets. In addition to the qualities you selected in creating the template for your professional image, you will also need to master other "soft skills" that translate into a positive attitude and are an important element of your professional reputation. One of the greatest challenges that you will encounter as a makeup professional is the diverse personalities of your clients. Your client may be tired, stressed, overworked, unhappy, sad, nervous, or angry—and it will be your attitude and professional image that will shape the outcome of your makeup session. With this in mind, always remember that your job is to first satisfy the makeup needs of your clients and then navigate the positive or negative aspects of the makeup session. Think of yourself as a chameleon: Your ability to change your colors and adapt to your environment (within the bounds of your professional and personal ethics) will serve to grow your career for years to come (**Figure 19–5**). ☑ **LO3**

© Natali Glado/www.Shutterstock.com

▲ **Figure 19–5 Your ability to adapt to your environment is beneficial to your career.**

Adapting Your Attitude Using Image Enhancers.

Our attitude is the platform from which we view life and through which life views us. In the professional world, it is a rare occasion when we are given a "do over". It is imperative that you maintain the professional image you are creating; however, we are human and from time to time we all need an attitude adjustment. The **image enhancers**, or behaviors that improve the quality of your professional image through specific methods for conducting and representing yourself, detailed in this section will help you deliver the best professional image every day in every way.

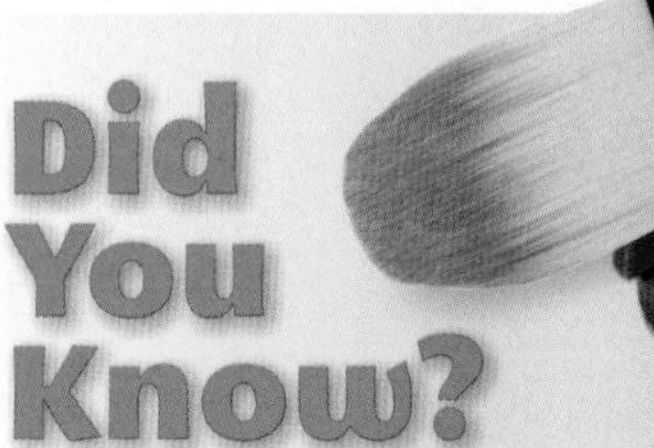

Chameleons are famous for their ability to change color. This ability serves as a form of communication, a response to environment, and as a defense against predators.

Image Enhancer #1: Communication Skills

Communication skills, also known as *soft skills*, are personal attributes that enhance an individual's interactions, job performance, and career prospects. Your ability to effectively communicate will dramatically contribute to your level of success.

- Hiring managers tend to hire those they *like*.
- Hiring managers tend to hire those who are like *themselves*.
- Hiring managers make hiring decisions within the *first 5 minutes*.

As a makeup artist, your artistic eye and technical skill are essential; however; the makeup profession is a people-oriented business, and your ability to communicate will have the greatest impact on your career. As a makeup professional, it is your responsibility and duty to understand and in return to be understood. Communication determines the results you get, so consequently if you are not getting the results you want, then you need to change the methods you use to communicate.

As a professional makeup artist it is important to be able to express yourself while also comprehending what a client is saying or feeling. This skill will allow you to communicate your vision to your client effectively and ensure that their expectations and needs are met. Effective communication between the makeup artist and the client can be the difference between a satisfied client and success or an unhappy client and failure.

Speaking Clear communication begins with you, the makeup professional. As you may recall from Chapter 6, Client Consultation, communication is the act of successfully sharing information between two people (or groups of people), so that the information is effectively and clearly understood. It is your responsibility as a professional to be able to explain to the client what you will be doing and how you will be doing it in a professional, educated manner (**Figure 19–6**). Spend some time paying attention to the way that you speak and the words that you choose to use. Specifically note your use of slang terms, incorrect grammar, your voice quality, and your tone. Oftentimes it is not what you say, but how you say it that has the most meaning.

▲ **Figure 19–6 Always communicate clearly and in a professional manner with your client.**

A terrific learning tool is to record yourself interacting with a client. After the session, play the recording back and listen to how you sounded, what you said, and the words that you chose to use. Carefully analyze your verbal communication and develop ways in which it can be improved upon and implement the changes immediately. In many cases people do not realize how they sound until they actually hear themselves speak.

Listening Although effective speaking is important in professional communication, listening can be even more important. Listening is a key communication skill for makeup artists. You may have a vision for a client that you think would look fantastic, but it very well may not be what the client is envisioning at all. Listen closely to what your client is saying, take their wishes into account, and then use that information in conjunction with your professional skills to deliver the perfect result. Your confident, knowledgeable suggestions will help create the expected result for both you and your client.

Eighty-five percent of success comes from your ability to communicate while only 15 percent of your success is attributed to your technical skills.

Listening is a skill, and one that can require practice. The key to being a good listener is never to interrupt while a client is talking, letting them finish their thoughts, and never assuming you know what they are thinking or saying. Once your client has finished speaking, repeat back to them what it is that you heard them say (this is the reflective listening technique you learned in Chapter 6, Client Consultation). This process will guarantee that you both have the same idea and expectations.

Activity

Take 15 minutes and sit and watch the people around you. Observe how they interact with others and see if you can identify five positive and five negative nonverbal behaviors. As a makeup professional your awareness of your own actions will strengthen your awareness of your clients and everyone around you. These skills will enhance your ability to interact with different personalities and in different professional settings.

Nonverbal Communication Ninety-eight percent of all communication is unconscious. **Nonverbal communication** is the communication expressed by body language, eye contact, facial expressions, and gestures. Look around wherever you are and if possible observe the unconscious communication from those around you—take notice of anything you see from rolling eyes to sighs, fidgets, quizzical looks, smiles, frowns, or nods. "Actions speak louder than words" is a well-known saying and one you have probably heard before. The more you work with people, the more adept you will become at reading body language. Tone of voice, facial expression, posture, and even eye movement and expression will become an invaluable tool in indicating for you whether or not you are on track with your clients and meeting their needs.

As a professional, you will need to be acutely aware of your own body language and the message it is sending to your client. Your posture, tone of voice, facial expressions, and most importantly—your confidence—will indicate the level of your professionalism to clients, coworkers, colleagues, and employers.

Nonverbal actions that send a negative message:

- Avoiding eye contact
- Not smiling
- Tapping your foot
- Crossing your arms
- Standing with shoulders slouched
- Chewing your lip
- Furrowing your brows

Image Enhancer #2: Customer Service

As a makeup professional you are in the service business, and therefore are providing a service for clients to purchase. Your customers will range from employers to colleagues to clients looking for a makeup application. It is up to you to provide every potential customer with the best experience possible. Think of customer service as providing a memorable experience which the person receiving your services wants to experience over and over again. Good customer service meets the client's expectations, whereas *great* customer service exceeds your clients expectations. How do we exceed our client's expectations? By creating an experience they will never forget and are pleased to have received (**Figure 19–7**).

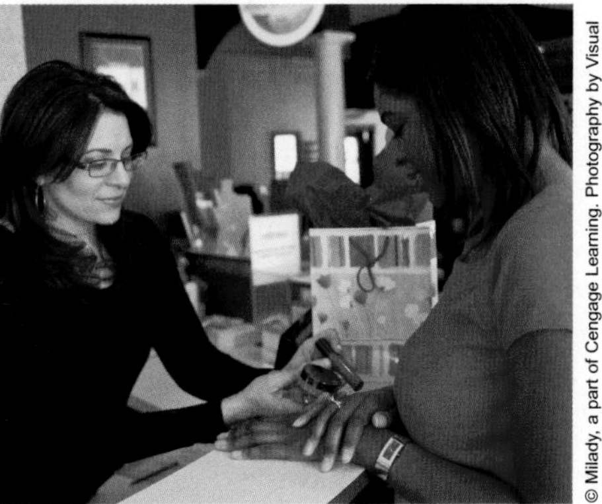

▲ **Figure 19–7 Effective customer service is key.**

Did You Know?

Seven percent of communication is verbal (involves actual words), 55 percent of communication is visual (body language, eye contact), and 38 percent is tonal (pitch, speed, volume, tone of voice). To communicate effectively as a professional, project strong body language imbued with confidence, competence, and charisma.

Think of a time when you experienced great customer service. What happened that made it special? What feelings were you left with? With this memory in mind, write down what great customer service experience you want to create for your employers, colleagues, and especially your clients...Think BIG and BOLD and remember that great customer service leads to great experiences and great experiences lead to more clients and a more successful YOU!

People tell one friend about good customer service and ten friends about bad customer service. With the popularity of social media, that number can easily quadruple.

It is your job to deliver results that exceed the needs and expectations of your clients. When your clients walk away from their makeup application satisfied, happy, and feeling beautiful, you have a client for life. Every customer is a learning experience and an opportunity to not only fine-tune your makeup skills, but to enhance your communication soft skills. To exceed your clients' expectations, you must combine your professional image, a positive attitude, and the information you obtain during the consultation process into one complete service package. Once you begin to make this process part of every makeup application you perform, you will easily exceed client expectations every time and promote a professional image and reputation that fosters success.

Image Enhancer #3: Ethics

You may often hear someone described as an ethical person. What exactly does this mean? **Ethics** are the moral principles by which we live and work. Ethics refers to doing what is right and being honest, forthcoming, and committed. In the beauty business, having a strong **work ethic** means taking pride in your work and committing yourself to consistently doing a good job for your clients, employer, and the salon or spa team. A solid work ethic incorporates doing what is right and being honest with staying motivated, displaying integrity, practicing good communication skills, and being enthusiastic in all of your endeavors.

- **Motivation** is having the drive to take the necessary actions to achieve a short- or long-term goal. Although motivation can come from external sources—parental or peer pressure, for instance—the best motivation is internal, such as the desire to perfect your makeup artistry skills. Motivation and drive will place opportunity all around you.
- **Integrity** is staying committed to a strong code of moral and artistic values. Integrity is the compass that keeps you on course over the length of your career.
- **Good technical and communication skills.** While you may excel in either technical or communication skills, you must develop both to reach the level of success you desire. Being able to employ good communication skills will always ensure that expectations are clear and correct results are delivered.
- **Enthusiasm and passion** are the flame that lights the fire! Never lose your eagerness to learn, grow, and expand your skills and knowledge. The makeup and beauty business evolves every day. New products, styles, techniques, and trends are constantly emerging onto the market place. A successful makeup artist is not only aware of new technologies and trends, but is also immersed in the details and incorporates these dynamic elements into their professional practice.

Many businesses create a mission statement that establishes the values that an individual or institution lives and works by, as well as future goals. Take a few moments and write your own mission statement based upon your personal code of ethics. Choose five practices or beliefs that are important to you and your work behavior and that represent the "professional you." Add these to your top 10 professional qualities as an integral part of your professional image (**Figure 19–8**).

Sample list of key points in a personal mission statement:

- To always be honest
- To always be prompt
- To always communicate clearly
- To always be respectful
- To always look at every challenge as an opportunity to grow

© Tyzhnenko Dmitry/www.Shutterstock.com

▲ **Figure 19–8** **Take a moment to write down your personal mission statement.**

Image Enhancer #4: Time Management

Whether you are hired as independent contractor or an employee, you are expected to show up on time at a given location to deliver a service. Being on time is a critical component of being a professional. We would not stay in practice or in demand very long if we were unable to be on time and balance that time with each client wisely. On the job, punctuality is a professional responsibility. Oftentimes your role will not be independent, even if you are an independent contractor. There will always be other professionals—hairdressers, stylists, directors, photographers, etc.—that are relying on you and your ability to manage your schedule. If you run late you will impact the entire team of individuals that also have a job to do. Remember: This is not a dinner party, and fashionably late will not cut it when a groom is waiting or millions of dollars are at stake on a production shoot. In the beauty business, time is money. Poor time-management skills will adversely affect your professional image and can have a catastrophic effect on your professional reputation and future success.

Makeup artists are hired to produce results and make sure their clients look magnificent. Although this is a critical role, most contractors or employers will finalize your commitment to them and then move on to other pressing concerns. This means you are on your own. This is your opportunity to exceed expectations and show who you are and what you are capable of delivering. Make it your practice to always arrive early, with your supplies and accessories clean and ready to use. Plan for the job to start on time and possibly exceed the estimated timeframe. If you are working as an employee, you will want to arrive at least 15 minutes early to the salon or spa. If you are working on location, for instance on a bride or a production, also arrive at least 15 minutes before your appointment or call-time to allow you to get your bearings and set up your station.

HERE'S A TIP

As a makeup professional you are responsible for your time management! Sometimes, certain predicaments or instances arise that are unforeseen and unavoidable and we do run late. If this happens, communicate with those it will affect immediately and be prepared to offer solutions to make up for the lost time.

Image Enhancer #5: Budgeting and Money Management

Regardless of whether you are employed as a regular employee or work on a contract basis, as a professional it is your responsibility to budget and manage your money. It is a much simpler task to manage money when you have a set, steady income. However, many makeup artists will be hired as independent contractors and work from job-to-job. This offers amazing flexibility, opportunity, experience, and excitement; on the other hand, this type of employment does not always offer a set income that you can base a budget upon.

Regardless of the employment structure, the best way to survive financially is to have a budget that clearly defines necessary expenses. After managing basic living expenses, you will want to explore financial options to secure long-term security and provide a cushion for times when work may be slow. Begin by making a complete list of monthly expenses. (Refer to **Table 19–1** for an example.) This will provide you with a bottom-line figure of how much you need to earn to pay your bills, purchase food, and meet transportation needs. The wise professional will then add 6 months of living expenses to that number to be placed into savings or investments. One of the most common mistakes made by people is living above and beyond their actual income. It is much easier to live according to the guidelines of a set budget and find that you have a little extra to spend each month than to impulsively overextend yourself and then worry about where the funds to meet upcoming expenses will come from.

HERE'S A TIP

Financial Planning only takes a few hours ... but it will make an enormous difference to your financial security ... spend some time on a class to learn about money and money management.

HERE'S A TIP

If you wear it to the beach or the night club; it is not professional attire. Before you leave the house, ask yourself: Is my appearance giving the impression that I am a serious, qualified, and educated professional?

Image Enhancer #6: Appearance

Fashion is, naturally, a creative outlet for the makeup artist. As makeup professionals our appearance is a great vehicle for self-expression. Being in the beauty business gives us more creative freedom when it comes to our appearance, and the makeup artist is often expected to present a professional appearance that is both fashionably put-together and trendy. It is when we go a little beyond the boundaries in our quest for individual expression that we may get into trouble. Do you recall the 7/11 rule? Within 7 seconds someone will establish 11 impressions of you. One of those first 11 impressions is a direct result of your appearance.

Carefully consider the job and venue where you are about to work. You would not arrive at a wedding in a black leather miniskirt, boots, and a black lace top with a studded necklace. However, if you have been hired to do the makeup for a hot new rock star and her backup singers, such attire may be perfectly acceptable. Regardless of the venue in which you are working, the most important factor to remember is that you are presenting yourself as a professional, and you are your own best advertising. First impressions speak volumes about the professional standards that you adhere to and practice. Professional and appropriate attire should be the premise behind every appearance you make (**Figure 19–9**).

Figure 19–9 Carefully consider your style decisions.

TABLE 19–1 INCOME AND EXPENSE WORKSHEET			
INCOME			
Income	**Monthly**	**Income**	**Monthly**
Wages/Salary		Child Support	
Tips		Alimony	
Bonuses		Misc.	
		TOTAL:	
EXPENSES			
Expenses	**Monthly**	**Expenses**	**Monthly**
Housing:		**Personal:**	
Rent/Mortgage		Clothing	
HOA		Dry Cleaning/Laundry	
Home Repairs/Improvements		Cosmetics/Styling Products	
Insurance Home/Renters		Child Care/Babysitter	
Transportation:		Continuing Education	
Car Payment		School Tuition	
Insurance		School Supplies	
Gas/Oil		Magazines/Books	
Repairs		Memberships (Gym/Clubs)	
Bus/Subway Fare		Fun/Blow Money	
Utilities:		**Entertainment:**	
Electric		Movies	
Gas		Vacation	

▲ Table 19–1 **Income and Expense Worksheet.**

(Continued)

EXPENSES			
Expenses	**Monthly**	**Expenses**	**Monthly**
Water		Music	
Trash/Sewer		Sporting Activities	
Cable		**Savings:**	
Internet		Savings Account	
Home Phone		Emergency Fund	
Cell Phone		401K/Stocks/Bonds	
Food:		**Gifts:**	
Grocery		Donations	
Restaurants		Contributions	
Coffee/Sodas/Vending Machines		Gifts (Birthday/Christmas)	
Debts:		**Other Expenses:**	
Credit Card			
Credit Card			
Credit Card			
Student Loans			
Medical:			
Insurance			
Doctor Bills			
Dentist			
Optometrist			
Medications			

▲ Table 19–1 (Continued)

EXPENSES			
Expenses	**Monthly**	**Expenses**	**Monthly**
		TOTAL EXPENSES:	
		NET MONTHLY INCOME: (Total Monthly Income less Total Monthly Expenses)	

▲ Table 19–1 **(Continued)**

The best way to determine an appropriate dress code is to place yourself in your client's or prospective employer's position. If you were them, how would you expect your makeup artist to dress? Your image and look is as crucial, if not more so, than the image and look your are being hired to create. In many instances, an employer will specify a required dress code, but until a position is secured, your choice of attire is a direct reflection of you and your commitment to your profession.

Image Enhancer #7: Hygiene

This may seem obvious and not worthy of mention. Who doesn't shower or brush their teeth? However, you need to keep in mind that hygiene does not begin and end at home. As a professional makeup artist, your attention to daily ongoing proper hygiene is a basic component of your professional image and a contributing factor to your success in the beauty field. It is very often minor details—such as attention to daily ongoing personal hygiene—that will have the greatest impact, both positive and negative, on another person's impression of you.

Personal hygiene is the daily maintenance of cleanliness and healthfulness through certain sanitary practices. Proper hygiene practices include:

- Daily grooming—showering, washing, and styling of hair.
- Clean and well-manicured nails.
- Dental hygiene—clean teeth and fresh breath. Keep a toothbrush with you and brush after meals as you are often only inches from a client's face. Keep mints in your makeup kit for you and your client.
- Clean, ironed, matching clothes.
- Body scents, the use of deodorant, and an awareness of the strength of fragrances. Fragrance is very subjective, and what smells good to one person may be unappealing to another. If you must wear fragrance, keep it very light and off your wrists. As a makeup artist, your wrist is often under your client's nose.
- Proper skin care and healthy-appearing skin.

- The correct application of makeup.
- Moisturized hands.
- Avoiding smoking—the smell of smoke does not go away when you finish your cigarette; the odor lingers on your breath, on your skin, on your clothes, and in your hair. If you must smoke, do not smoke during work hours if at all possible. At a minimum, try not to smoke at least 30 minutes before any makeup application. If you must smoke during your work day, when finished brush your teeth, use mouthwash, and wash your hands. Spritz a fabric odor-eliminator on your clothes as this will help diminish the scent somewhat. Clients have been known to switch makeup artists simply because the smell of cigarette smoke was offensive to them.

Once again, place yourself in your client's position: What would you expect from an individual that you have hired, or who has been hired to do your makeup? What would your interpretation be of their nails, skin, hair, makeup, breath, clothing, and perfume? This is the standard you should be prepared to adhere to and actually exceed whenever you appear at a job venue. ☑ LO4

ENHANCING YOUR PROFESSIONAL IMAGE WITH CONTINUING EDUCATION

Regardless of your age, experience, or skill, there are always new products, cosmetic ingredients, and techniques emerging in the beauty industry. The most successful makeup artists stay informed and up-to-date on the cutting-edge of what is new and happening in the makeup arena. There are many ways to stay informed and to gain the experience that will position you at the forefront of your contemporaries.

▼ **Figure 19–10 Read magazines to stay current.**

© Raisa Kanareva/www.Shutterstock.com

Magazines

Both consumer and professional magazines will keep you informed and up-to-date. Reading consumer magazines such as *New Beauty, Vogue, Allure,* and others will keep you informed of all of the information that your clients are being exposed to. This is critical in order for you to be able to answer questions and concerns clients will have about new trends, techniques, products, and ingredients. Professional trade magazines are not consumer-based, and are specifically published to provide the professional makeup artist with exciting, new information. They include topics on techniques, ingredients, jobs, education, products, trends, colors, FDA issues, supplies, tools, brush types, and styles along with every other aspect of the makeup profession (**Figure 19–10**).

Some great magazines to check out include:

- *Make-Up Artist Magazine*
- *On Makeup Magazine*
- *[BEAUTY]launchpad*
- *InStyle*
- *Beauty Fashion*
- *Cosmetic World*
- *WWD (Women's Wear Daily)*

The Internet

Internet technology has opened access to information at an entirely new level. The Internet offers numerous Web sites through which you can gain information on any given topic that you may need or want. Simply allocate a small amount of time, as little as once a month even, to search new topics and trends in the makeup industry.

Some great sites to check out include:

- www.stylenetwork.com
- www.khake.com
- www.fashiontrendsetter.com
- www.powdergroup.com
- www.makeup411.com

Volunteer

Volunteering your professional makeup services will not only enhance your techniques and skills, it is also an amazing way to network and expose your name and have your work well known in a community. Above all else, volunteering gives a gift to someone in need that is less fortunate, and it speaks volumes about the type of professional that you have become. Volunteer services are available for many different events and situations.

Here are a few ideas for volunteer opportunities:

- Women's shelters
- Hospitals
- Events for cancer patients
- Teenage girls' homes
- Wedding expo's
- Parent–Teacher associations (PTA)
- High school health events
- High school career events

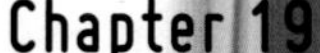

Working as an Intern or Assistant

Many of the major cosmetic companies hire interns on a regular basis. Although these may be unpaid positions, or have a very low pay rate, the experience is priceless. Companies that hire interns include MAC Cosmetics, L'Oréal, Avon, and Estée Lauder just to name a few.

Assisting is also another avenue to grow your skills and generate exposure. Seasoned professionals working in the film and television industry frequently hire assistants to prep, clean, and set up their workstations. The pay is usually minimal, but the exposure and experience are priceless.

Conference and Expo List:

- International Congress of Esthetics and Spa
- Midwest International Salon & Spa Expo
- International Beauty Expo
- Spa & Resort Expo
- International Esthetics, Cosmetics & Spa Conference
- Day Spa Expo & Business Forum
- International Make-Up Artist Trade show(IMATS)
- The Makeup Show

Conferences and Expos

There are over a dozen conferences across the United States that are specifically targeted to the beauty professional. Skin care, or esthetics conferences, always offer educational seminars and classes for makeup artists. Dates and locations may vary, but are usually set 1 year in advance, allowing makeup artists to schedule at least one conference into their schedule annually. There are increasingly more local and regional conferences being created to serve beauty professionals that are unable to travel to specific events in distant locations. Check with local beauty supply stores or distributors for educational classes as well.

Advanced Classes

There are many makeup academies and institutions across the United States that offer short one-day courses, week-long courses, and month(s)-long courses. Many also specialize in specialty areas such as theater makeup, airbrushing, camouflage makeup, television, runway, and print. Search trade magazines or the Internet for schools and programs that fit your needs. Before attending, be sure to ask for the references of graduates and instructors. You want to ensure that your time and money are well spent on a reputable class and institution. ☑ **LO5**

The world of makeup and beauty is incredibly exciting and the opportunities are limitless. The only thing that can hold you back is *you*. Additionally, your greatest asset in creating success is also *you*. Your professional image and how you present yourself to the world of makeup are the best marketing tools at your disposal. Making a name for yourself and achieving success in the beauty industry takes more than just skill—it takes passion, motivation, attitude, and a desire to be the best!

Review your template of the qualities and attitude enhancers that are the foundation for your professional image. How many of them do you currently practice? If you are missing a few, begin to cultivate those qualities now and start transforming yourself into the professional makeup artist you are meant to embody. The successes, joys, pleasures, and many benefits of being a professional makeup artist are yours for the taking.

Review Questions

1. Describe a professional image.
2. List examples of "extras" that should be included in the makeup toolbox.
3. What is the purpose of an on-line portfolio? A bound portfolio?
4. Why is a positive attitude important in shaping your professional image?
5. What is the key to being a good listener?
6. Why is it important to have a personal mission statement and code of ethics?
7. Why is it important to learn to budget money properly?
8. What are the seven image enhancers and why are they important?
9. List five methods through which you can practice continuing education.

Chapter Glossary

ethics	The moral principles by which we live and work.
image enhancers	Behaviors that improve the quality of your professional image through specific methods for conducting and representing yourself.
nonverbal communication	Communication expressed by body language, eye contact, facial expressions, and gestures.
on-line portfolio	An Internet display of your talents and work for potential customers and employers to evaluate your professional skills.
personal hygiene	Daily maintenance of cleanliness and healthfulness through certain sanitary practices.
professional image	Also known as professionalism; the impression projected by a person engaged in any profession, consisting of outward appearance and conduct exhibited in the workplace.
toolbox	An alternative term for professional makeup kit. Your makeup kit is a case containing all the supplies, tools, and implements needed to perform a professional makeup application.
work ethic	Taking pride in your work and committing yourself to consistently doing an excellent job for your clients, employer, and the salon or spa team.

Chapter 20 The Business of Makeup

Chapter Outline

Why Study the Business of Makeup?

The Earning Potential of a Professional Makeup Artist

Career Options

Getting the Job

Business Ownership

Making a Name for Yourself

Marketing

Getting Started

Learning Objectives

After completing this chapter, you will be able to:

- ☑ **LO1** Understand the scope of the earning potential of a professional makeup artist and the financial implications of being an employee or independent contractor.
- ☑ **LO2** Identify career options, employment opportunities, and employment demands.
- ☑ **LO3** Identify the components of a professional resume, the purpose and contents of a cover letter, and prepare for an interview.
- ☑ **LO4** Understand a business plan and business options.
- ☑ **LO5** Understand marketing techniques and resources in order to build your presence and reputation as a makeup artist.

Key Terms

Page number indicates where in the chapter the term is used.

blog
pg. 490

branding
pg. 488

business plan
pg. 486

client list
pg. 481

independent contractor
pg. 472

informational interview
pg. 475

kit fee
pg. 485

logo
pg. 488

makeup department head
pg. 477

private label
pg. 486

resume
pg. 481

retainer
pg. 480

union job
pg. 478

Career Profile

An expert in the field, Sally Henshaw has created a brand name that is complete and comprehensive. She has worked with and for high-end makeup lines including Dior and Lancôme, achieving a number of awards and earning titles such as "Instructor and Teacher of the Year" at the Makeup Academy. She attributes her success to focus and appreciation, advising her students and other aspiring artists to cultivate and maintain this type of attitude. Her commitment to makeup artistry and the industry has allowed her to establish her own makeup academy and author several makeup curriculums.

"I entered into the makeup business because of my love for art, design, and color. It created within me a burning desire to study all aspects of the esthetic world. The esthetics industry led me to create beauty through the art of makeup. I saw before and after photos of corrective makeup and I took them as an invitation. I wanted to learn everything I could to help women truly feel as beautiful as they are, both inside and outside. Makeup school was my answer.

"I was fortunate to find a direction that sparked my interest. As a makeup artist, the work that I am most proud of is my work in corrective makeup. Educating women on how to apply corrective makeup is some of my greatest work. Seeing and witnessing these women looking their best is the most rewarding feeling I have from all my years in the cosmetic industry. These women immediately take on a aura of confidence and experience sincere happiness knowing they will be able to replicate the design at home.

"My work in the industry has spanned a number of genres and I have had the pleasure of applying it across diverse areas of makeup artistry. During my career in the makeup industry I have achieved a number of accomplishments over the years such as: Celebrity Makeup Artist; Lancôme Institute de Beauté —Esthetician; National Makeup Artist, Christian Dior; Instructor and Teacher of the Year, Makeup Academy; Regional Trainer for account executives and top performers in cosmetic lines; owning my own makeup academy; authoring numerous cosmetic curriculums.

"My advice to any aspiring or established makeup artist is to specialize in one area and focus on that—become the best you can be. Work, study, and practice as much as you can. When you launch yourself into the world of makeup, take any jobs that are available, even if the monetary compensation is minimal or nonexistent, just so you can accumulate the experience and gain exposure. These experiences will give you a unique opportunity to perfect your skills. We all hit speed bumps that may temporarily slow us down; the important thing to remember is that these are learning experiences and sometimes opportunities in disguise. Stay professional, positive, and committed to your career and artistry. Always treat clients as you would a dear friend, and make it a point to overlook the negative and focus on the positive aspects in every situation."

Courtesy of Sally Henshaw-Eggleton

By now your professional image should be well established and you should be ready to begin your journey as a professional makeup artist. At this juncture, you might still be asking yourself "What area of the industry do I want to work in?" or "What type of 'artist' do I want to be?" These are excellent questions, and the information outlined in this chapter will help you select the path that is right for you. Keep in mind that almost everything you achieve is a stepping stone to the next level of advancement in your career. Success comes to those who work hard, hone their skills, and are willing to work their way up through the ranks. It is not realistic to think you will be the key makeup artist for a major motion picture right out of school. However, assisting the makeup team on a major motion-picture set or being the key on a small independent student film certainly is and are excellent goals and great accomplishments for a makeup artist just launching their career (**Figure 20–1**).

© Brian Chase/www.Shutterstock.com

▲ **Figure 20–1 Every opportunity is a stepping stone so remember to look your best.**

WHY STUDY THE BUSINESS OF MAKEUP?

Makeup artists should study and have a thorough understanding of the business of makeup because:

- It is important to further your understanding regarding what career paths fit your personality.
- It will enable you to construct realistic goals for your future.
- Your career is not only a representation of your skills and talent, it is also the cornerstone of your professional image.

Focus On

Dream Big, Think Realistic

"Be realistic and know that if you want to do the kind of work being done in New York and Hollywood, that is where you will need to live. Have a plan for your future but be prepared to change it."
—David Michaud

THE EARNING POTENTIAL OF A PROFESSIONAL MAKEUP ARTIST

Several factors influence the earning potential of a makeup artist. Factors that influence the salary range include type of client, type of work, frequency of work, and geographic location. The income of a makeup artist can be very lucrative, especially if you offer your services as an independent contractor. It is not uncommon for makeup artists performing bridal or prom applications to charge anywhere from $50 to $500 per service—and sometimes even more depending on your geographic location.

Concurrent with the authoring of this edition of *Milady Standard Makeup*, according to the U.S. Department of Labor's Bureau of Labor Statistics, the average hourly wage for a makeup artist in the field of performing arts (theatrical and performance) is about $25 per hour and $51,000 annually. In the film and video industry, the average hourly

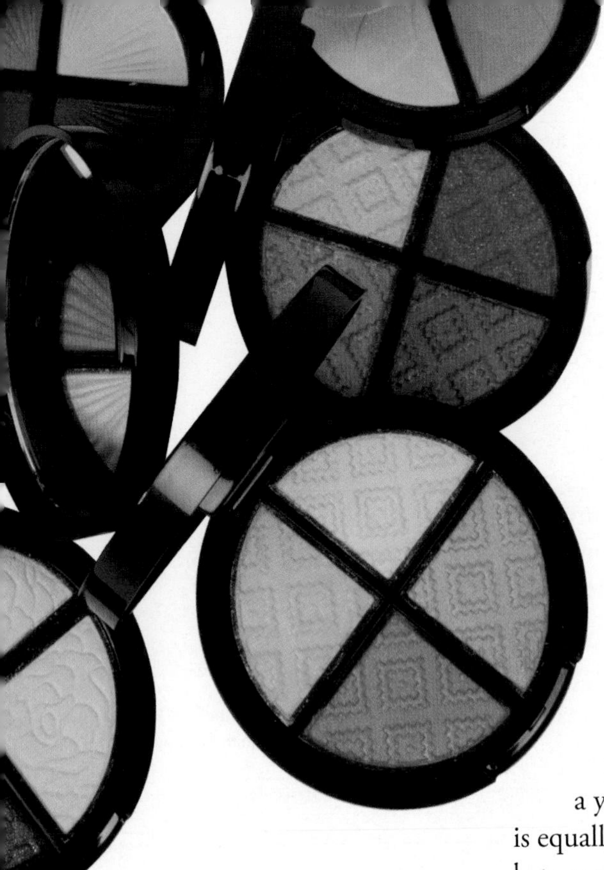

wage for makeup artists is $39 per hour and upwards of $80,000 annually. A freelance makeup artist working for film or television can earn as much as $500 per day, and a highly experienced makeup artist working in these industries can command anywhere from $2,000 to $5,000 per day. For a makeup artist who performs only personal-care services and is generally working in a salon or spa setting as an employee, the average hourly wage is about $13 per hour and $25,000 annually.

Your earning potential is entirely up to you and your goals, and as in any profession, the more advanced your skills and the more demand there is for your talent, the more you can charge for your services.

Employee versus Independent Contractor

The career options for a makeup artist are endless, and where you begin is not necessarily where you will find yourself even after a year or two. When deciding which career path is best for you, it is equally important to understand the legal and financial implications between being an employee versus an independent contractor.

Either career path will impact your lifestyle, and the right information is essential in deciding which career path is right for you. Both have risks and rewards. Also, you do not necessarily have to choose one or the other; you can work part time as an employee and also take on independent contract work. This is yet another example of one of many alluring aspects in the makeup industry—flexibility and freedom.

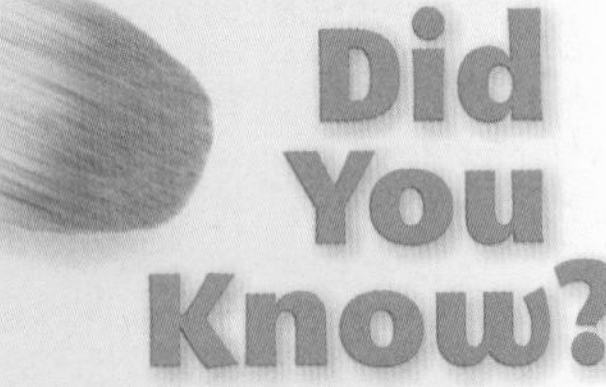

Did You Know?

Bobbi Brown began as an assistant to a New York makeup artist in 1979 and quickly worked her way up to doing makeup for models at photoshoots for *Glamour* and *Vogue magazines.* In 1990, she and a friend invested $10,000 each into manufacturing and marketing the lipstick line Bobbie Brown Cosmetics. After just 4 years their company was achieving close to $20 million in sales annually!

Employee

When starting out, working as an employee can be beneficial as you make a name for yourself, hone your skills, establish your professional image, grow your reputation, and build the 6-month cash reserve which you learned about in Chapter 19, Your Professional Image.

Working as an employee requires you to work a predetermined schedule. When you become an employee, you will be expected to conform to a set of rules and meet specific standards. You may find yourself needing to achieve certain revenue goals and sales quotas set by your employer. Working as an employee offers the security of a steady income and often includes health benefits, paid vacation time, and additional training.

Independent Contractor

An **independent contractor** is someone who sets his or her own fees, controls his or her own hours, has his or her own business card, and pays his or her own taxes. As an independent contractor, you really work for yourself. As exciting as working for yourself may seem and can be, there are important legal and tax ramifications that you alone will be responsible for and must be prepared to meet. As an independent contractor, you are a nonemployee service provider that must act in accordance with

Internal Revenue Service (IRS) guidelines; be able to control the means and methods by which you accomplish your work; be responsible for adhering to all laws set forth by the applicable licensing board; and meet any and all local, state, and federal rules and regulations that apply to small business owners in your trade.

The use of independent contractors is widespread in the makeup industry. Be cautious when accepting employment under this status and do your homework. A makeup artist who meets the lawful IRS definition of an independent contractor is considered self-employed and is responsible for paying all of his or her own insurance, federal and state income taxes, plus an additional self-employment tax. It is sometimes beneficial to the independent contractor to engage the services of an accountant or bookkeeper. There are also a number of software programs easily available to you that can be of great assistance if you decide to work as an independent contractor or run your own business. Each of these options will allow you to best prepare for proper tax payments, estimates, and IRS guidelines.

As an independent makeup artist, you set your rates. Depending upon the service that you are providing, you can charge a per-person fee, a daily fee, or a set fee encompassing all aspects of a particular job. Having your own makeup business and working as an independent makeup artist is a terrific way to direct your career down the path of your choosing. You can hand-pick the events and jobs you want to work on or specialize in, the locations where you work, and the hours you are available. Working as an independent or freelance makeup artist, you have the opportunity to establish a name and reputation for yourself as an "in demand" makeup professional who is highly sought after. The possibilities are endless! ☑ LO1

CAREER OPTIONS

The makeup profession has emerged as one of the top categories in the beauty industry. The majority of the growth has arisen out of an enormous demand from women and men who are committed to looking younger, healthier, and as beautiful as they possibly can. New products and ingredients are released almost daily as cosmetic companies launch innovative and creative developments to meet the demands of this explosion in growth. The career paths for the makeup professional are extensive and diverse.

As a new makeup artist it is important to stay open-minded and receptive to the many opportunities that will come your way. A position in one area may quickly lead to success in another. The key to success in any makeup position is motivation, determination, and a commitment to continue to perfect your skills in order to advance your abilities and enhance your professional reputation.

The Makeup Counter

As a new makeup artist one of the surest ways to find gainful employment and garner experience is at the makeup counter in a department

Focus On

Creativity

"My advice for future aspiring artists is to be open to learning different styles and techniques. Don't be afraid to use products on different areas of the face and reach out to different brands. The industry has changed so much just in the last 15 years, so be confident in yourself and your abilities and unafraid of the unknown."
—Krissy Ferro, Ferro Cosmetics

Before your informational interview, set an appointment for a service. Experience firsthand what it is to be a client at this particular salon or spa. Observe the interaction of the management team, receptionist(s), stylist(s), makeup artist(s), and esthetician(s). Is this a place your clients would love? Is this the place you would like to work?

store, makeup boutique, or beauty bar. You will be hired either by a retail establishment or the cosmetic brand you will be representing. If hired by the cosmetic brand, your opportunities for advancement are much more diverse and can lead to a position within the organization as a trainer or national artist. Once hired, you will receive training regarding product knowledge along with educational updates and seminars on new ingredients, products, and seasonal color trends. This position will build your knowledge base about products and ingredients as well as enhance your skill set regarding colors, customer service, and application techniques. You will experience the benefits that come from creating a variety of makeup looks ranging from everyday makeup to prom to glamour to bridal and so much more.

To begin your journey behind the counter, select five cosmetic companies and/or retail establishments you would like to work at. Check both the cosmetic companies' and retail establishments' Web sites for career opportunities. Review your resume and then submit it—and follow up with a phone call. You can also visit the establishment in person with your resume in hand and ask to speak with the Makeup Department manager about hiring opportunities. A position as a makeup artist at a cosmetics' counter will also encourage you to stay on the cutting-edge of the latest trends, colors, and makeup products as you will regularly be demonstrating these looks for customers. It is also an excellent way to meet many people and build a following of loyal clients.

Compensation for a makeup artist at a cosmetics' counter is usually an hourly rate plus commission on products sold (and quite often an excellent discount on personal product purchases since it is easier to sell what you use and what you like!).

Salon or Spa

If you have a cosmetology or esthetics license, then a salon or spa is an excellent option for employment. Many salons and spas have a resident makeup artist on staff. After a full day of beauty treatments, or even a facial or haircut, a makeup application is the ideal way to send a client out the door. Makeup artists in a salon or spa are fortunate to have the opportunity to work on many different clients, create many different looks, and acquire retail sales skills in recommending makeup products and colors for home use. Quite often, salons and spas are the ideal place for brides, bridal parties, birthday parties, girls' night out, and prom makeovers. Working in a salon or spa can be the ideal environment for a new makeup artist to find the perfect multifaceted makeup experience.

Many salons and spas carry a particular brand of makeup and may even have exclusive sales rights in their area for that brand. If this is the case, it offers the makeup artist the opportunity to gain specialized education and experience with an exclusive brand.

To begin your journey working in a salon or spa, select the top three to five salons and/or spas in your area. Begin by calling the manager, owner, or networking with other beauty and wellness professionals who can connect you with someone who works at the salon or spa. Once you have made contact, ask for an informational interview. An **informational interview** is a scheduled meeting or conversation whose sole purpose is to gather information. During this meeting, you can ask for career and industry advice as well as gather information on the field and possibly find employment leads while also expanding your professional network. This is also an opportunity for you to determine if there is a comfortable fit between you and the organization where the informational interview is taking place.

As the health, wellness, and beauty industry has thrived throughout the last decade, the employment benefits have also expanded. Many salons and spas offer employees hourly rates, commission on retail sales, paid vacations, and health benefits. Another option available is to rent space in the salon or spa as an independent contractor.

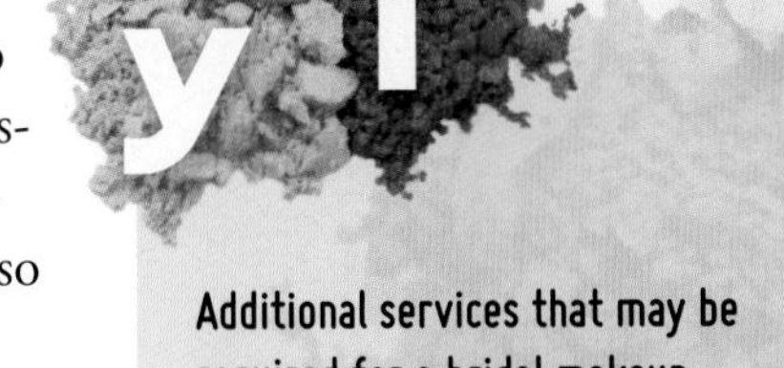

Additional services that may be required for a bridal makeup application (additional fees apply):

- Tattoo camouflage
- Body makeup
- Airbrush makeup
- Lash application
- Lash extensions
- Eyebrow design

Bridal Makeup

The bridal business is a multibillion dollar industry, and the wedding day can be the most important day in a woman's life. It is the job of the bridal makeup artist to enhance the bride's beauty without changing the way she looks.

If you like diverse locations, are comfortable with and enjoy the challenge of managing personalities under stress, and find satisfaction in making the most important day of a woman's life memorable then this could be a career option for you (**Figure 20–2**). Working in a salon, spa, or at a makeup counter is a great way to meet brides-to-be in order to begin establishing yourself and developing a professional reputation for this career path.

The bridal makeup artist can live anywhere and be very successful. Every city, no matter how large or small, has brides. Excellent resources for beginning your journey as a bridal makeup artist are the wedding professionals in your local area. These professionals include wedding planners, wedding photographers, florists, caterers, hairstylists, bridal stylists, and bridal shops. The best place to begin networking is at bridal expositions. Introduce yourself as a bridal makeup artist, and design your portfolio and business card to represent your work as a bridal makeup artist. Referrals and word of mouth are the best tools for a makeup artist to build their clientele and grow their professional reputation.

Bridal makeup fees vary depending on geography. The general range for fees is as follows:

- Bride on wedding day—$100 to $500
- Bride trial run—$35 to $200 (approximately 30 to 40 percent of the wedding day fee)
- Additional applications—$50 to $200 (individual makeup applications for other bridal party members)
- Full-day package—$700 to $2000 (this includes a makeup application for all bridal party members)

▼ Figure 20–2 **Bridal makeup will keep you working in diverse locations.**

A resource for brides looking to hire makeup artists for their wedding day is www.weddingmakeup.com. It is also a great place to see how other bridal makeup artists market themselves, and when you are ready, you too can join the roster.

Theater, Film, and Television

Theater, film, and television are a great niche for a makeup artist who is creative, innovative, and has an artistic eye for design. It is a stimulating, ever-changing environment that requires the willingness and flexibility to be away from home for weeks to months at a time, the stamina to work long hours, and the disposition and business skills to work as an independent contractor.

Theater

Makeup artists with an eye for meeting a creative vision are ideal for the world of theater. Plays and other theatrical productions, such as ballets and operas, rely on makeup artists to enhance and alter actors' features to meet the demands of the production's creative needs (**Figure 20–3**). Makeup artists may need to design a look that makes an actor or performer appear older or younger, or create special-effects makeup designs, such as scars or burns for example, through the use of specialized makeup, techniques, and prosthetics. A career in theater makeup requires some knowledge and educational background in theater with an emphasis in costuming and makeup. Many specialized schools and academies are available to assist makeup artists to develop skills for this career specialty.

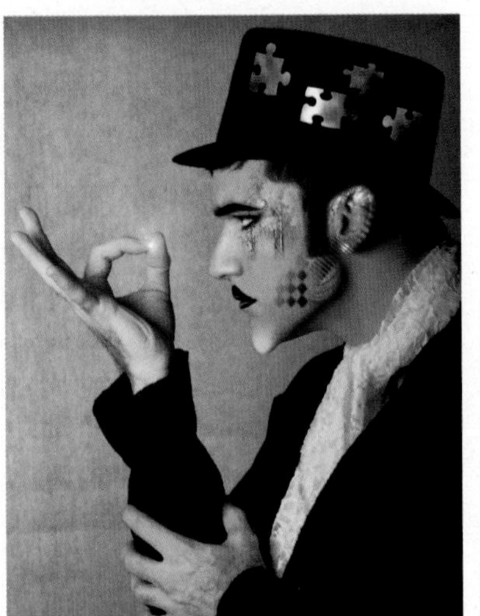

© CURAphotography/www.Shutterstock.com

▲ **Figure 20–3 Dramatic applications are perfect for the theater.**

Through a combination of experience and educational training, makeup artists working in the theater venue learn how to evaluate an entire performance, as well as any particular scene, so that the makeup designs seen on stage are not adversely affected by the theater's lighting and are visualized as authentic and believable by the audience.

To begin your journey as a theater makeup artist, call the theater department of your local college or university and inquire if they have classes in theater makeup. Ask if these courses are offered as continuing education or if you need to be a registered student. You can also call your local performing arts center and any local stores selling professional theater makeup. The Internet is also a great resource for researching and exploring career training and options for theater makeup. If this is an area of interest, ask to spend some time behind stage with makeup artists as either an assistant, or just ask if you can observe the amazing transformations that go on before an actor steps out on stage.

Makeup artists working in theater are most often independent contractors and paid either by the day or a contract price for the entire job. Depending upon your skill, experience, and expertise your daily pay rate can range from a few to hundreds or even to thousands of dollars.

Did You Know?

Costuming is a set of clothes—unusual or period—worn in a play by an actor or by an individual attending a special event such as a dress or costume ball.

Film and Television

Makeup artists in the film and television industry need to be as creative and flexible as those in theater. Studio or set lighting, attention to detail, and delivering a finished look that the viewer finds believable need to be taken into account. With the advances in technology and the advent of high-definition television and film, attention to the fine details of an individual's face are crucial. Texture, tone, blemishes, highlights, and contours are all essential factors in creating the desired look.

An excellent place to begin your journey as a makeup artist for film and television is working with student films. This is an excellent training ground as it provides the freedom to make mistakes, room to ask questions, and acts as a learning platform for both you and your future colleagues. Contact your local colleges, universities, and film schools and inquire about their film-studies programs, scour the Internet looking for assistant makeup jobs, and NETWORK. In the film industry, it is not only who you know but also who knows you.

Until you are completely comfortable with your skill level and the protocols of working in a theater production, local performing arts and theater groups, colleges, and universities are excellent starting points for offering your talents as a volunteer or as an assistant to the key makeup artist in their productions.

Since the investment in time, money, and talent is greater in this area than in most professions the producers, directors, production companies, publicists, key makeup artists, and so on are not apt to take risks on an unknown makeup artist. Your reputation, makeup skills, experience (no matter how limited or expansive), enthusiasm, and professional image are what will be used to evaluate you and determine whether or not you will be a good fit for a position. Once hired in any capacity and, you contribute positively to the production you will be hired again. If your contributions are questionable, you will quickly find yourself out of a job and your professional reputation in jeopardy. Makeup jobs in film and television are fiercely competitive; to give yourself a competitive edge present the right personality and place yourself at the center of the movie and television industry. In North America these hubs are located in Los Angeles, New York, Toronto, and Vancouver.

Careers in Theater, Film, and Television

Working in film and television is a tight-knit circle; however, once you have proven the kind of professional you are, being a makeup artist for film and television can be a lucrative career. The pay scale is the same as theater and is based on skill and experience.

The production of theater, film, and television programs requires a fine-tuned balance of teamwork. For the makeup crew on these productions, a team of makeup professionals work together on set to deliver the vision and results of the director and writer. Following is a description of the makeup crew and their respective roles. Depending on the size of the production, the roles and responsibilities can be interchangeable.

- The **makeup department head** manages the makeup department for the film, television, or theater production. They read the script;

meet with the director and screen writer; and they are responsible for the research, design, and execution of the makeup for each and every actor. They make hiring decisions in addition to maintaining budgets for salaries, supplies, materials, and special effects. The makeup department head is generally responsible for the primary actors' makeup applications as well.

WEB RESOURCES

For more information on special effects makeup resources visit:

www.theeffectslab.com

www.cinefex.com

- The **key makeup artist** is the person applying makeup to the secondary actors and is also the team member responsible for following the script and design guidelines with precision and accuracy. Filming or performing the same scene can take days, and it is the responsibility of the makeup artist to ensure there is continuity in the look of the makeup from one day to the next.
- The **third** and **fourth makeup artist** often appears on large productions; however, these are often revolving positions as crew is booked based on the number of actors in each scene. Makeup artists are often hired as "day players" to supervise the extras and other untitled characters.
- The **special effects makeup artist** uses wigs, makeup, prosthetics, molds, and other tools to create the desired look the script may demand. Think of movies such as *Lord of the Rings, Star Wars, Avatar*, or *The Lion King* stage production—it is the special effects makeup artist who takes us to fantasy land (**Figure 20–4**). Special effects makeup artists work in theaters, film and television productions, theme parks, cruise ships, and avant-garde fashion shows. You will need additional specialized training to meet the diverse requirements for creating the many and varied characters and looks that the special effects makeup artists creates.
- The **makeup assistant** has responsibilities and duties that vary depending upon the size of the production. Some of the duties and tasks include setting up workstations, maintaining workstations, cleaning brushes and product, stocking supplies, maintaining inventory, running errands, and assisting senior staff. On smaller productions, the makeup assistant will also apply makeup and prep actors.

▲ Figure 20–4 **Special effects makeup can be used from independent films to major motion pictures.**

Make-Up Artists & Hair Stylists Guild, I.A.T.S.E

If a career in theater, film, or television is one you would like to pursue, then understanding the rules and regulations of the Make-up Artists & Hair Stylists Guild is essential. Though it is not mandatory to join the union, work on large productions will most likely be what is called a **union job**, one where all the persons working on the production must be members of the Make-up Artists & Hairstylists Guild of the I.A.T.S.E. Smaller independent projects are not union and do not have the same requirements. To join the union you must have worked in Los Angeles or New York, and the terms to become a member in good standing will take at least 3 years and is often a 5-year process. There is a fee to join and union dues are paid annually. The union offers many benefits and protects your rights as a working makeup artist.

Fashion

Many makeup artists aspire to work in the world of fashion. Behind-the-scene of the world's top runway debuts, photoshoots, launches of new product lines, international season previews, and the high-fashion catwalk is a thrilling and exciting place to be. The makeup artist's job in this environment is to be efficient, creative, skilled, and poised to handle the high stress of working with the industry's top models and designers. The creation of the ultimate flawless look, often with a flare of extravagance, is an integral part of just another day's work. Fashion makeup artists are well informed on the newest trends in color and glamour and are capable of taking into account studio lighting, runway lighting, and any special effects that the designers or the production require and the audience will view.

The world of fashion requires teamwork, flexibility, creativity, and innovation—very much like the world of theater, film, and television; however, the one major difference is that the world of fashion moves at a much faster pace. A fashion show or photoshoot can take days, weeks, or months to prep depending on the extent of the production; that being said, it is "show day" that separates the professionals from the novices. Backstage is organized chaos as models are being readied for their turn on the catwalk or in front of the camera. You will be left to your own devices, expected to be prepared and capable of performing your tasks on time as needed. There is little-to-no room for error in the world of fashion makeup. The show must go on without a hitch and excuses are not tolerated. The world of fashion is fun, exhilarating, and exciting. If you thrive under pressure and chaos and love glamour, then this could be the career path for you. (Refer to Chapter 11, The Exciting World of High Fashion and High-Definition, for additional information.)

WEB RESOURCES

MAKE-UP ARTISTS & HAIR STYLISTS GUILD, I.A.T.S.E.

LOCAL 706, I.A.T.S.E.—Los Angeles

LOCAL798, I.A.T.S.E.—New York

Eligibility requirements for all classifications can be found on their respective Web sites under the tab "How to Join."

For detailed information on Local 706 Union in Los Angeles or Local 798 Union in New York visit their Web sites at:

www.local706.org/howTo.cfm

www.798makeupandhair.com

Getting Started in Fashion Makeup

The first thing needed to begin your journey as a fashion makeup artist is experience and a diverse portfolio of beauty and editorial photos that showcase your range of talent. An impeccable professional image is also a must. To get started in fashion makeup, here are a few suggestions to help you begin:

- Call photography schools and work with student photographers; offer your services in exchange for photos. This is an excellent way to build your portfolio at the same time.
- Volunteer your services as an assistant or intern until you feel confident enough to move to area fashion shows at local malls and department stores and work independently.
- Call fashion buyers and send them to your on-line portfolio or offer to drop your bound portfolio off so that they can review it at their convenience.
- Attend area fashion shows as an audience member and network while you are there.

Be willing to work hard and be open to all opportunities. Each job is your chance to shine and to network; make it a habit to ask for cards and offer yours, send notes to the people you work with, and keep in touch with those in the industry that you meet—you never know who your next job will come from. If you are serious about this career path, then geographic location will be a factor: many models and designers are located in New York, Los Angeles, Toronto, London, Paris, Milan, and Miami. It will require some research and investigation, but you will most likely need to be where the fashion industry is active and flourishing and the opportunities for a fashion makeup artist are greater.

Fashion makeup artists are hired as independent contractors and are compensated by the day or per job. However, there are some designers and photographers that work with one particular makeup artist throughout a season, or even for years, and keep them on **retainer**, a fixed sum of money that the client agrees to pay, in advance, to secure the services of the makeup artist as needed, when needed.

Educator

After a few years in the industry, once you have honed your skills and built a name for yourself, you can expand your professional expertise into the arena of education. Establish a relationship with an esthetics or cosmetology school and offer a variety of one-day, two-day, or even week-long makeup classes. Cosmetic companies have extensive education departments and are always looking for experienced educators to work locally, nationally, and internationally. This is an excellent way to give back to the field and help new makeup artists enhance their skills while building your reputation at the same time. One of the benefits of being an educator is that you will always be on the cutting edge of the industry since you will need to stay a step or two ahead of your students.

Getting Started in Education

To begin your journey as an educator you must be at the top of your game; young professionals are looking up to you as a mentor and guide. Your professional image, reputation, and skill level must be held in high esteem by industry professionals and your peers. At this stage of your career your client list, contacts, and resume will be substantial. Contact colleagues, friends, and acquaintances to let them know the direction you want to take—these are excellent resources to assist you in establishing yourself as an educator.

You can earn a substantial income by holding makeup classes and charging per person. One class with ten students paying $200 each will generate $2,000 for just that day. ✓ LO2

GETTING THE JOB

There are plenty of terrific jobs available to the makeup artist who is dedicated, hardworking, motivated, and talented. It will not matter whether you choose the route of independent contractor or employee, the methods for landing jobs in either role is very similar: networking, referrals, and perseverance are the key elements. The world's leading makeup artists were not born successful, nor did it happen for them overnight; they achieved success through determination, self-motivation, commitment, and persistence. These success stories were created by those makeup artists who used their time wisely, planned for their future, went the extra mile, and met everyday challenges confident in their abilities and skill. They owe their success to no one but themselves. If you want to enjoy similar success, you must prepare yourself and work for the opportunities that await you.

HERE'S A TIP

Get involved! Volunteering not only looks great on a resume, it also offers fabulous work experience. Volunteer for fundraisers, prom makeovers, health fairs, women's expos, or any place where you can make yourself visible!

Resume/Client List

In the world of a makeup professional your resume and client list are interchangeable. A **resume** is a written summary of education and work experience that highlights relevant accomplishments and achievements. It informs potential employers of your achievements and accomplishments in a simple and straightforward manner that can be easily reviewed at a glance (**Figure 20–5**). A **client list** refers to all the productions, events, and celebrity or notable clients you have worked on.

If you are a new makeup artist and have little work experience, then your resume should focus on your skills and accomplishments to date. The average employer spends little time reviewing a resume; the average is approximately 20 seconds. Those 20 seconds will determine whether or not an employer grants you an interview.

▼ **Figure 20–5 Review your resume before every interview.**

Resume Guidelines

Here are some basic guidelines to follow when preparing your professional resume:

- Keep it simple, and limit it to one page.
- Create a document and save it to your computer. More often than not you will be sending your resume electronically.
- Include your name, address, phone number, and e-mail address on both the resume/client list and your cover letter.
- List recent, relevant work experience (including celebrity/notable clients if applicable).
- List relevant education and the name of the institution from which you graduated, as well as relevant courses attended.
- List your professional skills and accomplishments.
- Focus on information that is relevant to the position you are seeking.
- Focus on achievements instead of detailing duties and responsibilities. Accomplishment statements enlarge your basic duties and responsibilities. Even if you have very little work experience or a small client base, you can focus on accomplishments and achievements while completing your education. Include information such as:

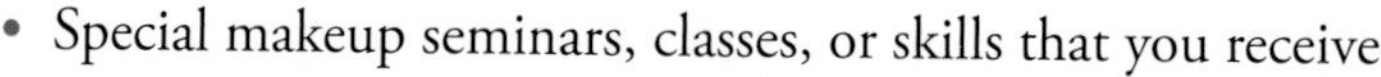

- Special makeup seminars, classes, or skills that you received
- Any awards or recognitions
- Various types of makeovers performed (bridal, prom, special occasion, fashion, etc.)
- Different types of products, tools, and techniques used
- Amount of return business (including school/clinic and client feedback)

WEB RESOURCES

For additional help in writing your resume and cover letter as well as job hunting visit Milady Beauty & Wellness Career Transitions at: www.milady.cengage.com/jobsearch/careertransitions.html or visit:

www.creativejobscentral.com/makeup-jobs

www.indeed.com

- Follow the employer's instructions when sending your resume. Do not deviate from their instructions as this will keep your resume from being seen.
- Print a hard copy on resume-quality paper, if needed. Resume-quality paper is a thicker stock of paper, between 16 and 24 lbs. It is best to choose subdued colors like white, ivory, buff, granite, or pale gray. (Your electronic resume should follow these same guidelines as well.) Texture should be a cotton fiber or a good-quality bond paper. The font should be Times New Roman or Arial. Avoid the temptation of using fancy fonts, added color, or artistic flairs; all these added flourishes succeed in achieving is making your resume difficult to read. The rule of thumb to follow when creating your resume/client list is "keep it simple."

Cover Letter

It is best to include a cover letter when sending your resume. Your cover letter demonstrates your professional image and answers the question "Why should I hire you?" The cover letter's purpose is to introduce you to your potential employer, give the reason why you are perfect for the job, detail how you can benefit the company and most of all, get you the interview. You must do your research about the company you are applying to so that you can deliver a perception of engaged readiness to join a functioning, successful team. If sending your cover letter electronically, follow the interviewer's instructions thoroughly, which will be either "include as attachment" or "include in body of e-mail."

Here are some important tips to follow before you begin writing your cover letter:

- Research the company.
- Check all spelling, punctuation, and grammar.
- Do not use abbreviations, emoticons, or all small caps.
- If printing, use the same paper as your resume.
- Keep it brief, half a page: one to two paragraphs should cover what you are trying to state.

Professional References

A professional reference is a person who can provide information about your job performance. It is a recommendation based on your professional image, work ethic, and skills. When choosing a person to give you a recommendation, choose people you know will speak highly of you. Ask them if they would be willing to be a reference for you and ask for a letter of recommendation. Most resume's state "references available upon request" at the end, and when a potential employer or client requests your references, send your list of professional references along with their letters as a separate document or cut and paste them in the body of an e-mail, depending on the interviewer's instructions.

Be sure to include the name, title, place of employment, e-mail address, and phone number of each professional reference along with their letter of recommendation. Start collecting professional references now. If you don't have your references available when a potential employer asks for them, it will be too late. If you are just starting out and are not sure where to begin to find professional references, ask your instructors and peers or colleagues you worked with on projects. When volunteering, ask the person in charge if they would write a reference when the event is over.

The Interview

Upon review of your resume and cover letter by a potential employer, the next step in getting the job is the actual interview. Once you have been granted an interview, write your interview time on your calendar or in your day planner. Do not miss your interview, do not be late, and whatever you do, do not call to reschedule.

As you learned in earlier chapters, first impressions are priceless. In 7 seconds someone will make 11 impressions about you without even speaking to you. Instantly your makeup, clothes, posture, fragrances, hair, jewelry, facial expression, and confidence will be evaluated and solidify your professional image in the mind of your beholder. The resume and cover letter are your first opportunity to impress a potential employer and set yourself apart from other candidates for the same position—the interview is the next, and you only have one chance to make a positive first impression (**Figure 20–6**).

▲ **20–6 Make your first impression count.**

Interview Preparation

Your appearance is crucial, especially since you are applying for a position in the image and beauty industry. Consider the following points as you prepare for the interview:

- Dress for success—consider the position and dress appropriately. Remember: if you would wear it to the beach or to a club, then don't wear it to the interview. Dress to fit into the work environment that you are looking to be hired at for employment.
- Hair, makeup, and nails should be a representation of what a professional makeup artist would expect. This is not the time to be excessively trendy or to express extreme individuality.
- Always introduce yourself with a firm handshake, a smile, and make eye contact.

- The manner in which you walk, stand, sit, and speak will display volumes about your ability to handle the position and yourself in a professional setting.
- Be prepared with an additional resume and cover letter inclusive with references.
- Bring your professional makeup portfolio.
- Bring a small makeup toolkit in case you are asked to perform a makeup application on the spot.
- Arrive at least 10 minutes early.
- Do not bring in your cell phone.
- Do not arrive with a cup of coffee or other beverages or food.
- Avoid smoking for at least 1 hour prior to the interview.

Interview Questions

Every interviewer has their own interview style, but there are certain questions commonly asked in almost every interview. Being familiar with these questions will allow you to reflect on your answers ahead of time and be prepared with complete and confident answers (**Figure 20–7**). Typical questions include the following:

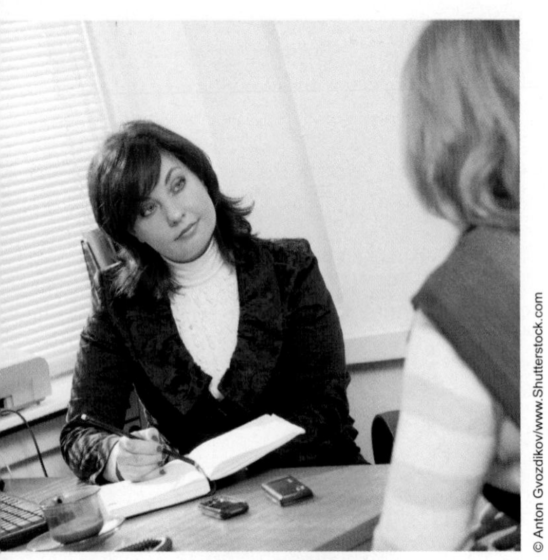

© Anton Gvozdikov/www.Shutterstock.com

▲ **Figure 20–7 Familiarize yourself with the common interview questions.**

- Why do you want to work here?
- What did you like best about your training?
- Are you punctual and regular in attendance?
- What skills do you feel are your strongest?
- What would you consider to be a weak area for you?
- What do you like most about makeup?
- Why did you get into the makeup profession?
- Describe what you feel a team player is.
- Do you consider yourself flexible? Please explain.
- Where do you see yourself in 3 years?
- What days and hours are you available for work?
- Are there any obstacles that would prevent you from keeping your commitment to your position? Please explain.
- Describe a difficult situation with a client or fellow student in school. How did you handle it?
- Do you consider yourself a salesperson?
- Would you be willing to attend our company's training program?
- Would you please describe ways that you provide excellent customer service?

You cannot be overprepared for an interview. The most important thing to remember is to be yourself; be confident, positive, and honest. Avoid any derogatory remarks or conversation regarding your education, classmates, prior employers, or past coworkers. Everything that you say is

TABLE 20-1 INTERVIEW QUERY QUESTIONS
(questions to ask the interviewer)

Employer	Independent Contractor
Is there a job description? May I review it?	Who is my main contact if I have questions about the job?
Is there an employee manual? May I review it?	What code of conduct is expected on the film set or production?
How long have your employees been with you?	How long is the production scheduled to run?
Does the business offer continuing education opportunities?	Do I need my kit and is there a **kit fee**? (A *kit fee* is for makeup supplies needed for a television, film, theater, or fashion production and is usually paid by the production company and requires receipts for all products purchased.)
What is the form of compensation? Does the company offer any type of benefits?	What is the compensation and how will I be paid? Weekly, biweekly, monthly?
When will the position be filled?	When will the position be filled?
May I contact you in a week regarding your decision?	May I contact you in a week regarding your decision?

▲ Table 20–1 **Interview Query Questions.**

a representation of the type of professional you are and the way that you will handle professional situations.

Very often a potential employer will ask if you have any questions. Be prepared with a few important questions that will influence your ability to do your job. Find out what the job expectations are and if the position truly is a good fit for you. **Table 20–1** outlines some questions that you might consider in preparing for an interview.

By obtaining the answers to some of your questions, you can compare the information you have gathered from other interviews and choose the one that offers the best package of income and career development.

Remember to follow up the interview with a thank-you note or e-mail. Be very brief, thank the interviewer for the time he or she spent with you, close with a positive statement pertaining to your desire for the position or the job, and state that you look forward to hearing from them soon. If the interviewer suggests that you call to learn about the employment decision, then by all means do so. ☑ LO3

In today's behavioral interviewing techniques, several existing team members may also interview the candidate in addition to the hiring manager.

BUSINESS OWNERSHIP

If your dream is to own your own business, you may be ready to jump full force into a business venture and open a makeup boutique or other type of retail makeup business. Many professional makeup artists have opened their own studios in which they offer their services and also retail exclusive lines or private label their own cosmetic line.

Private label products are typically manufactured or provided by one company for offer under another company's brand. They are often positioned as lower-cost alternatives to regional, national, or international brands. There are several excellent private-label companies that produce quality products, colors, and packages that can have your business name and logo stamped right on them. This is an amazingly exciting business venture, but it does require an investment of time, effort, and money.

Business Start Up

Starting a business is exhilarating and exhausting at the same time. However, if owning your own business is your passion, and you do it properly, it can be a huge success. To begin with, you will need to write a complete business plan as this will be required by a financial institution for acquiring a loan. Your business plan will also act as your guidebook for business operations.

A **business plan** is a strategy for understanding key elements in developing a business; it also serves as a guide to making informed business decisions. It is a formal statement of a set of business goals, the reasons your goals are attainable, and the plan for reaching those goals. It may also contain background information about the organization or the persons responsible for reaching those goals. Your business plan will be reviewed by financial institutions as a means of deciding on the viability and feasibility of the success of the business and its ability to repay any loan.

Preparing Your Business Plan

Before you begin your business plan sit down and ask yourself "What image do I want my business to project?" Your business image will represent you and the way you operate, market, advertise, and your vision of success. Consider the professional image for your business all the way from the design of the exterior and interior to your logo. Ask yourself "What is the experience I want my clients to have in my establishment, and what is it that I want them to say about me, my work, and my employees?"

Your business plan should include:

- ***Executive Summary***—A brief overview of the business concept and plan for success. It is the What, Why, Where, When, and How you are going to succeed.
- ***Mission Statement***—A mission statement defines the reason for a business's existence. It states the purpose of the company. It pro-

vides a sense of direction by defining guiding principles and clarifying goals. It should be relatively brief; three to five lines is standard. Create a mission statement that will act as description of the key strategic influences on your business such as the market you will serve, the kinds of services you will offer, and the quality level of the services provided. Your mission statement will also serve as your blueprint for operating your business.

- ***Vision Statement***—A vision statement is what you want your business to be, now and in the future. It is your framework for all goal setting and planning. It is your hopes and dreams for your business. It is your vision for what you are trying to build. Create a vision statement with your passion in mind and statements detailing how you can best serve your clients, your community, and the makeup profession.
- ***Start Up Expenses***—Inventory, equipment, and supplies.
- ***Construction Costs***—Build-out of the selected location.
- ***Marketing and Advertising Plan***—Appropriate strategies and funding for this critical business element.
- ***Competitive Strategy***—An action plan outlining how you will gain a competitive advantage over your competitors thru pricing, customer service, and products/services offered. In other words: why your clients will purchase your products and services over someone else.
- ***Salary/Payroll Expenses***—Dependent upon staff and employees.
- ***Leasing Expenses***—Selecting your location with visibility and accessibility in mind is one of the most important factors in choosing an ideal location. Your location should represent the image that you have created for your business. Lighting, parking, and safety are also important considerations.
- ***One-, Three-, and Five-year Financial Projections***—This is part of your overall budget.
- ***Licenses and License Fees***
- ***Insurance***
- ***Operational Plan***—An operational plan supports the business mission and vision statements. It is your plan on how you will manage the internal systems of your business. It covers human resources, finance and technology, and includes budgets and plans for staff, inventory, supplies, utilities, repairs, computers, software, etc. Questions to ask yourself when writing an operational plan for the next 1 to 3 years are:
  - Where are we now?
  - Where do we want to be?
  - How do we get there?

Upon completion of your business plan, you will have a well-defined picture of your concept and budget. The next step is to research local

You don't have to be a business owner to have a mission and vision statement. Create your own personal mission and vision statements to help guide you on your career path. Both of these statements will elevate your professional image and help you stay true to yourself as you navigate your makeup career.

WEB RESOURCES

Every state has a Small Business Bureau. This is a great resource to help entrepreneurs begin the process of putting together their business plan. They offer classes, grants, loans, and counseling and training. Visit www.sba.gov for detailed information.

regulations and state laws. Be sure to do your homework and ensure that your business is in compliance with all state and local laws and regulations. The best way to achieve this is by searching the Internet for guidelines or visiting your town hall and speaking to regional inspectors and officers. LO4

Focus On

Success

"Makeup artists can often be undervalued in a business setting, especially in the beginning of your career. Knowing how to value yourself in the workforce and knowing how to have your contractual agreements and other details in order before you begin a job is one key to a successful career."— Thom Cammer

MAKING A NAME FOR YOURSELF

Regardless of whether you collect a paycheck from an employer, are an independent contractor, or own your own business as a makeup artist, *you* are your business. Your skills, abilities, professional traits, and success are completely dependent upon you. You are the one who builds, maintains, and grows your business. This is the power of the makeup and beauty business: You have complete control over your growth, your success, and your business.

Branding Yourself

When starting out as a makeup artist it is important to think of your talent, skill, and professional image as a brand. Most artists find it difficult to "sell" themselves, so establishing your talent and skills as a "brand" will make it much easier and less intimidating to market and promote yourself. **Branding** is the character of your business and the personality and image you are projecting to potential clients and employers. Everything clients and potential employers see must make a statement of who you are and what you offer. A **logo** is a unique symbol of design used to identify a specific organization or brand.

Your logo, business card, Web site, portfolio, and makeup kit—in combination with your professional image, work ethic, skills, and talent—must work together to reflect, enhance, and support your brand through your networking and marketing efforts.

Review the career profiles throughout this book to distinguish how each featured makeup artist's brand appears to you, then check out their Web sites and portfolios to see how accurate your impressions are.

Defining Your Brand

Defining your brand is a journey of self-discovery. It can be difficult, time consuming, and uncomfortable. The image surrounding a makeup artist's brand is the principal source of your competitive advantage, and it is what will make you memorable.

The questions below will help you in defining your brand:

- What do you want to be known for?
- What do you want your clients and potential clients to think of you and your work?
- What kind of message do you want your marketing to say to your potential clients?
- What can you do better than your competition?
- Why should people hire you and work with you?

MARKETING

Marketing is how you convey your brand through promotions and advertising. Marketing sells your brand, and it is your brand that your customers will be attracted to and choose to buy.

Think of marketing as the method of attracting and retaining satisfied clients. It is the means for selling and promoting yourself. Your marketing efforts should be 24/7 as you begin your makeup career. The energy you put in marketing today will come back to you one-hundred fold in years to come.

Getting Started

Before you start branding and marketing yourself, you will need to have your Web site and portfolios ready for potential clients to view. Even if you have very few photos and no clients, begin the process of creating these two important marketing tools now as it takes time to research and develop what your "brand" will ultimately look like. Nowadays creating your own Web site can be quick, easy, and quite fun. Refer back to Chapter 19, Your Professional Image, if a refresher is needed on creating your portfolios. Think of your bound portfolio and on-line portfolio and Web site as your brick and mortar foundation. This is where you will send potential clients and employers to view your work. Remember that these are not only representations of your skills and talent, but also of your professional image. In addition to your work, you can post your resume and client list to your Web site as well as behind-the-scenes photos and videos of events, photoshoots, and makeovers you have worked upon. Only post photos and other materials that represent you and your work in the best possible light. If it is not appropriate for all visitors to the site, then do not post it. Collect testimonials and referrals from clients and people you have worked with and post these to your Web site or portfolio as well—this is where people will find you, and it is also where people will decide if they want to contact you.

Did You Know?

When you begin anything new it takes 10 units of energy to produce 1 unit of results; once you have mastered the task it takes 1 unit of energy to produce 10 units of results.

Business Cards

Business cards are an important part of promoting business and they help us swap information quickly and effectively. Create a memorable business card with your logo, Web site, or on-line portfolio information, phone, and e-mail or social media sites. Tell the world what you specialize in and how good you are at it (**Figure 20–8**). For those who are always connected to a smart phone or smart pad, applications are available that make swapping and sending information fun and easy. Check with your phone carrier for the latest developments in business card applications. Be creative and hand out business cards everywhere you go. You never know where you will find a potential client. And remember: regardless of marketing ideas and money spent, the finest and most effective means of advertising is still *word of mouth*.

▲ **Figure 20–8 Your own business card will set you apart from the competition.**

© Robbi/www.Shutterstock.com

Marketing Yourself: Where and to Whom

The number one secret you need to know if you want to grow your business in the shortest amount of time possible is: What are your clients telling their friends about you?

A recent survey conducted by the Professional Beauty Association (PBA) yielded some informative results that all makeup artists would do well to keep mind when planning marketing strategies. The top three ways, ordered from most often to least often, that clients find a service provider are listed below.

- Number one: recommendation/referral.
- Number two: location—you're in the neighborhood and convenient.
- Number three: advertisement.

Viral Marketing

The modern version of word of mouth is viral marketing, also known as *referral and recommendation.* It is the personal communication about a service or product between target clients and their friends, relatives, and associates. The viral marketing technique passes along your message to hundreds and even thousands of potential clients through social media sites and e-mail campaigns.

Viral marketing is a phenomenon because viruses are infectious agents—and these agents are clients who are so motivated about your services that they tell their friends and family, and for some clients that network can reach into the thousands.

Social Media

Social media is a platform to engage and communicate with a community of people and is an ideal vehicle for viral marketing. Social media allows you to bridge geographical and cultural distances to reach a variety of people, usually with the same interests.

Social media for business is similar yet very different from your personal page. It is a means to attract a following and have other people promote you and your business via viral marketing.

This is accomplished by providing content that is seen as valuable and relevant to your audience:

- Write a **blog**, which is an on-line journal or newsletter reflecting your knowledge, talent, and skills, with makeup and beauty tips and resources.
- Start a Beauty Tip of the Day.
- Network with cosmetic and beauty brands and give your personal review of new products.
- Start a makeup and cosmetic advice column.

WEB RESOURCES

- The Hair & Makeup Artist Network (HMAN) is an excellent resource to help you market yourself successfully: www.hmartistsnetwork.com
- www.styleseat.com is an on-line destination for beauty and wellness professionals and clients. Professionals can showcase their work and connect with new and existing clients.

A number of social media sites exist which makeup artists can use to promote their brand through social media marketing. Three well-known and popular sites readily available are Facebook, Yelp, and Twitter.

Facebook For the business person, Facebook enables you to have your business contacts, your profile, business groups, targeted prospects, and social media applications all under one on-line roof. Through Facebook's information sharing, you can find more opportunities to network with other professional artists and potential clients. Facebook's on-line structure utilizes viral threads at a macro level. The potential for reaching untapped resources and potential clients is almost limitless. If you have not done so yet, start following other makeup artists and makeup communities on Facebook and check out what they are doing and posting. Once you feel confident, set up your own business page on Facebook and start your own following.

Yelp The major benefit and main point of Yelp is the ease of communication most users experience. This site is a virtual "word-of-mouth" forum for the digital world. With Yelp communities popping up in most American cities and many other locations around the globe, it is becoming a simple matter to access "hot" spots on the Internet and view what other professionals and consumers alike are focusing on.

Yelp is not just reviews; there are events, event reminders, and special offers from businesses. A user can make friends with other yelpers, the same as with Facebook or MySpace. The friend feature allows you to send messages to other users or even "follow" them, which enables you to see a specific reviewer's posts on a business they have reviewed first in the default sort order of reviews. If you want to post your personal reviews from Facebook, you can import them directly from your Facebook profile to Yelp. User instructions and a full list of features for Yelp can be found via the site's home page.

Twitter When you sign-up with Twitter, you can use the service to post and receive messages with a network of contacts. Instead of sending a dozen e-mails or text messages, you send one message to your Twitter account and the service distributes it to all your friends. Members use Twitter to organize impromptu gatherings, carry on a group conversation, or just send a quick update to let people know what is currently going on. Twitter is an excellent way to maintain your presence with clients, contacts, and colleagues in the social media venue.

Marketing has changed over the years and will continue to change as technology and buying psychology evolve. It is just as important to keep up with marketing advances as it is to keep up with the latest trends, products, and new innovations in the beauty and makeup business.

Focus On

Social Media Marketing

"In today's market having a Web site is arguably as important as having a hard-copy portfolio. Invest in a Web site and combine it with social networking as soon as you can."—Jake Galvez

WEB RESOURCES

With technology advancing every day it is important to stay current with changes in social media, especially as it pertains to your business. A great resource for on-line marketing tools is www.hubspot.com. They have free webinars and e-books that are current and comprehensive with all the pertinent information needed to succeed in today's growing social media market.

Marketing Ideas

There are many cost-effective ways to market yourself as a professional makeup artist and quickly start to establish a client base.

- ***Public Relations Events.*** A great way to build your brand is to do publicity events. Exposing your talents and skill to the public by getting the press involved can really get your name out among the public. An excellent resource to assist in this endeavor is the book *Guerilla Publicity* (Adams Media, 2nd ed., 2008). Creating an effective and catchy press release that will attract the media's interest is important. For example: "Local makeup artist helps cancer patients look and feel more beautiful during their treatment and beyond."
- ***Volunteer.*** Perform complimentary makeovers for local newscasters and television personalities. Do demos or mini-classes at local cosmetology and esthetics schools and volunteer at women's shelters, local high schools, career fairs, cancer treatment centers, and hospitals.
- ***Advertise.*** Place a small add in a local paper, magazine, or newsletter around wedding season and prom time.
- ***Business Cards.*** Post your business cards at the local gym or fitness center.
- ***Establish Relationships.*** Nurture relationships with local bridal stores, wedding planners, florists, photographers, and hair salons.
- ***Cross Promote with Local Businesses.*** A very cost-effective way to market yourself is to partner with other local businesses in your area that share a similar client base to the one you service. Such businesses might include plastic surgeons, gyms, small clothing stores and boutiques, jewelry stores, Pilates studios, and so on.
- ***Chamber of Commerce.*** This is a key one. Are you a member? Are you active? Again, low-cost networking involves being out in the community meeting and greeting people. Going to mixers or even being on the board has you connecting with like-minded people and generates exposure for you and your brand.
- ***Trade Shows/Bridal Expos.*** Share a booth at a bridal show with a dress shop or photographer and do makeovers on the spot. These events are commonly held once a year, so the opportunity to present is limited. If your setup and presentation is correct, these events can provide an excellent return on your investment of time and money. One thing to remember is that poor planning and execution will be a waste of your hard-earned dollars as the booth fee for these events is paid in advance and is almost always nonrefundable.
- ***Local Corporations.*** Make a hit list of local corporations in your area; ones you want to target and then call on them with an offering of a group VIP package for the ladies. Consider developing and presenting an on-site "day of beauty" where you educate company personnel on various makeup applications and beauty

tips. This will not only help establish your professional name but enhance your reputation and professional image as well.

- ***Charity Events.*** These venues create exposure, support a good cause, and get you connected with many people.
- ***Gift Certificates.*** These are powerful tools in the business world. Gift certificates are a guarantee of additional revenue for the business. They are a great marketing tool to generate positive word of mouth. Offer them on your Web site for makeup lessons, makeup applications, brow design, and so forth. ☑ **LO5**

Focus On

A Dynamic Spirit

"Anyone interested in becoming a Makeup Artist needs to have a dynamic and passionate spirit and to be open to any and all learning experiences—education is key, you never stop learning. I believe that opportunities arise around every corner. Some of the fundamental characteristics needed are: passion, creativity, flexibility, efficiency, and timing. Being open and receptive to what life offers will open many wonderful and exciting doors to a variety of arenas in the beauty industry."—Peggy Ruelke

GETTING STARTED

The employment opportunities for the makeup artist are endless. You are about to set out on a new career full of excitement, opportunity, and unlimited potential. Your makeup career path can and will be whatever you make it.

Place careful consideration on your various employment opportunities and use your educational time to develop a feel for your passions, ambitions, and goals. Take each element in your career path one step at a time. Use every day to build up your experience, your knowledge, and your skills so that your confidence and ability continually shine through. Develop a dynamic portfolio that is supported by a sound resume. Keep your materials, information, and questions organized in order to ensure a high-impact interview.

Once you have secured a job, take the time and effort necessary to learn all that you can about your new position, responsibilities, and the establishment or production you will be serving. Keep up on changes in the makeup industry. Attend trade shows and expositions while taking advantage of as much continuing education offerings as you can manage. Become an active participant in efforts and events that support, promote, and advance the makeup industry. Work hard to represent your new vocation as the respected, fulfilling, and profitable profession that it has become.

Review Questions

1. What factors influence the salary potential of a professional makeup artist?
2. What is the difference between an employee and an independent contractor?
3. List at least six career and job opportunities for a makeup artist.
4. Describe the steps to take to begin a career path as a makeup artist behind a counter, as a salon or spa makeup artist, and as a bridal makeup artist.
5. Describe the role of a key makeup artist.
6. List the key points that should be included on a resume.
7. What is the purpose of a cover letter?
8. If a job interview is scheduled for noon, at what time should you arrive?
9. What topics should you avoid commenting upon during a job interview?
10. What is the purpose of a business plan?
11. Define the purpose of a mission statement and a vision statement.
12. Define branding.
13. What are the essential marketing tools you need before you start establishing a clientele?
14. What is the most effective means for securing clients and jobs?
15. What is viral marketing?
16. List at least seven ways to market yourself as a new makeup artist.

Chapter Glossary

blog	An on-line journal or newsletter reflecting your knowledge, talent, and skills.
branding	The character of your business and the personality and image you are projecting to potential clients and employers.
business plan	Strategy for understanding key elements in developing business; also serves as a guide to making informed business decisions.
client list	A list of all the productions and celebrity or notable clients you have worked on.
independent contractor	Someone who sets his or her own fees, controls his or her own hours, has his or her own business card, and pays his or her own taxes.
informational interview	A scheduled meeting or conversation whose sole purpose is to gather information.

Chapter Glossary *(continued)*

kit fee	Fee for makeup supplies needed for a television, film, theater, or fashion production and is usually paid by the production company and requires receipts for all products purchased.
logo	Unique symbol of design used to identify a specific organization or brand.
makeup department head	Manages the makeup department for the film, television, or theater production. They read the script, meet with the director and screen writer, and they are responsible for the research, design, and execution of the makeup for each and every actor. They make hiring decisions in addition to maintaining budgets for salaries, supplies, materials, and special effects. The makeup department head is generally responsible for the primary actors' makeup applications as well.
private label	Products or services typically manufactured or provided by one company for offer under another company's brand.
resume	A written summary of education and work experience that highlights relevant accomplishments and achievements.
retainer	Fixed sum of money that the client agrees to pay, in advance, to secure the services of the makeup artist as needed, when needed.
union job	A job in which all the persons working on the production must be members of the Make-up Artists & Hairstylists Guild of the I.A.T.S.E.

Appendix A: Resources

Publications

Brown, B. (2002). Beauty evolution: A guide to a lifetime of beauty. William Morrow: New York, NY.

Center for Disease Control and Prevention. (2008). Guidelines for Disinfection and Sterilization in Healthcare Facilities.

Jones, R. (2008). Looking younger: Makeovers that make you look as young as you feel. Fair Winds Press: Beverly, MA.

Schmaling, S. (2010). Milady's aesthetician series: Aging skin. Milady, a part of Cengage Learning: Clifton Park, NY.

Steinman, D.A. and Steinman, H.K (2002). Skin camouflage. *Atlas of Cosmetic Surgery*, Saunders Elsevier, Inc., Philadelphia, PA.

Websites

Alchin, L.K. (2008, March 20). *The elizabethan era.* Retrieved from http://www.elizabethan-era.org.uk/

Am*erican Academy of Dermatology* [Online]. http://www.aad.org/

Burchett, G. and Davis, C. (2004). Retrieved from http://www.tattooarchive.com/tattoo_history/burchett_george_charles.html

Cp historical overview. (n.d.). Retrieved from http://www.californiaperfumecompany.net/company/cal_historical_overview.html

Cylax by royal appointment. (n.d.). Retrieved from http://www.cyclax.com/

Global natural cosmetic sales approaching us $7 billion. (2007, September 18). Retrieved from http://www.organicconsumers.org/articles/article_7149.cfm

Illes, J. (2011). Beauty secrets of ancient egypt. Retrieved from http://www.touregypt.net/egypt-info/magazine-mag06012000-mag4.html

Long-lasting lipstick. (n.d.). Informally published manuscript, Lemelsen , MIT, Cambridge , MA. Retrieved from http://web.mit.edu/invent/iow/bishop.html

Mary Kay Inc. (n.d.). Retrieved from http://www.fundinguniverse.com/company-histories/Mary-Kay-Inc-Company-History.html

Teng, J. (2009). Colour cosmetics in asia pacific – Euromonitor International. Retrieved from http://www.in-cosmeticsasia.com/files/MARKEuromonitor_International_incosmetics_Asia_2009

The beauty: top 100. (2004). Retrieved from http://www.scribd.com/doc/3027409/Top-100-Cosmetic-Manufacturers

Appendix B: Conversions

U.S. Measurement-Metric Conversion Tables

The following tables show standard conversions for commonly used measurements in Milady Standard Makeup 1st Edition.

Conversion Formula for Inches to Centimeters: (number of) inches x 2.54 = centimeters

LENGTH	
INCHES	CENTIMETERS
⅛ inch (.125 inches)	0.317 centimeters
¼ inch (.25 inches)	0.635 centimeters
½ inch (.50 inches)	1.27 centimeters
¾ inch (.75 inches)	1.9 centimeters
1 inch	2.54 centimeters
2 inches	5.1 centimeters
3 inches	7.6 centimeters
6 inches	15.2 centimeters
12 inches	30.5 centimeters

Conversion Formula for U.S. Fluid Ounces to Milliliters:
(amount of) U.S. fluid ounce (fl. oz.) x 29.573 milliliters (ml)
Conversion Formula for U.S. Fluid Ounces to Liters:
(amount of) U.S. fluid ounce (fl. oz.) x .029573 liters (l)

VOLUME (LIQUID)	
U.S. FLUID ONCES	MILLILITERS/LITERS
1 fluid ounce (⅛ cup)	29. 57 milliliters/.02957 liters
2 fluid ounces (¼ cup)	59.14 milliliters/.05914 liters
4 fluid ounces (½ cup)	118.29 milliliters/.11829 liters
6 fluid ounces (¾ cup)	177.43 milliliters/.17743 liters
8 fluid ounces (1 cup)	236.58 milliliters/.23658 liters
16 fluid ounces (1 pint)	473.16 milliliters/.47316 liters
32 fluid ounces (1 quart)	946.33 milliliters/.94633 liters
33.81 fluid ounces (1 liter)	1,000 milliliters/1 liter
64 fluid ounces (½ gallon)	1,892.67 milliliters/1.8926 liters
128 fluid ounces (1 gallon)	3,785.34 milliliters/3.78534 liters

Conversion Formula for Degrees Fahrenheit (°F) to Degrees Celsius (°C): °C = (°F-32) x (5/9) ***

TEMPERATURE	
DEGREES FAHRENHEIT (°F)	DEGREES CELSIUS (°C)
32°	0°
40°	4.444°
50°	10°
60°	15.556°
70°	21.111°
80°	26.667°
98.6°	37°
200°	93.333°
300°	148.889°
400°	204.444°

*** If you have a Fahrenheit temperature of 40 degrees and you want to convert it into degrees on the Celsius scale: Using the conversion formula, first subtract 32 from the Fahrenheit temperature of 40 degrees to get 8 as a result. Then multiply 8 by five and divide by nine (8 x 5)/9 to get the converted value of 4.444 degrees Celsius.

Glossary/Index

A

Basal cell carcinoma, most common and least severe type of skin cancer; often characterized by light or pearly nodules, 70

Beach bride, a bride who has a wedding ceremony scheduled on the sands of a beach in close proximity to the water, 215

Becker, Alexander, 376

Bioburden, the number of viable organisms in or on an object or surface or the organic material on the surface of an object before decontamination or sterilization, 34

Birthmark. See Nevus

Black color, impact of, 103

Blemished skin, 304, 310–314

Blepharitis, eye condition characterized by chronic inflammation of the eyelid, 407

Blog, an on-line journal or newsletter reflecting your knowledge, talent, and skills, 490

Blondel, Clair, 208

Bloodborne pathogens, disease-causing microorganisms carried in the body by blood or body fluids; examples include hepatitis and HIV, 30–31

Blotting paper, a highly absorbent, thin paper used to absorb excess oil from the surface of the skin, leaving a smooth, matte finish, 88

Blush brush, 83

Boar bristles, 82

Body substance isolation (BSI), personal protective equipment is worn for contact with all body fluids, even if blood is not visible, 40

Botox®, a prescription medicine created using botulinum toxin; it is used to treat lines and wrinkles by paralyzing the muscles located at the site of injection, 326

Bow, Clara, 13

Branding, the character of your business and the personality and image you are projecting to potential clients and employers, 488

Bridal makeup, 475
  application procedure, 216, 229–234
  attending bridal expos, 492

Bronzer, 358

Broski, Staci, 448

Brow accessories, 86–87

Brow comb, a tool used to brush the eyebrow hairs into the desired position, creating a finely groomed look, 87

Brow cream, a thick, colored cream used for very sparse eyebrows in need of heavier coverage, 180

Brow gel, a makeup product specifically designed to work like a hair gel; it holds the brows in position and provides them with a beautiful, long-lasting, finished look, 180

Brow pencils, similar to an eyeliner pencil and are used to fill in sparse areas, define the brow, or completely re-create a brow, 180

Brow scissors, very small scissors with short, thin ends; they are used to trim long brow hairs that you do not want to remove completely, but that need to be shortened for proper shaping, 87

Brow shadows, also known as brow powders; used for creating a soft-looking eyebrow; they are applied with an angled brow brush, 180

Brow stencils, cut outs of various eyebrow shapes to guide the shaping of eyebrows, the removal of stray hairs, and the application of product, 180

Brush bristles, allergic reaction to, 82
  Brush cleaners, 86

Brushes, makeup, 90, 192, 194
  caring for, 38
  natural-hair bristles, 80–82
  synthetic, 82

three parts of, 79–80
types and uses, 82–86

BSI. *See* Body substance isolation

Buccinator muscle, thin, flat muscle of the cheek between the upper and lower jaw that compresses the cheeks and expels air between the lips, 60

Budgeting, 459–460. *See* also Money management

Bulla (plural: bullae), large blister containing a watery fluid; similar to a vesicle but larger, 64

Bündchen, Gisele, 164

Burn survivors, camouflage makeup for, 359, 362–364

Business
career options
bridal makeup, 475
educator, 480
fashion, 479–480
makeup counter, 473–474
salon or spa, 474–475
theater, film, and television, 476–478
earning potential, 471–473
getting started, 493
getting the job, 480–486
marketing, 489–493
ownership, 486–488
reasons to study, 471
reputation/branding yourself, 48

Business cards, 489, 492

Business plan, strategy for understanding key elements in developing business; also serves as a guide to making informed business decisions, 486
competitive strategy, 487
construction costs, 487
executive summary, 486
financial projections, 487
insurance, 487
leasing expenses, 487
licenses and license fees, 5, 487
marketing and advertising plan, 487
mission statement, 486
operational plan, 487
salary/payroll expenses, 487
start up expenses, 487
vision statement, 487

Byrne, Alex, 57

California Perfume Company, 12

Camel bristles, 82

Cammer, Thom, 274, 488

Camouflage makeup, the strategic layering of various colors and textures to hide pigmentation issues, 355
corrective techniques, 355–356
makeup appointment for, 361
procedures
birthmarks and tattoos, 360–361, 370–372, 394–396
burn survivors, 362–364
hyperpigmentation, 367–369
vitiligo, 365–366
reasons to study, 355
skin conditions requiring, 358
birthmarks, 360
burn survivors, 359
hyperpigmentation, 355, 360
tattoos, 361
vitiligo, 359
types of
airbrush, 357
bronzer, 358
color correctors, 357
highlighter, 358
liquid foundation, 356
mineral makeup, 357–358
pastes and creams, 356
setting powder, 358

Concentrate (disinfectant), 34

Confidence, as key quality, 450

Conjunctivitis (pinkeye), common bacterial infection of the eyes, extremely contagious, 68

Construction costs, 487

Consultation form, a questionnaire used to gather pertinent information about a client and her needs, 112–117
creating your own, 117
eyebrow shaping included in, 118

Contagious disease (communicable disease), also known as a communicable disease; disease that is spread by contact from one person to another person, such as the common cold, ringworm, conjunctivitis (pinkeye), viral infections, and natural nail or toe and foot infections, 28. *See* also Infection control

Contamination, the presence, or the reasonably anticipated presence, of blood or other potentially infectious materials on an item's surface or visible debris or residues such as dust, hair, and skin, 29

Contemporary style, represents a fresh, clean look with an edgy avant-garde feel featuring current ideas in style, fashion, and design, 240

Contour, to recede, minimize in apparent size, or draw attention away from a feature, 131

Contour brush, 85

Cool colors, colors that suggest coolness; they are dominated by blues, greens, violets, and blue-reds, 101

Corrective techniques, 355–356. *See* also Camouflage makeup

Corrugator muscle, muscle located beneath the frontalis and orbicularis oculi that draws the eyebrow down and wrinkles the forehead vertically, 59

Cosmetic treatment card, a form used to document the details of the application, including an evaluation of the client's features, the purpose for the visit, the colors and products used, the application techniques, and any other pertinent information that will be useful for future visits, 119

Couture style, breathes the beauty of Hollywood glamour and mystique with eye-catching elegant, yet subtle, trend-setting fashions, 240
couture makeup procedure, 246–247, 255–258

Cover letter, for resume, 482

Crayola© crayons, 105

Cream foundations, foundations that can be either water-based or oil-based; they are thicker in consistency than a liquid foundation and provide overall coverage with a smooth texture and deep tone, 130

Cream shadows, shadows that are lighter than stick shadows and do not dry to a powder, 174

Cream-to-cream shadows, shadows that begin as a smoothly blending cream and then dry as a light powder, 174

Creative, as key quality, 450

Creative direction and collaboration, 242

Cross-contamination, the spread of bacteria from one place, person, or product to another, 130

Crust, dead cells that form over a wound or blemish while it is healing; an accumulation of sebum and pus, sometimes mixed with epidermal material, 66

Customer service, 457–458

Cyclex Cosmetic, 12

Cysts, closed, abnormally developed sacs containing fluid, semifluid, or morbid matter, above, or below the skin, 67

Dual-action airbrush, an airbrush with two stages: it releases air when you press down on the lever, and it sprays makeup when you pull back on the lever, 378

Duncan, Michael Clark, 208

Dyspigmentation, hypopigmentation or hyperpigmentation caused by trauma, illness, or hormonal imbalance, 69, 324, 359
  camouflage makeup for, 360, 367–369
  makeup for men with, 283
  postinflammatory hyperpigmentation, 355

E

Earning potential, 471–473

Ears, pathogen entry through, 29

Eczema, an inflammatory, uncomfortable, and often chronic disease of the skin characterized by moderate to severe inflammation, scaling, and sometimes severe itching, 68

Educator, 480

Efficacy, the ability to produce an effect, 34

Egypt, ancient, 7–8

Elastin, protein base similar to collagen that forms elastic tissue, 63

Elizabeth II (queen), 12

Elizabethan Era, 9

Emollient based, water-in-oil or oil-in-water blends of ingredients that soften and smooth the skin, 130

England
  eighteenth century, 10
  Elizabethan Era, 9
  nineteenth century, 12
  Regency Era, 10–11
  Stuart Era, 9–10
  twentieth century, 12
  Victorian Era, 11–12

Enthusiasm, as key quality, 458

Environmental allergies, 117

Environmental Protection Agency (EPA), 23–24
  disinfectants registered with, 35

EPA. *See* Environmental Protection Agency

Epidermis, outermost and thinnest layer of the skin; it is made up of five sub-layers that work together to create the visual appearance of the skin, 61

Ethics, the moral principles by which we live and work, 458–459

Euromonitor International Colour Cosmetic Report, 16

Evening bride, a bride with a wedding ceremony scheduled from late afternoon through the evening hours, from 4 p.m. and later, 215

Even-set eyes, eyes that are perfectly balanced; the ideal eye shape for any face shape, 166

Everyday application
  alternative, 194–196
  procedure for, 197–203
  product checklist, 193
  reasons to study, 191
  special considerations, 196
  tool checklist, 191–192

Excoriation, skin sore or abrasion produced by scratching or scraping, 66

Executive summary, 486

Exposure incident, contact with nonintact (broken) skin, blood, body fluid, or other potentially infectious materials that is the result of the performance of an employee's duties, 43–44

Eye shadow, 173, 193
  applicators, 89
  brushes, 84

Federal agencies, 22–24

Ferro, Krissy, 21

Ferrule, the metal part of the brush that attaches the glued bristles to the handle and adds a certain amount of strength to the bristles, 80

Fiber-optic brush, 85

Fields, Megan, 404

Film makeup artist, 476–478

Financial planning, personal, 450, 459–460
Income and Expense Worksheet, 461–463

Financial projections, in business plan, 487

First impressions, 5, 103, 111–112

Fisher, Catherine "Kitty," 10

Fissure, a crack in the skin that penetrates the dermis. Examples are severely cracked and/or chapped hands or lips, 66

Five-o'clock shadow, a style created by not shaving for a day; currently a popular fashion look, 279

Flappers, northern, urban, single, young middle-class women in the 1920s that had their own jobs, disposable income, and independence, 13

Folliculitis, also known as folliculitis barbae, sycosis barbae, or barber's itch. Inflammation of the hair follicles caused by a bacterial infection from ingrown hairs. The cause is typically from ingrown hairs due to shaving or other epilation methods, 31

Foundation, a makeup product designed to even out skin tone and mild imperfections and provide a base for the makeup application, 128, 193, 195
for aging clients, 329
application techniques, 130–132
blending with skin tone, 119–120
types of, 129–130

Foundation brush, 83

Francis, Julia, 110

Freelance makeup artist, 4

French Restoration, 10

Friendly mutton chops, a combination of mutton chops and a moustache to create one continuous line of facial hair, 278–279

Friends Beauty Supply, North Hollywood, 452

Frisket film, an adhesive-backed paper and plastic combination that is used by airbrush artists to create templates (stencils), 382

Frontal bone, the bone that forms the forehead, 59

Frontalis, a muscle of the scalp, it is not considered a muscle of the eyebrow; but is responsible for raising the eyebrows, drawing the scalp forward, and causing wrinkles across the forehead, 60

Fu Manchu moustache, a style created by facial hair that grows over the lip and extends down each side of the mouth to the jaw area, 278

Full beard, a style in which hair covers all three basic areas: the upper lip, the chin, and the sides of the face. This style is typically trimmed at the neck area, at the lip line, and sides, 278–279

Fungi (singular: fungus), microscopic plant parasites that include molds, mildews, and yeasts; fungi can produce contagious diseases such as ringworm, 31

Fungicidal, capable of destroying fungi, 25

G

Galena, the dark blue-gray ore of lead that in ancient times was mined off the coast of the Red Sea (used to make mesdemet), 7

Galvez, Jake, 238

H

J

K

L

M

Mendhi makeup, the art of decorating the body with henna, 442–443

Mentalis muscle, muscle that elevates the lower lip and raises and wrinkles the skin of the chin, 60

Mesdemet, the first black eye shadow; it was created by the Egyptians using galena, 7–8

Mesopotamia, ancient, 8

Methicillin-resistant staphylococcus aureus (MRSA), initially appears as a skin infection such as pustules, rashes, and boils that can be difficult to cure. Without proper treatment, the infection becomes systemic and can have devastating consequences that can result in death, 28

Michaud, David, 354, 471

Microorganism, any organism of microscopic or submicroscopic size, 26, 31

Middle Ages, 8

Midwest International Beauty Expo, 466

Milars, Lydia, 298

Mildew, a type of fungus that affects plants or grows on inanimate objects but does not cause human infections, 31

Milia, benign keratin-filled cysts that can appear just under the epidermis and have no visible opening, 67

Milk/dairy allergy, 117

Mineral makeup, contains nonbacterial, finely ground particles from the earth; contains fewer chemicals and dyes than most traditional makeup; most are talc-free and less likely to cause allergic reactions, 129
- for camouflage, 357–358
- Ferro's, 21
- for men, 281
- for teens, 303

Mission statement, 459, 486

Mitchell, Christian, 434

Mod trend, 15

Model comp cards, cards that provide information including a given model's measurements and height; they also provide useful visual information that makeup artists can use as they develop a plan for creating a each model's overall look and makeup application, 242

Modern glamour style, makeup that enhances the individual's features with a timeless quality of beauty and always looks modern; red lips, pale eye shadow, and a defined upper eyelid, 240

Moisturizer, 128

Money management, 450, 459–460
- Income and Expense Worksheet, 461–463

Monroe, Marilyn. See Baker, Norma Jeane

Moorhouse, Farrah, 4

Morality, makeup and, 10–11

Morning bride, a bride with a wedding ceremony scheduled in the morning hours, prior to noon, 214

Mortuary makeup, the application of makeup on individuals that are deceased, 439–440

Mosquito bites, 65

Mousse foundation, a liquid product that comes in an aerosol or spray can, boosted by air (like whipped cream); it is light, easy to apply, and an excellent choice for any skin type, 130

Mouth
- lips as facial feature, 182–184
- pathogen entry through, 29
- perfect pout, 211, 220–222

MRSA. *See* Methicillin-resistant staphylococcus aureus

MSDS, 23. *See* Material Safety Data Sheet

Mukha Essentials, 78

Multiuse (reusable), items that can be cleaned, disinfected, and used on more than one person even if the item is accidentally exposed to blood or body fluid, 37

Mutton chops, a style characterized by wide swaths of sideburns growing down the sides of the face, almost touching the corners of the mouth. The mutton chop style was popularized in the 1970s by Elvis Presley, 278

N

Naimies Beauty Center, 452

Nars, François, 57

Nasal bones, the two bones that form the bridge of the nose, 58

Nasolabial folds, lines between the corners of the nose and the mouth, 199

Native Americans, cosmetics, 9

Natural hair, hair from a variety of animal sources, 80

Natural immunity, immunity that is partly inherited and partly developed through healthy living, 32

Natural makeup, for men, 284–289

Natural-hair brushes, brushes made from animal hairs or blends of animal hairs, 80

Navarro, Stephanie, 4

Needle, the part of the airbrush that controls the amount of makeup flowing through the nozzle, 378

Nettles, 65

Neutral colors, colors that do not complement or contrast any other color. Examples include brown and gray, 101

Neutralization, the color-theory method of concealing unwanted or uneven color on the skin, 386

Nevus (birthmark), small or large malformation of the skin due to abnormal pigmentation or dilated capillaries, 69
  camouflage makeup for, 360, 370–372

Niches, also known as birthmark; small or large malformation of the skin due to abnormal pigmentation or dilated capillaries, 435

Night-time wedding. *See* Evening bride

Nodule, a solid bump larger than .4 inches (1 centimeter) that can be easily felt, 70

Nonelectrical tools and implements, disinfecting, 38, 46–47

Nonpathogenic, harmless organisms that may perform useful functions and are safe to come in contact with since they do not cause disease or harm, 26

Nonporous, an item that is made or constructed of a material that has no pores or openings and cannot absorb liquids, 23

Nonstriated muscles, muscles that are involuntary and function automatically, without conscious will, 59

Non-thermogenic makeup, does not soak into the skin and is specifically manufactured for application to skin that has no heat or normal body temperature; can be applied in a light layer or as a heavy application to conceal imperfections, damage, bruises, scars, or other marks, 440

Nonverbal communication, communication expressed by body language, eye contact, facial expressions, and gestures, 457

Nose
  pathogen entry through, 29
  procerus muscle of, 60
  rosacea on, 67

Nozzle, one of the replaceable parts of the airbrush; it determines the size of the spray pattern, 378

Nylon, the firmest synthetic fiber that is used in makeup brushes; it is commonly used for eyebrow brushes as well as concealer and eyeliner brushes, 82

O

Oblong shaped face, 140

Occupational disease, illnesses resulting from conditions associated with employment, such as prolonged and repeated overexposure to certain products or ingredients, 29

Occupational Safety and Health Administration (OSHA), 22–23

Oil blotting papers, silky sheets that help to absorb oil without compromising the makeup, 252

Oil-based foundation, a foundation that contains more oil than water; best suited for dry or mature skin types, 129

On-line journal (blog), 490

On-line portfolio, an Internet display of your talents and work for potential customers and employers to evaluate your professional skills, 453

Operational plan, 487

Orbicularis oculi muscle, ring muscle of the eye socket; enables you to close your eyes, 59

Orbicularis oris muscle, flat band of muscle around the upper and lower lips that compresses, contracts, puckers, and wrinkles the lips, 60

Organic cosmetics, 15

Organized, as key quality, 450

OSHA. *See* Occupational Safety and Health Administration

Oval shaped face, 138–139, 276

Ownership, business, 486–488

P

Pale complexion, social significance of, 7–9

Palette, tool used to hold makeup that is scraped or removed from its containers, 88

Palor, a pale, colorless complexion or appearance, 10

Paper drape, 90

Paper palette, a palette made of disposable waterproof parchment paper or artist paper; it holds all the different products that you will use on an individual model, 247

Papillary layer, outer layer of the dermis, directly beneath the epidermis, 62

Papule, a raised bump, often red due to inflammation, and often sore due to the pressure of swelling; papules are frequently seen in acne; large sore bumps that do not have a head of pus, 64

Parabens, ingredients used a preservatives in cosmetics, 129

Paramedical makeup, a special branch of makeup artistry that routinely utilizes camouflaging techniques, 355

Parasites, organisms that grow, feed, and shelter on or in another organism (referred to as a host), while contributing nothing to the survival of that organism, 27, 31–32

Parasitic disease, disease caused by parasites, such as lice and mites, 29

Partial-lid (Asian) eyes, makeup procedure, 170–171

Pastes and creams, 356

Pathogenic, harmful microorganisms that can cause disease or infection in humans when they invade the body, 26, 31

Q

R

Raccoon bristles, 82

Real Color Wheel (RCW), 105

Receding hairline, anti-shine makeup for, 281–282

Red, impact of color, 103

Red clay, 8

References, on job performance, 482–483

Refillable brush, a brush with a reservoir handle that can be refilled with product: product and brush all in one, 86

Reflective listening, listening to the client and then repeating, in your own words, what you think the client is telling you, 118

Regency Era, 10–11

Regulations
- EPA, 23–24
- federal agencies, 22–24
- against making diagnosis, 26
- MSDS, 23
- OSHA, 22–23
- state agencies, 24
- Regulatory agencies, 23–24, 32

Renaissance, Italian, 9

Resting phase, when the face is not moving, 326

Resume, a written summary of education and work experience that highlights relevant accomplishments and achievements, 481
- cover letter with, 482

Retainer, fixed sum of money that the client agrees to pay, in advance, to secure the services of the makeup artist as needed, when needed, 480

Reticular layer, deeper layer of the dermis that consists of specialized proteins known as collagen and elastin, 62

Retractable brushes, brushes that retreat into the handle of the brush, 86

Reusable items. See Multiuse

Risorius muscle, muscle of the mouth that draws the corner of the mouth out and back, as in grinning, 60

Romans, ancient, 8

Rosacea, chronic redness and congestion appearing primarily on the cheeks and nose, characterized by redness, dilation of the blood vessels, and in some cases, formation of papules and pustules, 67

Round eyes, lovely large circles; they are also classified as protruding or bulging eyes, 167
- round Asian eyes makeup procedure, 168–170

Round shaped face, 140–141, 276

Ruelke, Peggy Sue, 190, 493

Runway makeup procedure, 290–293

S

Salary/payroll expenses, 487

Sales, of color cosmetics, 16. See also Business

Salicylic acid, a beta hydroxy acid ingredient that exfoliates, prevents bacterial growth, cleanses the pores, and helps prevent infection, 279

Salon, career at, 474–475

Sanitize, a chemical process for reducing the number of disease-causing germs on cleaned surfaces to a safe level, 25

Saturation, the pureness of a color or the dominance of a hue in a color, 102–103

Soft focus, an airbrush application method created by holding the airbrush 3 to 6 inches (7.5 to 15 centimeters) from the skin; color intensity and opacity can be enhanced by using consecutive passes, 382

Soul patch, a style achieved by confinement of the facial hair just below the lower lip; this style was very popular among the beatniks and jazz artists of the 1950s and 1960s, 278

SP. See Standard Precautions

Spa, career at, 474–475

Spa & Resort Expo, 466

Spatulas, 90

Special effects makeup, makeup technique used to make a person look older; younger; injured; alien; or of a different gender, age, or race; in other words, different from normal; used in the production of plays and movies to increase the believability of the characters, or create something that is otherwise considered not normal, 440–442

Special occasions, any occasion that holds importance to an individual such as birthdays, anniversaries, reunions, parties, weddings, or even a night out without the kids, 121, 210
- photography tips, 209–210
- prom makeup, 304–306, 314–318
- reasons to study makeup for, 209
- special looks for
  - candy apple glazed lips, 212, 226–228
  - defined (chiseled) cheek, 212, 223–225
  - perfect pout, 211, 220–222
  - smoky eyes, 211, 217–219
- weddings, 213–216
- basic bridal makeup application procedure, 216, 229–234

Spirilla, spiral or corkscrew-shaped bacteria that cause diseases such as syphilis and Lyme disease, 26

Sponges, 90

Spooly. *See* Mascara

Squamous cell carcinoma, a type of skin cancer more serious than basal cell carcinoma; characterized by scaly, red or pink papules or nodules; also appear as open sores or crusty areas; can grow and spread in the body, 70

Square shaped face, 141–142, 276

Squirrel bristles, 81

Stages of aging, 333–349

Standard definition television (SDTV), traditional analogue transmission with lower resolution, 249

Standard Precautions (SP), precautions such as wearing personal protective equipment to protect skin and mucous membrane where contact with a client's blood, body fluids, secretions (except sweat), excretions, nonintact skin, and mucous membranes is likely. Workers must assume that all blood and body fluids are potential sources of infection, regardless of the perceived risk, 40–43

Staphylococci, pus-forming bacteria that grow in clusters like bunches of grapes and are responsible for causing abscesses, pustules, and boils. Some types of staphylococci may not cause infections in healthy humans, 26

Start up expenses, 487

State regulations
- for disinfection, 24
- ingrown hair extraction, 280
- licensing, 5, 487
- scope of practice, 5, 127

T

U

V

Y

Z